Business Communication

Business Communication

Process and Product

Mary Ellen Guffey
Los Angeles Pierce College

Wadsworth Publishing Company
Belmont, California
A Division of Wadsworth, Inc.

Business Communications Editor: Kathy Shields
Development Editor: Mark Palmer
Editorial Assistant: Tamara Huggins
Production Editor: Deborah Cogan
Designer: Carolyn Deacy
Print Buyer: Randy Hurst
Art Editor: Kelly Murphy
Permissions Editor: Jeanne Bosschart
Copy Editor: Thomas Briggs
Photo Researchers: Photosynthesis; Roberta Broyer
Technical Illustrator: Precision Graphics
Cover Designer: Bill Reuter
Compositor: GTS Graphics
Printer: Arcata (Hawkins)

International Thompson Publishing
The trademark ITP is used under license

1 2 3 4 5 6 7 8 9 10—98 97 96 95 94

Printed in the United States of America

Library of Congress Cataloging-in-Publication Data

Guffey, Mary Ellen.
Business Communication: process and product / Mary Ellen Guffey.
p. cm.
Includes bibliographical references and index.
ISBN 0-534-92898-6
1. Business writing. 2. English language—Business English.
3. Business communication. I. Title.
HF5718.3.G838 1994
651.7—dc20 93-17784

About the Author

A practicing professional, Mary Ellen Guffey has been teaching business communication for over thirty years. She received a bachelor's degree, *summa cum laude,* in business education from Bowling Green State University; a master's degree in business education from the University of Illinois, where she held a fellowship; and a doctorate in economic and business education from the University of California, Los Angeles. Dr. Guffey is currently a professor of business and teaches business communication courses at Los Angeles Pierce College.

She is the author of *Business English,* Fourth Edition, which serves more students than any other book in its field, and *Essentials of Business Communication,* Second Edition, a highly successful text-workbook. Dr. Guffey also serves on the review boards of the *The Delta Pi Epsilon Journal* and *The Bulletin* of the Association of Business Communication.

A teacher's teacher and leader in the field, Dr. Guffey acts as a partner and mentor to hundreds of business communication instructors across the country. Her workshops, seminars, newsletters, articles, and teaching materials help novice and veteran business communication instructors achieve effective results in their courses.

Brief Contents

PART ONE • COMMUNICATION FOUNDATIONS 1

1 The Communication Process 3
2 Listening and Intercultural Communication 31

PART TWO • THE PROCESS OF WRITING 55

3 Analyzing, Anticipating, and Adapting 57
4 Researching, Organizing, and Composing 83
5 Revising, Proofreading, and Evaluating 113

PART THREE • LETTERS AND MEMOS 135

6 Direct Letters 137
7 Direct Memos 169
8 Negative News 193
9 Persuasive and Sales Messages 225
10 Goodwill and Special Messages 255

PART FOUR • REPORTS AND PROPOSALS 283

11 Report Planning and Research 285
12 Report Organization and Presentation 317
13 Typical Business Reports 347
14 Proposals and Formal Reports 377

PART FIVE • PRESENTATION SKILLS 421

15 Speaking Skills 423
16 Employment Messages 449

Appendix A Competent Language Usage Essentials: A Business Communicator's Guide 487
Appendix B Document Formats 509
Appendix C Data Documentation 523
Appendix D Correction Symbols 531
Key to C.L.U.E. Exercises 535
Notes 539
Acknowledgments 545
Index 549

Detailed Contents

PART I COMMUNICATION FOUNDATIONS 1

1 / The Communication Process 3

Sara Lee Corporation: Career Track Profile 4

Communication Power for Knowledge Workers 6

Today's Knowledge Society 6

Emphasis on Communication Skills 6

The Role of Communication 7

Career Skills: Five Common Myths About Writing on the Job 8

The Process of Communication and Its Barriers 8

Sending and Receiving Messages 9

Barriers to Interpersonal Communication 11

Overcoming Communication Barriers 13

Organizational Communication and Its Barriers 14

Functions 14

Forms 16

Flow 19

Barriers to Organizational Communication 20

Surmounting Organizational Barriers 22

Ethics: Four Ethical Guidelines Every Business Communicator Should Know 23

Strengthening Your Communication Skills 25

Summary of Learning Goals 25

Review and Discussion Questions 27

Activities and Problems 27

2 / Listening and Intercultural Communication 31

The Travelers: Career Track Profile 32
Strengthening Listening Skills 34
The Listening Process and Its Barriers 34
The Dynamics of Good Listening 36
Career Skills: Nine Poor Listening Habits That Can Sidetrack Your Career 37
Improving Your Listening Effectiveness 37
Checklist for Improving Listening 38
Creating Meaning from Nonverbal Messages 38
How the Eyes, Face, and Body Send Silent Messages 40
How Time, Space, and Territory Send Silent Messages 41
How Appearance Sends Silent Messages 42
Checklist for Improving Nonverbal Communication Skills 43
Developing Intercultural Sensitivity 44
Comprehending Cultural Diversity 44
Cultivating the Right Attitude 46
Cross Culture: Cultural and Ethical Dilemmas for Women Managers 47
Adapting Messages to Intercultural Audiences 48
Checklist for Improving Intercultural Sensitivity 50
Summary of Learning Goals 51
Review and Discussion Questions 52
Activities and Problems 52

PART II  THE PROCESS OF WRITING 55

3 / Analyzing, Anticipating, and Adapting 57

Lands' End: Career Track Profile 58
Approaching the Writing Process Systematically 60
The Basics of Business Writing 60
The 3-×-3 Writing Process 60
Phase 1: Preparing to Write 62
Analyzing the Task 62
Technology: Seven Ways Computers Can Make You a Better Business Writer 63
Anticipating the Audience 64
Adapting to the Task and Audience 65
Career Skills: Eight Easy Ways to Make Readers and Listeners Angry 71
Checklist for Adapting a Message to Its Audience 72
Adapting to Ethical and Legal Responsibilities 73

Five Common Ethical Traps 73
Goals of Ethical Business Communication 74
Tools for Doing the Right Thing 75
Language That Avoids Litigation 77
Summary of Learning Goals 78
Review and Discussion Questions 79
Activities and Problems 80

4 / Researching, Organizing, and Composing 83

Liz Claiborne: Career Track Profile 84
Researching Data and Generating Ideas 86
Formal Research Methods 86
Informal Research and Idea Generation 87
Researching Data and Generating Ideas on the Job 87
Organizing Data 89
Listing and Outlining 90
Grouping Ideas into Patterns 94
Composing the First Draft 96
Ethics: Communicator Motivation and the Ethics Underlying Messages 97
Creating Forceful Sentences 97
Drafting Effective Paragraphs 100
Checklist for Composing Sentences and Paragraphs 103
Writing in a Group 104
Collaboration Patterns 105
Obstacles to Collaboration 106
Summary of Learning Goals 107
Review and Discussion Questions 108
Activities and Problems 108

5 / Revising, Proofreading, and Evaluating 113

People *Magazine: Career Track Profile 114*
Revising Messages 116
Clarity: Keeping It Simple 116
Conciseness: Trimming the Fat 117
Vigor: Revising for Directness 119
Readability: Improving Comprehension 121
Career Skills: Applying the Fog Index to Determine Readability 123
Checklist for Revising Messages 124
Proofreading for the Finishing Touch 125
What to Watch For in Proofreading 125

Technology: Spell Checkers Are Wonderful, But . . . 126
How to Proofread Routine Documents 126
How to Proofread Complex Documents 127
Technology: Grammar and Style Checkers: Good and Bad News 128
Evaluating the Product 129
Summary of Learning Goals 129
Review and Discussion Questions 130
Activities and Problems 131

PART III LETTERS AND MEMOS 135

6 / Direct Letters 137

Ben & Jerry's Homemade: Career Track Profile 138
Strategies for Direct Letters 140
Characteristics of Good Letters 140
Using the Direct Pattern for Letters 142
Applying the 3-×-3 Writing Process to Direct Letters 143
Direct Request Letters 144
Requesting Information and Action 144
Placing Orders 145
Making Claims 147
Checklist for Writing Direct Requests 148
Direct Reply Letters 150
Complying with Requests 150
Acknowledging Customer Orders 154
Granting Adjustments and Claims 155
Checklist for Writing Direct Replies 158
Writing International Letters 160
Ethics: Greed Is Out; Ethics and Mission Statements Are In 161
Summary of Learning Goals 162
Review and Discussion Questions 162
Activities and Problems 163

7 / Direct Memos 169

Bank of America: Career Track Profile 170
Writing Direct Memos 172
Characteristics of Successful Memos 172
Writing Process for Memos 174
Organization of Memos 175

Forms of Memos 177
Standard Memos 177
Electronic Mail Memos 177
Technology: How E-Mail Is Changing World Communication 180
Kinds of Memos 181
Procedure and Information Memos 181
Career Skills: Avoiding Six Cardinal Sins in Writing Memos 182
Request and Reply Memos 183
Confirmation Memos 187
Checklist for Writing Direct Memos 187
Summary of Learning Goals 188
Review and Discussion Questions 189
Activities and Problems 189

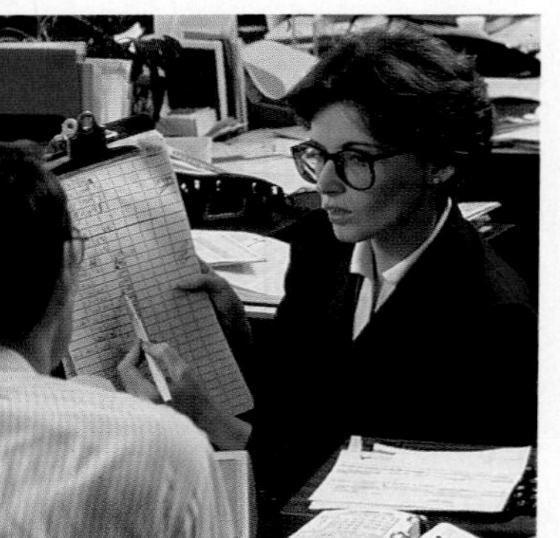

8 / Negative News 193

WordPerfect Corporation: Career Track Profile 194
Strategies for Breaking Bad News 196
Goals in Communicating Bad News 196
Using the Indirect Pattern to Prepare the Reader 196
Avoiding Three Causes of Legal Problems 196
Components of a Bad-News Message 198
When to Use the Direct Pattern 202
Applying the 3-×-3 Writing Process 202
Refusing Routine Requests 203
Rejecting Requests for Favors, Money, Information, and Action 203
Declining Invitations 204
Technology: Personalizing Form Letters 206
Checklist for Refusing Routine Requests 207
Sending Bad News to Customers 207
Handling Problems with Orders 208
Denying Claims 209
Refusing Credit 209
Checklist for Delivering Bad News to Customers 211
Managing Negative Organization News 212
Announcing Bad News to Employees 212
Saying No to Job Applicants 214
Checklist for Managing Negative Organization News 214
Cross Culture: Presenting Bad News in Other Cultures 215
Summary of Learning Goals 215
Review and Discussion Questions 216
Activities and Problems 217

9 / Persuasive and Sales Messages 225

Dean Witter Reynolds, Inc.: Career Track Profile 226
Strategies for Making Persuasive Requests 228
- Applying the 3-×-3 Writing Process to Persuasive Messages 228
- Blending the Components of a Persuasive Message 230

Career Skills: Seven Rules Every Persuader Should Know 232
- Being Persuasive but Ethical 234

Writing Successful Persuasive Requests 234
- Requesting Favors and Actions 235
- Persuading Within Organizations 237
- Requesting Adjustments and Making Claims 239

Checklist for Making Persuasive Requests 242
Planning and Composing Sales Messages 242
- Applying the 3-×-3 Writing Process to Sales Messages 242
- Crafting a Winning Sales Message 243

Checklist for Writing Sales Letters 248
Summary of Learning Goals 249
Review and Discussion Questions 249
Activities and Problems 250

10 / Goodwill and Special Messages 255

American Airlines: Career Track Profile 256
Goodwill Messages 256
- Suggestions for Writing Goodwill Messages 258
- Thanks 259
- Recognition 261
- Response 263
- Sympathy 263

Checklist for Writing Goodwill Messages 264
Special Business Messages 265
- Letters of Recommendation 265
- Performance Appraisals 269
- Warnings 269
- Operational Instructions 272

Ethics: Recognizing Sexual Harassment 273
- News Releases 274
- Announcements 274

Summary of Learning Goals 277
Review and Discussion Questions 278
Activities and Problems 279

PART IV REPORTS AND PROPOSALS 283

11 / Report Planning and Research 285

The Winters Group: Career Track Profile 286
Clarifying and Classifying Reports 288
Typical Business Reports 288
Functions of Reports 290
Direct and Indirect Patterns 290
Formats of Reports 291
Writing Style 296
Applying the 3-×-3 Writing Process to Reports 296
Analyzing the Problem and Purpose 297
Anticipating the Audience and Issues 299
Preparing a Work Plan 300
Researching Report Data 302
Locating Secondary Data 302
Generating Primary Data 305
Career Skills: Survey Sampling at a Glance 309
Documenting Data 310
Three Documentation Formats 310
Ethics: Avoiding Plagiarism and Using Quotations 311
Summary of Learning Goals 314
Review and Discussion Questions 314
Activities and Problems 315

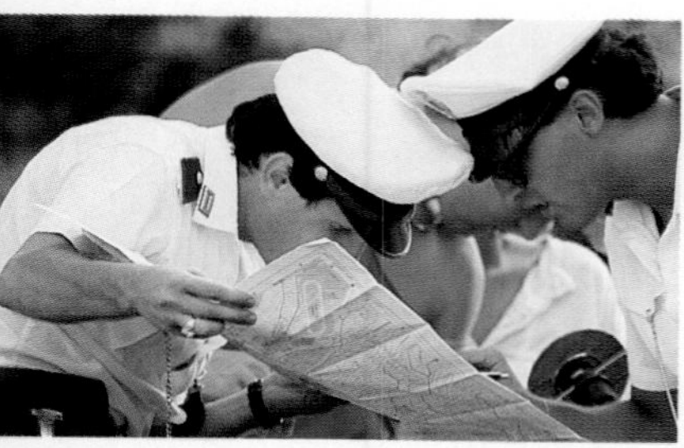

12 / Report Organization and Presentation 317

RAND: Career Track Profile 318
Interpreting Data 320
Tabulating and Analyzing Responses 320
Drawing Conclusions in Reports 325
Writing Report Recommendations 327
Organizing Data 328
Ordering Information Logically 329
Providing Reader Cues 330
Illustrating Data 334
Matching Visuals and Objectives 334
Technology: Using Your Computer to Produce Charts 337
Incorporating Visuals in Reports 341

Ethics: Making Ethical Charts and Graphics 342
Summary of Learning Goals 343
Review and Discussion Questions 344
Activities and Problems 345

13 / Typical Business Reports 347

Baltimore Orioles: Career Track Profile 348
Informational Reports 350
Periodic Reports 350
Situational Reports 352
Career Skills: Ten Tips for Designing Better Documents 356
Investigative Reports 357
Compliance Reports 357
Checklist for Writing Informational Reports 358
Analytical Reports 360
Justification/Recommendation Reports 360
Feasibility Reports 365
Yardstick Reports 368
Research Studies 369
Checklist for Writing Analytical Reports 372
Summary of Learning Goals 373
Review and Discussion Questions 374
Activities and Problems 374

14 / Proposals and Formal Reports 377

Hewlett-Packard: Career Track Profile 378
Preparing Formal and Informal Proposals 380
Components of Informal Proposals 380
Special Components of Formal Proposals 385
Checklist for Writing Proposals 386
Writing Formal Reports 387
Components of Formal Reports 387
Final Writing Tips 391
Putting It All Together 393
Checklist for Preparing Formal Reports 393
Summary of Learning Goals 408
Review and Discussion Questions 408
Activities and Problems 409

PART V  PRESENTATION SKILLS 421

15 / Speaking Skills 423

Walt Disney Imagineering: Career Track Profile 424
Oral Presentations 426
Preparing an Effective Oral Presentation 426
Organizing the Content 427
Career Skills: Nine Techniques for Gaining and Keeping Audience Attention 428
Planning Visual Aids and Handouts 431
Polishing Your Delivery 433
Career Skills: Stage Fright and the Fight-or-Flight Response 435
Adapting to International and Cross-Cultural Audiences 436
Ethics: The "Worst Deadly Sin" in a Presentation 437
Checklist for Preparing and Organizing Oral Presentations 438
Meeting and Conferences 439
Planning Meetings 439
Conducting Meetings 440
Participating in Meetings 441
Videoconferencing 441
Telephones and Voice Mail 442
Making Productive Telephone Calls 443
Receiving Productive Telephone Calls 444
Making the Best Use of Voice Mail 444
Summary of Learning Goals 445
Review and Discussion Questions 446
Activities and Problems 447

16 / Employment Messages 449

Residence Inn by Marriott: Career Track Profile 450
Preparing for Employment 452
Identifying Your Interests 452
Evaluating Your Qualifications 452
Choosing a Career Path 453
Searching the Job Market 454
Career Skills: Networking to Explore the Hidden Job Market 455
The Persuasive Résumé 456
Choosing a Résumé Style 456
Arranging the Parts 460
Applying the Final Touches 464
Ethics: Avoiding Writing an Unethical Résumé 465
Checklist for Writing a Persuasive Résumé 469

The Persuasive Letter of Application 470
Gaining Attention in the Opening 470
Building Interest in the Body 473
Motivating Action in the Closing 474
Final Tips 475
Checklist for Writing a Persuasive Letter of Application 475
Follow-up Letters and Other Employment Documents 476
Reference Request 476
Application Request Letter 477
Application or Résumé Follow-up Letter 477
Interview Follow-up Letter 477
Rejection Follow-up Letter 478
Application Form 478
Interviewing for Employment 479
Career Skills: Answering Ten Frequently Asked Interview Questions 480
Summary of Learning Goals 482
Review and Discussion Questions 483
Activities and Problems 483

Appendix A Competent Language Usage Essentials: A Business Communicator's Guide 487

Appendix B Document Formats 509

Appendix C Data Documentation 523

Appendix D Correction Symbols 531

Key to C.L.U.E. Exercises 535

Notes 539

Acknowledgments 545

Index 549

Preface

B*usiness Communication: Process and Product* introduces a unique teaching/learning package that solves a major problem for instructors and students today. It provides the atmosphere of an exciting real-life business environment for business communication—without sacrificing sound pedagogy. This means that students experience the enrichment of real people and real business situations while at the same time learning a hands-on process that they can carry with them to apply long after they leave the classroom.

Business Communication: Process and Product takes students inside some of the country's best-run and most respected organizations, such as Liz Claiborne, Ben & Jerry's, American Airlines, Bank of America, and Walt Disney Imagineering. More importantly, though, it balances this exposure with a well-developed and consistently applied process approach to communication. Students need more than real business settings in which to frame their learning. They need a process that outlines specific steps to follow in solving future communication problems, a tangible strategy they can apply in their careers. In addition to a process, we provide ample products of that process.

Features That Build Career Skills Quickly

Today's students know that they must have top-notch career skills to succeed in an increasingly competitive, diverse, and global business environment. This book includes numerous features that supply both process and product, the two keys to developing successful communication skills. Briefly described here, selected features are illustrated in the Visual Guide to the Book that follows.

3-×-3 writing process. This rational, comprehensive process outlines a plan that guides both oral and written composition. Developed in Chapters 3, 4, and 5, the process is then applied in all following chapters. Phase 1 includes analyzing, anticipating, and adapting. Phase 2 covers researching, organizing, and composing. Phase 3 presents revising, proofreading, and evaluating. In addition to explaining the writing process, these chapters teach basic writing techniques. They also provide plenty of reinforcement exercises, thus enabling students to develop facility with the working tools they will need on the job.

Career Track profiles. Each chapter begins with an interview of a front-line employee from a leading company. Personally conducted by the author, these interviews provide insights, tips, and, in many instances, role models for readers. Interviewees like Brian Finnegan at Lands' End and Renee Rodriguez at Sara Lee discuss their careers and supply practical advice for beginning business communicators. Because most interviewees are entry-level or mid-career employees and not CEOs or company presidents, readers can relate to their experiences and identify with them readily.

Process visualizers. Many model documents illustrate the 3-×-3 writing process in colorful graphics. Readers immediately see how the process relates to a specific letter, memo, or report. For today's visually oriented audiences, these process visualizers emphasize and demonstrate the most important part of the course—a strategy and basic pattern to follow in solving communication problems.

Career Track feature boxes. Twenty-eight colorful boxes discuss topics in four areas: ethics, cross-cultural issues, technology, and career skills. These enrichment boxes keep readers current with fast-paced articles providing career tips, communication strategies, and stimulating insights on current issues.

Spotlight on Communicators. Every chapter contains pictures of one or more professional and business leaders (such as Lee Iacocca, Bill Marriott, and Justice Sandra Day O'Connor) who comment on relevant communication strategies that helped them succeed.

Integration of ethics and cross-cultural issues. Instead of treating these topics in separate chapters or in appendixes, we introduce ethics and cross-cultural issues early and in all relevant chapters thereafter. Each chapter also includes one or more ethical questions to stimulate discussion and focus attention.

C.L.U.E.: Competent Language Usage Essentials. Students can review and reinforce grammar and language principles by using the C.L.U.E. program. This business writer's handbook contains 50 of the most used and abused writing concepts, along with frequently misspelled and misused words. Students can complete the diagnostic test and learning exercises independently. Instructors can also use the C.L.U.E. exercises at the ends of Chapters 1 through 10 for class instruction and review.

Complete but concise coverage. In just 16 succinct chapters (instead of 18 to 24 in other books), all the traditional business communication topics are covered. Additionally, students will find career communication extras like how to write performance appraisals, employee warnings, and letters of recommendation.

Powerful employment chapter. Practical and up-to-date model résumés, letters of application, and job-search suggestions led reviewer after reviewer to commend Chapter 16. Two veteran business communication professors said that this chapter was among the best they had ever seen in any textbook.

Efficient report treatment. In only four chapters, we present comprehensive report-writing techniques and fully formatted reports. Moreover, our long analytical report illustrates a real campus problem in which college students collect data, analyze solutions, draw conclusions, and make recommendations. Instead of a corporate problem far beyond the experience of students, this book shows a realistic problem typical of student research.

Textual Aids That Promote Learning and Retention

The message of this book centers on both process and product. To deliver that message most effectively to readers, we introduce a unique pedagogical program featuring **visualization.** More than ever, today's sophisticated audiences respond to visual cues. Moreover, visualization is an important part of learning theory, helping readers understand and retain concepts. Therefore, the following textual aids contain many elements that involve showing as well as telling:

- Dozens of fully formatted memos, letters, reports, résumés, and other documents
- Targeted annotations on model documents that direct the eye to specific strategies, applications, and examples (instead of unfocused marginal comments)
- Numerous bulleted items highlighting important concepts in the text
- Colorful graphics to emphasize important strategies, such as the components of a persuasive message
- Tips boxes to spotlight and summarize practical, "how-to" advice
- Over 100 color photos with provocative images and relevant captions
- Draft documents to stimulate discussion and provide revision practice
- Checklists that capsulize relevant concepts for rapid review
- Lively end-of-chapter activities with a variety of short and long cases and at least one collaborative problem for each chapter
- Up-to-date advice on communication technology and software so that students know what to expect in today's offices and how to best use current tools
- Learning goals coordinated with chapter summaries so that students can check their comprehension

Instructional Resources That Facilitate Dynamic Teaching

A rich variety of instructional resources supplement and support the book, giving every instructor working tools to create a dynamic, exciting, and effective course.

Instructor's resource manual. This helpful guide includes model course schedules, sample syllabi, teaching ideas, classroom management techniques, focus for chapter lectures, chapter outlines, answers for chapter review questions, suggested responses for discussion questions, and ideas for using chapter activities.

Student study guide. Promoting success in the course and in future careers, this hands-on study guide provides students with a variety of exercises and sample test questions that review chapter concepts and key terms. The study guide also helps students enrich their vocabularies, master frequently misspelled words, and develop language competency with bonus C.L.U.E. exercises. Nearly all exercises are self-checked so that students receive immediate feedback.

Test item file and software. Instructors may generate their own tests from a test-item file containing 50 questions for each chapter. These questions include true-false, multiple choice, and fill-in items. Questions are available in hard-copy test banks as well as on disks for either DOS or Macintosh environments.

Videotapes. Specially filmed to supplement the book, this set of five videotapes introduces each book part: communication foundations, the process of writing, letters and memos, reports and proposals, and presentation skills. Adopters may order these videotapes by calling their Wadsworth sales representatives.

Transparency acetates and masters. Written by the author, approximately 170 acetates and masters summarize, supplement, and highlight course concepts. One-, two-, and four-color acetates include text figures and lecture enrichment material. Additional transparency masters contain lecture outlines for every chapter and solutions to key problems. This complete package, one of the best transparency instructional programs in the field, is free to adopters.

Business communication newsletter and free teaching materials. All instructors adopting the book will receive a free subscription to the author's business communication newsletter published twice yearly. In addition to highlighting current issues and news of interest in the business communication course, the newsletter announces various free teaching materials that may be ordered directly from the author. These materials include items such as sample syllabi from professors across the country, extra case problems and solutions, certificates of achievement to be awarded to students, transparency teaching units, and many other helpful classroom materials.

Appreciation for Assistance

Probably no other new book has had a greater level of professional support in its development than has *Business Communication: Process and Product.* I am deeply grateful to the reviewers and other experts, listed on the next page, who contributed their pedagogic and academic expertise in shaping the book's final form.

In addition to these friends and colleagues, I sincerely thank the many professionals at Wadsworth for their invaluable assistance in publishing this state-of-the-art book. In particular, I would like to single out Larry Alexander, Kathy Shields, Carolyn Deacy, Kelly Murphy, Joy Westberg, Debbie Dennis, and especially Debbie Cogan, my caring and careful production editor. I also commend Tom Briggs, Lorraine Korkosz, Ron Lear, Bobbie Broyer, and Laurel Anderson for their editing, research, and proofreading assistance.

My heartfelt appreciation goes to Rolf Janke for launching this project four years ago; to Mark Palmer for contributing perceptive development ideas; to Marilyn Lammers, California State University, Northridge, for developing the test bank, composing the guide to electronic revision, and making other valuable contributions; and to Dr. Janet Adams, Mankato State University, for working with me to construct an exciting Instructor's Resource Guide.

Finally, I express my profound gratitude to my husband, Dr. George R. Guffey, Department of English, University of California, Los Angeles, for supplying love, strength, and wisdom.

Mary Ellen Guffey

Acknowledgments

I am grateful to the following professors who reviewed the manuscript or contributed other valuable information and support for this project:

Leslie Adams, Houston Baptist University
Virginia Allen, Joliet Junior College
Kehinde A. Adesina, Contra Costa College
Cynthia Anderson, Youngstown State University
Vanessa D. Arnold, University of Mississippi
Lois J. Bachman, Community College of Philadelphia
Rebecca Barksdale, University of Central Florida
Sandra Berill, Arkansas State University
Martha E. Bradshaw, Southeastern Louisiana University
Bernadine Branchaw, Western Michigan University
James F. Carey, Onondaga Community College
Randy E. Cone, University of New Orleans
James Conley, Eastern Michigan University
Jane G. Corbly, Sinclair Community College
Martha Cross, Delta State University
Linda Cunningham, Salt Lake Community College
Bertha Dee-Babcock, University of San Francisco
Dorothy Drayton, Texas Southern University
Margaret Erthal, Southern Illinois University at Edwardsville
Kerry J. Gambrill, Florida Community College
Judith L. Graham, Holyoke Community College
David Hamilton, Bemidji State University
Paul Hegele, Elgin Community College
Rovena L. Hillsman, California State University, Sacramento
Warren B. Humphrey, University of Central Florida
Edna Jellesed, Lane Community College
Diana K. Kanoy, Central Florida Community College
G. Scott King, Sinclair Community College
Suzanne P. Krissler, Orange County Community College
Linda L. Labin, Husson College
Suzanne Lambert, Broward Community College South
Marilyn L. Lammers, California State University, Northridge
Joyce N. Larsen, Front Range Community College
Barbara Lea, West Valley College
Sonia Maasik, University of California, Los Angeles
Bruce MacBeth, Clarion University of Pennsylvania
Diana S. McKowen, Indiana University at Bloomington
Maureen L. Margolies, University of Cincinnati, Raymond Walters College
Mary C. Miller, Ashland University
Nancy B. Moody, Sinclair Community College
Lin Nassar, Oakland Community College
Beverly H. Nelson, University of New Orleans
John P. Nightingale, Eastern Michigan University
Alexa B. North, Georgia State University
Rosemary Olds, Des Moines Area Community College
James S. O'Rourke IV, University of Notre Dame
Pamela A. Patey, Riverside Community College
Joan Policano, Onondaga Community College
Paula J. Pomerenke, Illinois State University
Karen Sterkel Powell, Colorado State University
Gloria Power, Delgado Community College
Richard G. Raspen, Wilkes University
Virginia L. Reynolds, Cleveland State University
Ruth D. Richardson, University of North Alabama
Terry D. Roach, Arkansas State University, Jonesboro
Linda Sarlo, Rock Valley College
Chris Saxild, Mt. Senario College
Joseph Schaffner, State University of New York at Alfred
Marilyn Simonson, Lakewood Community College
Charles L. Snowden, Sinclair Community College
Gayle A. Sobolik, California State University, Fresno
Ted D. Stoddard, Brigham Young University
Leslie S. Talley, University of Central Florida
Barbara P. Thompson, Columbus State Community College
Mary L. Tucker, Colorado State University
Doris A. Van Horn Christopher, California State University, Los Angeles
David Victor, Eastern Michigan University
John L. Waltman, Eastern Michigan University
Carol M. Williams, Pima County Community College District
Jane D. Williams, J. Sargeant Reynolds Community College
Rosemary B. Wilson, Washtenaw Community College
Beverly C. Wise, State University of New York at Morrisville
William E. Worth, Georgia State University

A Visual Guide to the Book

In successful business communication, process and product are closely related. This book presents a consistent, logical process approach that you can apply to solve communication problems and create successful communication products—both written and oral. And the manner of presentation is innovative. Author Mary Ellen Guffey introduces unique visualization techniques to involve you *actively* in learning communication skills and applying them effectively. In addition to state-of-the-art graphics, you'll find model documents and inside tips from some of the country's best-run and most-respected organizations.

Process is a strategy developed early and applied consistently throughout the book. Easy-to-follow models translate theory into concrete visuals so that you can see the process in action and apply it yourself. You'll learn to analyze a problem, organize your ideas logically, and express your ideas correctly and persuasively. **Product** represents the wide range of communication skills and applications today's successful business people must have at their command. Both process and product are presented visually for quick comprehension and lasting retention.

Chances to learn from the best—in the form of model documents—appear in every chapter. Among them are résumés that work for job hunters, memos that monitor operations and gain support, business letters that satisfy customers and deliver information, and reports that analyze problems and offer solutions.

On the next seven pages, you will find specific features of the book that will help you learn the essentials of successful business communication by mastering the principles, applying them consistently, and visualizing yourself as an effective business communicator.

EMPHASIS ON PROCESS VISUALIZATION

The 3-×-3 process, a practical and helpful approach to written and oral communication, is developed fully and applied consistently. With the book's strong graphics to guide you, you'll understand and remember this multi-stage process of *analyzing-anticipating-adapting, researching-organizing-composing,* and *revising-proofreading-evalulating.* After detailed discussion of each of these nine steps (in Chapters 3, 4, and 5), the 3-×-3 process is then applied to create communication products in all the chapters that follow. **Process visualizers** are colorful graphics that summarize the writing process and show how to apply it in solving specific problems. By consistent repetition and application of the process, you will learn and retain an invaluable problem-solving strategy you can take with you and use every day in your future career. Visualizing makes the process easy to understand and easy to remember.

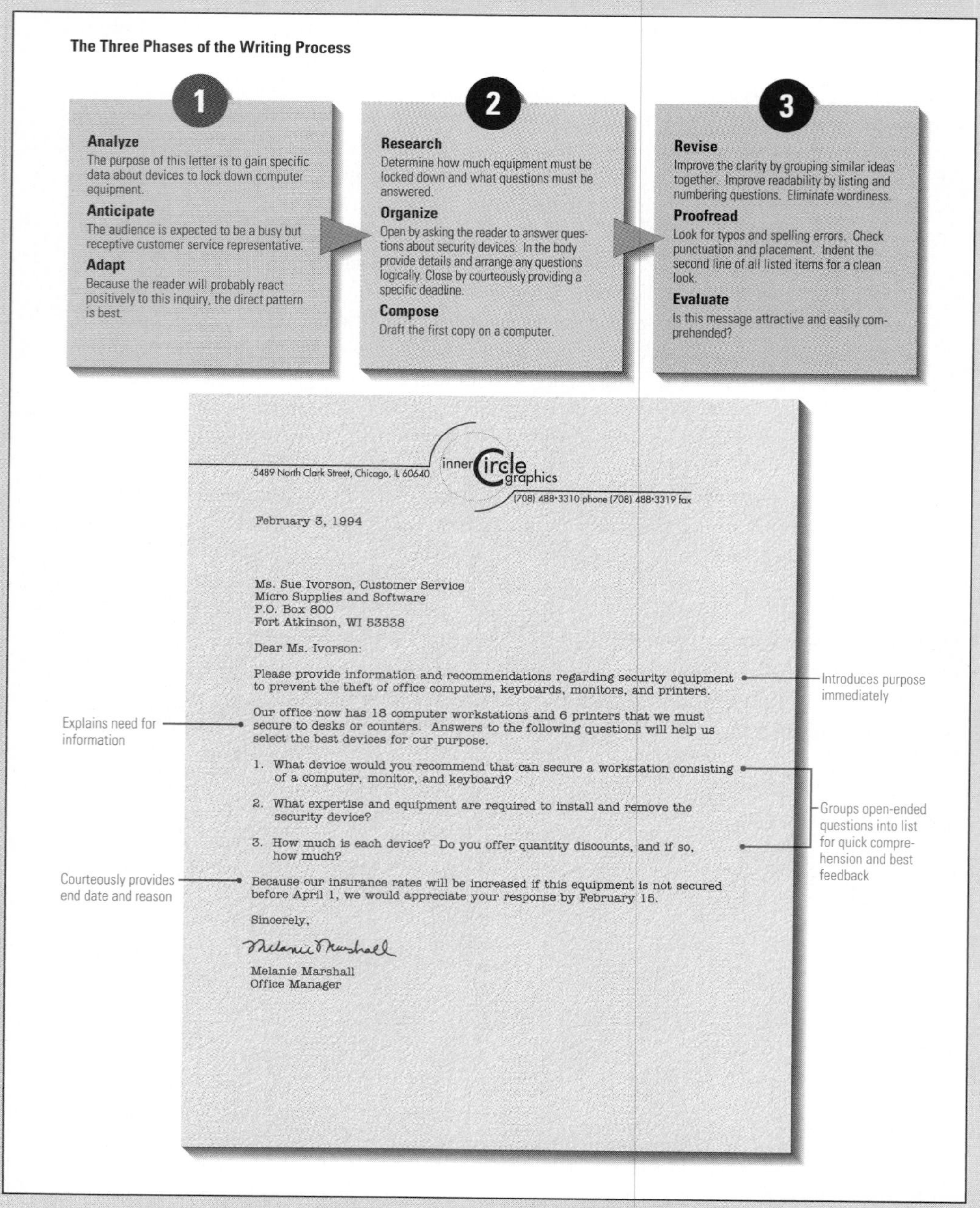

The Three Phases of the Writing Process
1
Analyze
The purpose of this letter is to gain specific data about devices to lock down computer equipment.
Anticipate
The audience is expected to be a busy but receptive customer service representative.
Adapt
Because the reader will probably react positively to this inquiry, the direct pattern is best.
2
Research
Determine how much equipment must be locked down and what questions must be answered.
Organize
Open by asking the reader to answer questions about security devices. In the body provide details and arrange any questions logically. Close by courteously providing a specific deadline.
Compose
Draft the first copy on a computer.
3
Revise
Improve the clarity by grouping similar ideas together. Improve readability by listing and numbering questions. Eliminate wordiness.
Proofread
Look for typos and spelling errors. Check punctuation and placement. Indent the second line of all listed items for a clean look.
Evaluate
Is this message attractive and easily comprehended?
inner circle graphics
5489 North Clark Street, Chicago, IL 60640
(708) 488-3310 phone (708) 488-3319 fax
Introduces purpose immediately
Explains need for information
Groups open-ended questions into list for quick comprehension and best feedback
Courteously provides end date and reason

February 3, 1994

Ms. Sue Ivorson, Customer Service
Micro Supplies and Software
P.O. Box 800
Fort Atkinson, WI 53538

Dear Ms. Ivorson:

Please provide information and recommendations regarding security equipment to prevent the theft of office computers, keyboards, monitors, and printers.

Our office now has 18 computer workstations and 6 printers that we must secure to desks or counters. Answers to the following questions will help us select the best devices for our purpose.

1. What device would you recommend that can secure a workstation consisting of a computer, monitor, and keyboard?
2. What expertise and equipment are required to install and remove the security device?
3. How much is each device? Do you offer quantity discounts, and if so, how much?

Because our insurance rates will be increased if this equipment is not secured before April 1, we would appreciate your response by February 15.

Sincerely,

Melanie Marshall

Melanie Marshall
Office Manager

ROLE MODELS AND RELEVANCE FOR CAREER SUCCESS

Career track profiles—in-depth interviews with successful business communicators—open each chapter. Since most of those profiled are front-line employees in entry-level or mid-career positions, you can relate to their "in-the-trenches" experiences easily. These interviewees discuss their careers and employers, offering practical advice that directly relates to the material covered in the chapter. As you discover how strong communication skills helped these communicators move into rewarding and often unexpected new careers, you can look to the profiles to inspire you and serve as role models for your own career track ascent.

People Magazine: Career Track Profile

Irreverent, informative, and always absorbing, *People* is one of the nation's favorite magazines. Celebrating its twentieth birthday, it ranks first among American magazines in advertising revenues, second in newsstand sales (behind *TV Guide*), and third in total readership, with 29 million readers.

People almost single-handedly elevated the concept of "personality" journalism—stories focusing on people and their behavior—into a legitimate and even essential part of American reporting. Nearly all consumer publications today feel the influence of *People* in their stories, sections, and columns. Unquestionably, what really interests people is other people. And it took *People* magazine to recognize this truth and capitalize on it.

"Readers don't have time for anything long or wordy in this busy, short-attention world. . . . Any writing that goes past one page had better be really important."

But no publication preserves the top spot year after year without delivering more than pictures and stories about people. Among insiders *People* reigns as queen of the "written" magazines. This means that every story is researched, written, checked, rewritten, rechecked, and revised by multiple levels of reporters, writers, editors, fact-checkers, copyeditors, and proofreaders. Editors boil down long files originally submitted by reporters into tightly written, fact-filled, fast-moving but concise articles. The multistage revision process results in finely polished, meaty writing. Not a word is wasted.

Associate editor Louise Lague is one of *People*'s expert writers who make every word count. She says her writing must be very concise, with many facts packed into every sentence. Although she was always interested in writing, she did not train to be a journalist. Louise graduated from Georgetown University in Washington, D.C. In her senior year recruiters asked what she had studied. When she replied, "French, Spanish, English, theology, philosophy, and history," they said, "What? No economics? No marketing? You're unfit for anything!" Three months later she found a job as a reporter and worked her way from newspapers to *People.*

In writing her stories, she always keeps the audience in mind. *People*'s readership about evenly divided between men and women, ave
She considers her readers sophisticated but
meaning must be comprehensible. Even short
if arranged cleverly and with wit. It doesn't
Louise's stories have to be readable and make
Prince Charles, Di, and the other royals, but no

Career track feature boxes—28 in all—keep you current with topics relevant to career success. These boxes provide communication strategies, career tips, and up-to-date information about effective business communication. Each box contains a **Career Track Application** that challenges you to apply what you have just learned so that you can be immediately productive on the job.

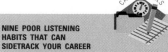

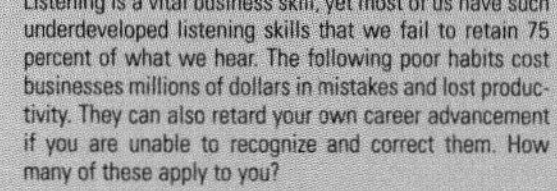

NINE POOR LISTENING HABITS THAT CAN SIDETRACK YOUR CAREER

Listening is a vital business skill, yet most of us have such underdeveloped listening skills that we fail to retain 75 percent of what we hear. The following poor habits cost businesses millions of dollars in mistakes and lost productivity. They can also retard your own career advancement if you are unable to recognize and correct them. How many of these apply to you?

- **Reacting to the speaker's appearance and speech mannerisms.** It's easy to be distracted by a speaker's looks, attire, age, or handicaps. Poor listeners refuse to make the effort to overcome personal biases that block objective reception.
- **Failing to control distractions.** Some listeners yield easily to external and internal distractions. They fail to control or block out surrounding noises, or they fail to resist thoughts that interfere with listening concentration.
- **Listening to evaluate rather than to understand.** Too often we listen only to determine if the speaker's ideas fit our frame of reference and beliefs. Listening for immediate evaluation interferes with hearing and understanding the speaker's ideas.
- **Daydreaming and pretending to listen.** We all know how to fix our gaze and look intently at the speaker while hearing nothing being said. This pseudolistening is one of the most serious of the bad listening habits.
- **Assuming the speaker wants input or advice.** Some listeners feel compelled to interrupt a speaker with comments like "Well, here's what I think about it" or "What you ought to do is . . ." Unless the speaker requests it, keep your advice to yourself.
- **Avoiding listening to anything difficult.** Many listeners prefer light, recreational listening. They automatically tune out heavy-duty topics. In doing so, they deprive themselves of the opportunity to learn something new and to develop listening techniques for coping with complex issues.
- **Waiting to jump in and grab the limelight.** Too many listeners are uncomfortable in the role; they much prefer to be speaking. The result? They fail to concentrate on what's being said, but instead are mentally preparing their next comments to be interjected at the first pause.
- **Pretending to understand.** Fear of appearing stupid, impolite, or uninformed may cause us to nod our heads in agreement when we don't really understand. Equally bad is presuming we already know what the speaker means, perhaps because we are familiar with the topic. In either case always ask clarifying questions to ensure that you understand.
- **Listening for facts only.** Failing to observe nonverbal cues can be crucial in one-to-one conversations. Poor listeners fail to pick up on voice intonation, eye movement, and body language. These cues help skillful listeners detect subtle meanings.

Career Track Application

During the next week complete two activities aimed at improving your listening skills. First, conduct a reality check. Ask your closest friends and family to evaluate your listening skills. And be grateful for their honest feedback! Second, evaluate your conversational style using the "50/50" rule. Do you listen 50 percent of the time?

rally occurs when the listener is waiting for the speaker's next idea. A final technique for improving retention is selective note-taking. Good listeners jot down key points, especially if they know they will be responsible for the information later. As Andrea Ciriello puts it, "Taking notes is a must."

Improving Your Listening Effectiveness

Positive attitude, involvement, openness, and retention are key factors that influence effective listening, but people who want to improve their listening skills usually need pointers or specific techniques. The following checklist provides tips to

Chapter 2
Listening and
Intercultural Communication
37

LEARNING FROM LEADERS

A who's who of business communication success is provided by Bank of America, Ben & Jerry's, Lands' End, Sara Lee, *People* Magazine, WordPerfect, American Airlines, the Baltimore Orioles, and other well-known companies and organizations who have contributed actual documents and inside information about their communication strategies to this book. What better way to see the connection between theory and practice? This inside look at real-world solutions to problems—as well as exposure to the kinds of documents that result—guarantees you interesting reading and realistic, insightful learning.

FIGURE 3.3 ● **Successful Customer Response Letter**

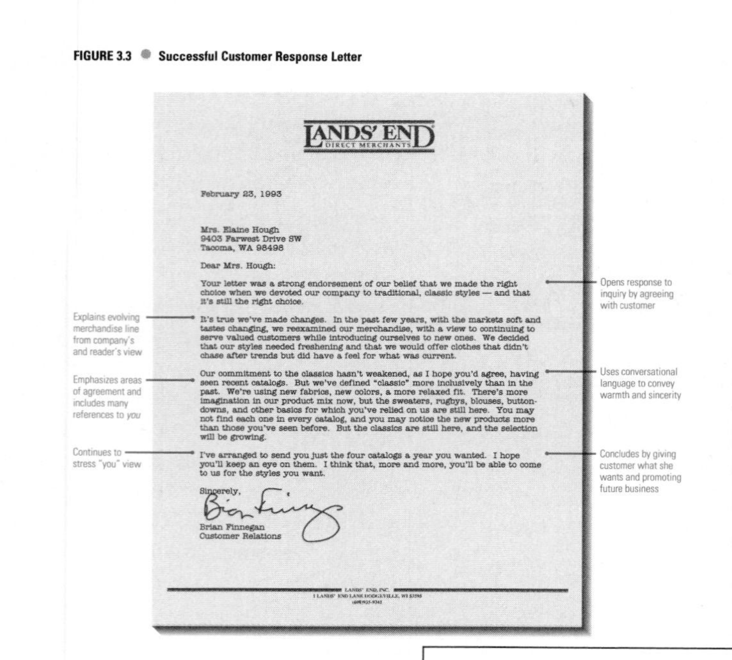

LANDS' END
DIRECT MERCHANTS

February 23, 1993

Mrs. Elaine Hough
9403 Farwest Drive SW
Tacoma, WA 98498

Dear Mrs. Hough:

Your letter was a strong endorsement of our belief that we made the right choice when we devoted our company to traditional, classic styles — and that it's still the right choice.

It's true we've made changes. In the past few years, with the markets soft and tastes changing, we reexamined our merchandise, with a view to continuing to serve valued customers while introducing ourselves to new ones. We decided that our styles needed freshening and that we would offer clothes that didn't chase after trends but did have a feel for what was current.

Our commitment to the classics hasn't weakened, as I hope you'd agree, having seen recent catalogs. But we've defined "classic" more inclusively than in the past. We're using new fabrics, new colors, a more relaxed fit. There's more imagination in our product mix now, but the sweaters, rugbys, blouses, button-downs, and other basics for which you've relied on us are still here. You may not find each one in every catalog, and you may notice the new products more than those you've seen before. But the classics are still here, and the selection will be growing.

I've arranged to send you just the four catalogs a year you wanted. I hope you'll keep an eye on them. I think that, more and more, you'll be able to come to us for the styles you want.

Sincerely,

Brian Finnegan
Customer Relations

"I/We" View	"You" View
I have scheduled your vacation to begin May 1.	You may begin your vacati
We have shipped your order by UPS, and we are sure it will arrive in time for the sales promotion January 15.	Your order will be delivere time for your sales promot
I'm asking all our employees to respond to the attached survey regarding working conditions.	Because your ideas count, the attached survey regard conditions.

FIGURE 6.7 ● **Adjustment Letter**

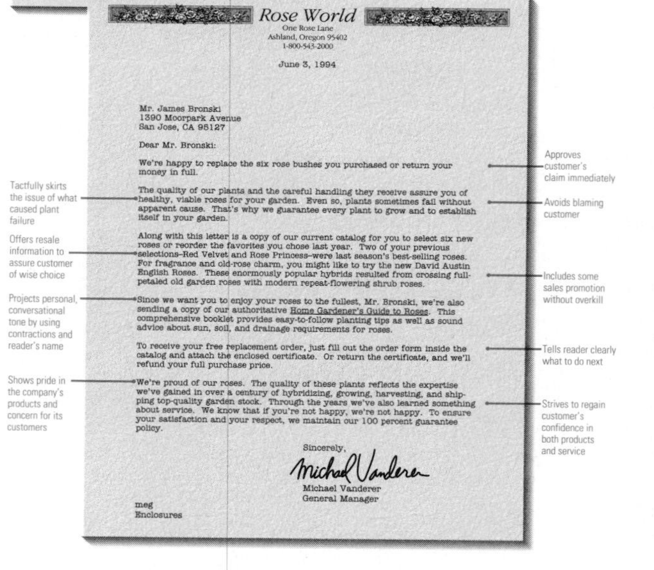

Tips for Letter Formatting

- Single-space business letters. Double-space between paragraphs.
- Place the date on line 13 or 2 lines below letterhead.
- Set margins so that letter looks centered on page.
- Leave three blank lines for the handwritten signature.
- Use a colon after the salutation and a comma after the complimentary close.
- Be consistent in letter format. For example, use full block with all lines starting at the left margin or modified block as shown here.

Rose World
One Rose Lane
Ashland, Oregon 95402
1-800-543-2000

June 3, 1994

Mr. James Bronski
1390 Moorpark Avenue
San Jose, CA 95127

Dear Mr. Bronski:

We're happy to replace the six rose bushes you purchased or return your money in full.

The quality of our plants and the careful handling they receive assure you of healthy, viable roses for your garden. Even so, plants sometimes fail without apparent cause. That's why we guarantee every plant to grow and to establish itself in your garden.

Along with this letter is a copy of our current catalog for you to select six new roses or reorder the favorites you chose last year. Two of your previous selections–Red Velvet and Rose Princess–were last season's best-selling roses. For fragrance and old-rose charm, you might like to try the new David Austin English Roses. These enormously popular hybrids resulted from crossing full-petaled old garden roses with modern repeat-flowering shrub roses.

Since we want you to enjoy your roses to the fullest, Mr. Bronski, we're also sending a copy of our authoritative Home Gardener's Guide to Roses. This comprehensive booklet provides easy-to-follow planting tips as well as sound advice about sun, soil, and drainage requirements for roses.

To receive your free replacement order, just fill out the order form inside the catalog and attach the enclosed certificate. Or return the certificate, and we'll refund your full purchase price.

We're proud of our roses. The quality of these plants reflects the expertise we've gained in over a century of hybridizing, growing, harvesting, and shipping top-quality garden stock. Through the years we've also learned something about service. We know that if you're not happy, we're not happy. To ensure your satisfaction and your respect, we maintain our 100 percent guarantee policy.

Sincerely,

Michael Vanderer
General Manager

meg
Enclosures

Sophisticated visualization techniques reinforce your understanding of the principles involved. Colorful pointers on the letters, memos, and reports lead to concise annotations that point out communication strategies and applications of theory. In addition, helpful **Tips** boxes appear with many of the documents, spotlighting and summarizing key procedures. These concise Tips boxes supply you with a valuable reference resource when you are on the job and need fast answers.

COMMUNICATION IN MANY FORMS

As a business communicator, you must be able to direct messages in different formats to diverse audiences. This book goes beyond traditional topics to provide **strategic coverage** in several crucial areas:

A full chapter is devoted to **memos,** the most commonly written business document. Examples include information, procedure, request, reply, and confirmation memos—plus an extensive discussion of electronic memos.

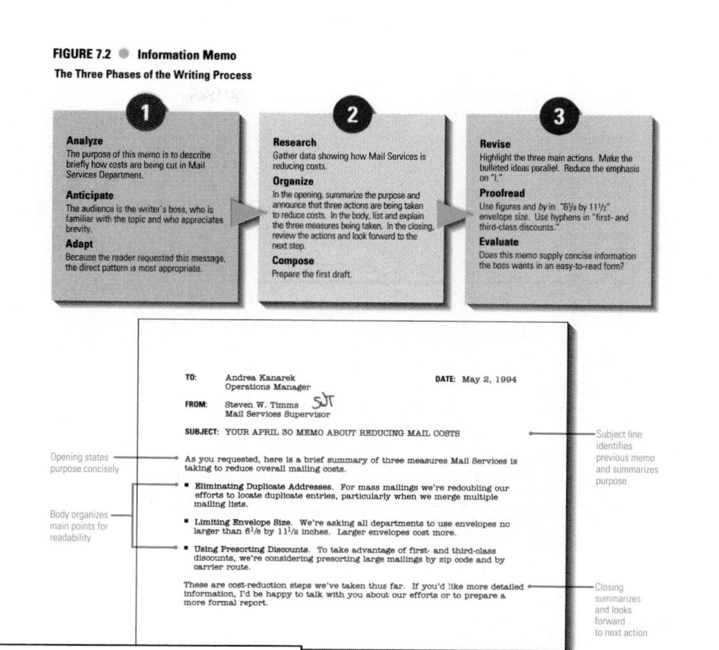

FIGURE 7.2 ● Information Memo

The Three Phases of the Writing Process

1
Analyze
The purpose of this memo is to describe briefly how costs are being cut in Mail Services Department.
Anticipate
The audience is the writer's boss, who is familiar with the topic and who appreciates brevity.
Adapt
Because the reader requested this message, the direct pattern is most appropriate.
2
Research
Gather data showing how Mail Services is reducing costs.
Organize
In the opening, summarize the purpose and announce that three actions are being taken to reduce costs. In the body, list and explain the three measures being taken. In the closing, review the actions and look forward to the next step.
Compose
Prepare the first draft.
3
Revise
Highlight the three main actions. Make the bulleted ideas parallel. Reduce the emphasis on "I."
Proofread
Use figures and *by* in "6⅛ by 11½" envelope size. Use hyphens in "first- and third-class discounts."
Evaluate
Does this memo supply concise information the boss wants in an easy-to-read form?

TO: Andrea Kanarek
Operations Manager

DATE: May 2, 1994

FROM: Steven W. Timms SWT
Mail Services Supervisor

SUBJECT: YOUR APRIL 30 MEMO ABOUT REDUCING MAIL COSTS

As you requested, here is a brief summary of three measures Mail Services is taking to reduce overall mailing costs.

- **Eliminating Duplicate Addresses.** For mass mailings we're redoubling our efforts to locate duplicate entries, particularly when we merge multiple mailing lists.
- **Limiting Envelope Size.** We're asking all departments to use envelopes no larger than 6⅛ by 11½ inches. Larger envelopes cost more.
- **Using Presorting Discounts.** To take advantage of first- and third-class discounts, we're considering presorting large mailings by zip code and by carrier route.

These are cost-reduction steps we've taken thus far. If you'd like more detailed information, I'd be happy to talk with you about our efforts or to prepare a more formal report.

Subject line identifies previous memo and summarizes purpose
Opening states purpose concisely
Body organizes main points for readability
Closing summarizes and looks forward to next action

nother computer—whether to the next desk or halfway around
s stored in the recipient's mailbox until accessed. These messages
dited, stored, deleted, or forwarded—and all without paper!
ica's organizations, communication by E-mail (called "messaging"
ou 'message' me?") is growing exponentially. The accompanying
discusses the reasons for its success and its effect on global

-mail is most effective in delivering simple messages; complex
bly be sent in hard-copy documents. As the technology improves,

FIGURE 16.7 ● Chronological Résumé

Although Jeffrey had little paid work experience off campus, his résumé looks impressive because of his relevant summer, campus, and extern experiences. He describes specific achievements related to finance, his career goal.

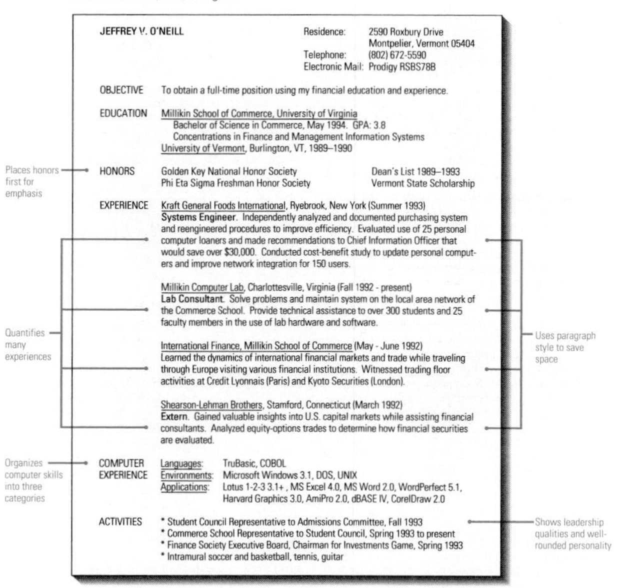

JEFFREY V. O'NEILL

Residence: 2590 Roxbury Drive
Montpelier, Vermont 05404
Telephone: (802) 672-5590
Electronic Mail: Prodigy RSBS78B

OBJECTIVE To obtain a full-time position using my financial education and experience.

EDUCATION Millikin School of Commerce, University of Virginia
Bachelor of Science in Commerce, May 1994. GPA: 3.8
Concentrations in Finance and Management Information Systems
University of Vermont, Burlington, VT, 1989–1990

HONORS Golden Key National Honor Society — Dean's List 1989–1993
Phi Eta Sigma Freshman Honor Society — Vermont State Scholarship

EXPERIENCE Kraft General Foods International, Ryebrook, New York (Summer 1993)
Systems Engineer. Independently analyzed and documented purchasing system and reengineered procedures to improve efficiency. Evaluated use of 25 personal computer loaners and made recommendations to Chief Information Officer that would save over $30,000. Conducted cost-benefit study to update personal computers and improve network integration for 150 users.

Millikin Computer Lab, Charlottesville, Virginia (Fall 1992 - present)
Lab Consultant. Solve problems and maintain system on the local area network of the Commerce School. Provide technical assistance to over 300 students and 25 faculty members in the use of lab hardware and software.

International Finance, Millikin School of Commerce (May - June 1992)
Learned the dynamics of international financial markets and trade while traveling through Europe visiting various financial institutions. Witnessed trading floor activities at Credit Lyonnais (Paris) and Kyoto Securities (London).

Shearson-Lehman Brothers, Stamford, Connecticut (March 1992)
Extern. Gained valuable insights into U.S. capital markets while assisting financial consultants. Analyzed equity-options trades to determine how financial securities are evaluated.

COMPUTER EXPERIENCE
Languages: TruBasic, COBOL
Environments: Microsoft Windows 3.1, DOS, UNIX
Applications: Lotus 1-2-3 3.1+ , MS Excel 4.0, MS Word 2.0, WordPerfect 5.1, Harvard Graphics 3.0, AmiPro 2.0, dBASE IV, CorelDraw 2.0

ACTIVITIES
* Student Council Representative to Admissions Committee, Fall 1993
* Commerce School Representative to Student Council, Spring 1993 to present
* Finance Society Executive Board, Chairman for Investments Game, Spring 1993
* Intramural soccer and basketball, tennis, guitar

Places honors first for emphasis
Quantifies many experiences
Organizes computer skills into three categories
Uses paragraph style to save space
Shows leadership qualities and well-rounded personality

the personal pronoun *I*. The abbreviated, objective style of a résumé precludes the use of personal pronouns. Use white, off-white, or buff-colored heavy bond paper (24-pound) and a first-rate printer.

After revising, proofread, proofread, and proofread again: for spelling and mechanics, for content, and for format. Then, have a knowledgeable friend or relative proofread it again. This is one document that must be perfect.

Finally, be sure to write your résumé yourself because no one knows you as well as you. Don't delegate the task to a résumé-writing service. Such services tend

A powerful employment communication chapter contains on-target advice for job-hunting, along with twice the number of model **résumés** found in other leading texts. And all model résumés are fully annotated.

Comprehensive, yet concise, material on **report-writing** is included, with 15 excellent, fully annotated models of reports and proposals. This book contains nearly three times as many complete and fully formatted reports as other leading texts.

Personnel communication is covered, including **performance appraisals,** which are increasingly important in business today. Employee warnings and operational instructions are also illustrated.

ETHICAL AND CROSS-CULTURAL CONSIDERATIONS

To help you recognize and apply ethical principles and intercultural sensitivity in all communication settings, Dr. Guffey integrates these concepts throughout the book. This integrative approach puts ethical conduct and cross-cultural tolerance in context, rather than isolating these increasingly important considerations from the reality of day-to-day business interactions. Discussion appears in the text wherever relevant, along with **Ethics** and **Cross-Culture boxes.** An **"Ethical Issues" question** for class discussion also appears in every chapter.

FOUR ETHICAL GUIDELINES BUSINESS COMMUNICATORS SHOULD KNOW

Pressures on people and on organizations today can create dilemmas that require, in addition to communication skills, an ability to make ethical decisions. Often, the dilemmas have no clear-cut right or wrong answers.

Assume that Carolyn Song and you are competing for a promotion to regional manager in Orlando, Florida. In the past year Carolyn has been quite successful at her work. Although you acknowledge that Carolyn is doing a good job, you have been with the company longer and believe you deserve the position. Moreover, you feel threatened by her; and frankly, you don't like her personally. This promotion is important to you not only professionally but personally: your elderly parents live in the Orlando area, and you want to be close by to help them out.

One day you happen to meet an old friend who has known Carolyn for some time. Over a cup of coffee you learn that Carolyn never graduated from the University of Texas, as stated on her résumé. In fact, she never attended college at all.

What should you do? Say nothing and, in effect, allow Carolyn to be rewarded for lying? Head straight to the vice president and expose the truth—which might, at the same time, conveniently eliminate a rival? Each action has potential consequences that make the decision difficult. Frequently, say ethicists, the "right" action is the one you can live with. But how do you arrive at that decision? Here are four simple guidelines that can help any business communicator make ethical choices:

- **Visualize the desired outcome.** What would you like to see happen as a result of resolving this issue? Will your choice produce the goal you seek?
- **Weigh the interests of all stakeholders.** Who will be affected by your choice? Consider the consequences for you, your fellow employees, your boss, the organization, your family, and the community. What effect will it have on Carolyn? Can you live with the consequences? Whose interests are most important?
- **Take the public-scrutiny test.** How would you feel about revealing your choice to your colleagues, friends, or spouse?
- **Balance your professional and personal goals.** Consider each choice and its effect on your career. Also consider its personal effects. Is there a choice that reconciles your professional goals with your personal values?

Career Track Application

Determine three or four actions you could take regarding Carolyn's dark secret. Then, evaluate each choice according to the four guidelines here. Be prepared to discuss your final choice and the reasoning behind it in class. Additional ethical guidelines will be presented in Chapter 3.

next day.[28] At Bank of America the CEO says, "We try to encourage a feedback process. We stress to [employees] that we care, we ask them to tell us what they think, and we always emphasize that we will give them an honest answer."[29]

Flattening the organizational structure. Businesses today their operations and eliminating layers of unnecessary manageme ing lines of communication. Toy-maker Mattel transformed itself control money loser" into a record-breaking money-maker by tak employees and cutting six layers from its organizational hierarc most effective ways of building responsiveness into organizatio layers of management," says Andrew S. Grove, CEO of comp Intel Corporation. "With fewer levels," he continues, "informatio urally and problems get solved faster."[31] In addition, because shorter distances, less distortion occurs.

CULTURAL AND ETHICAL DILEMMA FOR WOMEN MANAGERS

The international management consulting firm of Burns & McCallister finds itself in cultural hot water. The problem? It refuses to send female executives abroad to negotiate contracts in certain countries.

Despite its current bad publicity, Burns & McCallister has previously earned a reputation as a liberal firm that encourages the employment of women. Over 50 percent of its partners are female, and both *Working Woman* and *Working Mother* magazines have ranked it among the nation's top firms for women. It attracts women by offering exceptional benefits, such as flexible hours, family leave, home-based work, and part-time partner-track positions.

SILENT WOMEN. Why, then, does it send only male partners on certain assignments? In over fifty years of consulting, Burns & McCallister has learned that the cultures in certain countries do not allow women to be treated as they are in America. In some cultures, for example, women are not permitted to speak in a meeting of men. Although clerical help in these cultures might be female, contacts with clients must be through male partners or account executives.

Japan, for example, has a two-track hiring system with women represented in only 3 percent of all professional positions. Other women in the work force are uniformed office ladies who do the filing and serve tea. They generally are pressured to leave the work force when they marry in their mid-twenties. A recruiting brochure for Dentsu, a large Japanese advertising firm, pictured the typical Dentsu "Working Girl" and described only her attractive physical characteristics.[27] In America, such a sexist ad would infuriate women. But attitudes toward working women differ in other cultures.

COMPANY JUSTIFICATION. In defense of its ban on sending women to negotiate in certain cultures, the head of Burns & McCallister said: "Look, we're about as progressive a firm as you'll find. But the reality of international business is that if we try to use women, we don't get the job. It's not a policy on all foreign accounts. We've just identified certain cultures in which women will not be able to successfully land or work on accounts. This restriction does not interfere with their career track."

The National Organization for Women (NOW) argues that Burns & McCallister should apply its American standards throughout the world. Since women are not restricted here, they should not be restricted abroad. No special policy, especially one so discriminatory against women, should be instituted for cultures that vary from ours. Our culture treats women fairly, and other cultures should recognize and respect that treatment. Unless Burns & McCallister stands up for its principles, change can never be expected.

Career Track Application

Organize a debate or class discussion focused on these questions: On what grounds do you support or oppose the position of Burns & McCallister to prohibit women from negotiating contracts in certain cultures? Should Burns & McCallister sacrifice potential business to advance a high moral position? If the career advancement of women within the firm is not affected by the policy, should women care? Do you agree with NOW that change cannot occur unless Burns & McCallister takes a stand?

job descriptions now include statements such as "Must be able to interact with ethnically diverse personnel."

To improve tolerance, practice empathy. This means trying to see the world through another's eyes. It means being nonjudgmental, recognizing things as they are rather than as they "should be." It includes the ability to accept others' contributions in solving problems in a culturally appropriate manner. When Kal Kan Foods began courting the pets of Japan, for example, an Asian advisor suggested that the meat chunks in its Pedigree dog food be cut into perfect little squares. Why? Japanese pet owners feed their dogs piece by piece with chopsticks. Instead of insisting on what "should be" (feeding dogs chunky meat morsels), Kal Kan solved the problem by looking at it from another cultural point of view (providing neat small squares).[28]

Developing intercultural tolerance means practicing empathy, being nonjudgmental, and being patient.

INTEGRATED AIDS TO LEARNING

Dr. Guffey's experience as a successful teacher and textbook author shows throughout the book. She has included a number of carefully thought-out elements to help you understand and remember important concepts and techniques. **Learning goals** correlate with **chapter summaries** to focus your attention on the key points set forth in the chapter, thus enabling you to confirm that you have accomplished those goals.

CHAPTER 2

Listening and Intercultural Communication

LEARNING GOALS

After studying this chapter, you should be able to

1. **Explain the listening process and identify four elements of good listening**
2. **Specify and apply ten specific techniques that improve listening skills**
3. **Recognize the significance of nonverbal messages**
4. **Exercise ten specific suggestions to enhance nonverbal communication skills**
5. **Clarify pivotal American cultural values**
6. **Identify key attitudes that prevent intercultural miscommunication**
7. **Employ ten specific procedures for adapting messages to intercultural audiences**

dollar amounts to local currency, a
tional tone. In speaking English wi
use a few phrases in their language
choose simple English words, (c) w
(d) pause frequently and encourag
misunderstanding that occurs.

Chapter Review

1. What percent of most workers' communication time is spent listening? Of executives?

2. Define *lag time.*

3. Describe the four elements in the listening process.

4. Discuss five poor listening habits and how they can be overcome.

5. Name three specific things you can do to help yourself remember what a speaker says.

6. Define *nonverbal communication.*

7. When verbal and nonverbal messages disagree, which message does the receiver consider more truthful? Give an example.

8. How does good eye contact help a speaker/sender? How does it benefit a listener/receiver?

9. How can you ensure that the nonverbal and verbal messages you send are in agreement?

10. How does the appearance of a business document send nonverbal messages?

11. Describe five major elements of American culture.

12. What is *ethnocentrism?*

13. Describe five specific ways in which you can improve *oral* communication with a foreigner.

14. Describe five specific ways in which you can improve *written* communication with a foreigner.

15. What is a *stereotype?* Give examples.

Discussion

1. Since English is becoming the world's language and since America is a dominant military and trading force, why should Americans bother to learn about other cultures?

2. Discuss how listening skills are important to employees, supervisors, and executives. Who should have the best listening skills?

3. An international business consultant quipped that Asians spend money on entertainment while Americans spend money on attorneys. What are the implications of this statement for business communications?

4. Comment on the idea that body language is a science with principles that can be interpreted accurately by specialists.

5. Ethical Issue: In many countries government officials are not well paid, and "tips" (called "bribes" in America) are a way of compensating them. If such payments are not considered wrong in those countries, should you pay them as a means of accomplishing your business?

Activities

2.1 Bad Listening Habits

Concentrate for three days on your listening habits in class and on the job. What bad habits do you detect? Be prepared to discuss five bad habits and specific ways you could improve your listening skills. Your instructor may ask you to report your analysis in a memo.

2.2 Listening and Retention

Listen to a 30-minute segment of TV news using your normal listening habits. When you finish, make a list of the major items you remember, recording names, places, and figures. A day later watch the same 30-minute segment but put to use the good-listening tips in this chapter, including taking selective notes. When the segment is completed, make a list of the major items you remember. Which experience provided more information? What made a major difference for you?

52

Lively, realistic, and practical end-of-chapter activities include **chapter review questions, discussion topics, exercises,** and **problems.** Each chapter also provides at least one collaborative project to accustom you to the type of teamwork efforts often required in business today.

OTHER INTEGRATED AIDS TO LEARNING

Baseball players, notes playwright Neil Simon, get only three swings at a pitch and then they're out. In rewriting, however, "you get almost as many swings as you want and you know, sooner or later, you'll hit the ball." Although it takes real effort, revision allows the writer to work out the rough spots so that every message can score a hit.

ranges between 8.4 and 11.2.) By occasionally calculating the Fog Index of your writing, you can ensure that you stay within the 8–12 range. Remember that long sentences and long words—those over two syllables—make your writing foggy.

However, readability formulas don't always tell the full story. Although they provide a rough estimate, those based solely on word and sentence counts fail to measure meaningfulness. Even short words (like *skew, onus,* and *wane*) can cause trouble if readers don't recognize them. More important than length is a word's familiarity and meaningfulness to the reader. In Chapter 3 you learned to adapt your writing to the audience by selecting familiar words. Other techniques that can improve readability include well-organized paragraphs, transitions to connect ideas, headings, and lists.

The task of revision, summarized in the following checklist, is hard work. It demands objectivity and a willingness to cut, cut, cut. Though painful, the process is also gratifying. It's a great feeling when you realize your finished message is clear, concise, and readable.

Checklist for Revising Messages

- ✔ **Keep the message simple.** Express ideas directly. Don't show off or use fancy language.
- ✔ **Be conversational.** Include occasional contractions *(hasn't, don't)* and first-person pronouns *(I/we).* Use natural-sounding language.

Part II
The Process of Writing

124

This text includes many other features that are specifically designed to help you get full value from this book. Concise, yet insightful, **marginal notes** draw your attention to important material; informative **photo captions** advance ideas that are presented in the text; and **checklists** summarize text discussions to help you integrate, review, and apply concepts.

Job Applicants

job is one of life's major rejections. The blow is intensified by *nfortunately, you were not among the candidates selected for . . .).* he receiver's disappointment somewhat by using the indirect pat- important variation. In the reasons section it's wise to be vague in he candidate was not selected. First, giving concrete reasons may receiver *(Your grade point average of 2.7 was low compared with ndidates).* Second, and more important, providing extra informa- tal in a lawsuit. Hiring and firing decisions generate considerable To avoid charges of discrimination or wrongful actions, legal advi- zations to keep employment rejection letters general, simple, and

The following job refusal letter is tactful but intentionally vague. It implies that the applicant's qualifications don't match those needed for the position, but the letter doesn't reveal anything specific.

Shows appreciation. Doesn't indicate good or bad news.

To prevent possible lawsuits, gives no explanation. Places bad news in a dependent clause.

Ends with best wishes.

Dear Mr. Danson:

Thanks for letting us review your résumé submitted for our advertised management trainee opening.

We received a number of impressive résumés for this opening. Although another candidate was selected, your interest in our organization is appreciated. So that you may continue your search for a position at another organization, we are writing to you immediately.

We wish you every success in finding a position that exactly fits your qualifications.

The following checklist gives tips on how to communicate bad news within an organization.

Checklist for Managing Negative Organization News

- ✔ **Start with a relevant, upbeat buffer.** Open with a small bit of good news, praise, appreciation, agreement, understanding, or a discussion of facts leading to the reasons section.
- ✔ **Discuss reasons.** Except in job refusal letters, explain what caused the decision necessitating the bad news. Use objective, nonjudgmental, and nondiscriminatory language. Show empathy and fairness.
- ✔ **Reveal the bad news.** Make the bad news clear but don't accentuate it. Avoid negative language.
- ✔ **Close harmoniously.** End on a positive, friendly note. For job refusals, extend good wishes.

You've now studied the indirect method for revealing bad news and analyzed many examples of messages applying this method. As you observed, business writers generally try to soften the blow; however, they do eventually reveal the bad news. No effort is made to sweep it under the carpet or ignore it totally. In other cultures bad news may be more difficult to reveal. The accompanying Cross Culture box gives insights into how negative messages are treated abroad.

Part III
Letters and Memos

214

In addition, the **C.L.U.E. program,** a handy review and reference guide, appears as an appendix to the text. C.L.U.E. (an acronym for Competent Language Usage Essentials) focuses on frequently used and abused elements of grammar and usage, as well as words that are often misspelled or misused. You will feel more confident about the correctness of your language by brushing up your skills. Use the self-checked C.L.U.E. exercises within the guide itself or complete the exercises at the ends of Chapters 1 through 10.

Business Communication

Communication Foundations

1 The Communication Process

2 Listening and Intercultural Communication

The Communication Process

LEARNING GOALS

After studying this chapter, you should be able to

1. Explain the importance of communication skills for knowledge workers
2. Describe the communication process and its central objective
3. Recognize six barriers to interpersonal communication and methods for overcoming them
4. Identify the three functions of business communication
5. Contrast oral and written communication
6. Distinguish between formal and informal channels of communication
7. Recognize six barriers to organizational communication and methods for overcoming them

Sara Lee Corporation: Career Track Profile

"I never dreamed when I graduated from college that I would be doing what I'm doing now—and enjoying it so much," says Renee Rodriguez, administrator of creative services for Sara Lee Corporation in Chicago. Visions of cheesecake and poundcake pop up when we hear the name *Sara Lee,* but Sara Lee of the 1990s is much more than baked goods. The flourishing conglomerate has transformed itself into a consumer-goods superpower with 110,000 employees all over the globe. Sara Lee markets brand-name products such as Hanes and L'eggs hosiery, Playtex intimate apparel, and Coach leather goods. Although many operations are centered in the United States, Sara Lee ranks number four among U.S. consumer-products marketers in Europe; and it is aggressively expanding in Latin American and Pacific Rim countries.[1]

"Management not only talks to employees, but it also listens. And that's an important part of open communication here at Sara Lee."

Working at the corporate headquarters of a global company was not even a remote fantasy when Renee graduated from Beloit College in Wisconsin. Like many job seekers she didn't find a dream career immediately. She held clerical positions and developed her word processing and office skills at other companies before being hired by Sara Lee.

While working as a secretary in Corporate Affairs at Sara Lee, Renee started writing articles for Sara Lee's corporate newsletter. Increasingly, she tackled projects not generally associated with the position of secretary. And even though she learned a lot as she completed her administrative assignments, she decided to enroll at Northwestern University to broaden her skills with courses in newswriting and copyediting. While on the job she developed computer skills, teaching herself new programs as she needed them.

A year and a half after joining Corporate Affairs, Renee was named administrator of creative services, a newly created position. Among other duties she works to keep Sara Lee's lines of communication open. Given the massive number of employees located in the United States and abroad, Sara Lee faces an immense two-way communication task. Its managers need to communicate their plans and strategies in documents flowing downward to employees. At the same time these decision-makers must encourage the upward flow of ideas from employees to ensure successful operations and a mutual feeling of trust.

John H. Bryan, chief executive officer and chairman of the board of Sara Lee, understands all too well the value of communication skills as well as the need for promoting an open climate of communication within his organization. In underscoring his belief that communication skills are critical in career advancement, he says, "If I were designing a business school, communication would be the most important course in the curriculum."[2] Bryan feels just as strongly about maintaining a healthy climate for communication within the organization: "Sara Lee Corporation is committed to maintaining a corporate environment that fosters open communication, promotes the exchange of ideas, and increases understanding of our mission and corporate strategies."[3]

Sara Lee is expanding aggressively into international markets, recently tripling its bakery capacity in the United Kingdom. Much of its success abroad lies in its practice of listening to local managers who understand the culture and can communicate local preferences and market demands to company decision makers. Keeping communication channels open on the home front is one of the tasks of Renee Rodriguez.

Much of Renee's job centers on this commitment. She is editor of *News Updates,* the company newsletter, and co-editor of *Leeway,* the company's management magazine. She also manages "Time Out," a program of informal meetings between employees and upper management. Over coffee and sweet rolls (Sara Lee, of course) a corporate officer—sometimes even CEO John Bryan—discusses a topic in her or his area, enabling employees to keep up with what's happening in the organization. Acting as host and moderator of these get-togethers, Renee says, "Time Out meetings are extremely beneficial for both employees and management. Management not only talks to employees, but it also listens. And that's an important part of open communication here at Sara Lee."

Another program that helps Sara Lee maintain open communication is "RSVP." Employees anonymously submit questions and suggestions on topics such as day care, vacation policies, smoking rules, employee privileges, and rumors circulating within the company. Renee then researches answers and delivers responses using a number system that conceals the name of the inquirer. RSVP clears the air by enabling employees to ask "tough" questions without jeopardizing their positions or damaging relationships with immediate supervisors. This informal information conduit between management and employees helps to develop trust, one of the most important elements in successful management and good communication.[4]

Communication Power for Knowledge Workers

In many ways the experiences of Renee Rodriguez at Sara Lee reflect the bigger picture facing today's college students as they prepare for careers. She entered a vastly different employment environment from the agricultural economy of her great-grandparents and from the manufacturing economy of her grandparents and parents. The American economy now centers on service and information industries; according to some estimates 95 percent of all new jobs will be service- or information-related. Many of the jobs that will be available in five years do not even exist today.

Today's Knowledge Society

Knowledge workers are people who generate, process, and exchange information.

As the twenty-first century rapidly approaches, we become increasingly aware of an advanced society based on information and knowledge. Physical labor, raw materials, and capital are no longer the key ingredients in the creation of wealth. Now the vital raw material in our society, says futurist Alvin Toffler, is knowledge.[5] Tomorrow's wealth depends on the development and exchange of knowledge. Individuals entering the work force offer their knowledge, not their muscles. Knowledge workers, according to management guru Peter Drucker, get paid for their education and their ability to learn.[6] They engage in mind work. They deal with symbols: words, figures, and data. Currently, three out of four jobs involve some form of mind work, and that number will increase sharply in the future.

In her work at Sara Lee, Renee Rodriguez recognized quickly that she needed additional skills and knowledge. Similarly, millions of other traditional (18- to 24-year-old) and nontraditional (25 and older) students are flooding American colleges and universities—some to develop basic skills, others to enhance their abilities or to retrain for alternate professions. They are the work force of the future; they are knowledge workers. These people will find that their jobs increasingly involve generating, processing, and exchanging information.

Emphasis on Communication Skills

Employers value effective communication skills because good communicators make and save them money.

Most college students today don't need to be advised by a futurist that communication skills will be important to their career success. When they look through employment classified ads, they see job listings like those shown in Figure 1.1. The request for excellent communication skills is probably the most frequently seen requirement in job ads today. Employers and employees alike consistently rank communication skills at the top of the job skills list.[7] As American businesses expand into global markets, classified ads now often include requests for international communication skills.[8] Even in technical fields communication skills are demanded. The chief executives of the six largest public accounting firms put communication at the head of their list of three general skills needed to be successful in public accounting.[9] And corporations spend huge sums of money on trainers and consultants to improve employees' communication skills.

Why do employers take such an intense interest in communication skills? Organizations value these skills because good communicators (1) make them money and (2) save them money. Good communicators make money by performing well themselves and by motivating others to achieve. They are persuasive in promoting the organization's products, services, and reputation. Good communicators save money by communicating clearly the first time. Some authorities esti-

FIGURE 1.1 ● Classified Ads Seeking Knowledge Workers with Good Communication Skills

C-8 THE DAILY NEWS Tuesday, March 23, 1993

ASSISTANT FACILITY MANAGER
ERA Enterprises, a manufacturer of medical devices, offers outstanding opportunity. Assistant facility manager helps in the security, safety, and maintenance of the manufacturing facility. Must be familiar with state and federal regulations (OSHA, EPA) and have **excellent communication skills.**

FINANCIAL/REAL ESTATE PORTFOLIO ANALYST
You will review and analyze commercial/multi-family real property operating statements, rent rolls, loan agreements, and appraisals. Tasks include evaluating and writing detailed analyses of loans, developing and maintaining PC and mainframe data base, and analyzing economic and market data. Position demands **strong written communication skills. Writing sample required.**

ACCOUNT MANAGER

MARKETING ADMINISTRATIVE ASSISTANT
A leader in mass storage technology is seeking an adm. asst. to support the marketing team located at our corporate offices. Must be self-starter with secretarial skills including proficiency in PCs. **Must have excellent language skills and be able to communicate well with the public.** Please send résumé.

ACCOUNTING ANALYST
Major entertainment company seeks highly motivated accountant analyst to perform general ledger, statement, property, advertising, and other functions. Ideal candidate must have **strong oral and writing skills** to make presentations to all levels of management. Excellent benefits.

OFFICE PRODUCTS MARKETING
Looking for someone to help us sell our marketing concepts to businesses throughout the

ADMINISTRATIVE PERSONNEL ASSISTANT
Grow with our expanding cruise consultant business! Must be organized, personable, and well trained in WordPerfect and Lotus. **Communication skills a must! Will be tested.** AA degree in office technology preferred.

MANAGEMENT TRAINEE
One of the nation's leading companies is accepting résumés for trainees. Qualified candidates must have a bachelor's degree, **excellent writing and communication skills**, an ability to interface effectively with all levels of management and a diverse work staff, and leadership qualities.

INTERNATIONAL MARKETING COORDINATOR
Global computer electronics manufacturer seeks individual with marketing management training. The position requires **solid oral and written skills in English,** facility with other

SALES M
Leader in direc for person inter management. N Earning opportuni $50,000 after tr and benefits.

MANAGEME PROG
We need 3 individuals for ou trainee program. hiring and traini personnel, invento control, advertising ing of new p developing new s Retail experienc not necessary. to train you if yo Rapid advancem agement, where sales managers $45,000+.

ACCOUNTING S
Mulit-faceted co company paid sharing, 401K **2 year coll**

mate that one third of all documents are written merely to clarify earlier messages. That's a lot of wasted money when you consider that in 1991 the cost of dictating, transcribing, printing, and mailing an average business letter ranged from $12 to $18, depending on the method of transcription.[10]

Employees, too, appreciate the value of excellent communication skills. Such abilities enable them to complete their work efficiently and effectively—and to earn recognition and advancement. Probably the number one requirement for promotion to management is the ability to communicate. Corporate president Ben Ordover explains how he made executive choices: "Many people climbing the corporate ladder are very good. When faced with a hard choice between candidates, I used writing ability as the deciding factor. Sometimes a candidate's writing was the only skill that separated him or her from the competition."[11] And as individuals ascend the career ladder, oral and written communication skills become more important than technical skills. That's because managers spend most of their time communicating—supervising, delegating, evaluating, clarifying, and interacting.

● **Employees with good communication skills tend to climb the career ladder faster than those lacking such skills.**

Even though writing on the job is an important skill, myths and misconceptions about it persist, as discussed in the accompanying Career Skills box.

The Role of Communication

The mortar that holds together organizations—and the entire knowledge society—is communication. Without communication information could not be processed or exchanged; words and data would remain isolated facts. For example, when the Sara Lee Corporation wants to determine customer product satisfaction,

FIVE COMMON MYTHS ABOUT WRITING ON THE JOB

A myth is an unfounded belief or misconception. You may have seen movies or heard friends talk about some occupations, leading you to accept without scrutiny certain myths about writing on the job. These myths may affect the way you prepare for your career. Here are five common myths about writing and the facts that refute them.

MYTH. In technical fields like accounting you work with numbers—not words.
Fact. In truth 90 percent of all business transactions involve written correspondence.[12] Conducting business in any field—even in technical and specialized areas like computing, accounting, engineering, marketing, hotel management, and so forth—involves some writing. A study of professional, technical, and managerial workers found that they spent 23 percent of their time writing—more than one full day a week![13] Moreover, with promotions, writing tasks will increase.

MYTH. Secretaries will clean up your writing problems.
Fact. In today's world of tightened budgets, most businesspeople probably won't have a secretary. Although upper-level managers still have secretaries or assistants who may type their messages, many executives now write their own memos and letters on their computers because it's faster and more efficient. For those who do have administrative help, it's wise to remember that even the most highly skilled secretary cannot remedy fundamental problems in organization, emphasis, and tone.

MYTH. Technical writers do most of the real writing on the job.
Fact. Some companies employ technical writers to prepare manuals, documentation, and public documents like annual reports. Rarely, however, do these specialists write everyday messages (internal reports, letters, memos) for employees. Instead, sales representatives, programmers, accountants, engineers, technicians, and other professionals must rely on their own skills to communicate their ideas.

MYTH. Computers can fix any of your writing mistakes.
Fact. Today's style, grammar, and spell checkers are wonderful aids to business writers. They can highlight selected trouble areas and occasionally suggest revisions. What they can't do, though, is write the document and ensure its total accuracy. Spell checkers, for example, cannot distinguish between confusing words such as *their/there/they're* or *principal/principle.* Other checkers can't locate or correct most grammar, punctuation, style, tone, and organizational errors. Only trained writers can do that.

MYTH. Form letters will solve most of your writing problems.
Fact. Books and computer programs can provide dozens of ready-made letters or pattern paragraphs for which businesspeople merely fill in the blanks. When these letters are appropriate and well written, they can be useful timesavers. Often, however, such letters are poorly written and ill-suited for specific situations. Most messages demand that writers create their own original thoughts.

Career Track Application

Interview a specialist in your career area. What kinds of messages does she or he write? How often? After promotions, do these specialists have different writing tasks?

it conducts a survey. The survey is useless, however, until the data are analyzed and the results communicated to management. Only when words and data are translated into meaningful knowledge and communicated to decision-makers do they become valuable to the economy. Communication, then, is a central factor in the emerging knowledge society and a major consideration for anyone entering today's work force.

The Process of Communication and Its Barriers

Just what is *communication*? For our purposes communication is the *transmission of information and meaning from one individual or group to another.* The crucial element in this definition is *meaning.* Communication has as its central objective

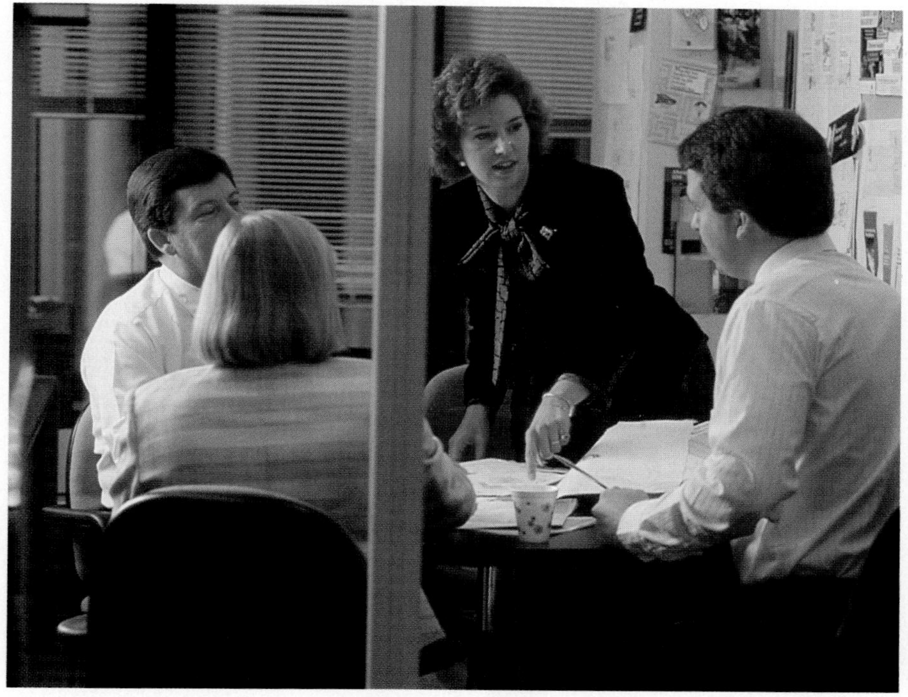

Performing a job well and being promoted depend greatly on your communication skills—your ability to explain ideas, lead meetings, convince customers, persuade management, and write clearly. Today's jobs focus increasingly on generating, processing, and exchanging information.

the transmission of meaning. The process of communication is successful only when the receiver understands an idea as the sender intended it. Both parties must agree not only on the information transmitted but also on the *meaning* of that information. This entire book is devoted to one objective: teaching you the skills of communication so that you can transmit meaning along with information. Let's look first at the process of communication and then at barriers that obstruct that process.

● **The object of communication is the transmission of meaning from sender to receiver.**

Sending and Receiving Messages

How does an idea travel from one person to another? Despite what you may have seen in some futuristic science fiction movies, we can't just glance at another person and transfer meaning directly from mind to mind. We engage in a sensitive process of communication that generally involves five steps, discussed here and depicted in Figure 1.2.

● **The communication process has five steps: idea formation, message encoding, message transmission, message decoding, and feedback.**

Sender has idea. The process of communication begins when the person with whom the message originates—the *sender*—has an idea. The form of the idea will be influenced by complex factors surrounding the sender: mood, frame of reference, background, culture, and physical makeup, as well as the context of the situation and many other factors. The way you greet people on campus, for example, depends a lot on how you feel, whom you are addressing (a classmate, a professor, a campus worker), and what your culture has trained you to say ("Hi," "Howdy," "How ya' doing?" or "Good morning").

The form of the idea, whether a simple greeting or a complex idea, is shaped by assumptions based on the sender's experiences. A manager sending a message to employees assumes they will be receptive, while direct-mail advertisers assume that receivers will give only a quick glance to their message. Ability to accurately predict how a message will affect its receiver and skill in adapting that message to its receiver are really the key factors in successful communication.

FIGURE 1.2 ● The Communication Process

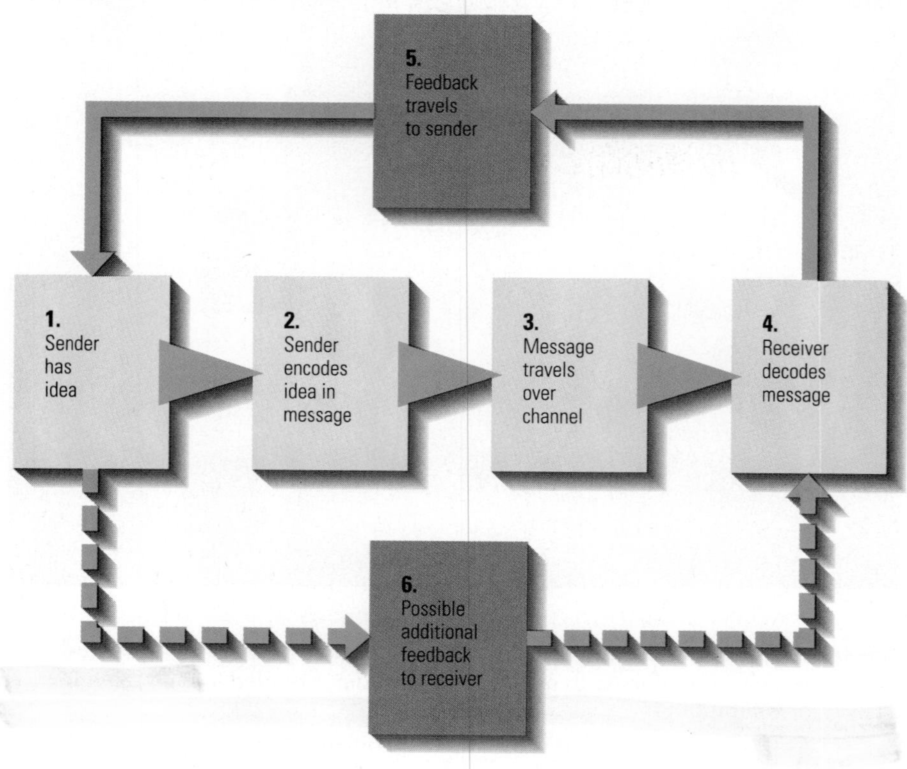

● **Encoding means converting an idea into words or gestures to convey meaning.**

Sender encodes idea in message. The next step in the communication process involves *encoding,* converting the idea into words or gestures that will convey meaning. A major problem in communicating any message verbally is that words have different meanings for different people. When misunderstandings result from missed meanings, it's called *bypassing.* You'll learn more about this communication obstacle shortly.

Recognizing how easy it is to be misunderstood, skilled communicators choose familiar words with concrete meanings on which both senders and receivers agree. In selecting proper symbols, senders must be alert to the receiver's communication skills, attitudes, background, experiences, and culture: How will the selected words affect the receiver? For example, a Dr. Pepper cola promotion failed miserably in Great Britain because American managers had not done their homework. They had to change their "I'm a Pepper" slogan after learning that *pepper* is British slang for *prostitute.*[14] Because the sender initiates a communication transaction, he or she has full responsibility for its success or failure. Choosing appropriate words or symbols is the first step.

● **Channels are the media—computer, telephone, letter, and so on—that transmit messages.**

Message travels over channel. The medium over which the message is physically transmitted is the *channel.* Messages may be delivered by computer, telephone, letter, memorandum, report, announcement, picture, spoken word, fax, or through some other channel. Because communication channels deliver both verbal and nonverbal messages, senders must choose the channel and shape the message carefully. A company may use its annual report, for example, as a channel to deliver many messages to stockholders. The verbal message lies in the report's financial and organizational news. Nonverbal messages, though, are conveyed by their appearance (glitzy versus bland), layout (ample white space versus tightly packed columns of print), and tone (conversational versus formal).

Anything that interrupts the transmission of a message in the communication process is called *noise.* Channel noise ranges from static that disrupts a telephone conversation to typographical errors in a letter that damage the credibility of the sender. Channel noise might even include the annoyance a receiver feels when the sender chooses an improper medium for sending a message, such as announcing a loan rejection via postcard. You'll learn more about choosing the proper channel or form for a message shortly, as well as ways of preventing noise from interfering with communication.

Receiver decodes message. The individual for whom the message is intended is the *receiver.* Translating the message from its symbol form into meaning involves *decoding.* Only when the receiver understands the meaning intended by the sender—that is, successfully decodes the message—does communication take place. Such success, however, is difficult to achieve because no two people share the same life experiences and because many barriers can disrupt the process.

Decoding can be disrupted internally by the receiver's lack of attention to or bias against the sender. It can be disrupted externally by loud sounds or illegible words. Decoding can also be sidetracked by semantic obstacles, such as misunderstood words or emotional reactions to certain terms. A memo that refers to all the women in an office as "girls," for example, may disturb its receivers so much that they fail to comprehend the total message.

Feedback travels to sender. The verbal or nonverbal response of the receiver is *feedback,* a vital part of the communication process. Feedback helps the sender know that the message was received and understood. If as a receiver you hear the message "How are you," your feedback might consist of words ("I'm fine") or body language (a smile or a wave of the hand). Although the receiver may respond with additional feedback to the sender (thus creating a new act of communication), we'll concentrate here on the initial message flowing to the receiver and the resulting feedback.

Senders can encourage feedback by asking questions such as *Am I making myself clear?* and *Is there anything you don't understand?* Senders can further improve feedback by timing the delivery appropriately and by providing only as much information as the receiver can handle. Receivers can improve the process by paraphrasing the sender's message with comments like *Let me try to explain that in my own words* or *My understanding of your comment is . . .*

The best feedback is descriptive rather than evaluative. For example, here's a descriptive response: *I understand you want to launch a chocolate chip cookie business.* Here's an evaluative response: *Your business ideas are always weird.* An evaluative response is judgmental and doesn't tell the sender if the receiver actually understood the message.

Barriers to Interpersonal Communication

The communication process is successful only when the receiver understands the message as intended by the sender. It sounds quite simple. Yet, it's not. How many times have you thought that you delivered a clear message, only to learn later that your intentions were totally misunderstood?

SPOTLIGHT ON COMMUNICATORS

As the founder of ASK, a $400 million computer software company in Silicon Valley, Sandra Kurtzig recognizes the power of encoding and decoding messages accurately. The best ideas in the world, she warns, are useless if they can't be communicated clearly and concisely to others.

Barriers to successful communication include bypassing, differing frames of reference, lack of language or listening skills, emotional interference, and physical distractions.

Most messages that we send reach their destinations, but many are only partially understood. You can improve your chances of communicating successfully by learning to recognize the barriers that are known to disrupt the process. These barriers occur at any stage in the process, from the sender's initial development of the message to the receiver's feedback. The most significant communication misunderstandings result from problems in these areas: bypassing, frame of reference, lack of language and listening skills, emotional interference, and physical distractions.

Bypassing. In the business world and in our personal lives, we depend almost totally on words to exchange ideas. Each of us attaches a little bundle of meanings to every word, and these meanings are not always similar. Bypassing happens when people miss each other with their meanings.[15] Let's say your boss asks you to "help" with a large customer mailing. When you arrive to do your share, you learn that you are expected to do the whole mailing yourself. You and your boss attached different meanings to the word *help*. Bypassing can lead to major miscommunication because people assume that meanings are contained in words. Actually, meanings are in people. For communication to be successful, the receiver and sender must attach the same symbolic meanings to their words.

Miscommunication often results when the sender's frame of reference differs markedly from the receiver's.

Frame of reference. Everything you see and feel in the world is translated through your individual frame of reference. This frame is formed by a combination of your experiences, education, culture, expectations, attitudes, personality, and many other elements. Because your frame of reference is unique, you will naturally perceive events differently from someone else. American owners attempting to modernize a Mexican assembly plant, for example, perceived failure when they saw a report indicating a slow pace of change. The Mexican managers, on the other hand, saw the report and congratulated themselves on their splendid progress. The owners' perceptions were colored by expectations and experiences rooted in a technological culture capable of rapid change. The Mexicans, recognizing the substantial hurdles to be overcome and conditioned by a slower-paced culture, perceived success in the achievements they had made. Lack of agreement about the meaning of the report resulted from the communicators' differing frames of reference. Wise business communicators, whether dealing with global or local audiences, strive to prevent communication failure by being alert to both their own frames of reference and those of others.

Lack of language skill. No matter how extraordinary the idea, it won't be understood or fully appreciated unless the communicators involved have good language skills. Each individual needs an adequate vocabulary, a command of basic punctuation and grammar, and skill in written and oral expression. Today's knowledge workers require especially fine-tuned skills because our economy increasingly revolves around the exchange of language-based information.

Lack of listening skill. Although most of us think we know how to listen, in reality many of us are poor listeners. Have you ever "faked" listening—made it appear you were paying attention when your mind was romping elsewhere? Nearly everyone has. This inattention to oral messages often prevents us from hearing them clearly and thus responding properly.

Emotional interference. Communication suffers when emotions cloud the mind. Shaping an intelligent message is difficult when you're feeling joy, fear, resentment, hostility, sadness, or some other strong emotion. It's especially hard to concentrate when anger muddies your ability to reason. When angry, senders and receivers drop those cooperative roles and become adversaries, so that the communication process deteriorates into name-calling or other counterproductive behavior.[16] To reduce the influence of emotions as a communication barrier, both senders and receivers should focus on the content of the message and try to remain objective.

Physical distractions. Faulty acoustics, noisy surroundings, or a poor telephone connection are physical distractions that may disrupt oral communication. Likewise, sloppy appearance, poor printing, careless formatting, and typographical errors can disrupt written messages.

Overcoming Communication Barriers

The road to communication success might appear to be filled with insurmountable obstacles. Effective communicators, however, have learned to overcome the barriers. Throughout this book you'll be taught countless techniques for becoming a successful communicator. Here are some suggestions for conquering barriers that disrupt interpersonal communication.

To overcome barriers, communicators must recognize communication's imperfections, adapt messages to receivers, improve language and listening skills, question preconceptions, and plan for feedback.

Realizing that the communication process is imperfect. Half the battle in communicating successfully is recognizing that the entire process is sensitive and susceptible to breakdown. Like a defensive driver anticipating problems on the road, a good communicator anticipates problems in encoding, transmitting, and decoding a message. Just knowing what can go wrong helps you prepare strategies to reduce misunderstandings.

Adapting your message to the receiver. Successful communicators focus on the receiver's environment and frame of reference. They ask themselves questions such as, How is that individual likely to react to my message? Does the receiver know as much about the subject as I do? What language level does that person understand? The better you are at anticipating these answers and viewing the message through the receiver's frame of reference, the more successful your communication will be.

Improving your language and listening skills. Misunderstandings are less likely if you arrange your ideas logically and use words precisely. Mark Twain was right when he said, "The difference between an almost-right word and the right word is like the difference between lightning and the lightning bug." But communicating is more than expressing yourself well. A large part of successful communication is listening. Management advisor Peter Drucker observes that "too many [executives] think they are wonderful with people because they talk well. They don't realize that being wonderful with people means *listening* well."[17]

Using words precisely and listening carefully help reduce miscommunication.

Questioning your preconceptions. Successful communicators continually examine their personal assumptions, biases, and prejudices. The more you pay attention to subtleties and know "where you're coming from" when you encode and decode messages, the better you'll communicate. An American software company, for example, failed unnecessarily in Japan because it simply translated its glossy brochure from English into Japanese. The Americans didn't realize that in Japan such brochures are associated with low-priced consumer products.[18] The software producer wrongly assumed that since glossy was upscale here, it would be perceived similarly in Japan.

Good communicators ask questions to stimulate feedback.

Planning for feedback. Finally, effective communicators create an environment for useful feedback. In oral communication this means asking questions such as "Do you understand?" and "What questions do you have?" as well as encouraging listeners to repeat instructions or paraphrase ideas. As a listener it means providing feedback that describes rather than evaluates. And in written communication it means asking questions and providing access: *Do you have my telephone number in case you have questions?* or *Please jot your answers down on my letter and return it in the enclosed envelope.*

Organizational Communication and Its Barriers

Within organizations the process of communication is even more sensitive. Potential problems are created whenever individuals interact. Further complicating the process are barriers created by the atmosphere and management levels within an organization. Some barriers are beyond your control, while others are not. Understanding the functions, forms, and flow of organizational communication will help you surmount its barriers.

Functions

Organizational communication—both internal and external—has three basic functions: to inform, to persuade, and to promote goodwill.

On the job you'll communicate internally and externally. Internally, you'll be exchanging ideas with superiors, coworkers, and subordinates. When these messages must be written, you'll probably choose E-mail or a printed memorandum, such as the American Airlines memo shown in Figure 1.3. When you are communicating externally with customers, suppliers, government, and the public, you will generally send letters on company stationery, such as American's letter also shown in Figure 1.3. Specifically, you'll be communicating to:

Internal Functions

- Issue and clarify procedures and policies
- Inform management of progress
- Persuade employees or management to make changes or improvements
- Coordinate activities and provide assistance
- Evaluate, compliment, reward, and discipline employees
- Get to know individuals personally

External Functions

- Answer inquiries about products or services
- Persuade customers to buy products or services
- Clarify supplier specifications and quality requirements
- Issue credit and collect bills
- Respond to regulatory agencies
- Promote a positive image of the organization

FIGURE 1.3 ● Internal and External Forms of Communication

Memo AmericanAirlines®

DATE: August 10, 1994

TO: Bob Markum

FROM: Tim Smith TM

SUBJECT: NEWS RELEASE ABOUT NASHVILLE CREW BASE

Enclosed is a draft of the news release announcing the Nashville crew base. Please look it over and make any changes you like. We've tried to keep it short and to the point. Captain Bill Baker has agreed to do the media conference late Tuesday morning since your schedule is so tight.

Because *Flagship News* is close to its deadline and would like to run a brief story on the announcement, I'll need your response by August 12. Thanks for your help.

Memorandums typically deliver written messages within organizations. They use a standard format and are concise and direct.

AmericanAirlines®

EXECUTIVE OFFICE

March 4, 1994

Ms. Christie Bonner
1792 Southern Avenue
Mesa, AZ 85202

Dear Ms. Bonner:

Congratulations for taking steps to overcome your fear of flying! Your eloquent words are testimony to the effectiveness of our AAir Born program; and more important, they underline how liberating the experience can be. I know the door is now open for you to enjoy many satisfying travel experiences.

Probably the most pleasant part of my responsibilities at American is receiving compliments from our customers about the service provided by our employees. I have passed along your kind words about those individuals who made such a difference to you in realizing your dream of flight. We appreciate the opportunity to recognize their fine performance.

On behalf of all of us associated with the AAir Born program, thank you very much, Ms. Bonner. We look forward to welcoming you aboard again soon.

Yours truly,

Janice Moore

Janice Moore
Staff Supervisor

Letters on company stationery communicate with outsiders. Notice how this one builds a solid relationship between American Airlines and a satisfied customer.

FIGURE 1.4 ● The Functions of Business Communication

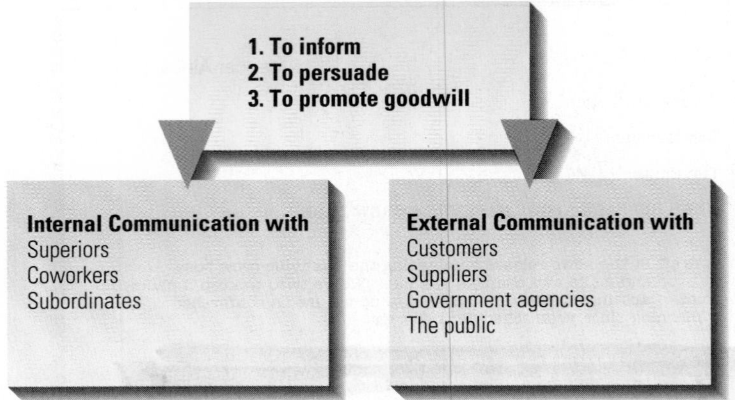

In all these tasks employees and managers use a number of communication skills: reading, listening, speaking, and writing. As college students, you have already begun to develop these skills. If, however, you're like most business undergraduates, you realize that you need to improve these skills to the proficiency level required for success in today's competitive job market. This book and this course will provide you with practical advice on how to do that.

Now, look back over the preceding lists of internal and external functions of communication in organizations. Although there appear to be a large number of diverse business communication functions, they can be summarized in three simple categories, as Figure 1.4 shows: (1) to inform, (2) to persuade, or (3) to promote goodwill.

Forms

● Organizational communication may be oral (two-way) or written (one-way).

Communication supports many organizational functions, both internal and external. The forms of that communication are oral (generally two-way) or, more often, written (one-way).

In small businesses much communication can be oral, often face-to-face. As organizations grow in complexity and number of members, however, more messages must be written. When Stephen Jobs and Steve Wozniak launched the enormously successful Apple Computer company in a garage, for example, they could talk with each other about their production ideas and marketing plans. But as the company ballooned into a computer colossus employing thousands, their forms of communication had to change. They were forced to use more impersonal means of exchanging information, such as memos, reports, bulletins, and newsletters. Their business also required them to keep written records for legal purposes. Although they didn't lose face-to-face contact totally, they could no longer run their business with oral communication only.

Oral, two-way communication. Probably the best way to transmit information meaningfully is orally. This communication form has many advantages. For one thing, it minimizes misunderstandings because communicators can immediately

FIGURE 1.5 ● Forms of Organizational Communication

Oral, Two-way Communication	Written, One-way Communication
Form	**Form**
Phone call	Announcement
Conversation	Memo, E-mail, fax
Interview	Letter
Meeting	Report, proposal
Conference	Newsletter
Advantages	**Advantages**
Immediate feedback	Permanent record
Nonverbal clues	Convenience
Warm feeling	Economy
Forceful impact	Careful message
Multiple input	Easy distribution

ask questions to clarify uncertainties. For another, it enables communicators to see each other's facial expressions and hear voice inflections, further improving communication. Oral communication is also an efficient way to develop consensus when many people must be consulted. Finally, most of us enjoy two-way interpersonal communication because it's easy, feels warm and natural, and promotes friendships.

● Oral communication minimizes misunderstandings, provides immediate feedback, permits consensus, and promotes friendships.

The main disadvantages of oral communication are that it produces no written record, sometimes wastes time, and may be inconvenient. When individuals meet face-to-face or speak on the telephone, someone's work has to be interrupted. And how many of us are able to limit a conversation to just business? Nevertheless, two-way communication has many interpersonal and organizational uses, summarized in Figure 1.5.

Written, one-way communication. Communication that travels one way is impersonal in the sense that two communicators cannot see or hear each other and cannot provide immediate feedback. Most forms of business communication—including announcements, memos, computer mail (E-mail), faxes, letters, newsletters, reports, proposals, and manuals—fall into this category.

● Written communication provides a permanent record, permits careful organization, is convenient and economical, and allows easy distribution.

Organizations rely on written communication for many reasons. It provides a permanent record, a necessity in these times of increasing litigation and extensive government regulation. Writing out an idea instead of delivering it orally enables communicators to develop an organized, well-considered message. Written documents are also convenient. They can be composed and read when the schedules of both communicators permit, and they can be reviewed if necessary.

Written messages have drawbacks, of course. They require careful preparation and sensitivity to audience and anticipated effect. Words spoken in conversation may soon be forgotten, but words committed to hard or soft copy become a public record—and sometimes an embarrassing one. Former IBM Chairman John Akers, for example, must have had second thoughts about his E-mail memo blasting managers for complacency and product defects. When leaked to the press, the memo shook up the financial world and damaged IBM's image and morale.

Another drawback to written messages is that they are more difficult to prepare. They demand good writing skills, and such skills are not inborn. The good news is that writing abilities can be learned. Because at least 90 percent of all business transactions involve written correspondence,[19] and because writing skills are so important to your business success, you will be receiving special instruction in becoming a good writer. Written messages have some drawbacks, but their uses, summarized in Figure 1.4, and their importance in business should not be underestimated.

In selecting a communication form, consider audience, organization, need for documentation, need for feedback, and formality level.

Selection of form. To choose the best communication form, ask yourself several questions:

- *Does this message require a written record?* If so, use a memo to send an interoffice message. Use a letter to communicate with a customer or other individual outside the organization. Write a report if considerable data are involved.
- *Do I need immediate feedback or multiple input?* Telephone calls or personal visits provide the fastest responses when immediate feedback is required. Group meetings and conferences are excellent for distributing information. They also work well when brainstorming for ideas and for building group consensus.
- *Does this message require careful organization and supporting documentation?* Complicated data or intricate procedures should be communicated in the form of long memos or reports, accompanied by visual aids.
- *How quickly does the message need to be delivered?* Urgent news often requires oral transmission. More routine messages can be sent in memos or letters.
- *How large and how far away is the audience?* A supervisor announcing a lunchtime fitness seminar to three employees in the same room could tell them personally. The same message aimed at 300 employees in four departments would require a less personal form of communication, such as a memo or a newsletter announcement.
- *How easily will my audience accept this message?* If management wants to convince employees that a new health care plan is better than the current plan, it may elect to present this message in small group sessions led by a compelling speaker. Persuasion and selling are most effective with face-to-face communication.
- *Do I need to show empathy, friendliness, or other feelings?* Face-to-face conversations, of course, allow communicators to express the most feeling—in giving both positive and negative news. When delivering bad news, such as criticizing or firing employees, many managers believe that the news should be delivered in person. When praising or giving a pat on the back, they feel that a written message shows thoughtfulness.
- *Does this message need the appearance of formality?* Some documents, such as proposals, contracts, and bylaws, gain credibility by looking formal. Disciplinary fact finding and grievance processing require formal documents. Sometimes, routine messages, such as ones granting credit or acknowledging orders for products, become more effective when conveyed via a formal, personally written letter rather than an informal postcard or an all-purpose form letter.

FIGURE 1.6 ● Formal Communication Channels

Flow

Selecting the best communication form demands some understanding of how messages and information flow through organizations. Both formal and informal communication channels exist. Dynamic, robust organizations like Sara Lee, Bank of America, and Xerox make use of both kinds of channels to encourage an open communication environment. A free exchange of information helps organizations solve problems, cut costs, better serve the public, and take full advantage of today's knowledge workers.

● Organizational communication may flow through formal or informal channels.

Formal channels. Formal channels of communication generally follow an organization's hierarchy of command, as shown in Figure 1.6. Information about policies and procedures originates with executives and flows down through managers to supervisors and finally to employees. Many corporations have formulated official communication policies that encourage regular open communication, suggest means for achieving it, and spell out responsibilities. Whether an organization has developed such a communication policy or not, official information among workers typically flows through formal channels in three directions: downward, upward, and horizontally.

● Formal communication usually flows downward from management to employees.

Downward flow. Information flowing downward generally moves from decision-makers, including the CEO and managers, through the chain of command to employees. This information includes job plans, policies, instructions, and procedures. Managers also provide feedback about employee performance and instill a sense of mission in achieving the organization's goals. One problem in downward communication is distortion resulting from long lines of communication. If, for example, the CEO in Figure 1.6 wanted to change an accounting procedure, he would probably not send a memo directly to the staff or cost accountants who would implement the change. Instead, he would relay his idea through proper formal channels—from the vice president for finance, to the accounting manager, to the senior accountant, and so on—until the message reached the affected employees. Obviously, the longer the lines of communication, the greater the chance that a message will be distorted. Indeed, a study of over 100 businesses where messages were transmitted through five levels of management revealed that only 20 percent of the given message reached its target audience.[20]

Feedback from employees forms the upward flow of communication in most organizations.

Upward flow. Information flowing upward provides feedback from employees to management. Subordinate employees describe progress in completing tasks, report roadblocks encountered, and suggest methods for improving efficiency. Channels for upward communication include memos, reports, departmental meetings, and suggestion systems. Ideally, the heaviest flow of information should be upward with information being fed steadily to decision-makers who can react and adjust quickly.

Horizontal flow. Lateral channels transmit information horizontally among workers at the same level, such as between the training supervisor and maintenance supervisor in Figure 1.6. These channels enable individuals to coordinate tasks, share information, solve problems, and resolve conflicts. Horizontal communication takes place through personal contact, memos, and meetings. However, most organizations have few established regular channels for the horizontal exchange of information.

Informal organizational communication transmits unofficial news through the grapevine.

Informal channels. Not all the information within an organization passes through formal channels; often, it travels in informal channels called the *grapevine.* These channels are based on social relationships in which individuals talk about work when they are having lunch, jogging, golfing, or carpooling to work. Alert managers find the grapevine an excellent source of information about employee morale and problems. Employees using the grapevine also consider it valuable for two reasons: (1) they can get information without formally having to admit that they need it, and (2) they can "think out loud" about problems, thus increasing their self-confidence and problem-solving ability.[21]

Researchers studying communication flow within organizations have revealed some unexpected facts about the grapevine. For one thing they have discovered that the grapevine can be a major source of information for members of an organization. Some studies suggest that as much as two thirds of an employee's information comes from informal channels.[22]

Noncontroversial information transmitted over the grapevine can be surprisingly accurate.

Another unanticipated finding is that the grapevine is accurate. Because almost all the information transmitted over the grapevine is oral, you'd expect it to be riddled with mistakes and distortions. Surprisingly, though, many researchers have found that, for noncontroversial company information transmitted over the grapevine, 75 to 90 percent of the details of messages were accurate.[23] Moreover, news traveling over the grapevine is transmitted quickly: one specialist found that it was the fastest channel for sending messages to employees.[24] News of a position opening up in a department, for example, often reaches other workers long before an official announcement travels down through formal channels.

Barriers to Organizational Communication

Both formal and informal communication within most organizations is less than perfect. Before we examine ways to improve it, let's pinpoint six specific barriers to organizational communication.

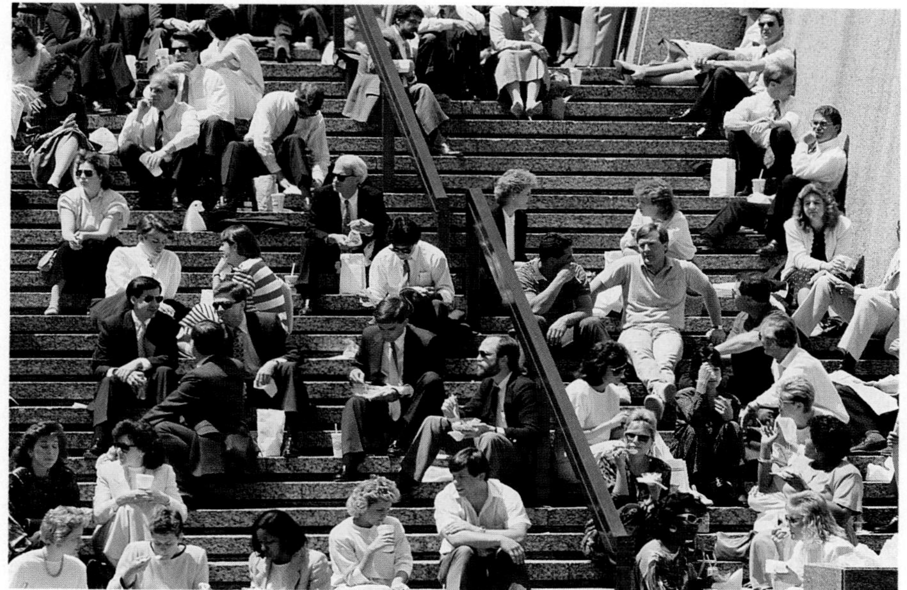

Lunching on the steps outside the office means a chance to sit in the sun and perhaps exchange news. Information transmitted among employees over informal communication channels travels quickly but may be incomplete or inaccurate. Studies show that workers prefer to learn company news from official, formal channels rather than through the grapevine.

Closed communication climate. An organization can enhance or inhibit communication by the environment it creates. In a closed climate, employees receive little organizational news. They don't know what's expected of them, and they feel that no one cares about them or listens to them. In the worst of such organizations, information is hoarded by top management, as if informing subordinates would weaken the control of management. Such a climate acts as a powerful communication barrier. In an open communication climate, like that at Sara Lee, management values employees and appreciates their need for organizational information. Hence, Sara Lee publishes regular employee newsletters, keeping employees informed of organizational goings-on. And because they feel free to communicate upward with a sense of influence, employees become part of the decision-making process.

Barriers to organizational communication include a closed communication climate, a top-heavy hierarchy, filtering, lack of trust, rivalry, and power and status issues.

Top-heavy organizational structure. Long lines of communication result when an organization has a top-heavy, multilevel structure. Because messages traveling upward or downward must pass through many managerial levels, distortion, delays in delivery, and alienation between senders and receivers often results. Each layer of management creates a roadblock to efficient communication. Assume, for example, that Juanita in Customer Service has a great idea for improving the company's product return procedures. She may never propose that idea if she knows that she must first submit it to her supervisor, who must then go through four more levels of management before the suggestion reaches a person who has the power to act on it.

Filtering. *Filtering* refers to the process of distorting, shortening, or lengthening messages as they travel through the communication network. Everyone who processes a message views it selectively through his or her own unique frame of reference. As a result, messages are *leveled* (some details are lost), *condensed* (facts are simplified), *sharpened* (selected details are highlighted), *assimilated* (confusions are clarified and interpreted), and *embellished* (details are added).[25] Filtering is most prevalent in organizations with long communication chains.

Filtering can cause distortion when messages are leveled, condensed, sharpened, assimilated, or embellished.

SPOTLIGHT ON COMMUNICATORS

General Electric CEO John F. Welch realizes the importance of trust in a corporation. People won't do their best, he observes, unless they believe they'll be treated fairly and without favoritism. To create that kind of trust, he advises laying out your values and then "walking the talk." Maintaining trust means doing what you say you will do, consistently, over time.

Lack of trust. Employees who trust their managers are likely to communicate openly. Employees cease trusting managers if they feel they are being tricked, manipulated, criticized, or treated impersonally. Of course, establishing trust is a reciprocal process: managers who trust their employees will receive trust in return and will believe that subordinates have the desire and ability to perform their jobs responsibly. This kind of trust goes a long way toward reducing communication barriers.

Rivalry. Employees competing for recognition and advancement may misrepresent or conceal information from one another and from management. They are reluctant to reveal information because they fear it might benefit a fellow employee at their expense. Thus, instead of speaking truthfully, rivals put a "spin" or "twist" on facts in an effort to protect their own interests and turf. James might, for example, discount, criticize, or misrepresent Sue's proposal to expedite customer orders. Although her plan has merit, he fears she may beat him out for the next promotion.

Unethical behavior resulting from rivalry can create barriers that distort the communication process. The accompanying Ethics box contains suggestions for dealing with ethical dilemmas.

Power and status. The very fact that one person (the boss) has power in an organization while all others (the subordinates) lack that power constitutes a potential roadblock to open communication. Many bosses are afraid to reveal difficulties, losses, or conditions that make them look weak. At the same time subordinates avoid disclosing information about lack of progress, frustrations, or disagreements among workers. They may even "color" their reports to convey the appearance of achievement.

Surmounting Organizational Barriers

Facing stiff global competition, many organizations now recognize that improved internal communication is a key to better employee performance and increased productivity. As *Fortune* magazine reports, "Internal communications—talk back and forth within the organization, up and down the hierarchy—may well be more important to a company's success than external communications. . . ." Free-flowing information within an organization enables management "to identify and attack problems fast, say, when customer service representatives first get an earful about some quality glitch, or sales[people] in the field encounter a new competitor."[26] Open lines of communication also create an environment of trust and employee goodwill. Here are specific ways in which organizations can reduce communication barriers.

● **Organizational communication barriers are greatly reduced when managers seek employee feedback.**

Encouraging an open environment for interaction and feedback. The climate an organization cultivates greatly influences communication. At Sara Lee small groups of employees are invited to talk with managers. At Chrysler, Lee Iacocca used to hold "town hall" meetings for 175 randomly selected employees. "I talk for five minutes, and then they get an hour and a half to knock my head in," he said.[27] CEO James Orr invites all 5,500 employees of the UNUM insurance company to "sound off" with messages to him over the company's E-mail system. Every night he reads the messages and sometimes answers with a personal call the

FOUR ETHICAL GUIDELINES BUSINESS COMMUNICATORS SHOULD KNOW

Pressures on people and on organizations today can create dilemmas that require, in addition to communication skills, an ability to make ethical decisions. Often, the dilemmas have no clear-cut right or wrong answers.

Assume that Carolyn Song and you are competing for a promotion to regional manager in Orlando, Florida. In the past year Carolyn has been quite successful at her work. Although you acknowledge that Carolyn is doing a good job, you have been with the company longer and believe you deserve the position. Moreover, you feel threatened by her; and frankly, you don't like her personally. This promotion is important to you not only professionally but personally: your elderly parents live in the Orlando area, and you want to be close by to help them out.

One day you happen to meet an old friend who has known Carolyn for some time. Over a cup of coffee you learn that Carolyn never graduated from the University of Texas, as stated on her résumé. In fact, she never attended college at all.

What should you do? Say nothing and, in effect, allow Carolyn to be rewarded for lying? Head straight to the vice president and expose the truth—which might, at the same time, conveniently eliminate a rival? Each action has potential consequences that make the decision difficult. Frequently, say ethicists, the "right" action is the one you can live with. But how do you arrive at that decision? Here are four simple guidelines that can help any business communicator make ethical choices:

- **Visualize the desired outcome.** What would you like to see happen as a result of resolving this issue? Will your choice produce the goal you seek?
- **Weigh the interests of all stakeholders.** Who will be affected by your choice? Consider the consequences for you, your fellow employees, your boss, the organization, your family, and the community. What effect will it have on Carolyn? Can you live with the consequences? Whose interests are most important?
- **Take the public-scrutiny test.** How would you feel about revealing your choice to your colleagues, friends, or spouse?
- **Balance your professional and personal goals.** Consider each choice and its effect on your career. Also consider its personal effects. Is there a choice that reconciles your professional goals with your personal values?

Career Track Application

Determine three or four actions you could take regarding Carolyn's dark secret. Then, evaluate each choice according to the four guidelines here. Be prepared to discuss your final choice and the reasoning behind it in class. Additional ethical guidelines will be presented in Chapter 3.

next day.[28] At Bank of America the CEO says, "We try to encourage a feedback process. We stress to [employees] that we care, we ask them to tell us what they think, and we always emphasize that we will give them an honest answer."[29]

Reducing layers of management shortens lines of communication.

Flattening the organizational structure. Businesses today are streamlining their operations and eliminating layers of unnecessary management, thus shortening lines of communication. Toy-maker Mattel transformed itself from an "out-of-control money loser" into a record-breaking money-maker by taking the advice of employees and cutting six layers from its organizational hierarchy.[30] "One of the most effective ways of building responsiveness into organizations is to eliminate layers of management," says Andrew S. Grove, CEO of computer chip–maker Intel Corporation. "With fewer levels," he continues, "information flows more naturally and problems get solved faster."[31] In addition, because messages travel shorter distances, less distortion occurs.

FIGURE 1.7 ● Barriers to the Communication Process

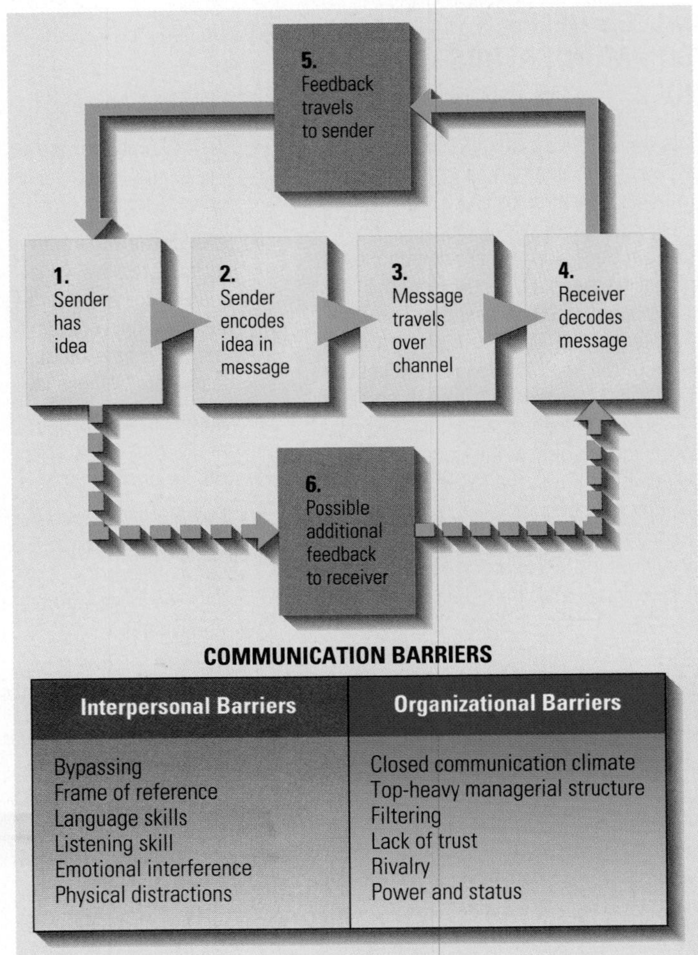

● **Horizontal communication improves morale and enriches an organization.**

Promoting horizontal communication. Horizontal communication builds bonds among employees, boosts morale, decreases turnover, and enriches the organization through exchange of ideas. At Lucasfilms, producers of the *Star Wars* trilogy and other films, managers felt that too little horizontal communication existed among editors, cinematographers, and artists. They opened the channels by forming softball teams limited to only one member from any one department. This forced individuals from different departments to start talking to one another.[32]

Establishing rumor-control centers. It's been estimated that at least 33 million fresh rumors circulate daily in American industries.[33] Many large organizations use telephone rumor-control systems to deal with inaccurate and/or injurious rumors. Employees can anonymously inquire about rumors at a central office. If the truth is known, callers learn immediately; if facts must be verified, employees can call back later to hear updates.

Providing ample information through formal channels. Studies show that most employees would rather receive company news through formal channels than from the grapevine.[34] The grapevine becomes less important in organizations where employees are regularly informed of company news. If employees receive a steady flow of information through meetings, newsletters, and announcements, unofficial channels carry only personal tidbits, such as who's dating whom. Recognizing the power of internal communication in today's competitive markets, increasing numbers of managers are talking candidly with employees, encouraging them to contribute ideas. Enlightened executives are using E-mail, videos, and satellite hookups to disseminate news of the organization.

Employees prefer to learn of organization news through official, formal channels.

Figure 1.7 summarizes two groups of obstacles that can sabotage interpersonal and organizational communication efforts.

Strengthening Your Communication Skills

You've just taken a brief look at the process of communication, its barriers, and its operation within organizations. This overview is the first step in strengthening your communication skills—your ability to read, listen, speak, and write. In addition to helping you feel confident in your personal life, these skills are exceptionally important in your professional life. Whether you get the job you seek and the promotions you deserve depends on many factors, some of which you can't control. But one factor that you do control is how well you communicate. Sara Lee CEO John Bryan recognized this when he said that communication skills are "about 99 percent developed." They are not inborn. Bryan contends that "the ability to construct a succinct memo, one that concentrates on the right issues, and the ability to make a presentation to an audience—these are skills that can be taught to almost anyone."[35]

Communication skills—reading, speaking, listening, writing—can be learned.

Communication skills can certainly be learned. This book and this course will help you become a better communicator through study of techniques, through observation of models, and through practice. Practice, of course, is most valuable when accompanied by appropriate feedback. You need someone like your instructor to tell you how to modify your responses so that you can improve.

We've designed this book and its Study Guide to provide you with the principles, process, models, and practice you need to become a successful business communicator.

Summary of Learning Goals

1. **Explain the importance of communication skills for knowledge workers.** Three out of every four future jobs will be filled by knowledge workers who can work effectively with words, figures, and data. These employees need excellent communication skills to be hired, to perform effectively on the job, and especially to be promoted into management.
2. **Describe the communication process and its central objective.** The sender encodes (selects) words or symbols to express an idea. The message is sent verbally over a channel (such as via letter, memo, or telephone call) or is expressed nonverbally, perhaps with gestures or body language. "Noise"—such as loud sounds, misspelled words, or other distractions—may interfere with the transmission. The receiver decodes (interprets) the message and

attempts to make sense of it. The receiver responds with feedback, informing the sender of the effectiveness of the message. The objective of communication is the transmission of meaning so that a receiver understand a message as intended by the sender.

3. **Recognize six barriers to interpersonal communication and methods for overcoming them.** *Bypassing* causes miscommunication because people have different meanings for the words they use. One's *frame of reference* creates a filter through which all ideas are screened, sometimes causing distortion and lack of objectivity. *Weak language skills* as well as *poor listening skills* impair communication efforts. *Emotional interference*—joy, fear, anger, and so forth—hampers the sending and receiving of messages. *Physical distractions*—noisy surroundings, faulty acoustics, and so forth—can disrupt oral communication.

   You can reduce or overcome these communication barriers if you (a) realize that the communication process is imperfect, (b) adapt your message to the receiver, (c) improve your language and listening skills, (d) question your preconceptions, and (e) plan for feedback.

4. **Identify the three functions of business communication.** Whether you are communicating internally or externally, the three primary functions are (a) to inform, (b) to persuade, and/or (c) to promote goodwill.

5. **Contrast oral and written communication.** Oral, usually two-way, communication provides immediate feedback, nonverbal clues, a warm feeling, and a forceful impact, as well as enabling multiple input. Written, usually two-way, communication provides a permanent record, convenience, economy, a careful message, and easy distribution.

6. **Distinguish between formal and informal channels of communication.** Formal channels of communication in organizations include policies, procedures, and directives flowing downward from management to employees. An informal channel is the grapevine, which carries unofficial news—both personal and organizational—among friends and coworkers.

7. **Recognize six barriers to organizational communication and methods for overcoming them.** A *closed communication climate* prevents the free flow of information between management and subordinates. *Top-heavy organization* inhibits communication because messages must flow through many levels of management. *Filtering* causes distortion as receivers screen messages through their own perceptions. *Lack of trust* makes communication impossible. *Rivalry* and competition for recognition may cause individuals to distort or conceal essential data. *Power and status* can interfere with clear communication when, for example, the boss avoids admitting poor judgment or when employees are silent about achievements or circumstances that reflect poorly on them.

   Many barriers to communication can be overcome if an organization (a) encourages an open environment for interaction and feedback among all employees, (b) flattens the organizational structure by removing some levels of management, (c) promotes horizontal communication so that employees know what other employees are doing, (d) establishes rumor-control mechanisms to keep employees fully informed, and (e) provides ample organizational information directly from management to employees.

Chapter Review

1. What percentage of new jobs are expected to be service or information related?

2. Give two reasons employers seek employees with good communication skills.

3. Define *communication,* and explain its most critical factor.

4. Describe five steps in the process of communication.

5. How can senders encourage and receivers provide effective feedback?

6. List six barriers to interpersonal communication. Be prepared to discuss each.

7. Name five things that you could do personally to reduce barriers in your communication.

8. What are the three main functions of organizational communication?

9. Identify five common myths about business writing.

10. What are the advantages of oral communication?

11. What are the advantages of written communication?

12. What are the chief differences between formal and informal channels of organizational communication?

13. Within an organization what kinds of information flow downward?

14. List six organizational barriers to communication. Be prepared to discuss each.

15. List five means of overcoming barriers to organizational communication.

Discussion

1. Comment on the complaint of some companies that the more information provided to employees, the more employees want.

2. Recall a time when you experienced a problem as a result of poor communication. Analyze the causes and possible remedies for the problem.

3. Research shows that the grapevine often carries accurate information. Why, then, is it considered so unreliable?

4. Describe the communication climate in an organization to which you belonged or for which you worked.

5. Ethical Issue: How would you respond if you heard through the grapevine that a fellow manager with whom you were competing for a promotion was suspected of falsifying an efficiency report so that his department's record looked better than it really was?

Activities

1.1 Communication Assessment: How Do You Stack Up?

You know more about yourself than anyone else. That makes you the best person to assess your present communication skills. Take an honest look at your current skills and rank them using the following chart. How well you communicate will be an important factor in your future career—particularly if you are promoted into management, as many college graduates are. For each skill, circle the number from 1 (indicating low ability) to 5 (indicating high ability) that best reflects your perception of yourself.

Writing Skills	**Low**				**High**
1. Possess basic spelling, grammar, and punctuation skills	1	2	3	4	5
2. Am familiar with proper memo, letter, and report formats for business documents	1	2	3	4	5
3. Can analyze a writing problem and quickly outline a plan for solving the problem	1	2	3	4	5
4. Am able to organize data coherently and logically	1	2	3	4	5
5. Can evaluate a document to determine its probable success	1	2	3	4	5

Reading Skills	**Low**				**High**
1. Am familiar with specialized vocabulary in my field as well as general vocabulary	1	2	3	4	5
2. Can concentrate despite distractions	1	2	3	4	5
3. Am willing to look up definitions whenever necessary	1	2	3	4	5
4. Am able to move from recreational to serious reading	1	2	3	4	5
5. Can read and comprehend college-level material	1	2	3	4	5
Speaking Skills					
1. Feel at ease in speaking with friends	1	2	3	4	5
2. Feel at ease in speaking before a group of people	1	2	3	4	5
3. Can adapt my presentation to the audience	1	2	3	4	5
4. Am confident in pronouncing and using words correctly	1	2	3	4	5
5. Sense that I have credibility when I make a presentation	1	2	3	4	5
Listening Skills					
1. Spend at least half the time listening during conversations	1	2	3	4	5
2. Am able to concentrate on a speaker's words despite distractions	1	2	3	4	5
3. Can summarize a speaker's ideas and anticipate what's coming during pauses	1	2	3	4	5
4. Provide feedback, like nodding, paraphrasing, and asking questions	1	2	3	4	5
5. Listen with the expectation of gaining new ideas and information	1	2	3	4	5

Now analyze your scores. Where are you strongest? Weakest? How do you think outsiders would rate you on these skills and traits? Are you satisfied with your present skills? The first step to improvement is recognition of a need. Put a check mark next to the five traits you feel you should begin working on immediately.

1.2 Memo

Write a memo of introduction to your instructor. Use this format:

TO: Title, Instructor's name DATE: Present
FROM: Your name
SUBJECT: INTRODUCTION AND COMMUNICATION ASSESSMENT

Begin your memo by describing your major and your entry-level and long-term employment goals. What communication skills do you think will be required of you when you reach your ultimate career position? Discuss your present strengths and weaknesses. Begin your final paragraph with "In addition to attending school, I like to . . ." Describe some activities you enjoy.

1.3 Want Ads

Conduct your own survey of advertisements for jobs in your field. Consult the Sunday edition of a large newspaper. How many of the ads mention communication skills? What job tasks do the advertisements describe? How many of them require communication skills? What conclusions would you draw? Clip several ads that seem especially interesting or promising and bring them to class for discussion.

1.4 Information Flow

Consider an organization to which you belong or a business where you've worked. How did members learn what was going on in the organization? What kind of information flowed through formal channels? What were those channels? What kind of information was delivered through informal channels? Was the grapevine as accurate as official channels? How could the flow of information be improved?

1.5 Communication Process

Review the communication process and its barriers as described in the text. Now imagine that you are the boss in an organization where you've worked and you wish to announce a new policy aimed at improving customer service. Examine the entire communication process from sender to feedback. How will the message be encoded? What assumptions must you make about your audience? What channel is best? How can you encourage feedback? What noise may interfere with transmission? What barriers should you expect? How can you overcome them? Your instructor may ask you to write a memo describing your responses to these questions.

1.6 Communication Forms

What is the best form for delivering information in the following situations? You may suggest a personal letter, memo, company newsletter, telephone call, face-to-face conversation, or some other form of communication. Be ready to discuss your reasons.

a. Informing many groups that your company cannot allow them to tour your bottling plant this summer because of remodeling

b. Asking your boss for permission to attend a two-day seminar to improve your job skills

c. Launching a major company campaign to encourage employees to submit more ideas for improving the way they do their jobs

d. Informing the winners of Employee-of-the-Month awards

e. Checking the references of a job candidate

f. Comparing the cost of purchasing diskettes from three local vendors

1.7 Document Analysis: Barriers to Communication

The following memo was actually written in a large business organization. Comment on its effectiveness, tone, and potential barriers to communication.

> TO: All Departmental Personnel
> SUBJECT: FRIDAY P.M. CLEAN-UP
>
> Every Friday afternoon starting at 3 p.m. there is suppose to be a departmental clean-up. This practice will commence this Friday and continue until otherwise specified.
>
> All CC162 employees will partake in this endeavor. This means not only cleaning his own area, but contributing to the cleaning of the complete department.
>
> Thank you for your cooperation.

1.8 Communication Barriers

For each of the following situations, what interpersonal and/or organizational barriers might the message senders anticipate? How could the senders overcome these barriers?

a. During a recession an executive with a prestigious Ivy League education must write to all employees persuading them to agree to temporary wage cuts.

b. An accountant wishes to explain to the marketing department why it must report monthly sales figures differently.

c. An administrative assistant has been asked to organize and publicize a departmental surprise party for the boss.

d. You try to summarize an instructor's lecture for a friend who was absent.

e. You are in charge of writing the company's annual report, which will be read by stockholders, suppliers, customers, management, and others.

1.9 Feedback

One of the most difficult tasks in communication is finding out if you were understood. What advice could you give a manager regarding feedback? Your instructor may ask you to write a one-page essay explaining your ideas.

1.10 Communication Failures

Communication is not successful unless the receiver understands the message as the receiver meant it. Analyze the following examples of communication failures. What went wrong?

a. A supervisor issued the following announcement: "Effective immediately the charge for copying services in Repro will be raised ½ to 2 cents each." Receivers scratched their heads.

b. The pilot of a military airplane about to land decided that the runway was too short. He shouted to his engineer, "Takeoff power!" The engineer turned off the engines; the plane crashed.

c. The following statements actually appeared in letters of application for an advertised job opening. One applicant wrote, "Enclosed is my résumé in response to Sunday's New York Times." Another wrote, "Enclosed is my résumé in response to my search for an editorial/creative position." Still another wrote, "My experience in the production of newsletters, magazines, directories, and on-line data bases puts me head and shoulders above the crowd of applicants you have no doubtedly been inundated with."

d. The following sign in English appeared in an Austrian hotel that catered to skiers: "Not to perambulate the corridors in the hours of repose in the boots of ascension."

C.L.U.E. Review 1

Each chapter includes an exercise based on Appendix A, "Competent Language Usage Essentials (C.L.U.E.)." This appendix is a business communicator's condensed guide to language usage, covering 50 of the most used, and abused, language elements. It also includes a list of 150 frequently misspelled words and a quick review of selected confusing words. The following exercise is packed with errors based on concepts and spelling words from the appendix. If you are rusty on these language essentials, spend some time studying the guidelines and examples in Appendix A. Then, test your skills with the chapter C.L.U.E. exercises. You will find the corrections for these exercises at the end of the appendix. Remember, these exercises contain *only* usage and spelling words from Appendix A.

On a separate sheet, edit the following sentences to correct faults in grammar, punctuation, spelling, and word use.

1. After he checked many statements our Accountant found the error in columne 2 of the balance sheet.
2. Because Mr. Lockwoods business owned considerable property. We were serprised by it's lack of liquid assets.
3. The mortgage company checked all property titles separatly, however it found no discrepancies.
4. When Ms. Diaz finished the audit she wrote 3 letters. To appraise the owners of her findings.
5. Just between you and I whom do you think could have ordered all this stationary.
6. Assets and liabilities is what the 4 buyers want to see, consequently we are preparing this years statements.
7. Next spring my brother and myself plan to enroll in the following courses marketing english and history.
8. Dan felt that he had done good on the exam but he wants to do even better when it's given again next Fall.
9. Our records show that your end of the month balance was ninety-six dollars and 30 cents.
10. When the principle in the account grows to large we must make annual withdrawals.

Listening and Intercultural Communication

LEARNING GOALS

After studying this chapter, you should be able to

1. Explain the listening process and identify four elements of good listening
2. Specify and apply ten specific techniques that improve listening skills
3. Recognize the significance of nonverbal messages
4. Exercise ten specific suggestions to enhance nonverbal communication skills
5. Clarify pivotal American cultural values
6. Identify key attitudes that prevent intercultural miscommunication
7. Employ ten specific procedures for adapting messages to intercultural audiences

The Travelers: Career Track Profile

"Much of my job centers on listening . . . a skill that definitely can be learned."

Two years after graduating from Seton Hall University in New Jersey, Andrea Ciriello was hired as a consumer information coordinator at The Travelers, one of the nation's largest insurance companies. Suddenly, she needed skills for which she had little training.

Andrea joined a company known for its corporate logo of a red umbrella and its reputation for stability and responsiveness to customers. Founded in 1864 for the purpose of "insuring travelers [thus, its name] against loss of life or personal injury while journeying by railway or steamboat," Travelers now offers life, property, casualty, and health insurance, as well as extensive investment services. It insures millions of Americans and hundreds of thousands of businesses; in fact, over 50 percent of Fortune 500 companies have some form of Travelers' coverage. Its umbrella of service covers so many operations that providing answers to callers on Travelers' toll-free consumer information line requires wide knowledge and special patience.

Acting as a resource person to consumer representatives fielding these calls, Andrea must constantly keep abreast of what's happening in the huge company. That means knowing the latest Standard & Poor's ratings of its subsidiaries, addresses and telephone numbers of field offices across the country, and details about new offerings, policy cancellations, and program changes. "In such a large company, a big part of my job is keeping the consumer reps up to date with the myriad of changes occurring continuously," says Andrea.

"My most challenging task, though, is working directly with callers. When I fill in for consumer reps or take referred calls (those that the reps can't answer), I talk with policyholders, agents, prospective customers, field office managers, and many others who need information. We handle consumer calls coming to the home office here in Hartford, Connecticut—even calls that must be redirected to our field offices throughout the country.

"Much of my job centers on listening—to my supervisor, to the customer reps, and especially to the callers. Strange how you can go through four years of college and not really learn how to listen. In my training here at Travelers, I was taught techniques that helped me greatly; listening is a skill that definitely can be learned. We have a training room equipped with a speaker phone so that everyone can hear a call. The most startling thing I witnessed was how one conversation could produce many different interpretations. When we listened to a customer's call, we often didn't hear the same thing at all. What did the customer actually want?

"One technique that helps me tremendously is the 'listen-to-report' principle. Whether I'm receiving instructions from my supervisor or hearing a policyholder's request, I treat the information as if I will have to explain it to someone else. I rarely rely on my memory; notes are much more dependable. When you know that you will have to report to someone else, you try very hard to get all the information straight; and taking notes is a must.

"Asking questions also helps clarify what's being said. Because people work from different pools of information, they sometimes mean something entirely different from what you think you hear. Often, our callers are confused about their insurance coverage. They may inquire about a group pension when, in fact, they mean an individual annuity. To draw out the correct information, I might ask, 'Is this a benefit through your company or did you purchase your policy from an agent?' The answer to that question helps me distinguish between the two kinds of coverage. Phrasing the question carefully elicits the information I need quickly.

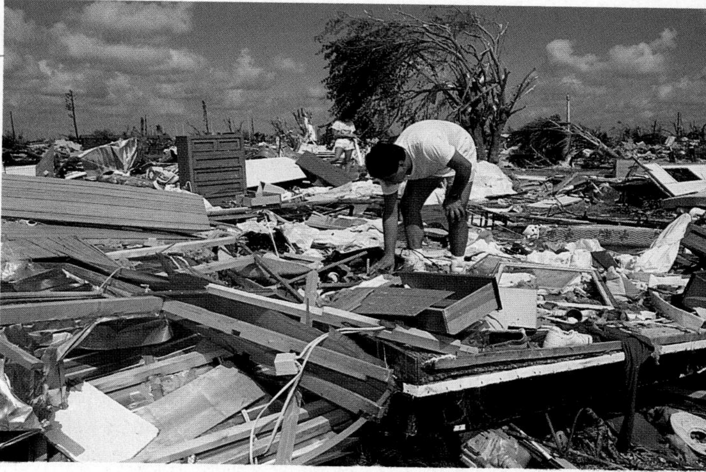

Hurricane Andrew in Florida caused intense suffering and billions of dollars in losses to individuals and insurance companies. The Travelers immediately sent teams of claims handlers to help its customers get back on their feet quickly. In addition to 300 permanent property-casualty claims adjusters and staff in Florida, it brought in more than 200 out-of-state adjusters. Listening to customers and being prepared in times of emergency has helped The Travelers spread its umbrella of protection to more than half of all Fortune 500 companies.

"Another technique that I've learned to use (both on the job and off) is echoing. By restating in my own words what the speaker said and asking for verification, I can find out if we agree. Because it's so easy to misunderstand what someone is trying to say, I like to repeat the speaker's main points—in a friendly, compassionate tone of voice. I might say, 'Let me check to see if I am understanding you clearly.' My questions can't sound like attacks, though, or the caller becomes defensive.

"One of the biggest problems for listeners is impatience. I must constantly work on my tendency to jump to hasty conclusions. It's important to hear the caller out, get all the facts, and clarify as the conversation progresses. I've learned that every story has two sides; it pays to be patient and cautious until the speaker finishes."

Another problem that Andrea faces is a distracting work environment. Telephones are constantly ringing (her telephone has two lines on it). She hears other conversations in the office, and she uses her computer to search for answers as she listens to callers' questions. Overcoming these distractions demands powerful concentration. "I clear my mind so that I hear only the person I'm talking with. Busy surroundings come with the territory here, but so does teamwork. I know that one of my coworkers will pick up a second call, allowing me to focus totally on what I'm hearing."

Andrea closes all business conversations with two important routines: (1) she confirms what was said by summarizing the significant points, and (2) she outlines what will happen next. These thoughtful steps, like her many other good listening techniques, help Andrea hear what speakers are really saying. Then she is able to convert the information she hears into meaning, which, of course, is the real goal of communication.[1]

Strengthening Listening Skills

Listening is a key personal and career skill.

Listening is one of the first requirements mentioned when employers describe crucial employment skills. Such skills open the door to promotion and career success. Listening powers such as those Andrea Ciriello developed on the job at Travelers, however, require training and discipline. The good news, though, is that these skills and attitudes are learnable. By developing your listening skills, you may well be tapping into one of your greatest resources for career and personal success.[2] This chapter discusses the listening process and its barriers; it also provides specific suggestions for improving listening techniques.

In Chapter 1 we examined the communication process primarily from the perspective of the sender, focusing on the importance of creating meaning in messages. Now we'll concentrate on the receiving end of communication, examining how to interpret meaning through verbal and nonverbal cues. In addition, this chapter describes how the already sensitive process of communication becomes even more complex when we communicate with people from diverse backgrounds and cultures.

Most workers spend 30 to 45 percent of their communication time listening;[3] executives, however, devote 60 to 70 percent of this time to listening.[4] When John Sculley became CEO at Apple Computer, he learned about some of his employees from the titles on their business cards. One card said "Hardware Wizard"; another announced "Software Evangelist"; still another proclaimed "Product Champion." After settling into his job, the new CEO decided that his title should reflect how he spent most of his time—"Chief Listener."[5]

Although executives and workers devote the bulk of their communication time to listening, research suggests that they're not very good at it. In fact, most of us are poor listeners. Some estimates indicate that only half the oral messages heard in a day are completely understood.[6] Experts say that we listen at only 25 percent efficiency. In other words, *we ignore, forget, distort, or misunderstand 75 percent of everything we hear.*

Reasons for inefficient listening include lack of training, competing sounds and stimuli, and the slowness of speech.

Such listening inefficiency may result from several factors. Lack of training is one significant reason. Few schools give as much emphasis to listening as to the development of reading, speaking, and writing skills. In addition, our listening skills may be less than perfect because of the large number of competing sounds and stimuli in our lives that interfere with concentration. Finally, we are inefficient listeners because of the slowness of speech. While most speakers talk at about 150 words per minute, listeners can process oral communication at over 400 words per minute. This lag time causes daydreaming, which in turn reduces listening efficiency.

Examining the process of listening, as well as its barriers, may shed some light on ways to improve your listening efficiency and retention.

The Listening Process and Its Barriers

Listening takes place in four stages, discussed here and illustrated in Figure 2.1. Like communication, listening can be obstructed by barriers, which may be grouped into two categories: mental and physical.

Perception. The listening process begins when you hear sounds and concentrate on them. Stop reading for a moment and become conscious of the sounds around you: Do you notice the hum of an electrical appliance, background sounds from a TV program, muffled traffic noise, or the murmur of distant voices? Until you

FIGURE 2.1 ● The Listening Process and Its Barriers

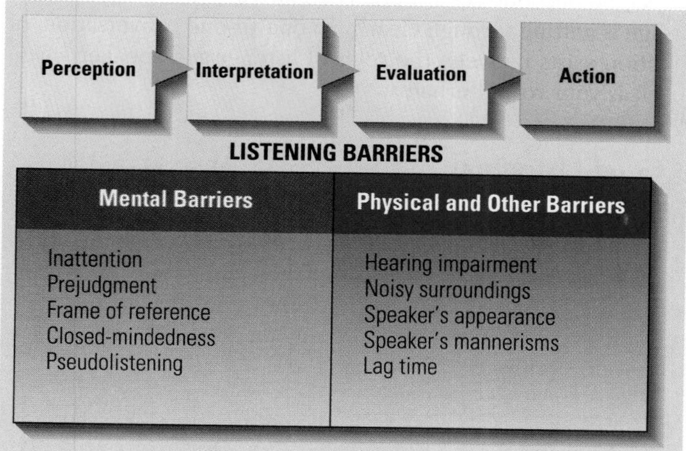

"tuned in" to them, these sounds went unnoticed. The conscious act of listening begins when you observe the sounds around you and select those you choose to hear. You tune in when (1) you sense that the message is important, (2) you are interested in the topic, or (3) you are in the mood to listen.

● **The four stages in the listening process are perception, interpretation, evaluation, and action.**

Perception is reduced by impaired hearing, noisy surroundings, inattention, and pseudolistening. Pseudolistening occurs when listeners "fake" it—when they look as if they are listening, but their minds are wandering far off.

Interpretation. Once you have focused your attention on a sound or message, you begin to interpret, or decode, it. As described in Chapter 1, interpretation of a message is colored by your cultural, educational, and social frame of reference. The meanings you attach to the speaker's words are filtered through your expectations and total life experiences. Thus, your interpretation of the speaker's meaning may be quite different from what the speaker intended because your frame of reference is different.

As Andrea Ciriello learned at Travelers, listeners can improve their chances of comprehending the message the sender intended by asking clarifying questions such as "Let me see if I am understanding you clearly."

Evaluation. After interpreting the meaning of a message, you analyze its merit and draw conclusions. To do this, you attempt to separate fact from opinion. Good listeners try to be objective; they avoid prejudging the message. In research with college students, one researcher determined that closed-mindedness and opinionated attitudes functioned as major barriers to listening. Certain students were not good listeners because their prejudices prevented them from opening up to a speaker's ideas.[7] The appearance and mannerisms of the speaker can also affect a listener's evaluation of a message. A juror, for example, might jump to the conclusion that an accused man is guilty because of his fierce expression or his substandard English. Thus, to evaluate a message accurately and objectively, you must (1) consider all the information, (2) be aware of your own biases, and (3) avoid jumping to hasty conclusions.

● **Evaluation involves separating fact from opinion and judging messages objectively.**

Action. Responding to a message may involve storing the message in memory for future use, reacting with a physical response (a frown, a smile, a laugh), or supply-

SPOTLIGHT ON COMMUNICATORS

Be "equal opportunity" listeners, advises Nancy K. Austin, management consultant and co-author of the best-selling book *A Passion for Excellence*. Such listening authorizes people to think. Attentive listening also conveys the nonverbal message that the speaker is smart and has important things to say, thus encouraging open communication. But good listeners, she says, must be all there—no sidelong glances, squirming, or signs of distraction. If your attention slips, try asking a few questions.

ing feedback to the speaker. Listener feedback is essential because it helps clarify the message so that it can be decoded accurately. Feedback also helps the speaker to find out if the message is getting through clearly. In one-to-one conversation, of course, no clear distinction exists between the roles of listener and speaker—you give or receive feedback as your role alternates.

The Dynamics of Good Listening

A large part of the process of becoming a good listener is the ability to recognize and correct existing poor habits, such as those discussed in the accompanying Career Skills box. Good listeners acknowledge their faults and resolve to correct them, a considerable task for most of us. You won't become a perfect listener overnight, but you can certainly begin the process by working on good listening dynamics such as a positive attitude, openness, involvement, and retention.

Positive attitude. Good listeners expect to learn something. In a sense they're listening selfishly. They're thinking, "What's in this for me? What can I learn that may help me?" They are willing to make the mental effort to listen hard because of the potential rewards. For example, college students listen closely to lectures to earn higher grades; employees listen carefully to instructions from supervisors so that they can do their jobs better and earn promotions; company representatives listen attentively to their customers to discover how to retain their business. The first step to good listening is acknowledging that listening is a valuable information-gathering activity.

Openness. Listening effectively requires an openness to new ideas. Good listeners are aware of internal feelings, attitudes, and prejudices that might block alternative views. In communicating with people from other cultures, good listeners try to look beyond their own narrow cultural values. They're tolerant and patient. Like Andrea Ciriello they understand that there are two sides to every story. Instead of tuning out with thoughts like "That's not the way we would do it where I come from" or "What a stupid idea," good listeners continue listening. Moreover, they are not distracted by a speaker's emotional words, offbeat appearance, or quirky speech habits. Considerable mental effort is required to concentrate on the message despite verbal and nonverbal "noise" in the communication process.

Involvement. Good listeners get involved in the listening process. They show commitment to the speaker nonverbally with steady eye contact, an alert body, and undivided attention. They refrain from distracting activities—fidgeting, playing with a pen or key, shifting in the chair, or trying to finish another task while listening. Recall how Andrea Ciriello blocked out all distractions to focus her attention on a caller. Good listeners also get involved by politely asking clarifying questions that do not attack the speaker. Instead of saying "But I don't understand how you could say that," a good listener seeks clarification by saying "Please help me understand by explaining more about . . ."

Good listening means maintaining a positive attitude, being open to new ideas, getting involved in the listening process, and working to retain information.

Retention. An important aspect of listening is retaining what is said. One way to increase retention, particularly of complex data, is to separate the central idea, key points, and details. Sometimes the speaker's points are easy to recognize; other times, the listener must supply the organization. Another way to improve retention is paraphrasing, which involves silently rephrasing and summarizing a message in your own words. Effective listeners do this during lag time—the pause that natu-

NINE POOR LISTENING HABITS THAT CAN SIDETRACK YOUR CAREER

Listening is a vital business skill, yet most of us have such underdeveloped listening skills that we fail to retain 75 percent of what we hear. The following poor habits cost businesses millions of dollars in mistakes and lost productivity. They can also retard your own career advancement if you are unable to recognize and correct them. How many of these apply to you?

- **Reacting to the speaker's appearance and speech mannerisms.** It's easy to be distracted by a speaker's looks, attire, age, or handicaps. Poor listeners refuse to make the effort to overcome personal biases that block objective reception.
- **Failing to control distractions.** Some listeners yield easily to external and internal distractions. They fail to control or block out surrounding noises, or they fail to resist thoughts that interfere with listening concentration.
- **Listening to evaluate rather than to understand.** Too often we listen only to determine if the speaker's ideas fit our frame of reference and beliefs. Listening for immediate evaluation interferes with hearing and understanding the speaker's ideas.
- **Daydreaming and pretending to listen.** We all know how to fix our gaze and look intently at the speaker while hearing nothing being said. This pseudolistening is one of the most serious of the bad listening habits.
- **Assuming the speaker wants input or advice.** Some listeners feel compelled to interrupt a speaker with comments like "Well, here's what I think about it" or "What you ought to do is . . ." Unless the speaker requests it, keep your advice to yourself.
- **Avoiding listening to anything difficult.** Many listeners prefer light, recreational listening. They automatically tune out heavy-duty topics. In doing so, they deprive themselves of the opportunity to learn something new and to develop listening techniques for coping with complex issues.
- **Waiting to jump in and grab the limelight.** Too many listeners are uncomfortable in the role; they much prefer to be speaking. The result? They fail to concentrate on what's being said, but instead are mentally preparing their next comments to be interjected at the first pause.
- **Pretending to understand.** Fear of appearing stupid, impolite, or uninformed may cause us to nod our heads in agreement when we don't really understand. Equally bad is presuming we already know what the speaker means, perhaps because we are familiar with the topic. In either case always ask clarifying questions to ensure that you understand.
- **Listening for facts only.** Failing to observe nonverbal cues can be crucial in one-to-one conversations. Poor listeners fail to pick up on voice intonation, eye movement, and body language. These cues help skillful listeners detect subtle meanings.

Career Track Application

During the next week complete two activities aimed at improving your listening skills. First, conduct a reality check. Ask your closest friends and family to evaluate your listening skills. And be grateful for their honest feedback! Second, evaluate your conversational style using the "50/50" rule. Do you listen 50 percent of the time?

rally occurs when the listener is waiting for the speaker's next idea. A final technique for improving retention is selective note-taking. Good listeners jot down key points, especially if they know they will be responsible for the information later. As Andrea Ciriello puts it, "Taking notes is a must."

Improving Your Listening Effectiveness

Positive attitude, involvement, openness, and retention are key factors that influence effective listening, but people who want to improve their listening skills usually need pointers or specific techniques. The following checklist provides tips to

● A three-step plan for improving your listening skills begins with recognizing your own bad listening habits.

help you become a better listener. To put these tips to work for you, try following this three-step plan:

- **Step 1: Identify your personal bad listening habits.** Do you pseudolisten? Do you tune out difficult topics? Are you more eager to refute than to learn?
- **Step 2: Select techniques to begin working on immediately.** Choose at least two suggestions from the checklist that you feel you could put to work as soon as possible.
- **Step 3: Create opportunities for practice.** During your next classroom lecture or meeting, write at the top of your note pad, "Today I'm here to listen and learn." Then concentrate on doing just that.

Checklist for Improving Listening

✔ **Stop talking.** Accept the role of listener by concentrating on the speaker's words, not on what your response will be.

✔ **Work hard at listening.** Become actively involved, and expect to learn something.

✔ **Block out competing thoughts.** Concentrate on the message, and don't allow yourself to daydream during lag time.

✔ **Control the listening environment.** Turn off the TV, close the windows, and move to a quiet location. Tell the speaker when you cannot hear.

✔ **Maintain an open mind.** Know your biases and try to correct for them. Be tolerant of less-abled and different-looking speakers.

✔ **Provide verbal and nonverbal feedback.** Encourage the speaker with comments like "Yes," "I see," "Okay," and "Uh huh," and ask polite questions. Look alert by leaning forward.

✔ **Paraphrase the speaker's ideas.** Silently repeat the message in your own words, sort out the main points, and identify supporting details. In conversation sum up the main points to confirm what was said.

✔ **Take selective notes.** If you are hearing instructions or important data, record the major points; then, verify your notes with the speaker.

✔ **Listen between the lines.** Observe nonverbal cues, and interpret the feelings of the speaker: What is really being said?

✔ **Capitalize on lag time.** Use spare moments to organize, review, anticipate, challenge, and weigh the evidence.

Creating Meaning from Nonverbal Messages

● Nonverbal cues can contain up to 93 percent of a message's meaning.

Understanding messages often involves more than merely listening to the spoken words. Nonverbal clues, in fact, can speak louder than words. Eye contact, facial expression, body movements, space, time, distance, appearance—all these nonverbal clues influence the way the message is interpreted, or decoded, by the receiver. In studies of interpersonal communication, researchers have found that

FIGURE 2.2 ● Elements in Message Meaning

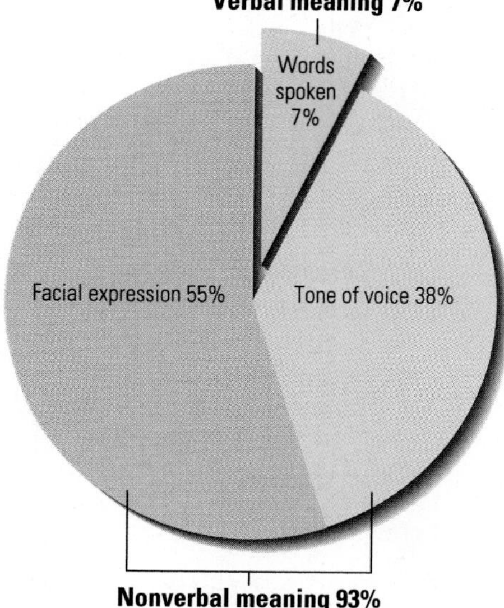

only 7 percent of the "attitudinal" meaning of a message comes from the words spoken. An astounding 93 percent of the meaning, as shown in Figure 2.2, results from nonverbal cues.[8]

● **The silent signals of nonverbal messages carry different meanings for various listeners.**

Nonverbal communication includes all unwritten and unspoken messages, both intentional and unintentional. These silent signals exert a strong influence on the receiver, yet interpreting them is by no means a science. Does a downward glance indicate modesty, embarrassment, or fatigue? Does a constant stare reflect coldness, insensitivity, or dullness?

Messages are especially difficult to decipher when the verbal and nonverbal codes contradict each other. How would you interpret the following?

- Kim assures the hostess that the eggplant moussaka is excellent but eats very little.
- Stewart protests that he's not really angry but slams the door when he leaves.
- Kyoko claims she's not nervous about the interview but perspires profusely.

● **When verbal and nonverbal messages clash, listeners tend to believe the nonverbal message.**

The nonverbal messages in these situations speak more loudly than the words uttered. As numerous studies indicate, when verbal and nonverbal messages conflict, receivers put more faith in the nonverbal cues. In one experiment speakers delivered a positive message but averted their eyes as they spoke. Listeners perceived the overall message to be negative. Moreover, listeners thought that gaze aversion suggested nonaffection, superficiality, lack of trust, and nonreceptivity.[9]

Successful communicators recognize the power of nonverbal messages. While it's unwise to attach arbitrary meanings to specific gestures or actions, some of the cues broadcast by body language are helpful in interpreting the general feelings and attitudes of the sender. For example, body language can suggest defensiveness, cooperation, nervousness, frustration, weakness, and power, as Figure 2.3 points out.

FIGURE 2.3 ● Body Language Cues

Defensiveness

Crossing arms, glancing sideways, touching or rubbing nose, rubbing eyes, buttoning coat, drawing away

Nervousness

Clearing throat, making "whew" sound, whistling, smoking, pinching flesh, fidgeting, covering mouth, jiggling money or keys, tugging ears, wringing hands

Cooperation

Leaning forward, opening hands, sitting on edge of chair, making hand-to-face gestures, unbuttoning coat

Power, Confidence

Making expansive movements, sitting upright, steepling hands, placing hands behind back or in coat pockets with thumbs out, acting affable, turning one's back, sitting in relaxed, almost sprawling position

Weakness, Insecurity

Making small movements, hunching over, pinching flesh, chewing pen, twiddling thumbs, biting fingernails, leaning forward with feet together on floor

Frustration

Taking short breaths, making "tsk" sound, wringing hands, clenching fists, pointing index finger, running fingers through hair, rubbing back of neck

How the Eyes, Face, and Body Send Silent Messages

Listeners are understandably confused when a speaker's nonverbal cues contradict the verbal message. Let's look more closely at the powerful effect eye contact, facial expressions, posture, and gestures have on communication.

● **Eye contact, facial expressions, and posture and gestures can all convey meaning.**

Eye contact. The eyes have been called the "windows to the soul." Even if communicators can't look directly into the soul, they consider the eyes to be the most accurate predictor of a speaker's true feelings and attitudes. Most of us cannot look another person straight in the eyes and lie. As a result, we tend to believe people who look directly at us. We have less confidence in—and actually distrust—those who cannot maintain eye contact. Sustained eye contact suggests trust and admiration; brief eye contact signifies fear or stress.

Good eye contact enables the message sender to determine if a receiver is paying attention, showing respect, responding favorably, or feeling distress. From the receiver's perspective good eye contact reveals the speaker's sincerity, confidence, and truthfulness. Since eye contact is a learned skill, however, you must be respectful of people who do not maintain it. You must also remember that nonverbal cues, including eye contact, have different meanings in various cultures. A New

York City department store manager, for example, fired a young Hispanic clerk suspected of pilfering. "She wouldn't meet my eyes when I questioned her," he told a union representative. "I knew she was lying." The union representative, himself Hispanic, explained, "What you don't understand is that a well-bred Hispanic girl will not make eye contact with a man who is not a relative. It's just considered too bold. . . . She'll look away or drop her eyes."[10]

Facial expression. The expression on a communicator's face can be almost as revealing of emotion as the eyes. Researchers estimate that the human face can display over 250,000 different expressions.[11] Although a few people can control these expressions and maintain a "poker face" when they want to hide their feelings, most of us display our emotions openly. Raising or lowering the eyebrows, squinting the eyes, swallowing nervously, clenching the jaw, smiling broadly—these voluntary and involuntary facial expressions supplement or entirely replace verbal messages.

Posture and gestures. Glance again at Figure 2.3 to see how important posture, gestures, and other body movements are in communicating attitudes and impressions. An individual's general posture can convey anything from high status and self-confidence to shyness and submissiveness. Leaning toward a speaker suggests attraction and interest; pulling away or shrinking back denotes fear, distrust, anxiety, or disgust.

Nonverbal messages often have different meanings in different cultures.

Similarly, gestures can communicate entire thoughts via simple movements. However, these nonverbal communicators may have different meanings in different cultures and can get you into trouble unless you know what the local customs are. In the United States, for example, forming the thumb and forefinger in a circle means everything's OK. In Germany and parts of South America the OK sign is an obscene reference. In England and Scotland tapping the nose says "You and I are in on the secret." In Wales it means "You're really nosy." In Holland pointing a finger at your forehead means "How clever!" In the rest of Europe the same gesture means "You're crazy" or "That's a crazy idea!"[12]

Tuning in on nonverbal messages requires an awareness of their existence and an appreciation of their importance. To take stock of how effective you are in nonverbal communication, ask a classmate to critique your use of eye contact, facial expressions, and body movements. Another way to analyze your nonverbal style is to videotape yourself making a presentation and study your performance. This way you can make sure your nonverbal cues send the same message as your words.

How Time, Space, and Territory Send Silent Messages

In addition to nonverbal messages transmitted by your body, three external elements convey information in the communication process: time, space, and distance.

People convey meaning in how they structure and organize time and how they order the space around themselves.

Time. How we structure and use time tells observers about our personality and attitudes. For example, when Maritza Perez, a banking executive, gives a visitor a prolonged interview, she signals her respect for, interest in, and approval of the visitor or the topic to be discussed. By sharing her valuable time, she sends a clear nonverbal message. Likewise, when David Ing twice arrives late for a meeting with a realtor, it could mean that the appointment is unimportant to David, that the realtor has low status, that David is a self-centered person, or that he has little self-discipline. These are assumptions that typical Americans might make. In other cultures and regions, though, punctuality is viewed differently. We'll look more closely at interpreting nonverbal cues from other cultures later in this chapter.

The way an office is arranged can send nonverbal messages about the openness of its occupant.

Space. How we order the space around us tells something about ourselves and our objectives. Whether the space is a bedroom, a dorm room, an office, or a department, people reveal themselves in the design and grouping of furniture within that space. Generally, the more formal the arrangement, the more formal and closed the communication environment. An executive who seats visitors in a row of chairs across from his desk sends a message of aloofness and desire for separation. An instructor who arranges chairs informally in a circle rather than in straight rows or a rectangular pattern conveys her desire for a more open, egalitarian exchange of ideas. A manager who creates an open office space with few partitions separating workers' desks seeks to encourage an unrestricted flow of communication and work among areas.

Territory. Each of us has certain areas that we feel are our own territory, whether it's a specific spot or just the space around us. Your father may have a favorite chair in which he is most comfortable, a cook might not tolerate intruders in his or her kitchen, and veteran employees may feel that certain work areas and tools belong to them.

We all maintain zones of privacy in which we feel comfortable. Figure 2.4 categorizes the four zones of social interaction among Americans, as formulated by anthropologist Edward T. Hall. If someone violates your territory, you feel uncomfortable and defensive, and you may even step back to reestablish your space. Nonverbally, you are sending messages revealing your feelings about the intruder. Again, the distance required for comfortable social interaction is largely controlled by culture, so one must be careful not to apply American norms universally.

How Appearance Sends Silent Messages

Your appearance and the appearance of your documents convey verbal and nonverbal meanings.

The physical appearance of a business document, as well as the personal appearance of an individual, transmits immediate and important nonverbal messages.

Appearance of business documents. The way a letter, memo, or report looks can have either a positive or a negative effect on the receiver. Envelopes—through their postage, stationery, and printing—can suggest routine, important, or junk mail. Letters and reports can look neat, professional, well organized, and attractive—or just the opposite. Sloppy, hurriedly written documents convey negative nonverbal messages regarding both the content and the sender. In succeeding chapters you'll learn how to create documents that send positive nonverbal messages through their appearance, format, organization, readability, and correctness.

Appearance of people. The way you look—your clothing, grooming, and posture—telegraphs an instant nonverbal message about you. Based on what they see, viewers make quick judgments about your status, credibility, personality, and potential. Because appearance is such a powerful force in business, some aspiring professionals are turning for help to image consultants (who charge up to $500 an hour!). As one human relations specialist observes, "If you don't look and act the part, you will probably be denied opportunities."[13]

What specific advice do image consultants give? Try to invest in conservative, professional-looking clothing and accessories; quality is much more important than

FIGURE 2.4 ● **Four Space Zones for Social Interaction**

Zone	Distance	Uses
Intimate	0 to 1½ feet	Reserved for members of the family and other loved ones.
Personal	1½ to 4 feet	For talking with friends privately. The outer limit enables you to keep someone at arm's length.
Social	4 to 12 feet	For acquaintances, fellow workers, and strangers. Close enough for eye contact yet far enough for comfort.
Public	12 feet and over	For use in the classroom and for speeches before groups. Nonverbal cues become important as aids to communication.

quantity. Avoid flashy garments, clunky jewelry, garish makeup, and overpowering colognes, because, as one image consultant remarks, "they speak volumes without your ever saying a word."[14] Pay attention to good grooming, including a neat hairstyle, body cleanliness, polished shoes, and clean nails. Project confidence in your posture—both standing and sitting.

Nonverbal communication can outweigh words in the way it influences how others perceive us. You can harness the power of silent messages by reviewing the tips in the following checklist, paying special attention to the last two.

● **The cues we send nonverbally are probably more important than those we send verbally.**

Checklist for Improving Nonverbal Communication Skills

- ✔ **Establish and maintain eye contact.** Remember that in America appropriate eye contact signals interest, attentiveness, strength, and credibility.
- ✔ **Use posture to show interest.** Encourage communication interaction by leaning forward, sitting or standing erect, and looking alert.
- ✔ **Reduce or eliminate physical barriers.** Move out from behind a desk or lectern; shorten lines of communication; arrange meeting chairs in a circle.
- ✔ **Improve your decoding skills.** Watch facial expressions and body language to understand the complete verbal and nonverbal message being communicated.
- ✔ **Probe for more information.** When you perceive nonverbal cues that contradict verbal meanings, politely seek additional clues (*I'm not sure I understand, Please tell me more about . . .*, or *Do you mean that . . .*).
- ✔ **Avoid assigning nonverbal meanings out of context.** Make nonverbal assessments only when you understand a situation or a culture.
- ✔ **Associate with people from diverse cultures.** Learn about other cultures to widen your knowledge and tolerance of intercultural nonverbal messages.
- ✔ **Appreciate the power of appearance.** Keep in mind that the appearance of your business documents, your business space, and yourself send immediate positive or negative messages to receivers.

SPOTLIGHT ON COMMUNICATORS

Isadore Sharp, chairman and founder of the Four Seasons luxury hotel chain, plans to extend operations worldwide. Especially aware of intercultural sensitivity, Four Seasons is looking for overseas managers with strong listening skills, alertness to body language, and open minds. In working abroad, Four Seasons managers must be able to suspend judgment because right and wrong may not be the same as they would be at home.

- ✔ **Observe yourself on videotape.** Ensure that your verbal and nonverbal messages are in sync by taping and evaluating yourself making a presentation.
- ✔ **Enlist friends and family.** Ask them to monitor your conscious and unconscious body movements and gestures to help you become a more effective communicator.

Developing Intercultural Sensitivity

Although we are not always accurate, we generally know how to interpret nonverbal cues (such as appearance, facial expression, and body language) from people who share our cultural upbringing. But the rules change when we communicate with people from other cultures. For example, think of how you show embarrassment—chances are you blush or lower your head. By contrast, when embarrassed, Japanese generally laugh or giggle, while Arabs stick out their tongues slightly.[15]

Understanding the meaning of a message requires special sensitivity and skills when business communicators are from different cultures. Negotiators for an American company learned this lesson when they were in Japan looking for a trading partner in Asia. The Americans were quite pleased after their first meeting with representatives of a major Japanese firm. The Japanese had nodded assent throughout the meeting and had not objected to a single proposal. The next day, however, the Americans were stunned to learn that the Japanese had rejected the entire plan. In decoding the nonverbal behavioral messages, the Americans made a typical mistake. They assumed the Japanese were nodding in agreement, as fellow Americans would. In this case, however, the nods of assent indicated comprehension—not approval.[16]

As world markets and economies become increasingly intertwined, Americans at home and abroad will be doing business with more people from other countries. Already, half of the 110,000 employees of the huge American Xerox company work on foreign soil, while over half of the employees of the giant Sony Corporation are not Japanese.[17] Moreover, America's population and work force are rapidly becoming more ethnically diverse. In your future work you may find that your employers, fellow workers, or clients are from other countries. You might even travel abroad for your employer or on your own. Learning more about the powerful effect that culture has on behavior will help you minimize misunderstanding in your dealings with people from other cultures.

Comprehending Cultural Diversity

Every country or region within a country has a unique common heritage, joint experience, and shared learning that produces its culture. This background gives its members a complex system of cultural values, traits, morals, and customs. It teaches them how to behave; it conditions their reactions. Comparing traditional American values with those in other cultures will broaden your worldview and help you develop the proper attitude for successful intercultural communication.

● The emerging global economy will require business communicators to work with people from other countries and cultures.

A typical American has habits and beliefs similar to those of other members of Western, technologically advanced societies. In the limited space here it's impossible to cover fully the infinite facets of Western culture. But we can outline some key American habits and values[18] and briefly contrast them with other cultural views. Remember, though, that these are generalizations, intended to help us form a broad perspective. They may not describe you or members of other cultures personally.

Individualism. Americans believe in individualism, an attitude of independence and freedom from control. They think that initiative and self-assertion result in personal achievement. They believe in individual action and personal responsibility, and they desire a large degree of freedom in their personal lives.

While Americans value individualism and personal responsibility, other cultures emphasize group- and team-oriented values.

Other cultures emphasize belonging to organizations, groups, and teams; they encourage acceptance of group values, duties, and decisions. They typically resist independence because it fosters competition and confrontation instead of consensus. In group-oriented cultures like that of Japan, for example, self-assertion and individual decisions are discouraged. "The nail that sticks up gets pounded down" is a common Japanese saying.[19] Business decisions are often made by all who have competence in the matter under discussion. In China managers also focus on the group rather than on the individual, preferring a "consultative" management style over an autocratic style.[20]

Formality. Americans place less emphasis on tradition, ceremony, and social rules than do people in some other cultures. They dress casually and are soon on a first-name basis with others. Their lack of formality is often characterized by directness. In business dealings Americans come to the point immediately; indirectness, they feel, wastes time, a valuable commodity.

While Americans value informality and straightforwardness, other cultures may value tradition and ceremony.

This informality and directness may be confusing abroad. In Mexico, for example, a typical business meeting begins with handshakes, coffee, and an expansive conversation about the weather, sports, and other light topics. An invitation to "get down to business" might offend a Mexican executive.[21] In Japan signing documents and exchanging business cards are important rituals. In Europe first names are never used without invitation. In Arab, South American, and Asian cultures, a feeling of friendship and kinship must be established before business can be transacted.

Communication style. Americans value straightforwardness, are suspicious of evasiveness, and distrust people who might have a "hidden agenda" or who "play their cards too close to the chest."[22] Americans also tend to be uncomfortable with silence and impatient with delays. Some Asian businesspeople have learned that the longer they delay negotiations, the more concessions impatient Americans are likely to make.

Americans tend to be direct and to understand words literally.

Americans also tend to use and understand words literally. Latins, on the other hand, enjoy plays on words; and Arabs and South Americans sometimes speak with extravagant or poetic figures of speech that may be misinterpreted if taken literally. Nigerians prefer a quiet, clear form of expression; and Germans tend to be direct but understated.[23]

Change. In cultures shaped by Western religious values, change is a phenomenon that can be influenced and even controlled. Change is accepted and planned for.

In other cultures change is perceived as inevitable, the natural evolution of people and society. Thus, the future cannot be altered; it is predetermined. To devout Moslems, for example, planning for the future is sacrilegious because such plans might circumvent the will of Allah. Managers of an American electronics company sent to Iran to establish a telephone switching station were aware of this belief. As a result, they trained Iranian employees in extensive troubleshooting techniques so that equipment problems would not be attributed to Allah.[24]

Americans may place different values on change and time orientation than do people in other cultures.

Time orientation. Americans consider time a precious commodity to be conserved. They correlate time with productivity, efficiency, and money. Keeping people waiting for business appointments wastes time and is also rude.

In other cultures time may be perceived as an unlimited and never-ending resource to be enjoyed. An American businessperson, for example, was kept waiting two hours past a scheduled appointment time in Latin America. She wasn't offended, though, because she was familiar with Hispanics' more relaxed concept of time.[25]

Although Asians are punctual, their need for deliberation and contemplation sometimes clashes with our desire for speedy decisions. They do not like to be rushed. A Japanese businessperson considering the purchase of American appliances, for example, asked for 5 minutes to consider the salesperson's proposal. The potential buyer crossed his arms, sat back, and closed his eyes in concentration. A scant 18 seconds later, the American launched into the sales pitch to the obvious bewilderment of the Japanese.[26]

Cultivating the Right Attitude

Being aware of your own culture and how it contrasts with others is an important first step in preventing intercultural misunderstanding. Avoiding ethnocentrism and stereotyping while developing tolerance further helps business communicators overcome cultural barriers.

Avoiding ethnocentrism. The belief in the superiority of one's own race is known as *ethnocentrism,* a natural attitude inherent to all cultures. If you were raised in America, the values described previously probably seem "right" to you, and you may wonder why the rest of the world doesn't function under the same sensible rules. An American businessperson in an Arab or Asian country might feel irritated at time spent over coffee or other social rituals before any "real" business is transacted. In these cultures, however, personal relationships must be established and nurtured before credible negotiations may proceed.

Learning about other cultures and respecting other cultural values helps you avoid ethnocentrism.

Ethnocentrism causes us to judge others by our own values. We expect others to react as we would, and they expect us to behave as they would. Misunderstandings naturally result. An American who wants to set a deadline for completion of a negotiation is considered pushy by an Arab. That same Arab, who prefers a handshake to a written contract, is seen as naive and possibly untrustworthy by the American. These ethnocentric reactions can be reduced through knowledge of other cultures and development of flexible, tolerant attitudes.

Consider the dilemma of the international consulting firm Burns & McCallister, described in the accompanying Cross Culture box. In refusing to send women to negotiate in certain countries, the company enraged some women's rights groups. But was Burns & McCallister actually respecting the cultures of those countries?

Developing tolerance. Working among people from different cultures demands tolerance and acceptance of diversity. People with closed views cannot look beyond their own ethnocentrism. But as global markets expand and as our own society becomes increasingly multiethnic, tolerance becomes especially significant. Some

CULTURAL AND ETHICAL DILEMMA FOR WOMEN MANAGERS

The international management consulting firm of Burns & McCallister finds itself in cultural hot water. The problem? It refuses to send female executives abroad to negotiate contracts in certain countries.

Despite its current bad publicity, Burns & McCallister has previously earned a reputation as a liberal firm that encourages the employment of women. Over 50 percent of its partners are female, and both *Working Woman* and *Working Mother* magazines have ranked it among the nation's top firms for women. It attracts women by offering exceptional benefits, such as flexible hours, family leave, home-based work, and part-time partner-track positions.

SILENT WOMEN. Why, then, does it send only male partners on certain assignments? In over fifty years of consulting, Burns & McCallister has learned that the cultures in certain countries do not allow women to be treated as they are in America. In some cultures, for example, women are not permitted to speak in a meeting of men. Although clerical help in these cultures might be female, contacts with clients must be through male partners or account executives.

Japan, for example, has a two-track hiring system with women represented in only 3 percent of all professional positions. Other women in the work force are uniformed office ladies who do the filing and serve tea. They generally are pressured to leave the work force when they marry in their mid-twenties. A recruiting brochure for Dentsu, a large Japanese advertising firm, pictured the typical Dentsu "Working Girl" and described only her attractive physical characteristics.[27] In America, such a sexist ad would infuriate women. But attitudes toward working women differ in other cultures.

COMPANY JUSTIFICATION. In defense of its ban on sending women to negotiate in certain cultures, the head of Burns & McCallister said: "Look, we're about as progressive a firm as you'll find. But the reality of international business is that if we try to use women, we don't get the job. It's not a policy on all foreign accounts. We've just identified certain cultures in which women will not be able to successfully land or work on accounts. This restriction does not interfere with their career track."

The National Organization for Women (NOW) argues that Burns & McCallister should apply its American standards throughout the world. Since women are not restricted here, they should not be restricted abroad. No special policy, especially one so discriminatory against women, should be instituted for cultures that vary from ours. Our culture treats women fairly, and other cultures should recognize and respect that treatment. Unless Burns & McCallister stands up for its principles, change can never be expected.

Career Track Application

Organize a debate or class discussion focused on these questions: On what grounds do you support or oppose the position of Burns & McCallister to prohibit women from negotiating contracts in certain cultures? Should Burns & McCallister sacrifice potential business to advance a high moral position? If the career advancement of women within the firm is not affected by the policy, should women care? Do you agree with NOW that change cannot occur unless Burns & McCallister takes a stand?

job descriptions now include statements such as "Must be able to interact with ethnically diverse personnel."

To improve tolerance, practice empathy. This means trying to see the world through another's eyes. It means being nonjudgmental, recognizing things as they are rather than as they "should be." It includes the ability to accept others' contributions in solving problems in a culturally appropriate manner. When Kal Kan Foods began courting the pets of Japan, for example, an Asian advisor suggested that the meat chunks in its Pedigree dog food be cut into perfect little squares. Why? Japanese pet owners feed their dogs piece by piece with chopsticks. Instead of insisting on what "should be" (feeding dogs chunky meat morsels), Kal Kan solved the problem by looking at it from another cultural point of view (providing neat small squares).[28]

● **Developing intercultural tolerance means practicing empathy, being nonjudgmental, and being patient.**

● **While Americans value directness, people from other cultures may strive for harmony and face-saving.**

In business transactions Americans usually assume that economic factors are the primary motivators of people. It's wise to remember, though, that strong cultural influences are also at work. Saving face, for example, is important in many parts of the world. Because Americans value honesty and directness, they come right to the point and "tell it like it is." Mexicans and Asians, on the other hand, are more concerned with preserving social harmony and saving face. They are indirect and go to great lengths to avoid the offense of saying no. The Japanese, in fact, have 16 different ways to avoid an outright no. The empathic listener recognizes the language of refusal and pushes no further.

Being tolerant also involves patience. If a foreigner is struggling to express an idea in English, avoid the temptation to finish the sentence and provide the word that you presume is wanted. When we put words in their mouths, our foreign friends often smile and agree out of politeness, but our words may in fact not express their thoughts. Thus, our impatience may prevent us from learning the communicator's true thoughts. Remaining silent is another means of exhibiting tolerance. Instead of filling every lapse in conversation, Americans should recognize that in Asian cultures people deliberately use periods of silence for reflection and contemplation.

● **Looking beyond stereotypes means seeing individual qualities.**

Moving beyond stereotypes. Our perceptions of other cultures sometimes cause us to form stereotypes about groups of people. A *stereotype* is an oversimplified pattern applied uncritically. For example, the Swiss are hard-working, efficient, and neat; Germans are formal, reserved, and blunt; Americans are loud, friendly, and impatient; Asians are gracious, humble, and inscrutable. These attributes may accurately describe cultural norms, but when applied to individual business communicators, such stereotypes create misconceptions and cause misunderstandings. As an American, are you loud, friendly, and impatient? Probably not, and you resent being lumped into this category. When you meet and work with people from other cultures, remember that they, too, resent being stereotyped. Look beneath surface stereotypes and labels to discover individual personal qualities.

Adapting Messages to Intercultural Audiences

Working successfully with people from other cultures requires a certain amount of sensitivity and adjustment. The following suggestions provide specific tips for minimizing oral and written miscommunication.

Suggestions for communicating orally. Although it's best to speak a foreign language fluently, many of us lack that skill. Fortunately, global business transactions are often conducted in English, though the level of proficiency may be limited among those for whom it is a second language. An executive with Ford-Europe said that Americans abroad make a big mistake in thinking that people who speak English always understand what is being said. "Comprehension can be fairly superficial," he warns. The following suggestions may help you better understand and be understood in English.

- **Learn foreign phrases.** Even if English is used, foreign nationals appreciate it when you learn greetings and a few phrases in their language. Practice the phrases phonetically so that you will be understood.

Presentations in an intercultural setting, especially to an audience that uses English infrequently, require sensitivity. Wise speakers use simple language, speak slowly, watch for eye messages, and encourage frequent feedback.

- **Use simple English.** Use simple words, and speak in short sentences (under fifteen words). Eliminate puns, sports and military references, slang, jargon (special business terms), and any words that can't be translated.
- **Observe eye messages.** Be alert to a glazed expression or wandering eyes—these tell you the listener is lost.
- **Encourage accurate feedback.** Ask probing questions, and encourage the listener to paraphrase what you say. Don't assume that a yes, a nod, or a smile indicates comprehension.
- **Check frequently for comprehension.** Avoid waiting until you finish a long explanation to request feedback. Instead, make one point at a time, pausing to check for comprehension, and don't proceed to B until A has been grasped.
- **Speak slowly and enunciate clearly.** However, don't raise your voice. Also, overpunctuate with pauses and full stops, and always write numbers for all to see.
- **Accept blame.** If a misunderstanding results, graciously accept the blame for not making your meaning clear.
- **Listen without interrupting.** Curb your inclination to finish sentences or to fill out ideas for the speaker. Keep in mind that Americans abroad are often accused of listening too little and talking too much.

After conversations or oral negotiations, confirm the results and agreements with follow-up letters. For proposals and contracts, engage a translator to prepare copies in the local language. Roger Axtell, international behavior expert, offers three other important pieces of advice: smile, smile, smile. He calls the smile the single most understood and most useful form of communication in either personal or business transactions.[29]

Suggestions for communicating in writing. Many of the suggestions for oral communication hold true for written documents as well. In addition, you may find it helpful to do some research in learning how documents are formatted and how letters are addressed and developed in the intended reader's country. We'll examine these topics further in later chapters.

● **Translate your message into the receiver's language if the document is important, if it will have many readers, or if you must be persuasive.**

Engage a translator if (1) your document is important, (2) your document will be distributed to many readers, or (3) you must be persuasive. As one international executive says, "You can buy in English, but you have to sell in the other person's language."[30]

In writing documents some simple guidelines will help you communicate effectively. Use short sentences and short paragraphs (under five lines). Include relative pronouns *(that, which, who)* for clarity in introducing clauses. Stay away from contractions (especially ones like *Here's the problem*). Use precise, simple words *(end* instead of *terminate, use* instead of *implement)*. Avoid idioms *(once in a blue moon)*, slang *(my presentation really bombed)*, acronyms *(ASAP* for *as soon as possible)*, abbreviations *(DBA* for *doing business as)*, and jargon *(input, output, bottom line)*.

Numbers can be particularly problematic in cross-cultural communication. For international trade it's a good idea to learn and use the metric system. In citing numbers use figures *(15)* instead of spelling them out *(fifteen)*. Always convert dollar figures into local currency. Moreover, avoid using figures to express the month of the year. In America, for example, March 5, 1995, might be written as 3/5/95, while in Europe the same date might appear as 5.3.95. For clarity always spell the month out.

Making the effort to communicate with sensitivity across cultures pays big dividends. "Much of the world wants to like us," says businessman and international consultant Kevin Chambers. "When we take the time to learn about others, many will bend over backward to do business with us."[31] The following checklist summarizes suggestions for helping you improve your intercultural sensitivity.

Checklist for Improving Intercultural Sensitivity

- ✔ **Study your own culture.** Learn about your customs, prejudices, and views and how they differ from those in other societies.
- ✔ **Curb ethnocentrism.** Avoid judging others by your personal views. Learn to recognize and tolerate other behavior as normal, rather than as right or wrong.
- ✔ **Look beyond stereotypes.** Remember, individuals are often unlike their cultural stereotypes, so forget preconceptions and probe beneath the surface.
- ✔ **Use plain English.** Speak and write in short sentences using simple words and standard English. Eliminate puns, slang, jargon, acronyms, abbreviations, and any words that cannot be easily translated.
- ✔ **Encourage accurate feedback.** In conversations ask probing questions, and listen attentively without interrupting. Don't assume that a yes or a smile indicates assent or comprehension.
- ✔ **Hire a translator.** When negotiations or documents are important and one or both of the communicators lack fluency in the other's language, engage a professional interpreter or translator.

✔ **Adapt to local expectations.** Shape your writing to reflect the reader's document styles, if appropriate. Express currency in local figures. Write out months of the year for clarity.

Summary of Learning Goals

1. **Explain the listening process and identify elements of good listening.** The listening process involves (a) perception of sounds, (b) interpretation of those sounds, (c) evaluation of meaning, and (d) action, which might include a physical response or storage of the message in memory for future use. Good listening demands a positive attitude, openness to new ideas, active involvement in the listening process, and retention of key ideas.
2. **Specify and apply ten specific techniques that improve listening skills.** Listeners can improve their skills by identifying their bad listening habits (such as talking too much), blocking out competing thoughts, becoming actively involved, controlling the listening environment, maintaining an open mind, providing verbal and nonverbal feedback, paraphrasing the speaker's ideas, taking selective notes, listening between the lines, and capitalizing on lag time.
3. **Recognize the significance of nonverbal communication skills.** Nonverbal cues, both intentional and unintentional, may provide as much as 93 percent of the meaning of a message. Good communicators are alert to silent messages sent by the eyes, face, and body as well as those sent by time, space, territory, and appearance.
4. **Exercise ten specific suggestions to improve nonverbal communication skills.** Skillful communicators improve their nonverbal skills by maintaining eye contact, looking alert, eliminating physical barriers that separate them from their listeners, improving their comprehension of nonverbal signals, evaluating nonverbal messages only in context, seeking feedback, associating with diverse people, recognizing the power of appearance, seeing themselves on videotape, and asking friends and family to monitor their body language.
5. **Clarify pivotal American cultural values.** Important American values that influence our worldview include (a) respect for individualism, independence, and self-assertion, (b) emphasis on informality and directness, (c) respect for material objects and business profits, (d) the perception that change can be controlled, and (e) the feeling that time is valuable and should be used carefully.
6. **Identify key attitudes that enhance intercultural communication.** Business communicators will be better able to overcome cultural barriers if they (a) avoid ethnocentrism, which causes us to judge others by our own cultural values, (b) develop tolerance and empathy in working with people from diverse cultures, and (c) look beneath surface stereotypes to discover each individual's personal qualities.
7. **Employ ten specific procedures for adapting messages to intercultural audiences.** In writing to individuals in other cultures, (a) observe their document formats and conventions, (b) hire a translator for important or persuasive messages, (c) use short words, sentences, and paragraphs, (d) convert

dollar amounts to local currency, and (e) adopt a more formal, less conversational tone. In speaking English with individuals from other cultures, (a) try to use a few phrases in their language, (b) speak slowly, use short sentences, and choose simple English words, (c) watch for comprehension in a listener's eyes, (d) pause frequently and encourage feedback, and (e) accept blame for any misunderstanding that occurs.

Chapter Review

1. What percent of most workers' communication time is spent listening? Of executives?

2. Define *lag time*.

3. Describe the four elements in the listening process.

4. Discuss five poor listening habits and how they can be overcome.

5. Name three specific things you can do to help yourself remember what a speaker says.

6. Define *nonverbal communication*.

7. When verbal and nonverbal messages disagree, which message does the receiver consider more truthful? Give an example.

8. How does good eye contact help a speaker/sender? How does it benefit a listener/receiver?

9. How can you ensure that the nonverbal and verbal messages you send are in agreement?

10. How does the appearance of a business document send nonverbal messages?

11. Describe five major elements of American culture.

12. What is *ethnocentrism*?

13. Describe five specific ways in which you can improve *oral* communication with a foreigner.

14. Describe five specific ways in which you can improve *written* communication with a foreigner.

15. What is a *stereotype*? Give original examples.

Discussion

1. Since English is becoming the world's language and since America is a dominant military and trading force, why should Americans bother to learn about other cultures?

2. Discuss how listening skills are important to employees, supervisors, and executives. Who should have the best listening skills?

3. An international business consultant quipped that Asians spend money on entertainment while Americans spend money on attorneys. What are the implications of this statement for business communications?

4. Comment on the idea that body language is a science with principles that can be interpreted accurately by specialists.

5. Ethical Issue: In many countries government officials are not well paid, and "tips" (called "bribes" in America) are a way of compensating them. If such payments are not considered wrong in those countries, should you pay them as a means of accomplishing your business?

Activities

2.1 Bad Listening Habits

Concentrate for three days on your listening habits in class and on the job. What bad habits do you detect? Be prepared to discuss five bad habits and specific ways you could improve your listening skills. Your instructor may ask you to report your analysis in a memo.

2.2 Listening and Retention

Listen to a 30-minute segment of TV news using your normal listening habits. When you finish, make a list of the major items you remember, recording names, places, and figures. A day later watch the same 30-minute segment but put to use the good-listening tips in this chapter, including taking selective notes. When the segment is completed, make a list of the major items you remember. Which experience provided more information? What made a major difference for you?

2.3 Silent Messages

Analyze the kind of silent messages you send your instructor, your classmates, and your employer. How do you send these messages? What do they mean? Be prepared to discuss them in small groups or in a memo to your instructor.

2.4 Body Language

What attitudes do the following body movements suggest to you? Do these movements always mean the same thing? What part does context play in your interpretations?

a. Whistling, wringing hands

b. Bowed posture, twiddling thumbs

c. Steepled hands, sprawling sitting position

d. Rubbing hand through hair

e. Open hands, unbuttoned coat

f. Wringing hands, tugging ears

2.5 Document Appearance

Select a business letter and envelope that you have received at home or work. Analyze their appearance and the nonverbal messages they send. Consider the amount of postage, method of delivery, correctness of address, kind of stationery, typeface(s), format, and neatness. What assumptions did you make when you saw the envelope? How about the letter itself?

2.6 Gender Differences

Many researchers in the field of nonverbal communication report that women are better at accurately interpreting nonverbal signals than are men. Conduct a class survey. On a scale of 1 (low) to 5 (high), how would you rank men in general on their ability to interpret the meaning of eye, voice, face, and body signals? Then rank women in general. Tabulate the class votes. Why do you think gender differences exist in the decoding of nonverbal signals?

2.7 American Culture

Your pen pal, who has never been to America, asks you to describe how the people behave. Based on your experiences, report to the class what you might say to your pen pal. Enlarge on the pivotal values of American culture presented in this chapter. Be prepared to write a letter if your instructor asks.

2.8 Negotiating Traps

Discuss the causes and implications of the following common mistakes made by Americans in their negotiations with foreigners:

a. Assuming that a final agreement is set in stone

b. Lacking patience and insisting that matters progress more quickly than the pace preferred by the locals

c. Assuming an interpreter is always completely accurate

d. Ignoring or misunderstanding the significance of rank

2.9 Global Economy

Fred Smith, CEO of Federal Express, says, "It is an inescapable fact that the U.S. economy is becoming much more like the European and Asian economies, entirely tied to global trade." Read local newspapers for a week and peruse national news magazines (*Time, Newsweek, Business Week,* and so forth) for articles that support or refute this assertion. Report your findings orally or in a memo to your instructor. This topic could be expanded into a long report for Chapter 13.

2.10 Collaborative Intercultural Panel

Find two or three students from other countries (possibly members of your class) who could report on differences between their cultures and American culture. Ask student travelers to report on their experiences abroad. In addition to individualism, formality, communication style, change, and time, consider such topics as importance of family, gender roles, and attitudes toward education, clothing, leisure time, and work. Conduct a panel discussion. (See Activity 14.6 in Chapter 14 for a sample report focused on an intercultural topic.)

C.L.U.E. Review 2

On a separate sheet edit the following sentences to correct faults in grammar, punctuation, spelling, and word use.

1. To avoid embarassing any employee the personell manager and myself has decided to talk personal to each individual.
2. 3 assistants were sent on a search and destroy mission in a conscious effort to remove at least fifteen thousand old documents from the files.
3. Electronic mail, now used by ¾ of Americas largest companys will transmit messages instantly.
4. An article entitled whats new with managers appeared in reader's digest which is read by 60,000,000 americans.

5. Your account is now sixty days overdue consequently we have only 1 alternative left.
6. The marketing managers itinirary listed the following three destinations seattle portland and eugene.
7. Each of the beautifully-printed books available at pickwick book company have been reduced to thirty dollars.
8. We reccommend therefor that a committee study our mail procedures for a 3 week period and submit a report of it's findings.
9. Their going to visit there relatives in columbus ohio over the memorial day holiday.
10. The hotel can acommodate three hundred convention guests but it has parking facilities for only one hundred cars.

II The Process of Writing

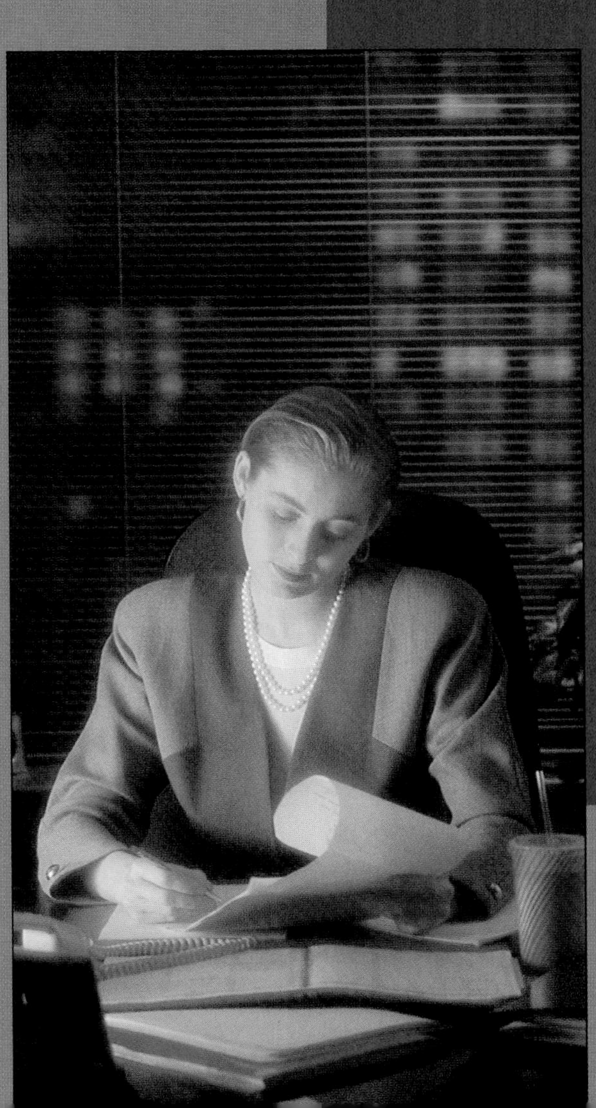

3 Analyzing, Anticipating, and Adapting

4 Researching, Organizing, and Composing

5 Revising, Proofreading, and Evaluating

Lands' End: Career Track Profile

"In college most of my papers gave back what I heard in lectures. . . . At Lands' End my writing has a specific purpose: responding to the customer."

If Lands' End were a person rather than one of the nation's leading catalog retailers, it would be a red-cheeked, salt-of-the-earth neighbor who wanders over on Saturday mornings. Coffee cup in hand, this cheerful friend is ready to chat or pitch in to help fix a broken bicycle. Lands' End fashioned its success largely by communicating a folksy image of small-town friendliness, old-fashioned values, and caring people.

Located in rural Dodgeville, Wisconsin, Lands' End works hard to live up to the image. It employs as many as 3,000 polite telephone operators, some of whom milk their cows and tend their farms before arriving at work. It's the catalog, though, that really sets the tone for the Lands' End image.

Offering classic casual clothing, Lands' End catalogs reach an amazing one out of every ten American households. They were among the earliest *magalogs*—catalogs so thick with articles and conversation that they rival magazines. Gary Comer, Lands' End founder, began writing catalog copy that connected on a personal level with customers, giving honest advice in a clear and unpretentious, yet intelligent, manner. The catalog created a warm glow and set up a dialogue with customers, many of whom view Lands' End as a friend. This attitude motivates customers to write letters—as many as 60,000 a year! And Lands' End answers every one, enlisting the help of company volunteers.

Correspondence that requires investigation and decisions, though, reaches the desk of Brian Finnegan in Customer Relations. Brian started at Lands' End five years ago as an operator. When he was promoted into Customer Relations, Brian recognized how different his writing tasks were from those he had in college (he graduated from Loras College in Dubuque, Iowa). "In college," he says, "most of my papers gave back what I heard in lectures or read in books. That's sure not what's happening here! At Lands' End my writing has a specific purpose: responding to the customer. Beyond answering their questions honestly and completely, I try to solidify the goodwill they feel toward us."

Brian sends out both good- and bad-news letters. "I write to customers on every conceivable topic. Sometimes they request that we add a product to the catalog. First, I check with our product managers to see if the item is already in the pipeline. Often it is, and I can tell the writer that great minds must think alike and the item will be appearing in future catalogs. Other times, I have to turn down requests, such as letters asking us to offer different sizes, other styles, or specialty lines like maternity clothes. And once in a while I must respond to a controversial matter.

"My goal is to be as responsive as possible. I always try to explain the 'why' behind a decision, especially when it's a negative answer. After all, when a customer takes the time to make a suggestion or inquiry, he or she deserves a full answer.

"The tone of a letter is very important. We have a style manual, but it covers mostly mechanical things like punctuation and capitalization. To get the right sound or tone to my letters, I occasionally read messages written by our CEO, Dick Anderson, who is a master communicator. He's had years of experience in writing advertising copy and working with customers. Unfailingly, his letters sound genuine and personal, yet professional.

Showing off its jersey polo shirts, Lands' End is one of the ever-increasing number of catalogs to feature people with disabilities. Motivated by both humanitarian and marketing concerns, many advertisers are taking a fresh look at this largely untapped market of consumers who live, love, and shop like everyone else. Sensitivity to others and language that includes rather than excludes are communication techniques that send positive nonverbal messages of tolerance and humanity. Such techniques are not only altruistic—they're also good business.

"My letters don't copy the catalog's style, which is chatty and familiar. Although I aim for warmth and informality, I still must show respect—and that requires some reserve. Usually I 'play off' the customer's letter; it tells me whether to be light or serious.

"Although it's almost second nature to me now, I follow a similar process for all my letters. Every situation begins with a problem: What does the customer want? I analyze both the problem and the writer. Sometimes I can respond to a letter without research, but most often I have to do some checking. I have freedom to go anywhere in the organization to get answers. For information I may call customer service, our buyers, or a product manager. After collecting the facts, I compose the letter at my computer. I don't use form letters because nearly every situation is unique.

"I try to avoid starting a letter with *Thank you for your letter.* I figure customers aren't interested in hearing how grateful we are up front; they really want answers to their questions. For most letters it's best to get right down to business at the beginning. After the opening I explain our decision and attempt to answer all the customer's concerns. The closing is the place for expressing appreciation. It's easy to fall into clichés at the end of a letter, such as *If you have any questions, do not hesitate to call me.* These meaningless endings waste the writer's final opportunity to say something sincere that reinforces a friendly feeling between writer and reader.

"After writing the first draft of a letter, I usually print a rough copy to proofread. Just reading the letter in sentences helps me hear whether the ideas are clear, concise, and natural. I revise and delete words, sometimes rearranging entire sentences. When I'm satisfied, I run a spell check and send the letter out. The payoff for me comes in feedback from grateful customers. It's surprising how many of them respond, even when I've had to send disappointing news."[1]

Approaching the Writing Process Systematically

Writing, like other goal-oriented activities, is easier when the writer follows a plan. Whether you're composing customer response letters like Brian Finnegan at Lands' End or preparing interoffice memos, reports, or oral presentations, the final product will be more effective and the act of producing it less stressful if you apply a systematic process.

The Basics of Business Writing

Business writing seeks to express, not impress; it is purposeful, economical, and reader-oriented.

Business writing differs from other writing you may have done. High school or college compositions and term papers probably required you to explain your feelings, display your knowledge, and meet a minimum word count. Business writing is as different from this kind of creative writing as night is from day. In the business world, you'll find that your writing needs to be:

- **Purposeful.** As Brian does at Lands' End, you will be writing to solve problems and convey information.
- **Economical.** You will try to present ideas clearly but concisely—excess verbiage is not rewarded.
- **Reader-oriented.** You will concentrate on looking at a problem from the reader's perspective instead of seeing it from your own.

These distinctions actually ease the writer's task. In writing most business documents, you won't be searching your imagination for creative topic ideas. Moreover, you won't be trying to dazzle readers with your extensive knowledge, powerful vocabulary, or graceful phrasing. The goal in business writing is to *express rather than impress.*

In many ways business writing is easier than creative writing, yet it still requires hard work, especially from beginners. But following a process, studying models, and practicing the craft can make nearly anyone a successful business writer. This book provides all three components: process, models, and practice. First, you'll focus on the process of writing.

The 3-×-3 Writing Process

The phases of the 3-×-3 writing process are analyzing, anticipating, and adapting; organizing, researching, and composing; and revising, proofreading, and evaluating.

This book divides the writing process into three distinct phases, as shown in Figure 3.1, with each phase further divided into three major activities. This 3-×-3 process provides you with a systematic plan for developing all your business communications—from simple memos and informational reports to corporate proposals and presentations.

The time spent on each phase varies with the deadline, purpose, and audience for the message. Let's consider how the 3-×-3 writing process might work in a typical business situation. Suppose you must write a letter to a department store buyer about a jeans order that your company cannot fill. The first phase prepares you to write and involves analyzing, anticipating, and adapting. In analyzing the situation, you decide to focus your letter on retaining the order. That can best be done by persuading the buyer to accept a different jeans model. You anticipate that the buyer will be disappointed that the original model is unavailable. What's more, she will probably be reluctant to switch to a different model. Thus, you must find ways to adapt your message to reduce her reluctance and convince her to switch.

FIGURE 3.1 ● **The 3-×-3 Writing Process**

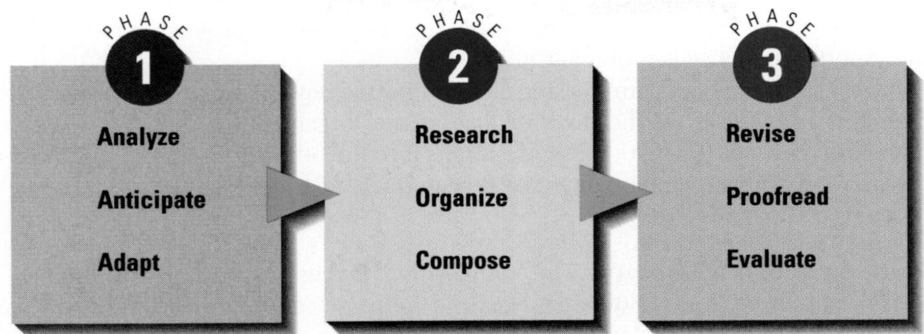

The second phase involves researching, organizing, and then composing the message. To collect facts for this letter, you would probably investigate the buyer's past purchases. You would check to see what jeans you have in stock that she might accept as a substitute. You might do some brainstorming or consult your colleagues for their suggestions about how to retain this order. Then, you would organize your information into a loose outline and decide on a strategy or plan for revealing your information most effectively. Equipped with a plan, you're ready to compose the first draft of the letter.

The third phase of the writing process involves revising, proofreading, and evaluating your letter. After writing the first draft, you'll revise the message for clarity, conciseness, tone, and readability. You'll proofread carefully to ensure correct spelling, grammar, punctuation, and format. Finally, you'll evaluate the message to see if it accomplishes your goal.

This process may seem a bit complicated for the daily messages that many businesspeople write. Does this same process apply to memos and short letters? And how do collaborators and modern computer technologies affect the process?

Adapting the process. Although good writers proceed through each phase of the writing process, some steps may be compressed for short, routine messages. Brief, everyday documents enlist the 3-×-3 process, but many of the steps are performed quickly, without prolonged deliberation. For example, Phase 1 may take the form of a few moments of reflection. Phase 2 may consist of looking in the files quickly, jotting a few notes in the margin of the original document, and composing at your computer. Phase 3 might consist of reading a printout, running a spell check, and making a few changes. Longer, more involved documents—like persuasive memos, sales letters, management reports, proposals, and résumés—require more attention to all parts of the process.

● **The steps in the 3-×-3 writing process may be altered, compressed, and rearranged depending on the nature of the document and the experience of the writer.**

One other point about the 3-×-3 writing process needs clarification. It may appear that you perform one step and progress to the next, always following the same order. Most business writing, however, is not that rigid. Although writers perform the tasks described, the steps may be rearranged, abbreviated, or repeated. Some writers revise every sentence and paragraph as they go. Many find that new ideas occur after they've begun to write, causing them to back up, alter the organization, and rethink their plan. You should expect to follow the 3-×-3 process closely as you begin developing your business writing skills. With experience, though, you'll become like other good writers who alter, compress, and rearrange the steps as needed.

Collaborating with others. The composition process is changed when two or more people work together on a project. Collaborative composition may be necessary for (1) big tasks, (2) items with short deadlines, and (3) projects that require the expertise or consensus of many people.

Let's say four people are working on a committee report as a group. The group members may work together as they analyze and organize the data. Then, one member composes the first draft and submits it to the others for suggestions. This revision and evaluation phase might be repeated several times before the final document is completed.

Working with a computer. The composition process is further affected by today's computer tools. Software exists to help you generate ideas, conduct research in electronic databases, and organize facts into outlines. In fact, all phases of the writing process—including keyboarding, revision, and collaboration—are simplified and supported by word processing programs, discussed more fully in the accompanying Technology box.

Wonderful as these powerful technological tools are, however, they do not automatically produce effective letters and reports. They can neither organize data into concise and logical presentations nor shape ideas into persuasive arguments. Only a well-trained author can do that. Nevertheless, today's technology enhances every aspect of writing. Therefore, skill in using computers is essential for anyone whose job requires composition.

Phase 1: Preparing to Write

• By following the 3-×-3 writing process, you can reduce anxiety, write more efficiently, and craft better messages.

Whether you're writing with a team, composing by yourself, or preparing an oral presentation, the product of your efforts can be improved by following the steps described in the 3-×-3 writing process. Not only are you more likely to get your message across, but you'll feel less anxious and your writing will progress more quickly. The remainder of this chapter concentrates on the first phase of composition: analyzing, anticipating, and adapting.

Analyzing the Task

In analyzing the composition task, you'll first need to identify the purpose of the message and select the best channel or form in which to deliver it.

• Most business communication has both primary purposes (to inform or persuade) and secondary purposes (to promote goodwill).

Identifying your purpose. As you begin to compose a message, ask yourself two important questions: (1) Why am I sending this message? and (2) What do I hope to achieve? Your responses will determine how you organize and present your information.

Your message may have primary and secondary purposes. For college work your primary purpose may be merely to complete the assignment; secondary purposes might be to make yourself look good and to get a good grade. The primary purposes for sending business messages are typically to inform and to persuade. A secondary purpose is to promote goodwill: you (and your organization) want to look good in the eyes of your audience.

Most business messages do nothing more than *inform*—explain procedures, announce meetings, answer questions, and transmit findings. Some business messages, however, are meant to *persuade*—to sell products, convince managers, motivate employees, and win over customers.

SEVEN WAYS COMPUTERS CAN MAKE YOU A BETTER BUSINESS WRITER

Although computers and software programs cannot actually do the writing for you, they provide powerful tools for making the composition process easier and more efficient. Here are some of the ways your computer can help you with your writing.

- **Fighting Writer's Block.** Because word processors enable ideas to flow almost effortlessly from your brain to a screen, you can expect fewer delays resulting from writer's block. You can compose rapidly, and you can experiment with structure and phrasing, later retaining and polishing the most promising thoughts. Many writers "sprint" write, recording unedited ideas quickly, to start the writing process and also to brainstorm for ideas on a project. Then, they tag important ideas and use computer outlining programs to organize those ideas into logical sequences.
- **Collecting Information Electronically.** Much of the world's information is now stored in databases accessible by computer. If, for example, your company were introducing a new exercise bicycle, you could use an electronic directory to locate sporting goods stores, ranking them by total revenue and zip code to facilitate your sales strategy. Specialized databases store vast libraries of computerized financial, marketing, economic, government, and current events information. All you need is a computer, a modem, a telephone line, and a credit card to deliver mountains of data to your computer screen. Chapter 11 discusses electronic databases in greater detail.
- **Composing and Revising.** By freeing writers from tiresome typing and retyping, computers have become the favored composition medium among business communicators and other writers. Word processing features that especially appeal to business writers are *insert* (separates text and allows words to be added), *move* (shifts text to different positions), *undo* (rescues and returns deleted text), *search* (locates targeted words quickly), *math* (calculates rows and columns of figures), and *sort* (alphabetizes items). Footnoting, indexing, thesaurus, and other features further ease the writing task.
- **Detecting and Correcting Errors.** Nearly all word processing programs today provide features that catch and correct spelling and typographical errors. Poor spellers and weak typists universally bless their spell checkers for repeatedly saving them from humiliation. Still, writers must recognize that misused words *(effect/affect)* and confusing words *(its/it's)* will escape spell-check detection. Other writing tools include grammar and style checkers. These programs make suggestions about word usage, readability, jargon, and other writing problems.
- **Designing and Producing Professional-looking Documents.** Gone are the days when writers were forced to take their copy to printers for special typographical features. With most high-end word processing programs today, scalable font (for different character sizes and styles), italics, and boldface enable you to produce professional-looking titles, subheadings, captions, and footnotes. In addition, you can use bullets, circles, lines, boxes, arrows, and many other features to highlight ideas.
- **Adding Graphics for Emphasis.** Your letters, memos, and reports may be improved by the addition of graphs and artwork to clarify and illustrate data. Instead of cutting and pasting these items into a report and then photocopying the page, you can now create a diagram exactly where you want it. You can also import graphs, charts, or diagrams created in database, spreadsheet, graphics, and draw-and-paint programs. Moreover, ready-made pictures, called "clip art," can be used to symbolize or illustrate ideas.
- **Using Collaborative Software for Team Writing.** Assume you are part of a group preparing a lengthy proposal to secure a government contract. You expect to write one segment of the proposal yourself and help revise parts written by others. Special word processing programs with commenting and strikeout features allow you to revise easily and to identify each team member's editing. These collaborative programs, called "groupware," also include decision-support tools to help groups generate, organize, and analyze ideas more efficiently than in traditional meetings.

Career Track Application

Individually or in teams, identify specific software programs that perform the tasks described here. Prepare a table naming each program, its major functions, and its advantages and disadvantages for business writers in your field.

Before writing a letter or preparing a presentation, think carefully about your audience. Visualizing the receiver and anticipating a reaction to your message helps you determine the words to use, the amount of detail to include, the best method of organization, and many other important factors.

Choosing an appropriate form or channel for a message often depends on how sensitive the message is.

Selecting the form. After identifying the purpose of your message, you need to select the most appropriate form (communication channel). As you learned in Chapter 1, some information is most efficiently and effectively delivered in person. A phone call or a quick meeting could convey a message or solve a problem, thus saving the considerable cost of writing, producing, delivering, reading, and storing a business document. Written documents, of course, also have advantages. They are relatively cheap and easy to distribute to a large or distant audience, and they are usually more carefully crafted than oral messages. Moreover, they provide a permanent record confirming specifications, decisions, dates, and so forth.

For sensitive or controversial messages, however, a written record may be just what you want to avoid. To illustrate, consider what may turn out to be the world's most expensive memo. Written by Microsoft Corporation CEO Bill Gates, it was leaked to the press with disastrous results. News of Gates' private fears for his company sent Microsoft stock diving, thus costing Gates $315 million in the value of his own company stock holdings.[2] A better channel for a potentially dangerous message would be a private conversation or a meeting with key people. As Gates learned, selecting the best form for a message means paying attention to your purpose, its sensitivity, and the audience.

Anticipating the Audience

Visualizing the audience for a message helps you choose appropriate language.

Some messages miss the mark. Consider the following letter sent to a seven-year-old boy who had written to a chocolate company asking for a Milky Bar pencil case. "Due to the overwhelming response this promotion has generated, we have unfortunately run out of stock temporarily. We are, therefore, holding your application pending stock replenishment."[3] The chocolate company's representative had no sense of audience; as a result, the language was totally inappropriate.

A good writer anticipates the audience for a message: What is the reader like? How will that reader react to the message? One copywriter at Lands' End pictures his sister-in-law whenever he writes product descriptions for the catalog. By profiling your audience and shaping a message to respond to that profile, you are more likely to achieve your communication goals.

FIGURE 3.2 ● **Asking the Right Questions to Profile Your Audience**

Primary Audience

Who is my primary reader or listener?

What is my personal and professional relationship with that person?

How much does that person know about the subject?

What do I know about that person's education, beliefs, culture, and attitudes?

Should I expect a neutral, positive, or negative response to my message?

Secondary Audience

Who might see this message after the primary audience?

How do these people differ from the primary audience?

Profiling the audience. Visualizing your audience is a pivotal step in the writing process. The questions in Figure 3.2 will help you profile your audience. How much time you devote to answering these questions depends greatly on your message and its context. An analytical report that you compose for management or an oral presentation before a big group would, of course, demand considerable audience anticipation. On the other hand, a memo to a coworker or a letter to a familiar supplier might require only a few moments of planning. No matter how short your message, though, spend some time thinking about the audience so that you can tailor your words to your readers or listeners. "The most often unasked question in business and professional communication," claims a writing expert, "is as simple as it is important: HAVE I THOUGHT ENOUGH ABOUT MY AUDIENCE?"[4]

● **By profiling your audience before you write, you can identify the appropriate tone, language, and channel.**

Responding to the profile. Anticipating your audience helps you make decisions about shaping the message. You'll discover what kind of language is appropriate—whether you're free to use specialized technical terms, whether you should explain everything, and so on. You'll decide whether your tone should be formal or informal, and you'll select the most desirable channel. Imagining whether the receiver is likely to be neutral, positive, or negative will help you determine how to organize your message.

Another result of profiling your audience will be knowing whether a secondary audience is possible. If so, you'll provide more background information and be more specific in identifying items than would be necessary for the primary audience only. Analyzing the task and anticipating the audience assists you in adapting your message so that it will accomplish what you intend.

Adapting to the Task and Audience

After analyzing your purpose and anticipating your audience, you must convey your purpose to that audience. Adaptation is the process of creating a message that suits your audience.

One important aspect of adaptation is *tone.* Conveyed largely by the words in a message, tone reflects how a receiver feels upon reading or hearing a message.

Ways to adapt to the audience include choosing the right words and tone, spotlighting reader benefits, cultivating a "you" attitude, and using sensitive, courteous language.

For example, think how you would react to these statements:

> You must return the form by 5 p.m.
>
> Would you please return the form by 5 p.m.

The wording of the first message establishes an aggressive or negative tone—no one likes being told what to do. The second message is reworded in a friendlier, more positive manner. Poorly chosen words may sound demeaning, condescending, discourteous, pretentious, or demanding. Skilled communicators create a positive tone in their messages by using a number of adaptive techniques, some of which are unconscious. These include spotlighting receiver benefits, cultivating a *you* attitude, and avoiding gender, racial, age, and disability bias. Additional adaptive techniques include being courteous, using familiar words, and choosing precise words.

Empathic communicators envision the reader and focus on benefits to that reader.

Spotlighting receiver benefits. Focusing on the audience sounds like a modern idea, but actually one of America's early statesmen and authors recognized this fundamental writing principle over 200 years ago. In describing effective writing, Ben Franklin observed, "To be good, it ought to have a tendency to benefit the reader."[5] These wise words have become a fundamental guideline for today's business communicators. Expanding on Franklin's counsel, a contemporary communication consultant gives this solid advice to his business clients: "Always stress the benefit to the readers of whatever it is you're trying to get them to do. If you can show them how you're going to save *them* frustration or help them meet *their* goals, you have the makings of a powerful message."[6]

Adapting your message to the receiver's needs means putting yourself into their shoes. It's called empathy. Empathic senders think about how a receiver will decode a message. They try to give something to the reader, solve the reader's problems, save the reader's money, or just understand the feelings and position of the reader. Which of the following messages are more appealing to the reader?

Sender-focused	**Receiver-focused**
To enable us to update our stockholder records, we ask that the enclosed card be returned.	So that you may receive dividend checks and information related to your shares promptly, please return the enclosed card.
Our warranty becomes effective only when we receive an owner's registration.	Your warranty begins working for you as soon as you return your owner's registration.
We offer an audiocassette language course that we have complete faith in.	The sooner you order the audiocassette language program, the sooner the rewards will be yours.
The Human Resources Department requires that the enclosed questionnaire be completed immediately so that we can allocate our training resources funds.	You can be one of the first employees to sign up for the new career development program if you fill out the attached questionnaire and get it back to us immediately.

Effective communicators develop the "you" view—in a sincere, not manipulative or critical, tone.

Cultivating the "you" view. Notice how many of the previous receiver-focused messages included the word *you*. In concentrating on receiver benefits, skilled communicators naturally develop the "you" view. They emphasize second-person pronouns *(you, your)* instead of first-person pronouns *(I/we, us, our)*. Whether your goal is to inform, persuade, or promote goodwill, the catchiest words you can use are *you* and *your*. Compare the following examples.

FIGURE 3.3 ● Successful Customer Response Letter

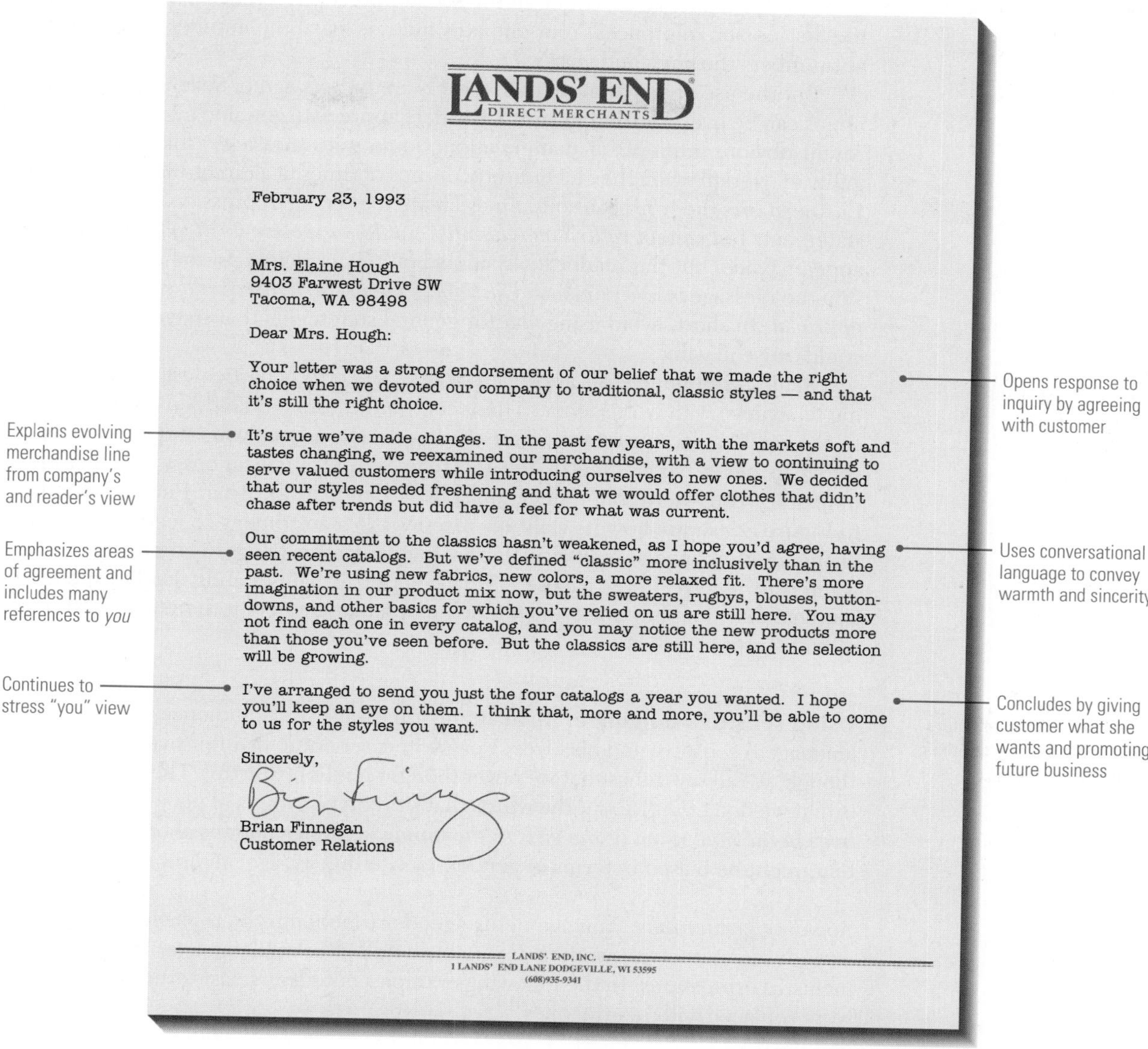

LANDS' END
DIRECT MERCHANTS

February 23, 1993

Mrs. Elaine Hough
9403 Farwest Drive SW
Tacoma, WA 98498

Dear Mrs. Hough:

Your letter was a strong endorsement of our belief that we made the right choice when we devoted our company to traditional, classic styles — and that it's still the right choice.

It's true we've made changes. In the past few years, with the markets soft and tastes changing, we reexamined our merchandise, with a view to continuing to serve valued customers while introducing ourselves to new ones. We decided that our styles needed freshening and that we would offer clothes that didn't chase after trends but did have a feel for what was current.

Our commitment to the classics hasn't weakened, as I hope you'd agree, having seen recent catalogs. But we've defined "classic" more inclusively than in the past. We're using new fabrics, new colors, a more relaxed fit. There's more imagination in our product mix now, but the sweaters, rugbys, blouses, button-downs, and other basics for which you've relied on us are still here. You may not find each one in every catalog, and you may notice the new products more than those you've seen before. But the classics are still here, and the selection will be growing.

I've arranged to send you just the four catalogs a year you wanted. I hope you'll keep an eye on them. I think that, more and more, you'll be able to come to us for the styles you want.

Sincerely,

Brian Finnegan
Customer Relations

LANDS' END, INC.
1 LANDS' END LANE DODGEVILLE, WI 53595
(608)935-9341

Opens response to inquiry by agreeing with customer
Explains evolving merchandise line from company's and reader's view
Emphasizes areas of agreement and includes many references to *you*
Uses conversational language to convey warmth and sincerity
Continues to stress "you" view
Concludes by giving customer what she wants and promoting future business

"I/We" View	**"You" View**
I have scheduled your vacation to begin May 1.	You may begin your vacation May 1.
We have shipped your order by UPS, and we are sure it will arrive in time for the sales promotion January 15.	Your order will be delivered by UPS in time for your sales promotion January 15.
I'm asking all our employees to respond to the attached survey regarding working conditions.	Because your ideas count, please complete the attached survey regarding working conditions.

• **Avoid overusing "you" or including it when it suggests blame.**

To see if you're really concentrating on the reader, try using the "empathy index." In one of your messages, count all the second-person references. Then, count all the first-person references. Your empathy index is low if the number of *I*'s and *we*'s outnumbers the *you*'s and *your*'s.

But the use of *you* is more than merely a numbers game. Second-person pronouns can be overused and misused. Readers appreciate genuine interest, but they resent obvious attempts at manipulation. Some sales messages, for example, are guilty of overkill when they include *you* dozens of times in a direct-mail promotion. Furthermore, the word can sometimes create the wrong impression. Consider this statement: *You cannot return merchandise until you receive written approval. You* appears twice, but the reader feels singled out for criticism. In the following version the message is less personal: *Customers may return merchandise with written approval.* In short, avoid using *you* for general statements that suggest blame and could cause ill will.

Skilled communicators are able to convey sincerity, a particularly difficult feeling to achieve with words alone. These communicators send hidden messages that say to readers and customers "You are important, I hear you, and I'm honestly trying to please you." One of the most successful organizations to achieve this empathic "you" view communication style is Lands' End. Brian Finnegan's letter in Figure 3.3 shows how he skillfully responds to a customer's concerns about the changing merchandise mix available in Lands' End catalogs. The customer also wanted to receive fewer catalogs. Brian's letter explains Lands' End's expanded merchandise line, but notice how much emphasis he puts on the reader and how often he uses "you."

• **Sensitive communicators avoid gender, racial or ethnic, and disability biases.**

Using sensitive language. In adapting a message to its audience, be sure your language is sensitive and bias-free. Few writers set out to be offensive. Sometimes, though, we all say things that we never thought might be hurtful. The real problem is that we don't *think* about the words that stereotype groups of people, such as *the boys in the mail room* or *the girls in the typing pool.* Be cautious about expressions that might be biased in terms of gender, race, ethnicity, age, and disability.

Avoiding gender bias. You can defuse gender timebombs by replacing words that exclude or stereotype women (sometimes called sexist language) with neutral, inclusive expressions. In the following examples note how sexist terms and phrases were replaced with neutral ones.

Gender-biased	**Improved**
female doctor, woman attorney, cleaning woman	doctor, attorney, cleaner
waiter/waitress, authoress, stewardess	server, author, cabin attendant
mankind, man-hour, man-made	humanity, working hours, artificial
office girls	office workers
the doctor . . . he	doctors . . . they
the teacher . . . she	teachers . . . they
executives and their wives	executives and their spouses
foreman, flag-man, workman	lead worker, flagger, worker

Gender-biased	Improved
businessman, salesman	businessperson, sales representative
Every employee must have his picture taken.	Every employee must have a picture taken.
	All employees must have their pictures taken.
	Every employee must have his or her picture taken.
	You *(or one)* must have a picture taken.

Generally, you can avoid gender-biased language by leaving out the words *man* or *woman*, by using plural nouns and pronouns, or by changing to a gender-free word *(person* or *representative).*

Avoiding racial or ethnic bias. You need indicate racial or ethnic identification only if the context demands it.

Racially or Ethnically Biased	Improved
An Indian accountant was hired.	An accountant was hired.
James Lee, an African American, applied.	James Lee applied.

Avoiding age bias. Again, specify age only if it is relevant, and avoid expressions that are demeaning or subjective.

Age-biased	Improved
The law applied to old people.	The law applied to people over 65.
Sally Kay, 55, was transferred.	Sally Kay was transferred.
spry old gentleman	man
little old lady	woman

Avoiding disability bias. Unless relevant, do not refer to an individual's disability. When necessary, use terms that do not stigmatize disabled individuals.[7]

Disability-biased	Improved
afflicted with, suffering from, crippled by	has
defect, disease	condition
confined to a wheelchair	uses a wheelchair
She has a handicap.	She is disabled.

These examples give you a quick look at a few problem expressions. The real key to bias-free communication, though, lies in your awareness and commitment. Always be on the lookout to be sure that your messages do not exclude, stereotype, or offend people.

Expressing yourself positively. Certain negative words create ill will because they appear to blame or accuse readers. For example, opening a letter to a customer with *You claim that* suggests that you don't believe the customer. Other

SPOTLIGHT ON COMMUNICATORS

Katie Couric, co-host of the "Today" show and former Pentagon reporter, does her homework before she conducts interviews. Disarmingly cheerful and humorous, she can also be hard-hitting and uncompromising in her blunt questioning of newsmakers. Yet she always strives to be positive, courteous, and fair—important characteristics of every good communicator.

loaded words that can get you in trouble are *complaint, criticism, defective, failed, mistake,* and *neglected.* Often the writer is unconscious of the effect of these words. Take a look at the accompanying Career Skills box to see eight easy ways to make your readers and listeners angry. To avoid these angry reactions, restrict negative words and try to find positive ways to express ideas. You provide more options to the reader when you tell what can be done instead of what can't be done.

Negative	**Positive**
You failed to include your credit card number so we can't mail your order.	We'll mail your order as soon as we receive your credit card number.
Your letter of May 2 claims that you returned a defective headset.	Your May 2 letter describes a headset you returned.
You cannot park in Lot H until April 1.	You may park in Lot H starting April 1.
You won't be sorry that . . .	You will be happy that . . .
The problem cannot be solved without the aid of top management.	With the aid of top management, the problem can be solved.

Being courteous. Maintaining a courteous tone involves not just guarding against rudeness but also avoiding words that sound demanding or preachy. Expressions like *you should, you must,* and *you have to* cause people to instinctively react with "Oh, yeah?" One remedy is to turn these demands into rhetorical questions that begin with *Will you please* . . . Giving reasons for a request also softens the tone.

Less Courteous	**More Courteous**
You must complete this report before Friday.	Will you please complete the report by Friday.
You should organize a car pool in this department.	Organizing a car pool will reduce your transportation costs and help preserve the environment.

Even when you feel justified in displaying anger, remember that losing your temper or being sarcastic will seldom accomplish your goals as a business communicator—to inform, to persuade, and to create goodwill. When you are irritated, frustrated, or infuriated, keep cool and try to defuse the situation. Concentrate on the real problem. What must be done to solve it?

● **Even when you are justifiably angry, courteous language is the best way to achieve your objectives.**

You May Be Thinking This	**Better to Say This**
This is the second time I've written. Can't you get anything right?	Please credit my account for $843. My latest statement shows that the error I noted in my letter of June 2 has not been corrected.
Am I the only one who can read the operating manual?	Let's review the operating manual together so that you can get your documents to print correctly next time.
Hey, don't blame me! I'm not the promoter who took off with the funds.	Please accept our sincere apologies and two complimentary tickets to our next event. Let me try to explain why we had to substitute performers.

Simplifying your language. In adapting your message to your audience, whenever possible use short, familiar words that you think they will recognize. Don't, however, avoid a big word that (1) conveys your idea efficiently and (2) is appro-

EIGHT EASY WAYS TO MAKE READERS AND LISTENERS ANGRY

Communicators in all career areas run the risk of angering receivers by using certain expressions that have hidden meanings. Here are techniques and expressions to avoid because they are guaranteed to offend your audience.

- **Call them stupid (even if done unintentionally):**

  If you had read the instruction booklet . . .

  You are probably ignorant of the fact that . . .

- **Suggest that they are lying (even if you don't say so directly):**

  You claim that you returned the item.

  According to you, the item stopped working.

- **Issue commands and orders:**

  You must comply with our regulations.

  We expect you to complete all portions of the form.

- **Confuse a person's name or gender:**

  Dear Ms. Lee: We understand, Mr. Lee, that . . .

  Dear Phoung: As a lady of fine tastes, you . . .

- **Indicate that they are complainers:**

  You complain that . . .

  We have received your complaint describing . . .

- **Blame them:**

  Obviously you overlooked . . .

  You forgot to . . .

  You neglected to . . .

  You failed to . . .

- **Write in a language that requires interpretation:**

  When your financial status ameliorates, your application will be given expeditious scrutiny.

  Because of current electronic compositional instrumentation, you need no longer fear exposure of your grammatical foibles.

- **Issue ultimatums:**

  This will be the last memo sent on this subject. Anyone dressing inappropriately faces immediate disciplinary action!

  Either comply with the regulations or face the consequences!

Career Track Application

Collect actual memos, letters, or other documents that illustrate unintentionally offensive language. Bring the documents to class for discussion and revision.

priate for the audience. Your goal is to shun pompous and pretentious language. One communication expert advises writers to use "GO" words. If you mean *begin,* don't say *commence* or *initiate.* If you mean *give,* don't write *render.*[8] By substituting everyday, familiar words for unfamiliar ones, as shown here, you help your audience comprehend your ideas quickly.

● **The simpler the language, the better.**

Unfamiliar	Familiar
commensurate	equal
interrogate	question
mandate	require
materialize	appear
remunerate	pay
terminate	end

At the same time, be selective in your use of jargon. *Jargon* describes technical or specialized terms within a field. These terms enable insiders to communicate complex ideas briefly, but to outsiders they mean nothing. Personnel professionals,

SPOTLIGHT ON COMMUNICATORS

The hardest part of her job is making complicated financial information easy to read and understand, admits successful *Newsweek* columnist and financial advisor Jane Bryant Quinn. Diligent revision helps her clarify her thinking and her language. Whether writing about borrowing, investing, or insuring, she constantly adapts to her audience and looks for familiar language. "I'm always asking myself, 'Will the reader understand this word, this phrase?' "

for example, know precisely what's meant by "cafeteria plan" (a benefits option program), but most of us would be thinking about lunch. Geologists refer to *plate tectonics*, and physicians discuss *metastatic carcinomas*, but these terms mean little to most of us. Use specialized language only when the audience will understand it. And don't forget to consider secondary audiences: Will those potential readers understand any technical terms used?

Using precise, vigorous words. Strong verbs and concrete nouns give readers more information and keep them interested. Don't overlook the thesaurus (or the thesaurus program on your computer) for expanding your word choices and vocabulary. Whenever possible, use specific words as shown here.

Imprecise, Dull	Improved
a gain in profits	a jump in profits
	a 23 percent hike in profits
it takes memory	it hogs memory
	it demands 2 MG of ram
to think about	to identify, diagnose, analyze
	to probe, examine, inspect

By reviewing the tips in the following checklist, you can master the steps in preparing to write. As you review these tips, remember the three basics of preparing for the composition process: analyze, anticipate, and adapt.

Checklist for Adapting a Message to Its Audience

✔ **Identify the message purpose.** Ask yourself why you are communicating and what you hope to achieve. Look for primary and secondary purposes.

✔ **Select the most appropriate form.** Determine whether you need a permanent record or whether the message is too sensitive to put in writing.

✔ **Profile the audience.** Identify your relationship with the reader and your knowledge about that individual or group. Assess how much they know about the subject.

✔ **Focus on reader benefits.** Phrase your statements from the readers' viewpoint, not the writer's. Concentrate on the "you" view *(Your order will arrive, You can enjoy, Your ideas count).*

✔ **Avoid bias in gender and racial expressions.** Use bias-free words *(businessperson* instead of *businessman, working hours* instead of *man-hours).* Omit ethnic identification unless the context demands it.

✔ **Avoid bias in age and disability language.** Include age only if relevant. Avoid potentially demeaning expressions *(spry old gentleman),* and use terms that do not stigmatize disabled people *(he is disabled* instead of *he is a cripple* or *he has a handicap).*

✔ **Express ideas positively rather than negatively.** Instead of *Your order can't be shipped before June 1,* say *Your order can be shipped June 1.*

✔ **Use short, familiar words.** Use technical terms and big words only if they are appropriate for the audience *(end* not *terminate, required* not *mandatory).*

 **Search for precise, vigorous words.** Use a thesaurus if necessary to find strong verbs and concrete nouns (*announces* instead of *says, brokerage* instead of *business*).

Adapting to Ethical and Legal Responsibilities

The process of adaptation hits a sensitive chord when we confront ethical and legal issues. Is a message honest? Is an action ethical? Will the message cause a lawsuit?

Businesspeople in the 1990s are increasingly concerned with ethics. An estimated 95 percent of Fortune 500 corporations as well as many smaller companies have now adopted ethics statements or codes of conduct.[9] Moreover, business organizations are sponsoring ethics workshops, conducting ethics simulations, and hiring ethics counselors/facilitators. What caused this explosion of ethical awareness? According to one poll, many companies "listed the goal of being socially responsible as their primary reason for incorporating ethics into their organizations."[10] Businesses also recognize that ethical practices make good business sense. Ethical companies endure less litigation, less resentment, and less government regulation.[11] Equally important, ethical business managers and businesses "tend to be more trusted and better treated by employees, suppliers, stockholders, and consumers."[12] For individuals ethical behavior makes sense because once a reputation is tainted, trust can never be regained.

• Ethical conduct not only promotes social responsibility but also makes good business sense.

Just what is ethical behavior? Ethics author Mary E. Guy defines it as "that behavior which is the *right* thing to do, given the circumstances."[13] Ethical behavior involves four principles: honesty, integrity, fairness, and concern for others. "These four principles are like the four legs of a stool," explains ethics authority Michael Josephson. "If even one leg is missing, the stool wobbles, and if two are missing, the stool falls. It's not enough to pride yourself on your honesty and integrity if you're not fair or caring."[14] Consider a manager who would never dream of behaving dishonestly on the job or off. Yet this same manager forces a key employee to choose between losing her job and staying home with a sick child. The manager's lack of caring and failure to consider the circumstances creates a shaky ethical position that would be difficult to justify.

Five Common Ethical Traps

In making ethical decisions, business communicators commonly face five traps that can make choosing the right decision more difficult.[15]

• Recognizing five ethical traps can help communicators avoid them.

The false necessity trap. People act from the belief that they're doing what they *must* do. They convince themselves that they have no other choice, when in fact it's generally a matter of convenience or comfort. Consider the Beech-Nut Corporation's actions when it discovered that its supplier was providing artificial apple juice. Beech-Nut canceled its contracts but continued to advertise and sell the adulterated "apple" juice as a 100 percent natural product in its baby food line. Apparently falling into the false necessity trap, Beech-Nut felt it had no choice but to continue the deception.

The doctrine-of-relative-filth trap. Unethical actions sometimes look good when compared with the worse behavior of others. What's a little fudging on an expense account compared with the pleasure cruise the boss took and charged to

SPOTLIGHT ON COMMUNICATORS

Teresa McBride, National Minority Small Business Person of the Year, founded her Albuquerque-based computer consulting company on a firm basis of ethics, honesty, and trust. The youthful entrepreneur vows to deliver according to a customer's requirements—or she will refer the customer to someone who can, even a competitor. Emphasis on ethics helps explain the phenomenal success of her multimillion-dollar business and its recognition as the country's fastest-growing Hispanic-owned business.

the company as a business trip? On Wall Street many stockbrokers probably considered their minor deviations from ethical sales techniques to be insignificant, and therefore acceptable, when compared to the major crimes of junk-bond king Michael Milken and others.

The rationalization trap. In falling into the rationalization trap, people try to explain away unethical actions by justifying them with excuses. Consider employees who "steal" time from their employers—taking long lunch and coffee breaks, claiming sick leave when not ill, and completing their own tasks on company time. It's easy to rationalize such actions: "I deserve an extra-long lunch break because I can't get all my shopping done on such a short lunch hour" or "I'll just write my class report at the office because the computer printer is much better than mine, and they aren't paying me what I'm worth anyway."

The self-deception trap. Applicants for jobs often fall into the self-deception trap. They are all too willing to inflate grade-point averages or exaggerate past accomplishments to impress prospective employers. One applicant, for example, claimed experience as a broker's assistant at a prestigious securities firm. A background check revealed that he had interviewed for the securities job but was never offered it.[16] Another applicant claimed that in his summer job he was "responsible for cross-corporate transferral of multidimensional client receivables." In other words, he moved boxes from sales to shipping. Self-deception can lead to unethical and possibly illegal behavior.

The ends-justify-the-means trap. Taking unethical actions to accomplish a desirable goal is a common trap. Consider a manager in a Medicare claims division of a large health insurance company who coerced clerical workers into working overtime without pay. The goal was the reduction of a backlog of unprocessed claims. Despite the worthy goal the means of reaching it was unethical.

Goals of Ethical Business Communication

Business communicators can minimize the danger of falling into ethical traps by setting specific ethical goals. Although the following goals hardly comprise a formal code of conduct, they will help business writers maintain a high ethical standard.

Telling the truth. Ethical business communicators do not intentionally make statements that are untrue or deceptive. We become aware of dishonesty in business when violators break laws, notably in advertising, packaging, and marketing. The Federal Trade Commission, for example, ordered Kraft Foods to cancel a deceptive advertisement claiming that each Kraft Singles processed cheese slice contained as much calcium as five ounces of milk, an untrue statement.[17]

Half-truths, exaggerations, and deceptions constitute unethical communication. But conflicting loyalties sometimes blur the line between right and wrong for businesspeople. Let's say you helped the marketing director, who is both your boss and your friend, conduct consumer research about a new company product. When you see the final report, you are astonished at how the findings have been distorted to show a highly favorable product approval rating. You are torn between loyalty to your boss (and friend) and loyalty to the company. Tools for helping you solve such ethical dilemmas will be discussed shortly.

Labeling opinions. Sensitive communicators know the difference between facts and opinions. *Facts* are verifiable and often are quantifiable; *opinions* are beliefs held with confidence but without substantiation. It's a fact, for example, that women are starting new businesses twice as fast as men.[18] It's an opinion, though, that increasing numbers of women are abandoning the corporate employment arena to start these businesses. Such a statement can't be verified. Stating opinions as if they were facts is unethical.

Facts are verifiable; opinions are beliefs held with conviction.

Being objective. Ethical business communicators recognize their own biases and strive to keep them from distorting a message. Suppose you are asked to investigate microcomputers and write a report recommending a brand for your office. As you visit stores and watch computer demonstrations, you discover that an old high school friend is selling Brand X. Because you always liked this individual and have faith in his judgment, you may be inclined to tilt your recommendation in his direction. However, it's unethical to misrepresent the facts in your report or to put a spin on your arguments based on friendship. To be ethical, you could note in your report that you have known the person for ten years and that you respect his opinion. In this way, you have disclosed your relationship as well as the reasons for your decision. Honest reporting means presenting the whole picture and relating all facts fairly.

Writing clearly. The ethical business communicator feels an obligation to write clearly so that the reader understands easily and quickly. Some states have even passed "Plain English" laws that require businesses to write policies, warranties, and contracts in language comprehensible to average readers. Plain English means short sentences, simple words, and clear organization. Writers who intentionally obscure the meaning with long sentences and difficult words are being unethical.

"Plain English" laws require simple, understandable language in policies, contracts, warranties, and other documents.

A thin line separates unethical composition from inefficient composition. Some might argue that writers who send wordy, imprecise messages requiring additional correspondence to clarify the meaning are acting unethically. However, the problem may be one of experience and skill rather than ethics. Although such messages waste the time and resources of both senders and receivers, they are not unethical unless the *intent* is to deceive.

Giving credit. As you probably know, using the written ideas of others without credit is called *plagiarism.* Ethical communicators give credit for ideas by (1) referring to originators' names within the text, (2) using quotation marks, and (3) documenting sources with endnotes, footnotes, or internal references. (You'll learn how to do this in Chapter 13.) One student writer explained his reasons for plagiarizing material in his report by rationalizing, "But the encyclopedia said it so much better than I could!" This may be so, yet such an argument is no justification for appropriating the words of others. Quotation marks and footnotes could have saved the student. In school or on the job, stealing ideas or words from others is unethical.

Tools for Doing the Right Thing

In composing messages or engaging in other activities on the job, business communicators can't help being torn by conflicting loyalties. Do we tell the truth and risk our jobs? Do we show loyalty to friends even if it means bending the rules?

Talking with a coworker whose advice you value can be an important tool in resolving ethical problems. When you are torn by conflicting loyalties or responsibilities, discuss your concerns with someone you trust.

Acting ethically means doing the right thing—given the situation.

Should we be tactful or totally honest? Is it our duty to make a profit or to be socially responsible? Acting ethically means doing the right thing *given the circumstances.* Each set of circumstances requires analyzing issues, evaluating choices, and acting responsibly.

Resolving ethical issues is never easy, but the task can be made less difficult if you know how to identify key issues. The following questions may be helpful.

- *Is the action you are considering legal?* No matter who asks you to do it nor how important you feel the result will be, avoid anything that is prohibited by law. Giving a kickback to a buyer for a large order is illegal, even if you suspect that others in your field do it and you know that without the kickback you will lose the sale.

Business communicators can help resolve ethical issues through self-examination.

- *How would you see the problem if you were on the opposite side?* Looking at all sides of an issue helps you gain perspective. Consider the issue of mandatory drug testing among employees. From management's viewpoint such testing could stop drug abuse, improve job performance, and lower health insurance premiums. From the employees' viewpoint mandatory testing reflects a lack of trust of employees and constitutes an invasion of privacy. By weighing both sides of the issue, you can arrive at a more equitable solution.
- *What are alternate solutions?* Consider all dimensions of other options. Would the alternative be more ethical? Under the circumstances, is the alternative feasible? Can an alternate solution be implemented with a minimum of disruption and with a high degree of probable success? In the situation involving your boss's distortion of consumer product research, you could go to the head of the company and tell what you know. A more tactful alternative, however, would be to approach your boss and ask if you misunderstood the report's findings or if an error might have been made.
- *Can you discuss the problem with someone whose advice you trust?* Suppose you feel ethically bound to report accurate information to a client—even though your boss has ordered you not to do so. Talking about your dilemma with a coworker or with a colleague in your field might give you helpful insights and lead to possible alternatives.

- *How would you feel if your family, friends, employer, or coworkers learned of your action?* If the thought of revealing your action publicly produces cold sweats, your choice is probably not a wise one. Losing the faith of your friends or the confidence of your customers is not worth whatever short-term gains might be realized.

Perhaps the best advice in ethical matters is contained in the Golden Rule: Do unto others as you would have others do unto you. The ultimate solution to all ethics problems is treating others fairly.

Language That Avoids Litigation

Ethics questions are perplexing because few written rules exist to guide us. Legal questions are equally confusing because, although laws exist, they are not always interpreted consistently. And in our current business environment, lawsuits abound, many of which center on the use and abuse of language. You can protect yourself and stay out of court by knowing what's legal and by adapting your language accordingly. Four information areas generate the most lawsuits: investments, safety, marketing, and human resources.[19]

Careful communicators should familiarize themselves with information in four information areas: investments, safety, marketing, and human resources.

Investment information. Writers describing the sale of stocks or financial services must follow specific laws written to protect investors. Any messages—including letters, newsletters, and pamphlets—must be free from misleading information, exaggerations, or half-truths. One company in Massachusetts inadvertently violated the law by declaring that it was "recession-proof." After going bankrupt, the company was sued by angry stockholders claiming that they had been deceived. Another company, Lotus Development Corporation, caused a flurry of lawsuits by withholding information that revealed problems in a new version of its 1-2-3 program. Stockholders sued, charging that managers had deliberately concealed the bad news, thus keeping stock prices artificially high. Experienced financial writers know that careless language and even poor timing may provoke litigation.

Safety information. Writers describing potentially dangerous products worry not only about being sued but also about protecting people from physical harm. Warnings must do more than suggest danger; they must also clearly tell people how to use the product safely and motivate them to do so. Clearly written safety messages avoid vague, abstract, and unfamiliar words. They include presentation techniques, such as headings and bullets—devices you'll learn more about in coming chapters.

Warnings on dangerous products must be written especially clearly.

Marketing information. Sales and marketing messages are illegal if they falsely advertise prices, performance capability, quality, or other product characteristics, or deceive the buyer in any way. A Southern California entrepreneur, for example, promoted a Band-Aid-like device, Le Patch, as "a dramatic breakthrough in weight control technology." When worn around the waist, Le Patch was supposed to reduce appetite. The claims, however, could not be proved; and the promoter was charged with misrepresenting the product. Sellers of services must also be cautious about the language they use to describe what they will do. Letters, reports, and proposals that describe services to be performed are interpreted as contracts in

Sales and marketing messages must not make claims that can't be verified.

court. Therefore, language must not promise more than intended. Here are some dangerous words (and recommended alternatives) that have created misunderstandings leading to lawsuits.[20]

Dangerous Word	Court Interpretation	Recommended Alternative
inspect	to examine critically; to investigate and test officially; to scrutinize	review study tour the facility
determine	to come to a decision; to decide; to resolve	evaluate assess analyze
assure	to render safe; to make secure; to give confidence; to cause to feel certain	to facilitate; to provide further confidence; to enhance the reliability of

The safest recommendations contain positive, job-related information.

Human resources information. The vast number of lawsuits relating to employment makes this a treacherous area for business communicators. In evaluating employees in the workplace, avoid making unsubstantiated negative comments. It's also unwise to assess traits *(she is unreliable)* because they require subjective judgment. Concentrate instead on specific incidents *(in the last month she missed four work days and was late three times).* Defamation lawsuits have become so common that some companies no longer provide letters of recommendation for former employees. To be safe, give recommendations only when the former employee authorizes the recommendation and when you can say something positive. Stick to job-related information.

Statements in employee handbooks also require careful wording, because the courts might rule that such statements are "implied contracts." Consider the following handbook remark: "We at Data Corporation show our appreciation for hard work and team spirit by rewarding everyone who performs well." This seemingly harmless statement could make it difficult to fire an employee because of the implied employment promise.[21]

In adapting messages to meet today's litigious business environment, be sensitive to the rights of others and to your own rights. The key elements in this adaptation process are awareness of laws, sensitivity to interpretations, and careful use of language.

Summary of Learning Goals

1. **Explain the three phases of writing.** Phase 1 involves analyzing the message, anticipating the audience, and considering ways to adapt the message to the audience. Phase 2 involves researching the topic, organizing the material, and composing the message. Phase 3 involves revising, proofreading, and evaluating the message.
2. **Analyze the purpose of a writing task and anticipate its audience.** An important part of preparation for writing is determining your purpose and knowing what you hope to achieve. Equally important is profiling your primary and secondary audiences so that you will know what adaptations to make.

3. **Use various writing techniques to adapt a message to its audience.** Skilled writers strive to (a) spotlight reader benefits, (b) look at the message from the reader's perspective (the "you" view), (c) use sensitive language that avoids gender, racial, ethnic, and disability biases, (d) state ideas positively and courteously, and (e) use short, familiar, and precise words.
4. **Recognize five common ethical traps.** Five ethical pitfalls to avoid are (a) the false necessity trap, in which people feel they have only one choice; (b) the doctrine-of-relative-filth trap, whereby unethical actions look acceptable when compared with worse behavior of others; (c) the rationalization trap, in which people justify unethical actions with excuses; (d) the self-deception trap, whereby people convince themselves that unethical behavior is acceptable; and (e) the ends-justify-the-means trap, in which unethical methods are used to achieve a worthy goal.
5. **Specify the goals of an ethical business communicator.** Ethical business communicators strive to (a) tell the truth, (b) label opinions so that they are not confused with facts, (c) be objective and avoid distorting a message, (d) write clearly and avoid obscure language, and (e) give credit when using the ideas of others.

Chapter Review

1. Describe the components in each stage of the 3-×-3 writing process.

2. Name three instances when business communicators might collaborate on a writing project.

3. What are three ways in which business writing differs from other writing?

4. What is *empathy,* and how does it apply to business writing?

5. Discuss the effects of first- and second-person pronouns.

6. What unspoken message does a reader perceive from the words *You claim that . . .* ?

7. What is gender-biased language? Give examples.

8. When should a writer include racial or ethnic identification, such as *Ellen Lee, an Asian, . . .* ?

9. What is *jargon* and when is it appropriate for business writing?

10. What's wrong with using words like *commence, mandate,* and *interrogate*?

11. Name four ways that businesses today are showing their concern for ethics.

12. How would you describe *ethical behavior*?

13. Discuss five thinking traps that block ethical behavior.

14. What four information areas generate the most lawsuits?

15. How can business communicators protect themselves against litigation?

Discussion

1. How can the 3-×-3 writing process help the writer of a business report as well as the writer of an oral presentation?

2. Comment on the idea that the most important step in composition is in audience analysis.

3. Discuss the following statement: "The English language is a landmine—it is filled with terms that are easily misinterpreted as derogatory and others that are blatantly insulting. . . . Being fair and objective is not enough; employers must also appear to be so."[22]

4. How are the rules of ethical behavior that govern businesses different from those that govern your personal behavior?

5. Ethical Issue: Suppose your superior asked you to change year-end financial data, and you knew that if you didn't, you might lose your job. What would you do if it were a small amount? A large amount?

Activities

3.1 Document for Analysis

Discuss the following memo, which is based on an actual document sent to employees. How could you apply what you learned in this chapter to improving this memo?

> TO: All Employees Using HP 5000 Computers
>
> It has recently come to my attention that a computer security problem exists within our organization. I understand that the problem is twofold in nature:
>
> a. You have been sharing computer passwords.
> b. You are using automatic log-on procedures.
>
> Henceforth, you are prohibited from sharing passwords for security reasons that should be axiomatic. We also must forbid you to use automatic log-on files because they empower anyone to have access to our entire computer system and all company data.
>
> Enclosed please find a form that you must sign and return to the aforementioned individual, indicating your acknowledgement of and acquiescence to the procedures described here. Any computer user whose signed form is not returned will have his personal password invalidated.

3.2 Analyzing Audiences

Using the questions in Figure 3.2, write a brief analysis of the audience for each of the following communication tasks.

a. Your letter of application for a job advertised in your local newspaper. Your qualifications match the job description.

b. A memo to your boss persuading her to allow you to attend a computer class that will require you to leave work early two days a week for ten weeks.

c. An unsolicited sales letter promoting life insurance to a targeted group of executives.

d. A letter from the municipal water department explaining that while the tap water may taste and smell bad, it poses no threats to health.

e. A letter from a credit card organization refusing credit to an applicant.

3.3 Ethics Survey

How do your ethics compare with those of businesspeople across the country? Complete the following survey and then compare your responses with the results obtained from readers of *Business Month* magazine.[23] Be prepared to discuss your responses in class.

a. Corporate ethics should be as important a priority as profits.

☐ Strongly agree ☐ Agree ☐ Undecided ☐ Disagree ☐ Strongly disagree

b. In an overzealous attempt to help their companies, officials at two generic drug makers lied to the FDA. Is this kind of dishonesty ever acceptable?

☐ Yes, because ____________________

☐ No, because ____________________

c. It's okay to bend the rules if the survival of your job is at stake.

☐ Always ☐ Often ☐ Occasionally ☐ Never

d. How would you rank the following infractions, where 1 represents the most offensive and 5 the least offensive infraction?

_____ cheating on an expense report

_____ playing dirty tricks on a competitor

_____ taking credit for someone else's accomplishment

_____ paying bribes in a country where it's the accepted custom

_____ lying to protect a friend

e. Although he voted to deny shareholders a lucrative $200-a-share takeover offer, Time Inc.'s CEO entered into a different merger deal guaranteeing himself a 10-year contract for at least $14.6 million. Was this ethical?

☐ Yes ☐ No ☐ Don't know

3.4 Reader Benefits and "You" View

Revise the following sentences to emphasize the reader's perspective and the "you" view.

a. Our safety policy forbids us from renting power equipment to anyone who cannot demonstrate proficiency in its use.

b. We take pride in announcing a new schedule of low-cost flights to Hawaii.

c. So that we may bring our customer records up to date and eliminate the expense of duplicate mailings, we are asking you to complete the enclosed card.

d. Our fifty years of experience in direct-mail advertising will enable us to help you dazzle your customers.

e. I give my permission for you to attend the two-day workshop.

f. We're requesting all employees to complete the enclosed questionnaire so that we may develop a master schedule for summer vacations.

g. I think my background and my education match the description of the manager trainee position you advertised.

h. We are offering an in-house training program for employees who want to improve their writing skills.

i. We are pleased to announce an arrangement with IBM that allows us to offer discounted computers in the student bookstore.

j. We have approved your application for credit.

k. We are pleased to announce that we have selected you to join our trainee program.

l. Because we need to clear out all old model VCRs to make space for the new ones, we're offering savings up to 50 percent.

m. We will reimburse you for all travel expenses.

n. To enable us to continue our policy of selling name brands at discount prices, we cannot give cash refunds on returned merchandise.

o. We offer a free catalog of computer and office supplies that saves money and shopping time for readers.

3.5 Language Bias

Revise the following sentences to eliminate gender, racial, age, and disability stereotypes.

a. A skilled secretary proofreads her boss's documents and catches any errors he makes.

b. The award went to Jean Kim, a Korean-American.

c. Because she is confined to a wheelchair, we look for restaurants without stairs.

d. Each worker has his assigned parking place.

e. Some theaters have special prices for old people.

f. How many man-hours will the project require?

g. James is afflicted with arthritis, but his crippling rarely interferes with his work.

h. Debbie Sanchez, 24, was hired; and Tony Morris, 57, was promoted.

i. All conference participants and their wives are invited to the banquet.

j. Our company encourages the employment of handicapped people.

k. Representing the community are a businessman, a lady attorney, and a female doctor.

l. A salesman would have to use all his skills to sell those condos.

m. Their child suffers from cerebral palsy.

n. Every homeowner should check his policy carefully.

o. We have an excellent Hispanic computer technician.

3.6 Positive Expression

Revise the following statements to make them more positive.

a. We can't send you a catalog until our next set is printed June 15.

b. In your letter you claim that you returned a defective headset.

c. Although you apparently failed to read the operator's manual, we are sending you a replacement blade for your food processor. Next time read page 18 carefully so that you will know how to attach this blade.

d. We can't process your application because you neglected to insert your social security number.

e. Construction cannot begin until the building plans are approved.

f. Because of a mistake in its address, your letter did not arrive until January 3.

g. In response to your complaint, we are investigating our agent's behavior.

h. It is impossible to move forward without community support.

i. Customers are ineligible for the 10 percent discount unless they show their membership cards.

j. You won't be disappointed with your new credit card.

3.7 Courteous Expression

Revise the following messages to show greater courtesy.

a. You must sign and return this form immediately.

b. This is the last time I'm writing to try to get you to record my January 6 payment of $500 to my account. Anyone who can read can see from the attached documents that I've tried to explain this to you before.

c. As manager of your department, you will have to get your employees to use the correct forms.

d. To the Staff: Can't anyone around here read instructions? The operating manual for our copy machine very clearly describes how to remove jammed paper on page 12. But I'm the only one who ever does it, and I've had it! No more copies will be made until you learn how to remove jammed paper.

e. If you had listened to our agent more carefully, you would know that your policy does not cover accidents outside the United States.

3.8 Familiar Words

Revise the following sentences to avoid unfamiliar words.

a. Your remuneration for a day's work will be $50.

b. Pursuant to your invitation, we will interrogate our manager.

c. Recent laws mandate equal remuneration for men and women who perform equal tasks.

d. In a dialogue with the manager, I learned that you plan to terminate our agreement.

e. Did the steering problem materialize subsequent to our recall effort?

f. Once we ascertain how much it costs, we can initiate the project.

3.9 Precise Words

From the words in parentheses, select the most precise, vigorous words.

a. Please try to *(contact, reach, telephone)* me as soon as you arrive.

b. He is *(engaged by, associated with, employed by)* the Dana Corporation.

c. We plan to *(acknowledge, publicize, applaud)* the work of exemplary employees.

d. The splendid report has *(a lot of, many, a warehouse of)* facts.

e. The board of directors thought the annual report was *(good, nice, helpful)*.

For the following sentences provide more precise alternatives for the italicized words.

f. Management is (a) *looking* for a (b) *better* way to solve the problem.

g. The CEO (a) *said* that only (b) *the right kind of* applicants should apply.

h. After (a) *reading* the report, I decided it was (b) *bad*.

i. Marci said the movie was (a) *different* but her remarks weren't very (b) *clear* to us.

j. I'm (a) *going* to Little Rock tomorrow, and I plan to (b) *find out* the real problem.

k. Most (a) *people* don't have much (b) *feeling toward* brand names unless the brands are heavily promoted.

l. The (a) *news* made us feel particularly (b) *positive*.

3.10 Legal Language

To avoid possible litigation, revise the italicized words in the following sentences taken from proposals.

a. We will *inspect* the building plans before construction begins.

b. Our goal is to *assure* completion of the project on schedule.

c. We will *determine* the amount of stress for each supporting column.

C.L.U.E. Review 3

On a separate sheet edit the following sentences to correct faults in grammar, punctuation, spelling, and word use.

1. If I was you I would schedule the conference for one of these cities Atlanta Memphis or Nashville.

2. The committees next meeting is scheduled for May fifth at three p.m., and should last about two hours.

3. Were not asking you to altar the figures, we are asking you to check there accuracy.

4. Will you please fax me a list of our independant contractors names and addresses?

5. The vacation calender fills up quick for the Summer months, therefore you should make your plans early.

6. After the inspector issues the waver we will be able to procede with the architects plan.

7. If we can't give out neccessary information what is the point in us answering the telephone.

8. Every new employee will receive their orientation packet, and be told about their parking priviledges.

9. About eighty-five percent of all new entrants into the workforce in the 1990s is expected to be: women, minorities and immigrants.

10. Our Vice President in the Human Resources Development Department asked the Manager and I to come to her office at three-thirty p.m.

Researching, Organizing, and Composing

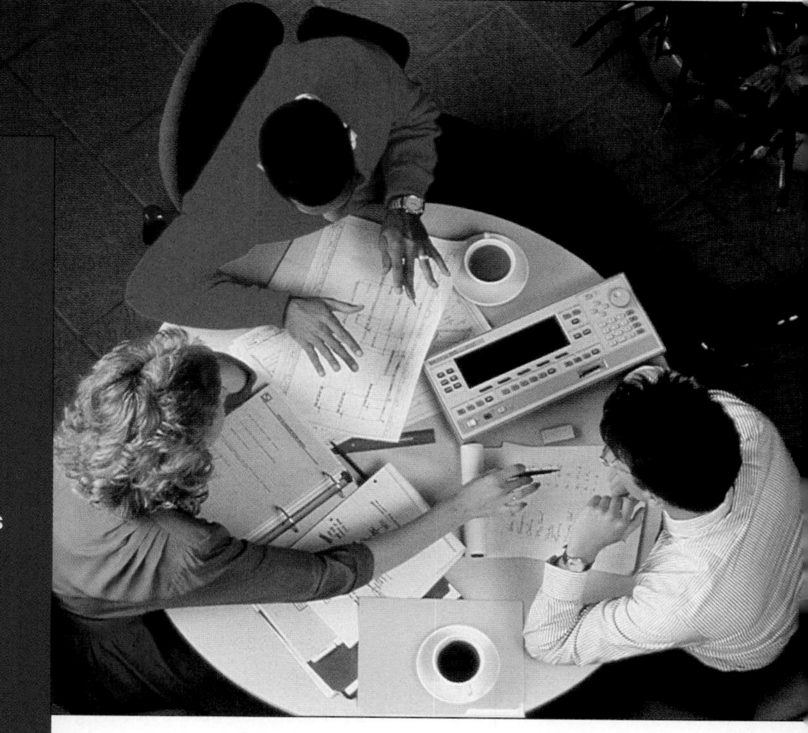

LEARNING GOALS

After studying this chapter, you should be able to

1. Contrast formal and informal research methods
2. Organize ideas into alphanumeric or decimal outlines
3. Compare direct and indirect patterns of idea organization
4. Explain techniques for creating forceful sentences
5. Explain how to write effective paragraphs
6. Describe how to reduce problems characteristic of collaborative writing

Liz Claiborne: Career Track Profile

"Everything I do requires communication and organizational skills."

Over the past decade Liz Claiborne, Inc., has quietly become the largest women's apparel company in the world. It's one of only two companies started by a woman to crack the Fortune 500. Moreover, it consistently ranks in the top ten of Fortune's list of "America's Most Admired Corporations." Liz Claiborne has remained amazingly successful—and has even expanded into new markets—during one of the deepest retailing slumps in the country's history. Staying alive in the fickle fashion industry is no easy task, even in good times.

Liz Claiborne's success results largely from recognizing and capitalizing on important lifestyle changes sweeping America. Mix-and-match styles at comfortable prices suit America's increasingly female work force just fine. Its success formula is simple: "Straightforward fashion that's designed for women who have more important things to think about than what to wear. No gimmicks. No surprises." Industry experts describe the line as "accessible" rather than "aspirational."

Liz Claiborne evolved from a basic sportswear business into one of the nation's most successful businesses by listening to its customers. At the company's headquarters in North Bergen, New Jersey, $10 million worth of IBM computers work round the clock to crunch sales data, revealing what's hot and what's not. Executives and 150 specialists also interview customers across the country, who consistently say, "We want style, quality, fit, *and* value."

Reinforcing the accessibility of its clothing is an open corporate spirit, where equality and teamwork flourish. Open doors and first names prevail. In fact, all 7,000 employees are listed alphabetically *by first name* in the company directory. Although the atmosphere is informal, the staff is action- and success-oriented.

Susanne Tully joined the rapidly expanding Liz Claiborne enterprise fresh out of college nine years ago. But Susanne wasn't a traditional college grad. She had worked for many years as a secretary before deciding she needed a change. Susanne quit her job, entered Montclair State College in New Jersey, and began a grueling program of full-time studies as well as full-time employment. While her friends were off on ski trips, she was writing term papers. "The whole upside-downness of my life seemed unbearable at the time," reveals Susanne, "but I've never second-guessed that decision once."

In the New Jersey headquarters Susanne began as administrative assistant to the chief

financial officer. Eventually, she became a manager with responsibility for recruiting college graduates, running internships, reporting on equal employment opportunity and affirmative action programs, and coordinating special events. She's also editor and chief contributor to *Liz Biz,* the internal company newspaper. "My biggest surprise," says Susanne, "was the large degree of responsibility I was given and the small amount of guidance—no mentor to guide the way."

Consistently recognized as one of America's best-managed and most-admired companies, Liz Claiborne, Inc., depends on its computerized information network to learn what's selling and what isn't throughout the country. Up-to-the-minute reports are produced by its SURF network (System Updated Retail Feedback). With immediate data on sales, styles, sizes, and colors, division heads can adjust orders, inventories, and plans accordingly.

One major responsibility is college recruiting, which often begins with efforts to correct a misconception. "Lots of college students don't know that Liz Claiborne is much more than fashion. I'm looking for people to place in operations management, accounting, finance, information systems, marketing, and merchandising—in addition to those in design and computer-aided design." On campuses Susanne gives presentations, attends job fairs, and conducts preliminary interviews. Back in the office she corresponds with and keeps track of hundreds of applicants, as well as informing the numerous company divisions and various departments within those divisions of progress in filling their requests.

"Everything I do requires communication and organizational skills," reports Susanne. "Before writing anything, I assemble the necessary information and decide what action should be taken. I never start writing a document until I know where I'm going so that I can say it in as few words as possible. We don't stand on formality here; our whole internal structure is informal. We try to generate as little paper as possible, so we're very conservative with words. If it can be said in one paragraph, or, better yet, taken care of with a telephone call—that's what we do. For letters going outside, though, we're not quite so casual. I try to personalize every letter, and that requires some thought and preparation."

For routine tasks—internal memos, familiar letters, periodic reports—Susanne gets ready to write by collecting background information from meetings, files, or previous correspondence. "That information is usually easily organized," she says, "because it's familiar to me and the data is obvious. Concentrating on the end result is important. If I'm asking for something, I always tell when I need it—politely, of course—and try to make it easy for the recipient to do."

More challenging assignments require greater organizational skills and more creativity from Susanne. Often, she has to research facts, generate ideas, and organize them into a logical presentation or program—without any previous model to build on.[1]

Researching Data and Generating Ideas

Before writing, conduct formal or informal research to collect or generate necessary information.

Business communicators like Susanne Tully face daily challenges that require data collection, idea generation, and organization. These activities are part of the second phase of the writing process, which includes researching, generating ideas, and organizing.

No smart businessperson would begin writing a message before collecting all the needed information. We call this collection process "research," a rather formal-sounding term. For simple documents, though, the procedure can be quite informal. Research is necessary before beginning writing because the data you collect help shape the message. Discovering significant information after a message is half completed often means starting over and reorganizing. To avoid frustration and inaccurate messages, collect information that answers a primary question:

- *What does the receiver need to know about this topic?*

When the message involves action, search for answers to secondary questions:

- *What is the receiver to do?*
- *How is the receiver to do it?*
- *When must the receiver do it?*
- *What will happen if the receiver doesn't do it?*

Whenever your communication problem requires more information than you have in your head or at your fingertips, you must conduct research. This research may be formal or informal.

Formal Research Methods

Formal research may involve searching libraries and electronic databases or investigating primary sources (interviews, surveys, and experimentation).

Long reports and complex business problems generally require some use of formal research methods. Let's say you are a market specialist for Coca-Cola, and your boss asks you to evaluate the impact of private-label or generic soft drinks (the bargain-basement-brand knockoffs sold at Kmart and other outlets). Or, let's assume you must write a term paper for a college class. Both tasks require more data than you have in your head or at your fingertips. To conduct formal research, you could:

- **Search manually.** You'll find helpful background and supplementary information through manual searching of resources in public and college libraries. These traditional sources include periodical indexes for lists of newspaper, magazine, and journal articles, along with the card catalog for books. Other manual sources are book indexes, encyclopedias, reference books, handbooks, dictionaries, directories, and almanacs.
- **Access electronically.** Like other facets of life, the research process has been changed considerably by the computer. Much of the printed material just described is now available on compact discs or from mainframe databases that can be accessed by computer. College and public libraries subscribe to retrieval services that permit you to access thousands of bibliographic or full-text databases.
- **Investigate primary sources.** To develop firsthand, primary information for a project, go directly to the source. For the Coca-Cola report, for example, you would find out what consumers really think by conducting interviews or sur-

veys, by putting together questionnaires, or by organizing focus groups. Formal research includes scientific sampling methods that enable investigators to make accurate judgments and valid predictions.

- **Experiment scientifically.** Another source of primary data is experimentation. Instead of merely asking for the target audience's opinion, scientific researchers present choices with controlled variables. Assume, for example, that Coca-Cola wants to determine at what price and under what circumstances consumers would switch from Coca-Cola to a generic brand. The results of such experimentation would provide valuable data for managerial decision making.

Because formal research techniques are particularly necessary for reports, you'll learn more about these techniques in Part IV.

Informal Research and Idea Generation

Most routine tasks—such as familiar memos, letters, and informational reports—require data that you can collect informally. For some projects, though, you rely more on your own ideas instead of—or in addition to—researching existing facts. Here are some techniques for collecting informal data and for generating ideas:

- **Look in the files.** Before asking others for help, see what you can find yourself. For many routine messages you can often find previous documents to help you with content and format.
- **Talk with your boss.** Get information from the individual making the assignment. What does that person know about the topic? What slant should be taken? What other sources would he or she suggest?
- **Interview the target audience.** Consider talking with individuals at whom the message is aimed. Often, they can provide clarifying information that tells you what they want to know and how you should shape your remarks.
- **Conduct an informal survey.** Gather unscientific but helpful information via questionnaires or telephone surveys. In preparing a memo report predicting the success of company van pools, for example, circulate a questionnaire asking for employee reactions.
- **Brainstorm for ideas.** Alone or with others, discuss ideas for the writing task at hand, and record at least a dozen ideas without judging them. Small groups are especially fruitful in brainstorming because people spin ideas off one another.
- **Develop a cluster diagram.** Prepare a cluster diagram (discussed in the next section) to help you generate and organize ideas. Clustering allows your mind to open up and free associate.

Researching Data and Generating Ideas on the Job

Let's follow Susanne Tully at Liz Claiborne to see how she collected data and generated ideas for two projects—one simple and one complex.

Writing an informational memo. The first is an informational memo, shown in Figure 4.1, to all employees describing a photo contest sponsored by Liz Claiborne. For this memo Susanne began by brainstorming with her staff, other employees, and her boss to decide on a photo contest theme. After naming a

SPOTLIGHT ON COMMUNICATORS

Generating ideas is a top priority for Gerry Laybourne, president of the cable television network Nickelodeon/Nick at Nite. Three techniques work for her: being unafraid of making mistakes or looking silly, refusing to censor ideas, and brainstorming with her staff. Because she feels that many heads are better than one, she encourages brainstorming and follows it up with team-centered management.

FIGURE 4.1 ● Informational Memo

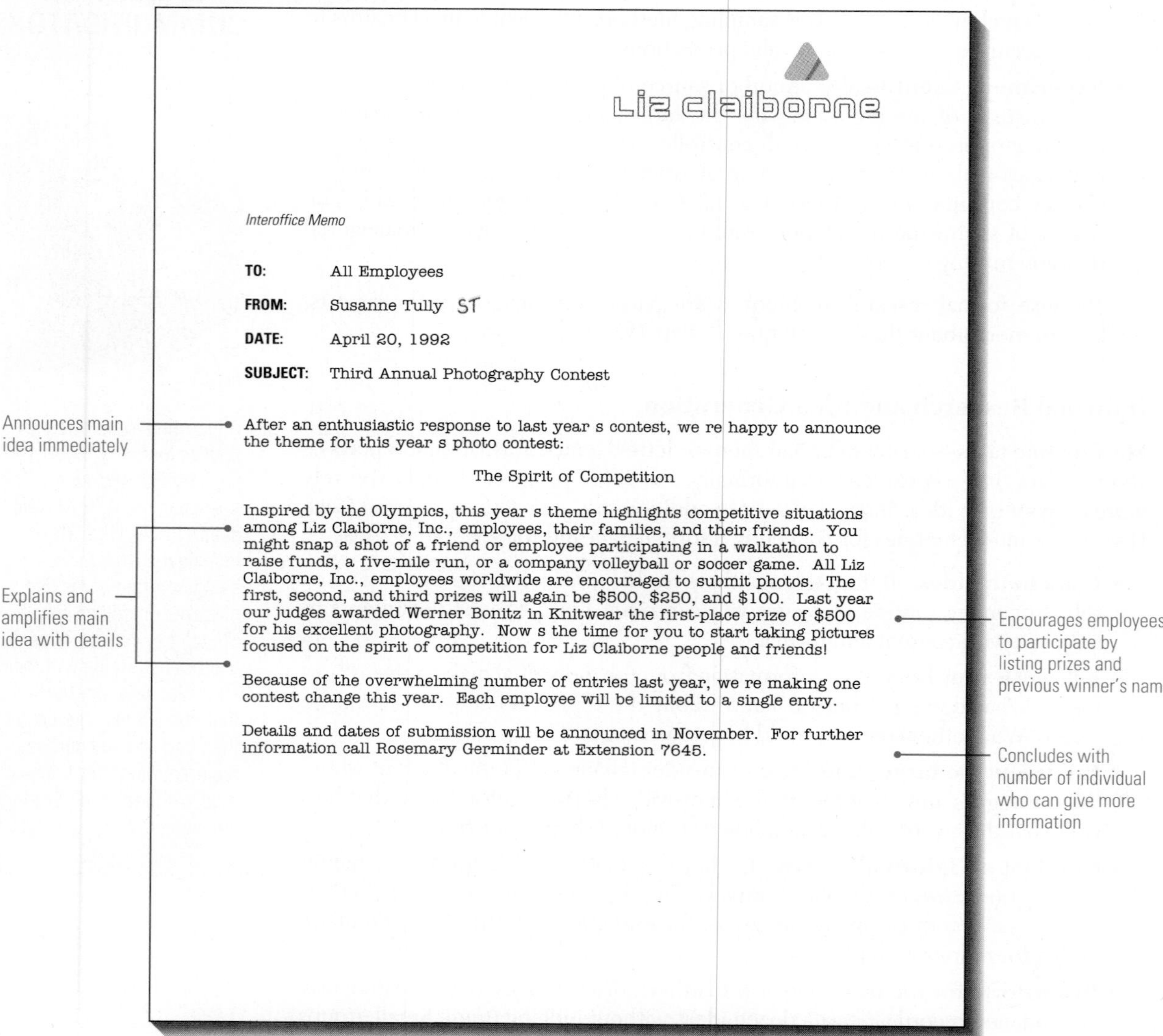

Liz claiborne
Interoffice Memo
TO: All Employees
FROM: Susanne Tully ST
DATE: April 20, 1992
SUBJECT: Third Annual Photography Contest
After an enthusiastic response to last year s contest, we re happy to announce the theme for this year s photo contest:
The Spirit of Competition
Inspired by the Olympics, this year s theme highlights competitive situations among Liz Claiborne, Inc., employees, their families, and their friends. You might snap a shot of a friend or employee participating in a walkathon to raise funds, a five-mile run, or a company volleyball or soccer game. All Liz Claiborne, Inc., employees worldwide are encouraged to submit photos. The first, second, and third prizes will again be $500, $250, and $100. Last year our judges awarded Werner Bonitz in Knitwear the first-place prize of $500 for his excellent photography. Now s the time for you to start taking pictures focused on the spirit of competition for Liz Claiborne people and friends!
Because of the overwhelming number of entries last year, we re making one contest change this year. Each employee will be limited to a single entry.
Details and dates of submission will be announced in November. For further information call Rosemary Germinder at Extension 7645.
Announces main idea immediately
Explains and amplifies main idea with details
Encourages employees to participate by listing prizes and previous winner's name
Concludes with number of individual who can give more information

theme, "The Spirit of Competition," inspired by the Olympics, she consulted the files to see who had won prizes in last year's contest. She also double-checked with management to ensure that the prize money—$500, $250, and $100—remained the same. Then she made the following quick scratch list outlining the points she wanted to cover in her memo.

Photo Contest Memo

1. Announce theme; give examples
2. Encourage all employees worldwide to participate
3. Review prizes; name last year's winner
4. Limit: one entry each
5. Details in November; call Rosemary for more info

Many business messages, like Susanne's finished memo, require only simple data collection and idea generation techniques.

Preparing a recruitment brochure. Susanne's second project, though, demanded both formal and informal research, along with considerable creativity. She needed to produce a recruitment brochure that explained career opportunities for college students at Liz Claiborne. She had definite objectives for the brochure: it should be colorful, exciting, concise, lightweight (because she had to carry stacks of them to college campuses!), and easily updated. Moreover, she wanted the brochure to promote Liz Claiborne, describing its progressive benefits, community involvement, career potential, and corporate values program (called "Priorities").

Some of her thoughts about this big project are shown in the cluster diagram in Figure 4.2. Cluster diagraming sparks our creativity; it encourages ideas to spill forth because the process is unrestricted. From the jumble of ideas in the initial cluster diagram, main categories—usually three to five—are extracted. At this point some people are ready to make an outline; others need further visualization, such as a set of subclusters, shown in Figure 4.3. Notice that four major categories (Purpose, Content, Development, and Form) were extracted from the initial diagram. These categories then became the hub of related ideas. This set of subclusters forms the basis for an outline, to be discussed shortly.

● **Cluster diagraming helps generate ideas and reveal relationships between ideas.**

To collect data for this project, Susanne employed both formal and informal research methods. She studied recruiting brochures from other companies. She talked with college students to ask what information they looked for in a brochure. She conducted more formal research among the numerous division presidents and executives within her company to learn what really went on in all the departments, such as Information Systems, Operations Management, Production, and Design. She also had to learn the specific educational and personality requirements for careers in those areas. Working with an outside consultant, she prepared a questionnaire, which was used in personal interviews with company executives. The interviews included some open-ended questions, such as "How did you start with the company?" It also contained more specific questions about the number of employees in their departments, intended career paths, degree requirements, personality traits desired, and so forth. Organizing the mass of data collected was the next task.

Organizing Data

The process of organization may begin before you collect data, as it did for Susanne Tully, or occur simultaneously with data collection. For complex projects, organization may be on-going. Regardless of when organization occurs, its primary goals are grouping and patterning. Well-organized messages group similar items together; ideas follow a sequence that helps the reader understand relationships and accept the writer's views. Unorganized messages proceed free-form, jumping from one thought to another. Such messages fail to emphasize important points. Puzzled readers can't see how the pieces fit together, and they become frustrated and irritated. Many communication experts regard poor organization as the greatest failing of business writers.

● **Well-organized messages group similar ideas together so that readers can see relationships and follow arguments.**

This section introduces two simple techniques that can help you organize data: the scratch list and the outline. (Chapter 12 presents additional advice for organizing data in reports.) This section also covers two common patterns for arranging business messages—direct and indirect.

FIGURE 4.2 ● Using Cluster Diagram to Generate Ideas for Liz Claiborne College Recruiting Brochure

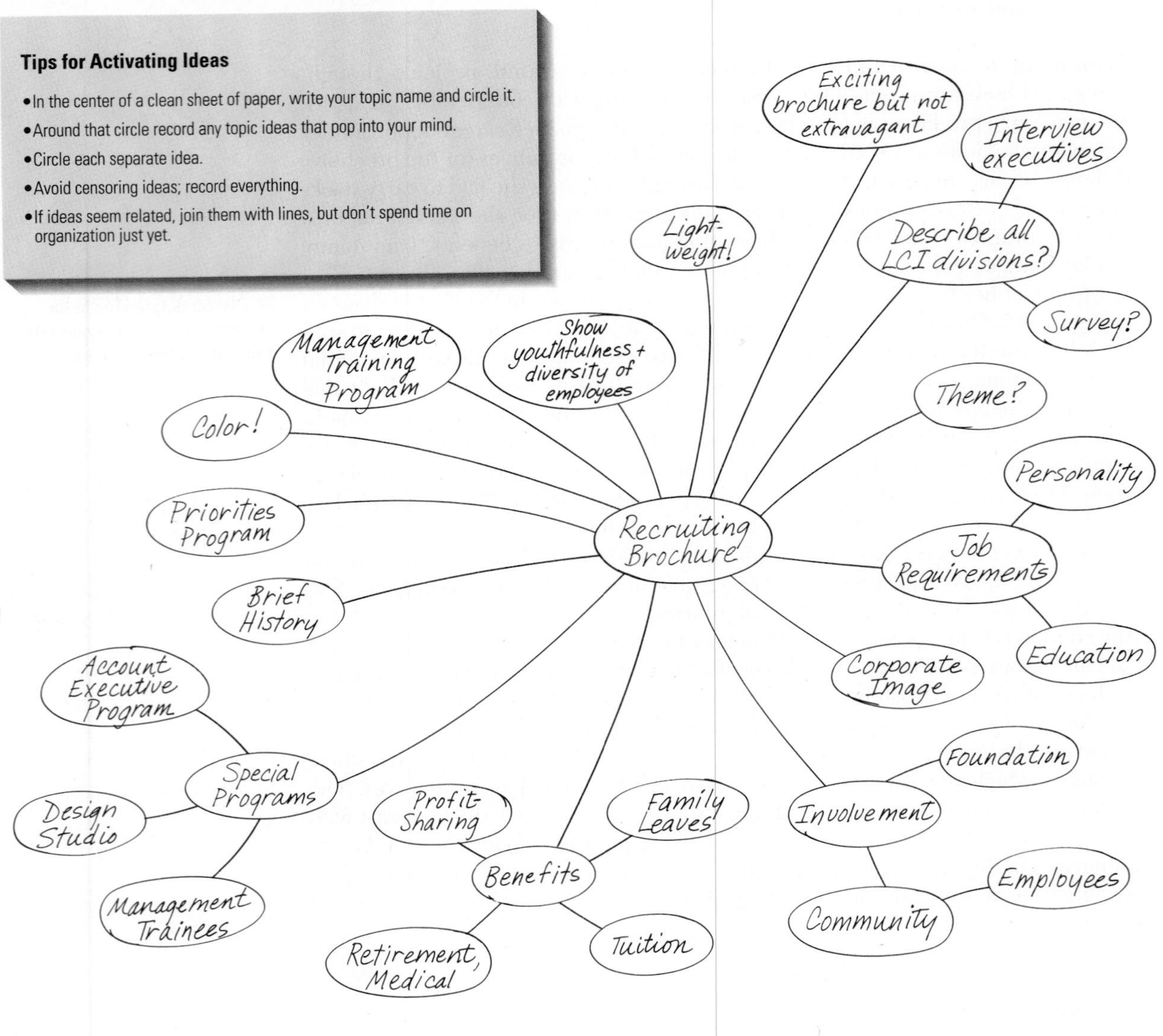

Listing and Outlining

In developing simple messages, some writers make a quick scratch list of the topics they wish to cover, as Susanne Tully did for her memo in Figure 4.1. Writers often jot this scratch list in the margin of the letter or memo to which they are responding—and the majority of business messages are written in response to other documents. These writers can then dictate or compose a message at their computers directly from the scratch list.

Most writers, though, need to organize their ideas—especially if the project is complex—into a hierarchy, such as an outline. Figure 4.4 shows two outline for-

FIGURE 4.3 ● Organizing Ideas from Cluster Diagram into Subclusters

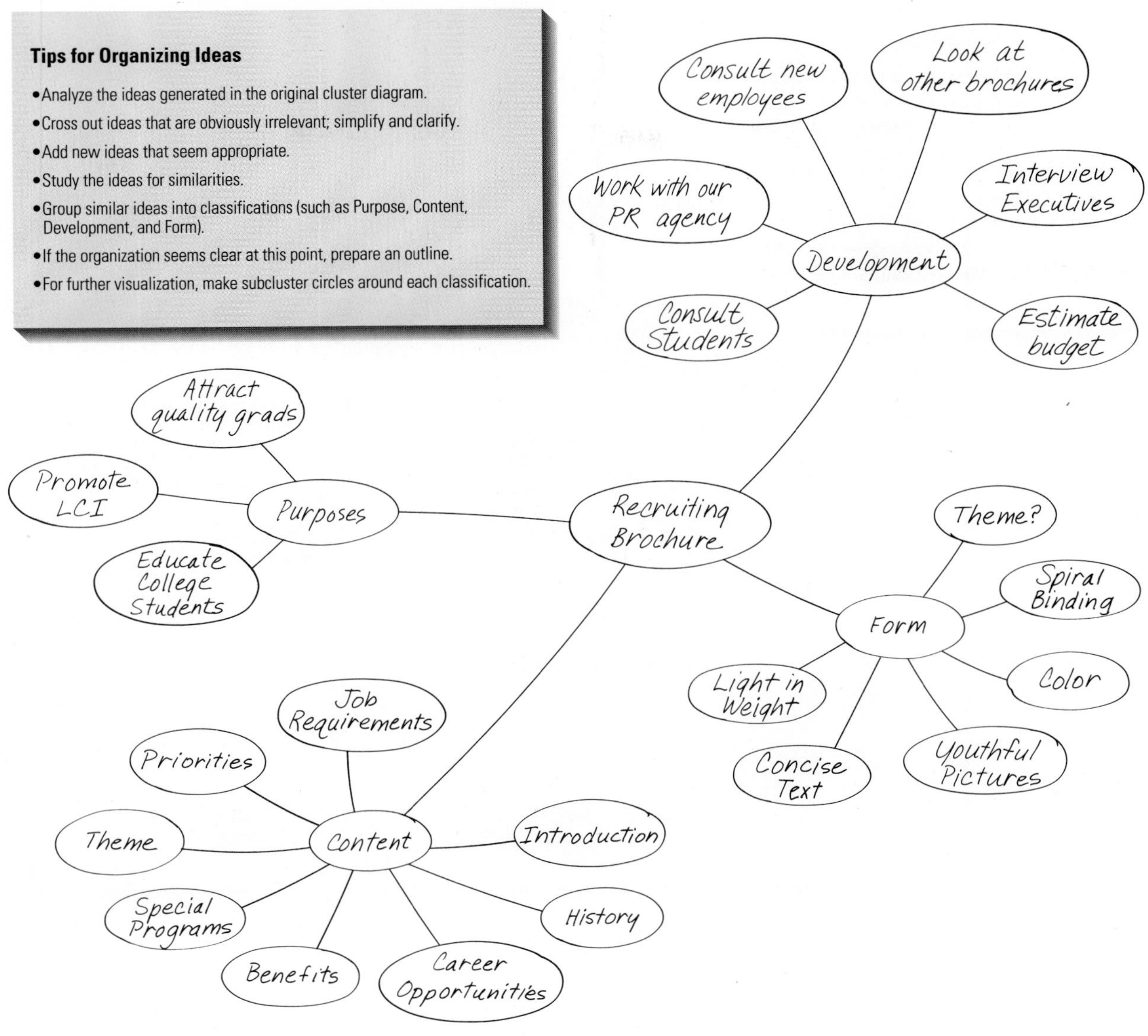
Tips for Organizing Ideas
•Analyze the ideas generated in the original cluster diagram.
•Cross out ideas that are obviously irrelevant; simplify and clarify.
•Add new ideas that seem appropriate.
•Study the ideas for similarities.
•Group similar ideas into classifications (such as Purpose, Content, Development, and Form).
•If the organization seems clear at this point, prepare an outline.
•For further visualization, make subcluster circles around each classification.
Consult new employees
Look at other brochures
Work with our PR agency
Interview Executives
Development
Consult Students
Estimate budget
Attract quality grads
Promote LCI
Purposes
Recruiting Brochure
Theme?
Educate College Students
Spiral Binding
Form
Light in Weight
Color
Job Requirements
Concise Text
Youthful Pictures
Priorities
Theme
Content
Introduction
Special Programs
History
Benefits
Career Opportunities

mats: alphanumeric and decimal. The familiar alphanumeric format uses Roman numerals, letters, and numbers to show major and minor ideas. The decimal format, which takes a little getting used to, has the advantage of showing how every item at every level relates to the whole. Both outlining formats force you to focus on the topic, identify major ideas, and support those ideas with details, illustrations, or evidence. Many computer outlining programs now on the market make the mechanics of the process a real breeze.

● Alphanumeric outlines show major and minor ideas; decimal outlines show how ideas relate to one another.

The hardest part of outlining is grouping ideas into components or categories—ideally three to five in number. If you have more than five components, look

FIGURE 4.4 ● Two Outlining Formats

Tips for Making Outlines

- Define the main topic (purpose of message) in the title
- Divide the main topic into major components or classifications (preferably three to five). If necessary, combine small components into one larger category.
- Break the components into subpoints.
- Don't put a single item under a major component; if you have only one subpoint, integrate it with the main item above it or reorganize.
- Strive to make each component exclusive (no overlapping).
- Use details, illustrations, and evidence to support subpoints.

Format for Alphanumeric Outline

Title: Major Idea, Purpose

I. First major component
  A. First subpoint
    1. Detail, illustration, evidence
    2. Detail, illustration, evidence
  B. Second subpoint
    1.
    2.
II. Second major component
  A. First subpoint
    1.
    2.
  B. Second subpoint
    1.
    2.
III. Third major component
  A.
    1.
    2.
  B.
    1.
    2.

(This method is simple and familiar.)

Format for Decimal Outline

Title: Major Idea, Purpose

1.0 First major component
  1.1 First subpoint
    1.1.1 Detail, illustration, evidence
    1.1.2 Detail, illustration, evidence
  1.2 Second subpoint
    1.2.1
    1.2.2
2.0 Second major component
  2.1 First subpoint
    2.1.1
    2.1.2
  2.2 Second subpoint
    2.2.1
    2.2.2
3.0 Third major component
  3.1
    3.1.1
    3.1.2
  3.2
    3.2.1
    3.2.2

(This method relates every item to the overall outline.)

for ways to combine smaller segments into broader topics. The following example shows how a portion of the Liz Claiborne brochure subcluster (Figure 4.3) can be organized into an alphanumeric outline.

I. Introduction
  A. Brief history of Liz Claiborne
    1. Founding, Fortune 500 status
    2. Product lines
  B. Corporate environment
    1. System of values: "Priorities"
    2. Team spirit; corporate image
II. Career opportunities
  A. Operations management
    1. Traffic
    2. International trade and corporate customs
    3. Distribution

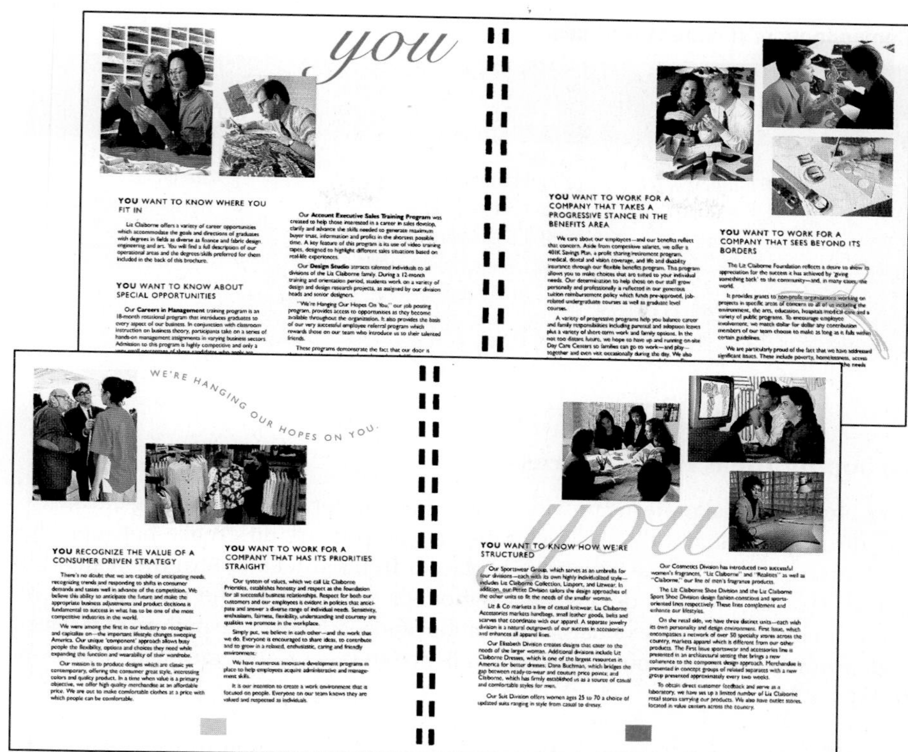

In organizing this Liz Claiborne recruitment brochure, Susanne Tully and her staff achieved coherence and readability by converting each topic from the outline into a consistent, reader-centered heading. Notice the emphasis on "you," an important lesson for every business communicator to learn.

B. Accounting and finance
   1. General accounting
   2. Internal audit
   3. Treasury and risk management
C. Special opportunities
   1. Management training program
   2. Account executive sales training program
   3. Design studio

Notice that each major category is divided into at least two subcategories, which in turn are fleshed out with examples, details, statistics, case histories, and other data. In moving from major point to subpoint, you are progressing from large abstract concepts to small concrete ideas. And each subpoint could be further subdivided with more specific illustrations if you desired. You can determine the appropriate amount of detail by considering what your audience (primary and secondary) already knows about the topic and how much persuading you must do.

The topic and the communication channel determine how ideas are grouped into components.

How you group ideas into components depends on your topic and your channel of communication. The finished Liz Claiborne recruitment brochure, shown above, required careful editing so that each component fit into the page layout. Business documents, on the other hand, do not have rigid page constraints and usually contain typical components arranged in traditional patterns, as shown in Figure 4.5.

Thus far, you've seen how to collect information, generate ideas, and prepare an outline. How you order the information in your outline, though, depends on what pattern or strategy you choose.

FIGURE 4.5 ● Typical Major Components in Business Outlines

Letter or Memo	Procedure	Informational Report	Analytical Report	Proposal
I. Opening II. Body III. Close	I. Step 1 II. Step 2 III. Step 3 IV. Step 4	I. Introduction II. Facts III. Summary	I. Introduction/Problem II. Facts/Findings III. Conclusions IV. Recommendations (if requested)	I. Introduction II. Proposed solution III. Staffing IV. Schedule, cost V. Authorization

Grouping Ideas Into Patterns

● Business messages typically follow either the direct pattern, with the main idea first, or the indirect pattern, with the main idea following explanation and evidence.

Two organizational patterns provide plans of action for typical business messages: the direct pattern and the indirect pattern. The primary difference between the two patterns is where the main idea is placed. In the direct pattern the main idea comes first, followed by details, explanation, or evidence. In the indirect pattern the main idea follows the details, explanation, and evidence. The pattern you select is determined by how you expect the audience to react to the message, as shown in Figure 4.6.

The direct pattern for receptive audiences. In preparing to write any message, you need to anticipate the audience's reaction to your ideas and frame your message accordingly. When you expect the reader to be pleased, mildly interested, or at worst neutral, use the direct pattern. That is, put your main point—the purpose of your message—in the first or second sentence. Notice how long it takes the sender to get to the main idea of this message:

> As you know, the Management Council has been considering the possibility of starting an internship program for college students here at LaserPro. Such a program might attract better-qualified prospective job candidates than our present system. It would enable us to begin training students and would also help develop a sense of loyalty toward LaserPro before those students finish their education. But such a program would require considerable research and promotion before it could be implemented. We have, therefore, voted to begin a pilot program starting next fall.

● Frontloading saves the reader time, establishes the proper frame of mind, and prevents frustration.

To open more directly, this message would read, *The Management Council has voted to begin a college internship pilot program starting next fall,* with explanation and details following. This direct method, also called *frontloading,* has at least three advantages:

- **Saves the reader's time.** Many of today's businesspeople can devote only a few moments to each message. Those messages that take too long to get to the point may lose their readers along the way.
- **Sets a proper frame of mind.** Learning the purpose up front helps the reader put the subsequent details and explanations in perspective. Without a clear opening, the reader may be thinking, "Why am I being told this?"
- **Prevents frustration.** Readers forced to struggle through excessive verbiage before reaching the main idea become frustrated with and resentful toward the writer. Poorly organized messages create a negative impression of the writer.

FIGURE 4.6 ● Audience Response Determines Pattern of Organization

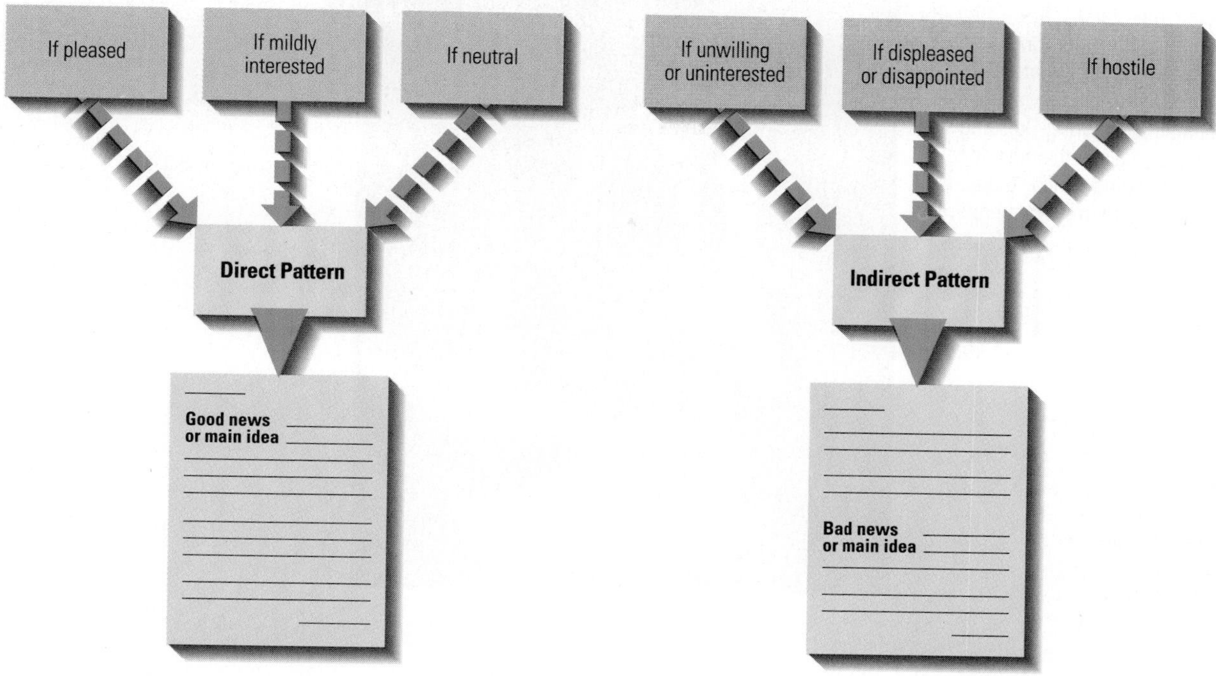

This frontloading technique works best with audiences that are likely to be receptive to or at least not disagree with what you have to say. Typical business messages that follow the direct pattern include routine requests and responses, orders and acknowledgements, nonsensitive memos, and informational reports. All these messages have one element in common: none has a sensitive subject that will upset the reader.

The indirect pattern for unreceptive audiences. When you expect the audience to be uninterested, unwilling, displeased, or perhaps even hostile, the indirect pattern is more appropriate. In this pattern don't reveal the main idea until after you have offered explanation and evidence. This approach works well with three kinds of messages: (1) bad news, (2) ideas that require persuasion, and (3) sensitive news, especially when being transmitted to superiors. The indirect pattern has these benefits:

● The indirect pattern is appropriate when the audience may be uninterested in, displeased by, or hostile to the message.

- **Respects the feelings of the audience.** Bad news is always painful, but the trauma can be lessened when the receiver is prepared for it.
- **Ensures a fair hearing.** Messages that may upset the reader are more likely to be read when the main idea is delayed. Beginning immediately with a piece of bad news or a persuasive request, for example, may cause the receiver to read no further.
- **Minimizes the negative reaction.** A reader's overall reaction to a negative message is generally improved if the news is delivered gently.

Typical business messages that could be developed indirectly include letters and memos that refuse requests, deny claims, and disapprove credit. Persuasive requests, sales letters, sensitive messages, and some reports also benefit from the

Skilled communicators save their time (and that of their readers!) by organizing their ideas into logical patterns before sitting down at the computer to write. Deciding where to place the main idea and grouping similar thoughts together are important prewriting tasks.

indirect strategy. You'll learn more about how to use the indirect pattern in Chapters 8 and 9. The indirect strategy causes some communicators concern because it seems devious. For further discussion of this issue, see the accompanying Ethics box.

In summary, business messages may be organized directly, with the main idea first, or indirectly, with the main idea delayed. Although these two patterns cover many communication problems, they should be considered neither universal nor inviolate. Every business transaction is distinct. Some messages are mixed: part good news, part bad; part goodwill, part persuasion. In upcoming chapters you'll practice applying the direct and indirect patterns in typical situations. Then, you'll have the skills and confidence to evaluate communication problems and vary these patterns depending on the goals you wish to achieve.

Composing the First Draft

When composing the first draft, write quickly and save revision for later.

Once you've researched your topic, organized the data, and selected a pattern of organization, you're ready to begin composing. Communicators who haven't completed the preparatory work often suffer from "writer's block" and sit staring at a piece of paper or at the computer screen. It's difficult to get started without organized ideas and a plan. Composition is also easier if you have a quiet environment in which to concentrate. Businesspeople with messages to compose set aside a given time and allow no calls, visitors, or other interruptions. This is a good technique for students as well.

As you begin composing, keep in mind that you are writing the first draft, not the final copy. Experts advise that you write quickly, getting your thoughts down now and refining them in later versions.[2] This method works especially well for those composing on a computer because it's simple to make changes at any point

ETHICS

COMMUNICATOR MOTIVATION AND THE ETHICS UNDERLYING MESSAGES

You may worry that the indirect organizational strategy is unethical since a writer deliberately delays the main idea. But let's put that strategy into context. Assume that you are writing a letter denying credit to a customer. Instead of bluntly announcing the denial, you begin by explaining the reasons necessitating the denial. Then, you present the bad news. By delaying bad news, you soften the blow somewhat, as well as ensure that your reasoning will be read while a receiver is still receptive. Your motives are not to deceive the reader or to hide the news; instead, your goal is to be a compassionate, yet effective communicator.

The key to ethical communication lies in the motives of the sender. Unethical communicators *intend to deceive.* The following are selected news items for you to consider. Although you can't read the minds of those involved, examine these cases and think about the ethics of the communicators. Is it ethical communication? Did they intend to deceive or not?

- Victoria's Secret offers free $10 gift certificates. However, when customers try to cash the certificates, they find they are required to make a minimum purchase of $50 worth of merchandise.[3]
- An advertisement (by Comb Authorized Liquidators) lists IBM PS/2 computers (IBM Quality! IBM Durability! IBM Reliability!) at a remarkably low price of $698. The advertisement describes a color monitor, enhanced keyboard, expansion slots, and hard drive, along with many other features. Buried in the text is this statement: "Factory renewed by IBM."[4] In other words, the machines are used.
- TV and print advertisements proclaim Volvo's durability when a monster truck named "Bear Foot" roars across the tops of parked cars, flattening every one except a Volvo 240. However, the Volvo used in the car-crushing exhibition in Austin, Texas, is actually reinforced with steel to withstand being run over. Moreover, although the ads re-create a Vermont truck rally, they do not identify the action as a dramatization.[5]
- Advertisements for the Discover credit card assert that it does not charge interest on cash advances. It does, however, charge stiff transaction fees.[6]
- Trans World Airlines advertises a $149 round-trip fare to Puerto Rico, but barely mentions requirements for a hotel stay or car rental.[7]

Career Track Application

Assume that one of your tasks for a national chain of copy stores is writing advertisements. One national ad on which you work shouts in huge letters, "SAME-DAY DELIVERY." You know, however, that such service is available only when customers bring in their copy before 10 a.m. What would you do?

of the composition process. If you are handwriting the first draft, double-space so that you have room for changes.

Creating Forceful Sentences

As you create your first draft, you'll be working at the sentence level of composition. Although you've used sentences all your life, you may be unaware of how they can be shaped and arranged to express your ideas most forcefully. First, let's review some basic sentence elements.

Complete sentences have subjects and verbs and make sense.

SUBJECT VERB / SUBJECT VERB

This report is clear and concise. Our employees write many reports.

Clauses and phrases, the key building blocks of sentences, are related groups of words. Clauses have subjects and verbs; phrases do not.

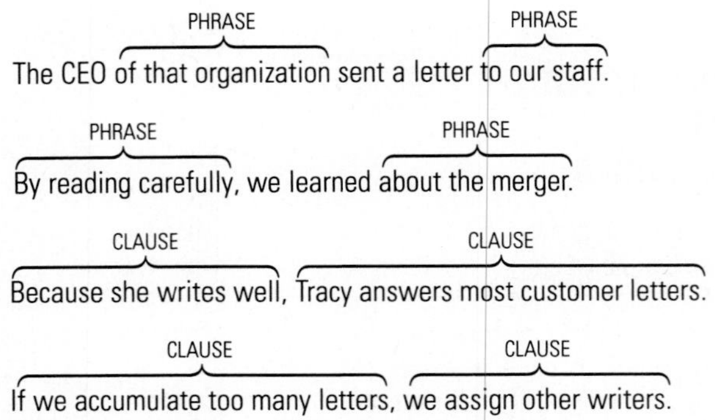

PHRASE
PHRASE
The CEO of that organization sent a letter to our staff.
PHRASE
PHRASE
By reading carefully, we learned about the merger.
CLAUSE
CLAUSE
Because she writes well, Tracy answers most customer letters.
CLAUSE
CLAUSE
If we accumulate too many letters, we assign other writers.

Clauses may be divided into two groups: independent and dependent. Independent clauses can stand alone; thus, every grammatically complete sentence contains at least one independent clause. Dependent clauses depend for their meaning on independent clauses; they cannot stand alone. In the two preceding examples the clauses beginning with *If* and *Because* are dependent. Dependent clauses are often introduced by words like *if, when, because,* and *as.*

INDEPENDENT CLAUSE

Tracy is a customer service representative.

DEPENDENT CLAUSE INDEPENDENT CLAUSE

When Tracy writes to customers, she uses simple language.

By learning to distinguish phrases, independent clauses, and dependent clauses, you'll be able to punctuate sentences correctly and avoid three basic sentence faults: the fragment, the run-on sentence, and the comma splice. In Appendix A, we examine these writing problems in greater detail. For now, however, let's look at some ways to make your sentences more readable and forceful.

● **Forceful sentences are short and stress important ideas.**

Using short sentences. Because your goal is to communicate clearly, you're better off limiting your sentences to about 20 words or fewer. The American Press Institute reports that reader comprehension drops off markedly as sentences become longer.[8] Thus, in crafting your sentences, keep the following correspondences between sentence length and comprehension in mind:

Sentence Length	Comprehension Rate
8 words	100%
15 words	90%
19 words	80%
28 words	50%

● **Sentences of twenty or fewer words have the most impact.**

Instead of stringing together clauses with *and, but,* and *however,* break some of those complex sentences into separate segments. Business readers want to grasp ideas immediately. They can do that best when thoughts are separated into short sentences. On the other hand, too many monotonous short sentences will sound "grammar schoolish" and may bore or even annoy the reader. Strive for a balance between longer sentences and shorter ones. Your computer software probably has the ability to point out long sentences and give you an average sentence length.

Emphasizing important ideas. You can stress prominent ideas in three ways. The first is to place an important idea at the beginning of a sentence. Notice how this sentence obscures the date of the meeting by burying it: *All production and* *administrative personnel will meet May 23, at which time we will announce a new plan of salary incentives.* To emphasize the date, start the sentence with it: *On May 23 all personnel will meet . . .* A secondary position of importance is the end of a sentence: *All personnel will meet to discuss salary incentives on May 23.* Remember this guideline when composing paragraphs as well; put the main idea at the start and then follow up with supporting material.

A second way to emphasize an important idea is to be sure that it acts as the subject in a sentence. Notice the difference between the sentences *Michelle wrote the environmental report* and *The environmental report was written by Michelle.* Michelle receives the emphasis in the first version; the report receives it in the second.

A third way to emphasize an idea is to place it in a short sentence. Important ideas can get lost when enveloped by numerous competing words. How quickly can you grasp the important idea in this sentence? *This announcement is to inform all employees and guests that the hotel's restaurant will be closed Thanksgiving Day, although we do plan to resume restaurant services Friday at 7 a.m.* To give impact to the main idea, present it in a short sentence: *The hotel's restaurant will be closed Thanksgiving Day.* Then, provide explanations and details.

Using the active voice. In the active voice the subject performs the action: *Brandon selected new computers.* In the passive voice the subject receives the action: *New computers were selected by Brandon.* Passive-voice sentences deemphasize the performer of the action. The performer is in a phrase *(by Brandon)* or is totally absent: *(New computers were selected).* If you suspect that a verb is passive but you're not sure, try the "by whom?" test: *New computers were selected [by whom?].* If you can fill in the performer of the action, the sentence is probably passive.

● Active-voice sentences are forceful and easy to understand.

What difference does it make if the verb is active or passive? Active-voice sentences are more direct because they reveal the performer immediately: they're easier to understand, more forceful, and shorter. Most business writing should be in the active voice.

Using the passive voice selectively. Although we prefer active verbs in business writing, passive verbs are useful in certain instances. For example, when the performer is unknown or insignificant, use passive voice: *Drug tests are given to all applicants.* Who performs the drug tests is unimportant. You can also use the passive voice to tactfully deflect attention away from the people involved: *Three totals were calculated incorrectly.* Notice that this sentence stresses the problem while concealing the person who committed the error.

● Passive-voice sentences are useful for tact and to direct attention to actions instead of people.

Avoiding dangling phrases. Verbal phrases must be immediately followed by the words they can logically describe or modify. When such phrases dangle without a clearly modified term, they confuse—and sometimes amuse—readers, as in these examples:

Dangling Modifier	**Improved**
Belching steam and hissing dangerously, the driver cautiously examined the overheated radiator. *(This sentence says the driver is belching steam and hissing dangerously.)*	Belching steam and hissing dangerously, the overheated radiator was examined cautiously by the driver.

Locked safely in the office vault, only the vice president had access to the corporate securities. *(Is the vice president locked in the vault?)*

Locked safely in the office vault, the corporate securities were accessible only to the vice president.

Try this trick for detecting and remedying dangling modifiers. Ask the question Who? or What? after any introductory verbal phrase. The words immediately following any verbal phrase should tell the reader *who* or *what* is performing the action. Try the Who? test on the previous danglers.

Another form of misplaced modifier is a phrase separated from the word(s) it describes. The solution is simply to move the misplaced phrase closer to the words it modifies.

Misplaced Modifier

The busy personnel director interviewed only candidates who had excellent computer skills in the morning. *(This sentence says the candidate's computer skills were effective only before lunch.)*

Improved

In the morning the busy personnel director interviewed only candidates who had excellent computer skills.

Drafting Effective Paragraphs

Effective paragraphs focus on one topic, link ideas to build coherence, and use transitional devices to enhance coherence.

From composing sentences, we progress to paragraphs. A paragraph is one or more sentences designated as a separate thought group. To avoid muddled and meaningless paragraphs, writers must recognize basic paragraph elements, conventional sentence patterns, and ways to organize sentences into one of three classic paragraph patterns. They must also be able to polish their paragraphs by linking sentences and using transitional expressions.

Discussing one topic. Well-constructed paragraphs discuss only one topic. They reveal the primary idea in a main sentence that usually, but not always, appears first. Other ideas, connected logically with transitional expressions (verbal road signs), support or illustrate that idea.

Organizing sentences into paragraphs. Paragraphs are usually composed of three kinds of sentences:[9]

- **Main sentence:** expresses the primary idea of the paragraph.
- **Supporting sentence:** illustrates, explains, or strengthens the primary idea.
- **Limiting sentence:** opposes the primary idea by suggesting a negative or contrasting thought; may precede or follow the main sentence.

These sentences may be arranged in three classic paragraph plans: direct, pivoting, and indirect.

The direct paragraph pattern is appropriate when defining, classifying, illustrating, or describing.

Using the direct paragraph plan. Paragraphs arranged in the direct plan begin with the main sentence, followed by supporting sentences. Most business messages use this paragraph plan because it clarifies the subject immediately. This plan is useful whenever you must define (a new product or procedure), classify (parts of a whole), illustrate (an idea), or describe (a process). Simply start with the main sentence; then strengthen and amplify that idea with supporting ideas, as shown here:

Main Sentence	A social audit is a report on the social performance of a company.
Supporting Sentences	Such a report may be conducted by the company itself or by outsiders who evaluate the company's efforts to produce safe products, engage in socially responsible activities, and protect the environment. Many companies publish the results of their social audits in their annual reports. Ben & Jerry's Homemade, for example, devotes a major portion of its annual report to its social audit. The report discusses Ben & Jerry's efforts to support environmental restoration. Moreover, it describes workplace safety, employment equality, and peace programs.

You can alter the direct plan by adding a limiting sentence if necessary. Be sure, though, that you follow up with sentences that return to the main idea and support it, as shown here:

Main Sentence	Flexible work scheduling could immediately increase productivity and enhance employee satisfaction in our entire organization.
Limiting Sentence	Such scheduling, however, is impossible for all employees.
Supporting Sentences	Managers would be required to maintain their regular hours. For many other employees, though, flexible scheduling permits extra time to manage family responsibilities. Feeling less stress, employees are able to focus their attention better at work; hence they become more relaxed and more productive.

Using the pivoting paragraph plan. Paragraphs arranged in the pivoting plan start with a limiting sentence that offers a contrasting or negative idea before delivering the main sentence. Notice in the following example how two limiting sentences about drawbacks to foreign service careers open the paragraph; only then do the main and supporting sentences describing rewards in foreign service appear. The pivoting plan is especially effective for comparing and contrasting ideas. In using the pivoting plan, be sure you emphasize the turn in direction with an obvious *but* or *however.*

● **The pivoting paragraph pattern is appropriate when comparing and contrasting.**

Limiting Sentences	Foreign service careers are certainly not for everyone. Many overseas posts are in remote countries where harsh climates, health hazards, security risks, and other discomforts exist.
Main Sentence	However, careers in the foreign service offer special rewards for the special people who qualify.
Supporting Sentences	Foreign service employees enjoy the pride and satisfaction of representing the United States abroad. They relish frequent travel, enriching cultural and social experiences in living abroad, and action-oriented work.

Using the indirect paragraph plan. Paragraphs arranged in the indirect plan start with the supporting sentences and conclude with the main sentence. This useful plan enables you to build a rationale, a foundation of reasons, before hitting the audience with a big idea—possibly one that is bad news. It enables you to explain your reasons and then in the final sentence draw a conclusion from them. Notice in the following example that the supporting sentences describe a scenario of computer use leading up to a new procedure that some readers may resent. The indirect plan works well for describing causes followed by an effect.

● **The indirect paragraph pattern is appropriate when delivering bad news.**

Supporting Sentences	Since 1986 we have actively supported the use of personal computers by sales reps. We now have over 1,000 computer users, and the number continues to grow. As a result of this dramatic growth, our expenses for software programming, testing, and duplication have become a major item in our budget. Last year we spent over $150,000 to deliver personal computer software to the field.
Main Sentence	As a result of escalating expenses, we've decided to standardize two elements in our computer use: 3.5-inch diskettes and hard-drive machines.

You'll learn more techniques for implementing these plans when you write letters, memos, and reports in subsequent chapters.

● **Coherent paragraphs link ideas by sustaining the main idea, using pronouns, dovetailing sentences, and using transitional expressions.**

Linking ideas to build coherence. Paragraphs are coherent when ideas are linked, that is, when one idea leads logically to the next. Well-written paragraphs take the reader through a number of steps. When the author skips from Step 1 to Step 3 and forgets Step 2, the reader is lost. You can use several techniques to keep the reader in step with your ideas.

Sustaining the key idea. This involves simply repeating a key expression or using a similar one. For example:

> Our philosophy holds that every customer is really a *guest.* All new employees to our theme parks are trained to treat *guests* as *VIPs.* These *VIPs* are never told what they can or cannot do.

Notice how the repetition of *guest* and *VIP* connects ideas.

Using pronouns. Familiar pronouns, such as *we, they, he, she,* and *it,* help build continuity, as do demonstrative pronouns like *this, that, these,* and *those.* These words confirm that something under discussion is still being discussed. For example:

> All new park employees receive a two-week orientation. *They* learn that every staffer has a vital role in preparing for the show. *This* training includes how to maintain enthusiasm.

Be careful with *this, that, these,* and *those,* however. These words usually need a noun with them to make their meaning absolutely clear. In the last example notice how confusing *this* becomes if the word *training* is omitted.

Dovetailing sentences. Sentences are "dovetailed" when an idea at the end of one connects with an idea at the beginning of the next. For example:

> New hosts and hostesses learn about the theme park and its *facilities.* These *facilities* include telephones, food services, bathrooms, and attractions, as well as the location of *offices.* Knowledge of administrative *offices* and internal workings of the company, such as who's who in administration, ensures that staffers will be able to *serve guests* fully. *Serving guests,* of course, is our No. 1 priority.

Dovetailing of sentences is especially helpful with dense, difficult topics. However, this technique should not be overused.

Using transitional expressions to build coherence. Transitional expressions are another excellent device for achieving paragraph coherence. These words, some of which are shown in Figure 4.7, act as verbal road signs to readers and

FIGURE 4.7 ● Transitional Expressions to Build Coherence

To Add or Strengthen	To Show Time or Order	To Clarify	To Show Cause and Effect	To Contradict	To Contrast
additionally	after	for example	accordingly	actually	as opposed to
again	before	for instance	as a result	but	at the same time
also	earlier	I mean	consequently	however	by contrast
besides	finally	in other words	for this reason	in fact	conversely
likewise	first	that is	so	instead	on the contrary
moreover	meanwhile	this means	therefore	rather	on the other hand
further	next	thus	thus	still	
furthermore	now	to put it another way	under the circumstances	though	
	previously			yet	
	then				

listeners. Transitional expressions enable the receiver to anticipate what's coming, to reduce uncertainty, and to speed up comprehension. They signal that a train of thought is moving forward, being developed, possibly detouring, or ending. Transitions are especially helpful in persuasive writing.

● **Transitional expressions help readers anticipate what's coming, reduce uncertainty, and speed comprehension.**

As Figure 4.7 shows, transitions can add and strengthen, show cause and effect, indicate time or order, contradict, clarify, and contrast ideas. Thus, you must be careful to select the best transition for your purpose. Look back at the examples of direct, pivoted, and indirect paragraphs to see how transitional expressions and other devices build paragraph coherence. Remember that coherence in communication rarely happens spontaneously; it requires effort and skill.

Composing short paragraphs. Although no rule regulates the length of paragraphs, business writers recognize the value of short paragraphs. Paragraphs with fewer than eight lines look inviting and readable, whereas long, solid hunks of print appear formidable. If a topic can't be covered in fewer than ten printed lines (not sentences), consider breaking it up into smaller segments.

● **Paragraphs with fewer than ten lines are attractive and readable.**

The following checklist summarizes the key points of writing a first draft.

Checklist for Composing Sentences and Paragraphs

For Effective Sentences

✔ **Use short sentences.** Keep in mind that sentences with fewer than 20 words are easier to read. Use longer sentences occasionally, but rely on short sentences.

✔ **Emphasize important ideas.** Place main ideas at the beginning of short sentences for emphasis.

- ✔ **Apply active and passive verbs carefully.** Use active verbs *(She wrote the letter* instead of *The letter was written by her)* most frequently; they immediately identify the doer. Use passive verbs to be tactful, to emphasize an action, or to conceal the performer.
- ✔ **Eliminate misplaced modifiers.** Be sure that introductory verbal phrases are followed by the words that can logically modify them. To check the placement of modifiers, ask Who? or What? after such phrases.

For Effective Paragraphs

- ✔ **Develop one idea.** Use main, supporting, and limiting sentences to develop a single idea within each paragraph.
- ✔ **Use the direct plan.** Start most paragraphs with the main sentence followed by supporting sentences. This direct plan is useful in defining, classifying, illustrating, and describing.
- ✔ **Use the pivoting plan.** To compare and contrast ideas, start with a limiting sentence; then, present the main sentence followed by supporting sentences.
- ✔ **Use the indirect plan.** To explain reasons or causes first, start with supporting sentences. Build to the conclusion with the main sentence at the end of the paragraph.
- ✔ **Build coherence by linking sentences.** Hold ideas together by repeating key words, using pronouns, and dovetailing sentences (beginning one sentence with an idea from the end of the previous sentence).
- ✔ **Provide road signs with transitional expressions.** Use verbal signals to help the audience know where the idea is going. Words like *moreover, accordingly, as a result,* and *thus* function as idea pointers.
- ✔ **Limit paragraph length.** Remember that paragraphs with fewer than eight printed lines look inviting. Consider breaking up longer paragraphs if necessary.

Writing in a Group

Business professionals increasingly work in teams that require collaborative writing.

The suggestions and techniques provided thus far suggest that writing is a solitary task—and it generally is. But not always. Nine of every ten business professionals report that they sometimes collaborate or work as part of a team to create documents.[10] Some business writers say that one fifth of all the writing they do is produced with a group.[11] Group writing is necessary when

- A task is too large or complex for one individual to complete
- A deadline is near
- A task requires varied viewpoints and expertise
- Agreement is needed from many people

Susanne Tully collaborated with graphics specialists, public relations experts, and editors in producing the Liz Claiborne recruitment brochure. This big project was more than she could handle alone and also required expertise that she lacked. Business communicators often find that their projects require a team effort.

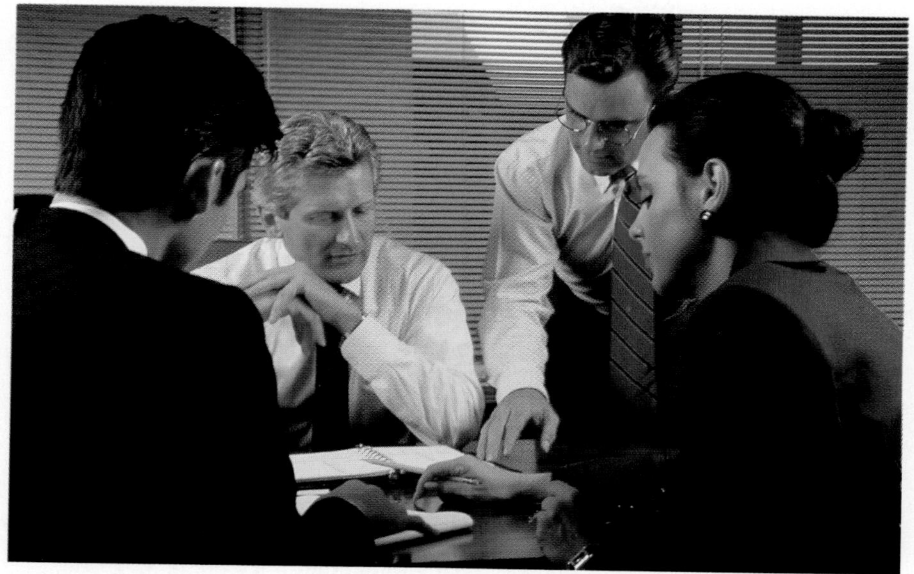

Many business projects require a group effort, particularly when the assignment is too large for one person or when many different viewpoints must be combined. Understanding an assignment thoroughly and establishing ground rules are two keys to working harmoniously and meeting deadlines on collaborative projects.

Collaboration Patterns

Whether you collaborate voluntarily (seeking advice and differing perspectives) or involuntarily (through necessity or by assignment), your on-the-job collaboration may fall into one of four patterns.

Collaboration may consist of a subordinate writing for a boss's approval or many people working on a project.

One author writing for someone else's approval. Subordinates often draft documents for the signature of their busy superiors. For example, your boss might ask you to draft a memo to all supervisors describing how to use a new computer program for preparing work schedules. Your boss talks with you about what to include, you write a draft, the boss reads and revises it, and you complete the final memo.

One author writing for a group. Suppose you're part of a task force named by the CEO to iron out a bonus plan for the sales force. Your group meets several times, and then they ask you, the best writer in the group, to complete the final report. You prepare a draft that the entire group discusses and edits. Then you compose the final version for all members to sign.

Many authors preparing individual segments of the document. Some documents require the input of many individuals. Assume that the president wants a report analyzing the effects of centralized customer service. Managers from several divisions—Sales, Customer Relations, and Personnel—write segments of the report describing how centralization would affect them. Then the segments are joined together into one document. This method can result in a poor product unless one skilled individual has authority to edit the final report to achieve consistency.

Many authors preparing the entire document. This collaboration pattern is the least efficient because all contributors must work together through some or all of the writing stages: analysis, adaptation, organizing, composing, revising, and evaluating. Such a combined effort, though, can produce a consistent, timely, and

SUCCESSFUL COLLABORATION REQUIRES GROUND RULES

Whenever people work together on written projects, trouble is likely to result unless ground rules are established. And those rules must be defined *before a single word is written.* Here are some of the more important responsibilities and duties that must be worked out in advance:

- Decide how you will establish the document's purpose and main issues (typically groups work together in this first phase to brainstorm and plan).
- Decide how you will write the first version (generally, groups divide the drafting of sections among themselves).
- Determine how to coordinate the project into a unified whole.
- Decide who is responsible for ensuring that the document meets the needs of its audience.
- Determine who is responsible for the accuracy of data.
- Name a chief arbiter who has final say on matters concerning format, structure, degree of formality, and writing style.
- Decide who will copyedit the document, eliminating typos and grammatical errors.
- Appoint someone to see that the document is produced carefully and on time.
- Determine who has authority and responsibility to approve the final draft.

Career Track Application

To better understand the problems resulting from group writing, work in teams of three or four on a single writing assignment (such as any of the collaboration projects listed in each chapter's problems). Work out your own ground rules in assigning responsibilities or apply those described here.

valuable document. Let's assume your organization has a short time in which to produce a proposal for a contract that means survival for the entire company. To complete the proposal, you and your coauthors work together for three straight days, actually hammering out every sentence. A variation on this pattern finds the team members gathering to analyze goals and organize the topic. Then they disperse to compose their individual segments, returning to work together in preparing the final version and revising it.

Obstacles to Collaboration

Although collaboration usually produces better documents because of the combined experience of the writers, the process has inherent problems. The most difficult obstacles involve differing personalities and styles of the group writers. Consider the following account of an ill-fated collaborative project.

> *The CEO of a Boston high-tech firm assembled a team of high-level executives to assist in the development of a corporate mission statement. The team included two vice presidents, four line managers, as well as the director of internal communications and several members of her group. This team interviewed the CEO, all his senior officers, and a large segment of employees, customers, and even some competitors. After amassing considerable data, the team was ready to write. The two vice presidents talked briefly and agreed to divide the task. Each would use his specific expertise to write a segment, and then the internal communications people would tie it together and smooth it out.*

Focusing on corporate culture, the vice president of human resources wrote in an informal, conversational style, using many anecdotes and quotations. The vice president of finance leaned heavily on profit projections. He was of the old school of writing: long, fastidiously impersonal sentences; scrupulous footnoting; and detailed numerical charts.

Although the combined draft was clearly too long, each man was unwilling to see changes or cuts made to his section. After the final editing was completed, each writer restored a few passages cut by the communications staff. The unacceptable end product looked like a portrait painted jointly by Andrew Wyeth and Andy Warhol.[12]

Successful group documents emerge from thoughtful preparation, clear definition of contributors' roles, commitment to a group-approved plan, and willingness to take responsibility for the final document. For help in establishing ground rules for group projects, see the Career Skills box on the facing page.

Summary of Learning Goals

1. **Contrast formal and informal research methods.** Formal research for long reports and complex problems may involve searching library data manually or electronically, as well as conducting interviews, surveys, focus groups, and experiments. Informal research for routine tasks may involve looking in company files, talking with your boss, interviewing the target audience, conducting informal surveys, brainstorming for ideas, and cluster diagraming.
2. **Organize ideas into alphanumeric or decimal outlines.** Outlining is a key component of organization. Divide the main topic into three to five major components. Break the components into subpoints consisting of details, illustrations, and evidence. For an alphanumeric outline arrange items using Roman numerals (I, II), capital letters (A, B), and numbers (1, 2). For a decimal outline show the ordering of ideas with decimals (1.0, 1.1, 1.1.1).
3. **Compare direct and indirect patterns of idea organization.** The direct pattern places the main idea first. This pattern is useful when audiences will be pleased, mildly interested, or neutral. It saves the reader's time, sets the proper frame of mind, and prevents reader frustration. The indirect pattern places the main idea after explanations. This pattern is useful for audiences that will be unwilling, displeased, or hostile. It respects the feelings of the audience, ensures a fair hearing, and minimizes negative reactions.
4. **Explain techniques for creating forceful sentences.** Sentences are most forceful when they are short (under 20 words). A main idea may be emphasized by making it the sentence subject, placing it first, and removing competing ideas. Forceful sentences use active verbs, although passive verbs may be necessary for tact or deemphasis. Forceful sentences avoid dangling phrases.
5. **Explain how to write effective paragraphs.** Direct paragraphs (main sentence followed by supporting sentences) are useful to define, classify, illustrate, and describe. Pivoting paragraphs (limiting sentence, main sentence, supporting sentences) are useful to compare and contrast. Indirect paragraphs (supporting sentences followed by main sentence) build a rationale and foundation of ideas before presenting the main idea. Paragraphs may be improved through use of coherence techniques and transitional expressions.

6. **Describe how to reduce problems characteristic of collaborative writing.** Collaborative writers must establish ground rules, including who will establish the document's purpose and priorities, who will be responsible for data accuracy, who will edit the document, who has responsibility for meeting the deadline, and who will approve the final draft.

Chapter Review

1. How does a writer "brainstorm"?

2. What is a cluster diagram, and when might it be useful?

3. Describe an alphanumeric outline.

4. Distinguish between the direct and indirect patterns of organization for typical business messages.

5. Why should most messages be "frontloaded"?

6. List some of the business messages that should be frontloaded.

7. List some of the business messages that should *not* be frontloaded—those that follow the indirect pattern.

8. Why should writers plan for revision? How can they do it?

9. Distinguish an independent clause from a dependent clause. Give examples.

10. Name three ways to emphasize important ideas in sentences.

11. Distinguish between active-voice sentences and passive-voice sentences. Give examples.

12. Describe three kinds of sentences used to develop ideas in paragraphs.

13. Describe three paragraph plans. Identify the uses for each.

14. What is coherence, and how is it achieved?

15. Describe four patterns in which group writing might occur in the workplace.

Discussion

1. Why is cluster diagraming considered an *intuitive* process while outlining is considered an *analytical* process?

2. Why is audience analysis so important in choosing the direct or indirect pattern of organization for a business message?

3. In what ways do you imagine that writing on the job differs from the writing you do in your academic studies? Consider process as well as product.

4. What are the ethics of group writing? How ethical is it for a subordinate to compose a document that a superior will sign? Is it ethical for one person to do most of the writing on a project that a team will take credit for?

5. Ethical Issue: Discuss the ethics of the indirect pattern of organization. Is it manipulative to delay presentation of the main idea in a message?

Activities

4.1 Document for Analysis

First, read the following memo to see if you can understand what the writer wants all Southeast Division employees to do. Then, discuss why this memo is so hard to read. How long are the sentences? How many passive-voice constructions can you locate? How effective is the paragraphing? Can you spot four dangling modifiers? In the next activity you'll improve the organization of this message.

To: All Southeast Division Employees

[1]Personal computers and all the software to support these computers are appearing on many desks of Southeast Division employees. [2]After giving the matter considerable attention, it has been determined by the Systems Development Department (SDD) that more control should be exerted in coordinating the purchase of hardware and software to improve compatibility throughout the division so that a library of resources may be developed. [3]Therefore, a plan has been developed by SDD that should be followed in making all future equipment selections and purchases. [4]To make best possible choice, SDD should be contacted as you begin your search because questions about personal computers, word processors, hardware, and software can be answered by our knowledgeable staff, who can also provide you with invaluable assistance in making the best choice for your needs at the best possible cost.

[5]After your computer and its software arrive, all your future software purchases should be channeled through SDD. [6]To actually make your initial purchase, a written proposal and a purchase request form must be presented to SDD for approval. [7]A need for the purchase must be established; benefits that you expect to derive resulting from its purchase must be analyzed and presented, and an itemized statement of all costs must be submitted. [8]By following these new procedures, coordinated purchasing benefits will be realized by all employees. [9]I may be reached at X466 if you have any questions.

4.2 Organizing Data

Use either a cluster diagram or an outline to organize the garbled message in Activity 4.1. Beyond the opening and closing of the message, what are the three main points the writer is trying to make? Should this message use the direct pattern or the indirect pattern? Your instructor may ask you to (1) discuss how this entire message could be revised or (2) actually rewrite it.

4.3 Collaborative Brainstorming

In teams of four or five, analyze a problem on your campus such as the following: unavailable classes, unrealistic degree requirements, lack of student intern programs, poor parking facilities, inadequate registration process, lack of diversity among students on campus, and so forth. Use brainstorming techniques to generate ideas that clarify the problem and explore its solutions. Each team member should prepare a cluster diagram to record the ideas generated. Either individually or as a team, organize the ideas into an outline with three to five main points and numerous subpoints. Assume that your ideas will become part of a letter to be sent to an appropriate campus official or to your campus newspaper discussing the problem and your solution.

4.4 Individual Brainstorming

Analyze a problem that exists where you work or go to school, such as long lines at the copy or fax machines, overuse of express mail services, understaffing during peak customer service hours, poor scheduling of employees, inferior or inflexible benefit package, outdated office or other equipment, or one of the campus problems discussed in Activity 4.3. Select a problem about which you have some knowledge. Assume your boss or department chair wants you to submit a short report analyzing the problem. Prepare a cluster diagram to develop ideas. Then, organize the ideas into an outline with three to five main points and numerous subpoints.

4.5 Outlining

The following topics will be part of a report that a consultant is submitting to a group of investors who requested information about starting a new radio station in Scottsdale, Arizona. Arrange the topics into a coherent alphanumeric outline. Clue: the items are already in the right order.

Problem: determining program format for new radio station KFSD-FM

Background: current radio formats available to listeners in Scottsdale

Background: demographics of target area (population, age, sex, income)

Survey results: music preferences

Survey finds that top two favorites are easy listening and soft rock

Next two favorites are country and rock

Other kinds of music mentioned in survey: classical, jazz

Survey results: newscast preferences

News emphasis: respondents prefer primarily national news but with some local items

Respondents say yes to news but only short, hourly newscasts

Analysis of findings: discussion of all findings in greater detail

Recommendations: hybrid format combining easy listening and soft rock

Recommendations: news in 3- to 5-minute newscasts hourly; cover national news but include local flavor

We recommend starting new station immediately.

Exercises

4.6 Sentence Elements

In the following sentences underscore and identify dependent clauses (DC), independent clauses (IC), and phrases (P). Circle subjects and verbs in clauses.

a. To please customers and make money, Stew Leonard opened a dairy store.

b. Although it grew to become the world's largest dairy store, Stew Leonard's opened with only eight items.

c. From the beginning of the business, Leonard aimed to make his store unusual and fun.

d. When customers shop, they find a petting zoo in the parking lot and free ice cream cones at the checkouts.

e. As Leonard sees it, the store attitude begins with him, and then it passes to his department managers.

4.7 Sentence Length

Break the following sentences into shorter sentences. Use appropriate transitional expressions.

a. If firms have a substantial investment in original research or development of new products, they should consider protecting those products with patents, although all patents eventually expire and what were once trade secrets can become common knowledge in the industry.

b. As soon as consumers recognize a name associated with a product or service, that name is entitled to legal protection as a trademark; in fact, consumers may even create a trademark where none existed or create a second trademark by using a nickname as a source indicator, such as the name "Coke," which was legally protected even before it had ever been used by the company.

c. Although no magic formula exists for picking a good trademark name, firms should avoid picking the first name that pops into someone's head; moreover, they should be aware that unique and arbitrary marks are best, while descriptive terms such as "car" or "TV repair" are useless, and surnames and geographic names are weak because they lack distinction and exclusivity.

4.8 Active and Passive Voice

In the following sentences convert passive-voice verbs to active-voice verbs. Add subjects if necessary. Be prepared to discuss which sentence version is more effective.

a. A decision to focus on customer service was made by the board.

b. First, the product line was examined to determine if it met customers' needs.

c. In the past, products had been built to the company's internal expectations of market needs.

d. When it was realized that changes were in order, a new product line was designed.

e. After just-in-time inventory procedures were introduced, our inventories were cut in half.

f. Our company was recently named "Vendor of the Year" by Texas Instruments.

Now convert active-voice verbs to passive-voice verbs, and be prepared to discuss which sentence version is more effective.

g. We cannot authorize repair of your VCR since you have allowed the warranty period to expire.

h. I cannot give you a cash refund for merchandise that you purchased over 60 days ago.

i. Kaiser Hospital does not accept patients who are not members.

j. You must submit all reports by Friday at 5 p.m.

k. Joan added the two columns instead of subtracting them, thus producing the incorrect total.

4.9 Misplaced Modifiers

Remedy any dangling or misplaced modifiers in the following sentences. Add subjects as needed, but retain the introductory phrases. Mark "C" if correct.

a. To stay in touch with customers, telephone contacts were encouraged among all sales reps.

b. By making sales reps a part of product design, a great deal of money was saved.

c. Addressing a large audience for the first time, my knees shook and my voice wobbled.

d. To receive a bachelor's degree, complete 120 units of study. *(Tricky!)*

e. Noxious fumes made the office workers sick coming from the storage tanks of a nearby paint manufacturer.

f. Using available evidence, it becomes apparent that the court has been deceived by the witness.

g. Having found the misplaced report, the search was ended.

h. The presidential candidate announced his intentions to run as a national candidate in his hometown of Blue Bell, Pennsylvania.

i. Although T-Mart is a self-service department store, every effort is made to give customers personalized, patient service. *(Tricky!)*

j. Ignoring the warning prompt on the screen, the computer was turned off resulting in the loss of data.

4.10 Transitional Expressions

Add transitional expressions to the following sentences to improve the flow of ideas (coherence).

a. Computer style checkers rank somewhere between artificial intelligence and artificial ignorance. They are like clever children: smart but not wise. Business writers should be fully aware of the limitations and the usefulness of style checkers.

b. Our computerized file includes all customer data. It provides space for name, address, and other vital information. It has an area for comments, a feature that comes in handy and helps us keep our records up-to-date.

c. No one likes to turn out poor products. We began highlighting recurring problems. Employees make a special effort to be more careful in doing their work right the first time. It doesn't have to be returned to them for corrections.

d. In-depth employment interviews may be structured or unstructured. Structured interviews have little flexibility. All candidates are asked the same questions in the same order. Unstructured interviews allow a free-flowing conversation. Topics are prepared for discussion by the interviewer.

e. Fringe benefits consist of life, health, and dental insurance. Some fringe benefits might include paid vacations and sick pay. Other fringe benefits include holidays, funeral leave, and emergency leave. Paid lunch, rest periods, tuition reimbursement, and child care are also sometimes provided.

f. Service was less than perfect for many months. We lacked certain intangibles. We didn't have the customer-specific data that we needed. We made the mistake of removing all localized, person-to-person coverage. We are returning to decentralized customer contacts.

4.11 Paragraph Organization

The following poorly written paragraphs follow the indirect plan. Locate the main sentence in each paragraph. Then revise each paragraph so that it is organized directly. Improve coherence by using the techniques described in this chapter.

a. Many of our customers limp through their business despite problems with their disk drives, printers, and peripherals. We cannot service their disk drives, printers, and peripherals. These customers are unable to go without this equipment long enough for the repair. We've learned that there are two times when we can get to that equipment. We can do our repairs in the middle of the night or on Sunday. All of our staff of technicians now works every Sunday. Please authorize additional budget for my department to hire technicians for night and weekend service hours.

b. Air express is one of the ways SturdyBilt power mowers and chain saws may be delivered. Air express promises two-day delivery but at a considerable cost. The cheapest method is for retailers to pick up shipments themselves at our nearest distribution center. We have distribution centers in St. Louis, Phoenix, and Los Angeles. Another option involves having our trucks deliver the shipment from our distribution center to the retailer's door—for an additional fee. These are the options SturdyBilt provides for the retailers purchasing our products.

C.L.U.E. Review 4

Edit the following sentences to correct faults in grammar, punctuation, spelling, and word use.

1. Although, we formally used a neighborhood printer for all our print jobs we are now saving almost five hundred dollars a month by using desktop publishing.

2. Powerful softwear however cannot garantee a good final product.

3. To develop a better sense of design we collected desireable samples from: books, magazines, brochures, and newsletters.

4. We noticed that, poorly-designed projects often was filled with cluttered layouts, incompatible typefaces, and to many typefaces.

5. Our layout design are usually formal but occassionally we use an informal layout design which is shown in figure six.

6. We ussually prefer a black and white design; because color printing is much more costly.

7. Expensive color printing jobs are sent to foreign countries, for example china italy and japan.

8. Jeffreys article which he entitled "The Shaping of a corporate image" was excepted for publication in "the journal of communication."

9. Every employee will persenally recieve a copy of his Performance Evaluation which the President said will be the principle basis for promotion.

10. We will print three hundred and fifty copies of the newsletter, to be sent to whomever is currently listed in our database.

Revising, Proofreading, and Evaluating

LEARNING GOALS

After studying this chapter, you should be able to

1. Revise a document to make it clear, conversational, and concise
2. Revise a document so that it is vigorous and direct
3. Recognize and apply techniques for improving readability
4. Proofread routine and complex documents
5. Evaluate a message to judge its success

People Magazine: Career Track Profile

Irreverent, informative, and always absorbing, *People* is one of the nation's favorite magazines. Celebrating its twentieth birthday, it ranks first among American magazines in advertising revenues, second in newsstand sales (behind *TV Guide*), and third in total readership, with 29 million readers.

People almost single-handedly elevated the concept of "personality" journalism—stories focusing on people and their behavior—into a legitimate and even essential part of American reporting. Nearly all consumer publications today feel the influence of *People* in their stories, sections, and columns. Unquestionably, what really interests people is other people. And it took *People* magazine to recognize this truth and capitalize on it.

"Readers don't have time for anything long or wordy in this busy, short-attention world. . . . Any writing that goes past one page had better be really important."

But no publication preserves the top spot year after year without delivering more than pictures and stories about people. Among insiders *People* reigns as queen of the "written" magazines. This means that every story is researched, written, checked, rewritten, rechecked, and revised by multiple levels of reporters, writers, editors, fact-checkers, copyeditors, and proofreaders. Editors boil down long files originally submitted by reporters into tightly written, fact-filled, fast-moving but concise articles. The multistage revision process results in finely polished, meaty writing. Not a word is wasted.

Associate editor Louise Lague is one of *People*'s expert writers who make every word count. She says her writing must be very concise, with many facts packed into every sentence. Although she was always interested in writing, she did not train to be a journalist. Louise graduated from Georgetown University in Washington, D.C. In her senior year recruiters asked what she had studied. When she replied, "French, Spanish, English, theology, philosophy, and history," they said, "What? No economics? No marketing? You're unfit for anything!" Three months later she found a job as a reporter and worked her way from newspapers to *People*.

In writing her stories, she always keeps the audience in mind. *People*'s readership, about evenly divided between men and women, averages 37 years of age and two years of college. She considers her readers sophisticated but unstuffy. "We don't talk down to them, yet the meaning must be comprehensible. Even short words and short sentences can be sophisticated if arranged cleverly and with wit. It doesn't have to be simple, simple, simple." Above all, Louise's stories have to be readable and make their points quickly and clearly. "I love covering Prince Charles, Di, and the other royals, but not everybody is intrigued by all the historical and

Shown with sons William and Harry, Princess Diana is a favorite *People* magazine subject. She has appeared on nearly twice as many *People* covers as any other celebrity. Because one of her magazine assignments is the British royal family, editor Louise Lague must be able to research, write, and edit articles about royal events quickly.

family details we uncover. With so little space, it's important to get to the point."

On the subject of clarity, she remarks, "I learned a long time ago that even if you know a lot of long words, current jargon, and foreign phrases, it doesn't make sense to use them if your goal is to make people understand what you're saying. Use them carefully. There's a big difference between 'soup du jour' and 'De gustibus non contendum.' Keep it very straight and very clear—almost as if you're writing a letter to your grandmother."

To improve the vigor of her writing, Louise slashes unnecessary words—especially adjectives and prepositional phrases—and shows action with colorful verbs. Here's the first version of one story idea: "Wynonna Judd had a cold, and she didn't feel well. She was afraid that the condition of her throat would affect the quality of her singing for her performance." Revised and condensed, the second version is enlivened with vivid verbs: "Sidelined by a cold, Wynonna Judd feared hoarseness would hamper her performance."

Whether she's writing stories or business memos, Louise begins with an outline. "I list all the main points that must be discussed—in any order. Then I give them numbers (1, 5, 3, 2, and so forth) to show a sequence. Next, I write the first version and try to get it all down in any form. Thank God for the computer! The next version is for taking things out." In the revision stage she strives to make her writing "short, short, and shorter." In recommending brevity, she admonishes, "Don't overexplain. Everyone thinks that because something is in black and white, it's perfectly clear. Not so! Too much information confuses. Main facts no longer stand out when too many words surround them."

Louise says that any writing—business or pleasure—that goes past one page had better be really important. And it needs to have a trick in the layout—bullets, boxes, paragraph headings, numbered lists, or the like—whenever possible. "Readers don't have time for anything long or wordy in this busy, short-attention world."

Although Louise Lague writes about celebrities and political figures for *People* magazine, her writing process and goals are quite similar to yours and those of other business writers. She's concerned with clarity, conciseness, directness, readability, and audience needs—just as you are. Like other good writers Louise achieves these goals through careful revision.[1]

Revising Messages

Because few writers can produce copy on the first attempt, revision is an important step in the writing process.

This chapter focuses on the final phase in the 3-×-3 writing process: revising, proofreading, and evaluating. Revising means improving the content and sentence structure of your message. Proofreading involves correcting its grammar, spelling, punctuation, format, and mechanics. Evaluating is the process of analyzing whether your message achieved its purpose. Although the composition process differs for individuals and situations, this final phase should occupy a significant share of the total time you spend on a message. Some experts recommend devoting about half the total composition time to revising and proofreading.[2]

Rarely is the first or even second version of a message satisfactory. One authority says, "Only the amateur expects writing perfection on the first try."[3] The revision stage is your chance to make sure your message really says what you mean. Many professional writers, like Louise Lague at *People* magazine, compose the first draft quickly without worrying about language, precision, or correctness. Then they revise and polish extensively. Other writers, however, prefer to revise as they go—particularly for shorter business documents.

Important messages—like those you send to customers or superiors or turn in to instructors for grades—deserve careful revision and proofreading. When you finish a first draft, plan for a cooling-off period. Put the document aside and return to it after a break, preferably after 24 hours or longer.

Whether you revise immediately or after a break, you'll want to examine your message critically. You should be especially concerned with ways to improve its clarity, conciseness, vigor, and readability.

Clarity: Keeping It Simple

One of the first revision tasks is assessing the clarity of your message. A clear message is one that is immediately understood. To achieve clarity, resist the urge to show off or be fancy. Remember Louise Lague's suggestion that you use the same unadorned style appropriate for letters to your grandmother. Remember, too, that you're not trying to impress a college instructor. In fact, the key difference between college essay writing and business writing is that business writing is straightforward and clear. It is not meant to show how much you know. Put simply, the goal of business writing is to *express,* not *impress*. This involves two simple rules: (1) keep it simple and (2) keep it conversational.

To achieve clarity, remember to KISS—Keep It Simple, Stupid!

Applying the KISS formula. Why do some communicators fail to craft simple, direct messages? For several reasons:

- Untrained executives and professionals worry that plain messages don't sound important.
- Subordinates fear that plain talk won't impress the boss.
- Unskilled writers create foggy messages because they've not learned how to communicate clearly.

Whatever the cause, you can eliminate the fog by applying the familiar KISS formula: *K*eep *I*t *S*imple, *S*tupid! One way to achieve clear writing is to use active-voice sentences that avoid negative, indirect, and pompous language.

Indirect	Improved
Employees have not been made sufficiently aware of the potentially adverse consequences involved regarding these chemicals.	Warn your employees about these chemicals.
To be sure of obtaining optimal results, it is essential that you give your employees the implements that are necessary for completion of the job.	To get the best results, give employees the tools they need to do the job.

Keeping it conversational. Clarity is further enhanced by language that sounds like conversation. This doesn't mean that your letters and memos should be chatty or familiar. Rather, you should strive to sound professional, yet not artificial or formal. This means avoiding legal terminology, technical words, and third-person constructions *(the undersigned, the writer)*. It also means sounding friendly and warm, just as you do in conversation. Thus, you may include occasional contractions *(can't, doesn't)* and first-person pronouns *(I/we)* in all but the most formal business reports. To determine if your writing is conversational, try the kitchen test. If it wouldn't sound natural in your kitchen, it probably needs revision. Note how the following formal sentences were revised to pass the kitchen test.

● To achieve a conversational tone, sound professional but not stilted.

Formal	Conversational
As per your verbal instruction, steps will be undertaken immediately to investigate your billing problem.	At your suggestion I'm investigating your billing immediately.
Our organization would like to inform you that your account has been credited in the aforementioned sum.	We're crediting your account for $78.

Conciseness: Trimming the Fat

Another revision task is making certain that a message makes its point in the fewest possible words. One of the shortest and most effective business letters ever written contained only nineteen words. Composed by business tycoon Cornelius Vanderbilt, the following masterpiece in brevity was sent to a pair of business associates who tried to swindle him while he vacationed in Europe:

● Main points are easier to understand in concise messages.

Gentlemen:

You have undertaken to cheat me. I won't sue you, for the law is too slow. I'll ruin you.

Yours truly,

Cornelius Vanderbilt

Messages without flabby phrases and redundancies are easier to comprehend and more forceful because main points stand out, as Vanderbilt's letter proves. Efficient messages also save the reader valuable time.

Concise writing begins with clear thinking. A famous Hollywood producer once said, "If you can't write your idea on the back of my calling card, you don't have a clear idea." Similarly, Procter & Gamble, the giant household products manufacturer, for years required all memos to be limited to one page.[4] The president returned long messages, urging writers to "boil it down to something I can grasp." Conciseness indicates clear thinking and total control over the material.

● Concise messages are the product of clear thinking and a solid grasp of the material.

SPOTLIGHT ON COMMUNICATORS

Sam Walton, one of America's most successful merchants, said, "If you had to boil down the Wal-Mart system to one single idea, it would probably be communication, because it is one of the real keys to our success." His brand of communication meant sharing management strategies with sales associates in straightforward, simple talk, as in his sales plan: "Buy it low, stack it high, sell it cheap."

But concise writing is not easy. As one expert copyeditor observes, "Trim sentences, like trim bodies, usually require far more effort than flabby ones."[5] To turn out slim sentences and lean messages, you do not have to be brusque, rude, or simple-minded. Instead, you must take time in the revision stage to "trim the fat." And before you can do that, you must learn to recognize it. Locating and excising wordiness involves (1) removing opening fillers, (2) eliminating redundancies, (3) reducing compound prepositions, and (4) purging empty words.

Removing opening fillers. Openers like *there is, it is,* and *this is* fill in sentences but generally add no meaning. These fillers reveal writers spinning their wheels until deciding where the sentence is going. Train yourself to question these constructions. About 75 percent can be eliminated, almost always resulting in more forceful and more efficient sentences.

Wordy	Improved
There are three things I want you to do.	I want you to do three things.
It is important to start meetings on time.	Starting meetings on time is important.

If the words *it* or *this* clearly refer to previous antecedents, their use is justified, of course.

Eliminating redundancies. Expressions that repeat meaning or include unnecessary words are redundant. To say *important essentials* is like saying "essential essentials" because *important* carries the same meaning as *essential.* Excessive adjectives, adverbs, and phrases often create redundancies. The following list represents a tiny segment of the large number of redundancies appearing in business writing today. What word in each expression creates the redundancy?

Redundancies to Avoid

advance warning	exactly identical	perfectly clear
alter or change	few in number	personal opinion
assemble together	free and clear	potential opportunity
basic fundamentals	grateful thanks	positively certain
collect together	great majority	proposed plan
consensus of opinion	integral part	serious interest
contributing factor	last and final	refer back
dollar amount	midway between	true facts
each and every	new changes	very unique
end result	past history	visible to the eye

Reducing compound prepositions. Many wordy prepositional phrases can be expressed in single words. In the following examples the shorter forms say the same thing much more efficiently.

Compound Preposition	Shorter Form
as to whether	whether
at a later date	later
at this point in time	now
at such time, at which time	when

Compound Preposition	Shorter Form
by means of, in accordance with	by
despite the fact that	although
due to the fact that, inasmuch as, in view of the fact that	because
for the amount of	for
in advance of, prior to	before
subsequent to	after
the manner in which	how
until such time as	until

Purging empty words. Familiar phrases roll off the tongue easily, but many contain expendable parts. Be alert to these empty words: *case, degree, the fact that, factor, instance, nature,* and *quality.* Notice how much better the following sentences sound when the empty words are removed:

> ~~In the case of~~ *USA Today* ~~the newspaper~~ improved its readability.
>
> Because of ~~the degree of~~ active participation by our sales reps, profits soared.
>
> We are aware ~~of the fact~~ that many managers need assistance.
>
> Except for ~~the instance of~~ Mazda, Japanese imports sagged.
>
> She chose a career in a field that was analytical ~~in nature.~~ *(Or, She chose a career in an analytical field.)*
>
> Student writing in that class is excellent ~~in quality.~~

Also avoid saying the obvious. In the following examples notice how many unnecessary words can be omitted:

> ~~When it arrived,~~ I cashed your check immediately. *(Announcing the check's arrival is unnecessary. That fact is assumed in its cashing.)*
>
> ~~We need printer cartridges; therefore,~~ please send me two dozen laser cartridges. *(The first clause is obvious.)*
>
> ~~This is to inform you that~~ the meeting will start at 2 p.m. *(Avoid unnecessary lead-ins.)*

Finally, look carefully at clauses beginning with *that, which,* and *who.* They can often be shortened without loss of clarity. Search for phrases, such as *it appears that,* that can be reduced to a single adjective or adverb, such as *apparently.*

> Changing the name of a ∧ *successful* company ~~that is successful~~ is always risky.
>
> All employees ~~who are among those~~ completing the course will be reimbursed.
>
> Our ∧ *final* proposal, ~~which was~~ slightly altered ~~in its final form,~~ finally won approval.
>
> We plan to schedule ∧ *weekly* meetings ~~on a weekly basis.~~

Vigor: Revising for Directness

Much business writing has been criticized as lifeless, cautious, and "really, really boring."[6] This boredom is caused not so much by the content as by wordiness and dull, trite expressions. You've already studied ways to improve clarity and concise-

SPOTLIGHT ON COMMUNICATORS

Even though he works in the complex field of data and information processing, executive Mike Simmons insists on simplicity. "I'm a nut on plain vanilla. . . . It took me years to learn how not to use acronyms to talk about our business." As chief information officer of Bank of Boston, he realizes that plenty of smart people don't know anything about data processing. To avoid irritating those people, he stresses simplicity, directness, and jargon-free communication.

● **Much business writing is plagued by wordiness and triteness.**

A new emphasis on readability in business contracts, policies, and other documents has sent researchers and writers back to the books. Instead of producing documents written in legalese, many companies are now emphasizing comprehensibility and plain English. Fidelity Investments, the nation's largest investment fund company, recently rewrote, reorganized, and redesigned its prospectus and other documents so that they are easier for customers to understand. Fidelity eliminated jargon, concentrated on using familiar words, and added graphics to emphasize important points.

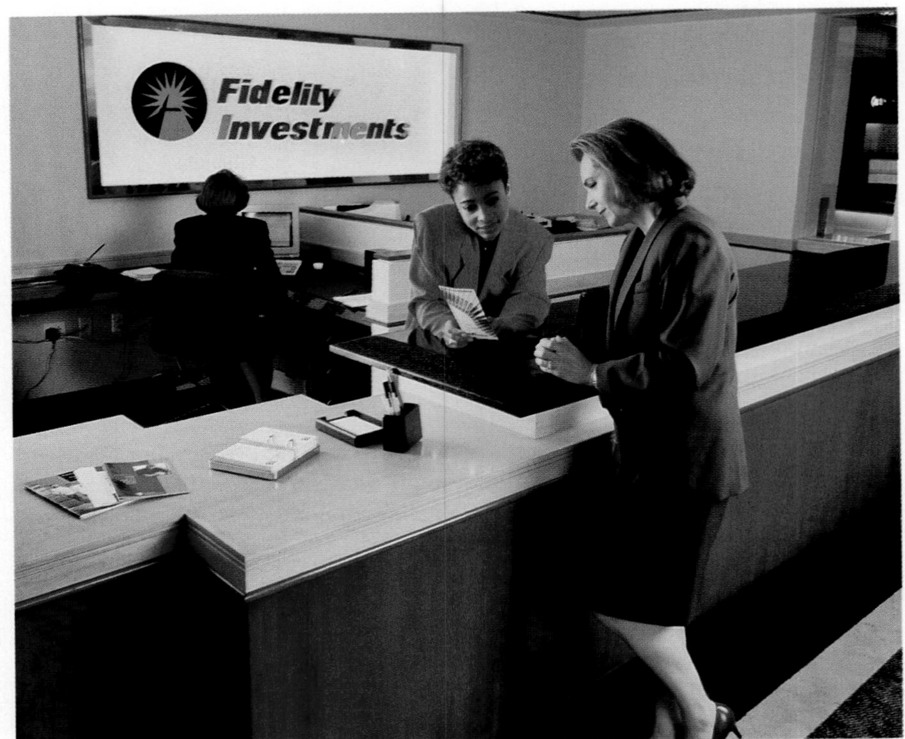

ness. You can also reduce wordiness and improve vigor by (1) kicking the noun habit and (2) dumping trite business phrases.

Overusing noun phrases lengthens sentences, saps verbs, and muddies the message.

Kicking the noun habit. Some writers become addicted to nouns, needlessly transforming verbs into nouns *(we make a recommendation of* instead of *we recommend).* This bad habit increases sentence length, drains verb strength, slows the reader, and muddies the thought. Notice how efficient, clean, and forceful the verbs below sound compared with their noun phrase counterparts.

Wordy Noun Phrase	Verb
conduct a discussion of	discuss
create a reduction in	reduce
engage in the preparation of	prepare
give consideration to	consider
is dependent on	depends
make an assumption of	assume
make a discovery of	discover
perform an analysis of	analyze
reach a conclusion about	conclude
take action on	act

Dumping trite business phrases. To sound "businesslike," many writers repeat the same stale expressions that other writers have used over the years. Your writing will sound fresher and more vigorous if you eliminate these phrases or find more original ways to convey the idea.

Trite Phrase	Improved Version
as per your request	as you request
pursuant to your request	at your request
enclosed please find	enclosed is
every effort will be made	we'll try
in accordance with your wishes	as you wish
in receipt of	have received
please do not hesitate to	please
thank you in advance	thank you
under separate cover	separately
with reference to	about

Readability: Improving Comprehension

To help receivers anticipate and comprehend ideas quickly, two special writing techniques are helpful: (1) parallelism, which involves balanced writing, and (2) highlighting, which makes important points more visible. And to ensure that your document is readable, consider applying the Fog Index, a readability measure.

• Comprehension can be enhanced through parallelism and graphic highlighting.

Developing parallelism. As you revise, be certain that you express similar ideas in balanced or parallel construction. For example, the phrase *clearly, concisely, and correctly* is parallel because all the words end in *-ly.* To express the list as *clearly, concisely, and with correctness* is jarring because the last item is not what the receiver expects. Instead of an adverb, the series ends with a noun. To achieve parallelism, match nouns with nouns, verbs with verbs, phrases with phrases, and clauses with clauses. Avoid mixing active-voice verbs with passive-voice verbs.

• Parallelism means matching nouns with nouns, verbs with verbs, phrases with phrases, and so on.

Nonparallel	Improved
The policy affected all vendors, suppliers, and those involved with consulting.	The policy affected all vendors, suppliers, and consultants. *(Series matches nouns.)*
Good managers analyze a problem, collect data, and alternatives are evaluated.	Good managers analyze a problem, collect data, and evaluate alternatives. *(Series matches verb forms.)*

Be alert to a list or series of items; the use of *and* or *or* should signal you to check for balanced construction. When elements cannot be balanced fluently, consider revising to subordinate or separate the items.

Nonparallel	Improved
Foreign service employees must be able to communicate rapidly, concisely, and be flexible in handling diverse responsibilities.	Foreign service employees must be able to communicate rapidly and concisely; they must also be flexible in handling diverse responsibilities.

Applying graphic highlighting. One of the best ways to improve comprehension is through graphic highlighting techniques. Spotlight important items by setting them off with

• Graphic devices such as lists, bullets, headings, and white space spotlight important ideas.

- Letters, like (a), (b), and (c), within the text
- Numerals, like 1, 2, and 3, listed vertically

- Bullets—black squares, raised periods, or other figures
- Headings
- Capital letters, underscores, boldface, and italics

Ideas formerly buried within sentences or paragraphs stand out when targeted with one of these techniques. Readers not only understand your message more rapidly and easily but also consider you efficient and well organized. In the two sentences following, notice how highlighting with letters makes the three items more visible and forceful. Numerals are also appropriate, particularly to indicate numbered groups or a sequence.

Original	**Highlighted**
Nordstrom attracts upscale customers by featuring quality fashions, personalized service, and a generous return policy.	Nordstrom attracts upscale customers by featuring (a) quality fashions, (b) personalized service, and (c) a generous return policy.

Lists offset from the text and introduced with bullets have a strong visual impact.

If you have the space and wish to create even greater visual impact, you can list items vertically and use bullets. Capitalize the word at the beginning of each line. Don't add end punctuation unless the statements are complete sentences. In the following items notice how each one begins with an *-ing* verb. Parallel construction is very important whenever you itemize ideas.

Several factors contribute to our successful service program:

- Setting and broadcasting goals for the organization
- Instilling an understanding of what quality service means
- Conducting customer surveys

Headings help writers to organize information and enable readers to absorb important ideas.

Headings benefit both the writer and the reader. They force the writer to organize carefully so that similar data are grouped together. And they help the reader separate major ideas from details. Moreover, headings enable a busy reader to skim familiar or less important information. They also provide a quick preview or review. Although headings appear more often in reports, they are equally helpful in complex letters and memos. Here, they informally summarize items within a message:

Our staff is developing a policy that eliminates as many barriers as possible to an international assignment for dual-career couples. Thus far, the policy has these unique conditions.

Dislocation allowance. The dislocated spouse receives a one-time payment of 33 percent of the last three months' gross taxable income up to $10,000.

Premove visit. Spouses may receive a loss-of-earnings payment up to $4,000 to cover any premove visit to the foreign assignment.

Language and other training. While on assignment, the spouse may be reimbursed for language training and any schooling that advances the spouse's career.

Too much graphic highlighting can clutter a document and reduce comprehension.

To highlight individual words, use capital letters, underlining, bold type, or italics. Be careful with these techniques, though, because they SHOUT at the reader. Consider how the reader will react.

The following chapters supply additional ideas for grouping and spotlighting data. Although highlighting techniques can improve comprehension, they can also clutter a message if overdone. Many of these techniques also require more space, so use them judiciously.

APPLYING THE FOG INDEX TO DETERMINE READABILITY

One way to calculate the "readability" of a document is by applying the Gunning Fog Index. Here's how you can figure it manually for the business letter shown here. (This same calculation can be performed by many computer software programs.)

- **Step 1: Select the passage.** Choose a continuous passage of between 100 and 130 words.
- **Step 2: Count the total words.** Count numbers, dates, and abbreviations as separate words. Our business letter sample has 110 words.
- **Step 3: Count the sentences.** Count all independent clauses separately. For example, *He applied, and he was hired* counts as two sentences. Our sample has seven sentences, marked with superscript numbers.
- **Step 4: Find the average sentence length.** Divide the total number of words by the number of sentences (110 ÷ 7 = 16 words).
- **Step 5: Count the number of long words.** A word is *long* if it has three or more syllables. Exclude (a) capitalized words, (b) compound words formed from short words *(nevertheless)*, and (c) verbs made into three syllables by the addition of *-ed* or *-es (located, finances)*. In our sample the long words are underlined.
- **Step 6: Find the percentage of long words.** Divide the number of long words by the number of total words (10 ÷ 110 = .09 or 9 percent).
- **Step 7: Add the results.** Add the average sentence length (16) and the percentage of long words (9). The result is 25.
- **Step 8: Multiply.** Multiply by .04 (25 × .04 = 10). The reading level of this letter is 10.

Dear Mrs. Lawrence:

[1]Yes, I can meet with you Thursday, April 3, at 10 a.m. to discuss possible ways to finance the purchase of a new home in San Diego. [2]Before we meet, though, you might like to consider two possible plans.

[3]The first plan finances your purchase with a swing loan, which has a fixed interest rate for a short period of time. [4]A second plan requires you to refinance your present residence. [5]We have located five programs from three different institutions that would do this. [6]Enclosed is a summary of these five plans.

[7]I look forward to seeing you Thursday to find a way for you to own a home in San Diego.

Sincerely,

The reading level of this short letter is 10, indicating appropriate writing for a business message. Your goal should be to keep your writing between the levels of 8 and 12. Two factors that most influence reading level are sentence length and word length.

Career Track Application

Compare the reading levels of several publications. Calculate the Fog Index for short passages from two of your college textbooks, your local newspaper, a business document (letter, memo, report), and an insurance policy. Discuss in class the appropriateness of the reading levels for each document.

Measuring readability. Experts have developed methods for measuring how easy, or difficult, a message is to read. Probably the best known is Robert Gunning's Fog Index, which measures long words and sentence length to determine readability. The accompanying Career Skills box shows you how to apply eight steps in figuring the Fog Index for a piece of writing, such as the sample business letter shown.

Readability formulas like the Fog Index are based on word and sentence lengths.

Our calculation indicates that this sample letter is written at a reading grade level of 10. The foggier a message, the higher its reading level. Magazines and newspapers that strive for wide readership keep their readability between levels 8 and 12. (*USA Today* is 10.6, *The New York Times* is 12.6,[7] and *People* magazine

Baseball players, notes playwright Neil Simon, get only three swings at a pitch and then they're out. In rewriting, however, "you get almost as many swings as you want and you know, sooner or later, you'll hit the ball." Although it takes real effort, revision allows the writer to work out the rough spots so that every message can score a hit.

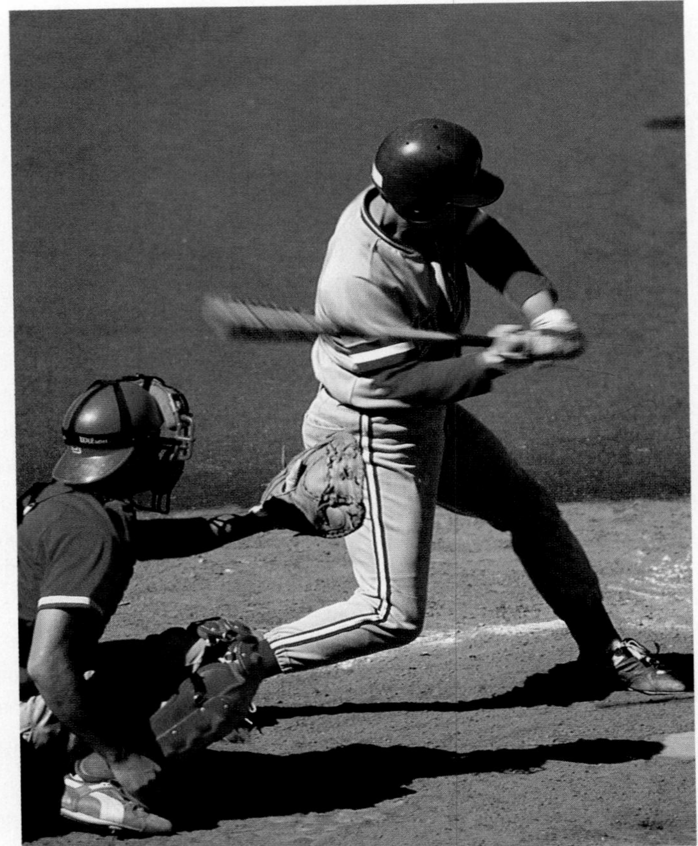

ranges between 8.4 and 11.2.) By occasionally calculating the Fog Index of your writing, you can ensure that you stay within the 8–12 range. Remember that long sentences and long words—those over two syllables—make your writing foggy.

However, readability formulas don't always tell the full story. Although they provide a rough estimate, those based solely on word and sentence counts fail to measure meaningfulness. Even short words (like *skew, onus,* and *wane*) can cause trouble if readers don't recognize them. More important than length is a word's familiarity and meaningfulness to the reader. In Chapter 3 you learned to adapt your writing to the audience by selecting familiar words. Other techniques that can improve readability include well-organized paragraphs, transitions to connect ideas, headings, and lists.

The task of revision, summarized in the following checklist, is hard work. It demands objectivity and a willingness to cut, cut, cut. Though painful, the process is also gratifying. It's a great feeling when you realize your finished message is clear, concise, and readable.

Checklist for Revising Messages

✔ **Keep the message simple.** Express ideas directly. Don't show off or use fancy language.

✔ **Be conversational.** Include occasional contractions *(hasn't, don't)* and first-person pronouns *(I/we)*. Use natural-sounding language.

- ✔ **Avoid opening fillers.** Omit sentence fillers like *there is, it is,* and *this is* to produce more direct expression.
- ✔ **Shun redundancies.** Eliminate words that repeat meanings, such as *mutual cooperation.* Watch for repetitious adjectives, adverbs, and phrases.
- ✔ **Tighten your writing.** Check phrases involving *case, degree, the fact that, factor,* and other words that unnecessarily increase wordiness. Avoid saying the obvious.
- ✔ **Don't convert verbs to nouns.** Keep your writing vigorous by avoiding the noun habit *(analyze* not *make an analysis of).*
- ✔ **Avoid trite phrases.** Keep your writing fresh, direct, and contemporary by skipping such expressions as *enclosed please find* and *pursuant to your request.*
- ✔ **Strive for parallelism.** Help receivers anticipate and comprehend your message by using balanced writing *(planning, drafting, and constructing* not *planning, drafting, and construction).*
- ✔ **Highlight important ideas.** Use graphic techniques such as letters, numerals, bullets, headings, capital letters, underlining, boldface, or italics to spotlight ideas and organization.
- ✔ **Test readability.** Check your writing occasionally to identify its reading level. Remember that short, familiar words and short sentences help readers comprehend.

Proofreading for the Finishing Touch

Once you have the message in its final form, it's time to proofread it. Don't proofread earlier because you may waste time checking items that eventually are changed or omitted.

Proofreading before a document is completed is generally a waste of time.

What to Watch For in Proofreading

Careful proofreaders check for problems in these areas:

- **Spelling.** Now's the time to consult the dictionary. Is *recommend* spelled with one or two *c*'s? Do you mean *affect* or *effect*? Use your computer spell checker, but don't rely on it totally. See the accompanying Technology box to learn more about the benefits and hazards of computer spell checkers.
- **Grammar.** Locate sentence subjects; do their verbs agree with them? Do pronouns agree with their antecedents? Review the C.L.U.E. principles in Appendix A if necessary.
- **Punctuation.** Make sure that introductory clauses are followed by commas. In compound sentences put commas before coordinating conjunctions *(and, or, but, nor).* Double-check your use of semicolons and colons.
- **Names and numbers.** Compare all names and numbers with their sources because inaccuracies are not immediately visible. Especially verify the spelling of the names of individuals receiving the message. Most of us immediately dislike someone who misspells our name.
- **Format.** Be sure that your document looks balanced on the page. Compare its parts and format with those of standard documents shown in Appendix B. If you indent paragraphs, be certain that all are indented.

SPELL CHECKERS ARE WONDERFUL, BUT...

Nearly all high-end word processing programs now include spell checkers. Also called dictionaries, these programs compare your typed words with those in the computer's memory and mark all discrepancies.

Spell checkers find a great many—but not all—word use and spelling errors. One study of college writing found that 75 percent of the students' spelling and usage errors would have been found by spelling software.[8] Doubtless, students are thankful for such assistance! But the flip side of the story is that 25 percent of the errors were *not* found. How this might happen is illustrated by the following poem:

I have a spell checker
That came with my PC.
It plainly marks four my review
Mistakes I cannot sea.
I've run this poem threw it,
I'm sure your pleased too no.
Its letter perfect in it's weigh—
My checker tolled me sew.[9]

The lesson to be learned here is that you can't rely totally on any spell checker. Misused words will not be highlighted because the spell checker doesn't know what meaning you have in mind. That's why you're wise to print out every message and proofread it word by word. Proofreading is the only way you can detect keyboarding errors, like *they* for *the* or *prepared* for *prepare*. Double-check confusing duos like *than/then, personal/personnel,* and *principle/principal.*

Career Track Application

Run a paper from this or another class through a spell checker. Then have a friend or classmate proofread it to see what the computer missed.

How to Proofread Routine Documents

Most routine documents require a light proofreading. You may be working with a handwritten or a printed copy or on your computer screen. If you wish to print a copy, make it a rough draft (don't print it on letterhead stationery). In time you may be able to produce a "first-time-final" message, but beginning writers seldom do.

For handwritten or printed messages, read the entire document. Watch for all of the items just described. Use standard proofreading marks, shown in Figure 5.1, to indicate changes.

● **For both routine and complex documents, it's best to proofread from a printed copy, not on a computer screen.**

For computer messages you can read the document on the screen, preferably in WYSIWYG mode (what you see is what you get). Use the down arrow to reveal one line at a time, thus focusing your attention at the bottom of the screen. A safer proofreading method, however, is reading from a printed copy. You're more likely to find errors and to observe the tone. "Things really look different on paper," observes Louise Lague at *People* magazine. "Don't just pull a letter out of the printer and stick it in an envelope. Read every sentence again. You'll catch bad line endings, strange page breaks, and weird spacing. You can also get a totally different feeling about what you've said when you see it in print. Sometimes you can say something with a smile on your face; but if you put the same thing in print, it won't work."[10]

FIGURE 5.1 ● Proofreader's Marks

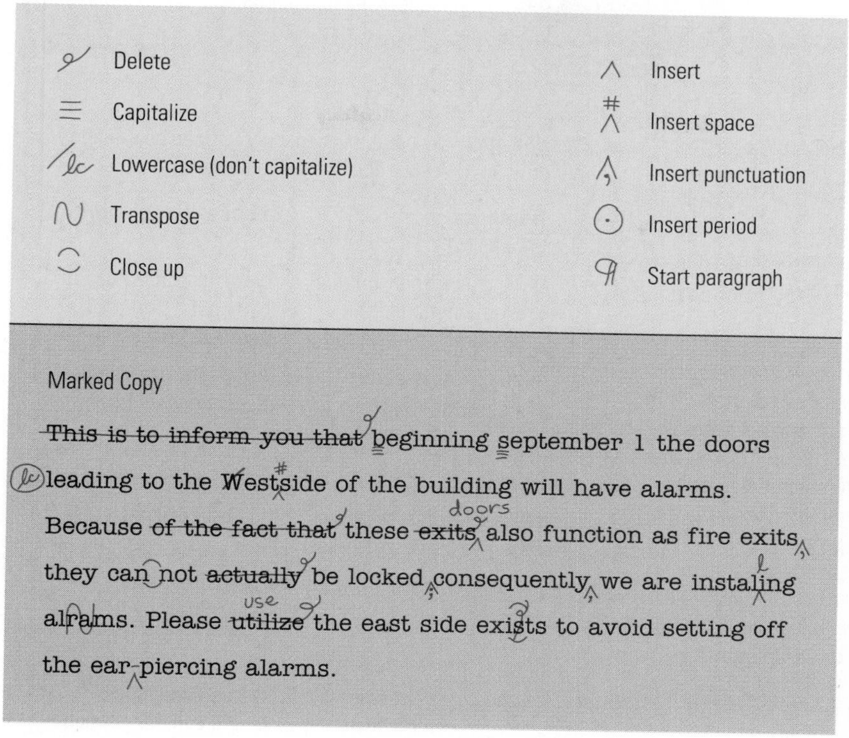

Mark	Meaning	Mark	Meaning
ℊ/	Delete	∧	Insert
≡	Capitalize	# ∧	Insert space
/lc	Lowercase (don't capitalize)	∧ ,	Insert punctuation
∩∪	Transpose	⊙	Insert period
⌒ ⌣	Close up	¶	Start paragraph

Marked Copy

This is to inform you that beginning september 1 the doors leading to the Westside of the building will have alarms. Because of the fact that these exits also function as fire exits they can not actually be locked consequently we are instaling alrams. Please utilize the east side exists to avoid setting off the ear piercing alarms.

How to Proofread Complex Documents

● **Complex documents should be proofread at least twice.**

Long, complex, or important documents demand more careful proofreading using the following techniques:

- Print a copy, preferably double-spaced, and set it aside for at least a day. You'll be more alert after a breather.
- Allow adequate time to proofread carefully. A common excuse for sloppy proofreading is lack of time.
- Be prepared to find errors. One student confessed, "I can find other people's errors, but I can't seem to locate my own." Psychologically, we don't *expect* to find errors, and we don't *want* to find them. Overcome this obstacle by anticipating errors and congratulating, not criticizing, yourself each time you find one.
- Read the message at least twice—once for word meanings and once for grammar/mechanics. For very long documents (book chapters and long articles or reports), read a third time to verify consistency in formatting.
- Reduce your reading speed. Concentrate on individual words rather than ideas.
- For documents that must be perfect, have someone read the message aloud. Spell names and difficult words, note capitalization, and read punctuation.
- Use standard proofreading marks, shown in Figure 5.1, to indicate changes.

GRAMMAR AND STYLE CHECKERS: GOOD AND BAD NEWS

Like most of us, you probably welcome any aid that improves your writing. Leading word processing programs—WordPerfect for Windows, Microsoft Word for Windows, and Microsoft Word for the Macintosh—now have built-in grammar and style checkers that are almost as easy to use as spell checkers. That's the good news.

The bad news is that they may be limited in the accuracy of "errors" they detect. Analyzing written material is complicated, and most grammar and style checkers tend to offer inappropriate suggestions along with useful advice. Moreover, no grammar and style checker is currently able to evaluate the quality of a person's writing. Despite these drawbacks, though, many writers find them useful.

Just how do they operate? Generally, you keyboard and save a document. Then you simply press a "hot key" or make a selection from the word processing menu to begin the checking program. As the checker flags each "problem," you read the suggestions and decide whether to revise. On the right are sample suggestions made by three leading grammar and style checker programs. Notice that the decision to revise is still up to the writer.

Checkers can flag certain sentence fragments, passive-verb constructions, wordy phrases, unfamiliar words, and clichés. They can also calculate readability level, average sentence and paragraph length, and number of difficult words. Such programs are especially good at mechanical tasks. But don't rely on them to solve all your writing problems. They aren't that sophisticated.

Most leading grammar and style checkers recognize documents created in a number of word processing programs for Macintosh, DOS, and Windows environments. They compare your writing to a set of "rules" and then flag errors that do not follow the rules. Many programs also allow you to customize the rules to your writing needs (business, technical, journalistic, fiction, and so forth).

As you can see from our examples, grammar and style checks don't correct anything. They merely make suggestions. Although such checkers are useful for pinpointing elements that may need revision, only *you* can be the final authority on how your document should be written.

Sentence	**Checker Suggestion**
Grammatik	
John was responsible for implementation of the program.	Try using a form of "carry out," "set up," "use," or "tool."
Although management anticipates changes.	"Although" can't begin an independent clause.
RightWriter	
San Francisco is only 325 miles away as the crow flies.	Reconsider the use of the cliché "as the crow flies."
Although management anticipates changes.	Consider replacing "anticipates" with the correct form of the simpler "expect." Is this a complete sentence? If so, is a comma missing?
Correct Grammar	
An error was found in the report.	This verb group [was found] may be in the passive voice.
This idea is first and foremost in our minds.	Wordy. Consider "first," "foremost," or "primarily" instead.

Career Track Application

Use a word processing program with a built-in grammar and style checker in preparing letters and memos for this class. Analyze the suggestions made by the checker. Revise your documents using your judgment about what changes improve message effectiveness.

● **Computer programs can help analyze writing, calculate readbility, and locate some grammar errors.**

You may want to try a computer program that analyzes certain aspects of your writing style. These style checkers identify such writing characteristics as use of passive voice, trite phrases, split infinitives, and wordy expressions, as well as readability level. Some even locate selected grammar errors. At this point, however, these software programs are probably most useful in learning environments where an instructor is available to interpret and discuss the recommendations. For more discussion of grammar and style checkers, see the Technology box above .

FIGURE 5.2 ● **The Complete 3-×-3 Writing Process**

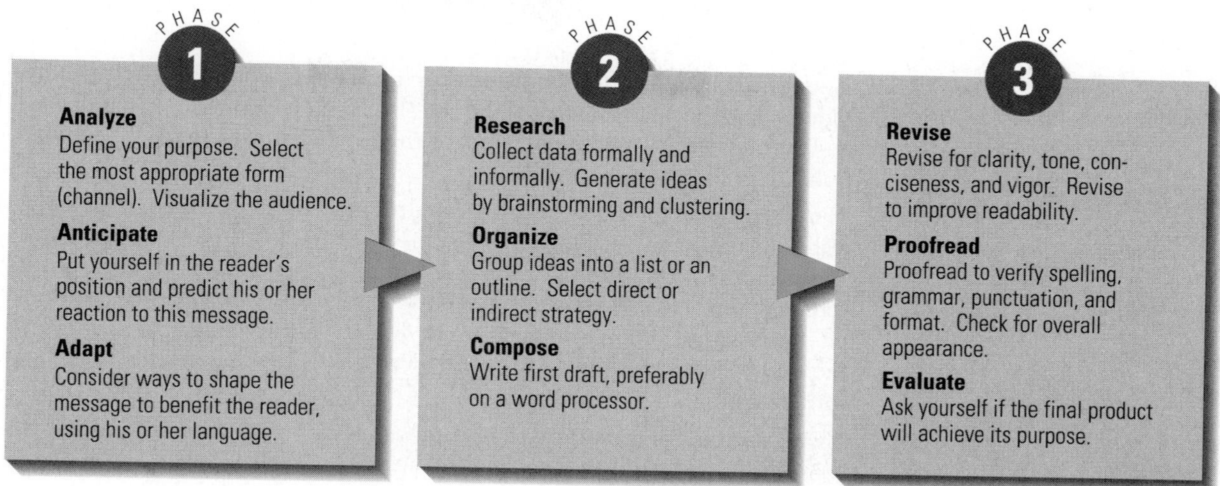

PHASE 1
Analyze
Define your purpose. Select the most appropriate form (channel). Visualize the audience.
Anticipate
Put yourself in the reader's position and predict his or her reaction to this message.
Adapt
Consider ways to shape the message to benefit the reader, using his or her language.
PHASE 2
Research
Collect data formally and informally. Generate ideas by brainstorming and clustering.
Organize
Group ideas into a list or an outline. Select direct or indirect strategy.
Compose
Write first draft, preferably on a word processor.
PHASE 3
Revise
Revise for clarity, tone, conciseness, and vigor. Revise to improve readability.
Proofread
Proofread to verify spelling, grammar, punctuation, and format. Check for overall appearance.
Evaluate
Ask yourself if the final product will achieve its purpose.

Evaluating the Product

As part of applying finishing touches, take a moment to evaluate your writing. How successful will this message be? Does it say what you want it to? Will it achieve your purpose? How will you know if it succeeds?

● **A good way to evaluate messages is through feedback.**

As you learned in Chapter 1, the best way to judge the success of your communication is through feedback. Thus, you should always encourage the receiver to respond to your message. This feedback will tell you how to modify future efforts to improve your communication technique.

Your instructor will also be evaluating some of your writing. Although any criticism is painful, try not to be defensive. Look on these comments as valuable advice tailored to your specific writing weaknesses—and strengths. Many businesses today spend hundreds of dollars per employee bringing in communication consultants to improve writing skills. You're getting the same training in this course. Take advantage of this chance—one of the few you may have—to improve your skills. The best way to improve your skills is through instruction, practice, and evaluation.

In this class you have all three elements: instruction in the writing process (summarized in Figure 5.2), practice materials, and someone willing to guide and evaluate your efforts. Because it's almost impossible to improve your skills alone, grab this chance. Multimillionaire Malcolm Forbes, founder of *Forbes* magazine, wisely observed, "The best place to learn to write is in school. If you're still there, pick your teachers' brains!"[11]

Summary of Learning Goals

1. **Revise a document to make it clear, conversational, and concise.** Clear documents use active-voice sentences and simple words and avoid negative expressions. Clarity is further enhanced by language that sounds like conversation, including occasional contractions and first-person pronouns *(I/we)*. Conciseness can be achieved by excluding opening fillers *(There are)*, redundancies *(basic essentials)*, and compound prepositions *(by means of)*.

2. **Revise a document so that it is vigorous and direct.** Vigorous, direct messages avoid wordy noun phrases *(conduct a discussion of)* and trite expressions *(please do not hesitate to).*

3. **Recognize and apply techniques for improving readability.** Two techniques that can improve readability are balanced constructions (parallelism) and spotlighting of important items with graphic devices (letters, numerals, bullets, headings, and so forth).

4. **Proofread routine and complex documents.** In proofreading documents, watch for problems in the following: spelling, grammar, punctuation, names and numbers, and format. Proofread routine documents line by line on the screen or, better yet, from a printed copy. For complex documents, proofread after a breather. Allow adequate time, reduce your reading speed, and read the document three times—for word meanings, for grammar/mechanics, and for formatting.

5. **Evaluate a message to judge its success.** Encourage feedback so that you can determine whether your communication achieved your goal. Welcome advice from your instructor on how to improve your writing skills.

Chapter Review

1. Approximately how much of the total composition time should be spent revising, proofreading, and evaluating?

2. What is the KISS method? What three ways can it apply to business writing?

3. What is a redundancy? Give an example. Why should writers avoid redundancies?

4. Why should communicators avoid openings such as *there is*?

5. What shorter forms could be substituted for the expressions *by means of, despite the fact that,* and *at this point in time*?

6. Why should a writer avoid the opening *This memo is to inform you that our next committee meeting is Friday*?

7. Why should a writer avoid an expression like *We hope you will give consideration to our proposal*?

8. What's wrong with businesslike expressions such as *enclosed please find* and *as per your request*?

9. Discuss five ways to highlight important ideas.

10. What two characteristics increase the Fog Index of written matter?

11. What is parallelism, and how can it be achieved?

12. Name six specific items to check in proofreading. Be ready to discuss methods you find useful in spotting these errors.

13. In proofreading, what major psychological problem do you face in finding errors? How can you overcome this barrier?

14. List four or more techniques for proofreading complex documents.

15. How can you overcome defensiveness when your writing is criticized constructively?

Discussion

1. Why is it difficult to recommend a specific process that all writers can follow in composition?

2. Discuss this statement by writing expert William Zinsser: "Plain talk will not be easily achieved in corporate America. Too much vanity is on the line."

3. To be conversational, should business writing be exactly like the way we talk? Support your opinion.

4. Why should the proofreading process for routine documents differ from that for complex documents?

5. **Ethical Issue:** What advice would you give in this ethical dilemma? Lisa is serving as interim editor of

the company newsletter. She receives an article written by the company president describing, in abstract and pompous language, the company's goals for the coming year. Lisa thinks the article will need considerable revising to make it readable. Attached to the president's article are complimentary comments by two of the company vice presidents. What action should Lisa take?

Activities

5.1 Document for Analysis

Revise the following memo to improve its clarity, conciseness, vigor, and readability. How many wordy constructions can you spot?

> To: All Management
>
> This memo is addressed to all members of management to advise you that once a year we like to remind management of our policy in relation to the matter of business attire. In this policy there is a recommendation that all employees should wear clothing that promotes a businesslike atmosphere and meets requirements of safety.
>
> Employees who work in offices and who, as part of their jobs, meet the public and other outsiders should dress in a professional manner, including coat, tie, suit, dress, and so forth. In areas of industrial applications, supervisors may prohibit loose clothing (shirttails, ties, cuffs) that could become entangled in machinery that moves.
>
> Where it is necessary, footwear should provide protection against heavy objects or sharp edges at the level of the floor. In the manufacturing and warehousing areas, prohibited footwear includes the following: shoes that are open toe, sandals, shoes made of canvas or nylon, tennis shoes, spiked heels, and heels higher than 1½ inches.
>
> Each and every manager has the responsibility for the determination of suitable business attire, and employees should be informed of what is required.

5.2 Document for Analysis

Use proofreading marks to indicate needed corrections in the following letter. Check spelling, typos, grammar, punctuation, names and numbers, and format.

> Dear Ms. Willis,
>
> We appreciate you interest in employe leasing through U.S. Staff Network. Our programs and our service has proved to be powerful management tools for business owners, like you.
>
> Our seventeen year history, Ms. Williams, provide the local service and national strength neccesary to offer the best employee leasing programs available, we save business owners time, and money, employee hassles and employer liability.
>
> Your employees' will receive health care benifits, retirement plan choices and a national credit union. As a small business owner you can eliminate personel administration. Which involves alot of goverment paperwork today.
>
> Whether you have one or 1,000 employees and offer no benefits to a full-benefits package employee leasing will get you back to the basics of running your business more profitably. I will call you to arrange a time to meet, and talk about your specific needs.
>
> Cordially,

5.3 Computing Fog Index

As an in-class project or for homework, do the following: (1) Compute the Fog Index for the following letter. (2) Then revise the letter using proofreading marks. Reduce its length and improve its readability by eliminating redundancies, wordiness, and trite expressions. Use simple, clear words. Shorten sentences. (3) Prepare a clean copy of the revised letter. (4) Finally, calculate the Fog Index for your revision.

> Dear Mr. Sato:
>
> Pursuant to your request, the undersigned is transmitting to you herewith the attached materials and documents with regard to the improvement of security in your business. To ensure the improvement of your after-hours security, you should initially make a decision with regard to exactly what you contemplate must have protection. You are, in all probability, apprehensive not only about your electronic equipment and paraphernalia but also about your company records, information, and data.
>
> Inasmuch as we feel you will want to obtain protection for both your equipment and data, we will make suggestions for taking a number of judicious steps to inhibit crime. First and foremost, we recommend that you install defensive lighting. A consultant for lighting, currently on our staff, can design both outside and inside lighting, which brings me to my second point. Exhibit security signs, due to the fact that nonprofessional thieves are often as not deterred by posted signs on windows and doors. As my last and final

recommendation, you should install space alarms, which are sensors that look down over the areas that are to receive protection, and activate bells or additional lights, thus scaring off intruders.

After reading the enclosed materials, please call me to further discuss the protection of your business.

Sincerely,

5.4 Interview

To learn more about on-the-job writing, interview someone—preferably in your field of study. Ask questions like these: What kind of writing do you do? What kind of planning do you do before writing? Where do you get information? Do you brainstorm? Make lists? Do you compose with pen and paper, a computer, or a dictating machine? How long does it take you to compose a routine one- or two-page memo or letter? Do you revise? How often? Do you have a preferred method for proofreading? When you have questions about grammar and mechanics, what or whom do you consult? Does anyone read your drafts and make suggestions? Can you describe your entire composition process? Do you ever work with others to produce a document? How does this process work? What makes writing easier or harder for you? Have your writing methods and skills changed since you left school? Your instructor may ask you to present your findings orally or in a written report.

Exercises

5.5 Clarity

Revise the following sentences to make them direct, simple, and conversational.

a. It has been determined by the staff that our process of check verification for customers must be simplified.

b. A request that we are making to managers is that they not spend all their time in their departments and instead visit other departments one hour a month.

c. It is the personal opinion of this writer that when deadlines have the characteristics of negotiation, they are no longer effective.

d. Our organization is honored to have the pleasure of extending a welcome to you as a new customer.

e. Please be advised that it is our intention to make every effort to deliver your order by the date of your request, April 1.

f. Enclosed herewith are the report and brochures to which you refer in your esteemed letter of the 12th.

g. It has been established that the incontestable key to the future success of this organization is a deep and firm commitment to quality.

h. It is our suggestion that you do not attempt to move forward until you seek and obtain approval of the plan from the department head prior to beginning the project.

i. Experience has indicated that employees who have had the opportunity to attend training sessions benefit most greatly when those sessions are not overly long.

j. If doubt is entertained regarding an optimal solution to the problem of acquiring new equipment, may I suggest that we refer the problem to a committee.

5.6 Conciseness

Suggest shorter forms for the following expressions.

a. for the purpose of

b. in reference to

c. in regard to

d. without further delay

e. on a yearly basis

f. in the event that

g. a report for which you have no use

h. an accountant who took great care

i. arranged according to the alphabet

j. a program that is designed to save money

5.7 Conciseness

Revise and shorten the following sentences.

a. There are four reasons that explain the sudden sales spurt for our product.

b. As per your suggestion, we will not attempt to make alterations or changes in the blueprints at this point in time.

c. It is perfectly clear that meetings held on a weekly basis are most effective.

d. Despite the fact that the bill seemed erroneous, we sent a check in the amount of $150.

e. We have received your letter, and we are pleased to send the pamphlets you request.

f. All accounts that are overdue must be sent a last and final notice before January 1.

g. There are numerous benefits that can result from a good program that focuses on customer service.

h. Because of the degree of active employee participation, we are of the opinion that the stock bonus plan will be successful.

i. At this point in time in the program, I wish to extend my grateful thanks to all the support staff who helped make this occasion possible.

j. There is a short questionnaire enclosed that is designed to help us take action on the proposed environment plan.

k. In accordance with your wishes, we are sending you under separate cover two contract forms.

l. Although the sales returns for July are high in number, experience has indicated that this is not an unusual condition for summer.

m. This is to inform you that quality should be our first and foremost goal.

n. It is important to give consideration to the fact that people do change.

o. For each and every single customer who complains, there are 10 to 15 other ones out there who are not bothering to speak up about their dissatisfaction or unhappiness.

p. Our consultants can assist you in answering questions which you have about carpet care.

q. It is our expectation that we will see increases in sales when the reps learn the new system.

r. Those who functioning as suppliers may not have a full understanding of the problem.

s. Except in the instance of Fat-Burger, most fast-food chains are aware of the fact that many consumers want choices on the menu that are healthful.

t. Two weeks in advance of its planned date of release, the announcement regarding our relocation was leaked to the press.

u. This is just to let you know that applications will be accepted at a later date for employees who are at the entry level.

v. Did he give you any indication as to whether he was coming?

w. There are many words that can be eliminated through revision that is carefully done.

5.8 Vigor

Revise the following sentences to reduce noun conversions, trite expressions, and other wordiness.

a. We must make the assumption that you wish to be transferred.

b. Please give consideration to our latest proposal, despite the fact that it comes into conflict with the original plan.

c. The committee reached the conclusion that a great majority of students had a preference for mail-in registration.

d. Please conduct an investigation of employee turnover in that department for the period of June through August.

e. After we engage in the preparation of a report, our recommendations will be presented in their final form before the Executive Committee.

f. There are three members of our staff who are making every effort to locate your lost order.

g. Whether or not we make a continuation of the sales campaign is dependent upon its success in the city of Houston.

h. If you need further assistance, please do not hesitate to call me at 889-1901.

i. Please forward any bills in connection with the construction, in accordance with our agreement, to the address of my attorney.

j. We are in receipt of your check in the dollar amount of $200.

5.9 Parallelism

Revise the following sentences to improve parallelism. If elements cannot be balanced fluently, use appropriate subordination.

a. Critics argue that American business is too concerned with machinery, capital, and operations that result in profitability.

b. Ensuring equal opportunities, the removal of barriers, and elimination of age discrimination are our goals.

c. Mr. Alvarez reads all incoming mail, and its distribution is made by him to all appropriate responders.

d. Last year Ms. Thompson wrote letters and was giving speeches to promote investment in her business.

e. Because of its air-conditioning and since it is light and attractive, I prefer this office.

f. For this position we assess oral and written communication skills, how well individuals solve problems, whether they can lead others, and we're also interested in interpersonal skills, such as cultural awareness and sensitivity.

5.10 Highlighting

Revise the following statements using highlighting techniques. Improve parallel construction and reduce wordiness if necessary.

a. Use a vertical list with numbers.

The Small Business Administration provides a variety of ways in which it aids small businesses. These services include loans (both private and government), helping out with the procurement of government contracts, and the provision of management training and consulting.

b. Use letters within the sentence.

The major benefits our organization offers include annual leave and sick leave, insurance for group life and medical expenses, and a private retirement fund.

c. Use a vertical list with bullets.

Our attorney made a recommendation that we take several steps to avoid litigation in regard to sexual harassment. The first step we should take involves establishing an unequivocal written statement prohibiting sexual harassment within our organization. The second thing we should do is make sure training sessions are held for supervisors regarding a proper work environment. Finally, some kind of procedure for employees to lodge complaints is necessary. This procedure should include investigation of complaints.

5.11 Proofreading

Use proofreading marks to mark spelling, grammar, punctuation, capitalization, and other errors in the following sentences.

a. To be elligible for this job, you must: (1) Be a U.S. citizen, (2) Be able to pass a through back ground investigation, and (3) Be available for world wide assignment.

b. Some businesses view "quality" as a focus of the organization rather then a atribute of there goods or services.

c. Its easy to get caught up in internal problems, and to overlook customers needs.

d. Incidently we expect both the ceo and the president to make speechs.

e. This is to inform you that wordiness destroys clarity therefore learn to cut the fat from your writing.

f. A clothing outlet opened at lakeland plaza in june, however business isslow.

C.L.U.E. Review 5

Edit the following sentences to correct faults in grammar, punctuation, spelling, and word use.

1. Business documents must be written clear to insure that readers comprehend the message quick.
2. We expect Mayor Wilson to visit the govenor in an attempt to increase the cities share of State funding.
3. The caller could have been him but we don't know for sure. Since he didn't leave his name.
4. The survey was sited in an article entitled "Whats new in softwear, however I can't locate it now.
5. All three of our companys auditors—Jim Lucus, Doreen Delgado, and Brad Kirby—critisized there accounting procedures.
6. Anyone of the auditors are authorized to procede with an independant action, however, only a member of the management counsel can alter policy.
7. Because our printer has been broke everyday this week; were looking at new models.
8. Have you all ready ordered the following? a dictionary a reference manual and a style book.
9. In the morning Mrs Williams ordinarilly opens the office, in the evening Mr Williams usualy closes it.
10. When you travel in england and ireland I advice you to charge purchases to your visa credit card.

Letters and Memos

6 Direct Letters

7 Direct Memos

8 Negative News

9 Persuasive and Sales Messages

10 Goodwill and Special Messages

Direct Letters

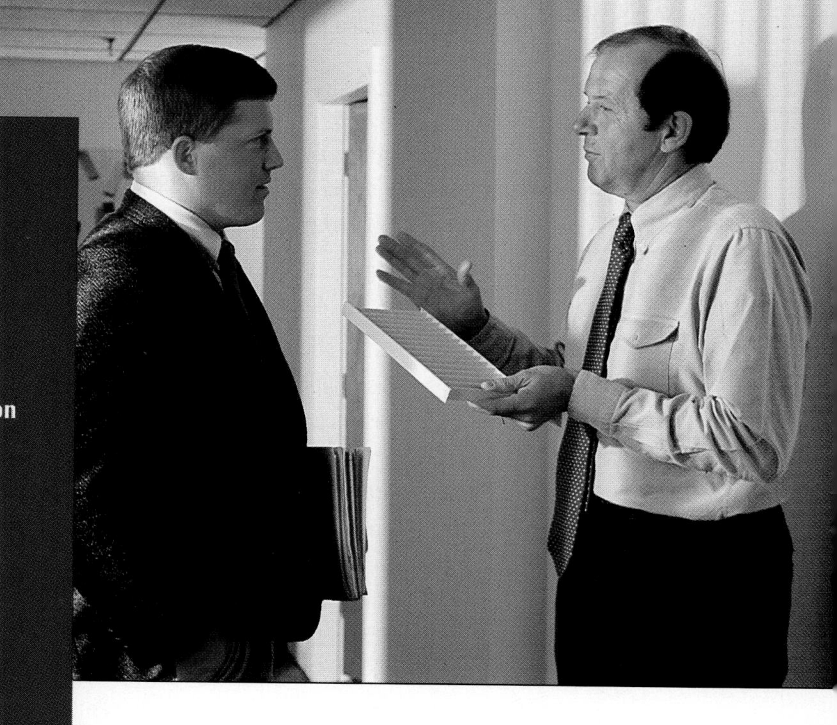

LEARNING GOALS

After studying this chapter, you should be able to

1. Describe the direct pattern for organizing letters
2. Write letters requesting information and action
3. Compose letters placing orders
4. Prepare letters making claims
5. Write letters complying with requests
6. Compose letters acknowledging customer orders
7. Prepare letters granting claims and making adjustments
8. Modify international letters to accommodate other cultures

Ben & Jerry's Homemade: Career Track Profile

> **"We never gloss over a problem, and we never invalidate a writer's concerns."**

Although it's not the country's biggest ice cream company, Ben & Jerry's Homemade is probably the most visible. In growing from a twelve-flavor miniparlor in Burlington, Vermont, into the country's second-largest maker of superpremium ice creams and frozen desserts, Ben & Jerry's has been showered with publicity. The flood of press notices flows not so much from its explosive business success or its funky flavor hits like Chunky-Monkey, Cherry Garcia, and Dastardly Mash. Of greater media interest is the new-age business philosophy of founders Ben Cohen and Jerry Greenfield. Unlike most entrepreneurs their aim is to build a successful business but, at the same time, be a force for social change.

Ben & Jerry's tries to operate in a way that improves local and global quality of life. It contributes 7½ percent of its pretax profits to charitable causes, ranging from cash grants for Vermont community groups to support for national progressive grass-roots causes. Equally important is its mission to create career opportunities, financial rewards, and a fun-filled work environment for employees. As Jerry says, "If it's not fun, why do it?"

Environmentally, Ben & Jerry's searches for innovative recycling, energy-saving, and waste-reclamation techniques to improve its own production and distribution procedures. Employees are encouraged to volunteer for "Green Teams," whose task is finding ways to improve the company's environmental impact.

Such a visible company with a popular national product and a strong social stance naturally generates a lot of letters. And Alice Blachly, consumer affairs coordinator, is one of the people who answer the mass of incoming correspondence at Ben & Jerry's.

After graduating from Swarthmore College with a degree in psychology and English, Alice worked for many years in a variety of jobs, including administrative assistant, nursery school teacher, and editor. One day an agency sent her on a temporary assignment to Ben & Jerry's. Although this job lasted only five days, she knew immediately that she wanted to stay. When the community relations department expanded, she submitted her résumé. For an employment test Alice responded to eight typical customer letters, and the test proved her writing skills and ingenuity to be just what the company wanted.

In answering customer correspondence, Alice generally works with three categories of letters: "fan" mail, information responses, and adjustments. Fan mail contains praise and testimonials: "tried the new Cherry Garcia Frozen Yogurt and . . . I want to go to Vermont and shake your sticky hands." To the fan letters Alice responds with handwritten cards or printed letters that promote good feelings and cement a long-lasting bond between Ben & Jerry's and its satisfied consumers. She wants customers to know their comments are appreciated.

Retaining the enthusiasm and support of Ben & Jerry's fans depends greatly on the cheerleading and charisma of co-founders Ben Cohen and Jerry Greenfield. Equally important, though, is their focus on integrating the company's financial and social goals and then communicating those goals clearly and directly to their three audiences: customers, employees, and stockholders. Letters to customers are a key channel of communication.

The letters from consumers seeking information or commenting on Ben & Jerry's social positions often require research. For example, a consumer worried that cottonseed oil, formerly contained in the nut-butter portion of Rainforest Crunch ice cream, might be contaminated by pesticides. Alice checked with company quality assurance experts and also investigated articles about cottonseed oil before responding. Other consumers wonder about Ben & Jerry's position on the treatment of cows by Vermont dairy farmers. "If we don't know the answers, we try to find out fast so that we can give accurate, current, and honest information. We never gloss over a problem, and we never invalidate a writer's concerns."

Adjustment letters are very important to Alice and the entire Ben & Jerry crew. These letters respond to consumer complaints, such as "My pint didn't have quite enough cookie dough" or "My frozen yogurt was icy." Alice gives adjustment letters first priority because Ben & Jerry's has not only high social principles but also high product standards. "We have trained consumers to expect the best," says Alice, "so they are disappointed when something goes wrong. And we are disappointed, too. We refund the purchase price, and we explain what caused the problem, if we know."

Like many successful companies Ben & Jerry's recognizes consumer letters as a gold mine of valuable product feedback. "A big part of my job," observes Alice, "goes beyond just answering mail. I pass on what I learn from consumers to our product people. Sometimes writers have great ideas for new flavors, packaging, and novelty products. You can be sure we want to hear them!"

In her letters Alice concentrates on two goals. First, she strives to answer clearly and completely all issues raised by the writer. As part of her revision process, she compares her printed letter with the customer's letter to be certain she has addressed every topic mentioned. A customer might write, for example, "I didn't get enough Heath® Bars in that last pint. By the way, have you considered a sugar-free ice cream? And we like your stand on peace." Each idea deserves a response.

Her second goal is to project a tone that shows respect for the writer's views. "Much is written about our company because of our sense of social responsibility. Consumers have put us up on a pedestal; if we stumble, we fall farther in their eyes. My letters explain our position, but we never try to change a writer's opinion." Alice Blachly's sensitive letters keep the lines of communication open between Ben & Jerry's and the outside world.[1]

Strategies for Direct Letters

Letters are a primary channel of communication for delivering messages *outside* an organization. In this book we'll divide letters into four groups: (1) direct letters communicating straightforward requests and replies (Chapter 6), (2) negative letters delivering refusals and bad news (Chapter 8), (3) persuasive letters containing sales and other messages (Chapter 9), and (4) special letters conveying goodwill and special messages (Chapter 10).

● **Direct letters to outsiders encourage product feedback, project a favorable company image, and promote future business.**

This chapter concentrates on direct, straightforward letters through which we conduct everyday business with outsiders. Such letters go to suppliers, government agencies, other businesses, and, most importantly, customers. At Ben & Jerry's and most other organizations, letters to customers receive a high priority because these messages encourage product feedback, project a favorable image of the company, and promote future business.

Publisher Malcolm Forbes understood the power of business letters when he said, "A good business letter can get you a job interview, get you off the hook, or get you money. It's totally asinine to blow your chances of getting *whatever* you want—with a business letter that turns people off instead of turning them on."[2] This chapter teaches you what turns readers on. You'll study the characteristics of good letters, techniques for organizing direct requests and responses, and ways to apply the 3-×-3 writing process. You'll also learn how to write six specific kinds of direct letters.

Characteristics of Good Letters

Although direct letters deliver straightforward facts, they don't have to sound and look dull or mechanical. At least three characteristics distinguish good business letters: clear content, a tone of goodwill, and correct form.

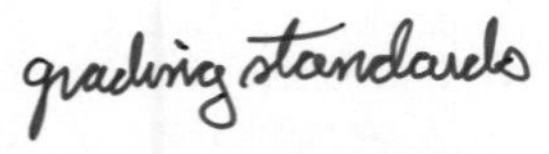

● **Clear letters feature short sentences and paragraphs, transitional expressions, familiar words, and active-voice verbs.**

Clear content. A clearly written letter separates ideas into paragraphs, uses short sentences and paragraphs, and guides the reader through the ideas with transitional expressions. Moreover, a clear letter uses familiar words and active-voice verbs. In other words, it incorporates all the writing techniques you studied in Chapters 3, 4, and 5.

One business observer estimated that "more than one third of business letters do nothing more than seek clarification of earlier correspondence."[3] A clear letter answers all the reader's questions or concerns so that no further correspondence is necessary. Recall, for example, how Alice Blachly at Ben & Jerry's double-checks all letters before sending them out to be certain that she has covered every point mentioned by the writer.

A tone of goodwill. Good letters, however, have to do more than deliver clear messages; they also must build goodwill. Goodwill is a positive feeling the reader has toward an individual or an organization. By analyzing your audience and adapting your message to the reader, your letters can establish an overall tone of goodwill.

● **Letters achieve a tone of goodwill by emphasizing a "you" view and reader benefits.**

To achieve goodwill, look for ways to present the message from the reader's perspective. In other words, emphasize the "you" view and point out benefits to the reader. In addition, be sensitive to words that might suggest gender, racial, age, or disability bias. Finally, frame your ideas positively because they will sound more

FIGURE 6.1 ● Business Letter Formatting

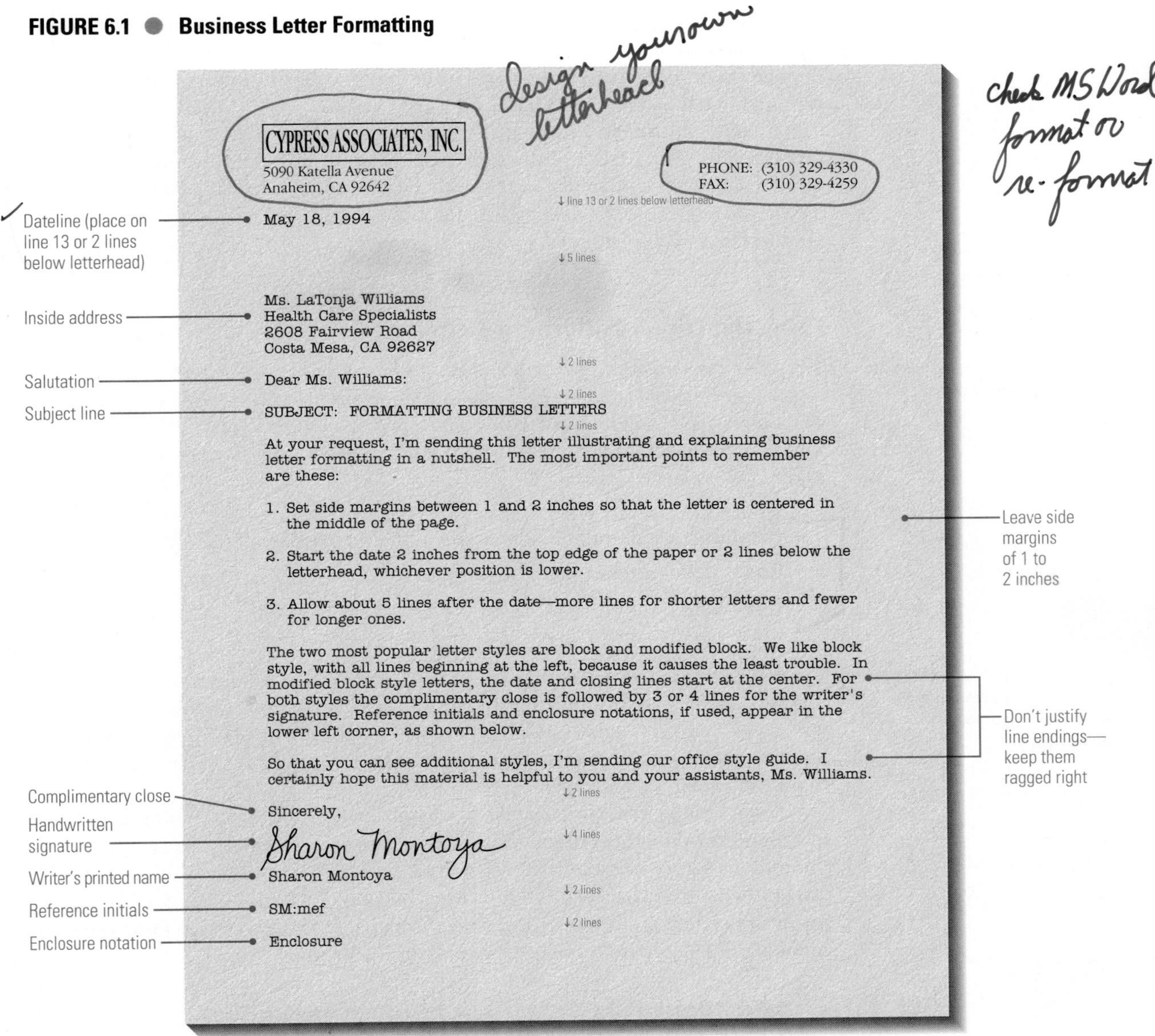

CYPRESS ASSOCIATES, INC.
5090 Katella Avenue
Anaheim, CA 92642

PHONE: (310) 329-4330
FAX: (310) 329-4259

May 18, 1994

Ms. LaTonja Williams
Health Care Specialists
2608 Fairview Road
Costa Mesa, CA 92627

Dear Ms. Williams:

SUBJECT: FORMATTING BUSINESS LETTERS

At your request, I'm sending this letter illustrating and explaining business letter formatting in a nutshell. The most important points to remember are these:

1. Set side margins between 1 and 2 inches so that the letter is centered in the middle of the page.
2. Start the date 2 inches from the top edge of the paper or 2 lines below the letterhead, whichever position is lower.
3. Allow about 5 lines after the date—more lines for shorter letters and fewer for longer ones.

The two most popular letter styles are block and modified block. We like block style, with all lines beginning at the left, because it causes the least trouble. In modified block style letters, the date and closing lines start at the center. For both styles the complimentary close is followed by 3 or 4 lines for the writer's signature. Reference initials and enclosure notations, if used, appear in the lower left corner, as shown below.

So that you can see additional styles, I'm sending our office style guide. I certainly hope this material is helpful to you and your assistants, Ms. Williams.

Sincerely,

Sharon Montoya

Sharon Montoya

SM:mef

Enclosure

pleasing and will give more information than negative constructions. And, of course, you must always be courteous.

Correct form. A business letter conveys silent messages beyond that of its printed words. The letter's appearance and format reflect the writer's carefulness and experience. A short letter bunched at the top of a sheet of paper, for example, looks as if it was prepared in a hurry or by an amateur.

● Appropriate letter formats send silent but positive messages.

For your letters to make a good impression, you need to select an appropriate format. The block style shown in Figure 6.1 is a popular format. Other letter formats are illustrated later in this chapter and shown in Appendix B. In the block style the parts of your letter—dateline, inside address, body, and so on—are set flush left on the page. Also, the letter is formatted so that it is centered on the page and framed by white space. Most letters will have margins of 1¼ to 2 inches, depending on how many words are in the body—shorter letters will have wider side margins than longer letters.

Finally, be sure to use ragged-right margins; that is, don't allow your word processor to justify the right margin and make all lines end evenly. Unjustified margins improve readability, say experts, by providing visual stops and by making it easier to tell where the next line begins. Study Figure 6.1 for more tips on making your letters look professional.

Using the Direct Pattern for Letters

Most business messages are direct requests or direct responses.

The everyday transactions of a business consist mainly of direct requests and responses. Because you expect the reader's response to be positive or neutral, you won't need special techniques to be convincing, to soften bad news, or to be tactful. Thus, in composing direct letters, you can organize your message, as shown in Figure 6.2, into three parts:

- **Opening:** a statement that announces the purpose immediately
- **Body:** details that explain the purpose
- **Closing:** a request for action or a courteous conclusion

Everyday business messages "frontload" by presenting the main idea or purpose immediately.

Frontloading in the opening. You should begin everyday messages in a straightforward manner by frontloading the main idea. State immediately why you are writing so that the reader can anticipate and comprehend what follows. Remember, every time a reader begins a message, he or she is thinking, "Why was this sent to me, and what am I to do?"

Some writers make the mistake of organizing a message in the same sequence in which they thought through the problem: they review the background, discuss the reasons for action, and then request an action. Most business letters, though, are better written "backwards." Don't get bogged down in introductory material, justifications, or old-fashioned "business" language; instead, reveal your purpose immediately. Compare these indirect and direct openers:

Indirect Opening	Direct Opening
Our company is experiencing difficulty in retaining employees. We also need help in screening job applicants. Our current testing program is unsatisfactory. I understand that you offer employee testing materials, and I have a number of questions to ask.	Please answer the following questions about your personnel testing materials.
My name is Mark Johnson, and I am interested in owning and operating one of your franchises in my area. Pursuant to this desire, I have many questions, but there's no point in asking them until I find out if you have a franchise available in my home town.	Do you have a franchise available in Mesa, Arizona?

Most simple requests can open immediately with a statement of purpose. Occasionally, however, complex requests may require a sentence or two of expla-

FIGURE 6.2 ● **Three-Part Direct Pattern for Requests and Responses**

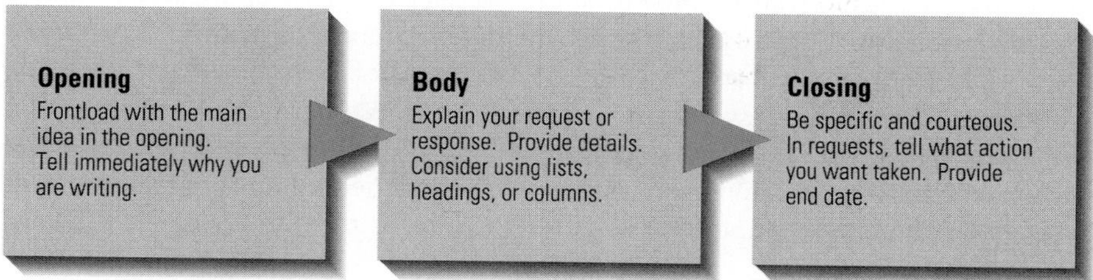

nation or background before the purpose is revealed. What you want to avoid, though, is delaying the purpose of the letter beyond the first paragraph.

Opening
Frontload with the main idea in the opening. Tell immediately why you are writing.
Body
Explain your request or response. Provide details. Consider using lists, headings, or columns.
Closing
Be specific and courteous. In requests, tell what action you want taken. Provide end date.

Explaining in the body. After a direct opening that tells the reader why you are writing, present details that explain your request or response. This is where your planning pays off, allowing you to structure the information for maximum clarity and readability. Here you should consider using some graphic devices to highlight the details: a numbered or bulleted list, headings, columns, or boldface or italic type.

● **The body explains the purpose for writing, perhaps using graphic devices to highlight important ideas.**

If you have considerable information, you'll want to develop each idea in a separate paragraph with effective transitions to connect them. The important thing to remember is to keep similar ideas together. The biggest problem in business writing is poor organization, and the body of a letter is where that failure becomes apparent.

Being specific and courteous in the closing. In the last paragraph of direct letters, readers look for action information: schedules, deadlines, activities to be completed. Thus, at this point, you should specify what you want the reader to do. If appropriate, include an end date—a date for completion of the action. If possible, give reasons for establishing the deadline. Research shows that people want to know why they should do something—even if the reasons seem obvious. Moreover, people want to be treated courteously *(Please answer these questions before April 1, when we must make a final decision),* not bossed around *(Send this information immediately).*

● **The closing courteously specifies what the receiver is to do.**

Applying the 3-×-3 Writing Process to Direct Letters

Although direct letters may be short and straightforward, they benefit from attention to the composition process. "If you force yourself to think through what you want to say and to whom you want to say it," observes a communication consultant in *Business Week,* "the writing task becomes infinitely easier."[4] Here's a quick review of the 3-×-3 writing process to help you think through its application to direct letters.

● **Before writing direct letters, make yourself analyze your purpose and anticipate the response.**

Analysis, anticipation, and adaptation. Before writing, spend a few moments analyzing your task and audience. Your key goals here are (1) determining your purpose, (2) anticipating the reaction of your audience, and (3) visualizing the audience. Too often, letter writers aren't sure of their purpose when they start writing. As Alice Blachly at Ben & Jerry's says, "If I'm having trouble with a letter and it's not coming out right, it's almost always because I haven't thought through exactly what I want to say."

SPOTLIGHT ON COMMUNICATORS

As top golfers visualize their swing just before they hit the ball, Mark H. McCormack visualizes his intended audience before writing business letters. The CEO of International Sports Management Group advises writers to think about how they want readers to react. Make sure you don't ask too much of them, he says, and then make it easy for them to respond—as you want them to.

Research, organization, and composition. Collect information and make a list of the points you wish to cover. For short messages such as an answer to a customer's inquiry, jot down notes on the document you are answering. For longer documents that require formal research, use a cluster diagram or the outlining techniques discussed in Chapter 4. When business letters carry information that won't upset the receiver, you can organize them in the direct manner described earlier. And be sure to plan for revision—a writer can seldom turn out an excellent message on the first attempt. For easier revision, keyboard your message on a word processor.

Revision, proofreading, and evaluation. When you finish the first draft, revise for clarity. The receiver should not have to read the message twice to grasp its meaning. Proofread for correctness. Check for punctuation irregularities, typos, misspelled words, or other mechanical problems. *Always* take time to run your spelling checker, if available. Finally, evaluate your product. Before any letter leaves her desk at Ben & Jerry's, Alice always rereads it and puts herself in the shoes of the reader: "How would I feel if I were receiving it?"

Direct Request Letters

Many of your business request letters will fall into one of three categories: (1) asking for information or action, (2) placing orders for products, or (3) making a claim requiring an adjustment when something has gone wrong. In this section you'll learn how to write good letters for each of these circumstances. Before you write any letter, though, consider its costs in terms of your time and work load. Whenever possible, don't write! Instead of asking for information, could you find it yourself? Would a telephone call or a brief visit to a coworker solve the problem quickly? If not, use the direct pattern to present your request efficiently.

Requesting Information and Action

A direct letter may open with a question or a polite request.

The majority of your business letters will request information or action. Suppose you have questions about a payroll accounting service your company is considering or you need to ask a customer to supply missing data from an order. For these direct messages put the main idea first. If your request involves several questions, you could open with a polite request, such as *Will you please answer the following questions about your payroll service.* Note that although this request sounds like a question, it's actually a disguised command. Since you expect an action rather than a reply, punctuate this polite command with a period instead of a question mark.

In the letter body explain your purpose and provide details. If you have questions, express them in parallel form so that they are balanced grammatically. To elicit the most information, pose open-ended questions *(What computer lock-down device can you recommend?)* instead of yes-or-no questions *(Do you carry computer lock-down devices?)*. If you are asking someone to do something, be sure your tone is polite and undemanding. Remember that your written words cannot be softened by a smile. When possible, focus on benefits to the reader *(To ensure that you receive the exact sweater you want, send us your color choice)*.

In the closing tell the reader courteously what is to be done. If a date is important, set an end date and explain why. Many request letters end simply with *Thank you,* forcing the reader to review the contents to determine what is expected and when. You can save the reader time by spelling out the action to be taken. Avoid other overused endings such as *Thank you for your cooperation* (trite), *Thank you in advance for . . .* (presumptuous), and *If you have any questions, do not hesitate to call me* (suggests that you didn't make yourself clear).

It's always appropriate to show appreciation, but try to do so in a fresh and efficient manner. For example, you could hook your thanks to the end date *(Thanks for returning the questionnaire before May 5, when we will begin tabulation)*. You might connect your appreciation to a statement developing reader benefits *(We are grateful for the information you will provide because it will help us serve you better)*. Or you could describe briefly how the information will help you *(I genuinely appreciate this information that will enable me to . . .)*. When possible, make it easy for the reader to comply with your request *(Note your answers on this sheet and return it in the postage-paid envelope)*. When Alice Blachly of Ben & Jerry's requests information from customers, she provides the company's toll-free number so that they can respond without having to write a letter.

● **Direct request letters maintain a courteous tone, spell out what needs to be done, and focus on reader benefits.**

Let's now analyze the first draft of a direct request letter written by office manager Melanie Marshall. She wants information about computer security devices, but the first version of her letter is confusing and inefficient. Melanie makes a common mistake: writing a message "backwards." Notice that her letter starts with the problem, telling the story from the writer's perspective, not the reader's.

Dear Ms. Ivorson:

Our insurance rates will be increased soon if we don't install security devices on our computer equipment. We have considered some local suppliers, but none had exactly what we wanted.

Starts with background information and explanation instead of request.

We need a device that can be used to secure separate computer components at a workstation including a computer, keyboard, and monitor. We currently own 18 computers, keyboard, and monitors, along with six printers.

Fails to organize information into logical order.

We wonder if professionals are needed to install your security devices. We're also interested in whether the devices can be easily removed when we need to move equipment around. We are, of course, very interested in prices and quantity discounts, if you offer them.

Confuses reader by jumping around among many topics. Fails to ask specific questions.

Thank you for your attention to this matter.

Ends with cliché. Fails to reveal what to do and when to do it.

Melanie's second version, shown in Figure 6.3, begins more directly. The opening sentence introduces the purpose immediately so that the reader quickly knows why the letter was sent. Melanie then provides background information. Most importantly, she organizes all her requests into specific questions, which are sure to bring a better result than her previous diffuse request. Study the 3-×-3 writing process in Figure 6.3 to see the plan Melanie followed in improving her letter.

Placing Orders

You may occasionally need to write a letter that orders supplies, merchandise, or services. Generally, such purchases are made by telephoning an order desk or by filling out a catalog form and faxing or mailing it to the vendor. Sometimes, however, you may not have a telephone number or an order form but only an address. To order items by letter, supply the same information that an order blank would

● **Letters placing orders specify items or services, quantities, dates, prices, and payment method.**

FIGURE 6.3 ● Direct Request Letter

The Three Phases of the Writing Process

1

Analyze
The purpose of this letter is to gain specific data about devices to lock down computer equipment.

Anticipate
The audience is expected to be a busy but receptive customer service representative.

Adapt
Because the reader will probably react positively to this inquiry, the direct pattern is best.

2

Research
Determine how much equipment must be locked down and what questions must be answered.

Organize
Open by asking the reader to answer questions about security devices. In the body provide details and arrange any questions logically. Close by courteously providing a specific deadline.

Compose
Draft the first copy on a computer.

3

Revise
Improve the clarity by grouping similar ideas together. Improve readability by listing and numbering questions. Eliminate wordiness.

Proofread
Look for typos and spelling errors. Check punctuation and placement. Indent the second line of all listed items for a clean look.

Evaluate
Is this message attractive and easily comprehended?

Format 6.3

inner circle graphics
5489 North Clark Street, Chicago, IL 60640
(708) 488•3310 phone (708) 488•3319 fax

February 3, 1994

Ms. Sue Ivorson, Customer Service
Micro Supplies and Software
P.O. Box 800
Fort Atkinson, WI 53538

Dear Ms. Ivorson:

Please provide information and recommendations regarding security equipment to prevent the theft of office computers, keyboards, monitors, and printers. — Introduces purpose immediately

Explains need for information — Our office now has 18 computer workstations and 6 printers that we must secure to desks or counters. Answers to the following questions will help us select the best devices for our purpose.

1. What device would you recommend that can secure a workstation consisting of a computer, monitor, and keyboard?

2. What expertise and equipment are required to install and remove the security device?

3. How much is each device? Do you offer quantity discounts, and if so, how much?

— Groups open-ended questions into list for quick comprehension and best feedback

Courteously provides end date and reason — Because our insurance rates will be increased if this equipment is not secured before April 1, we would appreciate your response by February 15.

Sincerely,

Melanie Marshall

Melanie Marshall
Office Manager

require. In the opening let the reader know immediately that this is a purchase authorization and not merely an information inquiry. Instead of *I saw a number of interesting items in your catalog*, begin directly with order language such as *Please send me by UPS the following items from your fall merchandise catalog*.

If you're ordering many items, list them vertically in the body of your letter. Include as much specific data as possible: quantity, order number, complete description, unit price, and total price. Show the total amount, and figure the tax and shipping costs if possible. The more information you provide, the less likely that a mistake will be made.

In the closing tell how you plan to pay for the merchandise. Enclose a check, provide a credit card number, or ask to be billed. Many business organizations have credit agreements with their regular suppliers that enable them to send goods without prior payment. In addition to payment information, tell when the merchandise should be sent and express appreciation. The following letter requesting personnel cards and envelopes for a human resources department illustrates the order letter pattern.

Ladies and gentlemen:

Please send by express mail the following items from your summer catalog.

Order letter opens directly with authorization for purchase, method of delivery, and catalog source.

250	No. OG-18 Payroll greeting cards	$102.50
250	No. OG-22 Payroll card envelopes	21.95
100	No. OM-01 Performance greeting cards	80.00
	Subtotal	$204.45
	Tax at 7%	14.31
	Shipping	24.00
	Total	$242.76

Uses orderly columns to make quantity, catalog number, description, and price stand out.

Calculates totals to prevent possible mistakes.

We would appreciate receiving these cards immediately since we are initiating an employee recognition program February 12. Enclosed is our check for $242.76. If additional charges are necessary, please bill my company.

Expresses appreciation and tells when items are expected. Identifies method of payment.

6.13, 6.14

Making Claims

Claims letters open with a clear problem statement, support the claim with specifics, and close with a statement of goodwill.

In business many things can go wrong—promised shipments are late, warranted goods fail, or service is disappointing. When you as a customer must write to identify or correct a wrong, the letter is called a "claim." Simple claims are those to which you expect the receiver to agree readily.

Most businesses today honestly want to satisfy their customers. The 1990s has been called the decade of quality—in terms of both products and service. To compete globally and to pump up local markets, American industry is particularly sold on the idea of improving service quality.[5] Like Ben & Jerry's, many organizations are increasingly aware of the importance of listening to consumers. Since it costs three times as much to win a new customer as it does to retain a current one, businesses especially want to hear what customers have to say. And they know that customers are quite perceptive. As one computer executive says, "Quite frankly, customers are actually wrong only about 2 percent of the time."[6]

Because you can expect a positive response when you have a legitimate claim or complaint, you should open a claim letter with a clear statement of the problem or with the action you want the receiver to take. You might expect a replacement, a refund, a new order, credit to your account, correction of a billing error, free repairs, free inspection, or cancellation of an order. When the remedy is obvious, state it immediately *(Please send us 24 Royal hot-air popcorn poppers to replace the 24 hot-oil poppers sent in error with our order shipped January 4).* When the remedy is less obvious, you might ask for a change in policy or procedure or simply for an explanation *(Because three of our employees with confirmed reservations were refused rooms September 16 in your hotel, would you please clarify your policy regarding reservations and late arrivals).*

Providing details without getting angry improves the effectiveness of a claim letter.

In the body of a claim letter, explain the problem and justify your request. Provide the necessary details so that the difficulty can be corrected without further correspondence. Avoid becoming angry or trying to fix blame. Bear in mind that the person reading your letter is seldom responsible for the problem. Instead, state the facts logically, objectively, and unemotionally; let the reader decide on the causes. Include copies of all pertinent documents such as invoices, sales slips, catalog descriptions, and repair records. When service is involved, cite names of individuals spoken to and dates of calls. Assume that a company honestly wants to please its customers—because most do. When an alternative remedy exists, spell it out *(If you are unable to send 24 Royal hot-air popcorn poppers immediately, please credit our account now and notify us when they become available).*

Conclude a claim letter with a courteous statement that promotes goodwill and expresses a desire for continued relations. If appropriate, include an end date *(We realize that mistakes in ordering and shipping sometimes occur. Because we've enjoyed your prompt service in the past, we hope that you will be able to send us the hot-air poppers by January 15).*

Written claims submitted promptly are taken more seriously than delayed ones.

Finally, in making claims, act promptly. Delaying claims makes them appear less important, as well as more difficult to verify. By taking the time to put your claim in writing, you indicate your seriousness. A written claim also starts a record of the problem should later action be necessary, so keep a copy of your letter.

Figure 6.4 shows a first draft of a hostile claim that vents the writer's anger but accomplishes little else. Its tone is belligerent, and it assumes that the company intentionally mischarged the customer. Furthermore, it fails to tell the reader how to remedy the problem. The revision tempers the tone, describes the problem objectively, provides facts and figures, and, most importantly, specifies exactly what the customer wants done.

To sum up, use the direct pattern with the main idea first when you expect little resistance to letters making requests. The following checklist reviews the direct strategy for information and action requests, orders, and adjustments.

Checklist for Writing Direct Requests

Information or Action Request Letters

- ✔ **Open by stating the main idea.** To elicit information, ask a question or issue a polite command *(Will you please answer the following questions . . .).*
- ✔ **Explain and justify the request.** In seeking information use open-ended questions structured in parallel, balanced form.
- ✔ **Request action in the closing.** Express appreciation, and set an end date if appropriate. Avoid clichés *(Thank you for your cooperation).*

Order Letters

- ✔ **Open by authorizing the purchase.** Use order language *(Please send me . . .),* designate the delivery method, and state your information source (such as a catalog, advertisement, or magazine article).

FIGURE 6.4 ● Direct Claim Letter

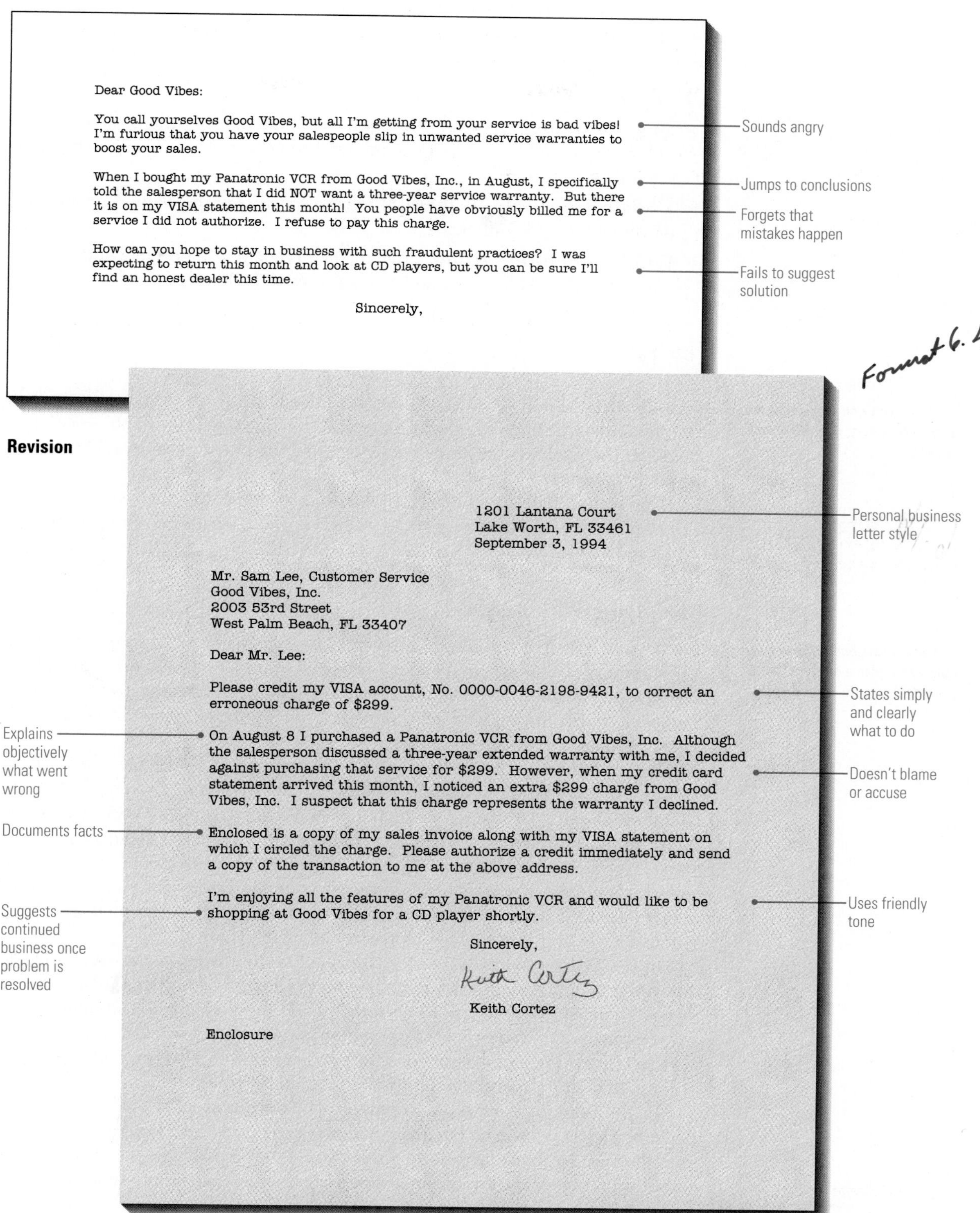

First Draft

Dear Good Vibes:

You call yourselves Good Vibes, but all I'm getting from your service is bad vibes! I'm furious that you have your salespeople slip in unwanted service warranties to boost your sales.

When I bought my Panatronic VCR from Good Vibes, Inc., in August, I specifically told the salesperson that I did NOT want a three-year service warranty. But there it is on my VISA statement this month! You people have obviously billed me for a service I did not authorize. I refuse to pay this charge.

How can you hope to stay in business with such fraudulent practices? I was expecting to return this month and look at CD players, but you can be sure I'll find an honest dealer this time.

Sincerely,

Sounds angry
Jumps to conclusions
Forgets that mistakes happen
Fails to suggest solution
Format 6. 4

Revision

1201 Lantana Court
Lake Worth, FL 33461
September 3, 1994

Mr. Sam Lee, Customer Service
Good Vibes, Inc.
2003 53rd Street
West Palm Beach, FL 33407

Dear Mr. Lee:

Please credit my VISA account, No. 0000-0046-2198-9421, to correct an erroneous charge of $299.

On August 8 I purchased a Panatronic VCR from Good Vibes, Inc. Although the salesperson discussed a three-year extended warranty with me, I decided against purchasing that service for $299. However, when my credit card statement arrived this month, I noticed an extra $299 charge from Good Vibes, Inc. I suspect that this charge represents the warranty I declined.

Enclosed is a copy of my sales invoice along with my VISA statement on which I circled the charge. Please authorize a credit immediately and send a copy of the transaction to me at the above address.

I'm enjoying all the features of my Panatronic VCR and would like to be shopping at Good Vibes for a CD player shortly.

Sincerely,

Keith Cortez

Keith Cortez

Enclosure

Personal business letter style
States simply and clearly what to do
Explains objectively what went wrong
Doesn't blame or accuse
Documents facts
Suggests continued business once problem is resolved
Uses friendly tone

✔ **List items in the body.** Include quantity, order number, description, unit price, extension, tax, shipping, and total costs.

✔ **Close with the payment data.** Tell how you are paying and when you expect delivery. Express appreciation.

Claim Letters

✔ **Begin with the purpose.** Present a clear statement of the problem or the action requested—such as a refund, replacement, credit, explanation, or correction of error.

✔ **Explain objectively.** In the body tell the specifics of the claim. Provide copies of necessary documents.

✔ **End by requesting action.** Include an end date if important. Add a pleasant, forward-looking statement. Keep a copy of the letter.

Direct Reply Letters

● **When you can respond favorably to requests, use the direct pattern.**

Occasionally, you will receive requests for information or action. In these cases your first task is deciding whether to comply. If the decision is favorable, your letter should let the reader know immediately by using the direct pattern and frontloading the good news.

This section focuses on direct reply letters in three situations: (1) complying with requests for information or action, (2) acknowledging orders, and (3) granting claims and adjustments.

Complying With Requests

● **Letters responding to requests may open with a subject line to identify the topic immediately.**

Often, your messages will respond favorably to requests for information or action. A customer wants information about a product. A supplier asks to arrange a meeting. Another business inquires about one of your procedures or about a former employee. In complying with such requests, you'll want to apply the same direct pattern you used in making requests.

The opening of a direct reply letter might contain a subject line, which helps the reader recognize the topic immediately. Usually appearing two lines below the salutation, the subject line refers in abbreviated form to previous correspondence and/or summarizes a message (*Subject: Your Letter of August 5 About Award Programs*). It often omits articles (*a, an, the*), is not a complete sentence, and does not end with a period. Knowledgeable business communicators use a subject line to refer to earlier correspondence so that in the first sentence, the most emphatic spot in a letter, they are free to emphasize the main idea.

In the first sentence deliver the information the reader wants. Avoid wordy, drawn-out openings such as *I have before me your letter of August 5, in which you request information about . . .* More forceful and more efficient is an opener that answers the inquiry (*Here is the information you wanted about . . .*). When agreeing to a request for action, announce the good news promptly (*Yes, I will be happy to speak to your business communication class on the topic of . . .*).

In the body of your reply, supply explanations and additional information. Because a letter written on company stationery is considered a legally binding contract, be sure to check facts and figures carefully. If a policy or procedure needs authorization, seek approval from a supervisor or executive before writing the let-

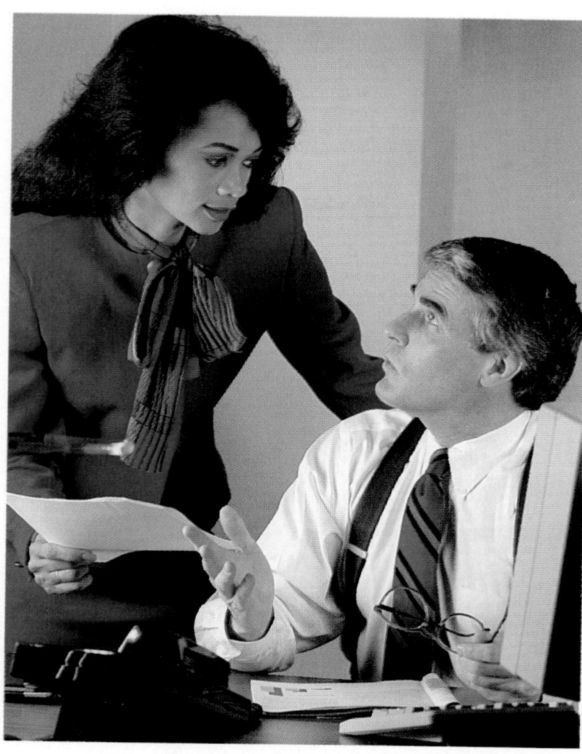

Before answering nonroutine requests, you may need to confer with coworkers and superiors to decide how to respond. Once you decide to comply with a request, announce the good news directly in the first sentence of your reply. In letters to customers you may provide extra information about products and services.

ter. When answering a group of questions or providing considerable data, arrange the information logically and make it readable by using lists, tables, headings, boldface, italics, or other graphic devices.

When customers or prospective customers inquire about products or services, your response should do more than merely supply answers. You'll also want to promote your organization and products. Often, companies have particular products and services they want to spotlight. Thus, when a customer writes about one product, provide helpful information that satisfies the inquiry, but consider using the opportunity to introduce another product as well. Be sure to present the promotional material with attention to the "you" view and to reader benefits *(You can use our standardized tests to free you from time-consuming employment screening).* You'll learn more about special techniques for developing sales and persuasive messages in Chapter 9.

Responding to customer inquiries provides a good opportunity to promote your business.

In concluding, make sure you are cordial and personal. Refer to the information provided or to its use *(I hope this data about our experiences helps you solve your microcomputing disk storage problems).* If further action is required, describe the procedure and help the reader with specifics *(The Small Business Administration publishes a number of helpful booklets. Its address is . . .).*

In replying to a customer's request for information, the writer in Figure 6.5 begins with a subject line that immediately identifies the topic and refers to previous correspondence. He uses the first sentence to present the most important information. Then he itemizes his list of responses to the customer's questions. If he had written these responses in paragraph form, they would have been less emphatic and more difficult to read. He goes on to describe and promote the product, being careful to show how it would benefit the customer. And he concludes by referring specifically to pages in an enclosed pamphlet and providing a number for the customer's response.

FIGURE 6.5 ● Customer Reply Letter

The Three Phases of the Writing Process

1

Analyze
The purpose of this letter is to provide helpful information and to promote company products.

Anticipate
The reader is the intelligent owner of a small business who needs help with personnel administration.

Adapt
Because the reader requested this data, she will be receptive to the letter. Use the direct pattern.

2

Research
Gather facts to answer the business owner's questions. Consult brochures and pamphlets.

Organize
Prepare a scratch outline. Plan for a fast, direct opening. Use bulleted answers to the business owner's three questions.

Compose
Write the first draft on computer. Strive for short sentences and paragraphs.

3

Revise
Eliminate jargon and wordiness. Look for ways to explain how the product fits the reader's needs. Revise for "you" view.

Proofread
Double-check the form of numbers *(July 12, page 6, 8 to 5 EST).*

Evaluate
Does this letter answer the customer's questions and encourage an order?

Office Headquarters, Inc.
443 Tecumseh Avenue, Garden City, New York 11530

July 15, 1994

Ms. Jessica White
White-Rather Enterprises
1349 Century Boulevard
Wichita Falls, TX 76308

Dear Ms. White:

SUBJECT: YOUR JULY 12 INQUIRY ABOUT PERSONNEL RECORD-KEEPING SYSTEM

Identifies previous correspondence and subject

Puts most important information first

Yes, we do offer a personnel record-keeping system specially designed for small businesses. I'm happy to answer your three questions about this system.

Lists answers to sender's questions in order asked

1. Our Personnel Manager system provides standard employee application forms that meet current government regulations.

2. The system includes an interviewer's guide for structured employee interviews, as well as a scripted format for checking references by telephone.

3. Yes, you can update your employees' records easily without the need for computer programs, hardware, or training.

Emphasizes "you" view

Our Personnel Manager system was specially designed to provide you with expert forms for interviewing, verifying references, recording attendance, evaluating performance, and tracking the status of your employees. We even provide you with step-by-step instructions and suggested procedures. You can treat your employees as if you had a professional human resources specialist on your staff.

Links sales promotion to reader benefits

Helps reader find information by citing pages

On page 6 of the enclosed pamphlet you can read about our Personnel Manager system. To receive samples of these items or to ask questions about their use, just call 1-800-354-5500. Our specialists are eager to help you weekdays from 8 to 5 EST.

Makes it easy to respond

Sincerely,

Mark E. Austin

Mark E. Austin
Senior Marketing Representative

Enclosure

FIGURE 6.6 ● **Direct Reply From Ben & Jerry's**

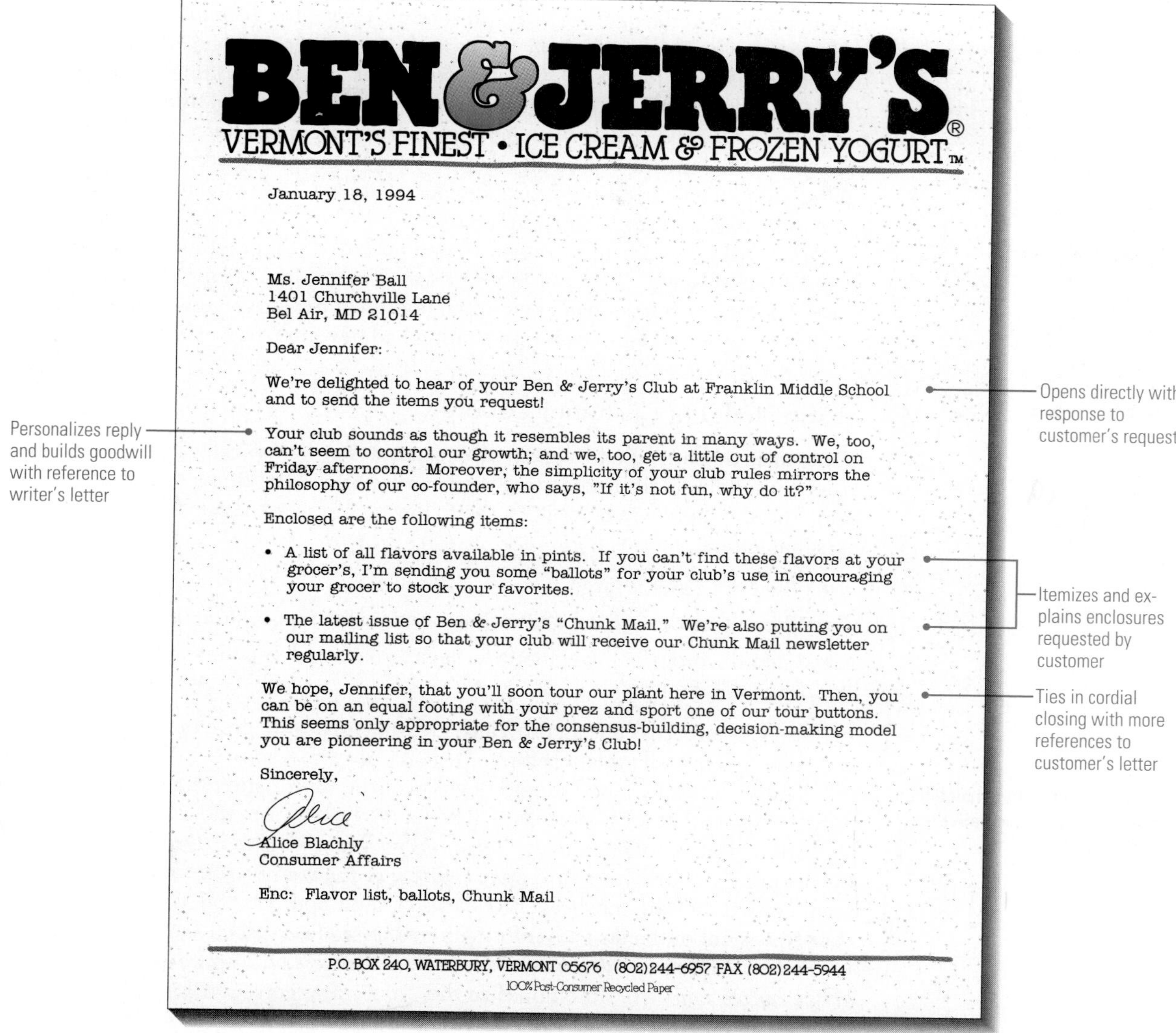

BEN & JERRY'S®
VERMONT'S FINEST • ICE CREAM & FROZEN YOGURT™

January 18, 1994

Ms. Jennifer Ball
1401 Churchville Lane
Bel Air, MD 21014

Dear Jennifer:

We're delighted to hear of your Ben & Jerry's Club at Franklin Middle School and to send the items you request!

Your club sounds as though it resembles its parent in many ways. We, too, can't seem to control our growth; and we, too, get a little out of control on Friday afternoons. Moreover, the simplicity of your club rules mirrors the philosophy of our co-founder, who says, "If it's not fun, why do it?"

Enclosed are the following items:

- A list of all flavors available in pints. If you can't find these flavors at your grocer's, I'm sending you some "ballots" for your club's use in encouraging your grocer to stock your favorites.
- The latest issue of Ben & Jerry's "Chunk Mail." We're also putting you on our mailing list so that your club will receive our Chunk Mail newsletter regularly.

We hope, Jennifer, that you'll soon tour our plant here in Vermont. Then, you can be on an equal footing with your prez and sport one of our tour buttons. This seems only appropriate for the consensus-building, decision-making model you are pioneering in your Ben & Jerry's Club!

Sincerely,

Alice Blachly
Consumer Affairs

Enc: Flavor list, ballots, Chunk Mail

P.O. BOX 240, WATERBURY, VERMONT 05676 (802) 244-6957 FAX (802) 244-5944
100% Post-Consumer Recycled Paper

Opens directly with response to customer's request
Personalizes reply and builds goodwill with reference to writer's letter
Itemizes and explains enclosures requested by customer
Ties in cordial closing with more references to customer's letter

A direct reply letter written by Alice Blachly, shown in Figure 6.6, responds to a request from a young Ben & Jerry's customer. Alice announces the letter's purpose immediately and also establishes rapport with the reader by describing similarities between the reader's Ben & Jerry's club and its parent organization. The body of the letter includes a bulleted list and an explanation of the items Alice is sending. Notice how Alice uses this opportunity to promote business by enclosing "ballots," on which consumers suggest to local grocers favorite ice cream flavors to be stocked. The cordial, personalized closing concludes a direct reply letter that is sure to build goodwill and promote future business while delivering the information sought.

The direct pattern is also appropriate for messages that are mostly good news but may have some negative elements. For example, a return policy has time limits;

In mixed-news messages the good news should precede the bad.

an air fare may contain holiday restrictions; a speaker can come but not at the time requested; an appliance can be repaired but not replaced. When the message is mixed, emphasize the good news by presenting it first *(Yes, I would be delighted to address your marketing class on the topic of . . .)*. Then, explain why a problem exists *(My schedule for the week of October 10 takes me to Washington and Philadelphia, where I am . . .)*. Present the bad news in the middle *(Although I cannot meet with your class at that time, perhaps we can schedule a date during the week of . . .)*. End the message cordially by returning to the good news *(Thanks for the invitation. I'm looking forward to arranging a date in October when I can talk with your students about careers in marketing)*.

Your goal is to present the negative news clearly without letting it become the focus of the message. Thus, you want to spend more time talking about the good news. And by placing the bad news in the middle of the letter, you deemphasize it. You'll learn other techniques for presenting bad news in Chapter 8.

Acknowledging Customer Orders

Companies that are able to ship all of a customer's order typically acknowledge the order by sending a printed card. These cards confirm the items ordered and tell when the shipment will be sent. In the following instances, though, it pays to send personal letters

- When the order is large
- When the order is from a first-time or an infrequent customer
- When the order has irregularities, such as back-ordered items, delivery delays, or missing items

In these special cases you can use a letter to build goodwill, promote your products, and cement a friendly relationship.

Order reply letters identify up front when and how delivery will be made.

Your order reply letter should begin with the information the customer most wants: when and how the delivery will be made. Don't waste the reader's time with an obvious statement such as *We have received your order of December 1.* Even the seemingly courteous expression *Thank you for your recent order* doesn't tell readers what they are most eager to learn. To show appreciation, you might couple your statement of thanks with information about delivery, such as *Thanks for your December 1 order, which was sent by Federal Express on December 4 and should arrive by December 6.* To emphasize the "you" view, consider this opening: *Your computer paper and printer ribbons were sent by UPS, and you should be receiving them by December 4, two days ahead of your deadline.*

The body of an order reply letter discusses relevant details and promotes new products or presents resale information.

In the body of the letter, discuss details of the order, including any irregularities. If an item is unavailable, must be sent from another location, or is back-ordered, discuss this negative news as positively as possible *(Although the ribbon cartridges for your printer must be sent from our Denver warehouse, you should receive them within two weeks)*. The middle of the letter is also an appropriate place for promoting new products or for presenting resale information. *Resale* is a marketing technique that reassures customers that their choices were good ones by emphasizing a product's best features, popularity, economy, and usefulness. A resale statement such as *The ribbons you have selected are the best we make* confirms the customer's discrimination and good judgment. Whereas resale information emphasizes a product that the customer has already selected, *sales promotion* focuses on additional products the customer may want. Both kinds of information are most effective when customers see how they can benefit from the products.

In the conclusion you'll want to make a personalized statement that shows reader benefits, expresses appreciation, offers further help, or conveys the expectation of continued good relations. For example: *Thanks for your order, Mr. Waters. If you have any questions about installing the ribbon cartridges or ordering other office supplies, give our experts a call at 1-800-555-3241.*

In the following case a bicycle helmet manufacturer could have acknowledged an order merely by sending a printed card or a form letter. Instead, this smart manufacturer seized the opportunity to welcome a new customer, resell the products already ordered, and promote a new line. Notice how the letter defuses the bad news that part of the order will be delayed.

Dear Ms. Brown:

In less than one week, your sporting goods store will have your order of ProTec bicycle helmets for adults. These adult helmets were shipped by UPS on October 12.

Reveals when and how shipment will arrive.

Because the youth helmets you ordered have become very popular as holiday gift items, we are temporarily out of stock. We expect a shipment by October 17 and will send them to you immediately. You won't be billed, of course, until they are sent.

Presents bad news in positive manner. Explains why item is delayed. Maintains "you" view.

As a new customer, you may be interested to know that the ProTec bike helmets you ordered are tops in the field. They received the highest rating by *Consumer Reports* in tests comparing 15 of the best-known models. Because of their impact protection and the strength of their straps and buckles, they will provide your customers with what is probably the safest bike helmet made today.

Builds customer's confidence in product with resale information. Creates bond with reader by offering special data for the new customer.

It's estimated that fewer than 10 percent of the nation's 85 million bike riders wear helmets. Why such resistance? Some of your customers have probably told you that helmets are uncomfortable and look "nerdy." However, a new generation of helmets has done away with hard-shell designs. Your customers will marvel at the new thin, semirigid shell helmets made by Race Team. They're light, safe, and incredibly colorful. Enclosed is literature describing the all-new Race Team fashion helmets, now offered at low introductory prices.

Recognizes weakness in market and ties it in with promotion of new product. Takes advantage of this customer's already identified interest in bike helmets to cultivate desire for new bike helmet.

We genuinely appreciate your order for ProTec helmets. To add the customer-pleasing fashion line of Race Team helmets to your inventory or to ask questions about your current order, just call 1-800-310-BIKE.

Closes with thanks and offers of help. Promotes future business.

6.21
6.22

Granting Adjustments and Claims

● Businesses generally respond favorably to claims because of legal constraints and the desire to maintain customer goodwill.

Even the best-run and best-loved businesses occasionally receive claims or complaints from consumers. Most businesses grant claims and make adjustments promptly—they replace merchandise, refund money, extend discounts, send coupons, and repair goods. Businesses make favorable adjustments to legitimate claims for two reasons. First, consumers are protected by contractual and tort law for recovery of damages.[7] Thus, for example, if you find an insect in a package of frozen peas, the food processor of that package is bound by contractual law to replace it. And if you suffer injury, the processor may be liable for damages. Second, and more obviously, most organizations genuinely want to please their customers and maintain goodwill to encourage repeat business.

Wise business organizations recognize customer complaints as an important source of feedback. These organizations listen carefully to the reasons for dissatisfaction and then jump at the chance to remedy the problem.

In reality, however, few customers take the time to complain. "If you have one customer who complains," says James W. Beltran, customer advocate for *Reader's Digest,* "there are 10 or 15 others out there who are dissatisfied, but who aren't bothering to complain."[8] Unless a business knows what's wrong, of course, it can't

At smart companies customer service is an art. L. L. Bean representatives are trained to ask complaining customers what will satisfy them—and then to do what the customers ask. If employees don't want to comply with customers' requests, they must clear their decisions with higher levels of management. Just the opposite is true in most companies, where employees must ask management to approve customers' requests. At L. L. Bean, only a director can say no to a customer, and that doesn't happen very often.

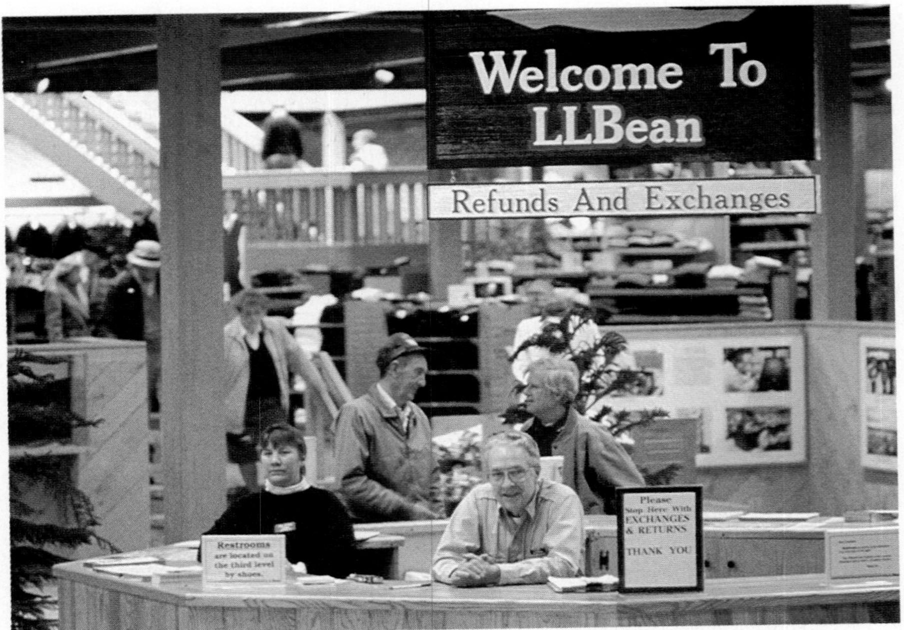

fix the problem. Another important reason for welcoming complaints relates to repeat business. Bill Shea, director of Customer Service at the multimillion-dollar catalog company L. L. Bean, says, "Research shows that customers who complain tend to be your most loyal customers and have a greater propensity for ordering from you again. If they have problems and don't bother to complain, they usually won't bother to reorder, either."[9]

Favorable responses to customer claims follow the direct pattern; unfavorable responses follow the indirect.

In responding to customer claims, you must first decide whether to grant the claim or not. Unless the claim is obviously fraudulent or represents an excessive sum, you'll probably grant it. When you say yes, your adjustment letter will be good news to the reader, so you'll want to use the direct pattern. When your response is no, the indirect pattern is appropriate. Chapter 8 discusses the indirect pattern for conveying negative news.

You'll have three goals in adjustment letters:

- Rectifying the wrong, if one exists
- Regaining the confidence of the customer
- Promoting further business

Opening sentences to positive adjustment letters tell the good news quickly.

The opening of a positive adjustment letter should approve the customer's claim immediately. Notice how quickly the following openers announce the good news:

> The enclosed $250 refund check demonstrates our desire to satisfy our customers and earn their confidence.
>
> You will be receiving shortly a new Techtronic cordless telephone to replace the one that shattered when dropped recently.
>
> Please take your Sanyo cassette tape deck to A-1 Appliance Service, 220 Orange Street, Pasadena, where it will be repaired at no cost to you.
>
> You're right! We agree that the warranty on your American Standard Model UC600 dishwasher should be extended for six months.

In making an adjustment, avoid sounding resentful or grudging. Once you decide to grant a claim, do so willingly. Remember that a primary goal in adjustments is future business. Statements that sound reluctant *(Although we generally refuse to extend warranties, we're willing to make an exception in this case)* may cause greater dissatisfaction than no response at all.

Adjustment letters seek to right wrongs, regain customer confidence, and promote further business.

In the body of an adjustment letter, your goal is to win back the confidence of the customer. You can do this by explaining what caused the problem (if you know) or by describing the measures you are taking to avoid recurrences of the problem, such as in the following:

> In preparing our products, we take special care to see that they are wholesome and free of foreign matter. Approved spraying procedures in the field control insects when necessary during the growing season. Our processing plants use screens, air curtains, ultraviolet lights, and other devices to exclude insects. Moreover, we inspect and clean every product to ensure that insects are not present.

Notice that this explanation does not admit error. Many companies sidestep the issue of responsibility because they feel that such an admission damages their credibility or might even encourage legal liability. Others admit errors indirectly *(Oversights may sometimes occur)* or even directly *(Once in a while a product that is less than perfect goes out)*. The major focus of attention, however, should be on explaining how diligently you work to avoid disappointing your customers.

Another sticky issue is whether to apologize. A study of adjustment letters received by consumers showed that half the letters contained apologies, either in the opening or in the closing.[10] Most business writing experts, however, advise against apologies, contending that they are counterproductive and merely remind the customer of unpleasantness related to the claim. If you do apologize, do it early and briefly. Do not apologize if you are not to blame or if the error is minor. Since you are agreeing to the claim, your focus should be on how you are complying with the request.

Concentrate on how you are complying with the request, not on apologizing.

The language of adjustment letters must be particularly sensitive, since customers are already upset. Here are some don'ts:

- Don't use negative words *(trouble, regret, misunderstanding, fault, error, inconvenience, you claim)*.
- Don't blame customers—even when they may be at fault.
- Don't blame individuals or departments within your organization; it's unprofessional.
- Don't make unrealistic promises; you can't guarantee that the situation will never reoccur.

To regain the confidence of your reader, consider including resale information. Describe a product's features and any special applications that might appeal to the reader. Promote a new product if it seems appropriate.

To close an adjustment letter, assume that the problem has been resolved and that future business will continue. You might express appreciation that the reader wrote, extend thanks for past business, refer to your desire to be of service, or mention a new product. Here are a variety of effective adjustment letter closings for various purposes:

> You were most helpful in informing us of this situation and permitting us to correct it. We appreciate your thoughtfulness in writing to us.
>
> Thanks for writing. Your satisfaction is important to us.

We hope that this refund check convinces you that service to our customers is our No. 1 priority. Our goal is to earn your confidence and continue to justify that confidence with quality products and excellent service.

Your cordless telephone will come in handy when you're playing and working outside this summer. For additional summer enjoyment take a look at the portable CD player on page 37 of the enclosed catalog. We value your business and look forward to your future orders.

The tone of an adjustment letter should suggest that the writer is on the customer's side.

The adjustment letter in Figure 6.7 offers to replace dead rose bushes. It's very possible that grower error caused the plants to die, yet the letter doesn't blame the customer. Notice, too, how resale and sales promotion information is introduced without seeming pushy. Most importantly, the tone of the letter suggests that the company is in the customer's corner and wants to do what is right.

Although the direct pattern works for many requests and replies, it obviously won't work for every situation. With more practice and experience, you'll be able to alter the pattern and apply the writing process to other communication problems. The following checklist summarizes the process of writing direct replies.

Checklist for Writing Direct Replies

Complying with Requests

- ✔ **Use a subject line.** Identify previous correspondence and the topic of this letter.
- ✔ **Open directly.** In the first sentence deliver the information the reader wants (*Yes, I can meet with your class* or *Here is the information you requested*). If the message is mixed, present the best news first.
- ✔ **In the body provide explanations and additional information.** Arrange this information logically, perhaps using a list, headings, or columns. For prospective customers build your company image and promote your products.
- ✔ **End with a cordial, personalized statement.** If further action is required, tell the reader how to proceed and give helpful details.

Acknowledging Customer Orders

- ✔ **Open with delivery information.** Tell when and how delivery will be made.
- ✔ **In the body give details of the order.** Discuss any irregularities, such as delays or back-ordered items. Use resale information to reassure customers of their wise choices. Consider sales promotion to highlight other products.
- ✔ **Close positively.** Show appreciation, offer help, and/or anticipate future orders.

Granting Claims and Adjustments

- ✔ **Open with approval.** Comply with the customer's claim immediately. Avoid sounding grudging or reluctant.
- ✔ **In the body win back the customer's confidence.** Explain the cause of the problem or describe your ongoing efforts to avoid such difficulties. Focus on your efforts to satisfy customers rather than on admitting blame or apologizing. Avoid negative words, accusations, and unrealistic promises. Consider including resale and sales promotion information.
- ✔ **Close positively.** Express appreciation to the customer for writing, extend thanks for past business, anticipate continued orders, refer to your desire to be of service, and/or mention a new product if it seems appropriate.

FIGURE 6.7 ● Adjustment Letter

Tips for Letter Formatting

- Single-space business letters. Double-space between paragraphs.
- Place the date on line 13 or 2 lines below letterhead.
- Set margins so that letter looks centered on page.
- Leave three blank lines for the handwritten signature.
- Use a colon after the salutation and a comma after the complimentary close.
- Be consistent in letter format. For example, use full block with all lines starting at the left margin or modified block as shown here.

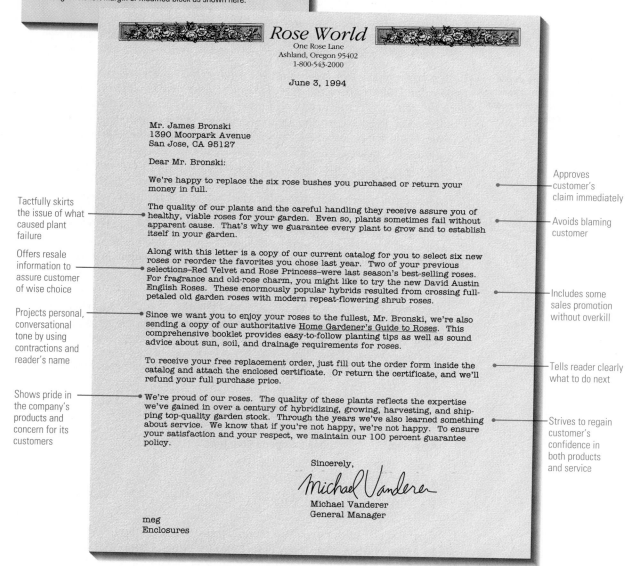

Rose World
One Rose Lane
Ashland, Oregon 95402
1-800-543-2000

June 3, 1994

Mr. James Bronski
1390 Moorpark Avenue
San Jose, CA 95127

Dear Mr. Bronski:

We're happy to replace the six rose bushes you purchased or return your money in full. *(Approves customer's claim immediately)*

The quality of our plants and the careful handling they receive assure you of healthy, viable roses for your garden. Even so, plants sometimes fail without apparent cause. That's why we guarantee every plant to grow and to establish itself in your garden. *(Tactfully skirts the issue of what caused plant failure)* *(Avoids blaming customer)*

Along with this letter is a copy of our current catalog for you to select six new roses or reorder the favorites you chose last year. Two of your previous selections–Red Velvet and Rose Princess–were last season's best-selling roses. For fragrance and old-rose charm, you might like to try the new David Austin English Roses. These enormously popular hybrids resulted from crossing full-petaled old garden roses with modern repeat-flowering shrub roses. *(Offers resale information to assure customer of wise choice)* *(Includes some sales promotion without overkill)*

Since we want you to enjoy your roses to the fullest, Mr. Bronski, we're also sending a copy of our authoritative Home Gardener's Guide to Roses. This comprehensive booklet provides easy-to-follow planting tips as well as sound advice about sun, soil, and drainage requirements for roses. *(Projects personal, conversational tone by using contractions and reader's name)*

To receive your free replacement order, just fill out the order form inside the catalog and attach the enclosed certificate. Or return the certificate, and we'll refund your full purchase price. *(Tells reader clearly what to do next)*

We're proud of our roses. The quality of these plants reflects the expertise we've gained in over a century of hybridizing, growing, harvesting, and shipping top-quality garden stock. Through the years we've also learned something about service. We know that if you're not happy, we're not happy. To ensure your satisfaction and your respect, we maintain our 100 percent guarantee policy. *(Shows pride in the company's products and concern for its customers)* *(Strives to regain customer's confidence in both products and service)*

Sincerely,

Michael Vanderer

Michael Vanderer
General Manager

meg
Enclosures

Writing International Letters

The letter-writing suggestions you've just studied work well for correspondence in this country. You may wish, however, to modify the organization, format, and tone of letters going abroad.

American businesspeople appreciate the efficiency and straightforwardness of directness in letters. Moreover, American business letters tend to be informal and conversational. Foreign correspondents, however, may look upon such directness and informality as inappropriate, insensitive, and abrasive. Letters in Japan, for example, may begin with deference, humility, and references to nature:

> Allow us to open with all reverence to you:
>
> The season for cherry blossoms is here with us and everybody is beginning to feel refreshed. We sincerely congratulate you on becoming more prosperous in your business.[11]

International letters should conform to the organizational, format, and cultural conventions of the receiver's country.

Letters in Germany commonly start with a long, formal lead-in, such as *Referring to your kind inquiry from the 31st of the month, we take the liberty to remind you with this letter*. . .[12] Italian business letters may refer to the receiver's family and children. And French correspondents would consider it rude to begin a letter with a request before it is explained. French letters also typically include an ending with this phrase (or a variation of it): *I wish to assure you [insert reader's most formal title] of my most respectful wishes [followed by the writer's title and signature].*[13] Foreign letters are also more likely to include passive-voice constructions *(your letter has been received),* exaggerated courtesy *(great pleasure, esteemed favor),* and obvious flattery *(your eminent firm).*[14]

Foreign letters may also use different formatting techniques. Whereas American business letters are typewritten and single-spaced, in other countries they may be handwritten and single- or double-spaced. Address arrangements vary as well, as shown in the following:

German	Japanese
Herr [title, Mr., on first line]	Ms. Atsuko Takagi [title, name]
Deiter Woerner [name]	5-12 Koyo-cho 4 chome [street, house number]
Fritz-Kalle-Strasse 4 [street, house number]	Higashinada-ku [city]
6200 Wiesbaden [postal district, city]	Tokyo 194 [prefecture, postal district]
Germany [country]	Japan [country]

Dates and numbers can be particularly confusing, as shown here:

American	Some European Countries
June 3, 1995	3rd of June 1995
6/3/95	3.6.95
$5,320.00 U.S.	$5,320,00 U.S.

To be safe, spell out the names of months instead of using figures. Verify sums of money and identify the currency unit. Before sending a letter abroad, review the section "Developing Intercultural Sensitivity" in Chapter 2.

Because the placement and arrangement of letter addresses and closing lines vary greatly, you should always research local preferences before writing. For important letters going abroad, it's also wise to have someone familiar with local customs read and revise the message. An American graduate student learned this

GREED IS OUT; ETHICS AND MISSION STATEMENTS ARE IN

As our nation emerges from the profit-oriented 1980s, business has rediscovered values and social responsibility. Greed is out; ethics are in. Scrambling to do the right thing, businesses and their employees are actively engaged in such activities as working with the homeless and tutoring underprivileged children. Many businesses are also reevaluating their product lines and investments to enhance quality of life and the environment.

To spell out their goals, companies are increasingly developing codes of ethics and mission statements. Such statements are not easily written because they require consensus and commitment. The employees and directors of Ben & Jerry's, for example, worked for over a year to hammer out the concise and meaningful three-part statement of mission shown here.

Not everyone, however, agrees with the trend toward the strong social stances of some public corporations. Respected economist Milton Friedman, a Nobel laureate, contends, "Few trends could so thoroughly undermine the very foundations of our free society as the acceptance by corporate officials of a social responsibility other than to make as much money for their stockholders as possible."[15] As you read Ben & Jerry's mission statement in this box, consider how its writers confronted the issue raised by economist Friedman.

Career Track Application

Analyze the Ben & Jerry's mission statement in terms of applying it. If you were an employee at Ben & Jerry's, how would it affect your actions if you worked in production, marketing, or accounting? How do you think it affects Alice Blachly in Consumer Affairs? Do you see any contradictions in the statement that might force compromises for the company and its employees? As a shareholder, how would you feel if a percentage of profits went to a foundation for charity but no dividends were paid? As a consumer, how would you feel about paying more for a product so that charitable causes could be supported?

Ben & Jerry's is dedicated to the creation and demonstration of a new corporate concept of linked prosperity. Our mission consists of three interrelated parts:

Product Mission: To make, distribute and sell the finest quality all-natural ice cream and related products in a wide variety of innovative flavors made from Vermont dairy products.

Social Mission: To operate the company in a way that actively recognizes the central role that business plays in the structure of society by initiating innovative ways to improve the quality of life of a broad community: local, national and international.

Economic Mission: To operate the company on a sound financial basis of profitable growth, increasing value for our shareholders and creating career opportunities and financial rewards for our employees.

Underlying the mission of Ben & Jerry's is the determination to seek new and creative ways of addressing all three parts, while holding a deep respect for individuals, inside and outside the company, and for the communities of which they are a part.

lesson when she wrote a letter, in French, to a Paris museum asking for permission to do research. She received no response. Before writing a second time, she took the letter to her French tutor. "No, no, mademoiselle! It will never do! It must be more respectful. You must be very careful of individuals' titles. Let me show you!" The second letter won the desired permission.

Summary of Learning Goals

1. **Describe the direct pattern for organizing letters.** Letters carrying positive or neutral messages should be organized with the main idea in the opening, explanations in the body, and courteous words in the closing.
2. **Write letters requesting information and action.** The opening immediately states the purpose of the letter, perhaps asking a question. The body explains and justifies the request. The closing tells the reader courteously what to do and shows appreciation.
3. **Compose letters placing orders.** The opening introduces the order and authorizes a purchase *(Please send me the following items . . .).* The body lists the desired items including quantity, order number, description, unit price, and total price. The closing describes the method of payment, tells when the merchandise should be sent, and expresses appreciation.
4. **Prepare letters making claims.** The opening describes the problem clearly or tells what action is to be taken. The body explains and justifies the request without anger or emotion. The closing, which might include an end date, contains a pleasant statement that expresses a desire for continued relations.
5. **Write letters complying with requests.** A subject line identifies previous correspondence, while the opening immediately delivers the good news. The body explains and provides additional information. The closing is cordial and personalized.
6. **Compose letters acknowledging customer orders.** The opening tells when and how the delivery will be made. The body discusses details of the order, including any irregularities. It may include resale or sales promotion information. The closing includes a personalized statement that demonstrates reader benefits, appreciation, helpfulness, and/or expectation of continued good relations.
7. **Prepare letters granting claims and making adjustments.** The opening immediately grants the claim without sounding grudging. To regain the confidence of the customer, the body may explain what went wrong and how the problem will be rectified. However, it may avoid accepting responsibility for any problems. The closing expresses appreciation, extends thanks for past business, refers to a desire to be of service, and/or mentions a new product.
8. **Modify international letters to accommodate other cultures.** Letters going to individuals in some cultures, such as Japan and Europe, should probably use a less direct organizational pattern and be more formal in tone. They should also be adapted to appropriate regional letter formats.

Chapter Review

1. What channel of communication is used to deliver messages *outside* an organization? *Inside* an organization?

2. Messages are considered routine when they are expected to elicit what kind of reader reaction?

3. Which letter format style is most popular?

4. Briefly, name five ways to develop goodwill in a letter.

5. Describe the three parts of a direct-pattern letter.

6. Why are open-ended questions better than yes-or-no questions? Give an example of each.

7. For order letters what information goes in the opening? In the body? In the closing?

8. What is a *claim*?

9. What is the value of a subject line?

10. Why is accuracy especially important in letters written on company stationery?

11. Distinguish between *resale* and *sales promotion* information.

12. In what three instances does it make sense to acknowledge an order with a personal letter?

13. Why do smart companies welcome complaints?

14. What are a writer's three goals for adjustment letters?

15. Name four things to avoid in adjustment letters.

Discussion

1. What's wrong with using the indirect pattern for writing routine requests and replies? If in the end the reader understands the message, why make a big fuss over the organization?

2. Is it insensitive to include resale or sales promotion information in an adjustment letter?

3. Why is it important to regain the confidence of a customer in an adjustment letter? How can it be done?

4. How are American business letters different from those written in other countries? Why do you suppose this is so?

5. Ethical Issue: Let's say you've drafted a letter to a customer in which you apologize for the way the customer's account was fouled up by the accounting department. You show the letter to your boss, and she instructs you to remove the apology. It admits responsibility, she says, and the company cannot allow itself to be held liable. You're not an attorney, but you can't see the harm in a simple apology. What should you do? Refer to the section "Tools for Doing the Right Thing" in Chapter 3 to review the five questions you might ask yourself in trying to do the right thing.

Exercises

6.1 Direct Openings

Revise the following openings so that they are more direct.

a. Pursuant to your letter of June 3, I am writing in regard to your inquiry about sliding mirror doors. We produce a variety of styles and finishes, all with heavy-duty tracking systems and shatter-resistant safety mirrors.

b. Please allow me to introduce myself. I am Lisa Gomez, and I am writing to inquire about the mountain bike that I saw on the cover of your magazine, *Mountain Bike Action,* in April. This bike interests me, and I'd like to know what kind it is and where I can find out more about it.

c. Because I've lost your order blank, I have to write this letter. I hope that it's all right to place an order this way. I am interested in ordering a number of things from your summer catalog, which I still have although the order blank is missing.

d. Your letter of March 21 has been referred to my desk for response. In your letter you inquire about the mountain bike featured on the cover of our magazine in April. That particular bike is a Series 70 Paramount and is manufactured by Schwinn.

e. I am pleased to receive your inquiry regarding the possibility of my acting as a speaker at the final semester meeting of your business management club on May 21. The topic of personnel interviewing interests me and is one on which I think I could impart helpful information to your members. Therefore, I am responding in the affirmative to your kind invitation.

f. Thank you for your recent order of November 2. We are sure you will enjoy the letterhead stationery that you ordered from our summer catalog. Your order is currently being processed and should leave our printing facility in Denver early next week. We use UPS for all deliveries in southern California. Because you ordered stationery with engraving, it cannot be shipped until October 4. You should not expect it before October 9.

g. We have just received your letter of December 13 regarding the unfortunate troubles you are having with your Hitachi videocassette recorder. In your letter you ask if you may send the VCR to us for inspection. Although we normally handle all service requests through our local dealers, in your circumstance we are willing to take a look at your unit here at our Torrance plant. Therefore, please send it to us so that we may determine what's wrong.

6.2 Subject Lines

Write efficient subject lines for each of the messages in Exercise 6.1. Add dates and other information if necessary.

6.3 Letter Formatting

On a sheet of paper draw two rectangles about 4 by 6 inches. Within these rectangles show where the major parts of letters go: letterhead, dateline, inside address, salutation, body, complimentary close, signature, and author's name. Use lines to show how much space each part would occupy. Illustrate two different letter styles, such as block and personal business style. Be prepared to discuss your drawings. Consult Appendix B for format guidelines.

6.4 Draft Document: Letter Requesting Information

Analyze the following letter. List its weaknesses. If your instructor directs, revise the letter.

> Dear Sir:
>
> Because we are one of the largest banking systems in the country, we receive hundreds of résumés from job candidates every day. We need help in sorting and ranking candidates by categories, such as job classification, education, work history, skill, and experience.
>
> Recently, I was reading *Personnel* magazine, and the March issue has a story about your new software program called Resumix. It sounds fascinating and may be the answer to our problem. We would like more information about this program, which is supposed to read and sort résumés.
>
> In addition to learning if the program can sort candidates into the categories mentioned earlier, I'm wondering if the program can read all the different type fonts and formats that candidates use on their résumés. Another important consideration for us is training and troubleshooting. If we need help with the program, would you supply it?
>
> Thank you for your cooperation.
>
> Sincerely,

6.5 Draft Document: Claim Request

Analyze the following letter. List its weaknesses. If your instructor directs, revise the letter.

> Gentlemen:
>
> I don't think I should be charged twice for a flight I took only once! When I made my reservation to fly from San Francisco to Los Angeles, I didn't know my father would get sick and require hospitalization on September 19. As a result, I could not make the trip on September 20 as I had originally planned.
>
> I finally did make the trip on September 30. But WestAir charged me $169 again! Your booking agent refused to look at the letter from my father's doctor describing the hospitalization. She said I had to write to headquarters. I still have my tickets from the September 20 flight, so you know I didn't use them. My travel agent says that I'm entitled to a refund. So why did I have to pay twice?
>
> I'm all for deregulation of the airline industry, but what happened to compassion and integrity?
>
> Angrily yours,

6.6 Draft Document: Favorable Adjustment Letter

Analyze the following letter. List its weaknesses. If your instructor directs, revise the letter.

> Dear Mrs. Winston:
>
> Thank you for your letter of May 18 in which you complain that you are receiving two issues of *Popular Electronics* each month.
>
> We have checked into the matter and ascertained that the misunderstanding resulted when you placed an order under the name of Mrs. Wendy Winston. You claim that this new subscription was made as part of your daughter's magazine fund-raising program at her school. You must be aware that the entire circulation operation of a large magazine is computerized. Obviously, a computer cannot distinguish between your current subscription for Mrs. H. C. Winston and a new one for another name.
>
> But we think we've straightened the problem out. We're extending your subscription for 14 months. That's a bonus of two issues to make up for the double ones you've received. However, we can't prevent you from receiving one or two more double issues.
>
> Sincerely,

Problems

6.7 Request Letter: Tell Me More

Select an advertisement from a newspaper or magazine that describes a product or service that interests you. Write a letter that asks for information not provided in the ad, such as price, availability, warranty, service, or restrictions. Ask at least four significant questions. Attach a copy of the ad to your letter.

6.8 Request Letter: June Move

Write to a realtor in a distant city. Assume that you have a family of four and will be changing jobs in June. Ask the realtor about houses or apartments in your price range. Inquire about availability, taxes, and desirable locales. Describe your needs. Provide enough information to ensure that you'll receive a useful response. You plan to visit the realtor and look at listings in April.

6.9 Request Letter: Assist from Dormans

Assume that you are Brian Wilson, personnel manager, First Bank of Colorado. Your bank employs over 8,000 workers in the state. At your Denver location you hire about a hundred people each year and you process internal transfers for another hundred. Processing all those applications has become increasingly burdensome. At a recent professional meeting you met Lawrence V. Moore, manager of placement at Dorman Manufacturing Company. He told you briefly about a computer system he had developed that enabled him to make the entire personnel task more manageable. He indicated that he would be happy to tell you more about his system if you would write him at Box 12A, Golden, Colorado 80613. Ask Mr. Moore to describe how his system allows candidates to be ranked on a variety of requirements (such as experience, skills, and education). You wonder about weighting of job requirements. For example, if certain skills are much more important than experience, how does his system handle this? You're very concerned about current rulings requiring that all candidates for a particular job be evaluated using the same scale. You understand that his system promotes such consistency, but you wonder how. When candidates are interviewed, how does his system allow them to be ranked, especially on such subjective traits as communication skills and ability to work in a team environment? Ask for any other information you feel would be helpful.[16]

6.10 Request Letter: Be Your Own Boss

Your rich uncle has just agreed to provide financial backing for you to start your own business. Fortunately, you recently read an article about the hottest small business franchises, complete with addresses for more information. Write to one of the following: Gift Baskets International, VIP Event Planning, Silk Plant City, Auto Detailing Specialists, Americana Bed and Breakfast Inns, Mobile Disk Jockeys, Wertz Self-Service Storage, I-Don't-Believe-It's-Yogurt, Yummy Donut Shops, BigMouth (voice-mail services), Videotaping Pros, Smyth Secretarial/Word Processing Services, PIP Printing, or Starmaker Image Consultants. Request information regarding start-up costs, equipment requirements, training, advertising support, potential customers, profit sharing, and growth potential. Your questions will be determined by the kind of franchise you select. Provide an appropriate address.

6.11 Order Letter: Dracula in London

In your local newspaper (supply name and date) you see an ad listing close-out prices on hundreds of computer games. The prices are so good you decide to place an order—either for yourself or for gifts. Because no order blank or toll-free telephone number is supplied, you write a letter to Discount Computer Sales, 2981 East 58th Street, New York, NY 11205 ordering the following games: Dracula in London (No. RVGA4.3) for $10.95; Duke Nukem (No. TVGA2.3) for $12.95; Hugo's Horror House (No. EVGA4.2) for $10.95; and Robomaze II (No. WVGA3.2) for $12.95. No tax is charged because it's out of state. The shipping cost is $6.50 for UPS or $11.50 for Federal Express. Figure the total and include it in your order.

6.12 Order Letter: Florida AV Supplies

As audiovisual supervisor for TechData, Inc., write a letter ordering the following supplies from Norfolk Suppliers, 301 Norview Avenue, Norfolk, VA 23514. You need 20 Kodak slide trays (No. A41-7829) at $13.78 each; 1,000 foil-back slide labels (No. A41-1632) at $10.76 for 1,000; and 1 double-decker slide file (No. A41-5492) at $24.55. You saw these items advertised in the September issue of *Visuals* magazine. Because you need these items for an immediate project, ask for two-day UPS delivery service at a cost of $16. Request that the invoice be sent to Rita Kemp, Purchasing Department, TechData, Inc., 2400 Hollywood Boulevard, Pembroke Pines, FL 33024.

6.13 Claim Letter: Windows That Won't Stretch

Assume you are Linda Jurado, owner of Linda's Interiors. Recently you completed a kitchen remodeling that required double-glazed, made-to-order oak windows. You ordered them from Bella Windows, 200 Main Street, Bella, IA 50218. When they arrived, your carpenter gave you the bad news: the windows were cut ⅝ inch too small—instead of 47⅞ inches, they were only 47¼ inches wide. In his words, "No way can I stretch those windows to fit these openings!" You waited three weeks for these windows, and your clients want them installed immediately. To please them, you had your carpenter rebuild the opening, but he charged you an extra $214 for his labor. You feel that Bella Windows should reimburse you for this amount since it was their error. In fact, you actually saved them a bundle of money by not returning the windows. Write a claim letter that requests a payment to you. Enclose a copy of your original order showing your measurements and your carpenter's bill. Perhaps you should also include a copy of Bella's invoice. You are a good customer of Bella, having used their quality windows on many other jobs. You're confident that they will grant this claim.

6.14 Claim Letter: Mouldy Grout Is Missing

You're mad! You purchased two $35 tickets to a concert featuring King Fisher and his Mouldy Grout band at Five Flags Lake Point Park. When you arrived for the concert May 25, neither King nor the Grout appeared. Three decidedly not-ready-for-prime-time groups filled in. You had been looking forward to this concert for seven weeks. You're angry and disappointed and feel that you've been taken. After the concert started, you stayed through two acts to see if the talent might improve. It didn't. It seems to you that you remember seeing newspaper advertisements publicizing the Mouldy Grout performance as recently as the day of the concert. As you left the Five Flags parking lot, you saw a small poster describing a change in the talent for the evening's concert.

Two weeks later you're still angry. You decide to write to Five Flags Lake Point Park, P.O. Box 4300, Sandusky, OH 45320 requesting a refund of the purchase price for two $35 tickets.

6.15 Claim Letter: The Real Thing

Select a product or service that has disappointed you. Write a claim letter requesting a refund, replacement, explanation, or whatever seems reasonable. Generally, such letters are addressed to customer service departments. For food product claims you should include bar-code identification from the package, if possible. Your instructor may ask you to actually mail this letter. Remember that smart companies want to know what their customers think, especially if a product could be improved. When you receive a response, share it with your class.

6.16 Collaborative Request Response: McDonald's Goes Green

Karen Capatosto, director of Customer Service for McDonald's Corp., has received a letter from an environmentalist wanting to know what McDonald's is doing to reduce the huge amounts of waste products that its restaurants generate. This inquiry argues that these wastes not only deplete world resources but also clog our already overburdened landfills.

Karen thinks that this is a good opportunity for her student interns to sharpen their reasoning and writing skills on the job. She asks you and the other interns to draft a response to the inquiry telling how McDonald's is cleaning up its act. Here are some of the facts that Karen supplies your group.

Actually, McDonald's has been quite active in its environmental efforts. Working with the Environmental Defense Fund, McDonald's has initiated a series of 42 resolutions that are cutting by more than 80 percent the huge waste stream from its 12,000 restaurants. McDonald's efforts meant making changes in packaging, increasing their recycling campaign, trying more composting, and retraining employees. McDonald's was one of the food industry leaders in abandoning the polystyrene "clamshell" box for hamburgers and sandwiches. Formerly using an average of 20 pounds of polystyrene a day per restaurant, McDonald's now uses only 10 percent of that figure.

McDonald's suppliers have been asked to use corrugated boxes that contain at least 35 percent recycled content. Moreover, suppliers will be asked to make regular reports to McDonald's that measure their progress in reaching new waste-reduction goals. Other environmental efforts include testing a starch-based material in consumer cutlery to replace plastic forks, knives, and spoons. Many restaurants have also begun trial composting of egg shells, coffee grounds, and food scraps. McDonald's is also starting a nationwide program for recycling corrugated boxes. In addition, the company is testing reusable salad lids and shipping pallets, pump-style bulk dispensers for condiments, and refillable coffee mugs.

McDonald's has retrained its restaurant crews to give waste reduction equal weight with other priorities, such as quickness, cleanliness, and quality service. The company is trying to reduce the waste both behind the counter (which accounts for 80 percent of the total waste) and over the counter. Although this letter draft should be addressed to Bruce W. Quinn, 1762 Evergreen Road, Waterloo, IA 50704, it may be used for other customer inquiries as well.[17]

6.17 Response Letter: You Can Account on Us

Assume that you are Marsha Morrison, manager of Account-on-Us, an agency that supplies temporary and permanent accounting and bookkeeping personnel. Respond to the letter of Diane Morantz, Morantz Investment Properties, 3040 Martin Luther King Drive, Shreveport, LA 71107, who inquired about your service. Ms. Morantz wants to find a full-charge bookkeeper, and she sent a description of the job she has available. She asked several questions, the first of which related to your fee. Tell her that the fee is based on the annual salary—you charge 1 percent per thousand of the annual salary. Enclose your fee schedule so that she can see what you're talking about. Her next question dealt with the candidate's qualifications. Assure Ms. Morantz that you test all applicants for accounting knowledge and that you contact all previous employers. Her last question focused on a guarantee. You offer a thirty-day guarantee. If during the first thirty days of employment the employee does not perform satisfactorily, you will find a replacement or refund the fee on a prorated basis, depending on the number of days worked.

Since you specialize in accounting and bookkeeping personnel, you attract qualified candidates. Nevertheless, you administer rigorous theory and applications tests; then, you select only the top performers. Seldom does any employer exercise your thirty-day guarantee. Your service can take the hassle out of hiring new employees since you do all the testing, screening, and reference checking. You have a file of satisfied local employers who have used your service. Tell her that you will call her next week (give specific date) to discuss background data on potential candidates. Along with your fee schedule, send Ms. Morantz your booklet entitled "How to Help a New Employee Get Off to a Good Start." Refer her to pages 4–5 where she can read ten tips for improving an employee's first week on the job.

6.18 Response Letter: Answering Real Customers

In a job you currently hold or one you've had in the past, consider the kinds of inquiries that customers, suppliers, or other outsiders typically make. What information do they want? Prepare a response letter using data with which you are familiar. Include answers to at least three significant questions. How can you develop reader benefits? What resale or sales promotion information can you use? Use the title of the person who would normally be answering these inquiries.

6.19 Order Response: Dusky Blue Is Worth Waiting For

Acknowledge the September 16 order of the Concoran Company, 12790 Beamer Road, Houston, TX 77088. You are sending them three Micron microfiche readers by Interstate Express; they should arrive in two weeks (give expected date). However, the 5 ten-drawer microform file cases in the order must be special-ordered because of the dusky blue color selected. These file cases will be shipped from Pennsylvania. Manufacturing takes three weeks and shipping will require another two weeks. Encourage the Concoran people to consider your acid-free microfiche envelopes (for temporary storage of microfiche records). You also have a special rate on microfiche file folder guides. These have DuPont Mylar tabs; a package of 50 has been reduced from $31.99 to $25.99. The file cases they ordered are your best high-grade steel, and the baked enamel finish—no matter which of the 15 fashion colors they order—is extremely durable, withstanding heavy-duty office use. If Concoran wants the file cases a little faster, it should call your Traffic Department at (522) 689-2120 to discuss ways to expedite shipping.

6.20 Order Response: Drying Wet Heads at MillionHairs

Send a letter to MillionHairs Salon, 2605 Pinebloom Drive, Roswell, GA 30076 acknowledging its February 4 order for hair dryers. Tell MillionHairs that you are shipping ten Turbo pistol-grip styling dryers by UPS with arrival expected about February 9. You won't, however, be able to send immediately the new Euro Air Diffusers they ordered. This device has unique styling "fingers" that lift and separate curly, permed, or fine hair to bring out natural texture. Because salons are snapping them up, you have run out. You expect a new supply in two weeks, and you will ship then, if that's OK with MillionHairs. To sell to their customers, MillionHairs might be interested in your Neon Combo pack, which includes a brightly colored fanny pack that holds their hair essentials while they are biking or at the beach. It includes a 1250-watt dryer, a ¾-inch curling iron, a spiral curling iron, and a hair brush—all color-coordinated in neon green or pink. This take-along hair care product makes a great gift.

6.21 Adjustment Letter: Tearful Inquiry

As Rod Furtado, manager, Consumer Affairs, Grant Laboratories, respond to the letter you received from Tina Gambrell, 4981 Fitzgerald Road, Simi Valley, CA 93067. Ms. Gambrell said that she has used Opti-Tears before without incident. A recent purchase, however, hurt her eyes and caused painful tears when she used it to lubricate her contact lenses. She returned her bottle of Opti-Tears and wants you to test it. Because Grant Laboratories welcomes customer letters, you appreciate Ms. Gambrell's inquiry. You are, naturally, very concerned when your customers experience eye discomfort in using your products. Let her know that Opti-Tears particularly appreciates her efforts in returning the bottle so that its laboratories can analyze the product for conformance to specifications. Opti-Tears continually evaluates its products, and results of this analysis provide useful information. Promise her that you'll send her results of the analysis when they become available. Send her several complimentary bottles of Adapettes Especially for Sensitive Eyes. This product contains a special ophthalmic lubricating solution that is formulated without preservatives. Individuals who have reacted to other products have had no problems with Adapettes.

6.22 Adjustment Letter: We'll Have to Eat This One

As Thomas T. Thompson, vice president, Customer Operations, Bella Windows, respond to Linda Jurado, owner of Linda's Interiors, 230 San Antonio Drive, Austin, TX 78715 (Problem 6.13). She asks for reimbursement of $214 for the extra amount she paid to have her oak windows installed. You check the invoice and the order and discover that your company did indeed cut the windows the wrong size. Now you must decide what to do. You can send her the money, but you'd rather give her a credit toward her next order—to encourage her repeat business. Give her a choice. Would she prefer a check for $214 or a credit of $350 toward her next order?

Tell her how Bella Windows prides itself on its quality-control procedures. All custom orders are verified when they are received, cut to order by expert wood artisans in the factory, and inspected before being shipped. Inform her that the mistake was certainly yours, though, and you realize that you need to redouble your efforts in scrutinizing custom orders. As the factory manager Leo said after seeing her letter and the original order, "She's right. Don't know what went wrong, but we'll have to eat this one." Leo was surprised—and thankful—that she kept the windows.

Remind her of your comprehensive line of traditional and European-style kitchen and bath cabinetry. Your cabinets come in hardwoods such as oak, cherry, hickory, and maple; you offer up to six finishes. You now manufacture high-tech laminate cabinets as well. Enclose a copy of your booklet, "Functional and Elegant Cabinets From Bella." You think she'll like the section on planning a social kitchen.

6.23 Adjustment Letter: Red Roses for a Blue Customer

Assume you are Barbara L. Hunt, vice president, Customer Service, First Atlantic Savings, 1340 Old Trenton Road, Trenton, NJ 08692. An irate bank customer—Michelle A. Marrinan, 340 Gateway Drive, Trenton, NJ 08644—calls to say that your bank humiliated her by bouncing six of her checks. Ms. Marrinan had deposited $11,500 to her account on December 1 and began writing checks on that deposit about four days later. Every one of her checks bounced, and she's furious. You look into the problem and find that the check she deposited was drawn on a California bank. For its protection First Atlantic has a policy prohibiting withdrawals from a large deposit until the deposit check has cleared the bank on which it was drawn. In this case it took eleven days for Ms. Marrinan's deposit to clear. Generally, it takes only five to seven days. You don't know why this check took so long.

Your tellers are trained to tell a customer making a large deposit that the amount will not be credited to the account until it clears its maker bank. Your teller apparently slipped up in warning Ms. Marrinan. You can understand why she is so mad. Not only did all those checks bounce, damaging her reputation, but the people to whom she wrote the checks also had to pay processing fees to their banks. Ms. Marrinan wants First Atlantic to write letters of apology to each person who received one of the checks explaining why the check bounced. She also wants you to pay any processing fees involved.

You think this situation points up a real need to change your bank's policy. For all future large deposits, you want a bank official to place a telephone call immediately to the issuing bank to verify the check. This should reduce the "hold" time on deposits. In the meantime, you wish to do everything possible to placate Ms. Marrinan, a valued bank customer. You decide to write her at once, agreeing that First Atlantic will send letters of explanation to her six payees. First Atlantic will also pay all processing fees caused by the bounced checks. But more than that, you are sending her a dozen red roses to let her know that First Atlantic cares about its customers.[18]

6.24 International Inquiry: Coming to America

Assume that you are Brad Young, assistant registrar, at the college or university you attend (or one with which you are familiar). You have been asked to respond to an inquiry from Ms. Harui Yamaguchi. She wants to come to America to attend college. She seeks information about an educational program at your institution (select the program in which you are enrolled or another). She also wants to know the tuition costs for international students and whether your institution has any special groups for international students. Write a supportive and informative letter to Ms. Harui Yamaguchi, 3-13 Tsukiji 5-chome (street, house number), Chuo-ku (city), Tokyo 104 (prefecture, postal district), Japan. Her letter was in English and she included a self-addressed envelope, but you can tell that she's not fluent in the language. In a separate memo to your instructor, describe how you adapted your message to this reader.

6.25 International Inquiry: Info to Germany

You are Denise Moore, customer service representative for an organization where you have worked or one with which you are familiar. Write a letter to Wolfgang Schleuter, Steinberg 21 (street address), 5840 Dortmand (district and city), Germany. Mr. Werner wants information about one of your products or services. He's considering buying it or distributing it in his country. His inquiry was in English, but you guess he's not expert at the language. In a separate memo to your instructor, describe how you adapted your message to this reader.

C.L.U.E. Review 6

Edit the following sentences to correct faults in grammar, punctuation, spelling, and word use.

1. The extrordinary increase in sales is related to us placing the staff on a commission basis and the increase also effected our stock value.
2. She acts as if she was the only person who ever received a complement about their business writting.
3. Karen is interested in working for the U.S. foreign service. Since she is hopping to travel.
4. Major Hawkins whom I think will be elected has all ready served three consecative terms as a member of the gulfport city counsel.
5. After Mr. Freeman and him returned from lunch the customer's were handled more quick.
6. Our new employees cafeteria, which opened six months ago has a salad bar that everyone definitly likes.
7. On Tuesday Ms Adams can see you at two p.m., on Wednesday she has a full skedule.
8. His determination courage and sincerity could not be denied however his methods were often questioned.
9. After you have checked the matter farther report to the CEO and I.
10. Mr. Garcia and her advised me not to dessert my employer at this time. Although they were quite sympathetic to my personel problems.

Direct Memos

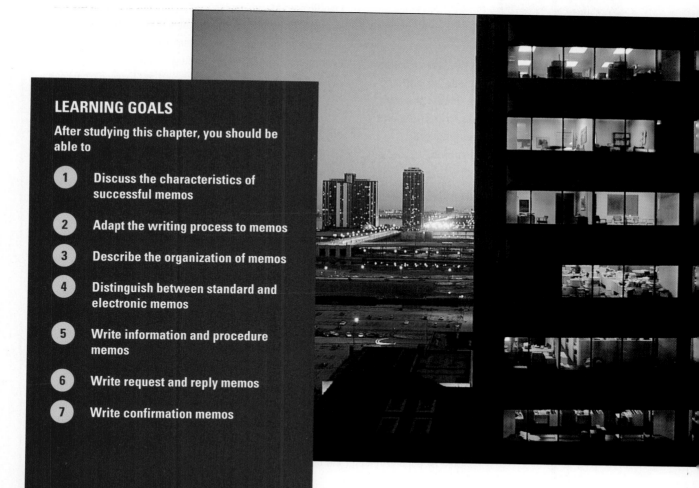

LEARNING GOALS

After studying this chapter, you should be able to

1. Discuss the characteristics of successful memos
2. Adapt the writing process to memos
3. Describe the organization of memos
4. Distinguish between standard and electronic memos
5. Write information and procedure memos
6. Write request and reply memos
7. Write confirmation memos

Bank of America: Career Track Profile

In the late 1980s once-prosperous Bank of America fell upon tough times. Suffering from staggering loan losses, deteriorating capital, and two takeover attempts, the California banking giant seemed doomed. Refusing to crumble, Bank of America slashed operating costs and sold some of its real estate crown jewels to raise capital.

The bank also went back to basics. Instead of courting risky global loans, Bank of America concentrated on local mortgage and consumer business for growth. Attractive, simple packages, such as a combined checking/savings account, spurred customer deposits. Chairman Richard M. Rosenberg conceded the simplicity of the bank's strategy, saying this is "no rocket-science stuff." Profits surged, and Bank of America gradually emerged as one of the country's best-managed and most profitable banks. *Business Week* applauded the turnaround, declaring that "banking's basket case has become Wall Street's darling."

"I've learned that the few moments it takes me to make an outline actually save me time in the long run. And listed items really make for easy reading and comprehension."

Then, in a stunning move, Bank of America further strengthened its position by combining with its principal competitor, Security Pacific National Bank. This merger created the nation's largest bank in terms of capital reserves and number of branches and ATM outlets. But the new banking superpower faces the gigantic task of consolidating operations while at the same time continuing its emphasis on local banking and customer service.

Kenneth Kim is one of the front-line employees implementing Bank of America's retail lending and consumer deposit strategies. Born in Korea, Ken is like many college students today who must work long hours as they complete their degree requirements. He started with Security Pacific and is now one of thousands of employees being integrated into the new 2,400-branch organization. Four days a week (including Saturdays), he serves customers as a new accounts and loan officer. Two days a week he attends classes at Los Angeles Pierce College and also at California State University, Northridge, to complete his degree in economics and business administration.

On the job Ken sometimes works the "platform," an open area where bank customers sit in comfortable chairs and discuss their accounts or loans. But he also devotes considerable time to "back-office" tasks that include writing letters to customers and memos within the organization. Some Bank of America messages are sent by E-mail, but the majority are transmitted by paper. Although the bank provides hundreds of models for customer letters, little help is available for writing memos. Most of Ken's memos involve requests for information, responses to requests, or procedural instructions.

Ken's experience at Bank of America has taught him valuable lessons about writing on the job, particularly internal messages. He writes a memo only if absolutely necessary. "It takes me at least an hour to write a good memo. I don't want to waste my time if it's something I could take care of over the telephone." However, when a permanent record is required for banking records, the memo must be written.

Ken is also concerned about the audience for his writing. "When you talk to someone, you have facial expressions to help carry the meaning. But writing depends wholly on the words, and it's very easy to be misunderstood. I'm careful about being funny, facetious, or ironic in writing. Humor is better in person." Ken also observes the management line of command. "It's not a good idea to write to someone above my immediate boss without my boss's approval."

Downsizing, mergers, and consolidations of banks—along with scores of other industries in the last decade—have resulted in leaner, meaner organizations. Such reorganization often means that remaining employees must work more efficiently and rely more heavily on technology for assistance. Interpersonal skills are still vital to work the "platform" in a bank, but equally important are technical skills for back-office tasks.

One of Ken's strengths is his ability to apply what he learned in his business communication class to his job. "I try to organize my ideas by concentrating on the body of the message first. In giving or requesting information, I like to use lists. I number the items, especially for procedures, such as describing how to enter information into the computer. If the items are not steps, I use bullets or asterisks to introduce each." Ken outlines the body and then writes the introduction and conclusion last. "I've learned that the few moments it takes me to make an outline actually save me time in the long run. And listed items really make for easy reading and comprehension."

Another technique Ken employs is having another employee read an important memo or letter. "It takes the pressure off me. I go to a colleague who is a good writer, and he tells me if my message sounds 'right.' It's funny, but I don't always find my own mistakes—ones that I would have found in someone else's writing."

Although his part-time work lengthens his degree program, Ken feels that his experience is like gold. As you will learn in Chapter 16, a great way to land a full-time job after college is to take a part-time position in the field of your major. While Ken works his way through college, he's acquiring precious experience. And he's also able to apply the concepts from many of his courses so that they are not merely theoretical. When he's ready for a permanent position, he'll have both experience and a degree—not a bad example to follow.[1]

Writing Direct Memos

- The most common forms of business communication today are memorandums and computer networks.

In a large number of today's organizations, employees spend more time writing memos, computer mail messages, and other internal notes than writing to individuals outside the business.[2] Executives devote as much as 22 percent of their time to reading and writing memos.[3]

Newly hired employees also make extensive use of internal communication. A study of recent graduates recruited by Fortune 500 companies found that the most-used forms of communications—including both internal and external messages—were memorandums and computer networks.[4]

Developing skill in writing internal messages brings you two important benefits. First, well-written documents are likely to achieve their goals. Second, such documents enhance your image within the organization. Individuals identified as competent, professional writers are noticed and rewarded; most often, they are the ones promoted into management positions.

This chapter concentrates on direct memos. These straightforward messages open with the main idea first because their topics are not sensitive and require little persuasion. You'll study the characteristics, writing process, organization, and forms for preparing procedure, information, request, reply, and confirmation memos.

Characteristics of Successful Memos

- Direct memos inform employees, request data, give responses, confirm decisions, and provide directions.

Because memos are standard forms of communication within most organizations, they may become your most common business communication medium. These indispensable messages inform employees, request data, supply responses, confirm decisions, and give directions. Good memos generally share certain characteristics.

TO, FROM, DATE, SUBJECT headings. Memos contain guide-word headings, often printed on special interoffice memo stationery, as shown in Figure 7.1. The guide words help readers immediately identify the date, origin, destination, and purpose of a message. You'll learn more about the form of memos shortly.

Single topic. Good memos generally discuss only one topic. Limiting the topic helps the receiver act on the subject and file it appropriately. A memo, for example, that discusses a computer printer problem and also requests permission to attend a conference runs the risk of 50 percent failure. The reader may respond to the printer problem but forget about the conference request.

Conversational tone. The tone of interoffice memos is expected to be conversational because the communicators are usually familiar with one another. This means using occasional contractions (*I'm, you'll*), ordinary words, and first-person pronouns (*I/we*). Beware, however, of overusing *I*. Many organizations today want individuals who can work as part of a team. One experienced advertising executive recalls the first memo he put together for his boss. "I thought it was 'the end' in terms of creative problem solving. I eagerly awaited his reaction. When the memo arrived back on my desk, it had no comment and only three corrections. They were small, but I still feel their impact today. In three places I used the word 'I.' In each case, he crossed out the 'I' and wrote in 'We.' It was my first and most important lesson in teamwork."[5]

FIGURE 7.1 ● Interoffice Memo Formatting

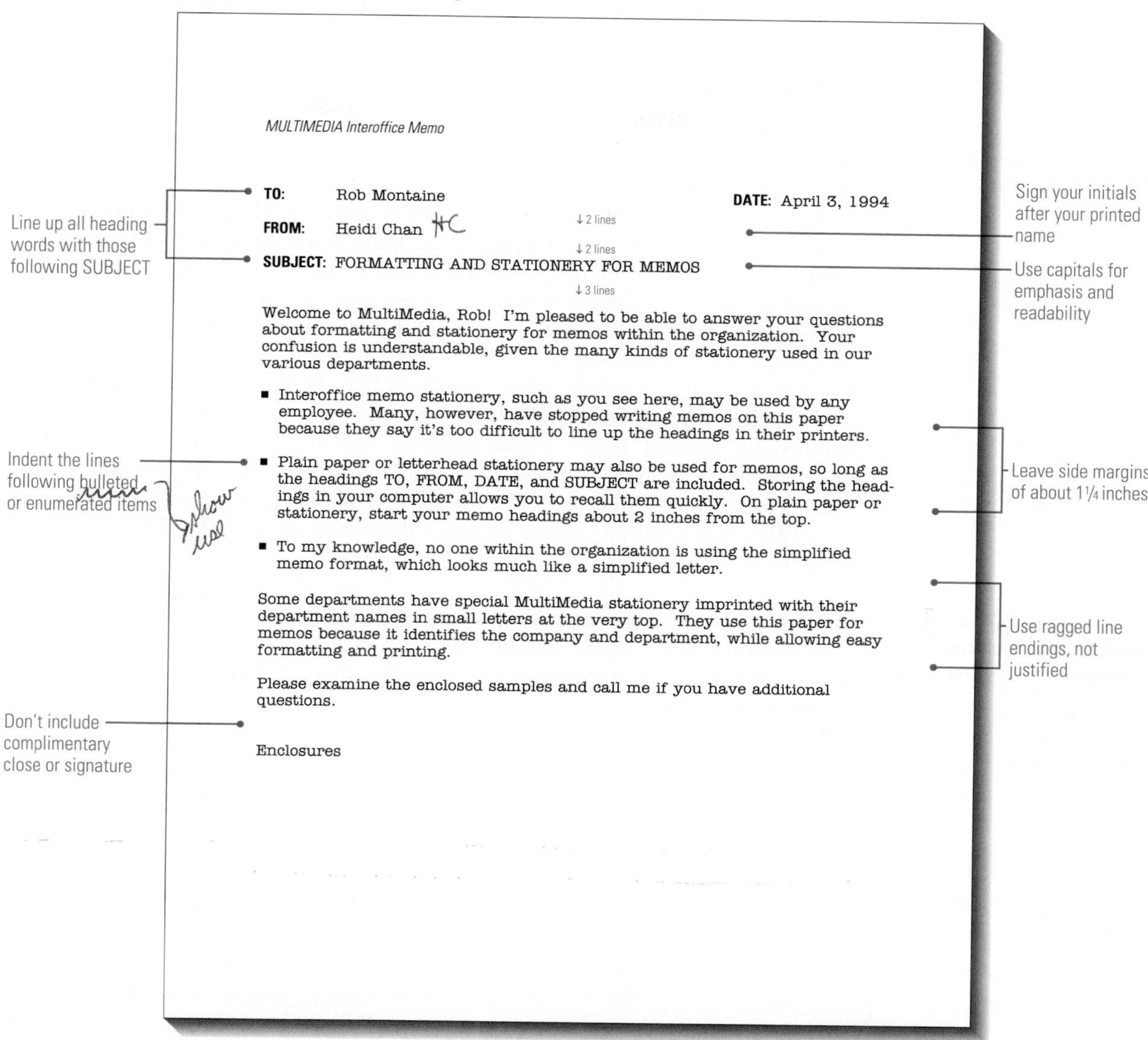

MULTIMEDIA Interoffice Memo

TO: Rob Montaine **DATE:** April 3, 1994

FROM: Heidi Chan HC

SUBJECT: FORMATTING AND STATIONERY FOR MEMOS

Welcome to MultiMedia, Rob! I'm pleased to be able to answer your questions about formatting and stationery for memos within the organization. Your confusion is understandable, given the many kinds of stationery used in our various departments.

- Interoffice memo stationery, such as you see here, may be used by any employee. Many, however, have stopped writing memos on this paper because they say it's too difficult to line up the headings in their printers.
- Plain paper or letterhead stationery may also be used for memos, so long as the headings TO, FROM, DATE, and SUBJECT are included. Storing the headings in your computer allows you to recall them quickly. On plain paper or stationery, start your memo headings about 2 inches from the top.
- To my knowledge, no one within the organization is using the simplified memo format, which looks much like a simplified letter.

Some departments have special MultiMedia stationery imprinted with their department names in small letters at the very top. They use this paper for memos because it identifies the company and department, while allowing easy formatting and printing.

Please examine the enclosed samples and call me if you have additional questions.

Enclosures

↓ 2 lines
↓ 2 lines
↓ 3 lines
Line up all heading words with those following SUBJECT
Indent the lines following bulleted or enumerated items
Don't include complimentary close or signature
Sign your initials after your printed name
Use capitals for emphasis and readability
Leave side margins of about 1¼ inches
Use ragged line endings, not justified

Conciseness. As functional forms of communication, routine memos contain only what's necessary to convey meaning and be courteous. Often, they require less background explanation and less attention to goodwill efforts than do letters to outsiders. Be particularly alert to eliminating wordiness. Avoid opening fillers *(there is, it is)*, long lead-ins *(I am writing this memo to inform you that)*, and wordy phrases *(because of the fact that)*.

● **Effective memos contain guide-word headings, focus on a single topic, are concise and conversational, and use graphic highlighting.**

Graphic highlighting. To make important ideas stand out and to improve readability, memo writers make liberal use of graphic highlighting techniques. The content of many informational, procedural, and confirmation memos lends itself to numbered or bulleted items, headings, tables, and other techniques you studied in Chapter 5. Such techniques make facts stand out.

Writing Process for Memos

Memo writing requires careful preparation and follows the 3-X-3 writing process.

Like letters and other messages, good memos require careful preparation. Although they often seem routine, it's wise to remember that they may travel farther than you expect. Consider the market researcher in Illinois, new to her job and eager to please her boss, who was asked to report on the progress of her project. Off the top of her head, she prepared a quick summary of her work and delivered her handwritten memo to her boss. Later that week the vice president of Marketing asked her boss how the project was progressing and was given the market researcher's hurried memo. The resulting poor impression was difficult for the new employee to overcome.

Careful writing takes time—especially at first. By following a systematic plan and practicing your skill, however, you can speed up your efforts and greatly improve the product. Bear in mind, moreover, that the effort you make to improve your communication skills can pay big dividends. Frequently, your speaking and writing abilities determine how much influence you'll have in your organization. As with other writing tasks, memo writing follows the familiar three-phase writing process.

Analyzing the purpose of a message helps determine whether a permanent record is required.

Analysis, anticipation, and adaptation. In Phase 1 you'll need to spend some time analyzing your task before writing. It's amazing how many of us are ready to put our pens or computers into gear before engaging our minds. Ask yourself three important questions:

- *Do I really need to write this memo?* A phone call or a quick visit to a nearby coworker might solve the problem—and save the time and expense of a written message. On the other hand, as Ken Kim has learned, some memos are needed to provide a permanent record.
- *Why am I writing?* Know why you are writing and what you hope to achieve. This will help you recognize what the important points are and where to place them.
- *How will the reader react?* Visualize the reader and the effect your message will have. Consider ways to shape the message to benefit the reader.

Research, organization, and composition. In Phase 2 you'll want to check the files, gather documentation, and prepare your message. Make an outline of the points you wish to cover. For short messages you can jot down notes on the document you are answering. Be sure to prepare for revision because excellence is rarely achieved on the first effort. Remember that a word processor makes writing and especially rewriting much easier.

Revision, proofreading, and evaluation. Careful and caring writers revise their messages, proofread the final copy, and make an effort to evaluate the success of their communication.

- **Revise for clarity.** Viewed from the receiver's perspective, are the ideas clear? Do they need more explanation? If the memo is passed on to others, will they need further explanation? Consider having a colleague critique your message, as Ken Kim does at Bank of America.

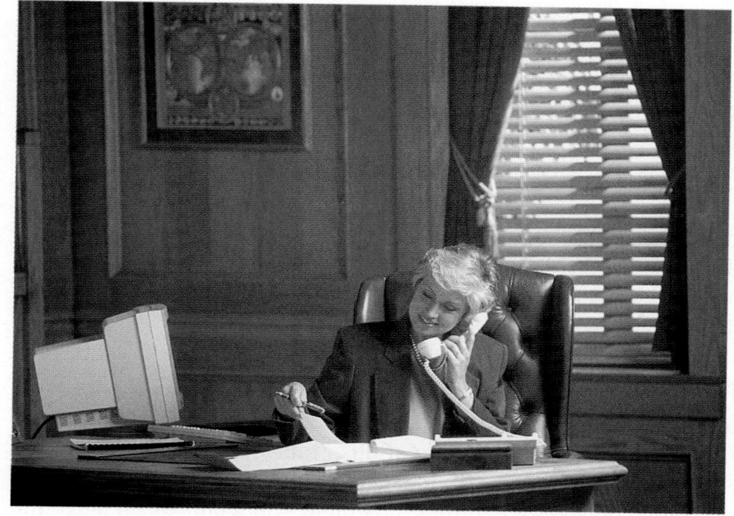

The writing process for memos—as for all documents—begins with analysis. Do you really need to send this message? A phone call might save the time and expense of a written message. But when you must deliver clear instructions or make a lasting record, plan to write. The time executives spend writing, revising, and reading memos can add up to one full month a year.

- **Proofread for correctness.** Are the sentences complete and punctuated properly? Do you have any typos or misspelled words? Remember to run your word processing spelling checker and to proofread your printout before sending it.
- **Plan for feedback.** How will you know if this message is successful? You can improve feedback by making it easy for the receiver to respond, with comments such as *Just initial your approval on this memo, return it to me, and I'll get started immediately.*

Organization of Memos

Direct memos—those that deliver good news or routine information—generally contain four parts: (1) a subject line that summarizes the message, (2) an opening that reveals the main idea immediately, (3) a body that explains and justifies the main idea, and (4) an action closing.

Direct memos contain a SUBJECT line, an opener stating the main idea, a body with explanation and justification, and an action closing.

Subject line. In letters a subject line is optional; in memos it is mandatory. The subject line should summarize the central idea. It provides quick identification for the reader and for filing. As you learned in Chapter 6, the subject line is usually written in an abbreviated style, often without articles *(a, an, the)*. It need not be a complete sentence, and it does not end with a period. It should be concise but provide enough information to be clear, as shown here:

SUBJECT: Staff Meeting May 3, 9 a.m., Room 10 (rather than simply *Meeting*)

SUBJECT: Proposal for Spring Marketing Plan (rather than *Proposal*)

SUBJECT: Instructions for Operating New Copy Machine (rather *Copy Machine*)

Opening. Most internal communication covers nonsensitive information that can be handled in a straightforward manner. "The memos that grab me tell right away what the writer has in mind," says corporate executive Doris Margonine.[6] Begin by frontloading; that is, reveal the main idea immediately. Even though the purpose of the memo is summarized in the subject line, that purpose should be restated—and amplified—in the first sentence. Some readers skip the subject line and plunge right into the first sentence. Notice how the following indirect memo openers can be improved by frontloading.

Most direct memos convey nonsensitive information and thus frontload the main idea in the opening.

SPOTLIGHT ON COMMUNICATORS

Described as a communicator who is as direct as the thrust of a piston, automobile industry leader Lee Iacocca advises young executives to be straightforward and precise in communicating their ideas. Anyone who can make a point in a clear, simple manner is a cut above the rest, he says.

Indirect Opening	**Direct Opening**
For the past six months the Human Resources Development Department has been considering changes in our employees' benefit plan.	Please review the following proposal regarding employees' benefits, and let me know by May 20 if you approve these changes.
As you may know, employees in Document Production have been complaining about eye fatigue as a result of the overhead fluorescent lighting in their center.	If you agree, I'll order six high-intensity task desk lamps at $189 each for use in the Document Production Center.

Body. The body of a memo provides more information about the reason for writing. It explains and discusses the subject logically. Design your data for easy comprehension by using numbered lists, headings, tables, and other graphic highlighting techniques. Compare the following versions of the same message. Observe how the graphic devices of columns, headings, and white space make the main points easy to comprehend.

Hard-to-read Paragraph Version

Effective immediately are the following air travel guidelines. Between now and December 31, only account executives may take company-approved trips. These individuals will be allowed to take a maximum of two trips, and they are to travel economy or budget class only.

Improved Version with Graphic Highlighting

Effective immediately are the following air travel guidelines:

Who may travel:	Account executives only
How many trips:	A maximum of two trips
By when:	Between now and December 31
Air class:	Economy or budget class only

Closing. Memos generally end with (1) action information, dates, or deadlines; (2) a summary of the message; or (3) a closing thought. Here again the value of thinking through the message before actually writing it becomes apparent. This is where readers look for deadlines and action language. An effective memo closing might be, *Please submit your report by June 15 so that we can have your data before our July planning session.*

In more complex memos a summary of main points may be an appropriate closing. If no action request is made and a closing summary is unnecessary, you might end with a simple concluding thought (*I'm glad to answer your questions* or *This sounds like a useful project*). Although you needn't close memos with goodwill statements such as those found in letters to customers or clients, some closing thought is often necessary to prevent a feeling of abruptness. Closings can show gratitude or encourage feedback with remarks such as *I sincerely appreciate your cooperation* or *What are your ideas on this proposal?* Other closings look forward to what's next, such as *How would you like to proceed?* As with routine letters, avoid trite expressions. Overused endings such as *Please let me know if I may be of further assistance* sound mechanical and insincere.

Putting it all together. Now let's put it all together. The following memo is the first draft of a message Steven Timms, Mail Services supervisor, wrote to his supervisor. Although it contains solid information, the message is so wordy and poorly organized that the reader will have trouble grasping its significance.

> MEMO TO: Andrea Kanarek
>
> This memo is in response to your recent inquiry about mail costs. Your message of April 30 said that you wanted a brief explanation of what is being done in Mail Services to cut back on overall costs. I can tell you that I've been doing many things to cut costs.
>
> For one thing, I'm trying very hard to locate duplicate names and addresses inadvertently included in our mailing lists. This problem is particularly difficult when we merge multiple mailing lists. Another thing I'm doing relates to envelope size. Departments that use envelopes larger than 6⅛ by 11½ are costing us a lot of money, which they do not realize. Therefore, I am making a proposal to all departments to limit envelope size.
>
> Finally, I'm looking into the possibility of presorting some of our first- and third-class mail. Mailings that are presorted are charged less.

Repeats information the reader already knows. Fails to open with information the reader wants.

Fails to help reader see the three main points. Overuses "I." Uses wordy expressions, such as "making a proposal" instead of *proposing*.

Fails to provide any form of conclusion.

Steven's revised message appears in Figure 7.2. To improve readability, he used bullets and boldfaced headings that emphasize the three actions he's taking to cut costs in his department. Notice, too, that he developed a more conversational tone and deemphasized "I" in his second version. Compare the revision with Steven's first draft. Which memo will make a better impression on his boss?

Forms of Memos

Memos in today's offices may appear in two forms: (1) hard-copy standard memos (printed on paper) or (2) electronic mail (E-mail) memos (sent over computer networks). Although many larger companies are rapidly installing E-mail networks, smaller organizations still rely on standard memos printed and distributed on paper.

• Memos may be transmitted by hard copy or E-mail.

Standard Memos

Most memos printed on paper begin with TO, FROM, DATE, and SUBJECT. Some organizations provide stationery with these printed guide words (see Figure 7.1). Aligning the text that follows the guide words, however, can be difficult on today's computers and printers. Employees using computers may prefer to skip the printed memo stationery and type in the guide words themselves, as Steven Timms did in his memo in Figure 7.2. You can simplify the process by storing a master form to be recalled any time you begin a memo.

• Master formats stored in word processors are useful in standard memos.

The position of the date varies; it could appear first, in the middle, or after the subject line. Some memos, especially in large organizations, include additional guide words, such as *Routing, Department, Floor,* or *Reference File.* When memos are addressed to groups of people, their names may be listed under the word *Distribution* in the heading or in the lower left corner.

Unlike business letters, memos are usually unsigned. Instead, writers initial the *FROM* line. Close friends may add salutations *(Dear Jan)* and signatures to personalize their memos, but generally memos do not include these items. For additional information about formatting memos, consult Appendix 2.

Electronic Mail Memos

Instead of using paper to send memos, increasing numbers of businesspeople are turning to computers and E-mail, as illustrated in Figure 7.3. E-mail requires computers, modems, and software to send messages electronically over networks connected by telephone lines and satellites. Almost instantaneously, a keyboarded

FIGURE 7.2 ● Information Memo

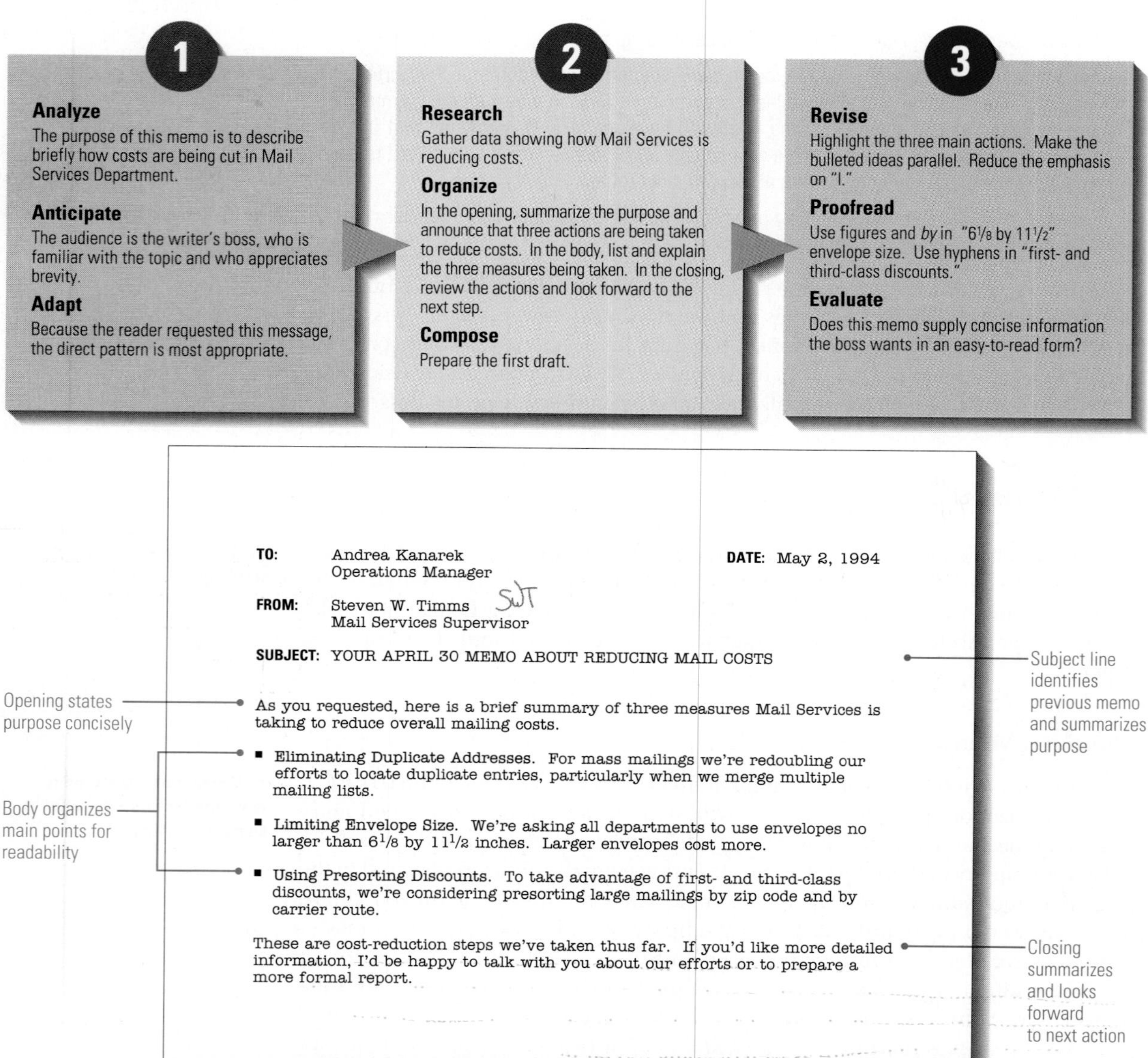

The Three Phases of the Writing Process
1
Analyze
The purpose of this memo is to describe briefly how costs are being cut in Mail Services Department.
Anticipate
The audience is the writer's boss, who is familiar with the topic and who appreciates brevity.
Adapt
Because the reader requested this message, the direct pattern is most appropriate.
2
Research
Gather data showing how Mail Services is reducing costs.
Organize
In the opening, summarize the purpose and announce that three actions are being taken to reduce costs. In the body, list and explain the three measures being taken. In the closing, review the actions and look forward to the next step.
Compose
Prepare the first draft.
3
Revise
Highlight the three main actions. Make the bulleted ideas parallel. Reduce the emphasis on "I."
Proofread
Use figures and by in "6⅛ by 11½" envelope size. Use hyphens in "first- and third-class discounts."
Evaluate
Does this memo supply concise information the boss wants in an easy-to-read form?
Subject line identifies previous memo and summarizes purpose
Opening states purpose concisely
Body organizes main points for readability
Closing summarizes and looks forward to next action

TO: Andrea Kanarek
Operations Manager

DATE: May 2, 1994

FROM: Steven W. Timms SWT
Mail Services Supervisor

SUBJECT: YOUR APRIL 30 MEMO ABOUT REDUCING MAIL COSTS

As you requested, here is a brief summary of three measures Mail Services is taking to reduce overall mailing costs.

- Eliminating Duplicate Addresses. For mass mailings we're redoubling our efforts to locate duplicate entries, particularly when we merge multiple mailing lists.
- Limiting Envelope Size. We're asking all departments to use envelopes no larger than $6^1/8$ by $11^1/2$ inches. Larger envelopes cost more.
- Using Presorting Discounts. To take advantage of first- and third-class discounts, we're considering presorting large mailings by zip code and by carrier route.

These are cost-reduction steps we've taken thus far. If you'd like more detailed information, I'd be happy to talk with you about our efforts or to prepare a more formal report.

● Use E-mail to deliver simple messages and hard copy for more complex messages.

memo travels to another computer—whether to the next desk or halfway around the world—and is stored in the recipient's mailbox until accessed. These messages may be printed, edited, stored, deleted, or forwarded—and all without paper!

Within America's organizations, communication by E-mail (called "messaging" as in "Why don't you 'message' me?") is growing exponentially. The accompanying Technology box discusses the reasons for its success and its effect on global communication.

Currently, E-mail is most effective in delivering simple messages; complex data should probably be sent in hard-copy documents. As the technology improves,

FIGURE 7.3 ● Sending Memos

Using Paper

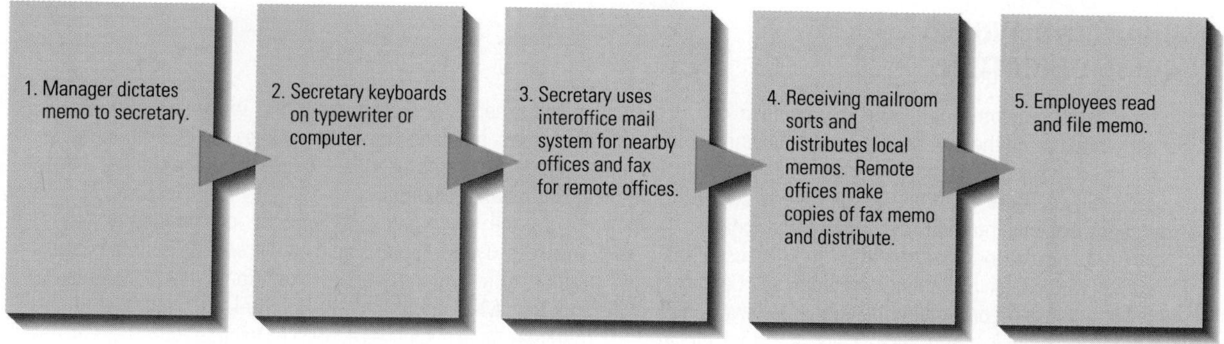

1. Manager dictates memo to secretary.
2. Secretary keyboards on typewriter or computer.
3. Secretary uses interoffice mail system for nearby offices and fax for remote offices.
4. Receiving mailroom sorts and distributes local memos. Remote offices make copies of fax memo and distribute.
5. Employees read and file memo.

Using Electronic Mail

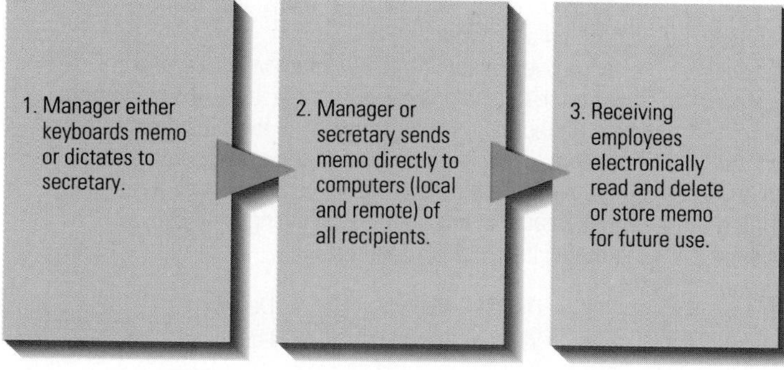

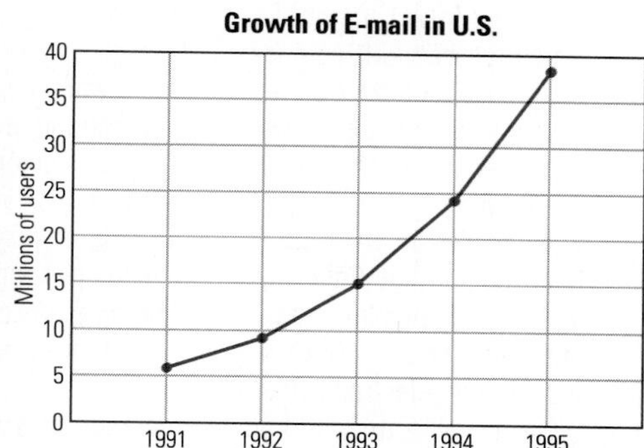

1. Manager either keyboards memo or dictates to secretary.
2. Manager or secretary sends memo directly to computers (local and remote) of all recipients.
3. Receiving employees electronically read and delete or store memo for future use.

Growth of E-mail in U.S.

however, E-mail may replace the traditional method altogether. In the meantime, although E-mail messages are often short, they require the same planning and care as conventional communication. Prudent writers take the time to organize their thoughts, compose carefully, and revise as needed.

Simplicity and economy are especially important in E-mail messages. The small size of many computer monitors makes short sentences and small paragraphs most readable. Writers will also want to curb any tendencies toward stylistic elegance. But they should beware as well of going too far in the direction of informality. One researcher found that E-mail writers used "much more emotional language than when they communicated in other ways, up to and including language used in locker rooms."[7] E-mail business communicators may forget that these messages reflect on themselves and that privacy is in no way guaranteed.

Actually, few guidelines exist for E-mail users. Two suggestions, however, are offered by Robert H. Anderson, who co-authored a report entitled "Toward an Ethic and Etiquette for Electronic Mail."[8] His advice?

● **Writers of E-mail messages should be careful in expressing emotion and must realize that messages are permanent.**

- **Be careful about expressing emotion.** Humor and irony are easily misinterpreted when the receiver can't see a grin or hear a chuckle.
- **Assume that messages are forever.** An electronic message "seems very transitory, but it lives on in somebody's archives."[9] This means that any message sent to another computer can be stored there indefinitely. And even when

HOW E-MAIL IS CHANGING WORLD COMMUNICATION

"E-mail is like a clothespin. Once you figure it out, you can't hang your clothes without it," says industry expert Frank Heart.[10] And it hasn't taken long for millions of businesspeople to figure out that E-mail speeds delivery of messages not only internally but also internationally.

It's not unusual for managers in Germany to use E-mail to confer with design and sales staffs in Israel, California, and Hong Kong. Globe-girdling electronic highways (networks) free communicators almost entirely from the restraints of time and distance.

Let's say, for instance, that you want to communicate with your friend Tom in Japan. You would log on to your local area network, compose a message, and enter Tom's electronic address. Add a few more keystrokes, and your message travels instantly to Tom's electronic mailbox on the other side of the world. If Tom is at his computer keyboard when your message is deposited in his "in box," he will be alerted by a beep and a computer screen announcement that a message for him has just arrived. Two or three minutes later, he can, following a procedure similar to the one you have just employed, place an answer in your own electronic mailbox.

To be able to send and receive such messages, you have three basic E-mail delivery options:

- Public membership networks, such as CompuServe, Prodigy, or America Online
- Private business networks using E-mail software, such as IBM's *PROFS* (popular for mainframes), Digital's *All-In-One* mail program (for minicomputers), and Lotus's *cc:Mail* (the leader among PCs)
- Hybrid service networks, like InfoNet, Bitnet, and InterNet

The advantage of E-mail is obvious: quick, inexpensive, interactive communication. Its rapid growth, say many experts, is transforming the workplace. For one thing, it's breaking down hierarchies by making upper managers more accessible. It's also speeding the pace of business and research.

On the down side, problems of incompatibility may frustrate users. For example, a person with access to many different networks (like CompuServe, GEnie, FidoNet, MCIMail, the Well, Unix-to-Unix Copy, and Bitnet) may need numerous addresses because gateways between these networks are unavailable. Other problems involve lack of privacy, poor security, and ambiguous ownership. Who, for example, owns information "published" on a network?

Moreover, many of the expressive cues present in face-to-face communication (notably, body language and voice inflection) are missing in E-mail environments. Therefore, users have developed their own substitute images, called "emoticons," to accompany their electronic words. Read and interpret the following examples by turning them clockwise 90 degrees:

:-)	Happy, smiley	>:>	Devilish
;-)	Winking, smiley	:-D	Laughing
:-(	Sad, frowning	:-@	Screaming
%-)	Confused	:-/	Skeptical
>:<	Angry	:-P	Nyahhh!

Career Track Application

Conduct a class discussion centered on the topic of E-mail. Who is already using E-mail personally and/or on the job? What for? Is E-mail appropriate for personal messages on the job? Is it safe for transmitting confidential information? Should company guidelines for use be set up?

you think you have erased a message from your own computer, it may remain on your hard disk drive, as Colonel Oliver North and his accusers discovered during the Iran-Contra affair.

Writers of memos, both electronic and hard-copy, run other risks. For advice on specific pitfalls to avoid in crafting memos, see the accompanying Career Skills box.

Planning for the arrival of special guests includes the exchange of many procedure and information memos within the host organization. Communication about unusual events, as well as everyday business, can be carried out by sending E-mail messages or traditional hard copy memos.

Kinds of Memos

Although many different kinds of memos are written to conduct the operations of any organization, their functions can generally be grouped into three categories: (1) procedure and information memos, (2) request and reply memos, and (3) confirmation memos.

Procedure and Information Memos

Procedure and information memos typically flow downward and convey clear information about daily operations.

Most internal memos describe procedures and distribute information. These messages typically flow downward from management to employees and relate to the daily operation of an organization. These nonsensitive messages follow the overall memo plan: clear subject line, direct opening, explanation, and closing. They have one primary function: conveying your idea so clearly that no further explanation (return memo, telephone call, or personal visit) is necessary.

In writing information and procedure memos, be careful of tone. Today's managers seek employee participation and cooperation, but they can't achieve that rapport if they sound like dictators or autocrats. Avoid making accusations and fixing blame. Rather, explain changes, give reasons, and suggest benefits to the reader. Assume that employees want to contribute to the success of the organization and to their own achievement. Remember, too, that saying something negatively *(Don't park in Lot A)* is generally less helpful than saying it positively *(Park in Lot B until Lot A is repaired)*.

The following procedure memo about large printing bills is disappointing both in content and tone.

MEMO TO: Staff Members

Lately, very large expenditures for printing jobs have been submitted, particularly bills being paid to PrintMasters. These bills are suspiciously large and can no longer be honored without careful scrutiny.

Fails to reveal the purpose of the memo (new procedures). Uses accusatory language.

AVOIDING SIX CARDINAL SINS IN WRITING MEMOS

Used carefully, memos deliver vital information and serve valuable functions within organizations. Used inappropriately, they only create problems and reduce productivity. Here are six cardinal sins you'll want to avoid in composing memos on the job:

- **Using an open memo—known as a shotgun or blister memo—to criticize a person or a department.** Shooting it out in a memo can trigger feuds that hurt even those not directly targeted. In the end the initial gunner may be the individual who gets shot down. If you are angry or emotional when writing, don't send the message immediately. Set it aside. After a cooling-off period, you'll probably see the situation differently. When delivering criticism, try to do it in person.
- **Distributing a memo universally.** Resist the urge to send your memo—no matter how artfully crafted—to the entire staff for their edification and enjoyment. Address only the individuals directly involved. If a message requires no reply, put *Information Only* at the top or near the subject line.
- **Expecting confidential memos to remain a secret.** Don't write anything that you couldn't say publicly. When your memo (or E-mail) leaves your computer, it's no longer under your control. And marking a document "Personal" or "Confidential" may actually attract attention. Remember that sensitive topics should be discussed in person.
- **Requiring readers to locate previous correspondence.** It's inconsiderate and inefficient to ask readers to locate documents that may be filed or difficult to find. Help readers by attaching copies of relevant reference materials or by providing brief summaries.
- **Forgetting to make it easy for readers to respond.** You can save your readers' time (and your organization's money) by encouraging them to jot a response down on your memo and return it. Be sure to indicate exactly what information or action you expect.
- **Copying your predecessor's style.** Unless your predecessor was an exceptionally fine writer, you're probably better off developing a writing style that fits your personality. Remember that today's writing is warmer and less formal than the style of messages in the past.

Career Track Application

Collect and analyze memos from your work, your school, and your friends. Do any seem to commit the sins described here? Throughout your course collect memos and other internal documents for class discussion.

Concentrates on what should *not* be done instead of what should be done. Word choice *(must stop, is now required)* conveys authoritarian tone.

Henceforth, all employees may not send out printing jobs without prior written notice. Using PrintMasters as our sole source must stop. Therefore, authorization is now required for all printing. Two copies of any printing order must be submitted to Kelly before any job is commenced. Please see Kelly if you have any questions.

Sounds insincere.

Thank you for your cooperation.

The following improved version of this memo delivers essentially the same message. It reflects, however, a more cooperative tone and illustrates clear thinking and expression.

MEMO TO: Staff

Opening reveals purpose immediately and offers brief explanation.

To improve budget planning and to control costs, please follow the new procedures listed below in submitting future requests for outside printing jobs.

Body uses conversational language in justifying reasons for change in procedures.

In our business, of course, printing is a necessary expenditure. However, our bills seem very high lately, particularly those from PrintMasters. The following procedures should help protect us from being overcharged:

1. Determine your exact printing specifications for a particular job.
2. Secure two estimates for the job.
3. Submit the written estimates to Kelly.
4. Place the order after receiving approval.

Following these new procedures will result in more competitive pricing and perhaps may even provide you with new creative printing options.

Listing of steps in chronological order tells readers exactly how to implement the new procedure. Beginning each numbered item with a verb improves readability and comprehension.

Provides additional justification for the new procedures.

The preceding procedure memo applies a direct strategy in telling how to complete a task. Information memos also use that straightforward approach in supplying details about organization activities, services, and actions. The following memo describes five child-care options. Notice how the information was designed for maximum visual impact and readability. Imagine how it would have looked if it had been presented in one or two big paragraphs.

MEMO TO: Staff

Members of your employee council have met with representatives from management in considering the following four options to provide child care.

1. *On-site day-care centers.* This option accommodates employees' children on the premises. Weekly rates would be competitive with local day-care facilities. This option is most costly but is worth pursuing, particularly if local facilities are deficient.
2. *Off-site centers in conjunction with other local employers.* We are looking into the possibility of developing central centers to be shared with nearby firms.
3. *Neighborhood child-care centers.* We would contract with local centers to buy open slots for employees' children, perhaps at a discount.
4. *Sick-child services.* This plan would provide employees with alternatives to missing work when children are ill. We are investigating sick-child programs at local hospitals and services that send workers to employees' homes to look after sick children.

As soon as we gather more information about these options, we will pass that data along to you.

Straightforward opening immediately sets forth the purpose from the reader's viewpoint.

Since these items reflect no particular order, they could have been bulleted, presenting a slightly cleaner appearance than a numbered list.

Ends with forward-looking statement. No action is required.

Request and Reply Memos

In requesting routine information or action within an organization, the direct approach works best. Generally, this means asking for information or making the request without first providing elaborate explanations and justifications. Remember that readers are usually thinking, "Why me? Why am I receiving this?" Readers can understand the explanation better once they know the request.

● **Request and reply memos follow the direct pattern in seeking or providing information.**

If you are seeking answers to questions, you have two options for opening the memo: (1) Ask the most important question first, followed by an explanation and then the other questions. (2) Use a polite command, such as *Please answer the following questions regarding . . .*

In the body of the memo, you can explain and justify your request or reply. When many questions must be asked, list them, being careful to phrase them similarly. Be courteous and friendly. In the closing include an end date (with a reason, if possible) to promote a quick response. For simple requests some writers encourage their readers to jot responses directly on the request memo. This practice saves everyone time.

The following request memo seeks information from managers about the use of temporary office workers. It begins with a polite command followed by numbered questions. Notice that the writer develops reader's benefits by describing how the data collected will be used to help the reader. Notice, too, the effort to promote the feeling that the writer is part of a team working together with employees to achieve their common goals.

MEMO TO: Department Managers

Opens with polite command.

Please answer the questions below about the use of temporary help in your department.

Explains the purpose concisely.

With your ideas we plan to develop a policy that will help us improve the process of budgeting, selecting, and hiring temporaries.

Lists parallel questions for easy reading and comprehension.

1. What is the average number of temporary office workers you employ each month?
2. What is the average length of a temporary worker's assignment in your department?
3. What specific job skills are you generally seeking in your temporaries?
4. What temporary agencies are you now using?

Includes end date, along with reason; makes it easy for reader to respond.

Just write your answers on this sheet, and return it to me before January 20. By the end of the month, we plan to have an improved policy that will help you fill your temporary employment needs as efficiently as possible.

In replying to simple requests that require no file copies, you can simply pen your remarks on the original memo and return it. For more complex answers, use the direct approach outlined earlier.

Writers sometimes fall into bad habits in answering memos. Here are some trite and long-winded openers that are best avoided:

In response to your message of the 15th . . . *(States the obvious.)*

Thank you for your memo of the 15th in which you . . . *(Suggests the writer can think of nothing more original.)*

I have before me your memo of the 15th in which you . . . *(Unnecessarily identifies the location of the previous message.)*

Pursuant to your request of the 15th . . . *(Sounds old-fashioned.)*

This is to inform you that . . . *(Delays getting to the point.)*

Please refer to your memo of . . . *(Asks reader to search for original document. Always supply a copy if necessary or summarize its points.)*

● **Direct opening statements can also be cheerful and empathic.**

Instead of falling into the trap of using one of the preceding shop-worn openings, start directly by responding to the writer's request. If you agree to the request, show your cheerful compliance immediately. Consider these good-news openers:

Yes, I will be glad to . . . *(Sends message of approval by opening with "Yes.")*

Here are answers to the questions you asked about . . . *(Sounds straightforward, businesslike, and professional.)*

You're right in seeking advice about . . . *(Opens with two words that every reader enjoys seeing and hearing.)*

We are happy to assist you in . . . *(Shows writer's helpful nature and goodwill.)*

The information you requested is shown on the attached . . . *(Gets right to the point.)*

After a direct and empathic opener, provide the information requested in a logical and coherent order. If you're answering a number of questions, arrange your answers in the order of the questions. In the favorable reply shown in Figure 7.4, information describing dates, speakers, and topics is listed in columns with headings. Although it requires more space than the paragraph format, this arrangement vastly improves readability and comprehension.

In providing additional data, use familiar words, short sentences, short paragraphs, and active-voice verbs. When alternatives exist, make them clear. Consider

FIGURE 7.4 ● **Reply Memo**

Tips for Memo Formatting

- Set one tab to line up all entries evenly after SUBJECT.
- Leave two blank lines between SUBJECT line and first line of memo text.
- Single-space all but the shortest memos. Double-space between paragraphs.
- For memos printed on plain paper, leave a top margin of 2 inches for full-page memos and 1 inch for half-page memos.
- Use 1¼-inch side margins.
- If a memo requires two pages, use a second-page heading that includes the addressee's name, page number, and date.
- Handwrite your initials after your typed name.

check on screen

Interoffice Memo

TO: Chris Kennedy
Vice President

DATE: September 4, 1994

FROM: Rick Estrada RE
Marketing Director

SUBJECT: SCHEDULING MANAGEMENT COUNCIL SPEAKERS

In response to your request, I'm happy to act as program chair for this year's luncheon meetings of the management council. Here's a tentative lineup of speakers I've scheduled for the first three meetings.

Date	Speaker	Topic
November 14	Dr. Helene Gardner Psychologist, USC	Successful Performance Appraisals
January 12	Mr. Jorge A. Rivera President, Rivera & Associates	Conducting Legal Employment Interviews
March 13	Ms. Lynn Hampton-Lee Consultant	Avoiding Sexual Harassment

As you suggested, I consulted other members of the council regarding an honorarium for the speakers. Frank Selby, Maria Lupo, Luke Chomsky, and I agreed that $200 was a reasonable sum to offer. The three speakers listed above seemed to consider $200 an acceptable amount.

For the last meeting in May, we have two topic possibilities. Which program would you prefer?

(1) Ethics in the Contemporary Office

(2) Time Management for Today's Managers

Because other members of the council were evenly divided between the choices, they wanted you to make the final decision. Just circle the program you prefer on the memo copy I've attached. Once I receive your choice, I'll begin looking immediately for a suitable speaker.

ftf
Enclosure

Announces good news directly and cordially

Lists data in columns with headings for easy reading

Uses short, active-voice sentences

Highlights choices with (1) and (2)

Anticipates need for two copies of memo

Makes it easy for reader to respond

WordPerfect Corporation: Career Track Profile

"People want to know that they are being taken seriously and that their requests are understood."

In little over a decade, WordPerfect Corporation swamped the competition and rose to the top of the word processing market. Nestled at the foot of snow-peaked mountains in Orem, it has become one of Utah's largest and most stable employers. Darin Richins considered himself a "lucky guy" to land a job with WordPerfect soon after graduating from Brigham Young University.

As a media specialist Darin publicizes products, oversees public relations specialists, and makes presentations to management and the press about product strategies and information. He also responds to "escalated" user-support problems. Actually, few problems reach an escalated or intensified status at WordPerfect because of its total commitment to customer service. "WordPerfect's support operation," says industry expert Amy Wohl, "is the biggest and the best. They take good care of everybody. They don't [even] ask you if you're a customer, because they figure if you aren't one now, next time out you will be." This kind of world-class service propelled WordPerfect into its no. 1 status. "WordStar was in there before us," admits founder Alan C. Ashton, "and I think they could have had the whole market if they'd paid more attention to customers."

WordPerfect certainly leads the industry in paying attention to customers. Each day 850 operators patiently answer the questions of over 20,000 callers who inquire about their computer software. For waiting callers, professional disc jockeys (called WordPerfect "hold" jockeys) play specially selected music. They intersperse talk with music, giving ski and weather news and also telling callers how long the wait will be and how many others are waiting. To ensure that callers don't have to wait too long, traffic is monitored by an elaborate cable TV system. When a red bar begins to spread across the screen, indicating a buildup of callers on hold, more operators are added immediately.

WordPerfect listens not only to customers but also to community members. Darin explains: "We think of community members as our users, too. Every corporation has a challenge in its community to be portrayed as a good corporate citizen. Because WordPerfect is a highly successful and very visible industry here in the Utah Valley, we receive an enormous number of financial requests. Naturally, we have to be selective. Some requests must be turned down." Darin also occasionally writes to users conveying bad news about "product

SUBJECT: Lack of Communication

I shouldn't have to tell you how much we depend on our community volunteers. Without them, many of our programs would fail.

Selections would have to be subject to our staffing needs within individual departments. For example, if everyone wanted the same day, we could not allow everyone to take it. In that case, we would allow the employee with the most seniority to have the day off.

Before we institute the new plan, though, we wanted to see what employees thought about this. Is it better to continue our current companywide uniform floating holiday?

Or should we try an individual floating holiday? Please let us know what you think as soon as possible.

Problems

7.6 Information Memo: Excellence in Georgia

After a depressing year of bad news and poor profits, Georgia Power was eager to find ways to improve employee morale. Its president, Bill Dahlberg, dreamed up an award program he calls "Everybody Has a Customer." This program would encourage employees to recognize fellow employees for outstanding effort and excellent achievement on the job.

You think that the award should be a certificate, with room for a picture of the awardee. You arrange for Polaroid cameras to be purchased and distributed to all locations. When an employee wishes to make an award, the awarder fills out the certificate and takes two pictures. For maximum visibility you think that one certificate should go to the awardee and another should be posted in the central entrance hall—on an employee bulletin board of honor. The program is to begin April 1. To make this program successful, you need to enlist the support of all managers. They, in turn, should inform and encourage employees to participate.

As vice president of Human Resources Development, write a memo to all managers describing the program and asking for their help. Tell them to discuss the program with their employees and distribute flyers you've had prepared. Encourage them to make comments and suggestions.[12]

7.7 Collaborative Information Memo: Holiday Partying

You feel that your department should have a Christmas or holiday party this year. After considerable urging, your boss finally agrees to allow one, so long as you and the other employees plan the event and share the costs with the company. You consult most of the people in your department and find that they'd like a Christmas dinner party at a local restaurant. In teams of four or five, work out details, such as date and time, type of dress, costs, guests, exchange of gifts, and entertainment. Then write a memo to your boss, Brian Lockwood, describing your plans and asking his permission to proceed. Be sure to make it easy for him to read and respond to your memo.

7.8 Procedure Memo: Ticket-Free Parking

Assume that you are Tran Crozier, director of the Human Resources Division of IBM at Franklin Lakes, New York. Both day- and swing-shift employees need to be reminded of the parking guidelines. Day-shift employees must park in Lots A and B in their assigned spaces. If they have not registered their cars and received their white stickers, the cars will be ticketed.

Day-shift employees are forbidden to park at the curb. Swing-shift employees may park at the curb before 3:30 p.m. Moreover, after 3:30 p.m. swing-shift employees may park in any empty space—except those marked Tandem, Handicapped, Van Pool, Car Pool, or Management. Day-shift employees may loan their spaces to other employees if they know they will not be using the space.

One serious problem is lack of registration (as evidenced by white stickers). Registration is done by Employee Relations. Any car without a sticker will be ticketed. To encourage registration, Employee Relations will be in the cafeteria May 12 and 13 from 11:30 a.m. to 1:30 p.m. and from 3 p.m. to 5 p.m. to take applications and issue white parking stickers.

Write a memo to employees that reviews the parking guidelines and encourages them to get their cars registered. Use itemization techniques and strive for a tone that fosters a sense of cooperation rather than resentment.

7.9 Procedure Memo: Hot Calls in August

Play the part of Sally Chernoff, division sales manager of DataCom Electronics. The company's long-distance telephone bills have been skyrocketing. Sales reps use the telephone to make "hot" calls—to close deals or to persuade hard-sells. However, Paul Wilson, vice president of Sales, is not sure that the cost of these calls is worth the return. He suggested sharply reducing or even eliminating *all* long-distance calls made by sales reps, but you want to collect information first. You propose a plan.

For the month of August, all sales reps are to place their long-distance calls through the company operator (rather than dialing direct). They are to keep a log of all calls, including the date, time, city, and reason for call. In September you'd like them to give you that telephone log. Then you can analyze the data and perhaps solve this telephone budget crisis. Privately, you hope that the cumbersome procedure will, by itself, decrease the number of calls.

Write a memo to all sales reps describing this procedure. Attach a telephone log. Include reader benefits and itemization techniques.

7.10 Request Memo: Visiting Computers

Revise the following poorly expressed memo.

TO: Keisha Wilson DATE: Current
FROM: Douglas Rockland
SUBJECT: Computer Visit

Please refer to my memo of May 20 in which I raised the possibility of a visitation to be made by you to Berkshire

Furniture Company. As I discussed in my memo, my friend Jim Ling is president at Berkshire; and he was telling me how his new multiuser computer system was solving some of the same problems that we face. I've arranged for you to tour their organization Thursday, June 4, at 1 p.m.

I am interested in a number of things, which we can talk about in my office Monday, June 8 at 10 a.m. after you return from your tour. One problem is connection of terminals from their factory to their order department. How do they do it? Another question I have relates to their accounting department and executive offices. Are these areas on the same computing system? The last thing I want you to be sure to find out about is how this computer system tracks shipments to customers.

Thank you for your cooperation.

7.11 Reply Memo: Rescheduling Interviews

Your boss, Fred Knox, had scheduled three appointments to interview applicants for an accounting position. All these appointments were for Friday, October 7. However, he now must travel to Philadelphia on that weekend. He asks you to reschedule all the appointments for one week later. He also wants a brief summary of the background of each candidate.

You call each person and arrange these times. Paul Scheffel, who has been an accountant for 15 years with Bechtel Corporation, agreed to come at 10:30 a.m. Mark Cunningham, who is a CPA and a consultant to many companies, will come at 11:30. Geraldine Simpson, who has a B.A. degree and 8 years of experience in payroll accounting, will come at 9:30 a.m. You're wondering if Mr. Knox forgot to include Don Stastry, operations personnel officer, in these interviews. Mr. Stastry usually is part of the selection process.

Write a memo to Mr. Knox including all the vital information he needs.

7.12 Confirmation Memo: Dream Vacation

Play the role of Jack Mendoza. You had a vacation planned for September 2 through 16. But yesterday your wife suggested delaying the vacation for several weeks so that you could travel through New England when the fall colors are most beautiful. She said it would be the vacation of her dreams, and you agree. Perhaps you could change your vacation dates. Alas, you remember that you're scheduled to attend the Hampshire marketing exhibit September 29–30. But maybe Melanie Grasso would fill in for you and make the presentation of the company's newest product, JuiceMate. You see your boss, Mas Watanabe, in the hall and decide to ask if you can change your vacation to September 28 through October 12. To your surprise, he agrees to the new dates. He also assures you that he will ask Melanie to make the presentation—and encourage her to give a special demonstration to the Dana Corporation, which you believe should be targeted.

Back in your office, you begin to worry. What if Mas forgets about your conversation? You can't afford to take that chance. Write a confirmation memo that summarizes the necessary facts—and also conveys your gratitude.

C.L.U.E. Review 7

Edit the following sentences to correct all language faults, including grammar, punctuation, spelling, and word use.

1. Mr. Krikorian always tries however to wear a tie and shirt that has complimentary colors.
2. The federal trade commission are holding hearings to illicit information about IBMs request to expand marketing in twenty-one city's.
3. Consumer buying and spending for the past 5 years, is being studied by a Federal team of analysts.
4. Because we recommend that students bring there own supplies; the total expense for the trip should be a miner amount.
5. Wasnt it Mr Cohen not Ms Lyons who asked for a tuition waver.
6. As soon as we can verify the figures either my sales manager or myself will call you, nevertheless, you must continue to disperse payroll funds.
7. Our human resources department which was formerally in room 35 has moved it's offices to room 5.
8. We have arranged interviews on the following dates, Wednesday at 330 pm Thursday at 1030 am and Friday at 415 pm.
9. The Post Dispatch our local newspaper featured as its principle article a story entitled, Smarter E-Mail is here.
10. Every one on the payroll, which includes all dispatchers and supervisers were cautioned to maintain careful records everyday.

enhancement" (requests asking WordPerfect to write special programs to make software perform specific functions).

When Darin must say no to customers or to community members, he prefers to break the bad news personally on the telephone. Often, though, a letter is required. In writing these bad-news letters, Darin begins by expressing appreciation or showing that he understands the request. If a request can't be granted, he explains why, trying to convey to the reader WordPerfect's position. When alternatives exist, he presents them, closing his letter on a positive note.

"For me, the most important thing to remember in working with negative news," says Darin, "is listening to customers and making sure I understand what they are asking. People want to know that they are being taken seriously and that their requests are understood. Usually, a short letter gives the wrong impression; it carries the message that we didn't adequately examine their request. A longer letter gives me a chance to explain our position and also reflects the hidden message that we value the reader enough to take the time to explain."

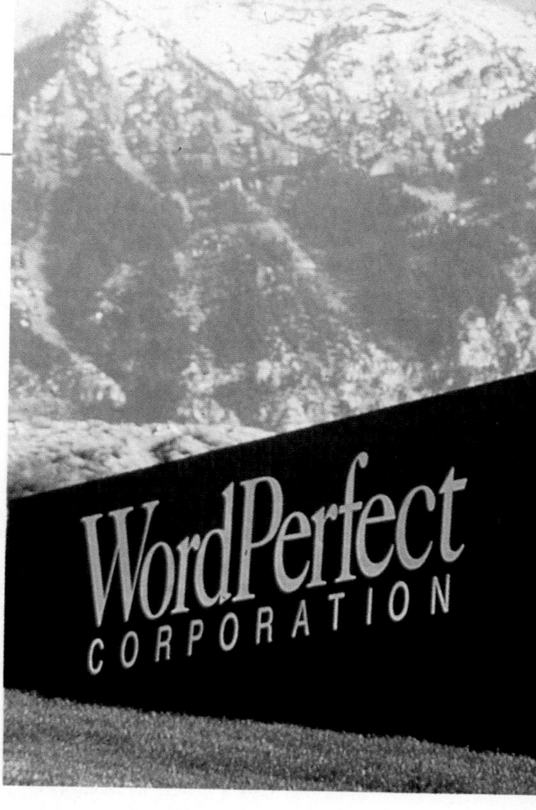

As a premier producer of word processing software, WordPerfect devotes a good deal of its resources to communication and support. About one fourth of its employees work in problem resolution, information services, customer support, and SWAT (Strategic WordPerfect Assistance Team) positions.

When Darin started at WordPerfect two years ago, he brought with him good training in communication and writing basics from his courses at BYU. What he needed to learn on the job was a technical vocabulary to describe WordPerfect's products and operations—the jargon that insiders used regularly. He acquired this knowledge by talking with coworkers and by cramming WordPerfect literature. "Those first months on the job demanded heavy homework," remembers Darin. "In developing my own letter-writing style, I reviewed textbook examples and studied trade publications. To learn how formal to be and to absorb the WordPerfect image, I examined documents that crossed my desk and analyzed letters in our huge files."

Darin particularly admires the image that WordPerfect has achieved. "This company has built a prominent reputation on its reliability and integrity. People expect us to be truthful. Even with bad news to announce, we don't try to cover it up or avoid it. When our *WordPerfect for Windows* was delayed, we were up front with our distributors and customers. Industry was crying for a windows word processor from WordPerfect, but it took us longer to develop than we expected. We explained that the newer technology was hard for us to gauge. And we're convinced that our honest explanations saved us customers and helped us retain the reputation on which WordPerfect was founded."[1]

Strategies for Breaking Bad News

● The sting of bad news can be reduced by giving reasons and communicating sensitively.

Breaking bad news is a fact of business life for Darin Richins and most other communicators. Because bad news disappoints, irritates, and sometimes even angers receivers, such messages must be written carefully. As Richins suggests, the bad feelings associated with disappointing news can be reduced if (1) the reader knows the reasons for the rejection and (2) the bad news is revealed with sensitivity. You've probably heard people say, "It wasn't so much the bad news that I resented. It was the way I was told!"

This chapter concentrates on how to use the indirect pattern in delivering negative messages. You'll apply that pattern to messages that refuse routine requests, deliver bad news to customers, and deal with negative organization news. But you'll also learn to identify four instances when the direct pattern may be preferable in announcing bad news.

Goals in Communicating Bad News

● In communicating bad news, key goals include getting the receiver to accept it, maintaining goodwill, and avoiding legal liability.

As a business communicator who must deliver bad news, you have many goals. First, you want to make the reader understand and *accept* the bad news. The indirect pattern helps in achieving these objectives. Second, you want to promote and maintain a good image of yourself and your organization. This goal is especially challenging since you are delivering bad news. Third, you want to make the message so clear that additional correspondence is unnecessary. Finally, you want to avoid creating legal liability or responsibility.

These are ambitious goals, and we're not always successful in achieving them all. The patterns you're about to learn, however, provide the beginning communicator with strategies and tactics that many writers have found successful in conveying disappointing news sensitively and safely. With experience, you'll be able to vary these patterns and adapt them to your organization's specific writing tasks.

Using the Indirect Pattern to Prepare the Reader

● The indirect pattern softens the impact of bad news by giving reasons and explanations first.

Revealing bad news indirectly shows sensitivity to your reader. Whereas good news can be revealed quickly, bad news must be broken gradually. By preparing the reader, you soften the impact. A blunt announcement of disappointing news might cause the receiver to stop reading and toss the message down. The indirect strategy enables you to keep the reader's attention until you have been able to explain the reasons for the bad news. The indirect plan consists of four parts, as shown in Figure 8.1:

- **Buffer**—a neutral or positive opening that does not reveal the bad news
- **Reasons**—an explanation of the causes for the bad news before disclosing it
- **Bad news**—a clear but understated announcement of the bad news that may include an alternative or compromise
- **Close**—a personalized, forward-looking, pleasant statement

Avoiding Three Causes of Legal Problems

Before we examine the components of a bad-news message, let's look more closely at how you can avoid exposing yourself and your employer to legal liability in writing negative messages. Although we can't always anticipate the consequences of

FIGURE 8.1 ● **Four-Part Indirect Pattern for Bad News**

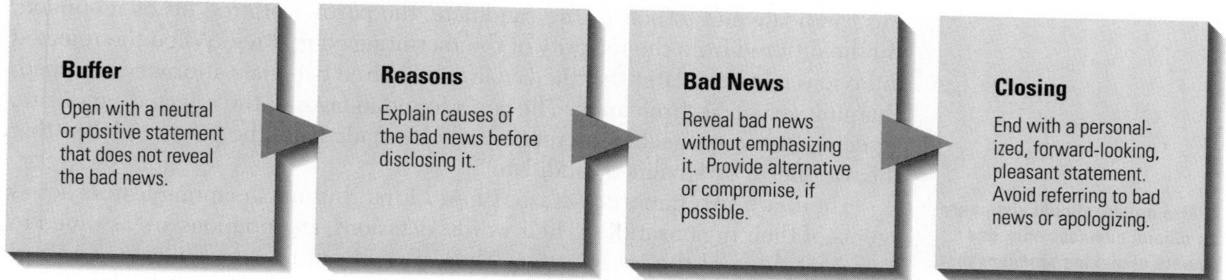

our words, we should be alert to three causes of legal difficulties: (1) abusive language, (2) careless language, and (3) the "good-guy syndrome."

Buffer
Open with a neutral or positive statement that does not reveal the bad news.
Reasons
Explain causes of the bad news before disclosing it.
Bad News
Reveal bad news without emphasizing it. Provide alternative or compromise, if possible.
Closing
End with a personalized, forward-looking, pleasant statement. Avoid referring to bad news or apologizing.

Abusive language. Calling people names (such as "deadbeat," "crook," or "quack") can get you in trouble. *Defamation* is the legal term for any false statement that harms an individual's reputation. When the abusive language is written, it's called *libel;* when spoken, it's *slander.* To be actionable (likely to result in a lawsuit), abusive language must be (1) false, (2) damaging to one's good name, and (3) "published"—that is, spoken within the presence of others or written. Thus, if you were alone with Jane Doe and accused her of accepting bribes and selling company secrets to competitors, she couldn't sue because the defamation wasn't published. Her reputation was not damaged. But if anyone heard the words or if they were written, you might be legally liable. Obviously, competent communicators avoid making unproven charges and letting their emotions prompt abusive language.

● **Abusive language becomes legally actionable when it is false, harmful to person's good name, and "published."**

Careless language. As the marketplace becomes increasingly litigious, we must be certain that our words communicate only what we intend. Take the case of a factory worker injured on the job. His attorney subpoenaed company documents and discovered a seemingly harmless letter sent to a group regarding a plant tour. These words appeared in the letter: "Although we are honored at your interest in our company, we cannot give your group a tour of the plant operations as it would be too noisy and dangerous." The court found in favor of the worker, inferring from the letter that working conditions were indeed hazardous.[2] The letter writer did not intend to convey the impression of dangerous working conditions, but the court accepted that interpretation.

This case points up two important cautions. First, be careful in making statements that are potentially damaging or that could be misinterpreted. Be wary of explanations that convey more information than you intend. Second, be careful about what documents you save. Attorneys may demand, in pursuing a lawsuit, all company files pertaining to a case. Even documents marked "Confidential" or "Personal" may be used.

The good-guy syndrome. Most of us hate to have to reveal bad news—that is, to be the bad guy. To make ourselves look better, to make the reader feel better, and to maintain good relations, we are tempted to make statements that are legally dangerous. Consider the case of a law firm interviewing job candidates. One of the firm's partners was asked to inform a candidate that she was not selected. The partner's letter said, "Although you were by far the most qualified candidate we interviewed, unfortunately, we have decided we do not have a position for a person

● **Avoid statements that make you feel good but may be misleading or inaccurate.**

of your talents at this time." To show that he personally had no reservations about this candidate and to bolster the candidate, the partner offered his own opinion. But he differed from the majority of the recruiting committee. When the rejected interviewee learned later that the law firm had hired two male attorneys, she sued, charging sexual discrimination. The court found in favor of the rejected candidate, agreeing that a reasonable inference could be made from the partner's letter that she was the "most qualified candidate."[3]

● Use organizational stationery for official business only, and beware of making promises that can't be fulfilled.

There are two important lessons here. First, business communicators act as agents of their organizations. Their words, decisions, and opinions are assumed to represent those of the organization. Thus, if you want to communicate your personal feelings or opinions, use plain paper (rather than company letterhead) and sign your name without title or affiliation. Second, volunteering extra information can lead to trouble. Thus, avoid supplying data that could be misused, and avoid making promises that can't be fulfilled. Don't admit or imply responsibility for conditions that caused damage or injury. Even apologies *(We're sorry that a faulty bottle cap caused damage to your carpet)* may suggest liability.

In Chapter 3 we discussed four information areas that generate the most lawsuits: investments, safety, marketing, and human resources. In this chapter we'll make specific suggestions for avoiding legal liability in writing responses to claim letters, credit letters, and personnel documents. You may find that in the most critical areas (such as collection letters or hiring/firing messages) your organization provides language guidelines and form letters approved by legal counsel. As the business environment becomes more perilous, we must be not only sensitive to the reader but also keenly aware of risks to ourselves and to the organizations we represent.

Components of a Bad-News Message

Legal issues aside, let's move on to the central focus of this chapter—how to deliver a bad-news message using the indirect pattern. The message will have four parts as shown in Figure 8.2: buffer, reasons, bad news, and closing.

● To reduce negative feelings, use a buffer opening for sensitive bad-news messages.

Buffering the opening. A buffer is a device to reduce shock or pain. To buffer the pain of bad news, begin with a neutral or positive statement that makes the reader continue reading. The buffer should be relevant and concise and provide a natural transition to the explanation that follows. The individual situation, of course, will help determine what you should put in the buffer. Here are some possibilities for opening bad-news messages.

Best news. Start with the part of the message that represents the best news. For example, in a memo that announces a new service along with a cutback in mail room hours, you might write, *To ensure that your correspondence goes out with the last pickup, we're starting a new messenger pickup service at 2:30 p.m. daily beginning June 1.*

Compliment. Praise the receiver's accomplishments, organization, or efforts. But do so with honesty and sincerity. For instance, in a letter declining an invitation to speak, you could write, *The Thalians have my sincere admiration for their fund-raising projects on behalf of hungry children. I am honored that you asked me to speak Friday, November 5.*

FIGURE 8.2 ● **Delivering Bad News Sensitively**

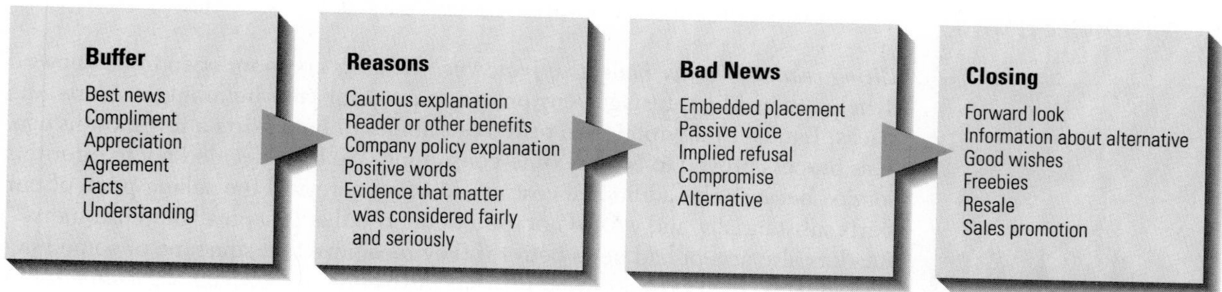

Appreciation. Convey thanks to the reader—for doing business, for sending something, for conveying confidence in your organization, for expressing feelings, or simply for providing feedback. Suppose you had to draft a letter that refuses employment. You could say, *I appreciated learning about your qualifications and the professional secretaries program at Valley College in our interview last Friday.* Avoid thanking the reader, however, for something you are about to refuse.

● **Openers can buffer the bad news with compliments, appreciation, agreement, relevant facts, and understanding.**

Agreement. Make a relevant statement with which both reader and receiver can agree. A letter that rejects a loan application might read, *We both realize how much the export business has been affected by the relative strength of the dollar in the past two years.*

Facts. Provide objective information that introduces the bad news. For example, in a memo announcing cutbacks in the hours of the employees' cafeteria, you might say, *During the past five years the number of employees eating breakfast in our cafeteria has dropped from 32 percent to 12 percent.*

Understanding. Show that you care about the reader. Notice how in this letter to customers announcing a product defect, the writer expresses concern: *We know that you expect superior performance from all the office products you order from Quill. That's why we're writing personally about the Exell printer ribbons you recently ordered.*

Good buffers avoid revealing the bad news immediately. Moreover, they do not convey a false impression that good news follows. Additionally, they provide a natural transition to the next bad-news letter component—the reasons.

Presenting the reasons. The most important part of a bad-news letter is the section that explains why a negative decision is necessary. As part of your planning before writing, you analyzed the problem and decided to refuse a request for specific reasons. Before disclosing the bad news that may upset the reader, try to explain those reasons.

● **Bad-news messages should explain reasons before stating the negative news.**

Being cautious in explaining. If the reasons are not confidential and if they will not create legal liability, you can be specific: *Growers supplied us with a limited number of patio roses, and our demand this year was twice that of last year.* In refusing a speaking engagement, tell why the date is impossible: *On January 17 we have a*

SPOTLIGHT ON COMMUNICATORS

Millionaire publisher Malcolm Forbes recognized that being agreeable while disagreeing is truly an art. He advised being positive and "nice." Contrary to the cliché, genuinely nice people most often finish first or very near it. He suggested using the acid test, particularly for a bad-news message. After you finish, read it *out loud*. You'll know if it sounds natural, positive, and respectful.

board of directors meeting that I must attend. Don't, however, make unrealistic or dangerous statements in an effort to be the "good guy."

Citing reader or other benefits if plausible. Readers are more open to bad news if it helps them. In refusing a customer's request for free hemming of skirts and slacks, Lands' End wrote: "We tested our ability to hem skirts a few months ago. This process proved to be very time-consuming. We have decided not to offer this service because the additional cost would have increased the selling price of our skirts substantially, and we did not want to impose that cost on all our customers."[4] Readers also accept bad news better if they recognize that someone or something else benefits, such as other workers or the environment: *Although we would like to consider your application, we prefer to fill managerial positions from within.* Avoid trying to show reader benefits, though, if they appear insincere: *To improve our service to you, we're increasing our brokerage fees.*

Explaining company policy. Readers resent blanket policy statements prohibiting something: *Company policy prevents us from making cash refunds* or *Contract bids may be accepted from local companies only* or *Company policy requires us to promote from within.* Instead of hiding behind company policy, gently explain why the policy makes sense: *We prefer to promote from within because it rewards the loyalty of our employees. In addition, we've found that people familiar with our organization make the quickest contribution to our team effort.* By offering explanations, you demonstrate that you care about readers and are treating them as important individuals.

Choosing positive words. As you learned in Chapter 3, the words you use affect a reader's response. Remember that the objective of the indirect pattern is holding the reader's attention until you've had a chance to explain the reasons justifying the bad news. To keep the reader in a receptive mood, avoid expressions that might cause the reader to tune out. Be sensitive to negative words like *claim, error, failure, fault, impossible, mistaken, misunderstand, never, regret, unwilling, unfortunately,* and *violate.*

Showing that the matter was treated seriously and fairly. In explaining reasons, demonstrate to the reader that you take the matter seriously, have investigated carefully, and are making an unbiased decision. As Darin Richins at WordPerfect points out, "Readers are much more accepting of bad news when they feel that they have been treated fairly." Avoid passing the buck or blaming others within your organization. Such unprofessional behavior makes the reader lose faith in you and your company.

Techniques for cushioning bad news include positioning it strategically, using the passive voice, implying the refusal, and suggesting alternatives or compromises.

Cushioning the bad news. Although you can't prevent the disappointment that bad news brings, you can reduce the pain somewhat by breaking the news sensitively. Be especially considerate when the reader will suffer personally from the bad news. A number of thoughtful techniques can cushion the blow.

Positioning the bad news strategically. Instead of spotlighting it, sandwich the bad news between other sentences, perhaps among your reasons. Don't let the refusal begin or end a paragraph—the reader's eye will linger on these high-visibility spots. Another technique that reduces shock is putting a painful idea in a subordinate clause: *Although another candidate was hired, we appreciate your interest in our organization and wish you success in your job search.* Subordinate clauses often begin with words like *although, as, because, if,* and *since.*

Using the passive voice. Passive-voice verbs enable you to depersonalize an action. Whereas the active voice focuses attention on a person *(We don't give cash refunds),* the passive voice highlights the action *(Cash refunds are not given because . . .).* Use the passive voice for the bad news.

Accentuating the positive. As you learned in Chapter 3, messages are far more effective when you describe what you can do instead of what you can't do. Rather than *We will no longer allow credit card purchases,* try a more positive appeal: *We are now selling gasoline at discount cash prices.*

Implying the refusal. It's sometimes possible to avoid a direct statement of refusal. Often, your reasons and explanations leave no doubt that a request has been denied. Explicit refusals may be unnecessary and at times cruel. In this refusal to contribute to a charity, for example, the writer never actually says no: *Because we will soon be moving into new offices in Glendale, all our funds are earmarked for moving and furnishings. We hope that next year we'll be able to support your worthwhile charity.* The danger of an implied refusal, of course, is that it is so subtle that the reader misses it. Be certain that you make the bad news clear, thus preventing the need for further correspondence.

Suggesting a compromise or an alternative. A refusal is not so depressing—for the sender or the receiver—if a suitable compromise, substitute, or alternative is available. In denying permission to a class to visit a historical private residence, for instance, this writer softens the bad news by proposing an alternative: *Although private tours of the grounds are not given, we do open the house and its gardens for one charitable event in the fall.*

You can further reduce the impact of the bad news by refusing to dwell on it. Present it briefly (or imply it), and move on to your closing.

Closing pleasantly. After explaining the bad news sensitively, close the message with a pleasant statement that promotes goodwill. The closing should be personalized and may include a forward look, an alternative, good wishes, freebies, resale information, or an off-the-subject remark.

● Closings to bad-news messages might include a forward look, an alternative, good wishes, freebies, and resale or sales promotion information.

Forward look. Anticipate future relations or business. A letter that refuses a contract proposal might read: *Thanks for your bid. We look forward to working with your talented staff when future projects demand your special expertise.*

Alternative. If an alternative exists, end your letter with follow-through advice. For example, in a letter rejecting a customer's demand for replacement of landscaping plants, you might say: *I will be happy to give you a free inspection and consultation. Please call 746-8112 to arrange a date for my visit.*

Good wishes. A letter rejecting a job candidate might read: *We appreciate your interest in our company, and we extend to you our best wishes in your search to find the perfect match between your skills and job requirements.*

Freebies. When customers complain—primarily about food products or small consumer items—companies often send coupons, samples, or gifts to restore confidence and to promote future business. In response to a customer's complaint about a frozen dinner, you could write, *Your loyalty and your concern about our frozen entrees is genuinely appreciated. Because we want you to continue enjoying our healthful and convenient dinners, we're enclosing a coupon that you can take to your local market to select your next Green Valley entree.*

Resale or sales promotion. When the bad news is not devastating or personal, references to resale information or promotion may be appropriate: *The computer workstations you ordered are unusually popular because of their stain-, heat-, and scratch-resistant finishes. To help you locate hard-to-find accessories for these workstations, we're enclosing our latest catalog, in which you'll find surge suppressors, multiple outlet strips, security devices, and PC tool kits.*

Avoid endings that sound canned, insincere, inappropriate, or self-serving or that invite further correspondence *(If you have any questions, do not hesitate . . .).* Don't refer to the bad news, and in general don't apologize. Apologies tend to be counterproductive; they undermine your decision and may unwittingly suggest legal responsibility. To review these suggestions for delivering bad news sensitively, take another look at Figure 8.2.

When to Use the Direct Pattern

● **The direct pattern is appropriate when the receiver might overlook the bad news, when directness is preferred, or when firmness is necessary.**

Most bad-news letters are best organized indirectly, beginning with a buffer and reasons. The direct pattern, with the bad news first, may be more effective, though, in situations like the following:

- **When the receiver may overlook the bad news.** With the crush of mail today, many readers skim messages, looking only at the opening. If they don't find substantive material, they may discard the message. Rate increases, changes in service, new policy requirements—these critical messages may require boldness to ensure attention.
- **When organization policy suggests directness.** Some companies expect all internal messages and announcements—even bad news—to be straightforward and presented without frills.
- **When the receiver prefers directness.** Busy managers may prefer directness. Such shorter messages enable the reader to get in the proper frame of mind immediately. If you suspect that the reader prefers that the facts be presented straightaway, use the direct pattern.
- **When firmness is necessary.** Messages that must demonstrate determination and strength should not use delaying techniques. For example, the last in a series of collection letters that seek payment of overdue accounts may require a direct opener.

Applying the 3-×-3 Writing Process

● **The 3-x-3 writing process is especially important in crafting bad-news messages because of the potential consequences of poorly written messages.**

Thinking through the entire process is especially important in bad-news letters. Not only do you want the receiver to understand and accept the message, but you want to be careful that your words say only what you intend. Thus, you'll want to apply the familiar 3-×-3 writing process to bad-news letters.

Analysis, anticipation, and adaptation. In Phase 1 you need to analyze the bad news so that you can anticipate its effect on the receiver. If the disappointment will be mild, announce it directly. If the bad news is serious or personal, consider techniques to reduce the pain. Adapt your words to protect the receiver's ego. Instead of *You neglected to change the oil, causing severe damage to the engine,* switch to the passive voice: *The oil wasn't changed causing severe damage to the engine.* Choose words that show you respect the reader as a responsible, valuable person.

Research, organization, and composition. In Phase 2 you can gather information and brainstorm for ideas. Jot down all the reasons you have that explain the bad news. If four or five reasons prompted your negative decision, concentrate on the strongest and safest ones. Avoid presenting any weak reasons; readers may seize on them to reject the entire message. After selecting your best reasons, outline the four parts of the bad-news pattern: buffer, reasons, bad news, closing. Flesh out each section as you compose your first draft.

Revision, proofreading, and evaluation. In Phase 3 you're ready to switch positions and put yourself into the receiver's shoes. Have you looked at the problem from the receiver's perspective? Is your message too blunt? Too subtle? Does the message make the refusal, denial, or bad-news announcement clear? Prepare the final version, and proofread for format, punctuation, and correctness.

Refusing Routine Requests

Every business communicator will occasionally have to say *no* to a request. As discussed in the chapter-opening profile, Darin Richins at WordPerfect takes the time to personalize any refusal he must write. Depending on how you think the receiver will react to your refusal, you can use the direct or the indirect pattern. If you have any doubt, use the indirect pattern.

Rejecting Requests for Favors, Money, Information, and Action

The reasons-before-refusal pattern works well when turning down requests for favors, money, information, or action.

Most of us prefer to be let down gently when we're being refused something we want. That's why the reasons-before-refusal pattern works well when you must turn down requests for favors, money, information, action, and so forth.

Let's say you must refuse a request from Mark Stevenson, one of your managers, who wants permission to attend a conference. You can't let him go because the timing is bad; he must be present at budget-planning meetings scheduled for the same two weeks. Normally, you'd try to discuss this with Mark in person. But he's been traveling among branch offices recently, and you haven't been able to catch him in. Your first inclination might be to send a quickie memo, as shown below, and "tell it like it is."

MEMO TO: Mark Stevenson

We can't allow you to attend the conference in September, Mark. Perhaps you didn't know that budget-planning meetings are scheduled for that month.

Announces the bad news too quickly and painfully.

Your expertise is needed here to help keep our telecommunications network on schedule. Without you, the entire system—which is shaky at best—might fall apart. I'm sorry to have to refuse your request to attend the conference. I know this is small thanks for the fine work you have done for us. Please accept my apologies.

Gives reasons, but includes a potentially dangerous statement about the "shaky" system. Overemphasizes the refusal and apology.

In the spring I'm sure your work schedule will be lighter, and we can release you to attend a conference at any time.

Makes a promise that might be difficult to keep.

follows. In this case that main clause contains an alternative that draws attention away from the refusal.

Notice, too, that this refusal does not offer apologies. The writer has done nothing for which to be sorry. Moreover, an apology emphasizes the pain of the

Problems with customer orders can sometimes be resolved by telephone. Large companies, though, more often rely on written messages. If the message contains any good news, begin with that. For messages that are primarily disappointing, use the indirect method, beginning with a buffer and an explanation.

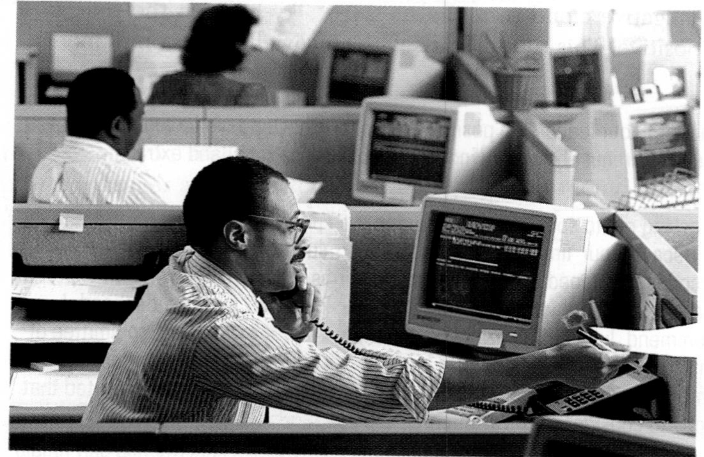

Handling Problems with Orders

● **In handling problems with orders, the indirect pattern is appropriate unless the message has some good-news elements.**

Not all orders can be filled as received. Suppliers may be able to send only part of an order or none at all. Substitutions may be necessary, or the delivery date may be delayed. Suppliers may suspect that all or part of the order is a mistake; the customer may actually want something else. In writing to customers about problem orders, it's generally wise to use the direct pattern if the message has some good-news elements. But when the message is disappointing, the indirect pattern is more appropriate.

Let's say you represent Patelle Toys, and you're scrambling for business in a slow year. A big customer, Child Land, calls in August and asks you to hold a block of your best-selling dolls. Like most vendors you require a deposit on large orders. September rolls around, and you still haven't received any money from Child Land. You must now write a tactful letter asking for the deposit—or else you will release the dolls to other buyers.[5] The problem, of course, is delivering the bad news without losing the customer's order and goodwill. Another challenge is making sure the reader understands the bad news. Do you think the resale and sales promotion emphases in the following letter dilute or obscure the bad news?

Dear Mr. Jones:

Includes appreciation and resale while establishing the facts.

We appreciate your interest in our Wendy Walkalong dolls. We've been holding a block of 500 of these top-selling dolls for you since August.

Reasons justify the coming bad news. Instead of focusing on the writer's needs *(we have a full warehouse and we need your deposit),* the reasons concentrate on motivating the reader. After the reasons, the bad news is clearly spelled out.

As we approach the holidays, the demand for all our dolls—including Wendy Walkalong—is increasing. Toy stores from Florida to California are asking us to ship these dolls. One reason the Wendy Walkalong is moving out of our warehouses so quickly is its low unit price, which makes it an economical gift item and a fast mover in an otherwise slow market. As soon as we receive your deposit of $4,000, we'll have this popular item on its way to your stores. Without a deposit by September 20, though, we must release this block to other retailers. Use the enclosed envelope to send us your check immediately. You can begin showing the hit doll Wendy Walkalong in your stores by November 1.

Closing uses sales promotion in suggesting another product. It also looks ahead to more business.

Please glance through the enclosed catalog for other toy items to stock this season. Many retailers have told us that Baby Thumbelina, a moderately priced cuddle doll (shown on page 23), is walking right off their shelves. We look forward to your check as well as to continuing to serve all your toy needs.

Cindy Scott software.

Denying Claims

Customers occasionally want something they're not entitled to or that you can't grant. They may misunderstand warranties or make unreasonable demands. Because these customers are often unhappy with a product or service, they are emotionally involved. Letters that say no to emotionally involved receivers will probably be your most challenging communication task. As publisher Malcolm Forbes observed, "To be agreeable while disagreeing—that's an art."[6]

In denying claims, the reasons-before-refusal pattern sets an empathic tone and buffers the bad news.

Fortunately, the reasons-before-refusal plan helps you be empathic and artful in breaking bad news. Obviously, in denial letters you'll need to adopt the proper tone. Don't blame customers, even if they are at fault. Avoid "you" statements that sound preachy *(You would have known that cash refunds are impossible if you had read your contract).* Use neutral, objective language to explain why the claim must be refused. Consider offering resale information to rebuild the customer's confidence in your products or organization.

In Figure 8.4 the writer denies a customer's claim for the difference between the price the customer paid for speakers and the price he saw advertised locally (which would have resulted in a cash refund of $151). While the catalog service does match any advertised lower price, the price-matching policy applies *only* to exact models. This claim must be rejected because the advertisement the customer submitted showed a different, older speaker model.

The letter to Matthew Tyson opens with a buffer that agrees with a statement in the customer's letter. It repeats the key idea of product confidence as a transition to the second paragraph. Next comes an explanation of the price-matching policy. The writer does not assume that the customer is trying to pull a fast one. Nor does he suggest that the customer is a dummy who didn't read or understand the price-matching policy. The safest path is a neutral explanation of the policy along with precise distinctions between the customer's speakers and the older ones. The writer also gets a chance to resell the customer's speakers and demonstrate what a quality product they are. By the end of the third paragraph, it's evident to the reader that his claim is unjustified.

Refusing Credit

As much as companies want business, they can extend credit only when payment is likely to follow. Credit applications, from individuals or from businesses, are generally approved or disapproved on the basis of the applicant's credit history. This record is supplied by a credit-reporting agency, such as TRW Information Services. After reviewing the applicant's record, a credit manager applies the organization's guidelines and approves or disapproves the application.

Goals when refusing credit include maintaining customer goodwill and avoiding actionable language.

If you must deny credit to prospective customers, you have four goals in conveying the refusal:

- Avoiding language that causes hard feelings
- Retaining customers on a cash basis
- Preparing for possible future credit—without raising false expectations
- Avoiding providing information that could cause a lawsuit

Because credit applicants are likely to continue to do business with an organization even if they are denied credit, you'll want to do everything possible to encourage that patronage. Thus, keep the refusal respectful, sensitive, and upbeat. To avoid possible litigation, some organizations give no explanation of the reasons

FIGURE 8.4 ● **Denying a Claim**

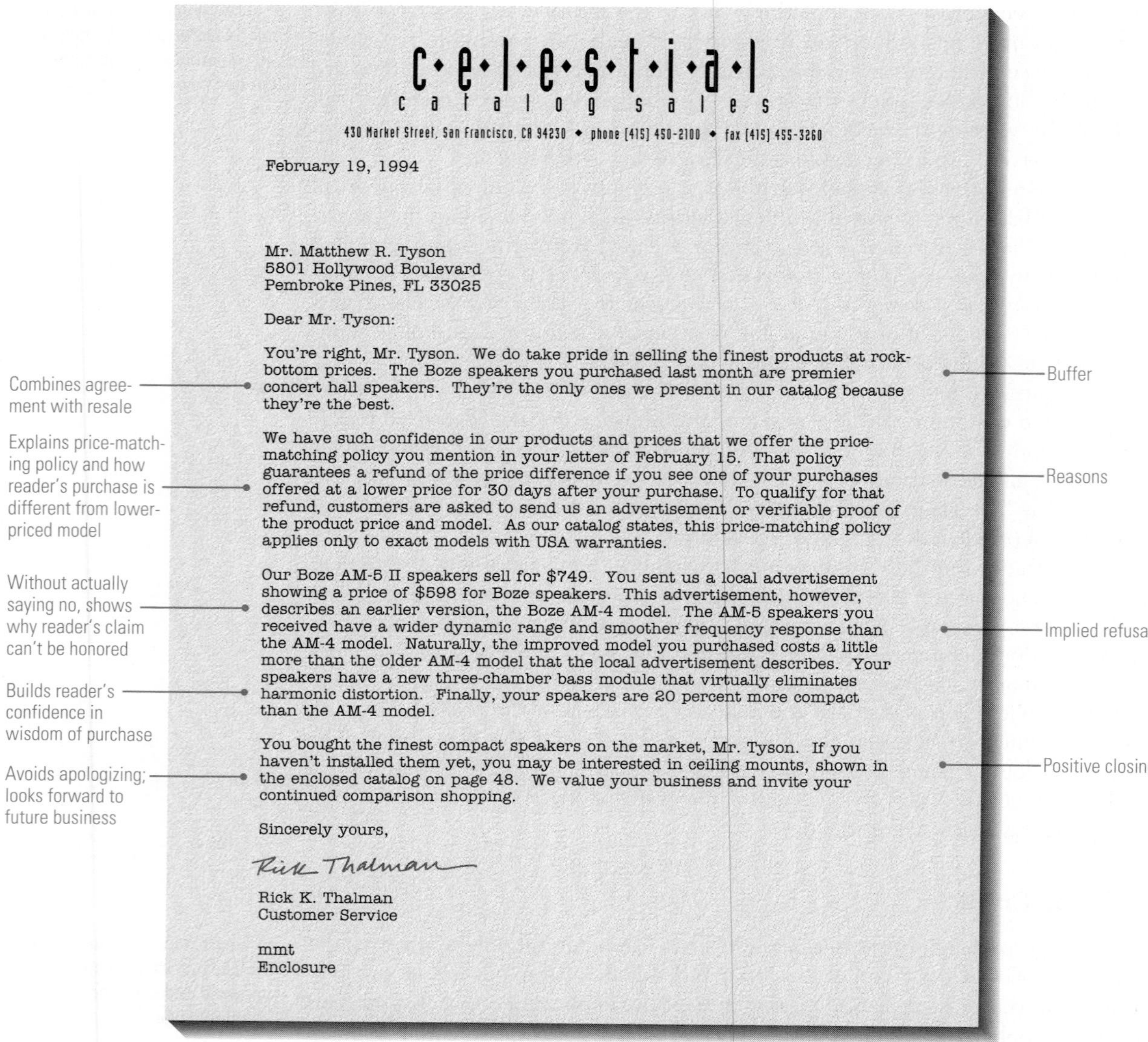

c•e•l•e•s•t•i•a•l
catalog sales

430 Market Street, San Francisco, CA 94230 • phone (415) 450-2100 • fax (415) 455-3260

February 19, 1994

Mr. Matthew R. Tyson
5801 Hollywood Boulevard
Pembroke Pines, FL 33025

Dear Mr. Tyson:

You're right, Mr. Tyson. We do take pride in selling the finest products at rock-bottom prices. The Boze speakers you purchased last month are premier concert hall speakers. They're the only ones we present in our catalog because they're the best.

We have such confidence in our products and prices that we offer the price-matching policy you mention in your letter of February 15. That policy guarantees a refund of the price difference if you see one of your purchases offered at a lower price for 30 days after your purchase. To qualify for that refund, customers are asked to send us an advertisement or verifiable proof of the product price and model. As our catalog states, this price-matching policy applies only to exact models with USA warranties.

Our Boze AM-5 II speakers sell for $749. You sent us a local advertisement showing a price of $598 for Boze speakers. This advertisement, however, describes an earlier version, the Boze AM-4 model. The AM-5 speakers you received have a wider dynamic range and smoother frequency response than the AM-4 model. Naturally, the improved model you purchased costs a little more than the older AM-4 model that the local advertisement describes. Your speakers have a new three-chamber bass module that virtually eliminates harmonic distortion. Finally, your speakers are 20 percent more compact than the AM-4 model.

You bought the finest compact speakers on the market, Mr. Tyson. If you haven't installed them yet, you may be interested in ceiling mounts, shown in the enclosed catalog on page 48. We value your business and invite your continued comparison shopping.

Sincerely yours,

Rick Thalman

Rick K. Thalman
Customer Service

mmt
Enclosure

Combines agreement with resale
Explains price-matching policy and how reader's purchase is different from lower-priced model
Without actually saying no, shows why reader's claim can't be honored
Builds reader's confidence in wisdom of purchase
Avoids apologizing; looks forward to future business
Buffer
Reasons
Implied refusal
Positive closing

for the refusal. Instead, they provide the name of the credit-reporting agency and suggest that inquiries be directed to it. Here's a credit refusal letter that uses a buffer but does not explain the reasons for the denial. Notice how the warm tone reassures the reader that she is respected and that her patronage is valued. The letter implies that her current credit condition is temporary, but it does not raise false hopes by promising future credit.

Dear Ms. Margolis:

Buffer identifies application and shows appreciation for it.

We genuinely appreciate your application of January 12 for a Fashion Express credit account.

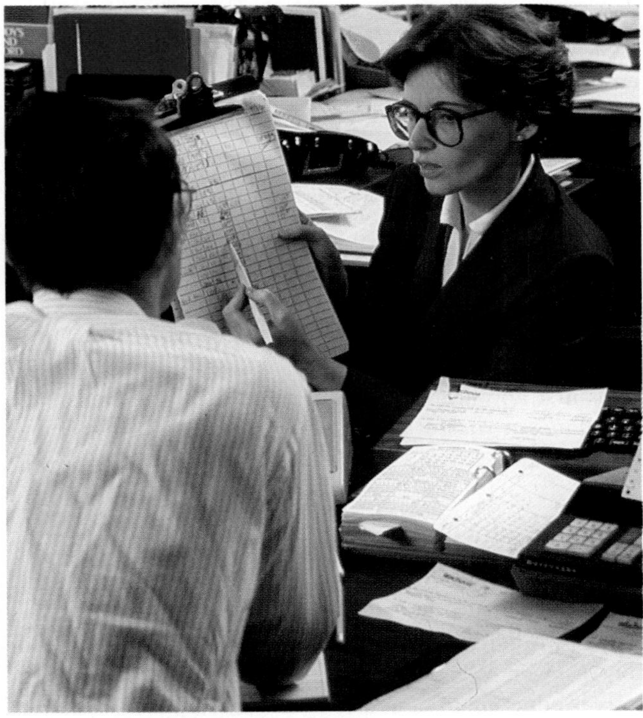

Bad news is easier to break when you can do it in person and when you have facts and reasons to justify it. The challenge to writers is explaining the facts, while at the same time showing empathy and sincerity. In sending bad news to customers, try to show them that they are respected and that their patronage is prized.

After receiving a report of your current credit record from TRW Information Services, we find that credit cannot be extended at this time. To learn more about your record, you may call a TRW credit counselor at (212) 356-0922. We've arranged for you to take advantage of this service for 60 days from the date of this letter at no charge to you.

Long sentence and passive voice deemphasize bad news. To prevent possible litigation, offers no reasons for denial.

Thanks, Ms. Margolis, for the confidence you've shown in Fashion Express. We invite you to continue shopping at our stores, and we look forward to your reapplication in the future.

Closes cordially and looks forward to continued patronage.

Some businesses do provide reasons explaining credit denials *(Credit cannot be granted because your firm's current and long-term credit obligations are nearly twice as great as your firm's total assets).* They may also provide alternatives, such as deferred billing or cash discounts. When the letter denies a credit application that accompanies an order, the message may contain resale information. The writer tries to convert the order from credit to cash.

Whatever form the bad-news letter takes, it's a good idea to have the message reviewed by legal counsel because of the litigation landmines awaiting unwary communicators in this area. The following checklist provides tips on how to craft effective bad-news letters.

Checklist for Delivering Bad News to Customers

- ✔ **Begin indirectly.** Express appreciation (but don't thank the reader for something you're about to refuse), show agreement on some point, review facts, or show understanding.
- ✔ **Provide reasons.** Except in credit denials, justify the bad news with objective reasons. Use resale if appropriate to restore the customer's confidence. Avoid blaming the customer or hiding behind company policy. Look for reader benefits.

- **Present the bad news.** State the bad news objectively or imply it. Although resale or sales promotion is appropriate in order letters, it may offend in claim or credit refusals.
- **Close pleasantly.** Suggest action on an alternative, look forward to future business, offer best wishes, refer to gifts, or use resale sensitively. Don't apologize, and don't mention the bad news.

Managing Negative Organization News

A tactful tone and a reasons-first approach help preserve friendly relations with customers. These same techniques are useful when delivering bad news to employees and when rejecting job applicants.

Announcing Bad News to Employees

Internal bad-news memos should use the indirect pattern to convey news that adversely affects employees.

Bad news within organizations might involve declining profits, lost contracts, harmful lawsuits, public relations controversies, and changes in policy. Whether you use a direct or an indirect pattern in delivering that news depends primarily on the anticipated reaction of the receiver. When bad news affects employees personally—such as cutbacks in pay, reduction of benefits, or relocation plans—you can generally lessen its impact and promote better relations by explaining reasons before revealing the bad news.

The first version of the following memo, which announces a substantial increase in the cost of employee health care benefits, suffers from many problems.

MEMO TO: Staff

Hits readers with bad news without any preparation.

Beginning January 1 your monthly payment for health care benefits will be increased to $109 (up from $42 last year).

Offers no explanation of why health care costs are rising. Action sounds arbitrary. Fails to take credit for absorbing previous increases.

Every year health care costs go up. Although we considered dropping other benefits, Midland decided that the best plan was to keep the present comprehensive package. Unfortunately, we can't do that unless we pass along some of the extra cost to you. Last year the company was forced to absorb the total increase in health care premiums. However, such a plan this year is inadvisable.

Sounds defensive; fails to provide reasons.

We did everything possible to avoid the sharp increase in costs to you this year. A rate schedule describing the increases in payments for your family and dependents is enclosed.

The improved version of this bad-news memo, shown in Figure 8.5, uses the indirect pattern. Notice that it opens with a relevant, upbeat buffer regarding health care—but says nothing about increasing costs. For a smooth transition, the second paragraph begins with a key idea from the opening ("comprehensive package"). The reasons section discusses rising costs with explanations and figures. The bad news ("you will be paying $109 a month") is clearly presented but embedded within the paragraph. Throughout, the writer strives to show the fairness of the company's position. The ending, which does not refer to the bad news or apologize, emphasizes how much the company is paying and what a wise investment it is. Notice that the entire memo demonstrates a kinder, gentler approach than that shown in the first draft. Of prime importance in breaking bad news to employees is providing clear, convincing reasons that explain the decision.

Most organizations involved in a crisis (serious performance problems, major relocation, massive layoffs, management shakeup, or public controversy) prefer to

FIGURE 8.5 ● **Announcing Bad News to Employees**

The Three Phases of the Writing Process

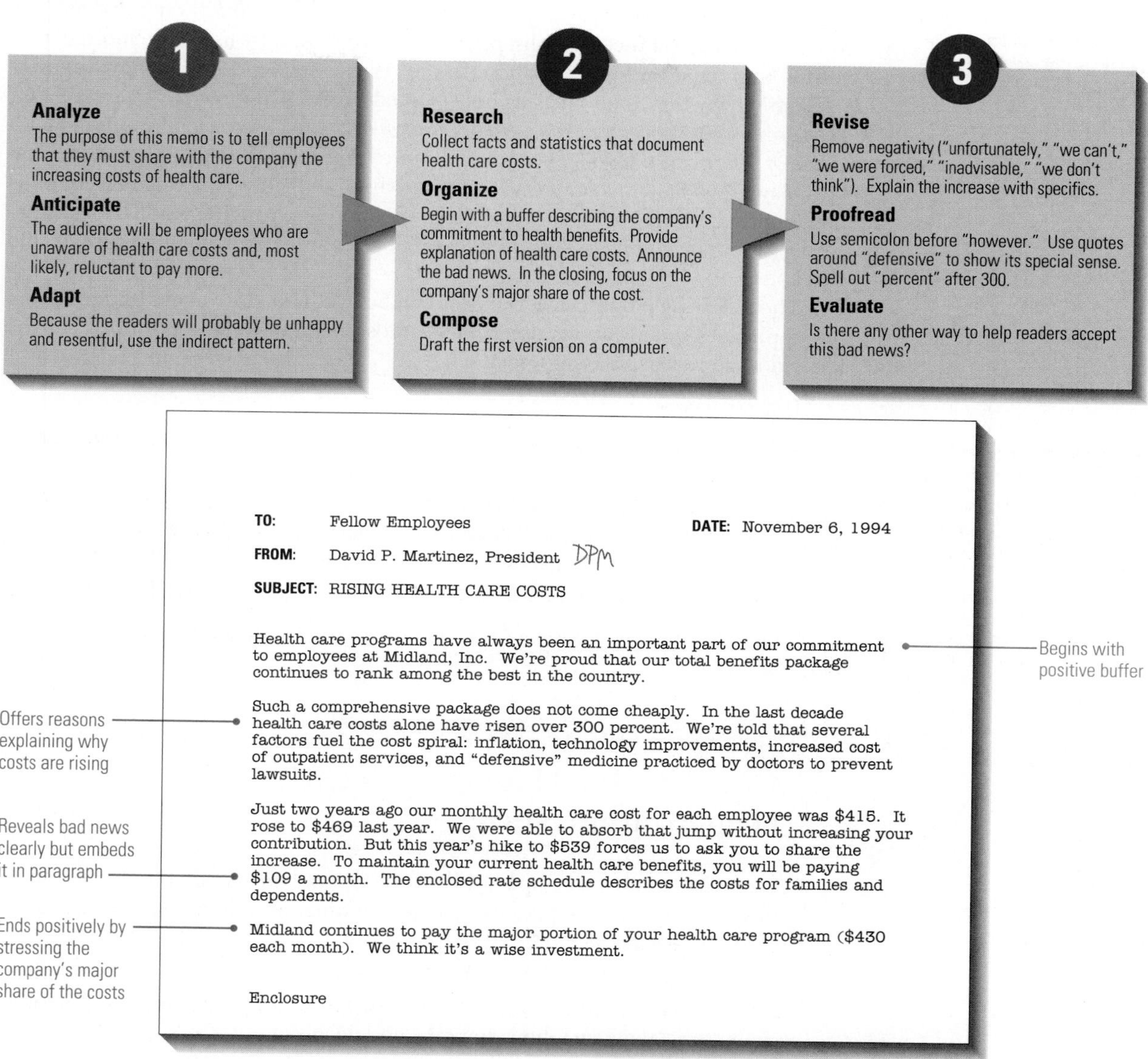

1
Analyze
The purpose of this memo is to tell employees that they must share with the company the increasing costs of health care.
Anticipate
The audience will be employees who are unaware of health care costs and, most likely, reluctant to pay more.
Adapt
Because the readers will probably be unhappy and resentful, use the indirect pattern.
2
Research
Collect facts and statistics that document health care costs.
Organize
Begin with a buffer describing the company's commitment to health benefits. Provide explanation of health care costs. Announce the bad news. In the closing, focus on the company's major share of the cost.
Compose
Draft the first version on a computer.
3
Revise
Remove negativity ("unfortunately," "we can't," "we were forced," "inadvisable," "we don't think"). Explain the increase with specifics.
Proofread
Use semicolon before "however." Use quotes around "defensive" to show its special sense. Spell out "percent" after 300.
Evaluate
Is there any other way to help readers accept this bad news?
Begins with positive buffer
Offers reasons explaining why costs are rising
Reveals bad news clearly but embeds it in paragraph
Ends positively by stressing the company's major share of the costs

TO: Fellow Employees　　　DATE: November 6, 1994

FROM: David P. Martinez, President DPM

SUBJECT: RISING HEALTH CARE COSTS

Health care programs have always been an important part of our commitment to employees at Midland, Inc. We're proud that our total benefits package continues to rank among the best in the country.

Such a comprehensive package does not come cheaply. In the last decade health care costs alone have risen over 300 percent. We're told that several factors fuel the cost spiral: inflation, technology improvements, increased cost of outpatient services, and "defensive" medicine practiced by doctors to prevent lawsuits.

Just two years ago our monthly health care cost for each employee was $415. It rose to $469 last year. We were able to absorb that jump without increasing your contribution. But this year's hike to $539 forces us to ask you to share the increase. To maintain your current health care benefits, you will be paying $109 a month. The enclosed rate schedule describes the costs for families and dependents.

Midland continues to pay the major portion of your health care program ($430 each month). We think it's a wise investment.

Enclosure

communicate the news openly to employees, customers, and stockholders. Instead of letting rumors distort the truth, they explain the organization's side of the story honestly and early. Morale can be destroyed when employees learn of major events affecting their jobs through the grapevine or from news accounts—rather than from management. For example, Exxon's poor handling of the *Valdez* oil spill—including delaying release of information and downplaying the environmental damage—harmed employee morale, angered stockholders, and lost the company thousands of customers.

● **Organizations can sustain employee morale by communicating bad news openly and honestly.**

Saying No to Job Applicants

● **Letters that deny applications for employment should be courteous and tactful but free of specifics that could trigger lawsuits.**

Being refused a job is one of life's major rejections. The blow is intensified by tactless letters (*Unfortunately, you were not among the candidates selected for . . .*). You can reduce the receiver's disappointment somewhat by using the indirect pattern—with one important variation. In the reasons section it's wise to be vague in explaining why the candidate was not selected. First, giving concrete reasons may be painful to the receiver (*Your grade point average of 2.7 was low compared with GPAs of other candidates*). Second, and more important, providing extra information may prove fatal in a lawsuit. Hiring and firing decisions generate considerable litigation today. To avoid charges of discrimination or wrongful actions, legal advisors warn organizations to keep employment rejection letters general, simple, and short.

The following job refusal letter is tactful but intentionally vague. It implies that the applicant's qualifications don't match those needed for the position, but the letter doesn't reveal anything specific.

Dear Mr. Danson:

Shows appreciation. Doesn't indicate good or bad news.

Thanks for letting us review your résumé submitted for our advertised management trainee opening.

To prevent possible lawsuits, gives no explanation. Places bad news in a dependent clause.

We received a number of impressive résumés for this opening. Although another candidate was selected, your interest in our organization is appreciated. So that you may continue your search for a position at another organization, we are writing to you immediately.

Ends with best wishes.

We wish you every success in finding a position that exactly fits your qualifications.

The following checklist gives tips on how to communicate bad news within an organization.

Checklist for Managing Negative Organization News

- ✔ **Start with a relevant, upbeat buffer.** Open with a small bit of good news, praise, appreciation, agreement, understanding, or a discussion of facts leading to the reasons section.
- ✔ **Discuss reasons.** Except in job refusal letters, explain what caused the decision necessitating the bad news. Use objective, nonjudgmental, and nondiscriminatory language. Show empathy and fairness.
- ✔ **Reveal the bad news.** Make the bad news clear but don't accentuate it. Avoid negative language.
- ✔ **Close harmoniously.** End on a positive, friendly note. For job refusals, extend good wishes.

You've now studied the indirect method for revealing bad news and analyzed many examples of messages applying this method. As you observed, business writers generally try to soften the blow; however, they do eventually reveal the bad news. No effort is made to sweep it under the carpet or ignore it totally. In other cultures bad news may be more difficult to reveal. The accompanying Cross Culture box gives insights into how negative messages are treated abroad.

PRESENTING BAD NEWS IN OTHER CULTURES

To minimize disappointment, Americans generally prefer to present negative messages indirectly. Other cultures may treat bad news differently.

In Germany, for example, business communicators occasionally use buffers but tend to present bad news directly. In Latin countries the question is not how to organize negative messages but whether to present them at all. It's considered disrespectful and impolite to report bad news to superiors. Thus, reluctant employees may fail to report accurately any negative message to their bosses.

In Asian cultures harmony and peace are sought in all relationships. Disrupting the harmony with bad news is avoided. Saying no is particularly difficult, even in situations where we would expect no hard feelings to result. Notice how evasive, polite, and charming a Beijing newspaper is in rejecting an article submitted by a British journalist:

> *We have read your manuscript with boundless delight. If we were to publish your paper, it would be impossible for us to publish any work of a lower standard. And as it is unthinkable that, in the next thousand years, we shall see its equal, we are, to our regret, compelled to return your divine composition, and beg you a thousand times to overlook our short sight and timidity.*

To prevent discord, Japanese communicators use a number of techniques to indicate no—without being forced to say it. In conversation they may respond with silence or with a counter question, such as "Why do you ask?" They may change the subject or tell a white lie to save face for themselves and for the questioner. Sometimes the answer sounds like a qualified yes: "I will do my best, but if I cannot, I hope you will understand," "Yes, but . . . ," or "yes" followed by an apology. All these responses should be recognized as no. In Thailand the negativism represented by a refusal is completely alien; the word *no* does not exist.

In many cultures negative news is offered with such subtleness or in such a positive light that it may be overlooked or misunderstood by literal-minded Americans. To understand the meaning of what's really being communicated, we must look beyond an individual's actual words, considering the communication style, culture, and situation as well.

Career Track Application

Interview fellow students or work colleagues who are from other cultures. How is negative news handled? How would typical individuals refuse a request for a favor, for example? How would a business refuse credit to customers? Is directness practiced? Report your findings to the class.

Summary of Learning Goals

1. **Explain and apply the four-part pattern for revealing bad news.** Begin with a buffer, such as a compliment, appreciation, a point of agreement, objective information, understanding, or some part of the message that represents good news. Then explain the reasons that necessitate the bad news, trying to cite benefits to the reader or others. Choose positive words, and clarify company policy if necessary. Announce the bad news strategically, mentioning a compromise or alternative if possible. Close pleasantly with a forward-looking goodwill statement.
2. **Identify causes of legal problems in business writing.** Abusive language is libelous and actionable when it is false, damages a person's reputation, and

is "published"—spoken within the presence of others or written. Even careless language (saying a manufacturing plant is "dangerous," for instance) can result in litigation. Moreover, any messages written on company stationery represent that company and can be legally binding.

3. **Apply the writing process to negative news messages.** Begin by analyzing the effect the message will have on the receiver. Gather information and analyze the reasons that prompted the bad news. To deliver serious or personal bad news, generally use the indirect plan. In revising, put yourself in the receiver's shoes and evaluate your letter.
4. **Refuse routine requests using the indirect pattern.** When you must refuse requests for favors, money, information, action, and other proposals, use the reasons-before-refusal pattern. Open with a buffer, provide reasons, announce the refusal sensitively, suggest possible alternatives, and end with a positive, forward-looking comment.
5. **Send bad news to customers while retaining their business.** In addition to using the indirect pattern, consider including resale material (reassuring the customer of a wise choice) or sales promotion (pushing a new product). Be careful of tone; use neutral, objective language and avoid blaming customers.
6. **Announce negative organization news sensitively.** When breaking bad news to employees, use the indirect pattern but be sure to provide clear, convincing reasons that explain a decision. In refusing job applicants, however, keep letters short, general, and tactful.

Chapter Review

1. Describe the four parts of the indirect message pattern.

2. How can business documents in an organization's file become part of a lawsuit?

3. What is a buffer?

4. Why should a writer give reasons before revealing bad news?

5. Name four or more ways to deemphasize bad news when it is presented.

6. What is the most important difference between direct and indirect letters?

7. Name four times when the direct pattern should be used for bad news.

8. Name four kinds of routine requests that businesses must frequently refuse.

9. Why should you be especially careful in cushioning the refusal to an invitation?

10. What is the major difference between bad-news messages for customers and those for other people?

11. List four goals a writer seeks to achieve in writing messages that deny credit to prospective customers.

12. Why should a writer be somewhat vague in the reasons portion of a letter rejecting a job applicant?

13. When organizations must reveal a crisis (such as the Exxon *Valdez* disaster), how should they communicate the news to employees, customers, stockholders, and the public?

14. What techniques might a Japanese communicator use to avoid saying no?

15. To avoid possible litigation in a letter refusing credit, what technique can be used in explaining reasons for the denial?

Discussion

1. Under what circumstances would form letters be appropriate for delivering bad news?

2. Discuss the contention that all letters addressed to customers or prospective customers should contain resale or sales promotion information.

3. Consider times when you have been aware that others have used the indirect pattern in writing or speaking to you. How did you react?

4. Discuss the ethics and legality of using company stationery to write personal letters.

5. Ethical Issue: In considering negative organization news, should companies immediately reveal grave illnesses of key executives? Or should executives be entitled to keep their health a private matter? Does it matter if the company is public or private?

Exercises

8.1 Organizational Patterns

Identify which organizational pattern you would use for the following messages: direct or indirect.

a. A letter refusing a request by a charitable organization to use your office equipment on the weekend.

b. A memo from the manager denying an employee's request for special parking privileges. The employee works closely with the manager on many projects.

c. An announcement to employees that a fitness specialist has canceled a scheduled lunchtime talk and cannot reschedule.

d. A letter from a bank refusing to fund a company's overseas expansion plan.

e. A form letter from an insurance company announcing new policy requirements that many policyholders may resent. If policyholders do not indicate the plan they prefer, they may lose their insurance coverage.

f. A letter from an amusement park refusing the request of a customer who was unhappy with a substitute concert performer.

g. The last in a series of letters from a collection agency demanding payment of a long-overdue account. The next step will be hiring an attorney.

h. A letter from a computer company refusing to authorize repair of a customer's computer on which the warranty expired six months ago.

i. A memo from an executive refusing a manager's plan to economize by purchasing reconditioned copiers. The executive and the manager both appreciate efficient, straightforward messages.

j. A letter informing a customer that the majority of the customer's recent order will not be available for six weeks.

8.2 Passive-Voice Verbs

Revise the following sentences to present the bad news with a passive-voice verb.

a. We will no longer be accepting credit cards for purchases.

b. No one is allowed to park in the yellow zone.

c. Our technicians cannot service your VCR.

d. We are unable to grant your request for a loan.

8.3 Subordinating Bad News

Revise the following sentences to position the bad news in a subordinate clause. (Hint: Consider beginning the clause with *Although*.) Use passive-voice verbs for the bad news.

a. We cannot refund your purchase price, but we are sending you two coupons toward your next purchase.

b. We appreciate your interest in our organization. Unfortunately, we are unable to extend an employment offer to you at this time.

c. It is impossible for us to ship your complete order at this time. However, we are able to send the four oak desks now; you should receive them within five days.

8.4 Implying Bad News

Revise the following statements to *imply* the bad news. Use passive-voice verbs and subordinate clauses to further deemphasize the bad news.

a. I already have an engagement in my appointment calendar for the date you mention. Therefore, I am unable to speak to your group. However, I would like to recommend another speaker who might be able to address your organization.

b. Because of the holiday period, all our billboard space was used this month. Therefore, we are sorry to say that we could not give your charitable group free display space. However, next month, after the holidays, we hope to display your message as we promised.

c. We cannot send you a price list nor can we sell our equipment directly to customers. Our policy is to sell only through dealers, and your dealer is Stereo City, located on Grove Street in Oklahoma City.

8.5 Evaluating Bad-News Statements

Discuss the strengths or weaknesses of the following bad-news statements.

a. It's impossible for us to ship your order before May 1.

b. Frankly, we like your résumé, but we were hoping to hire someone a little younger who might be able to stay with us longer.

c. I'm thoroughly disgusted with this entire case, and I will never do business with shyster lawyers like you again.

d. We can assure you that on any return visit to our hotels you will not be treated so poorly.

e. We must deny your credit application because your record shows a history of late payments, nonpayment, and irregular employment.

f. *(In a confidential company memo:)* I cannot recommend that we promote this young lady into any position where she will meet the public. Her colorful facial decoration, as part of her religion, may offend our customers.

8.6 Document Analysis: Refusal of a Favor Request

Analyze the following letter. List its weaknesses. If your instructor directs, revise it.

> Dear Mr. Waters:
>
> Unfortunately, we cannot allow you to apply the lease payments you've been making for the past ten months toward the purchase of your Sako 600 copier.
>
> Company policy does not allow such conversion. Have you ever wondered why we can offer such low leasing and purchase prices? Obviously, we couldn't stay in business long if we agreed to proposals such as yours.
>
> You've had the Sako 600 copier for ten months now, Mr. Waters, and you say you like its versatility and reliability. Perhaps we could interest you in another Sako model—one that's more within your price range. Do give us a call.

8.7 Document Analysis: Negative News for Customers

Analyze the following letter. List its weaknesses. If your instructor directs, revise it.

> Dear Charge Customers:
>
> This letter is being sent to you to announce the termination of in-house charge accounts at Golden West Print and Frame Shop. We are truly sorry that we can no longer offer this service.
>
> Because some customers abused the privilege, we must eliminate local charge accounts. We regret that we must take this action, but we found that carrying our own credit had become quite costly. To continue the service would have meant raising our prices. As a small but growing business, we decided it was more logical to drop the in-house charges. As a result, we are forced to begin accepting bank credit cards, including VISA and MasterCard.
>
> Please accept our apologies in trimming our services somewhat. We hope to see you soon when we can show you our new collection of museum-quality gilded wood frames.

8.8 Document Analysis: Saying No to a Job Applicant

Analyze the following letter. List its weaknesses. If your instructor directs, revise it.

> Dear Mr. Franklin:
>
> Ms. Sievers and I wish to thank you for the pleasure of allowing us to interview you last Thursday. We were delighted to learn about your superb academic record, and we also appreciated your attentiveness in listening to our description of the operations of the Maxwell Corporation.
>
> However, we had many well-qualified applicants who were interested in the advertised position of human resources assistant. As you may have guessed, we were particularly eager to find a minority individual who could help us fill out our Affirmative Action goals. Although you did not fit one of our goal areas, we enjoyed talking with you. We hired a woman graduate of Texas Technical University who had most of the qualities we sought.
>
> Although we realize that the job market is difficult at this time, you have our heartfelt wishes for good luck in finding precisely what you are looking for.

Problems

8.9 Request Refusal: The Answer is No

In an organization to which you belong or one where you have worked, identify a request that must be refused in writing. Do customers or organizations solicit contributions of money, time, products, or equipment? Do customers request actions that can't be taken? Do officers or members of a student organization want favors or actions that can't be granted? Must the organization refuse to participate in some event? Write a tactful letter refusing the request.

8.10 Request Refusal: Ascending Sales Stars

Dustin Ronzonni, a magazine editor, asks your organization, Panatronics International, for confidential information regarding the salaries and commissions of your top sales representatives. The magazine, *Marketing Monthly*, plans to spotlight young sales professionals "whose stars are ascending." You've got some great young superstars, as well as many excellent mature sales representatives. Frankly, the publicity would be great. You would agree in a minute except that (1) you don't want to be forced to pick favorites among your sales reps and (2) you can't reveal private salary data. Every sales rep operates under an individual salary contract. During salary negotiations several years ago, an agreement was reached in which both sales staff members and management agreed to keep the terms of these individual contracts confidential. Perhaps the editor would be satisfied with a list that ranks your top sales reps for the past five years. You could also send a fact sheet describing your top reps. You notice that three of the current top sales reps are under the age of thirty-five. Write a refusal that retains the goodwill of *Marketing Monthly,* 145 Fifth Avenue, New York, NY 10011.

8.11 Invitation Refusal: A Dog of a Company

Your boss, John A. Berman, CEO, International Paper Co., has just been voted Paper Industry Man of the Year by the American Paperwork Association. To receive the award, though, he has to agree to present the keynote address to the association at its February 18 meeting in Boston. It's impossible for him to attend since he'll be in Japan scouting for new paper company acquisitions. Mr. Berman is determined that IP should become less dependent on U.S. markets. He's particularly interested in expanding into specialty paper items, such as photographic papers. In fact, his wise acquisitions and aggressive management style explain why he's being singled out for this award. As one company director said, "Berman has taken a company that was a dog in the industry and made it into the best." Although Mr. Berman would like to attend, he cannot. He wants you, his assistant, to write to the American Paperwork Association refusing the invitation. It's unlikely, but if the APA could reschedule the meeting in March, Mr. Berman could attend. He's unavailable in April and May. For Mr. Berman's signature prepare a draft of the refusal letter addressed to Roberta A. Wexler, Executive Secretary, American Paperwork Association, 3981 Rosslyn Road, Arlington, VA 22209.[7]

8.12 Request Refusal: Mountain Bike Race Regrets

As president of CycleTech, you must refuse a request from the North American Biking Association. This group wants your company to become a major sponsor of the first annual Durango World Mountain Bike Championship—to the tune of $25,000! This is one tune you can't dance to. The stakes are just too high. You applaud the NABA for its proactive stance in encouraging families to participate in the sport of mountain biking. The NABA was also instrumental in opening up ski resorts to mountain bikers during the summer months. Actually, you'd like to support the Durango World Mountain Bike Championship. There's no doubt that such races increase interest in mountain biking and ridership. You have sponsored some bike races in the past, but for small amounts—usually under $500—which paid for trophies. But the NABA wants to offer large cash prizes and pay the expenses of big-name champions to enter.

You are a small Eugene, Oregon, company, and all your current profits are being ploughed into research to compete with the Japanese imports. You're very proud of your newly introduced brake pads and trigger-action shift levers. But these kinds of engineering breakthroughs are costly. You don't have the big bucks the NABA wants. You wouldn't mind taking an ad in their program or contributing $500 toward trophies. But that's the limit. Write a refusal to Joe W. Breeze, North American Biking Association, 8310 Montague Expressway, San Jose, CA 95131.

8.13 Request Refusal: Fragrance from Local Botanicals

Your home fragrance company, Aromatix, is riding a wave of popularity and explosive growth. Specializing in natural potpourris using only botanicals (dried flowers, leaves, pods, seeds, and other plant parts), you have become an industry leader. One of your projected markets is fragrant bath products—and perhaps perfume in the more distant future.

The manager of your Shakopee, Minnesota, production plant, Annette Buchanan, has written a memo to you asking if she can make a four-week trip to Europe and Asia in April. Specifically, she wants to visit India (for bakuli pods), Pakistan (for red rose buds), Bulgaria (for sloe berries), and France (for lavender flowers and other exotic dried flora). As an aside, she also mentioned visiting Hampton Farms, Manchester, Ohio, which cultivates scented geraniums used in various fragrances.

You must refuse the European/Asian portion of Annette's request for many reasons. You don't want her to be gone for four weeks in April, when your staff will be brainstorming ideas for new package designs. In addition, the trip would set a bad precedent. You've turned down the requests of other managers for European and Asian trips because, frankly, you don't think the benefits outweigh the considerable expense of travel abroad. Your company is pleased with the work of local nationals acting on your behalf. These representatives have been able to supply quality botanicals from overseas at reasonable prices. You feel that Americans are at a disadvantage in negotiations because they lack language skills.

You would, however, like Annette to inspect the scented geraniums in Ohio. Oils from these plants are critical in making naturally scented shower gels and body lotions. With the proliferation of elegant bath shops, these products could become hot items soon. You know Annette will be disappointed, and you hope she won't take this rejection personally. She's one of those rare managers who can combine management skills with creativity. You'd hate to lose her. She's made the Shakopee warehouse and distribution center a marvel of efficiency, computerizing the inventory so that you can locate and replenish items automatically. Moreover, it was Annette who came up with "microwave potpourri," one of the most successful new ideas in the industry. Popping a potpourri mix in the microwave causes its aromas to be released without the need for messy candles or awkward light bulbs. Her creativity is needed at the April design meetings. Therefore, as Jane Burke, Aromatix president (with headquarters in Chicago), write a memo to Annette Buchanan, operations manager, refusing the major portion of her request.

8.14 Claim Denial: Virus Infects Invaders

As Monty McAdams, director of marketing for Quixell, a software game manufacturer, you must respond to an angry customer, Donald V. Cruz. Mr. Cruz has reason to be upset. Your Galaxy Invaders program carried a computer virus, unknown to you at the time of distribution, that has infected his computer.

As soon as you learned about the virus two months ago, you stopped production and traced its source to a certain step in manufacturing. Your company, Quixell, doesn't know how the virus infected the manufacturing process; but you've corrected the problem, and your disks are now clean. Fortunately, only a small number of contaminated programs were distributed before detection. Some of the buyers have written to you, and you've been responding to each complaint individually.

Computer viruses are programs written to perform malicious tasks. They attach themselves secretly to data files and are then copied either by diskette or by a computer network. The particular virus contaminating your Galaxy Invaders program is called "Stoned III."[8] First reported in Europe just six months ago, it represents a new class of "stealth" viruses. They mask their location and are extremely difficult to detect. Quixell already has extensive virus-detection defenses, but this new virus slipped by. Quixell has just licensed special digital-signature software that will make it difficult for future viruses to spread undetected. But the new technology doesn't solve the current problem.

You doubt that your customers will sue over the virus. Courts in the past have generally found that if a company has been reasonably prudent in its production process, that company is not liable for damage caused by a third person (the individual who planted the virus). Nevertheless, you feel an obligation to do whatever is possible—within reason—to rectify the damage caused. Mr. Cruz wants Quizell to pay for a computer virus specialist to clean up his hard disk and restore it to its previous uncontaminated state. Such a solution is out of the question. It's much too expensive. Moreover, you can't be sure that his computer doesn't have problems that have nothing to do with the Invaders virus.

You are doing what other software manufacturers have done when faced with viruses—offer a clean disk and advice. You feel that Quixell is exceptional among software companies. Because of your vigilance and concern for product quality, you've never had a virus contaminate any of your 350 products—before Stoned III. You acted immediately to correct the problem, and you're trying to do the right thing now in helping the few customers who were affected. You have assigned a specialist on your staff, Roxanne Sawicky, to answer specific questions from affected customers. Her number is (415) 831-6690.

Write to Donald V. Cruz, 2360 Red River Road, Hope, AZ 72801, denying his request. Tell him that you're rushing him a clean copy of Galaxy Invaders. To remove the virus and clean up his hard disk, he should use the Integrity Anti-Virus program. It has special routines that will detect, remove, and prevent more than 400 viruses, including Stoned III. He can purchase this program by calling Integrity's toll-free number (1-800-555-4690).

8.15 Customer Bad News: The StairClimber or the LifeStep?

You are delighted to receive a large order from Susan Sweetman, Venice Beach Fitness Center, 4590 Lincoln Boulevard, Venice, CA 90063. This order includes two Lifecycle Trainers (at $1,295 each), four Pro Abdominal Boards (at $295 each), three Tunturi Muscle Trainers (at $749 each), and three Dual-Action StairClimbers (at $1,545 each).

You could ship immediately except for one problem. The Dual-Action StairClimber is intended for home use, not for gym or club use. Customers like it because they say it's more like scaling a mountain than climbing a flight of stairs. With each step, users exercise their arms to pull or push themselves up. And its special cylinders absorb shock so that no harmful running impact results. However, this model is not what you would recommend for gym use. You feel Ms. Sweetman should order your premier stairclimber, the LifeStep (at $2,395 each). This unit has sturdier construction and is meant for heavy use. Its sophisticated electronics provide a selection of customer-pleasing programs that challenge muscles progressively with a choice of workouts. It also quickly multiplies workout gains with computer-controlled interval training. Electronic monitors inform users of step height, calories burned, elapsed time, upcoming levels, and adherence to fitness goals. For gym use the LifeStep is clearly better than the StairClimber. The bad news is that the LifeStep is considerably more expensive.

You get no response when you try to telephone Ms. Sweetman to discuss the problem. Should you ship what you can, or hold the entire order until you learn whether she wants the StairClimber or the LifeStep? Or perhaps you should substitute the LifeStep and send only two of them. Decide what to do and write a letter to Ms. Sweetman.

8.16 Customer Bad News: College Bookstore Housecleaning

As the customer service manager of Randall House Publishing, you must refuse most of a shipment of books returned from the Everglades College Bookstore. Your policy is to provide a 100 percent return on books provided the books are returned prepaid in *new, unmarked,* and *resalable* condition. The return must be within twelve months of the original invoice date. Old editions of books must be returned within ninety days of your announcement that you will no longer be printing that edition. These conditions are published and sent with every order of books shipped.

The return shipment from the Everglades College Bookstore looks as if someone was housecleaning and decided to return all unsold books to you. Fourteen books are not your titles; return them. You could have accepted the 22 copies of Donner's *Introduction to Marketing*— if they were not imprinted with "Everglades College Bookstore," the price, and return instructions on the inside cover. The 31 copies of Hefferman's *College Writing Handbook* are second editions. Since you've been selling the third edition for fourteen months, you can't accept them. Five copies of Quigley's *Business Law* appear to be water-damaged; they're unsalable. From the whole mess it looks as if you'll be able to give them credit for 25 copies of Miller's *The Promotable Woman* (wholesale price $31). However, since Everglades sent no invoice information, you'll have to tack on a 15 percent service charge to cover the effort involved in locating the order in your records.

Write a letter to Richard M. Sanchez, manager, Everglades College Bookstore, Belle Glade, FL 32178, that retains his goodwill. Everglades has been a valued customer in the past. They've placed orders on time and paid on time. Tell Mr. Sanchez what is being returned and how much credit you are allowing. From the credit total, deduct $12.50 for return shipping costs.

8.17 Customer Claim Denial: Telling Time Under Water

As customer service representative Craig Garrison, you receive the following letter from a customer:

> Dear Rayco Watch Company:
>
> I'm sending back my Windsurfer V-2 watch. I received this watch as a gift for my birthday June 3, and I've been wearing it surfing and scuba diving for the past two weeks. I love all its features, but now it's stopped working. I thought this watch was supposed to be waterproof! My parents said it cost $96.20. Please refund this amount.
>
> Jerry Golden

The service department says the watch is water-damaged. Your technicians remind you that this watch is water-resistant—not waterproof. Apparently, it's undergone prolonged submersion. Mr. Golden admits that he's worn it scuba diving. You must refuse the claim. The Windsurfer V-2 is a fine watch, but it's meant for sailing and windsurfing, not for diving. As your advertisement says, "Wear the watch built for bad weather and good times." It contains many fine features for sailing enthusiasts: a rotating compass-points bezel for setting your course, dual time, tachymeter, stopwatch, calendar, alarm, microlight, and ventilated rubber band with wind conversion chart. But it's not intended for underwater wear.

For that purpose you would recommend one of your SportDiver models. Each of these is constructed with a rugged resin case and has a scratch-resistant plastic crystal that is guaranteed to maintain water resistance up to 150 feet. Tell Mr. Golden that you can't refund the full price, but you will give him 30 percent off the purchase price of a SportDiver model. Send him a current catalog and let him select one. Make it easy for him to respond. Write to Jerry Golden, 2390 Silver Strand Street, Redondo Beach, CA 90232.

8.18 Claim Denial: A Mess With Mouldy Grout

Assume you are Deborah Pool Dixon, manager, Promotions and Advertising, Six Flags Lake Point Park. You are upset by the letter you received from Jennifer Sledgeman, who complained that she was "taken" by Six Flags when you had to substitute performers for King Fisher and the Mouldy Grout band concert (see Problem 6.14). Explain to her that the concert was planned by an independent promoter. Your only obligation was to provide the theater facility and advertising. Three days before the event, the promoter left town, taking with him all advance payments from financial backers. As it turned out, many of the artists he had promised to deliver were not even planning to attend.

Left with a pretty messy situation, you decided on Thursday to go ahead with a modified version of the event since you had been advertising it and many would come expecting some kind of talent. At that time you changed your radio advertising to say that for reasons beyond your control, King Fisher and the Mouldy Grout band would not be appearing. You described the new talent and posted signs at the entrance and in the parking lot announcing the change. Contrary to Ms. Sledgeman's claim, no newspaper advertising featuring Fisher and Moldy Grout appeared on the day of the concert (at least you did not pay for any to appear that day). Somehow she must have missed your corrective radio advertising and signs at the entrance. You feel you made a genuine effort to communicate the changed program. In your opinion most people who attended the concert thought that Six Flags had done everything possible to salvage a rather unfortunate situation.

Ms. Sledgeman wants a cash refund of $70 (two tickets at $35 each). Six Flags has a no-money-back policy on concerts after the event takes place. If Ms. Sledgeman had come to the box office before the event started, you could have returned her money. But she stayed to see the concert. She claims that she didn't know anything about the talent change until after the event was well underway. This sounds unlikely, but you don't quarrel with customers. Nevertheless, you can't give her cash back. You already took a loss on this event. But you can give two complimentary passes to Six Flags Lake Point Park. Perhaps if Ms. Sledgeman and a friend return as guests under happier circumstances, they will look on Six Flags more positively.

8.19 Credit Refusal: No Job, No Loan

As Peter Quinette, credit manager, Columbia Auto City, you must refuse the credit application of Mark E. Victor, 340 Sugar Grove Avenue, Apt. 2-B, Springfield, OH 46430. His credit application shows that he has no current employment. Although his credit history from the Columbus Data Service looks reasonably good, without employment you can't grant him credit for an auto loan. One of the few rigid guidelines that Columbia maintains in credit applications is that the applicant must have a steady source of income, and Columbia's policy is to make this clear to applicants. After Mark finds employment, he could reapply. Another alternative is cosigning. If he finds a suitable cosigner, you might be able to make the loan. To do this, he needs to talk with you personally. Write to Mark telling him why you can't make the loan.

8.20 Credit Refusal: Waiting for the Boom Boxes

As Tyler Meadows, sales manager, Federated Sound Labs, you are delighted to land a sizable order for your new Panatronic CD boom boxes. This great little four-speaker sound system comes loaded with features including 32-track memory CD and disc-to-tape dubbing.

The purchase order is from High Point Electronics, a retail distributor in High Point, North Carolina. You send the order on to Tiffany Smythe, your credit manager, for approval of the credit application attached. To your disappointment, Tiffany tells you that High Point doesn't qualify for credit. Specifically, TRW Information Services reports that High Point has current and long-term credit obligations that are nearly twice as great as its total assets. Such a dismal financial picture means that it would be too risky to grant credit.

You decide to write to High Point with the bad news and an alternative. Suggest that High Point order a smaller number of the boom boxes. If it pays cash, it can receive a 2 percent discount. After High Point has sold these fast-moving units, it can place another cash order through your toll-free order number. With your fast delivery system, its inventory will never be depleted. High Point can get the units it wants now and can replace its inventory almost overnight.

Credit Manager Smythe tells you that your company generally reveals to credit applicants the name of your reporting service. You also give a general reason (such as *your credit obligations are nearly twice as great as your assets*) in explaining why an application has been refused. Write a credit refusal to E. A. Familian, High Point Electronics, 3590 Thomasville Road, High Point, NC 28001.

8.21 Collaborative Memo: Bad News for Employees

As one of the managers at Atlantic Health Services, you have been asked to meet with other managers to hammer out the details of a smoking policy. Last year's partial smoking ban is about to be revised. The Administrative Council, with the concurrence of the Executive Office, has agreed that, effective January 1, all work stations and offices should be smoke-free. What you must decide is whether restrooms, elevator areas, lobbies, hallways, stairwells, and cafeterias should also be smoke-free.

As an insurer and a provider of health care services, Atlantic is concerned with the well-being of its employees, their families, and its clients. It feels a responsibility to provide the most healthful work environment possible for employees. Increasing evidence suggests that secondary smoke is harmful to nonsmokers. Many organizations are now completely smoke-free.

In small student groups discuss how extensive the smoking ban should be. Then write a memo that announces the smoking policy to employees. You might add that Human Resources is investigating smoking cessation programs and the possibility of providing discounts for employees. When more information is available, you'll distribute it. Prepare a memo for Human Resources to send to all employees reflecting your smoking policy decision.

8.22 Bad News to Employees: Putting Off New Frames

As Martha Velazquez, manager of Human Resources for Laseronics, write a memo to all employees announcing changes in their vision care benefits and procedures. The message will contain a little good news and substantial bad news.

In the past employees could have vision examinations, along with new lenses and frames, once every twelve months. However, before employees could request eye examinations, they had to mail in a request and then wait for a benefit form to be sent. Then they filled out the benefit form and submitted it to Vision Service Program, the vision care provider. Eventually, members received authorization for eye care. You know how slow and irritating this procedure has been to employees. Now, VSP has a new method for requesting vision care. Employees may call a toll-free number, 1-800-346-2200, to obtain the benefit form. That's good news. Employees may also continue using the request form, if they choose.

The bad news is that, effective January 1, coverage for new frames will be changed from every twelve months to every twenty-four months (counting from the last date members received new frames). The frequency of vision examinations and lenses will remain the same (every twelve months). This reduction in benefits is necessitated by sharply increasing overall costs of vision care and by concessions made by the employees' union. The union opted for reduced vision care benefits instead of charging employees a fee to maintain the previous levels of care.

8.23 Saying No to a Job Applicant: See Us When You Have a Degree

As Andrea Mitchell, human resources vice president at Silicon Valley Enterprises, you must write to Cheryl Ann Fontana telling her that she was not selected for the position of administrative assistant. Cheryl Ann was one of the finalists for the advertised opening, but you decided to hire Richard Herringshaw because he knew Lotus, WordPerfect, and Word. He seemed to be more knowledgeable about computers than Cheryl Ann. On her résumé Cheryl had indicated that she was familiar with computing, but during the interview she revealed that she had completed only beginning courses. Moreover, Richard had finished an A.A. degree, while Cheryl Ann was still working on hers. When Cheryl completes more advanced courses and finishes her degree, you might be able to offer her something.

C.L.U.E. Review 8

Edit the following sentences to correct all language faults, including grammar, punctuation, spelling, and word confusions.

1. Your advertisement in the June second edition of the Boston Globe, caught my attention; because my training and experience matches your requirements.
2. Undoubtlessly the bank is closed at this hour but it's ATM will enable you to recieve the cash you need.
3. A flow chart detailing all sales' procedures in 4 divisions were prepared by our Vice President.
4. The computer and printer was working good yesterday, and appeared to be alright this morning; when I used it for my report.
5. If I was you I would be more concerned with long term not short term returns on the invested capitol.
6. We make a conscience effort by the way to find highly-qualified individuals with up to date computer skills.
7. If your résumé had came earlier I could have showed it to Mr. Sutton and she before your interview.
8. Deborahs report summary is more easier to read then David because she used consistant headings and efficient writing techniques.
9. At McDonald's we ordered 4 big macs 3 orders of french fries, and 5 coca-colas for lunch.
10. Because the budget cuts will severely effect all programs the faculty have unanimously opposed it.

Persuasive and Sales Messages

LEARNING GOALS

After studying this chapter, you should be able to

1. Explain the components of a persuasive message
2. Deliver a persuasive yet ethical argument
3. Request favors and action effectively
4. Write effective persuasive messages within organizations
5. Request adjustments and make claims successfully
6. Compose successful sales messages

Dean Witter Reynolds, Inc.: Career Track Profile

One of the hardest of all sales jobs is persuading people to invest their money in intangibles like stocks and bonds. Car salespeople have a real product that customers can touch and feel and drive, but securities salespeople must sell ideas and credibility and, most importantly, dreams. That's why it takes an unusually persuasive person to be a success in selling securities.

And René Nourse is one of those special people. In the Torrance, California, branch of Dean Witter Reynolds, Inc., one of the nation's top investment firms, she manages over 600 investor accounts and has become an associate vice president for investments. She also publishes a newsletter and conducts investment seminars. Because of her success and the image she projects, René was recently chosen from among 7,000 account executives to represent Dean Witter in a national advertising campaign.

"Facts and figures alone will never convince anyone. If you can't hook your facts to the dreams of the client, then all the statistics and charts in the world won't make any impression."

As an undergraduate at Oberlin College in Ohio, René majored in psychology and had no interest in the stock market or business in general. After graduation, though, she discovered that she liked selling; and she eventually worked her way from insurance to financial securities.

"Although I have my industry battle scars," laughs René, "I'm delighted to be with Dean Witter because of its supportive and noncompetitive internal atmosphere." Rather than working with corporations or portfolio funds, René focuses on individual investors. "That's where the excitement is," she notes. Most of her clients, with her advice, create their own stock portfolios, instead of investing in mutual funds, for which professional managers select the investments.

In helping people invest their money, René realizes the faith her clients put in her. "It's as if you have a person's entire life in your hands," she confesses. To develop such trust, she must be exceptionally credible. For René, credibility is partly established by referrals and testimonials; most of her new clients are referred from long-time clients. But she also establishes credibility with new clients by explaining her background, describing her experience with Dean Witter, and referring to her track record. "Without credibility," says René, "you're dead in the water! It's impossible to persuade anyone to do anything unless that person believes in you."

Although it deals with the stocks of thousands of companies traded on the New York Stock Exchange, Dean Witter Reynolds "measures success one investor at a time." One of the nation's top investment firms, Dean Witter serves over 2 million investors in over 400 locations. In working with individual investors, René Nourse recognizes the need to establish credibility before any persuasion can be effective.

Whether she's meeting one-on-one or addressing a large seminar group, René begins by applying two fundamental principles of persuasion—analyzing the audience and adapting to its needs. For her persuasion to be most effective, she must first find out what her clients really want. What are their dreams? To retire to a farm or to the shore? To provide college educations for their grandchildren? To take control of their money? Once she knows their goals, she must show them how to achieve those dreams. "I don't sell stocks," says René. "I sell people on their goals and the means with which to achieve them."

Like many persuasive people, René uses a number of techniques to get her message across. Linking a new concept to previous knowledge is especially effective. For example, she compares household budget planning to developing an overall investment plan because the principles underlying the two tasks are the same. Allotting portions of income to pay your rent, taxes, and food is much like allocating portions of your portfolio to growth, fixed-income, and income-generating investments.

René also knows that any good salesperson must be ready for objections. When clients say the stock market is too risky or too high to invest in, she's prepared to overcome their resistance. Armed with facts, figures, and graphs, she shows, for example, how a sum invested in the stock market in 1940 would have earned many times more than the same sum invested in a savings account, government securities, or bonds.

"But facts and figures alone will never convince anyone," says René. Other elements are much more important, including benefits to the client. "If you can't connect your facts to the dreams of the client, then all the statistics and charts in the world won't make any impression."

Additional critical factors in successful persuasion are honesty and enthusiasm. "Unless you know your product or service very well and unless you truly believe in it, don't try to sell it. People are very sensitive and intuitive. They're quick to detect insincerity."

Much of René's success in persuasion clearly results from her genuine enthusiasm for her product. "I feel so strongly that investing in stocks is one of the few ways you can make money in this country—aside from owning your own business—that all my clients immediately pick up on my sincerity."[1]

Strategies for Making Persuasive Requests

- **Successful persuasion results from a reasonable request and a well-presented argument.**

The ability to persuade is one of life's important skills. Persuading means using argument or discussion to change an individual's beliefs or actions. At Dean Witter, René Nourse uses many persuasive techniques to convince her clients to invest in securities. Doubtless you've used persuasion at home, at school, and on the job to convert others to your views or to motivate them to do what you want. The outcome of such efforts depends largely on the reasonableness of your request and the ability to present your argument. Business requests and sales messages work the same way.

When you think that your listener or reader is inclined to agree with your request, you can start directly with the main idea. But when the receiver is likely to resist, don't reveal the purpose too quickly. Like bad news, ideas that require persuasion benefit from preparation.

Assume you want a new, up-to-date office computer that is compatible with your home computer and other data sources. In a memo to your boss, Laura, who is likely to resist this request because of budget constraints, you wisely decide not to open with a direct request. Instead, you gain her attention and move to logical reasons supporting your request. This indirect pattern is effective when you must persuade people to grant you favors, accept your recommendations, make adjustments in your favor, or grant your claims.

- **Effective sales messages reflect thorough product knowledge, writer credibility, and specific reader benefits.**

The success of most sales messages, as René pointed out, rests on knowing your product well, developing credibility, and hooking your request to benefits for the receiver. In persuasive messages other than sales, you need to know precisely what you want the receiver to think or do. You also need to anticipate what appeals to make or "buttons to push" to motivate action. Achieving these goals in written messages requires special attention to the initial steps in the writing process.

Applying the 3-×-3 Writing Process to Persuasive Messages

Persuasion means changing people's views, and that's a difficult task. Pulling it off demands planning and perception. The 3-×-3 writing process provides you with a helpful structure for laying a foundation for persuasion. Of particular importance here are (1) analyzing the purpose, (2) adapting to the audience, (3) collecting information, and (4) organizing the message.

- **Persuasive messages require careful analysis of the purpose for writing.**

Analyzing the purpose. The purpose of a persuasive message is to convert the receiver to your ideas or to motivate action. A message without a clear purpose is doomed. Not only must you know what your purpose is and what response you want, but you must know these things when you start writing. Too often, ineffective communicators reach the end of a message before discovering exactly what they want the receiver to do. Then they must start over, giving the request a different "spin" or emphasis. Because your purpose establishes the strategy of the message, determine it first.

Let's return to your memo requesting a new computer. What exactly do you want your boss to do? Do you expect Laura to (1) meet with you so that you can show her how much computer time is lost with incompatible data, (2) purchase Brand X computer for you now, or (3) include your computer request in the department's five-year equipment forecast? By identifying your purpose up front, you can shape the message to point toward it. This planning effort saves considerable rewriting time and produces the most successful persuasive messages.

Adapting to the audience. While you're considering the purpose of a persuasive message, you also need to concentrate on the receiver. How can you adapt your request to that individual so that your message is heard? Zorba the Greek wisely observed, "You can knock forever on a deaf man's door." A persuasive message is equally futile—unless it meets the needs of its audience. In a broad sense, you'll be seeking to show how your request helps the receiver achieve some of life's major goals or fulfill key needs: money, power, comfort, confidence, importance, friends, peace of mind, and recognition, to name a few.

Effective persuasive messages focus on audience needs or goals.

On a more practical level, you want to show how your request solves a problem, achieves a personal or work objective, or just makes life easier for your audience. In your request for a new computer, for example, you could appeal to your boss's expressed concern for increasing productivity. If you were asking for a four-day work schedule, you could cite the need for improved efficiency and better employee morale.

To adapt your request to the receiver, consider these questions that the receiver will very likely be asking him- or herself:[2]

Why should I?	Says who?
Who cares?	So what?
What's in it for me?	What's in it for you?

Adapting to your audience means being ready to answer these questions. It means learning about the audience and analyzing why they might resist your proposal. It means searching for ways to connect your purpose with their needs. If completed before you begin writing, such analysis goes a long way toward overcoming resistance and achieving your goal. The accompanying Career Skills box presents additional strategies that can make you a successful persuader.

Researching and organizing data. Once you've analyzed the audience and considered how to adapt your message to their needs, you're ready to collect data and organize it. You might brainstorm and prepare cluster diagrams to provide a rough outline of ideas. For your computer request, if your strategy was to show that a new computer would increase your productivity, you would gather data to show how much time and effort could be saved with the new machine. To overcome resistance to cost, you would need information about prices. To ensure getting exactly the machine you desire, you would document models and features.

The key components of a persuasive request are gaining attention, showing the worth of the proposal, overcoming resistance, and motivating action.

The next step is organizing your data. Suppose you have already decided that your request will meet with resistance. Thus, you decide not to open directly with your request. Instead, you use the four-part indirect pattern, listed below and shown graphically in Figure 9.1:

- Gain attention
- Build interest
- Reduce resistance
- Motivate action

The indirect pattern discussed and illustrated here suggests a specific plan for making persuasive requests.

FIGURE 9.1 ● Four-Part Indirect Pattern for Persuasion

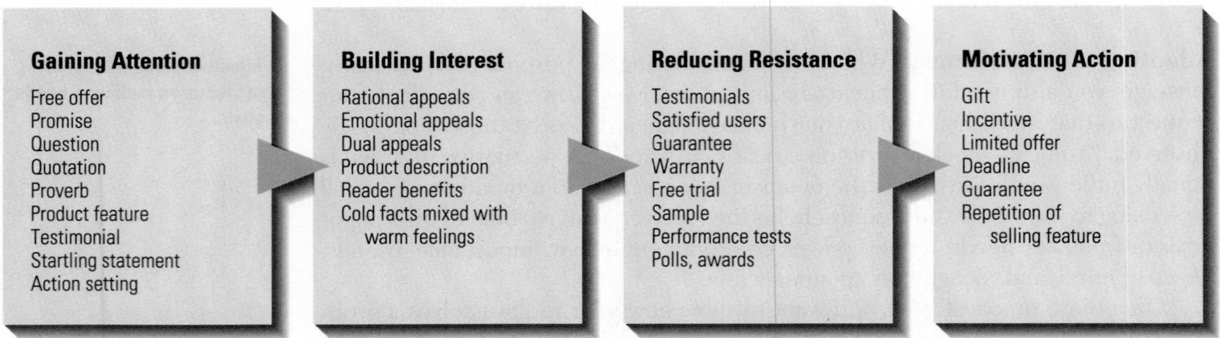

Gaining Attention
Free offer
Promise
Question
Quotation
Proverb
Product feature
Testimonial
Startling statement
Action setting
Building Interest
Rational appeals
Emotional appeals
Dual appeals
Product description
Reader benefits
Cold facts mixed with warm feelings
Reducing Resistance
Testimonials
Satisfied users
Guarantee
Warranty
Free trial
Sample
Performance tests
Polls, awards
Motivating Action
Gift
Incentive
Limited offer
Deadline
Guarantee
Repetition of selling feature

Blending the Components of a Persuasive Message

Although the indirect pattern appears to contain separate steps, successful persuasive messages actually blend these steps into a seamless whole. Moreover, the sequence of the components may change depending on the situation and the emphasis. Regardless of where they are placed, the key elements in persuasive requests are (1) gaining the audience's attention, (2) convincing them that your proposal is worthy, (3) overcoming resistance, and (4) motivating action.

● **Openers to persuasive requests should be brief, relevant, and engaging.**

Gaining attention. To grab attention, the opening statement in a persuasive request should be brief, relevant, and engaging. When only mild persuasion is necessary, the opener can be low-key and factual. If, however, your request is substantial and you anticipate strong resistance, provide a thoughtful, provocative opening. The following examples suggest possibilities.

- **Problem description.** In a recommendation to hire temporary employees: *Last month legal division staff members were forced to work 120 overtime hours, costing us $6,000 and causing considerable employee ill will.* With this opener you've presented a capsule of the problem your proposal will help solve.
- **Unexpected statement.** In a memo to encourage employees to attend an optional sensitivity seminar: *Men and women draw the line at decidedly different places in identifying what behavior constitutes sexual harassment.* Note how this opener gets readers thinking immediately.
- **Reader benefit.** In a proposal offering writing workshops to an organization: *For every letter or memo your employees can avoid writing, your organization saves $78.50.* Companies are always looking for ways to cut costs, and this opener promises significant savings.
- **Compliment.** In a letter inviting a business executive to speak: *Because our members admire your success and value your managerial expertise, they want you to be our speaker.* In offering praise or compliments, however, be careful to avoid obvious flattery.
- **Related fact.** In a memo encouraging employees to start car pooling: *A car pool is defined as two or more persons who travel to work in one car at least once a week.* An interesting, relevant, and perhaps unknown fact sets the scene for the interest-building section that follows.
- **Stimulating question.** In a plea for funds to support environmental causes: *What do Madonna, the Sequoia redwood tree, and the spotted owl have in*

common? Readers will be curious to find the answer to this intriguing question.

Building interest. After capturing attention, a persuasive request must retain that attention and convince the audience that the request is reasonable. To justify your request, be prepared to invest in a few paragraphs of explanation. Persuasive requests are likely to be longer than direct requests because the audience must be convinced rather than simply instructed. You can build interest and conviction through the use of the following:

The body of a persuasive request may require several paragraphs to build interest and reduce resistance.

- Facts, statistics
- Expert opinion
- Direct benefits
- Examples
- Specific details
- Indirect benefits

Showing how your request can benefit the audience directly or indirectly is a key factor in persuasion, as René Nourse recognized at Dean Witter. If you were asking alumni to contribute money to a college foundation, for example, you might promote *direct benefits* such as listing the donor's name in the college magazine or sending a sweatshirt with the college logo. Another direct benefit is a tax write-off for the contribution. An *indirect benefit* comes from feeling good about helping the college and knowing that students will benefit from the gift. Nearly all charities rely in large part on indirect benefits—the selflessness of givers—to promote their causes.

Reducing resistance. One of the biggest mistakes in persuasive requests is the failure to anticipate and offset audience resistance. How will the receiver object to your request? In brainstorming for clues, try *What if?* scenarios. Let's say you are trying to convince management that the employees' cafeteria should switch from paper and plastic plates and cups to ceramic. What if they say the change is too expensive? What if they argue that they are careful recyclers of paper and plastic? What if they contend that ceramic dishes would increase cafeteria labor and energy costs tremendously? What if they protest that ceramic is less hygienic? For each of these *What if?* scenarios, you need a counterargument.

Persuasive requests reduce resistance by addressing *What if?* questions and establishing credibility.

Unless you anticipate resistance, you give the receiver an easy opportunity to dismiss your request. Countering this resistance is important, but you must do it with finesse *(Although ceramic dishes cost more at first, they actually save money over time).* You can minimize objections by presenting your counterarguments in sentences that emphasize benefits: *Ceramic dishes may require a little more effort in cleaning, but they bring warmth and graciousness to meals. Most importantly, they help save the environment by requiring fewer resources and eliminating waste.* However, don't spend too much time on counterarguments, thus making them overly important. Finally, avoid bringing up objections that may never have occurred to the receiver in the first place.

Another factor that reduces resistance is credibility. Receivers are less resistant if your request is reasonable and if you are believable. When the receiver does not know you, you may have to establish your expertise, refer to your credentials, or demonstrate your competence. Even when you are known, you may have to establish your knowledge in a given area. René Nourse often supplies her biography to new Dean Witter clients so that they can see her qualifications and accomplishments. To establish your credibility in making a computer request to your boss, for example, you could describe visits to five showrooms where you tried 18 different models before determining the best one for your purposes.

SEVEN RULES EVERY PERSUADER SHOULD KNOW

Successful businesspeople create persuasive memos, letters, reports, and presentations that get the results they want. Yet, their approaches are all different. Some persuaders are gentle, leading readers by the hand to the targeted recommendation. Others are brisk and authoritative. Some are objective, examining both sides of an issue like a judge deciding a difficult case. Some move slowly and carefully toward a proposal, while others erupt like a volcano in their eagerness to announce a recommendation.

No single all-purpose strategy works for every persuasive situation because of the immense number of variables involved. You wouldn't, for example, use the same techniques in asking for a raise from a stern supervisor as you would use in persuading a close friend to see a movie of your choice. Different situations and different goals require different techniques. The following seven rules suggest various strategies—depending on your individual need.

- **Consider whether your views will create problems for your audience.** A student engineer submitted a report recommending a simple change at a waste-treatment facility. His recommendation would save $200,000 a year, but the report met with a cool reception. Why? His supervisors would have to explain to management why they had allowed a waste of $200,000 a year! If your views make trouble for the audience, think of ways to include the receivers in your recommendation if possible. Whatever your strategy, be tactful and empathic.
- **Don't offer new ideas, directives, or recommendations for change until your readers are prepared for them.** Receivers are threatened by anything that upsets their values or interests. The greater the change you suggest, the more slowly you should proceed. For example, if your boss is enthusiastic about a new marketing scheme (that would cost $50,000 to develop), naturally you will go slowly in shooting it down. If, on the other hand, your boss had little personal investment in the scheme, you could be more direct in your attack.
- **Select a strategy that supports your credibility.** If you have great credibility with your audience, you can proceed directly. If not, you might want to establish that credibility first. *Given* credibility results from position or reputation, such as that of the boss of an organization or a highly regarded scientist. *Acquired* credibility is earned. To acquire credibility, successful persuaders often identify themselves, early in the message, with the goals and interests of the audience (*As an owner of a small business like yourself . . .*). Another way to acquire credibility is to mention evidence or ideas that support the audience's existing views (*We agree that small business owners need more government assistance*). Finally, you can acquire credibility by citing authorities who rate highly with your audience (*Richard Love, recently named Small Businessperson of the Year, supports this proposal*).

● **Persuasive requests motivate action by specifying exactly what should be done.**

Motivating action. After gaining attention, building interest, and reducing resistance, you'll want to inspire the receiver to act. This is where your planning pays dividends. Knowing exactly what action you favor *before* you start to write enables you to point your arguments toward this important final paragraph. Here you will make your recommendation as specifically and confidently as possible—without seeming pushy. A proposal from one manager to another might conclude with, *So that we can begin using the employment assessment tests by May 1, please initial a copy of this memo and return it to me immediately.* In making a request, don't sound apologetic *(I'm sorry to have to ask you this, but . . .),* and don't supply excuses *(If you can spare the time, . . .).* Compare the following closings for a persuasive memo recommending training seminars in communication skills.

Too General

We are certain we can develop a series of training sessions that will improve the communication skills of your employees.

- **If your audience disagrees with your ideas or is uncertain about them, present both sides of the argument.** You might think that you would be most successful by revealing only one side of an issue—your side, of course. But persuasion doesn't work that way. You'll be more successful—particularly if the audience is unfriendly or uncertain—by disclosing *all* sides of an argument. This approach suggests that you are objective. It also helps the receiver remember your view by showing the pros and cons in relation to one another. Thus, if you want to convince the owners of a realty firm that an expensive new lockbox system is a wise investment, be truthful about any shortcomings, weaknesses, and limitations.
- **Win respect by making your opinion or recommendation clear.** Although you should be truthful in presenting both sides of an argument, don't be shy in supporting your conclusions or final proposals. You will, naturally, have definite views and should persuade your audience to accept them. The two-sided strategy is a means to an end, but it does not mean compromising your argument. One executive criticized reports from his managers because they presented much data and concluded, in effect, with "Here is what I found out and maybe we should do this or maybe we should do that." Be decisive and make specific recommendations.
- **Place your strongest points strategically.** Some experts argue that if your audience is deeply concerned with your subject, you can afford to begin with your weakest points. Because of its commitment, the audience will stay with you until you reach the strongest points at the end. For an unmotivated audience, begin with your strongest points to get them interested. Other experts feel that a supportive audience should receive the main ideas or recommendations immediately, to avoid wasting time. Whichever position you choose, don't bury your recommendation, strongest facts, or main idea in the middle of your argument.
- **Don't count on changing attitudes by offering information alone.** "If customers knew the truth about our costs, they would not object to our prices," some companies reason. Well, don't bet on it. Companies have pumped huge sums into advertising and public relations campaigns that provided facts alone. Such efforts often fail because learning something new (that is, increasing the knowledge of the audience) is rarely an effective way to change attitudes. Researchers have found that presentations of facts alone may strengthen opinions—but primarily for people who already agree with the persuader. The added information reassures them and provides ammunition for defending themselves in discussions with others.

Career Track Application

Consider a career-oriented problem in a current or past job: Customer service must be improved, workers need better training, inventory procedures are inefficient, equipment is outdated, worker scheduling is arbitrary, and so forth. Devise a plan to solve the problem. How could the preceding rules help you persuade a decision-maker to adopt your plan? In a memo to your instructor or in class discussion, outline the problem and your plan for rectifying it. Describe your persuasive strategy.

Too Timid

If you agree that our training proposal has merit, perhaps we could begin the series in June.

Too Pushy

Because we're convinced that you will want to begin improving the skills of your employees immediately, we've scheduled your series to begin in June.

Effective

May we work with you in improving the communication skills of your employees? Please call me at 439-2201 by May 1 to give your approval so that training sessions may start in June, as we discussed.

Note how the last opening suggests a specific and easy-to-follow action.

Figure 9.2 summarizes techniques to overcome resistance and craft successful persuasive messages.

FIGURE 9.2 ● **Components of a Persuasive Message**

Gaining Attention	**Building Interest**	**Reducing Resistance**	**Motivating Action**
Summary of problem Unexpected statement Reader benefit Compliment Related fact Stimulating question	Facts, figures Expert opinion Examples Specific details Direct benefits Indirect benefits	Anticipate objections Offer counterarguments Play *What if?* scenarios Establish credibility Demonstrate competence Show value of proposal	Describe specific request Sound confident Make action easy to take Don't apologize Don't provide excuses Repeat main benefit

Being Persuasive but Ethical

Business communicators may be tempted to make their persuasion even more forceful by fudging on the facts, exaggerating a point, omitting something crucial, or providing deceptive emphasis. Consider the case of a manager who sought to persuade employees to accept a change in insurance benefits. His memo emphasized a small perk (easier handling of claims) but deemphasized a major reduction in total coverage. Some readers missed the main point—as the manager intended. Others recognized the deception, however, and before long the manager's credibility was lost. A persuader is effective only when he or she is believable. If receivers suspect that they are being manipulated or misled, or if they find any part of the argument untruthful, the total argument fails.

● **Ethical business communicators maintain credibility and respect by being honest, fair, and objective.**

Persuasion becomes unethical when facts are distorted, overlooked, or manipulated with an intent to deceive. Of course, persuaders naturally want to put forth their strongest case. But that argument must be based on truth, objectivity, and fairness.

In prompting ethical and truthful persuasion, two factors act as powerful motivators. The first is the desire to preserve your reputation and credibility. Once lost, a good name is difficult to regain. An equally important force prompting ethical behavior, though, is your opinion of yourself. René Nourse and other stockbrokers admit that they're in the business to make money, but they still have to be able to look themselves in the mirror each morning.[3] René says, "We've gone through the '80s, when it was tough for morality. Now we're in the process of doing a complete turnaround; people are saying that honesty is what's really important. If you're unethical, you may make all the money in the world. But you won't retain family, friends, or lasting business relationships."

Writing Successful Persuasive Requests

● **The indirect pattern is appropriate when requesting favors and action, persuading within organizations, and requesting adjustments or making claims.**

Convincing someone to change a belief or to perform an action when that individual is reluctant requires planning and skill—and sometimes a little luck. When the request is in writing, rather than face to face, the task is even more difficult. The four-part indirect pattern, though, can help you shape effective persuasive appeals that (1) request favors and action, (2) persuade within organizations, and (3) request adjustments and make claims.

Requesting Favors and Actions

Persuading someone to do something that largely benefits you is not easy. Fortunately, many individuals and companies are willing to grant requests for time, money, information, special privileges, and cooperation. They allow these favors for a variety of reasons. They may just happen to be interested in your project, or they may see goodwill potential for themselves. Often, though, they comply because they see that others will benefit from the request. Professionals sometimes feel obligated to contribute their time or expertise to "pay their dues."

Requests for favors such as time, money, special privileges, or cooperation usually focus on indirect reader benefits.

You may find that you have few direct benefits to offer in your persuasion. Instead, you'll be focusing on indirect benefits, as the writer does in Figure 9.3. In asking a manager to speak before a marketing meeting, the writer has little to offer as a direct benefit other than a $300 honorarium. But indirectly, the writer offers enticements such as an enthusiastic audience and a chance to help other companies solve overseas marketing problems. This persuasive request appeals primarily to the reader's desire to serve his profession—although a receptive audience and an opportunity to talk about one's successes have a certain ego appeal as well. Together, these appeals—professional, egoistic, monetary—make a persuasive argument rich and effective.

As another example, consider the following persuasive message, which asks a company to participate in a survey requesting salary data—usually a touchy subject. Few organizations are willing to reveal how much they pay their employees. Yet, this request may succeed because of the explanation provided and the benefit offered (free salary survey data).

Dear Ms. Masi:

Has your company ever lost a valued employee to another organization that offered 20 percent more in salary for the same position? Have you ever added a unique job title but had no idea what compensation the position demanded?

Gains attention with two short questions that suggest problems the reader knows.

To remain competitive in hiring and to retain qualified workers, companies rely on survey data showing current salaries. My organization collects such data, and we need your help. Would you be willing to complete the enclosed questionnaire so that we can supply companies like yours with accurate salary data?

Discusses a benefit that leads directly to the frank request for help. Notice that the request is coupled with a reader's benefit.

Your information, of course, will be treated confidentially. The questionnaire takes but a few moments to complete, and it can provide substantial dividends for professional organizations that need comparative salary data.

Anticipates and counters resistance to confidentiality and time/effort objections.

To show our gratitude for your participation, we'll send you comprehensive salary surveys for your industry and your metropolitan area. Not only will you find basic salaries, you'll also learn about bonus and incentive plans, special pay differentials, expense reimbursements, perquisites such as a company car and credit card, and special payments like beeper pay.

Offers free salary data as a direct benefit. Describes the benefit in detail to strengthen its appeal.

Comparative salary data are impossible to provide without the support of professionals like you. Please complete the questionnaire and return it in the prepaid envelope before November 1, our fall deadline. You'll no longer be in the dark about how much your employees earn compared with others in your industry.

Appeals to professionalism. Motivates action with a deadline and a final benefit that relates to the opening questions.

Notice that the last paragraph gives details about how to comply with the request. It also takes advantage of an "emphasis spot" (the end of a letter) to provide a final benefit reminder echoing the opening questions.

An offer to work as an intern, at no cost to a company, would seem to require little persuasion. Actually, though, companies hesitate to participate in internship

FIGURE 9.3 ● Persuasive Favor Request

The Three Phases of the Writing Process

1

Analyze
The purpose of this letter is to persuade the reader to speak at a dinner meeting.

Anticipate
Although the reader is busy, he may respond to appeals to his ego (describing his successes before an appreciative audience) and to his professionalism.

Adapt
Because the reader will be uninterested at first and require persuasion, use the indirect pattern.

2

Research
Study the receiver's interests and find ways to relate this request to the reader's interests.

Organize
Gain attention by opening with praise or a stimulating remark. Build interest with explanations and facts. Show how compliance benefits the reader and others. Reduce resistance by providing ideas for the dinner talk. Motivate action by making it easy.

Compose
Prepare first draft on a computer.

3

Revise
Revise to show direct and indirect benefits more clearly.

Proofread
Use quotes around "R" to reflect their usage. In the fourth paragraph, use a semicolon in the compound sentence. Start all lines at the left for block-style letter.

Evaluate
Will this letter convince the reader to accept the invitation?

Dallas–Fort Worth Chapter
American Marketing Association
P.O. Box 3598
Dallas, TX 74209

January 28, 1994

Mr. Elliott P. Tarkanian
Marketing Manager, Western Division
Toys "R" Us, Inc.
Dallas, TX 75232

Dear Mr. Tarkanian:

One company is legendary for marketing American products successfully in Japan. [Piques reader's curiosity] [Gains attention]

That company, of course, is Toys "R" Us. The triumph of your thriving toy store in Amimachi, Japan, has given other American marketers hope. But this success story has also raised numerous questions. Specifically, how did Toys "R" Us circumvent local trade restrictions? How did you solve the complex distribution system? And how did you negotiate with all the levels of Japanese bureaucracy? [Builds interest]

The members of the Dallas–Fort Worth chapter of the American Marketing Association asked me to invite you to speak at our March 19 dinner meeting on the topic of "How Toys 'R' Us Unlocked the Door to Japanese Trade." By describing your winning effort, Mr. Tarkanian, you can help launch other American companies who face the same quagmire of Japanese restrictions and red tape that your organization overcame. [Notes indirect benefit] Although we can offer you only a small honorarium of $300, we can assure you of a big audience of enthusiastic marketing professionals eager to hear your war story. [Notes direct benefit]

Our relaxed group doesn't expect a formal address; they are most interested in what steps Toys "R" Us took to open its Japanese toy outlet. [Offsets reluctance by making the talk informal and easy to organize] [Reduces resistance] To make your talk easy to organize, I've enclosed a list of questions our members submitted. Most talks are about 45 minutes long.

Can we count on you to join us for dinner at 7 p.m. March 19 at the Cattleman's Inn in Grand Prairie? Just call me at (214) 860-4320 by February 15 to make arrangements. [Makes acceptance as simple as a telephone call] [Motivates action]

Sincerely,

Timothy W. Ellison

Timothy W. Ellison
Program Chair, AMA

TWE:grw
Enclosure

This bike race sponsored by Shaklee began with a persuasive request made orally and later firmed up in writing. Whether the request is made within an organization or externally, a persuader must be able to gain attention, build interest, reduce resistance, and motivate action. To justify a bike race, the writer connected Shaklee's health emphasis with the wholesome image of cyclists, each wearing clothing with prominent Shaklee logos.

programs because student interns require supervision, desk space, and equipment. They also pose an insurance liability threat.

In Figure 9.4 college student Melanie Harris seeks to persuade Software Enterprises to accept her as an intern. In the analysis process before writing, Melanie thought long and hard about what benefits she could offer the reader and how she could present them strategically. She decided that the offer of a trained college student's free labor was her strongest benefit. Thus, she opens with it, as well as mentioning the same benefit in the letter body and in the closing. After opening with the main audience benefit, she introduces the actual request ("Could you use the part-time services of a college senior . . . ?").

In the interest section, Melanie tells why she is making the request and describes its value in terms of direct and indirect benefits. Notice how she transforms obstacles (lack of equipment or desk space) into helpful suggestions about how her services would free up other staff members to perform more important tasks. She delays mentioning a negative (being able to work only 15 hours a week and only in the afternoon) until after building interest and reducing resistance. And she closes confidently and motivates action with reference to both direct and indirect benefits.

Persuading Within Organizations

Internal persuasive memos present honest arguments detailing specific reader benefits.

Instructions or directives moving downward from superiors to subordinates usually require little persuasion. Employees expect to be directed in how to perform their jobs. These messages (such as information about procedures, equipment, or customer service) follow the direct pattern, with the purpose immediately stated. However, employees are sometimes asked to perform in a capacity outside their work roles or to accept changes that are not in their best interests (pay cuts, job transfers, or reduced benefits). In these instances, a persuasive memo using the indirect pattern may be most effective.

The goal is not to manipulate employees or to seduce them with trickery. Rather, the goal is to present a strong but *honest* argument, emphasizing points

FIGURE 9.4 ● Persuasive Action Request

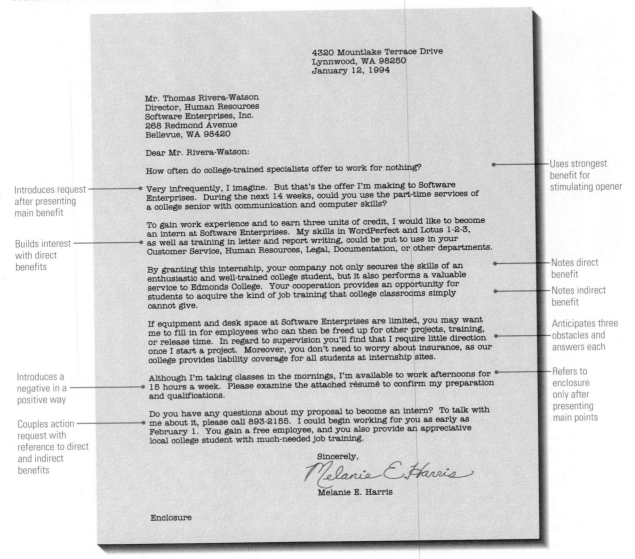

4320 Mountlake Terrace Drive
Lynnwood, WA 98250
January 12, 1994

Mr. Thomas Rivera-Watson
Director, Human Resources
Software Enterprises, Inc.
268 Redmond Avenue
Bellevue, WA 98420

Dear Mr. Rivera-Watson:

How often do college-trained specialists offer to work for nothing?

Very infrequently, I imagine. But that's the offer I'm making to Software Enterprises. During the next 14 weeks, could you use the part-time services of a college senior with communication and computer skills?

To gain work experience and to earn three units of credit, I would like to become an intern at Software Enterprises. My skills in WordPerfect and Lotus 1-2-3, as well as training in letter and report writing, could be put to use in your Customer Service, Human Resources, Legal, Documentation, or other departments.

By granting this internship, your company not only secures the skills of an enthusiastic and well-trained college student, but it also performs a valuable service to Edmonds College. Your cooperation provides an opportunity for students to acquire the kind of job training that college classrooms simply cannot give.

If equipment and desk space at Software Enterprises are limited, you may want me to fill in for employees who can then be freed up for other projects, training, or release time. In regard to supervision you'll find that I require little direction once I start a project. Moreover, you don't need to worry about insurance, as our college provides liability coverage for all students at internship sites.

Although I'm taking classes in the mornings, I'm available to work afternoons for 15 hours a week. Please examine the attached résumé to confirm my preparation and qualifications.

Do you have any questions about my proposal to become an intern? To talk with me about it, please call 893-2155. I could begin working for you as early as February 1. You gain a free employee, and you also provide an appreciative local college student with much-needed job training.

Sincerely,

Melanie E. Harris

Melanie E. Harris

Enclosure

Uses strongest benefit for stimulating opener

Introduces request after presenting main benefit

Builds interest with direct benefits

Notes direct benefit

Notes indirect benefit

Anticipates three obstacles and answers each

Introduces a negative in a positive way

Refers to enclosure only after presenting main points

Couples action request with reference to direct and indirect benefits

that are important to the receiver. In business, honesty is not just the best policy—it's the *only* policy. Especially within your own organization, people see right through puffery and misrepresentation. For this reason, the indirect pattern is effective only when supported by accurate, honest evidence.

Evidence also is critical when subordinates submit recommendations to their bosses. "The key to making a request of a superior," advises communication consultant Patricia Buhler, "is to know your needs and have documentation [facts, figures, evidence]." Another important factor is moderation. "Going in and asking for the world [right] off the cuff is most likely going to elicit a negative response," she adds.[4]

The following draft of a request for a copier fails to present convincing evidence of the need. Although the request is reasonable, the argument lacks credibility because of its high-pressure tactics and lack of proof.

TO: Nick Nostramos, Vice President DATE: April 12, 1994
FROM: Vanessa Ferguson, Marketing
SUBJECT: COPIERS

Although you've opposed copier purchases in the past, I think I've found a great deal on a copier that's just too good to pass up—if we act before May 1.

Begins poorly by reminding reader of negative past feelings.

Copy City has reconditioned copiers that they are practically giving away. If we move fast, they will provide many free incentives—like a free copier stand, free starter supplies, free delivery, and free installation.

Sounds high pressured and poorly conceived.

We must find a way to reduce copier costs in my department. At the present time we are making a total of 10,000 copies a month by sending secretaries or sales reps to Copy Quick, where we spend 5 cents a page and waste a lot of time. We're making at least eight trips a week, adding up to a considerable expense in travel time and copy costs.

Presents persuasive arguments illogically. Fails to tell exactly how much money could be saved.

Please give this matter your immediate attention and get back to me as soon as possible. We don't want to miss this great deal!

Doesn't suggest specific action for reader to take.

The preceding memo will probably fail to achieve its purpose. Although the revised version in Figure 9.5 is longer, it's far more effective. Remember that a persuasive message will typically take more space than a direct message because proving a case requires evidence. Notice that the subject line in Figure 9.5 tells the purpose of the memo without disclosing the actual request. By delaying the request until she's had a chance to describe the problem and discuss a solution, the writer prevents the reader's premature rejection.

The strength of this revision, though, is in the clear presentation of comparison figures showing how much money can be saved by purchasing a remanufactured copier. Although the organization pattern is not obvious, the revised memo begins with an attention-getter (frank description of problem), builds interest (with easy-to-read facts and figures), provides benefits, and reduces resistance. Notice that the conclusion tells what action is to be taken, makes it easy to respond, and repeats the main benefit to motivate action.

Requesting Adjustments and Making Claims

Persuasive adjustment letters make claims about damaged products, mistaken billing, inaccurate shipments, warranty problems, return policies, insurance snafus, faulty merchandise, and so on. Generally, the direct pattern is best for requesting adjustments (see Chapter 6). But if a past request has been refused or ignored or if you anticipate reluctance, then the indirect pattern is appropriate.

- **Effective adjustment letters make reasonable claims backed by solid evidence.**

In a sense, an adjustment letter is a complaint letter. Someone is complaining about something that went wrong. Some complaint letters just vent anger; the writers are mad, and they want to tell someone about it. But if the goal is to change something (and why bother to write except to motivate change?), then persuasion is necessary. Effective adjustment letters make a reasonable claim, present a logical case with clear facts, and adopt a moderate tone. Anger and emotion are not effective persuaders.

You'll want to open an adjustment letter with some sincere praise, an objective statement of the problem, a point of agreement, or a quick review of what you have done to resolve the problem. Then you can explain precisely what happened or why your claim is legitimate. Don't provide a blow-by-blow chronology of details; just hit the highlights. Be sure to enclose copies of relevant invoices, shipping orders, warranties, and payments. And close with a clear statement of what you want done: refund, replacement, credit to your account, or other action. Be sure to think through the possibilities and make your request reasonable.

FIGURE 9.5 ● Persuasive Memo

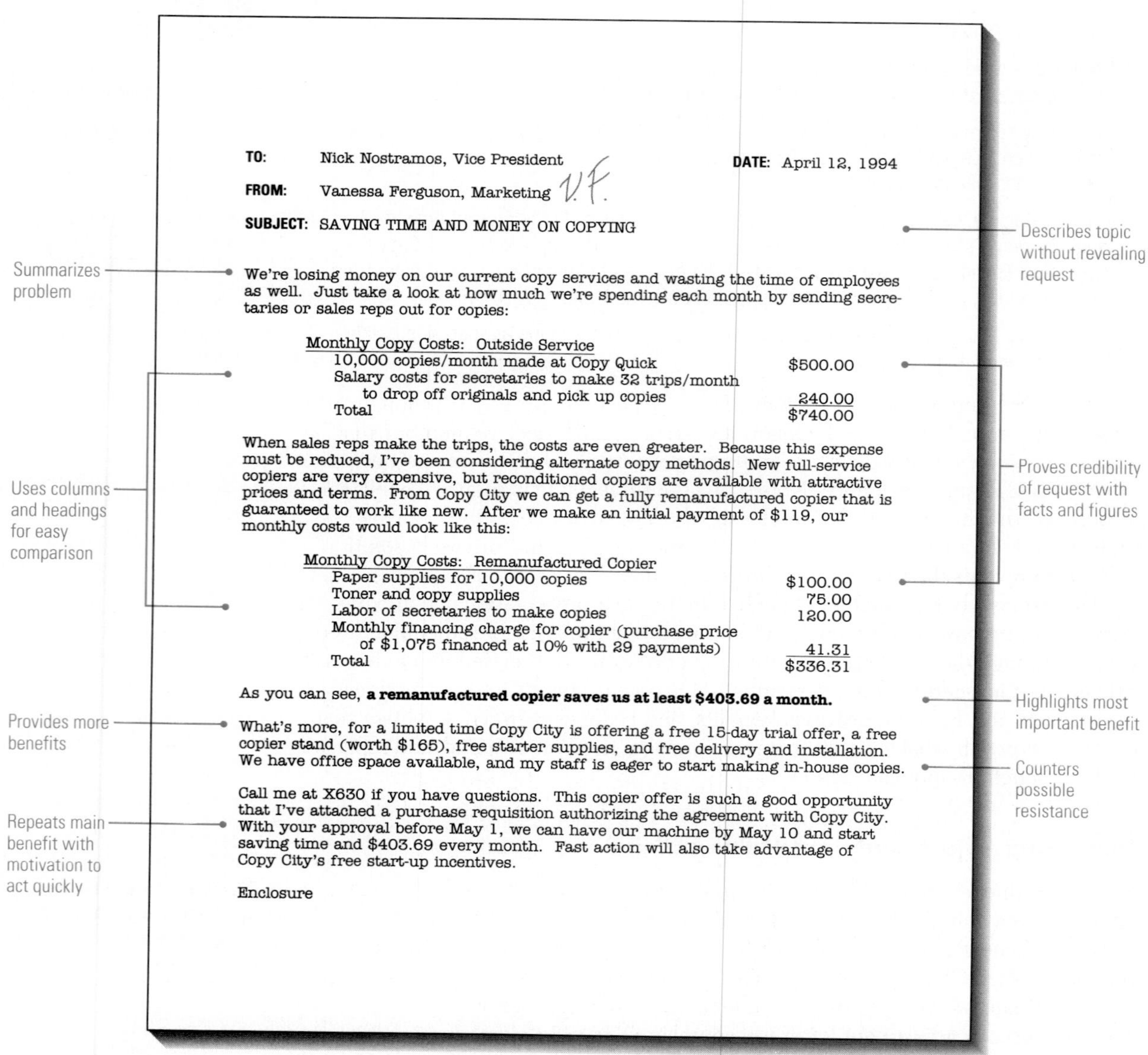

TO: Nick Nostramos, Vice President **DATE:** April 12, 1994

FROM: Vanessa Ferguson, Marketing *V.F.*

SUBJECT: SAVING TIME AND MONEY ON COPYING

We're losing money on our current copy services and wasting the time of employees as well. Just take a look at how much we're spending each month by sending secretaries or sales reps out for copies:

Monthly Copy Costs: Outside Service	
10,000 copies/month made at Copy Quick	$500.00
Salary costs for secretaries to make 32 trips/month to drop off originals and pick up copies	240.00
Total	$740.00

When sales reps make the trips, the costs are even greater. Because this expense must be reduced, I've been considering alternate copy methods. New full-service copiers are very expensive, but reconditioned copiers are available with attractive prices and terms. From Copy City we can get a fully remanufactured copier that is guaranteed to work like new. After we make an initial payment of $119, our monthly costs would look like this:

Monthly Copy Costs: Remanufactured Copier	
Paper supplies for 10,000 copies	$100.00
Toner and copy supplies	75.00
Labor of secretaries to make copies	120.00
Monthly financing charge for copier (purchase price of $1,075 financed at 10% with 29 payments)	41.31
Total	$336.31

As you can see, **a remanufactured copier saves us at least $403.69 a month.**

What's more, for a limited time Copy City is offering a free 15-day trial offer, a free copier stand (worth $165), free starter supplies, and free delivery and installation. We have office space available, and my staff is eager to start making in-house copies.

Call me at X630 if you have questions. This copier offer is such a good opportunity that I've attached a purchase requisition authorizing the agreement with Copy City. With your approval before May 1, we can have our machine by May 10 and start saving time and $403.69 every month. Fast action will also take advantage of Copy City's free start-up incentives.

Enclosure

Summarizes problem
Uses columns and headings for easy comparison
Provides more benefits
Repeats main benefit with motivation to act quickly
Describes topic without revealing request
Proves credibility of request with facts and figures
Highlights most important benefit
Counters possible resistance

● Adjustment requests should adopt a moderate tone, appeal to the receiver's sense of responsibility, and specify needed actions.

The tone of the letter is important. You should never suggest that the receiver intentionally deceived you or intentionally created the problem. Rather, appeal to the receiver's sense of responsibility and pride in its good name. Calmly express your disappointment in view of your high expectations of the product and of the company. Communicating your feelings, without rancor, is often your strongest appeal.

Brent Barry's letter, shown in Figure 9.6, follows the persuasive pattern as he seeks to return three answering machines. Notice that he uses simplified letter style (skipping the salutation and complimentary close) because he doesn't have a person's name to use in addressing the letter. Note also his positive opening; his calm, well-documented claims; and his request for specific action.

FIGURE 9.6 ● **Request for Adjustment**

Tips for Requesting Adjustments

- Begin with a compliment, point of agreement, statement of the problem, or brief review of action you have taken to resolve the problem.
- Provide identifying data.
- Prove that your claim is valid; explain why the receiver is responsible.
- Enclose document copies supporting your claim.
- Appeal to the receiver's fairness, ethical and legal responsibilities, and desire for customer satisfaction.
- Describe your feelings and your disappointment.
- Avoid sounding angry, emotional, or irrational.
- Close by telling exactly what you want done.

CHAMPION AUTOMOTIVES
309 Porterville Plaza, Lansing, Michigan 48914 (517) 690-3500

November 21, 1994

Customer Service
Raytronic Electronics
594 Stanton Street
Mobile, AL 36617

SUBJECT: CODE-A-PHONE MODEL 100S

Uses simplified letter style when name of receiver is unknown

Begins with compliment

Your Code-A-Phone Model 100S answering unit came well recommended. We liked our neighbor's unit so well that we purchased three for different departments in our business.

Describes problem calmly

After the three units were unpacked and installed, we discovered a problem. Apparently our office fluorescent lighting interferes with the electronics in these units. When the lights are on, heavy static interrupts every telephone call. When the lights are off, the static disappears.

We can't replace the fluorescent lights, so we tried to return the Code-A-Phones to the place of purchase (Office Mart, 2560 Haslett Avenue, Lansing, MI 48901). A salesperson inspected the units and said they could not be returned since they were not defective and they had been used.

Suggests responsibility

Stresses disappointment

Because the descriptive literature and instructions for the Code-A-Phones say nothing about avoiding use in rooms with fluorescent lighting, we expected no trouble. We were quite disappointed that this well-engineered unit—with its time/date stamp, room monitor, and auto-dial features—failed to perform as we hoped it would.

Tells what action to take

Appeals to company's desire to preserve good reputation

If you have a model with similar features that would work in our offices, give me a call. Otherwise, please authorize the return of these units and refund the purchase price of $519.45 (see enclosed invoice). We're confident that a manufacturer with your reputation for excellent products and service will want to resolve this matter quickly.

B.W. Barry

BRENT W. BARRY, PRESIDENT

BWB:ett
Enclosure

SPOTLIGHT ON COMMUNICATORS

To launch Pitney Bowes' new computerized mail system, Marketing Vice President Kathleen Synnott had to persuade both co-workers and customers that the new system made sense. Internally, her persuasion centered on economics, emphasizing the need for the company to reinvent its product. With customers, her sales message concentrated on benefits, showing how the new mail-meter system could allow mail of mixed sizes to be weighed, stamped, and prepared for the post office in minutes. She advises anyone selling a product to know it thoroughly.

The following checklist reviews pointers for helping you make persuasive requests of all kinds.

Checklist for Making Persuasive Requests

- ✔ **Gain attention.** In requesting favors, begin with a compliment, statement of agreement, unexpected fact, stimulating question, reader benefit, summary of problem, or candid plea for help. For claims also consider opening with a review of action you have taken to resolve the problem.
- ✔ **Build interest.** Prove the accuracy and merit of your request with solid evidence, including facts, figures, expert opinion, examples, and details. Suggest direct and indirect benefits for the receiver. Avoid sounding high-pressured, angry, or emotional.
- ✔ **Reduce resistance.** Identify what factors will be obstacles to the receiver; offer counterarguments. Demonstrate your credibility by being knowledgeable. In requesting favors or making recommendations, show how the receiver or others will benefit. In making claims, appeal to the receiver's sense of fairness and desire for goodwill. Express your disappointment.
- ✔ **Motivate action.** Confidently ask for specific action. For favors include an end date (if appropriate) and try to repeat a key benefit.

Planning and Composing Sales Messages

Direct-mail marketing, a rapidly growing multibillion-dollar industry, involves the sale of goods and services through letters, catalogs, brochures, and other messages delivered by mail. Professionals who specialize in direct-mail services have made a science of analyzing a market, developing an effective mailing list, studying the product, preparing a sophisticated campaign aimed at a target audience, and motivating the reader to act. You've probably received many direct-mail packages, often called "junk" mail. These packages typically contain a sales letter, a brochure, a price list, illustrations of the product, testimonials, and other persuasive appeals.

We're most concerned here with the sales letter: its strategy, organization, and evidence. Because sales letters are generally written by specialists, you may never write one on the job. Why, then, learn how to write a sales letter? In many ways, every letter we create is a form of sales letter. We sell our ideas, our organizations, and ourselves. Learning the techniques of sales writing will help you be more successful in any communication that requires persuasion and promotion. Furthermore, you'll recognize sales strategies, thus enabling you to become a more perceptive consumer of ideas, products, and services.

Applying the 3-×-3 Writing Process to Sales Messages

● **Successful sales messages require research on the product or service offered and analysis of the purpose for writing.**

Marketing professionals analyze every aspect of a sales message because consumers reject most direct-mail offers. Like the experts, you'll want to pay close attention to the preparatory steps of analysis and adaptation before writing the actual message.

Analyzing the product and purpose. Before writing a sales letter, you should study the product carefully. What can you learn about its design, construction, raw materials, and manufacturing process? About its ease of use, efficiency, durability, and applications? Be sure to consider warranties, service, price, and special appeals. At the same time, evaluate the competition so that you can compare your product's strengths against the competitor's weaknesses.

Now you're ready to identify your central selling points. One very effective marketing campaign centers totally on price: "If you paid full price, you didn't buy it at Crown Books." Another campaign focuses on service with a testimonial: "When we went looking for copiers, service was our number one concern . . . and Pitney Bowes was our number one choice." Analyzing your product and the competition helps you determine what to emphasize in your sales letter.

Another important decision in the preparatory stage involves the specific purpose of your letter. Do you want the reader to call for a free video and brochure? Fill out an order form? See a demonstration? Send a credit card authorization? Before you write the first word of your message, know what features of the product you will emphasize and what response you want.

Adapting to the audience. Blanket mailings sent "cold" to occupants generally produce low responses—typically only 2 percent. That means that 98 percent of us usually toss direct-mail sales letters directly into the garbage. But the response rate can be increased dramatically by targeting the audience through selected mailing lists. These lists can be purchased or compiled. Let's say you're selling fitness equipment. A good mailing list might come from subscribers to fitness or exercise magazines. By directing your message to a selected group, you can make certain assumptions about the receivers. You would expect similar interests, needs, and demographics (age, income, and other characteristics). With this knowledge you can adapt the sales letter to a specific audience.

SPOTLIGHT ON COMMUNICATORS

In writing winning sales messages, beware of impossible promises, warns Herb Kelleher, cofounder and CEO of Southwest Airlines. He believes his company has the quickest baggage delivery in the industry—only eight minutes from jetway to pickup. But when his marketing staff proposed making such a promise in the Southwest promotions, Kelleher balked. On rare occasions Southwest wouldn't be able to deliver, he reasoned, and broken promises are not easily forgotten.

Crafting a Winning Sales Message

Your sales message may promote a product, a service, an idea, or yourself. In each case the most effective messages will (1) gain attention, (2) build interest, (3) reduce resistance, and (4) motivate action. This is the same recipe we studied earlier, but the ingredients are different.

Gaining attention. One of the most critical elements of a sales letter is its opening paragraph. This opener should be short (one to five lines), honest, relevant, and stimulating. Marketing pros have found that eye-catching typographical arrangements or provocative messages, like the following, can hook a reader's attention:

Openers for sales messages should be brief, honest, relevant, and provocative.

- **Offer:** *A free trip to Hawaii is just the beginning!*
- **Promise:** *Now you can raise your sales income by 50 percent or even more with the proven techniques found in . . .*
- **Question:** *Do you yearn for an honest, fulfilling relationship?*
- **Quotation or proverb:** *Necessity is the mother of invention.*
- **Product feature:** *At last—a collection of personnel forms that help you both hire and manage employees, while complying with government regulations.*
- **Testimonial:** *"The* Journal *surprises, amuses, investigates, and most of all educates."* (*The New Republic* commenting on *The Wall Street Journal.*)
- **Startling statement:** *Let the poor and hungry feed themselves! For just $100 they can.*

SPOTLIGHT ON COMMUNICATORS

From San Francisco, Charles Schwab runs the nation's biggest discount stock brokerage firm. To sell his financial services, he makes both rational and emotional appeals. Rationally, he promises customers investment services at discount prices, sometimes undercutting industry giants by as much as 60 percent. Emotionally, he promises personalized, ethical service. His sincere soft-sell approach educates and assures investors, thus reducing resistance and fear.

- **Personalized action setting:** *It's 4:30 p.m. and you've got to make a decision. You need everybody's opinion, no matter where they are. Before you pick up your phone to call them one at a time, pick up this card: AT&T Teleconference Services.*

Other openings calculated to capture attention might include a solution to a problem, an anecdote, a personalized statement using the receiver's name, or a relevant current event.

Building interest. In this phase of your sales message, you should describe clearly the product or service. In simple language emphasize the central selling points that you identified during your prewriting analysis. Those selling points can be developed using rational or emotional appeals.

Rational appeals are associated with reason and intellect. They translate selling points into references to making or saving money, increasing efficiency, or making the best use of resources. In general, rational appeals are appropriate when a product is expensive, long-lasting, or important to health, security, and financial success. Emotional appeals relate to status, ego, and sensual feelings. Appealing to the emotions is sometimes effective when a product is inexpensive, short-lived, or nonessential. Many clever sales messages, however, combine emotional and rational strategies for a dual appeal. Consider these examples:

Rational Appeal

You can buy the things you need and want, pay household bills, pay off higher-cost loans and credit cards—as soon as you're approved and your Credit-Line account is opened.

Emotional Appeal

Leave the urban bustle behind and escape to sun-soaked Bermuda! All you need is your bathing suit, a little suntan lotion, and your Credit-Line card to recharge your batteries with an injection of sun and surf.

Dual Appeal

New Credit-Line cardholders are immediately eligible for a $100 travel certificate and additional discounts at fun-filled resorts. Save up to 40 percent while lying on a beach in picturesque, sun-soaked Bermuda, the year-round resort island.

A physical description of your product is not enough, however. Zig Ziglar, described as America's greatest salesperson, points out that no matter how well you know your product, no one is persuaded by cold, hard facts alone. In the end, he contends, "People buy because of the product benefits."[5] Your job is to translate those cold facts into warm feelings and reader benefits. Let's say a sales letter promotes a hand cream made with aloe and cocoa butter extracts, along with Vitamin A. Those facts become, "Nature's hand helpers—including soothing aloe and cocoa extracts, along with firming Vitamin A—form invisible gloves that protect your dry, rough skin against the hardships of work, harsh detergents, and constant environmental assaults."

Reducing resistance. Marketing pros use a number of techniques to overcome resistance and build desire. When price is an obstacle, consider these suggestions:

- Delay mentioning price until after you've created a desire for the product.
- Show the price in small units, such as the price per issue of a magazine.

Reputable muffler shops issue warranties that are explained to customers. Because the muffler-replacement industry has a history of ripping people off, Midas launched a successful $50 million ad campaign featuring genuine customer testimonials. Midas knows that consumers are skeptical when companies tout their own claims. But when satisfied customers offer praise, the claims carry more weight. Testimonials—especially from people who are like the audience—are a very effective technique for achieving credibility and for reducing resistance in sales and persuasive messages.

- Demonstrate how the reader saves money by, for instance, subscribing for two or three years.
- Compare your prices with those of a competitor.

In addition, you need to anticipate other objections and questions the receiver may have. When possible, translate these objections into selling points *(If you've never ordered software by mail, let us send you our demonstration disks at no charge).*

Techniques for reducing resistance include testimonials, guarantees, warranties, samples, and performance polls.

Other techniques to overcome resistance and prove the credibility of the product include the following:

- **Testimonials:** *"I learned so much in your language courses that I began to dream in French."—Holly Franker, Beaumont, Texas*
- **Names of satisfied users** (with permission, of course): *Enclosed is a partial list of private pilots who enthusiastically subscribe to our service.*
- **Money-back guarantee or warranty:** *We offer the longest warranties in the business—all parts and service on-site for two years!*
- **Free trial or sample:** *We're so confident that you'll like our software that we want you to try it absolutely free.*
- **Performance tests, polls, or awards:** *Last year our computer won customer satisfaction polls in the U.S., U.K., Germany, and France.*

Motivating action. All the effort put into a sales message is lost if the reader fails to act. To make it easy for readers to act, you can provide a reply card, a stamped and preaddressed envelope, a toll-free telephone number, or a promise of a follow-up call. Because readers often need an extra push, consider including additional motivators, such as the following:

Techniques for motivating action include offering a gift or incentive, limiting an offer, and guaranteeing satisfaction.

- **Offer a gift:** *You'll receive a free calculator with your first order.*
- **Promise an incentive:** *With every new, paid subscription, we'll plant a tree in one of America's Heritage Forests.*
- **Limit the offer:** *Only the first 100 customers receive free checks.*

watch in the water again. You were most disappointed when the V-2 stopped working. Its many features pleased you; you want another V-2. Address your follow-up letter requesting a replacement of the Windsurfer V-2 to Jackelyn Palmer, Customer Service Manager, Rayco Watch Company, 6250 Park Street, Fairfield, CT 06431.

9.16 Request for Adjustment: Angry Over Printer

As Becky W. Ellson, owner of a secretarial service, you are most unhappy with a printer you recently purchased. The salesperson promised that the Jetson Multiwriter II could produce proportional spacing at near letter quality. The printer does produce 10- and 12-pitch spacing, but not proportional spacing. You particularly need proportional spacing for preparing client grant proposals. After reading the manual carefully, you find no reference to proportional spacing. You decide to consult a friend who is a programmer; she says that this printer is incapable of producing proportional printing. You are very angry because the product has been misrepresented and because you have wasted enormous amounts of time and energy trying to make it work. You decide to control your anger and write to the manufacturer explaining your complaint without being too harsh. You want a full refund or a replacement printer that will generate proportional spacing with your IBM-compatible computer and your WordPerfect software program. Include your salesperson's name and a copy of the invoice. Write to Jetson, Inc., Office Products Division, 3530 Silverado, Torrance, CA 90321.

9.17 Sales Letter: Promoting Your Product or Service

Identify a situation in your current job or a previous one in which a sales letter is (was) needed. Using suggestions from this chapter, write an appropriate sales letter that promotes a product or service. Use actual names, information, and examples. If you have no work experience, imagine a business you'd like to start: word processing, student typing, pet grooming, car detailing, tutoring, specialty knitting, balloon decorating, delivery service, child care, gardening, lawn care, or something else. Write a letter selling your product or service to be distributed to your prospective customers. Be sure to tell them how to respond.

C.L.U.E. Review 9

Edit the following sentences to correct faults in grammar, punctuation, spelling, and word use.

1. 2 loans made to Consumer products corporation must be repaid within 90 days. Or the owners will be in default.
2. One loan was for property apprised at forty thousand dollars, the other was for property estimated to be worth ten thousand dollars.
3. Our Senior Marketing Director and the sales manager are quite knowledgable about communications hardware, therefore they are traveling to the Computer show in northern California.
4. We congradulate you on winning the award, and hope that you will continue to experience simular success, in the future.
5. Mr. Salazar left three million dollars to be divided among 4 heirs; one of whom is a successful manufacture.
6. If the CEO and him had behaved more professional the chances of a practicle settlement would be considerably greater.
7. Just inside the entrance, is the desk of the receptionist and a complete directory of all departments'.
8. Every new employee must recieve their permit to park in lot 5-A or there car will be sited.
9. When we open our office in Montreal we will need at least 3 people whom are fluent in french and english.
10. Most companys can boost profits almost one hundred percent by retaining just 5% more of there permenant customers.

Goodwill and Special Messages

LEARNING GOALS

After studying this chapter, you should be able to

1. Identify five characteristics of messages that deliver thanks, praise, or sympathy
2. Discuss three points to cover in thank-you notes for gifts
3. Specify six guidelines that a careful writer follows in writing employment recommendations
4. Explain the purposes of employee performance appraisals
5. List six topics to be covered in employee warnings
6. Describe six tips for writing news releases
7. Explain how to write clear operational instructions and announcements

American Airlines: Career Track Profile

Tim Smith's telephone rings constantly. That's not surprising, though, because over 25,000 unsolicited calls come in annually to the American Airlines corporate communications offices in Fort Worth where he is a media analyst. Some companies spend millions of dollars in public relations programs to get their telephones to ring. Not so at American.

Because it is the country's largest domestic airline, American attracts many inquiries from newspapers, magazines, radio and TV stations, and writers about the transportation industry. Recognizing the goodwill generated by a policy of open access to corporate news, American encourages the free flow of communication externally and internally.

"Service is our No. 1 product. To provide a high level of service, employees not only need to feel appreciated, but they must understand what's going on within the company."

Tim Smith is part of both efforts—getting information to outsiders and to insiders as well. Trained in journalism at the University of Florida in Gainesville, Tim was a broadcaster before joining American. As a corporate spokesperson, he writes letters, memos, news releases, and "talking points" (short policy statements) explaining American's programs and positions.

Internally, American works constantly to keep the lines of communication open between management and employees. Since customer relations play such an important role in an airline's success or failure, American strives to keep its employees informed and happy. As Tim says, "Service is our No. 1 product. To provide a high level of service, employees not only need to feel appreciated, but they must understand what's going on within the company."

Showing appreciation in a company with nearly 120,000 employees is no easy task. Individual managers may send short messages of thanks or congratulations to employees for jobs well done. And American Chairman Robert L. Crandall often writes individual notes expressing his personal thanks. But the company also has formal recognition programs that encourage supervisors to applaud the efforts of employees. One such program, AAchievers, rewards employees with points to be spent on company merchandise, trips, or other items.

Goodwill Messages

The work of Tim Smith at American Airlines revolves around developing goodwill for his company and writing special messages not ordinarily considered to be "business communication." Because these kinds of messages may play an important role in your personal success as well as that of your organization, this chapter provides

Another way that employees are recognized and encouraged to participate is through IdeAAs in Action, American's employee-suggestion program. Last year American was able to purchase a Boeing 757 jetliner with the savings realized by employee cost-cutting suggestions. Their ideas saved the company over $58 million in one year! In addition to recognition, employees' suggestions earn cash awards, prizes, and credits toward trips, furniture, and even college tuition.

Thanking people and employees is a company philosophy that starts with American's top management and trickles down to every level. Such encouragement and open communication keeps employees focused on their jobs and fulfills important human needs for recognition.

In addition to keeping employees informed, Tim functions as a conduit of information from American to the news media. His "talking points" and news releases cover topics like executive appointments, changes in service, industry issues, and company awards and innovations. In writing news releases, he says that his main goal is to get them read by the editors to whom they are sent. "We've done focus groups and learned that editors tend to read only the first sentence of a release. So you have to concentrate on getting the important ideas up front. And you also have to make sure you don't start out with a long, rambling sentence that goes off the Fog Index.

"Keeping it simple is key for any news release," says Tim. He suggests short, familiar words and a conversational tone. "People like to read quotations, but these words must sound the way people really talk and not unnatural or artificial."

He advises that a news release concentrate on no more than two or three points. "Including too many ideas tends to befuddle the reader and dilute your most important points." Although the first sentence should contain the main points, he cautions against packing it with every detail. Tim also advises against overdramatization and filling a story with "fluff" or meaningless facts that sound self-serving. "We never expect a news release to be published exactly as we wrote it," says Tim. "Yet we are often pleasantly surprised to see how many elements of a release do show up in print—if we've done a good job."[1]

As the nation's largest domestic airline, American is also one of the nation's biggest service providers. Maintaining a high level of service demands committed employees. No one knows this better than American: "The product we offer our customers bears the indelible image of our more than 100,000 employees." Developing employee involvement and commitment depends greatly on special efforts by the organization. Every successful organization uses goodwill and special messages to improve employee morale, as well as to forge strong ties with its customers.

many examples and writing tips. In addition to goodwill messages, you'll learn about letters of recommendation, performance appraisals, warnings, news releases, instructions, and announcements. These special messages follow no particular pattern. Each document is different, but the overall writing process you've learned, plus the specific tips provided here, will help you develop each document successfully.

Messages of thanks, recognition, and sympathy fulfill deep human needs.

Goodwill letters and memos express good wishes, warm feelings, and sincere thoughts to friends, customers, and employees. These messages can be among the most important that you write. Although such messages are not really necessary to make an organization run, they satisfy profound human needs. We all need to be accepted, remembered, consoled, appreciated, and valued. And goodwill messages fulfill these desires. Moreover, as American Airlines and many other companies know, such messages give you a competitive edge in establishing a positive organizational image and building solid employee loyalty. Goodwill messages include those that convey thanks, recognition, and sympathy.

Suggestions for Writing Goodwill Messages

Written goodwill messages—instead of phone calls or cards—provide a record that can be savored and treasured.

Goodwill messages seem to intimidate many communicators. Finding the right words to express feelings is thought to be more difficult than writing ordinary business documents. Writers tend to procrastinate when it comes to goodwill messages, or else they send a ready-made card or pick up the telephone. Remember, though, that the personal sentiments of the sender are always more expressive and more meaningful to readers than are printed cards or oral messages. Taking the time to write attaches more importance to our well-wishing. Notes also provide a record that can be reread, savored, and treasured.

In expressing thanks, recognition, or sympathy, you should always do so promptly. These messages are easier to write when the situation is fresh in your mind. They also mean more to the recipient. And don't forget that a prompt thank-you note carries the hidden message that you care and that you consider the event to be important.

The best goodwill messages—whether thanks, congratulations, praise, or sympathy—concentrate on the five S's:

- **Selfless.** Be sure to focus the message solely on the receiver—not the sender. Don't talk about yourself; avoid such comments as *I remember when I was promoted.*
- **Specific.** Personalize the message by mentioning specific incidents or characteristics of the receiver. Telling a colleague *Great speech* is much less effective than *Great story about McDonald's marketing in Moscow.* Take care to verify names and other facts.
- **Sincere.** Let your words show genuine feelings. Rehearse in your mind how you would express the message to the receiver orally. Then transform that conversational language to your written message. Avoid pretentious, formal, or flowery language (*It gives me great pleasure to extend felicitations on the occasion of your 20th anniversary with our firm).*
- **Spontaneous.** Keep the message fresh and enthusiastic. Avoid canned phrases (*Congratulations on your promotion, Thank you for the . . . , Good luck in the future).* Strive for directness and naturalness, not creative brilliance.
- **Short.** Although goodwill messages can be as long as needed, try to accomplish your purpose in only a few sentences. What's most important is remembering an individual; such caring does not require documentation or wordiness. Individuals and business organizations often use special note cards or stationery for brief messages.

Thanks

When someone has done you a favor or when an action merits praise, you need to extend thanks or show appreciation. Letters of appreciation may be written to customers for their orders, to hosts and hostesses for their hospitality, to individuals for kindnesses performed, or to colleagues for jobs well done.

Because the receiver will be pleased to hear from you, you can open directly with the purpose of your message. The letter in Figure 10.1 thanks a speaker who addressed a group of marketing professionals. Although such thank-you notes can be quite short, this one is a little longer because the writer wants to lend importance to the receiver's efforts. Notice that every sentence relates to the receiver and offers enthusiastic praise. And, by using the receiver's name along with contractions and positive words, the writer makes the letter sound warm and conversational.

Goodwill messages within organizations may not seem like business writing. American Airlines and many other organizations today, however, feel that employee recognition is an important factor in reaching corporate goals. Appreciating and respecting employees goes a long way toward maintaining employee morale. Satisfied workers mean higher productivity, better relations with customers, and increased staff loyalty.

Some organizations use special stationery or company greeting cards to convey good wishes. These cards carry imprinted messages like the following:

> Keep up the good work!
>
> It's a pleasure . . . to work with someone as special as you.
>
> Congratulations . . . on your accomplishment.
>
> Vacations are special . . . just like you; enjoy yours!
>
> Hang in there.

Inside these cards the writer pens a few personal comments. One company created special "Credit Cards" on which managers write spontaneous positive comments recognizing the efforts of employees.[2]

When your goodwill thoughts on the job require a more formal message than a card, you can use company letterhead stationery for letters to outsiders and memo forms or special notepaper for colleagues. The following messages provide models for expressing thanks for a gift, for a favor, and for hospitality.

To Express Thanks for a Gift

Thanks, Laura, to you and the other members of the department for honoring me with the elegant Waterford crystal vase at the party celebrating my twentieth anniversary with the company.

The height and shape of the vase are perfect to hold roses and other bouquets from my garden. Each time I fill it, I'll remember your thoughtfulness in choosing this lovely gift for me.

(1) Identifies the gift, (2) tells why you appreciate it, and (3) explains how you will use it.

To Send Thanks for a Favor

I sincerely appreciate your filling in for me last week when I was too ill to attend the planning committee meeting for the spring exhibition.

Without your participation much of my preparatory work would have been lost. It's comforting to know that competent and generous individuals like you are part of our team, Mark. Moreover, it's my very good fortune to be able to count you as a friend. I'm grateful to you.

Describes what the favor means to you. Avoids gushing *(How can I ever thank you enough!)* and doesn't overdo the superlatives *(You are positively the most wonderful human being alive!)*.

SPOTLIGHT ON COMMUNICATORS

A mere thank-you followed by general comments is rather hollow, says Andrew S. Grove, CEO of Intel, the nation's principal computer chip maker. He suggests making the thanks match the deed. Ask yourself what was special, unusual, extraordinary, or over and above the call of duty—and then describe it. Being specific, warm, and sincere are as important as the difference between a personal note and a computerized form letter.

FIGURE 10.1 ● Thank-you Letter for a Favor

The Three Phases of the Writing Process

1

Analyze
The purpose is to express appreciation to a business executive for presenting a talk before professionals.

Anticipate
The reader will be more interested in personalized comments than in general statements showing gratitude.

Adapt
Because the reader will be pleased, use the direct pattern.

2

Research
Consult notes taken during the talk.

Organize
Open directly by giving the reason for writing. Express enthusiastic and sincere thanks. In the body provide specifics. Refer to facts and highlights in the talk. Supply sufficient detail to support your sincere compliments. Conclude with appreciation. Be warm and friendly.

Compose
Write the first draft.

3

Revise
Revise for tone and warmth. Use the reader's name. Include concrete detail but do it concisely. Avoid sounding gushy or phony.

Proofread
Check the spelling of the receiver's name; verify facts. Check the spelling of *gratitude, patience, advice, persistence,* and *grateful.*

Evaluate
Does this letter convey sincere thanks?

Dallas–Fort Worth Chapter
American Marketing Association
P.O. Box 3598
Dallas, TX 74209

March 20, 1994

Mr. Elliott P. Tarkanian
Marketing Manager, Western Division
Toys "R" Us, Inc.
Dallas, TX 75232

Dear Elliott:

You have our sincere gratitude for providing the Dallas–Fort Worth chapter of the AMA with one of the best presentations our group has ever heard. — *Tells purpose and delivers praise*

Your description of the battle Toys "R" Us waged to begin marketing products in Japan was a genuine eye-opener for many of us. Nine years of preparation establishing connections and securing permissions seems an eternity, but obviously such persistence and patience pays off. We now understand better the need to learn local customs and nurture relationships when dealing in Japan. — *Personalizes the message by using specifics rather than generalities*

In addition to your good advice, we particularly enjoyed your sense of humor and jokes—as you must have recognized from the uproarious laughter. What a great routine you do on faulty translations! — *Spotlights the reader's talents*

We're grateful, Elliott, for the entertaining and instructive evening you provided our marketing professionals. Thanks! — *Concludes with compliments and thanks*

Cordially,

Timothy W. Ellison

Timothy W. Ellison
Program Chair, AMA

TWE:grw

People like to have their accomplishments and special events recognized by employers, co-workers, and friends. Whether done formally at a banquet or informally in a note, the recognition builds goodwill and self-esteem. Caring people send letters, notes, and memos to recognize achievements, awards, and special events in the lives of others.

To Extend Thanks for Hospitality

Jeffrey and I want you to know how much we enjoyed the dinner party for our department that you hosted Saturday evening. Your charming home and warm hospitality, along with the lovely dinner and sinfully delicious chocolate dessert, combined to create a truly memorable evening.

Most of all, though, we appreciate your kindness in cultivating togetherness in our department. Thanks, Jennifer, for being such a special person.

Offers praise for the (1) fine food, (2) charming surroundings, (3) warm hospitality, (4) excellent host and hostess, and (5) good company. Includes details to personalize the thoughts.

Recognition

Recognition means paying attention to accomplishments and significant events in the lives of friends, customers, and fellow workers. Caring individuals send letters, notes, or memos to congratulate individuals who receive honors, awards, and promotions. Thoughtful people also remember births, engagements, marriages, and other important events. On the job, considerate managers praise extraordinary effort, welcome new staff members, and honor retirees.

● Letters of recognition present timely, personalized messages on significant accomplishments or events.

In Figure 10.2 the president of a company recognizes and congratulates an employee who recently received an award. The important elements in giving recognition are timeliness (writing while the event is still current) and personalizing the message (including specific details).

The following messages provide recognition to a new employee and to a friend who was promoted.

To Greet a New Employee

Welcome to the Marketing Department. We're pleased, Jason, to have you join our family of product specialists.

Begins with simple, natural, and friendly welcome statement.

Please remember that Jerry and I—along with all the members of the department—are eager to explain our procedures and to make you feel at home. Once you get your feet on the ground, we'd like to introduce you to Charlie's, our favorite lunchtime restaurant. I'll call you to arrange a date next week.

Sounds spontaneous. Avoids dramatic, formal, or gushy words. Tries to be conversational, not businesslike.

We sincerely look forward to getting to know you and working with you.

FIGURE 10.2 ● Recognition Memo

Tips for Giving Recognition

- Send your congratulations promptly. Don't procrastinate until the moment has passed.
- Get the facts (and spelling) right in identifying the event.
- Tell why the event deserves special recognition.
- Give reasons to explain why you are pleased at the news.
- Focus your praise and compliments on the reader.
- Attach a clipping of any published account if available.

InterOffice Correspondence

DATACOM GENERAL, INC.
Office of the President

To: Terri Rae Young
Accounting Department

From: Jane Mangrum, President JM

Date: February 12, 1994

Subject: CONGRATULATIONS ON YOUR AWARD!

We just learned that you were named Volunteer of the Year by the Fort Lauderdale chapter of the Muscular Dystrophy Foundation, and we are very proud! On behalf of the management and your fellow employees at DataCom, please accept our heartfelt congratulations.

Opens directly by naming reason for recognition

Receiving this recognition is a great honor. It symbolizes your humanitarian concerns and your willingness to contribute your time and considerable talent in helping others who are less fortunate. We are very pleased for you, Terri Rae, and admire your efforts.

Concentrates on virtues of reader

Enclosed is a clipping from the Daily News describing your honor.

Shows thoughtfulness by including clipping

JM:rpy

Enclosure

To Recognize a Promotion

Congratulations, Lisa, on your recent promotion to the position of director of marketing in the Hertz car sales division! I'm delighted to learn of this well-deserved advancement. Your success, of course, was predictable, given your enthusiasm, sincerity, and perseverance. Best wishes for the continuation of a winning career.

In just a few sentences conveys thoughtfulness and good wishes.

Response

Should you respond when you receive a congratulatory note or a written pat on the back? By all means! These messages are attempts to connect personally; they are efforts to reach out, to form professional and/or personal bonds. Failing to respond to notes of congratulations and most other goodwill messages is like failing to say "You're welcome" when someone says "Thank you."[3] Responding to such messages is simply the right thing to do. Do avoid, though, minimizing your achievements with comments that suggest you don't really deserve the praise or that the sender is exaggerating your good qualities.

To Answer a Congratulatory Note

Thanks for your kind words regarding my award, and thanks, too, for sending me the newspaper clipping. I truly appreciate your thoughtfulness and best wishes.

Take the time to send a brief note in response to any goodwill message you receive.

To Respond to a Pat on the Back

Your note about my work made me feel good. I'm grateful for your thoughtfulness.

Accept praise gracefully.

Sympathy

Most of us can bear misfortune and grief more easily when we know that others care. Notes expressing sympathy, though, are probably more difficult to write than any other kind of message. Commercial "In sympathy" cards make the task easier—but they are far less meaningful. Grieving friends want to know what *you* think—not what Hallmark's card writers believe. To help you get started, you can always glance through cards expressing sympathy. They will supply ideas about the kinds of thoughts you might wish to convey in your own words. In writing a sympathy note, (1) refer to the death or misfortune sensitively, using words that show you understand what a crushing blow it is, (2) in the case of a death, praise the deceased in a personal way, (3) offer assistance without going into excessive detail, and (4) end on a reassuring, forward-looking note. Sympathy messages may be typed, although handwriting seems more personal. In either case, use note paper or personal stationery.

To Express Condolences

It is with deep sorrow, Dolores, that we learned of the death of your husband. Harold's kind nature and friendly spirit endeared him to all who knew him. He will be missed.

Mentions the loss tactfully and recognizes good qualities of the deceased.

Although words seem empty in expressing our grief, we want you to know that your friends at DataCom extend their profound sympathy to you. If we may help you or lighten your load in any way, you have but to call.

Assures receiver of your concern. Offers assistance.

We know that the treasured memories of your many happy years together, along with the support of your family and many friends, will provide strength and comfort in the months ahead.

Concludes on positive, reassuring note.

SPOTLIGHT ON COMMUNICATORS

Recognizing and appreciating employees is standard practice at Marriott, one of the nation's biggest employers. "Motivate them, train them, care about them, and make winners of them," says Bill Marriott. "We know that if we treat our employees correctly, they'll treat the customers right. And if the customers are treated right, they'll come back." Goodwill messages mean good business.

Checklist for Writing Goodwill Messages

General Guidelines: The Five S's

- ✔ **Be selfless.** Discuss the receiver, not the sender.
- ✔ **Be specific.** Instead of generic statements *(You did a good job)*, include special details *(Your marketing strategy targeting key customers proved to be outstanding)*.
- ✔ **Be sincere.** Show your honest feelings with conversational, unpretentious language *(We're all very proud of your award)*.
- ✔ **Be spontaneous.** Strive to make the message natural, fresh, and direct. Avoid canned phrases *(If I may be of service, please do not hesitate . . .)*.
- ✔ **Keep the message short.** Remember that, although they may be as long as needed, most goodwill messages are fairly short.

Giving Thanks

- ✔ **Cover three points in gift thank-yous.** (1) Identify the gift, (2) tell why you appreciate it, and (3) explain how you will use it.
- ✔ **Be sincere in sending thanks for a favor.** Tell what the favor means to you. Avoid superlatives and gushiness. Maintain credibility with sincere, simple statements.
- ✔ **Offer praise in expressing thanks for hospitality.** Compliment, as appropriate, the (1) fine food, (2) charming surroundings, (3) warm hospitality, (4) excellent host and hostess, and (5) good company.

Showing Recognition

- ✔ **Write promptly.** Don't procrastinate in recognizing accomplishments and significant events in the lives of friends, customers, and fellow workers.
- ✔ **Personalize the message.** Include specific details, anecdotes, and meaningful tidbits that show your thoughtfulness and feelings. Verify all facts and spellings.

Answering Congratulatory Messages

- ✔ **Respond to congratulations.** Send a brief note expressing your appreciation. Tell how good the message made you feel.
- ✔ **Accept praise gracefully.** Don't make belittling comments *(I'm not really all that good!)* to reduce awkwardness or embarrassment.

Extending Sympathy

- ✔ **Refer to the loss or tragedy directly but sensitively.** In the first sentence mention the loss and your personal reaction.
- ✔ **For deaths, praise the deceased.** Describe positive personal characteristics *(Howard was a forceful but caring leader)*.
- ✔ **Offer assistance.** Suggest your availability, especially if you can do something specific.
- ✔ **End on a reassuring, positive note.** Perhaps refer to the strength the receiver finds in friends, family, colleagues, or religion.

Special Business Messages

In addition to writing goodwill messages, you will probably be called on, in your business career, to compose various special messages. Particularly when you become a manager, you'll be writing letters of recommendation, performance appraisals, and, possibly, employee warnings. You may also have to compose operational instructions, news releases, and announcements. Even if these assignments seem distant to you now, you'll find them interesting to analyze. Although our advice is presented from a manager's perspective, it will be equally interesting to employees. For example, when your performance as an employee is being appraised, just what is the manager looking for or trying to accomplish?

Like goodwill messages these special messages follow no particular pattern. Each document is different, but the overall writing process you've learned, plus the specific tips provided here, will help you develop these messages successfully.

Letters of Recommendation

Letters of recommendation evaluate individuals. Although recommendations may be written to nominate people for awards and for membership in organizations, they are usually written by employers to appraise the performance of employees. The central concern in these messages is honesty. Thus, you must avoid puffing up the candidate's qualifications or distorting them to cover up weaknesses or to destroy the person's chances. Ethically and legally, we have a duty to the candidate as well as to other employers to describe that person truthfully and objectively.

Letters of recommendation present honest, objective evaluations of individuals and help match candidates to jobs.

We don't, however, have to endorse everyone who asks. Since recommendations are generally voluntary, we can—and should—resist writing letters for individuals we can't truthfully support. Ask these people to find other recommenders who know them better.

Some businesspeople argue that recommendations are useless because they're always positive. Despite the general avoidance of negatives, well-written recommendations do help match candidates with jobs. Hiring companies learn more about a candidate's skills and potential, thus enabling them to place the candidate properly.

For legal and ethical reasons, letters of recommendation should be written only for individuals whom the writer truly supports.

Legal and ethical issues. Regardless of the helpfulness of recommendations, a number of companies today, fearing lawsuits, prohibit their managers from recommending ex-employees. Instead, when these companies are asked about former employees, they provide only the essentials, such as date of employment and position held. Employers are gun-shy because former employees have sued—and won—charging defamation of character. Letters of recommendation carrying negative statements can damage reputations, thus preventing former employees from gaining employment.

Here's a case in point. In Florida Kenneth Stanbury applied for a new job after being fired as a project manager. In checking his references, the prospective company was told that Stanbury "seemed detail-oriented to the point of losing sight of the big picture." The recommender from his previous job went on to say that Stanbury "had a lot of knowledge and experience on big jobs . . . and that with a large staff might be very competent." The conclusion in this negative recommendation stated that Stanbury "no longer worked for [us] and that might say enough."

Stanbury did not get the job. Nor did he find employment elsewhere for three years. He did, however, win a lawsuit when the court learned that the "recommender" had made statements about Stanbury when that individual had never supervised, evaluated, read an evaluation of, or worked with Stanbury. The statements were based entirely on "general impressions" and on hearing people "talk about [Stanbury's] work on the job." In this case "rumor" and "gossip" were offered as fact. Because the writer neither qualified his statements nor disclosed their source, he misled the receiver. The court carefully noted, though, that its ruling did not indicate that "employers are at serious risk when providing employment references in the normal course of business."[4]

● **Because companies may be legally liable for withholding pertinent information, critical data should probably be communicated.**

Yet, companies that no longer allow references to be written for former employees face still another legal problem. Because silence can lead to bad hiring decisions, former employers can be sued for withholding pertinent information (if, for example, a past employer did not reveal information about a child molester who applied for work with a school). One executive admitted that he felt ethically bound to reveal serious deficiencies in former employees, even if his company prohibited the writing of recommendations. "When it comes to . . . anything that can cause really serious problems, I'll find a way to send up a red flag." Like many employers this executive believes that the consequences of withholding critical data "can just be too great—for the new employer, for its customers and other employees—and for us."[5]

Despite all the news about employment lawsuits, recent research suggests that the fear of litigation over recommendations is exaggerated. In fact, the number of defamation suits going to trial between 1965 and 1990 actually declined, and the average monetary award decreased.[6]

● **Good letters of recommendation provide confidential, truthful, and specific job-related information.**

Most businesspeople recognize that references serve a valuable purpose in conveying personnel data. Yet, they are cautious in writing them. Here are six guidelines that a careful writer can follow in writing recommendations:

- **Write only in response to requests.** Don't volunteer information, particularly if it's negative.
- **State that your remarks are confidential.** Remember that, while such a statement does not prevent legal review, it does suggest the intentions of the writer.
- **Provide only job-related information.** Avoid commenting on behavior or activities away from the job.
- **Avoid vague or ambiguous statements.** Keep in mind that imprecise, poorly explained remarks *(she left the job suddenly)* may be made innocently but could be interpreted quite differently.
- **Supply specific evidence for any negatives.** Support any damaging information with verifiable facts.
- **Stick to the truth.** Avoid making any doubtful statements. Truth is always a valid defense against libel or slander.

● **The body of a letter of recommendation should describe the candidate's job performance and potential in specific terms.**

How to write a recommendation. Recommendations often have three parts: opening, body, and conclusion. In the opening of an employment recommendation, you should give the name of the candidate and the position sought, if it is known. State that your remarks are confidential, and suggest that you are writing at the request of the applicant. Describe your relationship with the candidate, as shown here:

> Ms. Cindy Rosales, whom your organization is considering for the position of media trainer, requested that I submit confidential information on her behalf. Ms. Rosales worked under my supervision for the past two years in our Video Training Center.

The opening establishes the reason for writing and the relationship of the writer.

Letters that recommend individuals for awards may open with more supportive statements, such as *I'm very pleased to nominate Robert Walsh for the Employee-of-the-Month award. For the past sixteen months, Mr. Walsh served as staff accountant in my division. During that time he distinguished himself by . . .*

The body of an employment recommendation should describe the applicant's job performance and potential. Employers are particularly interested in such traits as communication skills, organizational skills, people skills, ability to work with a team, ability to work independently, honesty, dependability, ambition, loyalty, and initiative. In describing these traits, be sure to back them up with evidence. One of the biggest weaknesses in letters of recommendation is that writers tend to make global, nonspecific statements[7] (*He was careful and accurate* versus *He completed eight financial statements monthly with about 99 percent accuracy*). Employers prefer definite, task-related descriptions:

> As a training development specialist, Ms. Rosales demonstrated superior organizational and interpersonal skills. She started as a Specialist I, writing scripts for interactive video modules. After six months she was promoted to team leader. In that role she supervised five employees who wrote, produced, evaluated, revised, and installed 14 computer/videodisc training courses over a period of eighteen months.

A good recommendation describes general qualities ("organizational and interpersonal skills") backed up by specific evidence that illustrates those qualities.

Be especially careful to support any negative comments with verification (not *He was slower than other customer service reps* but *He answered 25 calls an hour, while most service reps average 40 calls an hour*). In reporting deficiencies, be sure to *describe* behavior (*her last two reports were late and had to be rewritten by her supervisor*) rather than *evaluate* it (*she is unreliable and her reports are careless*).

In the final paragraph of a recommendation, you should offer an overall evaluation. Indicate how you would rank this person in relation to others in similar positions. Many managers add a statement indicating whether they would rehire the applicant, given the chance. If you are strongly supportive, summarize the candidate's best qualities. In the closing you might also offer to answer questions by telephone. Such a statement, though, could suggest that the candidate has weak skills and that you will make damaging statements orally but not in print. Here's how our sample letter might close:

> Ms. Rosales is one of the most productive employees I have supervised. I would rank her in the top 10 percent of all the media specialists with whom I have worked. Were she to return to Bridgeport, we would be pleased to rehire her. If you need additional information, call me at (517) 440-3019.

The closing of a recommendation presents an overall ranking and may provide an offer to supply more information by telephone.

General letters of recommendation, written when the candidate has no specific position in mind, often begin with the salutation TO PROSPECTIVE EMPLOYERS. More specific recommendations, to support applications to known positions, address an individual. When the addressee's name is unknown, consider using the simplified letter format, shown in Figure 10.3, which avoids a salutation.

Figure 10.3 illustrates the entire writing process for preparing an employment letter of recommendation. After naming the applicant and the position sought, the letter describes the applicant's present duties. Instead of merely naming positive qualities (*personable, superior people skills, works well with a team, creativity,* and *initiative*), these attributes are demonstrated with specific examples and details.

FIGURE 10.3 ● Employment Recommendation Letter

The Three Phases of the Writing Process

1

Analyze
The purpose of this letter is to describe and evaluate the job performance of a former employee seeking a recommendation.

Anticipate
The reader wants information to help make a hiring decision.

Adapt
Because the reader will be interested and receptive, open directly with the purpose.

2

Research
Gather information about the candidate and the job sought.

Organize
Open by identifying the candidate, the position, and your relationship. State that your remarks are confidential and requested. In the body describe the candidate's job and accomplishments. Close by providing an overall evaluation.

Compose
Write the first draft.

3

Revise
Revise vague statements that might be misinterpreted. Remove any unsupported negative comments.

Proofread
Use commas after introductory clauses and in series. Use simplified letter style because the receiver's name is unknown.

Evaluate
Is this letter objective, truthful, and accurate? Is it fair to the candidate and to other candidates?

Good Samaritan Hospital
2404 Euclid Avenue
Cleveland, OH 44114

February 21, 1994

Vice President, Human Resources
Healthcare Enterprises
3529 Springfield Street
Cincinnati, OH 45890

RECOMMENDATION OF LANCE W. OLIVER

At the request of Lance W. Oliver, I submit this confidential information in support of his application for the position of assistant director in your Human Resources Department. Mr. Oliver served under my supervision as assistant director of Guest Relations at Good Samaritan Hospital for the past three years.

Mentions confidentiality of message

Identifies applicant and position

Tells relationship to writer

Mr. Oliver was in charge of many customer service programs for our 770-bed hospital. A large part of his job involved monitoring and improving patient satisfaction. Because of his personable nature and superior people skills, he got along well with fellow employees, patients, and physicians. His personnel record includes a number of "Gotcha" citations, given to employees caught in the act of performing exemplary service.

Supports general qualities with specific details

Mr. Oliver works well with a team, as evidenced by his participation on the steering committee to develop our "Service First Every Day" program. His most significant contributions to our hospital, though, came as a result of his own creativity and initiative. He developed and implemented a patient hotline to hear complaints and resolve problems immediately. This enormously successful telephone service helped us improve our patient satisfaction rating from 7.2 last year to 8.4 this year. That's the highest rating in our history, and Mr. Oliver deserves a great deal of the credit.

Describes and interprets accomplishments

We're sorry to lose Mr. Oliver, but we recognize his desire to advance his career. I am confident that his resourcefulness, intelligence, and enthusiasm will make him successful in your organization. I recommend him without reservation.

Summarizes main points and offers evaluation

Mary E. O'Rourke

MARY E. O'ROURKE, DIRECTOR, GUEST RELATIONS

MEO:rtd

Performance Appraisals

Many companies today review the performance of employees annually, semiannually, or quarterly. These appraisals have several purposes:

Performance appraisals help boost productivity, improve employee skills, identify future goals, and determine salaries, promotions, and duties.

- Encouraging employees to share in setting performance goals.
- Identifying employees' performance strengths and weaknesses.
- Determining whether employees are attaining their performance goals.
- Establishing an action plan for improving performance before the next evaluation.
- Providing management with a basis for determining salaries, promotions, and assignments.

Generally, the appraisal process begins when a manager and an employee sit down to develop the job description, standards, and objectives for the next review period. Then the manager observes the employee throughout the review period and prepares a written report evaluating the employee's performance. In a personal conference the manager and employee discuss the performance appraisal. Although appraisal practices and forms vary widely, most companies agree on one point. The primary focus should be on employee goal-setting and self-development. The manager encourages the employee to outline his or her personal plans for self-development.

Notice in Figure 10.4 that the evaluator spends more time on strengths than on weaknesses. In fact, most appraisals tend to be positive. When you must report negative performance, make sure you are objective, nonjudgmental, and nondiscriminatory. Avoid observations suggesting that decisions were affected by an employee's age, gender, race, or disability. To be most helpful and least actionable, stick to facts that can be verified.

Useful performance appraisals focus on employee goal-setting and self-development.

Dangerous	**More Objective**
Jane didn't get much done in the mornings because of her partying at night. She also had an arrogant attitude that caused considerable friction within the department.	Jane was late on an average of three mornings a week. She would not accept morning calls from customers. Moreover, three coworkers (see incident reports dated 3/15, 5/29, and 6/2) reported that her attitude made it difficult for them to work with her.

Performance appraisals are often prepared on forms like the one shown in Figure 10.4. For companies without forms, though, managers may write memos describing the strengths and weaknesses of an employee's performance. These memo reports might include headings such as *Quality of Work, Quantity of Work, Human Relations, Progress,* and *Personal Development Goals.*

Warnings

Managers must occasionally give employees written warnings that document problems in performance or work-related behavior.[8] Warnings are generally written at the time of the problem and are placed in an employee's personnel file. Causes for warnings include habitual tardiness or absenteeism, insubordination, low productivity, sexual harassment, or serious violations of company policy. Like performance

Warnings specify problems with performance or job-related behavior in firm yet sympathetic terms.

FIGURE 10.4 ● **Employee Performance Appraisal**

LASER PRODUCTS, INC.

EMPLOYEE PERFORMANCE APPRAISAL

Last Name	First Name	Employment Division	Job Title
Mattheson,	Jim	Consumer Services	Customer Service Rep II

Group	Appraisal Period
T-9880	June 1, 1993 - May 31, 1994

Type of Increase

___ **Merit** ___ **Promotion** ✓ **Merit and Promotion**

Effective Date of Increase June 1, 1994

Weekly Increase Recommended $50

I. PERFORMANCE

Quality of Work	Quantity of Work	Human Relations	Progress
A (B) C D E	A B (C) D E	(A) B C D E	A (B) C D E

Where is employee's performance most proficient?

The quality of Jim's telephone work with customers is superior. He shows remarkable patience in answering customers' questions. He listens carefully to customers' questions, clarifies requests and problems, and provides articulate, courteous answers. Because he knows our product line well, he gives comprehensive responses, often volunteering more information than the customer requested.

The quantity of his work is satisfactory. When working the telephone lines, he averages 69 customer calls a day, which is slightly below our goal of 75 calls a day. Although he takes a little longer than most reps on each call, he provides good answers and generally is able to solve customers' problems.

In human relations Jim is well above average. He is pleasant and cooperative in working with customers, fellow employees, and management. He takes direction easily and seems to get along well with the entire team.

Since his last review, Jim has made progress in two areas. First, he mastered our new Infomax computer program. In fact, he learned Infomax so quickly that I asked him to provide a demonstration for other customer service reps. Jim remains our expert on Infomax, and I am grateful for his enthusiastic support in implementing and trouble-shooting this new system. Second, Jim attended two 10-hour in-service training seminars covering customer service goals, handling complaints, and sharing experiences.

Focuses on employee's strengths

Quantifies observations whenever possible

Cites specific accomplishments

appraisals, warnings may be prepared on printed forms or written as memos. Here are tips for writing warnings:

- Describe the time, place, and details of the infraction or problem.
- Explain why the company objects to the behavior or what the effects of the problem are.
- Document details of prior occurrences of the problem.
- Itemize the steps necessary for the employee to correct the problem; include a schedule and deadline.
- Specify the action that management will take if the problem is not corrected.
- Tell when management will review the employee's progress.

Where does employee's performance need improvement?

When he switches to administrative work, which accounts for 25 percent of his assignment, Jim's performance falters somewhat. In working with correspondence, product mailings, and follow-ups, he has difficulty expressing his ideas in writing. Proofreaders return about half of his letters with spelling, grammar, and punctuation errors. Other customer service reps average a correction return rate of only 5 percent. Because he must rewrite so many of his documents, his productivity in this area is low.

Reports negatives with objective, nonjudgmental language

List employee's performance development goals and plans for the next evaluation period.

1. Jim will participate in an in-service training course in basic language skills.
2. He will also enroll in an evening college class in business writing.
3. Jim will reduce his correspondence correction return rate from 50 percent to 5 percent or less.
4. He will concentrate on increasing his customer-calls rate to reach the goal of 75 calls a day.

Establishes quantifiable goals

Overall Performance Rating (circle one).

A - Outstanding. Consistently exceeds job requirements. Sets example for others.
B - Excellent. Consistently meets job requirements and often exceeds them.
(C)- Good. Consistently meets job requirements.
D - Acceptable. Meets most job requirements but occasionally needs assistance.
E - Unsatisfactory. Well below job requirements. Immediate attention needed.

II. ATTENDANCE AND PUNCTUALITY

Is attendance and/or punctuality a problem to the extent that this increase is reduced or deferred? No

Expected date of next performance evaluation June 1, 1995

Signature of Evaluator Craig C. Binsky **Date** 6/1/94

Signature of Employee Jim Mattheson **Date** 6/1/94

The following warning memo projects a tone of firmness, yet shows some warmth and concern for the employee in the last sentence.

TO: Marilyn O'Riley

Addresses the employee directly.

FROM: John Pearson, Manager

SUBJECT: Attendance and Productivity Warning

Over the past year, Marilyn, your attendance has been irregular, affecting your job performance and productivity.

Identifies general problem.

For the six-month period of January to June of this year, you had 9 unauthorized absences and were late 16 times. From July to the end of the year you missed another 10 days and were late 14 times, according to our personnel records.

Presents specifics of infraction.

Describes the effect and implications of the employee's behavior.

Other customer service representatives have complained that they must carry a heavier load of calls and correspondence when you are missing. Morale in your department is declining, and some reps are asking if an additional person can be hired to handle the workload.

Cites prior dates when problem was communicated to employee.

At your performance review conferences June 4, 1993, and again January 7, 1994, you promised that your attendance would improve as soon as you settled temporary personal problems. I have not seen any change in your punctuality or attendance.

Tells exactly what the employee must do and sets deadline. States consequences if required behavior is not achieved.

To remain with our organization, Marilyn, you must have no unauthorized absence or tardiness in the next 3-month period. On March 3 I will review with you your attendance record and productivity. If they are unsatisfactory, we must release you and hire a new employee for your position. I sincerely hope you'll be able to stay with us, Marilyn.

Written warnings may also result from charges of sexual harassment. To be sure you understand what this term means and how casual comments might be misunderstood, read the accompanying Ethics box explaining sexual harassment.

Operational Instructions

Before writing operational instructions, learn about the process or product and the intended audience.

Business writers must occasionally describe how to perform an operation, such as filling out an expense report or ordering office supplies. The important thing to remember in writing instructions is that they must be so clear that readers know exactly what to do without asking questions.

To write good instructions, you'll want to divide the task into three segments: (1) planning to write, which involves practicing and observing the process, (2) describing the process, which includes the actual writing, and (3) following up, which means testing, evaluating, and revising the instructions.

Planning to Write Instructions

- **Learn about the process yourself.** Become familiar with the process. Try it repeatedly. Talk to experts.
- **Examine a parts list.** If you're describing a machine, use the exact wording your reader will see on the equipment.
- **Consider your audience.** Ask yourself, how much do they already know about the procedure? How sophisticated is their level of language?

Describing the Process

Effective operational instructions break the process into parts, number steps chronologically, include cautions and warnings, and incorporate necessary visuals.

- **Begin with a clear title.** Remember that the title should suggest the purpose of the instructions (not *Fax Machine* but *Operating Instructions for Fax Machine*).
- **Provide a short explanation.** Justify the reason for providing the instructions. You may wish to relate the instructions to a broader goal.
- **Divide the process into parts.** Separate the operation into major parts if necessary *(Reception of Fax Messages* and *Transmission of Fax Messages)*. Further divide the process into smaller units for step-by-step instruction.
- **Number the steps chronologically.** Begin with the logical starting point in the process and number each step.
- **Use active verbs in command language.** Instead of *The paper should be installed,* say *Install the paper.* Instead of *Make an adjustment to the document guide,* say *Adjust the document guide.*

ETHICS

RECOGNIZING SEXUAL HARASSMENT

Sexual harassment may be defined in many ways. According to Title VII of the Civil Rights Act, sexual harassment consists of unwelcome sexual advances, requests for sexual favors, and other verbal or physical conduct of a sexual nature when:

- Submission to such conduct is made either explicitly or implicitly a term or condition of employment.
- Submission to or rejection of such conduct by an individual is used as a basis for employment decisions affecting that person or third parties.
- Such conduct has the purpose of unreasonably interfering with an individual's work performance or creating an intimidating, hostile, or offensive working environment.

In a broader sense, according to communication experts, sexual harassment is anything that a victim believes is sexual harassment. The most notable case of alleged sexual harassment came in the Senate confirmation hearings for Supreme Court Justice Clarence Thomas. Attorney and law professor Anita Hill, a former colleague of Judge Thomas, testified that Thomas's sexual jokes and discussions of pornographic films at the office constituted sexual harassment

Even a well-intended compliment can be misconstrued. Suppose you say to a colleague, "That dress looks nice on your body." Although you may have intended it as a compliment to the person's fitness as well as to her taste in clothes, it would likely be taken as a sexual comment. Remember to anticipate the audience reaction before speaking. Learn to say simply, "That's a nice dress."

As you would with any communication, you'll want to be aware of a possible secondary audience. For example, what if the previous comment was overheard by your supervisor, who also thought it had sexual connotations? When that supervisor later writes performance appraisals or makes promotions, you may be considered risky.

During your career you'll probably find two groups in offices: those who tell off-color jokes or make comments with sexual innuendos and those that don't. It probably won't surprise you to learn that members of management rarely belong to the first group.

At this book's outset, we emphasized that effective communicators received better and more frequent promotions. Thus, it's in your own best interests to learn to think before you speak. Do you really need to share the off-color joke you heard last night? Does that compliment really need the sexual spin?

Career Track Application

Assume that last week you gave a colleague a compliment loaded with sexual innuendo. Tomorrow you must face the Human Resources director on charges of sexual harassment. Write one or two paragraphs describing why it was wrong and what you will do to avoid future problems.

- **Strive for parallel construction.** Try to express all the steps in the same grammatical way. Look back over the steps in this process description. Notice how each sentence after the bullet is expressed similarly.
- **Include cautions and warnings.** If necessary, alert users to possible damage to equipment or injury to themselves if steps are not followed.
- **Supply visuals if appropriate.** Keep in mind that complex tasks may require pictures, graphs, or diagrams to clarify the process.

Following Up

- **Review and revise.** Study the steps you have written and revise as needed. Decide whether you have provided the appropriate amount of detail.
- **Test the instructions.** Have someone else test the process to see if the instructions are operational.[9]

After writing operational instructions, you should review, revise, and test.

Compare the following two versions of brief instructions for writing a résumé. Notice how much more quickly you can understand the second version because every item is a command starting with an active verb.

Poor Instructions	**Good Instructions with Command Language**
1. Make a decision on a career goal.	1. Decide on a career goal.
2. Then your background must be analyzed.	2. Analyze your background.
3. Next make a description of your education.	3. Describe your education.
4. You should list your work experience.	4. List your work experience.

Now look at the instructions for operating a photocopy machine in Figure 10.5. Although these directions apply all the suggestions just listed, the real test occurs when readers try to follow the instructions. That's why it's a good idea to try out operational instructions on typical users before submitting the final version.

News Releases

Effective news releases feature an attention-getting opener, place key information up front, appeal to the target audience, and maintain visual interest.

News (press) releases announce information about your company to the media: new products, new managers, new facilities, participation in community projects, awards given or received, joint ventures, donations, or seminars and demonstrations. Naturally, you hope that this news will be published and provide good publicity for your company. But, as Tim Smith at American Airlines observed, this kind of largely self-serving information is not always appealing to magazine and newspaper editors or to TV producers. To get them to read beyond the first sentence, try these suggestions:

- Open with an attention-getting lead or a summary of the important facts.
- Include answers to the five W's and one H (who, what, when, where, why, and how) in the article—but not all in the first sentence!
- Appeal to the audience of the target media. Emphasize reader benefits written in the style of the focus publication or newscast.
- Present the most important information early, followed by supporting information. Don't put your best ideas last because they may be chopped off or ignored.
- Make the release visually appealing. Limit the text to one or two double-spaced pages with attractive formatting.
- Look and sound credible—no typos, no imaginative spelling or punctuation, no factual errors.

The most important ingredient of a press release, of course, is *news*. Articles that merely plug products end up in the circular file. The news release in Figure 10.6 emphasizes the most newsworthy aspects of an announcement introducing nutritious drinks and snacks for children.

Announcements

Like news releases, formal announcements include answers to the five W's: who, what, where, when, why.

Publicity for public events within business organizations usually takes the form of announcements. Formal announcements may be sent to printers for professional composition and typesetting. Today, though, individuals are likely to design and write their own notices on computers. Such messages may announce a speaker, a

FIGURE 10.5 ● Operational Instructions

Tips for Writing Instructions

- Know the process thoroughly.
- Write a clear title.
- Explain the purpose of the instructions.
- Separate the process into major segments.
- Number the steps.
- Start each step with a verb.
- Express all steps in the same form.
- Include warnings and visuals if appropriate.
- Test instructions on typical users.

HOW TO OPERATE THE CANON XL20 PHOTOCOPY MACHINE

Begins with clear title

The Canon XL20 copy machine located in the Reprographics Department on the second floor may be used by any employee making work-related copies. If everyone follows these instructions and uses the machine carefully, we can reduce service costs and also experience less downtime.

Explains why these instructions are important

Loading Paper

1. Remove Paper Tray 1 by pulling backward firmly.
2. Select about 250 sheets of 8½ x 11-inch xerographic paper and align the edges.
3. Insert the paper in the tray. Place paper edges under the retaining clips.
4. Return the paper tray to its drawer.

Numbers items in chronological order for systematic use

Divides process into two segments for quick reference

Making Copies

1. Press power switch to On. Wait for flashing ready indicator to become solid.
2. Place the original facing down on the copyboard glass. Center the copy.
3. Set the number of copies to be made by pressing the plus or minus key.
4. Press the Start key.

Starts each step with active verb in form of command

FIGURE 10.6 ● News Release

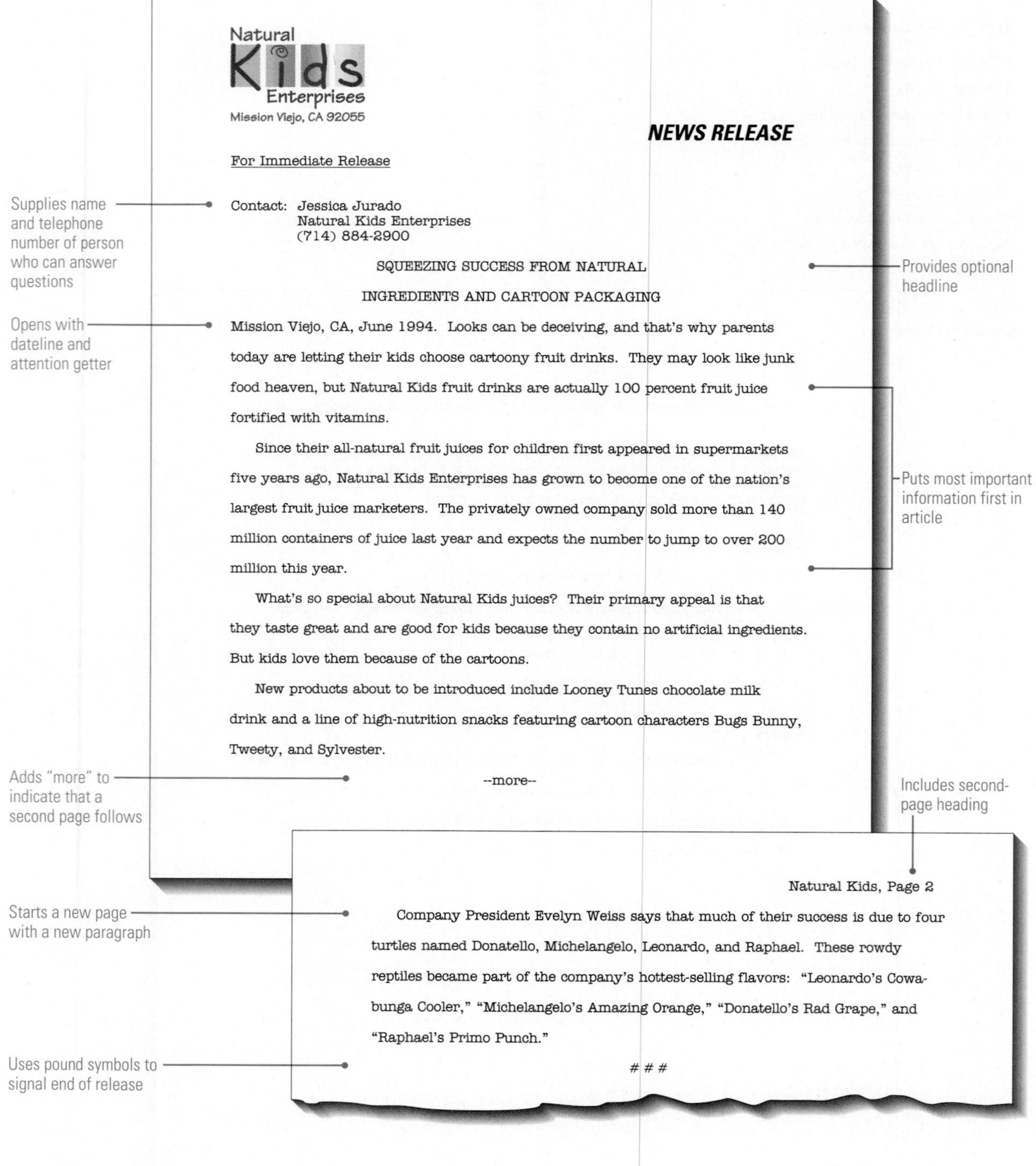

Natural
Kids
Enterprises
Mission Viejo, CA 92055
NEWS RELEASE
For Immediate Release
Contact: Jessica Jurado
Natural Kids Enterprises
(714) 884-2900
SQUEEZING SUCCESS FROM NATURAL
INGREDIENTS AND CARTOON PACKAGING
Mission Viejo, CA, June 1994. Looks can be deceiving, and that's why parents today are letting their kids choose cartoony fruit drinks. They may look like junk food heaven, but Natural Kids fruit drinks are actually 100 percent fruit juice fortified with vitamins.
Since their all-natural fruit juices for children first appeared in supermarkets five years ago, Natural Kids Enterprises has grown to become one of the nation's largest fruit juice marketers. The privately owned company sold more than 140 million containers of juice last year and expects the number to jump to over 200 million this year.
What's so special about Natural Kids juices? Their primary appeal is that they taste great and are good for kids because they contain no artificial ingredients. But kids love them because of the cartoons.
New products about to be introduced include Looney Tunes chocolate milk drink and a line of high-nutrition snacks featuring cartoon characters Bugs Bunny, Tweety, and Sylvester.
--more--
Natural Kids, Page 2
Company President Evelyn Weiss says that much of their success is due to four turtles named Donatello, Michelangelo, Leonardo, and Raphael. These rowdy reptiles became part of the company's hottest-selling flavors: "Leonardo's Cowabunga Cooler," "Michelangelo's Amazing Orange," "Donatello's Rad Grape," and "Raphael's Primo Punch."
# # #
Supplies name and telephone number of person who can answer questions
Opens with dateline and attention getter
Adds "more" to indicate that a second page follows
Starts a new page with a new paragraph
Uses pound symbols to signal end of release
Provides optional headline
Puts most important information first in article
Includes second-page heading

A news release or announcement for a grand opening, such as the successful Toys R Us opening in Japan, calls for careful, concise writing. Readers want to learn the who, what, where, when, and why of the event as quickly as possible.

company training program, the new location of a department, or some special event. Announcements may appear alone or within other messages, such as memos or letters.

Like news releases, announcements should include answers to the five W's: who, what, where, when, and why. To make them most readable and attractive, you might wish to center each line as shown here.

GRAND OPENING
Monday, August 1
Media Production Services
Now located in Room 202, South Wing
Photocopying, collating, brochures, binding, and other services

Summary of Learning Goals

1. **Identify five characteristics of messages that deliver thanks, praise, or sympathy.** Such messages should be selfless, specific, sincere, spontaneous, and short.
2. **Discuss three points to cover in thank-you notes for gifts.** Gift thank-yous should identify the gift, tell why you appreciate it, and explain how you will use it.
3. **Specify six guidelines that a careful writer follows in writing employment recommendations.** To avoid litigation, writers of recommendations should write only in response to specific requests from individuals, state that the remarks are confidential, provide only job-related information, avoid vague and ambiguous statements, supply specific evidence for any negative statements, and include only truthful statements.
4. **Explain the purposes of employee performance appraisals.** Performance appraisals are conducted to (1) encourage employees to share in setting

goals, (2) identify an employee's performance strengths and weaknesses, (3) determine whether employees are attaining their goals, (4) establish an action plan for improving before the next evaluation, and (5) provide management with a basis for determining salaries, promotions, and assignments.

5. **List six topics to be covered in employee warnings.** Employee warnings should (1) describe the time, place, and details of the infraction or problem, (2) explain why the company objects to the behavior, (3) document details of prior occurrences of the problem, (4) list the steps necessary to correct the problem, (5) specify the action that will be taken if the problem is not corrected, and (6) tell when the employee's progress will next be reviewed.

6. **Describe six tips for writing news releases.** Good news releases (1) open with an attention-getting lead or summary of the important facts, (2) answer the questions who, what, when, where, why, and how, (3) appeal to the audience of the target media, (4) present the most important information early, (5) make the release visually appealing, and (6) look and sound credible.

7. **Explain how to write clear operational instructions and announcements.** Clear instructions start with a clear title, explain the process in parts, number the steps chronologically, use active verbs in command language, strive for parallel construction, include cautions and warnings, and supply visuals if appropriate. Good announcements include answers to the five W's: who, what, where, when, and why.

Chapter Review

1. What human needs do goodwill messages satisfy?

2. List the five S's of goodwill messages. Be prepared to explain them.

3. What three topics should you include in a gift thank-you?

4. What four topics are usually covered in a hospitality thank-you?

5. What are the two most important elements in extending recognition?

6. List four topics often included in a message expressing sympathy to a friend who has lost a loved one.

7. Why are employers fearful of writing recommendations for former employees?

8. List six guidelines that careful recommenders follow to avoid lawsuits.

9. What should be discussed in the opening of a letter of recommendation?

10. What should be included in the body of a recommendation?

11. What goes in the conclusion of a recommendation?

12. What is the primary focus of a performance appraisal?

13. List six or more important items that should be included in a written warning.

14. Name three or more topics that an organization might feature in a press release.

15. How should you prepare for writing a set of operational instructions?

Discussion

1. Why are many writers reluctant to compose messages that deliver thanks, sympathy, or congratulations?

2. Why are written messages more meaningful than commercial cards or telephone calls?

3. Should you refuse to write a recommendation for an individual you can't recommend? Defend your answer.

4. Why are companies increasingly requiring regular employee performance appraisals?

5. Ethical Issue: Should businesses be obligated to write letters of recommendation evaluating the performance of former employees?

Exercises

10.1 Draft Document: Thank-you Letter

Analyze the following poor letter. Discuss its weaknesses. If your instructor directs, revise it. Add details.

> Dear Ms. Palko:
>
> Thanks for the guided tour of the Communications Services Center at Microtech, Inc. Everyone in our business communications class liked it. You must have spent a long time getting ready for us. We thought it was great! Everyone said how much they liked it. Especially the teleconferencing demo. Most of us had no idea how it worked. We also liked the electronic mail and voice mail systems. Thanks again.

10.2 Draft Document: Letter of Recommendation

Analyze the following poor letter. Discuss its weaknesses. If your instructor directs, revise it, adding needed information.

> To Whom It May Concern:
>
> I am happy to be able to recommend Mr. Quentin Ross. In his work for us, he was a good technician. He was responsible, creative, industrious, and always cooperative. Once in a while he was late, but we understood why.
>
> If we may be of further service, please call on us.

Problems

10.3 Thanks for a Gift: Thoughtful Boss

On your birthday your boss gives you an unexpected gift (such as a wallet, key case, fountain pen, or something similar). Write a thank-you note expressing your gratitude.

10.4 Thanks for a Favor: You're Special!

Express your appreciation to a fellow worker at your place of employment for performing a special favor for you: teaching you a procedure, showing you how to operate a piece of equipment, filling in during an emergency, helping you with a project, or just for offering encouragement and support when you needed it. If you are not employed, select an instructor or friend to thank for some special act.

10.5 Thanks for a Favor: Got the Job!

After completing your degree, you have taken a job in your field. One of your instructors was especially helpful to you when you were a student. This instructor also wrote an effective letter of recommendation that was instrumental in helping you obtain your job. Write a letter thanking your instructor.

10.6 Collaborative Thanks for a Favor: The Perfect Résumé.

Your business communication class was fortunate to have Thomas Fallo, author of *The Perfect Résumé,* speak to you about preparing résumés for today's competitive job market. Mr. Fallo provided the class with excellent tips for targeting jobs and defining an applicant's strengths. He showed an old-fashioned "tombstone" résumé and explained how to make today's résumés more persuasive. His special advice for college students and for women reentering the job market made a great deal of sense. You know that he did not come to plug his book; but when he left, most class members wanted to head straight for a bookstore to buy it. His talk was a big hit. Your professor asks the class to break into small groups so that each can draft a thank-you letter. Address the letter to Mr. Thomas Fallo, P.O. Box 3660, Sausalito, CA 94088.

10.7 Thanks for the Hospitality: Holiday Entertaining

Write a thank-you letter to your boss (supervisor, manager, vice president, president, or chief executive officer) or to the head of an organization to which you belong. Assume that you and other members of your staff or organization were entertained at an elegant dinner during the winter holiday season. Include specific details that will make your letter personal and sincere.

10.8 Recognition: Congratulations!

Write a note of congratulations to a coworker or friend in recognition of a special accomplishment: promotion, award, election to an office or special group, achievement of a goal, or some other significant event.

10.9 Recognition: Top Prof

After graduation you learn from a story in an alumni publication that one of your favorite college professors was named Professor of the Month. Write a letter expressing your good wishes.

10.10 Recognition: Old Friend, New Job

A friend of yours in Denver was just named marketing manager for Codex (they sell modems, telecommunications components, and networking systems). You've known her (or him) since childhood, but you had lost touch in the last five years. You saw your friend's picture and the accompanying story about the new position in your hometown's paper. Write your old friend a letter of recognition—and send the clipping.

10.11 Sympathy: To a Spouse

Imagine that a coworker was killed in an automobile accident. Write a letter of sympathy to his or her spouse.

10.12 Responding to Good Wishes: Saying Thank You

Write a short note thanking a friend who sent you good wishes when you recently completed your degree.

10.13 Letter of Recommendation: Technical Editor

As Taylor Watson, director, Documentation Division, write a letter recommending Derek R. Roth. Derek has been a technical editor in your division for four years. He's applying for a position of document administrator in the Research Department of Signal Labs (at a salary you can't match). You've always liked Derek; and it's easy to recommend him, much as you hate to see him go. Derek ranks among the top 10 percent of all the editors you've known. Under your supervision Derek generally worked with engineers in revising their reports. His job was to improve expression, revise poor organization, develop internal consistency, and correct grammatical errors—without antagonizing the report writer. He succeeded very well both in editing reports and in getting along with the engineers—no easy task considering how defensive the engineers could become when their writing was being revised ("attacked" is the word they used). But Derek's professional manner, his sincere and serious tone, and his obvious expertise elicited respect and willing cooperation from even the most reluctant engineers. They could see how much he was improving the quality of their reports.

Derek's language skills are superior. Because of his excellent general and technical vocabulary, you often assigned him to work with the engineers who had the weakest writing skills. He's also a meticulous proofreader. The documents he produces have about the lowest error rate of any technical writer in your department.

In addition to working with contextual material, he's had experience in art work from graphics to drafting. Your department uses Ventura desktop publishing software. Although Derek is not the best keyboarder with Ventura, he knows the system well enough to be able to produce quality design features. He's reliable, works well under pressure, and meets deadlines. Address the recommendation to Ms. Darcy Adams-Johnson, Director, Human Resources, Signal Labs, 13390 Beamer Road, Houston, TX 77099.

10.14 Letter of Recommendation: For Yourself

You've decided it's time to move on from your current job to a new position (select a realistic job for which you could apply). Step outside yourself for a moment; imagine that you are now your current supervisor. As supervisor write a letter of recommendation that describes your current duties and evaluates your accomplishments. Send this letter to Mr. Sam W. Engel, Vice President, Human Resources (name a company and add an address).

10.15 Performance Appraisal: Rating a Senior Secretary

As office manager for Rodeo Realty, you have to evaluate the six-month performance of Margaret Olson, senior secretary. Margaret prepares correspondence, reports, and announcements for six sales associates. She's a very fast keyboarder (over 80 words per minute), but sometimes her fingers fly too fast. She makes typos, especially in figure amounts, that are sometimes costly. Everyone likes Margaret, but all sales associates have learned to proofread her work very carefully. Two months ago your office sent out a new property listing that should have been for $1,200,000; Margaret omitted one of the zeros, causing a great deal of confusion.

Her sunny disposition makes Margaret popular among customers and staff. She has an excellent attendance record, having taken only one day of sick leave in the past year. Her output is outstanding; Margaret completes more work than any of your previous secretaries. When she uses the spell checker on her computer, her work has fewer typos. It seems, though, that she doesn't always use it. Margaret is reliable, conscientious, and eager to please. Her attitude is excellent.

When she started over a year ago, she knew little about the real estate business. She attended training seminars and learned realty jargon and procedures quickly. You would be totally satisfied with her performance if she were more accurate. Perhaps her eyes could be causing some of the problem; she's complained of eye fatigue and irritation from her contacts.

Write a performance report on Margaret, focusing on two sections of comments (see Figure 10.4): (1) Where is employee's performance most proficient, and (2) Where does employee's performance need improvement.

10.16 Performance Appraisal: Rating Yourself

Study the employee performance appraisal form shown in Figure 10.4. Imagine you are your own boss. In a job that you now hold or one you've had before, evaluate your own performance. Prepare two sections of the report: (1) Where is employee's performance most proficient, and (2) Where does employee's performance need improvement? Describe your job duties and rate your performance. Be honest!

10.17 Warning: Sleeping on the Job

As supervisor of Shipping and Receiving, write an employee warning memo to Richmond U. White. Rich is a shipping clerk who works a swing shift (from 4 p.m. to midnight). He was discovered sleeping on the job January 5 at 11 p.m. Sleeping on the job is a serious violation of company rules. Since he is the only clerk in the receiving area, one of his tasks is to guard the warehouse. In addition, he has paperwork to complete during his shift. In a previous performance review, his shift reports were noted as being "sketchy" and sometimes late. If he is found sleeping on the job again, he will be suspended or dismissed on the spot (you decide which). You would hate to see this happen since Rich has been with the company for five years.

10.18 Collaborative News Release: Attention Student Writers

As part of a team of college interns at Academic Software, you have been asked to prepare a press release describing a new product. Your press release will be sent to college newspapers; the content should be aimed at college students. Dr. Janet Adams, professor of communications at Mankato State University, founded College Software ten years ago because she realized that "computers could help students with their writing problems." With the aid of programmers, Dr. Adams developed a student style checker called EditWriter. It helps writers eliminate problems such as wordiness, poor usage, punctuation errors, and inappropriate gender-based language. The program actually helps both students and experienced writers improve their composition styles—but your current pitch is toward students.

EditWriter has many features. It covers over 16,000 common writing problems in 40 categories. It's menu-driven, fast, and easy to use. It comes with a 130-page manual that offers samples of incorrect and proper usage and mechanics. Best of all for students, it runs on low-end IBM computer systems; it requires only 256 KB of RAM and a monochrome monitor. Its output prints on nearly all printers.

Originally designed for college writing courses, EditWriter is especially adaptable for use in the classroom and in writing labs. Work sessions can be tailored to the level or interests of a particular class or an individual student. For students only, a half-price introductory offer of $45 is available. The program will be stocked at most college bookstores.

10.19 News Release: Heirloom Jeans

As Jeff Spiegel, public relations specialist, prepare a press release for Phoenix newspapers and TV and radio stations. Your company, Dollars for Denim (18402 North 32 Street, Phoenix, AZ 85031), buys used denim clothing. The market for old Levi Strauss jeans (preferably pre-1970) is booming in Japan. An authentic pair of 1950 Levi Strauss 501 jeans might fetch $2,000 in a Tokyo boutique. Apparently, the Japanese are obsessed with Western fashions, particularly the cowboy look. "They seem to have a longing for things from the Wild West," says Hideyuki Kawamura, manager of Delaware, a Tokyo specialty store.

At first, you collected old jeans quietly, so that you could keep the prices low. But as the demand grew, you had to go public. You're now willing to pay $50 to $200 for high-quality old jeans (1970–1985). Boys' sizes are particularly prized among Japanese men because they tend to be smaller than American men.

How can you tell really old Levis? Outside copper rivets held on the pockets in the 1930s. The rivets were moved inside in the late 1930s to 1960s. A real-leather patch marked 501 jeans in the 1950s.

You're looking for denim jeans or jackets without holes or stains. Although you dream of pre-1970s jeans, you are happy with even 5- and 10-year-old denim. Tokyo's collectors don't seem to care. As you've told reporters, "We'll buy denim anywhere. I've even bought jackets from people's backs as they're walking down the street."[10]

10.20 News Release: It's New!

In a company where you now work or for an organization you belong to, identify a product or service that could be publicized. Consider writing a press release announcing a new course at your college, a new president, new equipment, or a campaign to raise funds. Write an announcement for your local newspaper.

10.21 Instructions: Guide to New Employees

Your boss asks you to write instructions to operate a piece of equipment (such as a fax machine, copier, camera, or printer) or to describe a procedure (such as how to fill out expense reports). Your instructions will guide new employees. Use a real situation if possible. Include your instructions in a memo to your boss.

10.22 Collaborative Instructions: Registration Help

The Director of Admissions at your institution asks a group of student workers to help him revise the admission and registration instructions. He's heard complaints that the present instructions are unclear. Find these instructions in your class schedule or catalog. Write an improved version, including a title.

10.23 Instructions: Faxing It

The following instructions came with a new imported fax machine, the TurboFax 3200. Everyone in your office is eager to use the machine, but they can't understand the instructions. Write improved instructions that include a reminder that this machine is intended for office work only.

> For Transmission. Document is facing down for loading. Document guides adjusted to document width. Operator is inserting the leading butt of document into feeding slot. [With sheets of two or more pages, leading edges are forming a slope as the operator lightly inserts them into feeding position; bottom sheet is proceeding first.] Operator is then picking up telephone handset. With continuous dial tone, dialing other fax number. Other fax's answering tone signals. Operator is pressing START key. When start lamp twinkles on-off, operator is hanging up handset.

10.24 Announcement: Personnel Party

Prepare an announcement for a flyer. The Personnel Department is honoring and welcoming its new director, Mary K. Nakovey, at an open house, June 2, from 2 to 4 p.m., in its offices on the second floor. Encourage employees to drop by to greet Mary and their other friends in Personnel at this open house. Arrange the information in a centered format.

C.L.U.E. Review 10

Edit the following sentences to correct faults in grammar, punctuation, spelling, and word use.

1. U.S. exports has increased by seventy-six percent in the past five years; and our trade deficit has fell to it's lowest level since 1974.
2. After years of downsizing and restructuring the U.S. has now become one of the worlds most competitive producers in many industry's.
3. However many companies products still sell better at home then abroad; because these companys lack overseas experience.
4. Company's like Amway, discovered that there unique door to door selling method was very successful in japan.
5. The U.S. commerce department asked Mr. Sato and I to describe the marketing of: aircraft, high-tech products, and biomedical technology.
6. Some of the products most likely to suceed abroad are: blue jeans, coke, home appliances and prepared foods.
7. As american companys learn to accomodate global tastes they will be expanding into vast new markets in china, south america and europe.
8. The seminar emphasising exporting will cost three hundred dollars; which seems expensive for a newly-formed company.
9. The manager thinks that you attending the three day seminar is a good idea, however we must still check your work calander.
10. Exports from small companies has increased; thereby effecting this countrys trade balance positively.

Reports and Proposals

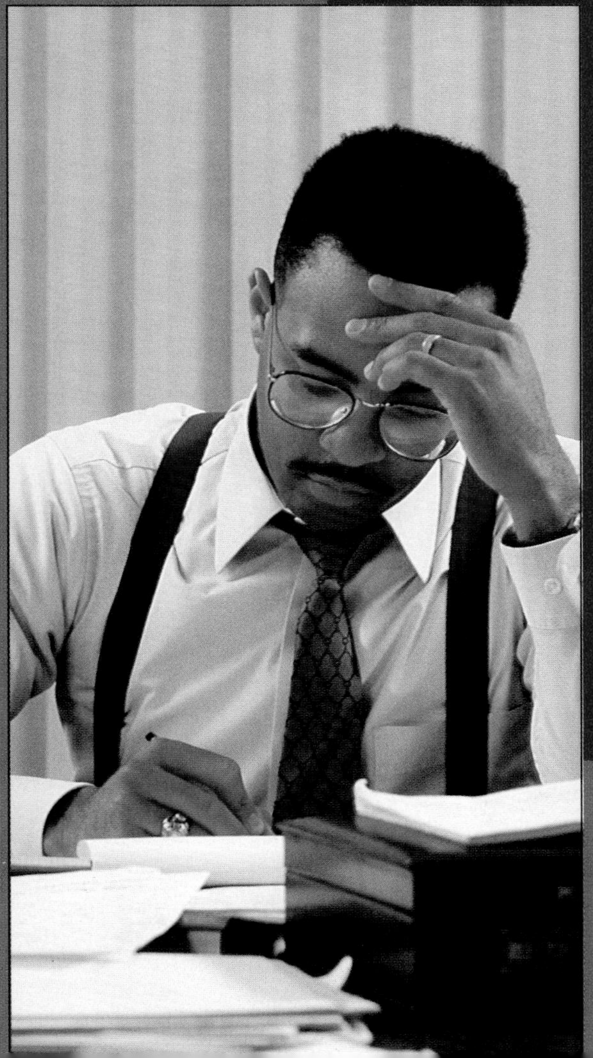

11 Report Planning and Research

12 Report Organization and Presentation

13 Typical Business Reports

14 Proposals and Formal Reports

Report Planning and Research

LEARNING GOALS

After studying this chapter, you should be able to

1. Describe nine typical business reports
2. Distinguish between informational and analytical reports
3. Identify four report formats
4. Apply the writing process to reports
5. Locate secondary and primary data
6. Document sources using traditional or contemporary formats

The Winters Group: Career Track Profile

"I could write some killer reports if I were back in college now," says Richard E. Eades, Jr., research analyst for a private consulting firm in Rochester, New York. Since graduating from the University of Rochester two years ago, Richard has had much opportunity to develop his research and report-writing skills at The Winters Group. This company specializes in survey research, focus groups, secondary research, and strategic planning for businesses. It also studies new product concepts, customer satisfaction levels, public opinion, and special markets such as minorities and the elderly.

"You can't sit down, type up a report, and send it out. It just doesn't work that way."

As a research analyst in a small firm, Richard does a bit of everything. He helps write proposals, develop questionnaire and survey instruments, collect data, and interpret findings. "The biggest difference between my college English papers and my current writing is that business writing is much more direct. Business executives don't have time for wordiness or fancy writing. I've learned to draft simple, straightforward sentences that make a point quickly. That meant unlearning the verbose style I had developed in college."

At The Winters Group most projects begin with a problem question posed by clients. How can we track customers' satisfaction with our products? How can we test our advertising agency's creative work? Should we introduce a new product? How can we monitor our competitors' activities?

After analyzing a client's problem, Winters Group researchers decide what underlying issues must be examined before reaching a solution. Recently, Richard worked on a project in which a public library requested help in enhancing its community image and expanding its base of financial support. "We explored the problem and isolated the major issues or subproblems requiring investigation," says Richard. "Then we prepared a proposal telling our objectives and laying out a solution. After the proposal was approved, we proceeded to collect data to help solve the problem. Most of our data came from focus groups of library advisory panels whose members discussed topics that we considered to be critical. My supervisor led the panel discussions, and I took notes and wrote the summary reports. For each report I extracted the key findings and drew conclusions based on those findings."

Richard works with both qualitative research (narrative responses from focus groups) and quantitative research (data processing results tabulated from customer satisfaction questionnaires). To analyze quantitative data, he begins with data processing printouts of tables and graphs. "A questionnaire may have ten questions," says Richard, "but the most important item is, say, No. 8: 'How likely are you to purchase this product?' I start with the data from

Mary-Frances Winters formed The Winters Group nearly a decade ago. Her company conducts research to solve problems such as that of a major corporation seeking to track customer satisfaction. The Winters Group developed a national survey program covering 25 of the corporation's key services. The resulting data enabled a team of Winters researchers to pinpoint geographic pockets of customer dissatisfaction. The client could then make tactical changes to improve its overall customer service.

that question, arranging all tables from most important to least important. Once I locate the 'key driver' motivating customer satisfaction, then everything begins to make sense. Writing flows easily once I understand what the data mean."

Richard's reports go through many revision stages. "You can't sit down, type up a report, and send it out. It just doesn't work that way. At first, it was difficult to revise my own writing. I didn't make many changes—because often I just couldn't think of a better way to say it. But the more I write, the more I see how to make improvements." Richard likes to finish a first draft by Friday, put it away, and not think about it at all over the weekend. On Monday he returns with a fresh eye. "Then I can see the main ideas more clearly, and I'm more willing to hack it up with drastic changes." Richard's supervisor critiques each revision, supplying expert advice on both content and form. Every report goes through many drafts for revising, editing, and proofreading. "If a client finds a mistake in a report—even a minor typo—she or he tends to doubt the accuracy of all our findings."

The writing style for reports at The Winters Group tends to be formal. To project professionalism and objectivity, its researchers avoid contractions, slang, jargon, or first-person pronouns *(I/we)*. Although most elements of their reports are formal, Winters Group researchers prefer short, simple sentences. As Richard points out, "Many of our clients speed-read these reports. They want to grasp the important points fast and move on. Long, complex sentences can't be read quickly."

Every project at The Winters Group begins with a work plan, detailed in a proposal to the client. The proposal describes the background of the problem to be investigated and outlines the objectives or purpose of the research. The proposal further specifies the scope of the study and tells what methods will be used to collect data. Most projects also include a timetable for the research and a completion date for the project. The final report to the client follows a consistent format: executive summary, background, methodology, key findings, conclusions, recommendations, and appendixes. "Having a consistent format," says Richard, "really simplifies my job. My mind can categorize the information immediately, and writing just follows naturally."

Richard's work is further eased by collaboration. "We work together on nearly every phase of a project. Three or four of us write survey questions together, bouncing ideas off each other and getting immediate feedback." Although only one person writes a final report, Richard says that many members of their team have worked together in analyzing research findings and drawing conclusions. "We work as a team to make sure that our findings are valid and that each report is errorless."[1]

Clarifying and Classifying Reports

Reports are a fact of life in American business. Although your career may not center on research and report writing, as does that of Richard Eades, you'll undoubtedly be called on to write reports at some time. American values and attitudes seem to prompt us to write reports. We analyze the pros and cons of problems, studying alternatives and assessing facts, figures, and details. We pride ourselves on being practical and logical; we solve problems by applying scientific procedures. For this kind of analysis, we need systematic information. And we often present this information in the form of reports.

This chapter examines categories, functions, organizational patterns, formats, and writing styles of reports. It also introduces the report-writing process and discusses methods of collecting and documenting data.

Effective business reports solve problems and answer questions systematically.

Because of their abundance and diversity, business reports are difficult to define. They may range from informal half-page trip reports to formal 200-page financial forecasts. Reports may be presented orally in front of a group or electronically on a computer screen. Some reports appear as words on paper in the form of memos and letters. Others are primarily numerical data, such as tax reports or profit-and-loss statements. Some seek to provide information only; others aim to analyze and make recommendations. Although reports vary greatly in length, content, form, and formality level, they all have one common purpose: *Business reports are systematic attempts to answer questions and solve problems.*

Typical Business Reports

In searching for answers and solving problems, organizations prepare thousands of different kinds of reports for managers, employees, customers, and the government. Many of these reports can be grouped into nine categories, briefly described below. Chapters 13 and 14 present "how-to" information and models for writing these reports.

Periodic, situational, investigative, and compliance reports often present data without interpretation.

Periodic operating reports. The most common reports in many organizations are written at regular intervals to monitor operations. These operating reports—like weekly activity reports from sales reps—answer questions about what employees are doing and how effectively the organization is achieving its mission. They monitor and control operations including production, sales, shipping, and customer service.

Situational reports. Unlike periodic reports, situational reports describe nonrecurring activities. This broad category includes trip, conference, and seminar reports, as well as progress reports for unusual activities, such as sponsoring a mountain bike–riding competition. Since situational reports describe one-time events, writers generally have no ready models to follow. Thus, these reports are usually more challenging, but also more creative, than periodic reports.

Investigative/informational reports. Reports that examine situations or problems and supply facts—with little in the way of interpretation or recommendations—are investigative. Assume, for example, that your boss asked you to research the Internal Revenue Service's position on the hiring of independent contractors. You would collect and organize facts into a logical, informational report. Now assume that your boss also wanted you to analyze the status of the independent contractors working for your organization and make recommendations about retaining them. Your report would become more analytical and would be classified differently.

Compliance reports. Prompted by the government, compliance reports answer such questions as "How much profit did your organization earn and what taxes do you owe?" These reports comply with laws and regulations that protect employees, investors, and customers. Such reports respond to government agencies like the Internal Revenue Service, the Securities and Exchange Commission, and the Equal Employment Opportunities Commission. A securities prospectus is a compliance report that answers questions from potential stockholders regarding company performance and finances.

Justification/recommendation reports. When managers and employees must justify or recommend something (like purchases, changes in operations, new programs, or personnel), they write justification or recommendation reports. These analytical reports usually travel upward to management, where the recommendations are approved or refused. In analyzing alternatives, interpreting findings, and making recommendations, these reports become important tools for managers in solving problems and making decisions.

● **Justification/recommendation, yardstick, and feasibility reports analyze alternatives, interpret findings, and often make recommendations.**

Yardstick reports. When a problem has two or more solutions, a helpful way to evaluate the alternatives is to establish consistent criteria—a "yardstick"—by which to measure the alternatives. For example, let's say that a company must decide whether to (1) continue using its outdated mainframe computers, (2) purchase networked personal computers, or (3) hire an outside agency to handle some of its computing needs. A yardstick report assesses the alternatives by applying the same criteria to each, such as cost, service, security, and reliability. Each alternative is measured against the criteria to find the best option.

Feasibility reports. Feasibility reports use analysis to predict whether projects or alternatives are practical or advisable. They answer questions such as "Should we open a branch office in Panama City?" Feasibility reports examine the benefits and problems connected with the project, as well as its costs and schedule for implementation. The emphasis is on whether to proceed with the venture.

Research studies. Business organizations sometimes commission research studies that examine problems thoroughly and scientifically. Researchers analyze a problem, suggest ways to solve it (called *hypotheses*), collect data about each possible solution, analyze that data, draw conclusions, and, if requested, make recommendations. The emphasis in these studies is on conducting objective research and interpreting the findings. For example, Richard Eades' research group was hired to study women of color and their feelings toward abortion, preventive health care, and civil and human rights issues.

● **Research studies examine problems thoroughly and scientifically, while proposals offer to solve problems.**

Proposals. As attempts to secure new business, proposals offer to solve problems, investigate ideas, or sell products and services. They are organized to answer the receiver's questions regarding the offer and its budget, schedule, and staffing. Another form of proposal is the business plan, a persuasive report that seeks to convince investors to fund a new company.

Functions of Reports

In terms of what they do, most of the reports just described can be placed in two broad categories: informational reports and analytical reports.

● **Informational reports simply present data without analysis or recommendations.**

Informational reports. Reports that present data without analysis or recommendations are primarily informational. Although writers collect and organize facts, they are not expected to analyze the facts for readers. A trip report describing an employee's visit to a trade show, for example, simply presents information. Other reports that present information without analysis involve routine operations, compliance with regulations, and company policies and procedures.

● **Analytical reports provide data, analyses, conclusions, and, if requested, recommendations.**

Analytical reports. Reports that provide data, analyses, and conclusions are analytical. If requested, writers also supply recommendations. Analytical reports may intend to persuade readers to act or to change their beliefs. Assume you're writing a feasibility report that compares several potential locations for a video rental shop. After analyzing and discussing alternatives, you might recommend one site, thus attempting to persuade readers to accept this choice.

Direct and Indirect Patterns

Like letters and memos, reports may be organized directly or indirectly. The reader's expectations and the content of a report determine its pattern of development, as illustrated in Figure 11.1. In long reports, such as corporate annual reports, some parts may be developed directly while other parts are arranged indirectly.

Direct pattern. When the purpose for writing is presented close to the beginning, the organizational pattern is direct. Informational reports, such as the letter report shown in Figure 11.2, are usually arranged directly. They open with an introduction, followed by the facts and a summary. In Figure 11.2 the writer explains a legal services plan. The report letter begins with an introduction. Then it presents the facts, which are divided into three subtopics identified by descriptive headings. The letter ends with a summary and a complimentary close.

Analytical reports may also be organized directly, especially when readers are supportive or are familiar with the topic. Many busy executives prefer this pattern because it gives them the results of the report immediately. They don't have to spend time wading through the facts, findings, discussion, and analyses to get to the two items they are most interested in—conclusions and recommendations. Figure 11.3 illustrates such an arrangement. This analytical memo report describes environmental hazards of a property that a realtor has just listed. The realtor is familiar with the investigation and eager to find out the recommendations. Therefore, the memo is organized directly.

You should be aware, though, that unless readers are familiar with the topic, they may find the direct pattern confusing. Many readers prefer the indirect pattern because it seems logical and mirrors the way we solve problems.

● **The indirect pattern is appropriate for analytical reports that seek to persuade or that convey bad news.**

Indirect pattern. When the conclusions and recommendations, if requested, appear at the end of the report, the organizational pattern is indirect. Such reports usually begin with an introduction or description of the problem, followed by facts and interpretation from the writer. They end with conclusions and recommendations. This pattern is helpful when readers are unfamiliar with the problem. It's also useful when readers must be persuaded or when they may be disappointed in

FIGURE 11.1 ● **Audience Analysis and Report Organization**

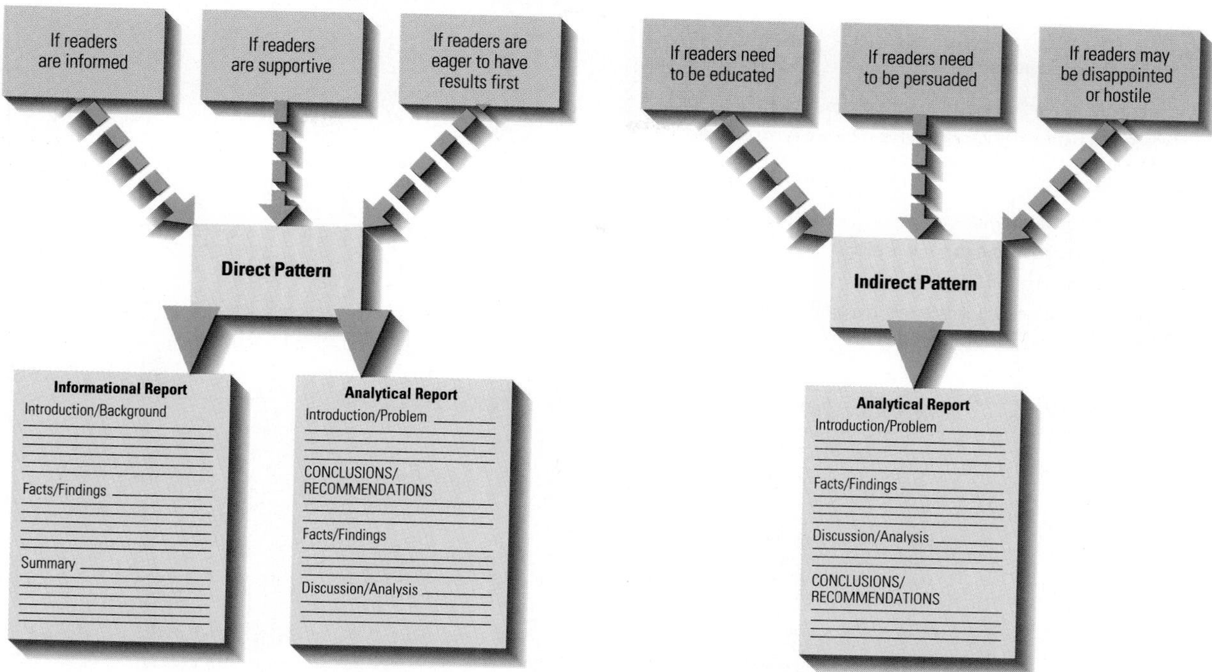

or hostile toward the report's findings. The writer is more likely to retain the reader's interest by first explaining, justifying, and analyzing the facts and then making recommendations. This pattern also seems most rational to readers because it follows the normal thought process: problem, alternatives (facts), solution.

Figure 11.4 shows a portion of an analytical report organized indirectly. Note how readers are introduced, in a background discussion, to the problem of vehicle emissions and smog. Then facts (research findings and proposed solutions to the problem) are presented and analyzed. Finally, the report concludes with recommendations suggesting solutions to the problem.

Formats of Reports

The format of a report is governed by its length, topic, audience, and purpose. After considering these elements, you'll probably choose from among the following four formats:

● **A report's format depends on its length, audience, topic, and purpose.**

- **Letter format.** Use letter format for short (say, ten or fewer pages) informal reports addressed outside an organization. Prepared on office stationery, a letter report contains a date, inside address, salutation, and complimentary close, as shown in Figure 11.2. Although they may carry information similar to that found in correspondence, letter reports usually are longer and show more careful organization than most letters. They also include headings.
- **Memo format.** For short informal reports that stay within organizations, memo format is appropriate. Memo reports begin with TO, FROM, DATE, and SUBJECT, as shown in Figure 11.3. Like letter reports, memo reports differ from regular memos in length, use of headings, and deliberate organization.

FIGURE 11.2 ● **Informational Report—Letter Format**

Tips for Letter Reports

- Use letter format for short informal reports sent to outsiders.
- Organize the facts section into logical divisions identified by consistent headings.
- Single-space the body.
- Double-space between paragraphs.
- Leave two blank lines above each side heading.
- Create side margins of 1 to 1¼ inches.
- Add a second-page heading, if necessary, consisting of the addressee's name, the date, and the page number.

Center for Consumers of Legal Services
P.O. Box 260
Richmond, VA 23219

Uses letterhead stationery for an informal report addressed to an outsider

September 7, 1994

Ms. Lisa Burgess, Secretary
Lake Austin Homeowners
3902 Oak Hill Drive
Austin, TX 78134

Dear Ms. Burgess:

As executive director of the Center for Consumers of Legal Services, I'm pleased to send you this information describing how your homeowners' association can sponsor a legal services plan for its members. After an introduction with background data, this report will discuss three steps necessary for your group to start its plan.

Presents introduction and facts without analysis or recommendations

Introduction

A legal services plan promotes preventive law by letting members talk to attorneys whenever problems arise. Prompt legal advice often avoids or prevents expensive litigation. Because groups can supply a flow of business to the plan's attorneys, groups can negotiate free consultation, follow-up, and discounts.

Two kinds of plans are commonly available. The first, a free plan, offers free legal consultation along with discounts for services when the participating groups are sufficiently large to generate business for the plan's attorneys. These plans actually act as a substitute for advertising for the attorneys. The second common type is the prepaid plan. Prepaid plans provide more benefits, but members must pay annual fees, usually of $200 or more a year. Over 30 million people are covered by legal services plans today, and a majority belong to free plans.

Since you inquired about a free plan for your homeowners' association, the following information describes how to set up such a program.

Arranges facts of report into sections with descriptive headings

Determine the Benefits Your Group Needs

The first step in establishing a free legal services plan is to meet with the members of your group to decide what benefits they want. Typical benefits include the following:

Free consultation. Members may consult a participating attorney—by phone or in the attorney's office—to discuss any matter. The number of consultations is unlimited, provided each is about a separate matter. Consultations are generally limited to 30 minutes, but they include substantive analysis and advice.

Free document review. Important papers—such as leases, insurance policies, and installment sales contracts—may be reviewed with legal counsel. Members may ask questions and receive an explanation of terms.

Identifies second and succeeding pages with headings

Ms. Lisa Burgess Page 2 September 7, 1994

Discount on additional services. For more complex matters, participating attorneys will charge members 75 percent of the attorney's normal fee. However, some organizations choose to charge a flat fee for commonly needed services.

Uses parallel side headings for consistency and readability

Select the Attorneys for Your Plan

Groups with geographically concentrated memberships have an advantage in forming legal plans. These groups can limit the number of participating attorneys and yet provide adequate service. Generally, smaller panels of attorneys are advantageous.

Assemble a list of candidates, inviting them to apply. The best way to compare prices is to have candidates submit their fees. Your group can then compare fee schedules and select the lowest bidder, if price is important. Arrange to interview attorneys in their offices.

After selecting an attorney or a panel, sign a contract. The contract should include the reason for the plan, what the attorney agrees to do, what the group agrees to do, how each side can end the contract, and the signatures of both parties. You may also wish to include references to malpractice insurance, assurance that the group will not interfere with the attorney-client relationship, an evaluation form, a grievance procedure, and responsibility for government filings.

Publicize the Plan to Your Members

Members won't use a plan if they don't know about it, and a plan will not be successful if it is unused. Publicity must be vocal and ongoing. Announce it in newsletters, meetings, bulletin boards, and flyers.

Persistence is the key. All too frequently, leaders of an organization assume that a single announcement is all that's needed. They expect members to see the value of the plan and remember that it's available. Most organization members, though, are not as involved as the leadership. Therefore, it takes more publicity than the leadership usually expects in order to reach and maintain the desired level of awareness.

Summary

A successful free legal services plan involves designing a program, choosing the attorneys, and publicizing the plan. To learn more about these steps or to order a $25 how-to manual, call me at (804) 355-9901.

Sincerely,

Richard M. Ramos

Richard M. Ramos, Esq.
Executive Director

pas

Includes complimentary close and signature

FIGURE 11.3 ● Analytical Report—Memo Format

Tips for Memo Reports

- Use memo format for most short (ten or fewer pages) informal reports within an organization.
- Leave side margins of 1 to 1¼ inches.
- Sign your initials on the FROM line.
- Use an informal, conversational style.
- For direct analytical reports, put recommendations first.
- For indirect analytical reports, put recommendations last.

Atlantic Environmental, Inc.

Interoffice Memo

TO: Kermit Fox, President **DATE:** March 7, 1994

FROM: Cynthia M. Rashid, Environmental Engineer CMR

SUBJECT: INVESTIGATION OF MOUNTAIN PARK COMMERCIAL SITE

For Allegheny Realty, Inc., I've completed a preliminary investigation of its Mountain Park property listing. The following recommendations are based on my physical inspection of the site, official records, and interviews with officials and persons knowledgeable about the site.

Recommendations

To reduce its potential environmental liability, Allegheny Realty should take the following steps in regard to its Mountain Park listing:

- Conduct an immediate asbestos survey at the site, including inspection of ceiling insulation material, floor tiles, and insulation around a gas-fired heater vent pipe at 2539 Mountain View Drive.
- Prepare an environmental audit of the generators of hazardous waste currently operating at the site, including Mountain Technology.
- Obtain lids for the dumpsters situated in the parking areas and ensure that the lids are kept closed.

Findings and Analyses

My preliminary assessment of the site and its immediate vicinity revealed rooms with damaged floor tiles on the first and second floors of 2539 Mountain View Drive. Apparently, in recent remodeling efforts, these tiles had been cracked and broken. Examination of the ceiling and attic revealed further possible contamination from asbestos. The insulation material surrounding the hot-water storage tank was in poor condition.

Located on the property is Mountain Technology, a possible hazardous waste generator. Although I could not examine its interior, this company has the potential for producing hazardous material contamination.

In the parking area large dumpsters collect trash and debris from several businesses. These dumpsters were uncovered, thus posing a risk to the general public.

In view of the construction date of the structures on this property, asbestos-containing building materials might be present. Moreover, this property is located in an industrial part of the city, further prompting my recommendation for a thorough investigation. Allegheny Realty can act immediately to eliminate one environmental concern: covering the dumpsters in the parking area.

Applies memo format for short, informal internal report

Uses first paragraph as introduction

Presents recommendations first (direct pattern) because reader is supportive and familiar with topic

Combines findings and analyses in short report

FIGURE 11.4 ● Portion of Analytical Report—Manuscript Format

Tips for Manuscript Reports

- Use manuscript format for long, complex, or formal reports and proposals.
- Print the report on plain paper.
- Allow side and bottom margins of 1 to 1¹/₄ inches.
- Display primary and secondary headings appropriately (see Chapter 12).
- Use single or double spacing depending on your organization's preferences.
- Document sources with appropriate citations.

REDUCING VEHICLE EMISSIONS
AND SMOG IN THE LOS ANGELES BASIN

Uses plain paper, title, and manuscript format for long, complex report

INTRODUCTION

Pacific Enterprises, Inc., is pleased to submit this report to the Air Resources Board of Los Angeles County in response to its request of April 18. This report examines the problem of vehicle emissions in the Los Angeles Basin. Moreover, it reviews proposed solutions and recommends a course of action that will lead to a significant reduction in the hydrocarbon and nitrogen oxide emissions of older vehicles.

Background and Discussion of Problem

The County of Los Angeles has battled dirty air for five decades. The largest stationary polluters (manufacturers, petroleum refineries, and electric power plants, for example) are no longer considered a major source of pollution. Today, the biggest smog producers are older automobiles, trucks, and buses. Newer vehicles, as a result of improved technology and government regulation, have sharply reduced their emissions. However, nearly 400,000 pre-1980 vehicles continue to operate on Southern California's streets and freeways. A recent state-funded study (Rutman 37) estimated that 50 percent of the smog generated in Southern California comes from these older vehicles.

Cites source of data with author reference

Yet, many of these vehicles are either undetected or exempted from meeting the clean-air standards. Little has been done to solve this problem because retrofitting these old cars with modern pollution control systems would cost more than many of them are worth. Two innovative solutions were recently proposed.

Uses single spacing to save paper and filing space

Reducing Smog by Eliminating Older Cars

Two large organizations, Unocal and Ford Motor Company, suggested a buy-out program to eliminate older cars. To demonstrate its effectiveness, the two firms bought more than 8,000 pre-1975 cars in the Los Angeles area for $700 each. These cars were junked, and buyers were encouraged to purchase newer and cleaner automobiles. One of

Organizes data indirectly, with recommendations last, to inform and persuade readers

RECOMMENDATIONS

Based on our findings and the conclusions discussed earlier, we submit the following recommendations to you:

1. Study the progress of Germany's attempt to reduce smog by retrofitting older vehicles with computer-controlled fuel management systems.
2. Invite Neutronics Enterprises in Carlsbad, California, to test its Lamba emission-control system at your El Monte test center.
3. Encourage Ford Motor Company and Unocal to continue their buy-out programs in exchange for temporary smog credits.

- **Manuscript format.** For longer, more formal reports, use manuscript format. These reports are usually printed on plain paper instead of letterhead stationery or memo forms. They begin with a title followed by systematically displayed headings and subheadings, as illustrated in Figure 11.4.
- **Printed forms.** Prepared forms are often used for repetitive data, such as monthly sales reports, performance appraisals, merchandise inventories, and personnel and financial reports. Standardized headings on these forms save time for the writer. Preprinted forms also make similar information easy to locate and ensure that all necessary information is provided.

Writing Style

Reports can be formal or informal depending on the purpose, audience, and setting.

Like other business messages, reports can range from informal to formal, depending on their purpose, audience, and setting. Research reports sent to clients, such as those Richard Eades wrote for The Winters Group, tend to be rather formal. Such reports must project an impression of objectivity, authority, and impartiality. But a report to your boss describing a trip to a conference would probably be informal.

An office worker once called a grammar hot-line service with this problem: "We've just sent a report to our headquarters, and it was returned with this comment, 'Put it in the third person.' What do they mean?" The hot-line experts explained that apparently management wanted a more formal writing style, using third-person constructions (*the company* or *the researcher* instead of *we* and *I*). Figure 11.5, which compares characteristics of formal and informal report-writing styles, can help you decide the writing style that's appropriate for your reports.

Applying the 3-×-3 Writing Process to Reports

The best reports grow out of a 7-step process beginning with analysis and ending with proofreading and evaluation.

Because business reports are systematic attempts to answer questions and solve problems, the best reports are developed methodically. The same 3-×-3 writing process that guided memo and letter writing can be applied to reports. Let's channel the process into seven specific steps:

- **Step 1:** Analyze the problem and purpose.
- **Step 2:** Anticipate the audience and issues.
- **Step 3:** Prepare a work plan.
- **Step 4:** Research the data.
- **Step 5:** Organize, analyze, interpret, and illustrate the data.
- **Step 6:** Compose the first draft.
- **Step 7:** Revise, proofread, and evaluate.

How much time you spend on each step depends on your report task. A short informational report on a familiar topic might require a brief work plan, little research, and no analysis of the data. A complex analytical report, on the other hand, might demand a comprehensive work plan, extensive research, and careful analysis of the data.

To illustrate the planning stages of a report, we'll watch Diane Camas develop a report she's preparing for her boss, Mike Rivers, at Mycon Pharmaceutical Laboratories. Mike asked Diane to investigate the problem of transportation for sales representatives. Currently, some Mycon reps visit customers (mostly doctors and

FIGURE 11.5 ● Report-writing Styles

	Formal Writing Style	Informal Writing Style
Use	Theses Research studies Controversial or complex reports (especially to outsiders)	Short, routine reports Reports for familiar audiences Noncontroversial reports Most reports for company insiders
Effect	Impression of objectivity, accuracy, professionalism, fairness Distance created between writer and reader	Feeling of warmth, personal involvement, closeness
Characteristics	Absence of first-person pronouns; use of third-person *(the researcher, the writer)* Absence of contractions *(can't, don't)* Use of passive-voice verbs *(the study was conducted)* Complex sentences; long words Absence of humor; figures of speech Reduced use of colorful adjectives, adverbs Elimination of "editorializing" (author's opinions, perceptions)	Use of first-person pronouns *(I, we, me, my, us, our)* Use of contractions Emphasis on active-voice verbs *(I conducted the study)* Shorter sentences; familiar words Occasional use of humor, metaphors Occasional use of colorful speech Acceptance of author's opinions and ideas

hospitals) using company-leased cars. A few reps drive their own cars, receiving reimbursements for use. In three months Mycon's leasing agreement for 14 cars expires, and Mike is considering a major change. Diane's task is investigating the choices and reporting her findings to Mike.

Analyzing the Problem and Purpose

The first step in writing a report is understanding the problem or assignment clearly. For complex reports it's wise to prepare a written problem statement. In analyzing her report task, Diane had many questions. Is the problem that Mycon is spending too much money on leased cars? Does Mycon wish to invest in owning a fleet of cars? Is Mike unhappy with the paperwork involved in reimbursing sales reps when they use their own cars? Does he suspect that reps are submitting inflated mileage figures? Before starting research for the report, Diane talked with Mike to define the problem. She learned several dimensions of the situation and wrote the following statement to clarify the problem—both for herself and for Mike.

● **Before beginning a report, identify the problem to be solved in a clear statement.**

> **Problem Statement:** The leases on all company cars will be expiring in three months. Mycon must decide whether to renew them or develop a new policy regarding transportation for sales reps. Expenses and paperwork for employee-owned cars seem excessive.

Diane further defined the problem by writing a specific question that she would try to answer in her report:

> **Problem Question:** What plan should Mycon follow in providing transportation for its sales reps?

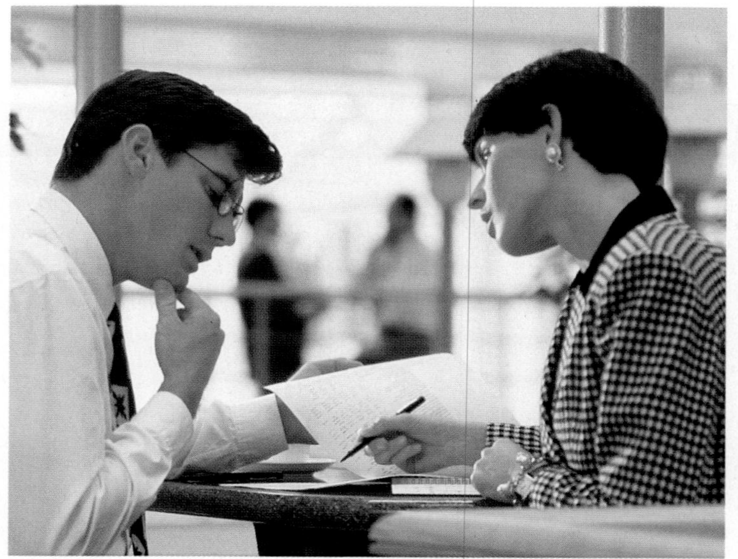

Smart researchers save themselves heartache and wasted time by determining the purpose of a report well before they start collecting data. Talking over the scope of a problem, the problem's significance, and any report limitations helps a researcher organize an entire project.

Now Diane was ready to concentrate on the purpose of the report. Again, she had questions. Exactly what did Mike expect? Did he want a comparison of costs for buying cars and leasing cars? Should she conduct research to pinpoint exact reimbursement costs when employees drive their own cars? Did he want her to do all the legwork, present her findings in a report, and let him make a decision? Or did he want her to evaluate the choices and recommend a course of action?

● A simple purpose statement defines the focus of a report.

After talking with Mike, Diane was ready to write a simple purpose statement for this assignment.

> **Simple Statement of Purpose:** To recommend a plan that provides sales reps with cars to be used in their calls.

Preparing a written purpose statement is a good idea because it defines the focus of a report and provides a standard that keeps the project on target. In writing useful purpose statements, choose active verbs telling what you intend to do: *analyze, choose, investigate, compare, justify, evaluate, explain, establish, determine,* and so on. Notice that Diane's statement begins with the active verb *recommend.*

Some reports require only a simple statement of purpose: *to investigate expanded teller hours, to select a manager from among four candidates, to describe the position of accounts supervisor.* Many assignments, though, demand additional focus to guide the project. An expanded statement of purpose considers three additional factors:

- **Scope.** What issues or elements will be investigated? To determine the scope, Diane brainstormed with Mike and others to pin down her task. She learned that Mycon currently had enough capital to consider purchasing a fleet of cars outright. Mike also told her that employee satisfaction was almost as important as cost effectiveness. Moreover, he disclosed his suspicion that employee-owned cars were costing Mycon more than leased cars. Diane had many issues to sort out in setting the boundaries of her report.
- **Significance.** Why is the topic worth investigating at this time? Some topics, after initial examination, turn out to be less important than originally thought. Others involve problems that cannot be solved, making a study useless. For

Diane and Mike the problem had significance because Mycon's leasing agreement would expire shortly and decisions had to be made about a new policy for transportation of sales reps.

- **Limitations.** What conditions affect the generalizability and utility of a report's findings? In Diane's case her conclusions and recommendations might apply only to reps in her Kansas City sales district. Her findings would probably not be reliable for reps in Seattle or Phoenix or Atlanta. Another limitation for Diane is time. She must complete the report in four weeks, thus restricting the thoroughness of her research.

Diane decides to expand her statement of purpose to define the scope, significance, and limitations of the report.

An expanded purpose statement considers scope, significance, and limitations.

> **Expanded Statement of Purpose:** The purpose of this report is to recommend a plan that provides sales reps with cars to be used in their calls. The report will compare costs for three plans: outright ownership, leasing, and compensation for employee-owned cars. It will also measure employee reaction to each plan. The report is significant because Mycon's current leasing agreement expires April 1 and an improved plan could reduce costs and paperwork. The study is limited to costs for sales reps in the Kansas City district.

After preparing a statement of purpose, Diane checked it with Mike Rivers to be sure she was on target.

Anticipating the Audience and Issues

Report writers must take into account both primary and secondary readers.

After defining the purpose, a report writer must think carefully about who will read the report. A major mistake is concentrating solely on a primary reader. Although one individual may have solicited the report, others within the organization may eventually read it, including upper management and people in other departments. A report to an outside client may first be read by someone who is familiar with the problem and then be distributed to others less familiar with the topic. Moreover, candid statements to one audience may be offensive to another audience. Diane could make a major blunder, for instance, if she mentioned Mike's suspicion that sales reps were padding their mileage statements. If the report were made public—as it probably would be to explain a new policy—the sales reps could feel insulted that their integrity was questioned.

As Diane considered her primary and secondary readers, she asked herself these questions:

- *What do my readers need to know about this topic?*
- *What do they already know?*
- *How will they react to this information?*
- *How can I make this information understandable and readable?*

Answers to these questions help writers determine how much background material to include, how much detail to add, whether to include jargon, what method of organization and presentation to follow, and what tone to use.

Major report problems should be broken into subproblems—or factored—to highlight possible solutions.

In the planning stages a report writer must also break the major investigative problem into subproblems. This process, sometimes called *factoring,* identifies issues to be investigated or possible solutions to the main problem. In this case Mycon must figure out the best way to transport sales reps. Each possible "solution" or issue that Diane considers becomes a factor or subproblem to be investigated. Diane came up with three tentative solutions to provide transportation to

SPOTLIGHT ON COMMUNICATORS

At Phelps County Bank in Rolla, Missouri, loan processor Peggy Laun helped implement a system of "upward evaluation." She saw a problem, conducted research, collected data, evaluated the results, and then proposed a system that enables employees to review their supervisors. Good research usually begins with a work plan designed to solve a specific problem.

sales reps: (1) purchase cars outright, (2) lease cars, or (3) compensate employees for using their own cars. These three factors form the outline of Diane's study.

Diane continued to factor these main points into the following subproblems for investigation:

What plan should Mycon use to transport its sales reps?

I. Should Mycon purchase cars outright?
   A. How much capital would be required?
   B. How much would it cost to insure, operate, and maintain company-owned cars?
   C. Do employees prefer using company-owned cars?

II. Should Mycon lease cars?
   A. What is the best lease price available?
   B. How much would it cost to insure, operate, and maintain leased cars?
   C. Do employees prefer using leased cars?

III. Should Mycon compensate employees for using their own cars?
   A. How much has it cost in the past to operate employee-owned cars?
   B. How much paperwork is involved in reporting expenses?
   C. Do employees prefer being compensated for using their own cars?

Each subproblem would probably be further factored into additional subproblems. These issues may be phrased as questions, as Diane did, or as statements. In factoring a complex problem, prepare an outline showing the initial problem and its breakdown into subproblems. Make sure your divisions are consistent (don't mix issues), exclusive (don't overlap categories), and complete (don't skip significant issues).

Preparing a Work Plan

After analyzing the problem, anticipating the audience, and factoring the problem, you're ready to prepare a work plan. Preparing a plan forces you to evaluate your resources, set priorities, outline a course of action, and establish a time schedule. Such a plan keeps you on schedule and also gives management a means of measuring your progress. A good work plan includes the following:

- Statement of the problem
- Statement of the purpose including scope, significance, and limitations
- Description of the sources and methods of collecting data
- Tentative outline
- Work schedule

A good work plan provides an overview of a project: resources, priorities, course of action, and schedule.

A work plan gives a complete picture of a project. Because the usefulness and quality of any report rests primarily on its data, you'll want to allocate plenty of time to locate sources of information. For firsthand information you might interview people, prepare a survey, or even conduct a scientific experiment. You'll probably also want to search—either manually or electronically—printed materials like books and magazines. Your work plan describes how you expect to generate or collect data. Since data collection is a major part of report writing, the next section of this chapter treats the topic more fully.

Figure 11.6 shows a complete work plan for a report that studies safety seals for a food company's products. This work plan is particularly useful because it outlines the issues to be investigated. Notice that considerable thought and discussion—and even some preliminary research—are necessary to be able to develop a useful work plan.

FIGURE 11.6 ● Work Plan for a Formal Report

Tips for Preparing a Work Plan

- Start early; allow plenty of time for brainstorming and preliminary research.
- Describe the problem motivating the report.
- Write a purpose statement that includes its scope, significance, and limitations.
- Describe data collection sources and methods.
- Divide the major problem into subproblems stated as questions to be answered.
- Develop a realistic work schedule citing dates for completion of major tasks.
- Review the work plan with whoever authorized the report.

Statement of Problem

Consumers worry that food and drug products are dangerous as a result of tampering. Our company may face loss of market share and potential liability if we don't protect our products. Many food and drug companies now offer tamper-resistant packaging, but such packaging is costly.

Statement of Purpose

The purpose of this study is to determine whether tamper-resistant packaging is necessary and/or feasible for our jams, jellies, and preserves. The study will examine published accounts of package tampering and evaluate how other companies have solved the problem. It will also measure consumers' interest in safety-seal packaging, as well as consumers' willingness to pay a slightly higher price for safety lids. We will conduct a market survey limited to a sample of 400 local consumers. Finally, the study will investigate a method for sealing our products and determine the cost for each unit we produce. This study is significant because safety seals could enhance the sales of our products and protect us from possible liability.

Defines purpose, scope, limits, and significance of report

Sources and Methods of Data Collection

Magazine and newspaper accounts of product tampering will be examined for the past 15 years. Articles describing tamper-resistant lids and other safe packaging devices for food and drug manufacturers will be studied. Moreover, our marketing staff will conduct a random telephone survey of local consumers, measuring their interest in safety seals. Finally, our production department will test various devices and determine the most cost-effective method to seal our product safely.

Describes primary and secondary data sources

Tentative Outline

I. Are consumers and producers concerned about product tampering?
   A. What incidents of tampering have been reported in the past 15 years?
   B. How did consumers react to tampered products causing harm?
   C. How did food and drug producers protect their products?
II. How do consumers react to safety seals on products today?
   A. Do consumers prefer food and drug products with safety seals?
   B. Would consumers be more likely to purchase our products if safety-sealed?
   C. Would consumers be willing to pay a few cents extra for safety seals?
III. What kind of safety seal is best for our products?
   A. What devices are other producers using—plastic "blister" packs, foil seals over bottle openings, or bands around lids?
   B. What device would work for our products?
   C. How much would each device cost per unit?
IV. Should we proceed with safety seals?

Factors problem into manageable chunks

Work Schedule

Investigate newspaper and magazine articles	Oct. 1-10
Examine safety-seal devices on the market	Oct. 8-18
Interview 400 local consumers	Oct. 8-24
Develop and test devices for our products	Oct. 15-Nov.14
Interpret and evaluate findings	Nov. 15-17
Compose first draft of report	Nov. 18-20
Revise draft	Nov. 21-23
Submit final report	Nov. 24

Estimates time needed to complete report tasks

SPOTLIGHT ON COMMUNICATORS

Premier management consultant and best-selling author Tom Peters recognizes the value of on-going research and reporting. He recommends collecting data not only about the performance of your own company but also about that of the competition. To stay abreast of rivals and their techniques, businesses must (1) collect data, (2) update them regularly, and (3) share them widely within the firm.

Although this tentative outline guides investigation, it does not determine the content or order of the final report. You may, for example, study five possible solutions to a problem. If two prove to be useless, your report may discuss only the three winners. Moreover, you will organize the report to accomplish your goal and satisfy the audience. Remember that a busy executive who is familiar with a topic may prefer to read the conclusions and recommendations before a discussion of the findings.

If the report is authorized by someone, be sure to review the work plan with that individual (your manager, client, or professor, for example) before proceeding with the project.

Researching Report Data

One of the most important steps in the process of writing a report is that of research. Because a report is only as good as its data, the remainder of this chapter describes how to find data and document it.

As you analyze a report's purpose and audience, you'll assess the kinds of data needed to support your argument or explain your topic. Do you need statistics, background data, expert opinions, group opinions, or organizational data? Figure 11.7 lists five forms of data and provides questions to guide you in making your research accurate and productive.

Data fall into two broad categories, primary and secondary. Primary data result from firsthand experience and observation. Secondary data come from reading what others have experienced and observed. Coca-Cola and PepsiCo, for example, produce primary data when they stage taste tests and record the reactions of consumers. These same sets of data become secondary after they have been published and, let's say, a newspaper reporter uses them in an article about soft drinks. Secondary data are easier and cheaper to develop than primary data, which might involve interviewing large groups or sending out questionnaires. Nearly every research project should begin with a search of secondary data. Often, something has already been written about your topic. Reviewing secondary sources can save time and effort and prevent you from "reinventing the wheel."

Locating Secondary Data

A logical place to begin any research project is by examining secondary data available in print and in databases. Your college, university, or municipal library should contain such data. If you are an infrequent library user, begin your research by talking with a reference librarian about your project. These librarians won't do the research for you, but they will steer you in the right direction. And they are very accommodating. Several years ago a *Wall Street Journal* poll revealed that librarians are among the friendliest, most approachable people in the working world.[2]

In locating secondary data, researchers find librarians a prime resource.

Some libraries also provide brochures and handouts and conduct workshops describing their cataloging and retrieval systems. For a business report you'll probably consult one or more of the following major sources of secondary information: (1) library catalogs; (2) periodicals and newspapers; (3) encyclopedias, dictionaries, and handbooks; and (4) electronic databases.

Library catalog. Libraries in the past indexed all their books on 3-by-5 cards alphabetized by author and/or by subject. Many libraries today, however, have

FIGURE 11.7 ● Selecting Report Data

Form of Data	Questions to Ask
Statistical	What is the source? How were these figures derived? In what form do I need the statistics? Must they be converted? How recent are they?
Background or historical	Has this topic been explored before? What have others said about it? What sources did they use?
Expert opinion	Who are the experts? Are their opinions in print? Can they be interviewed? Do we have in-house experts?
Individual or group opinion	Do I need to interview or survey people (such as consumers, employees, or managers)? Do good questionnaires already exist? Can parts of existing test instruments be used or combined?
Organizational	What are the proper channels for obtaining in-house data? Are permissions required? How can I find data about public and private companies?

computerized their card catalogs. Some systems are fully automated, showing the user not only whether a book is located in the library but also whether it is currently available. When you start to use a computer terminal to search for data, don't hesitate to request help from clerks or librarians. In using the library catalog system, remember that books provide excellent historical, in-depth data on a subject. For many business problems, however, books are inadequate because the material is outdated. Periodicals are more timely.

Periodicals and newspapers. Magazines, pamphlets, and journals are called *periodicals* because of their recurrent publication. Journals, by the way, are compilations of scholarly articles. Journals and other periodicals generally provide the most up-to-date information on a topic. To locate articles in general-interest magazines (such as *Time, Newsweek, The New Yorker,* and *U.S. News & World Report*), consult *The Readers' Guide to Periodical Literature.* To locate articles in business, industrial, and trade magazines and journals (such as *Business Week, Management Review, Barron's,* and *Forbes*), consult the *Business Periodicals Index.* Other indexes include the *Education Index, Applied Science and Technology Index,* and *Public Affairs Information Service Bulletin.* Business report writers usually find the *Business Periodicals Index* to be the most useful.

Newspapers from around the country and the world also supply current information, as well as being fascinating to read. Locating articles on a topic, however, is difficult unless you limit yourself to the newspapers that index their articles. Some indexes to consider are *Barron's Index, Index of the Christian Science Monitor, Los Angeles Times Index, National Observer Index, New York Times Index,* and *Wall Street Journal Index.* Most of these indexes are also available in print or electronically through the *National Newspaper Index.*

Encyclopedias, dictionaries, and handbooks. The reference section of a library contains special collections of helpful material. General encyclopedias include *Encyclopedia Americana, Concise Columbia Encyclopedia,* and *Encyclopedia Britannica.* Specialized encyclopedias include *Encyclopedia of American Economic History, Encyclopedia of Business Information Sources, Exporter's Encyclopedia,* and *Accountant's Encyclopedia.* The reference section may also house excellent dictionaries that function as encyclopedias, such as Prentice-Hall's *Encyclopedic Dictionary of Business.* Handbooks provide current data in specialized fields. For employment information consult the *Occupational Outlook Handbook* (published by the U.S. Department of Labor). Other handbooks include *Handbook of Auditing Methods, Handbook of Business Administration, Management Handbook, Sales Executives' Handbook,* and *Real Estate Handbook.*

Databases. Databases are collections of information usually accessed by computer. Your personal address book, however, with its alphabetized names and addresses, is a form of manual database. Vast amounts of data are now stored in computerized databases, making them huge electronic libraries. You can use them to conduct literature searches, check references, confirm statistics, quote experts, locate specific publications, and, in some instances, read entire documents. Because the computer can find items faster than even the most skilled researcher, these databases are rapidly becoming the principal source of secondary data today. In addition to speed, electronic databases provide access to stores of information that rival the holdings of the largest university and public libraries. Moreover, bibliographic data are constantly updated. Thus, database references are more current than printed indexes, which may lag as much as a year behind the publications they cite.

● **Much of the world's data are now stored in electronic databases.**

Kinds of databases. Databases can be grouped into three broad categories: in-house, statistical, and bibliographic. *In-house databases* consist of information related to the operations of a particular organization. Employees are able to access style manuals showing, for example, preferred spellings, document formats, and language usage. In-house systems also include user manuals for equipment, company policies and procedures, engineering drawings, and letters, memos, and specialized reports. *Statistical databases* hold huge stores of numerical data, such as census information, employment figures, stock and bond values, and indexes, like the Consumer Price Index. The U.S. Government supplies much of the statistics in databases. *Bibliographic databases* are most commonly used by researchers. They contain listings of books, magazine articles, newspaper stories, and other publications. They may show a title, a summary, or the full text of an article. These databases are rented to users who are charged for each minute of search time. Two popular databases for business users are BRS (Bibliographic Retrieval Services) and DIALOG Information Services. For information about service and rates, call 1-800-555-1212 to obtain their toll-free numbers.

● **Electronic databases may be in-house, statistical, or bibliographic.**

This furniture designer's report began with primary data generated by a survey of consumers. Because business reports typically address current problems, they rely heavily on primary data collected through surveys, interviews, and observation.

Accessing databases. Researchers access data through on-line or CD-ROM databases. *On-line* databases consist of information stored in remote mainframe computers. Subscribers access the data with their computers and modems. "On-line" means that one computer is connected by a telephone line (or hard wire) to another computer. Using an on-line database costs between $20 and $250 an hour, depending on the service and the time of day. *CD-ROM* (short for *C*ompact *D*isc, *R*ead *O*nly *M*emory) databases are stored on high-capacity discs that work on computers with special CD-ROM hard disk drives. These compact discs may include entire databases, such as ten years of *Time* magazine articles or a directory of all American business names and telephone numbers. Researchers using CD-ROM databases can find information immediately without paying for a telephone hookup to a remote mainframe computer. Users may also subscribe to services that update CD-ROM databases regularly. Your college or public library probably has the *Readers' Guide to Periodical Literature* on CD-ROM. Thus, you can sit at a computer terminal and electronically peruse countless titles of magazine articles.

● On-line databases may be accessed with a computer and a modem.

On the downside, searching commercial databases can be frustrating and expensive. You need skill in selecting *key words* (or *descriptors*), as well as experience in using a particular database. Thus, you may need to consult reference librarians or search professionals at first to provide assistance.

Generating Primary Data

Although you'll begin a business report by probing for secondary data, you'll likely also need primary data to give a complete picture. Because business reports typically solve specific current problems, they rely heavily on primary, firsthand data. If, for example, management wants to discover the cause of increased employee turnover in its Seattle office, it must investigate and collect information. Providing answers to business problems often means generating primary data through surveys, interviews, observation, or experimentation.

● Research projects often draw on primary data from surveys and interviews.

Surveys. Surveys collect data from groups of people. When companies develop new products, for example, they often survey consumers to learn their needs. The advantages of surveys are that they gather data economically and efficiently. Mailed surveys reach big groups nearby or at great distances. Moreover, people respond-

● Surveys yield efficient and economical primary data for reports.

ing to mailed surveys have time to consider their answers, thus improving the accuracy of the data.

Although mailed surveys may suffer low response rates, they are still useful in generating primary data.

Mailed questionnaires, of course, have disadvantages. Most of us rank them with junk mail, so response rates may be no higher than 10 percent. Furthermore, those who do respond may not represent an accurate sample of the overall population, thus invalidating generalizations from the group. Let's say, for example, that an insurance company sends out a questionnaire asking about provisions in a new policy. If only older people respond, the questionnaire data cannot be used to generalize what people in other age groups might think. A final problem with surveys has to do with truthfulness. Some respondents exaggerate their incomes or distort other facts, thus causing the results to be unreliable.

Nevertheless, surveys may be the best way to generate data for business and student reports. In preparing a survey, consider these pointers:

- **Explain why the survey is necessary.** In a cover letter or an opening paragraph, describe the need for the survey. Suggest how someone or something other than you will benefit. If appropriate, offer to send recipients a copy of the findings.
- **Consider incentives.** If the survey is long, persuasive techniques may be necessary. Response rates can be increased by offering money (such as a $1 bill), coupons, gift certificates, free books, or other gifts.
- **Limit the number of questions.** Resist the temptation to ask for too much. Request only information you will use. Don't, for example, include demographic questions (income, gender, age, and so forth) unless the information is necessary to evaluate responses.

Effective surveys target appropriate samples and ask a limited number of specific questions with quantifiable answers.

- **Use questions that produce quantifiable answers.** Check-off, multiple-choice, yes-no, and scale (or rank-order) questions (illustrated in Figure 11.8) provide quantifiable data that are easily tabulated. Responses to open-ended questions *(What should the bookstore do about plastic bags?)* reveal interesting, but difficult to quantify, perceptions.[3] To obtain workable data, give interviewees a list of possible responses (as shown in items 5–8 of Figure 11.8). For scale and multiple-choice questions, try to present all the possible answer choices. To be safe, add an "Other" or "Don't know" category in case the choices seem insufficient to the respondent. Many surveys use scale questions because they capture degrees of feelings. Typical scale headings are "agree strongly," "agree somewhat," "neutral," "disagree somewhat," and "disagree strongly."

The way a question is stated influences its response.

- **Avoid leading or ambiguous questions.** The wording of a question can dramatically affect responses to it, as shown in a *New York Times*/CBS national poll.[4] When respondents were asked "Are we spending too much, too little, or about the right amount on *assistance to the poor* [emphasis added]?" 13 percent responded "too much." When the same respondents were asked "Are we spending too much, too little, or about the right amount on *welfare* [emphasis added]?" 44 percent responded "too much." Because words have different meanings for different people, you must strive to use objective language and pilot test your questions with typical respondents. Stay away from questions that suggest an answer *(Don't you agree that the salaries of CEOs are obscenely high?)*. Instead, ask neutral questions *(Do CEOs earn too much, too little, or about the right amount?)*. Also avoid queries that really ask two or more things *(Should the salaries of CEOs be reduced or regulated by government legislation?)*. Instead, break them into separate questions *(Should the*

FIGURE 11.8 ● **Preparing a Survey**

The Three Phases of the Writing Process

1

Analyze
The purpose is to help the bookstore decide if it should replace plastic bags with cloth bags for customer purchases.

Anticipate
The audience will be busy students who will be initially uninterested.

Adapt
Because students will be unwilling to participate, the survey must be short and simple. Its purpose must be significant and clear.

2

Research
Ask students how they would react to cloth bags. Use their answers to form question reponse choices.

Organize
Open by explaining the survey's purpose and importance. In the body ask clear questions that produce quantifiable answers. Conclude with appreciation and instructions.

Compose
Write the first draft of the questionnaire.

3

Revise
Try out the questionnaire with small, representative group. Revise unclear questions.

Proofread
Read for correctness. Be sure that answer choices do not overlap and that they are complete. Provide "other" category if appropriate (as in No. 9).

Evaluate
Is the survey clear, attractive, and easy to complete?

North Shore College Bookstore
STUDENT SURVEY

The North Shore College Bookstore wants to do its part in protecting the environment. Each year we give away 45,000 plastic bags for students to carry off their purchases. We are considering changing from plastic to cloth bags or some other alternative, but we need your views.

Explains need for survey (use cover letter for longer surveys)

Please place checks below to indicate your responses.

1. How many units are you presently carrying?
   ___ 15 or more units
   ___ 9 to 14 units
   ___ 8 or fewer units

   ___ Male
   ___ Female

Uses groupings that do not overlap (not 9 to 15 and 15 or more)

2. How many times have you visited the bookstore this semester?
   ___ 0 times ___ 1 time ___ 2 times ___ 3 times ___ 4 or more times

3. Indicate your concern for the environment.
   ___ Very concerned ___ Concerned ___ Unconcerned

4. To protect the environment, would you be willing to change to another type of bag when buying books?
   ___ Yes
   ___ No

Indicate your feeling about the following alternatives.

Uses scale questions to channel responses into quantifiable alternatives, as opposed to posing an open-ended question

For major purchases the bookstore should	Agree	Undecided	Disagree
5. Continue to provide plastic bags.	___	___	___
6. Provide no bags; encourage students to bring their own bags.	___	___	___
7. Provide no bags; offer cloth bags at reduced price (about $3).	___	___	___
8. Give a cloth bag with each major purchase, the cost to be included in registration fees.	___	___	___
9. Consider another alternative, such as			

____

Allows respondent to add an answer in case choices provided seem insufficient

Please return the completed survey form to your instructor or to the survey box at the North Shore College Bookstore exit. Your opinion counts.

Tells how to return survey form

Thanks for your help!

salaries of CEOs be regulated by government legislation? Should the salaries of CEOs be reduced by government legislation?).

The larger the sample, the more accurate the resulting data is likely to be.

- **Select the survey population carefully.** Many surveys question a small group of people (a sample) and project the findings to a larger population. Let's say that a survey of your class reveals that the majority prefer Chicago-style pizza. Can you then say with confidence that all students on your campus (or in the nation) prefer Chicago-style pizza? To be able to generalize from a survey, you need to make the sample as large as possible. In addition, you need to determine if the sample is like the larger population. For important surveys you will want to consult books or experts in sampling techniques. The accompanying Career Skills box discusses basic sampling procedures.
- **Conduct a pilot study.** Try the questionnaire with a small group so that you can remedy any problems. For example, in the survey shown in Figure 11.8, a pilot study revealed that female students generally favored cloth book bags and were willing to pay for them. Male students opposed purchasing cloth bags. By adding a gender category, researchers could verify this finding. The pilot study also revealed the need to ensure an appropriate representation of male and female students in the survey.

Interviews with experts yield useful report data, especially when little has been written about a topic.

Interviews. Some of the best report information, particularly on topics about which little has been written, comes from individuals. These individuals are usually experts or veterans in their fields. Consider both in-house and outside experts for business reports. Tapping these sources will call for in-person or telephone interviews. To elicit the most useful data, try these techniques:

- **Locate an expert.** Ask managers and individuals working in an area whom they consider to be most knowledgeable. Check membership lists of professional organizations, and consult articles about the topic or related topics. Most people enjoy being experts or at least recommending them.
- **Prepare for the interview.** Learn about the individual you're interviewing as well as the background and terminology of the topic. Let's say you're interviewing a corporate communication expert about producing an in-house newsletter. You ought to be familiar with terms like *font* and software like Quark Express, Aldus Pagemaker, and Ventura. In addition, be prepared by making a list of questions that pinpoint your focus on the topic. Ask the interviewee if you may record the talk.
- **Make your questions objective and friendly.** Don't get into a debating match with the interviewee. And remember that you're there to listen, not to talk! Use open-ended, rather than yes-or-no, questions to draw experts out.
- **Watch the time.** Tell interviewees in advance how much time you expect to need for the interview. Don't overstay your appointment.
- **End graciously.** Conclude the interview with a general question, such as "Is there anything you'd like to add?" Express your appreciation, and ask permission to telephone later if you need to verify points.

Observation and experimentation. Some kinds of primary data can be obtained only through firsthand observation and investigation. How long does a typical caller wait before a customer service rep answers the call? How is a new piece of equipment operated? Are complaints of sexual harassment being taken seriously? Observation produces rich data, but that information is especially prone to charges of subjectivity. One can interpret an observation in many ways. Thus, to make observations more objective, try to quantify them. For example, record cus-

SURVEY SAMPLING AT A GLANCE

Let's assume your school wants to add a new eating facility on campus, and you've been asked to find out whether students want a fast-food hamburger stand or a health-food bar. Your first idea might be to survey *all* 20,000 students to ask what they prefer. Such a survey, however, would obviously require a lot of time and money. A better plan would be to question only a portion, or sample, of the student body. *Sampling* is the process used to select a small group of individuals to represent an entire population. Most samples can separated into two groups: probability samples and nonprobability samples.

PROBABILITY SAMPLES. In probability samples every person in the population has a known chance of being selected. Such samples allow researchers to estimate how closely the sample represents the population from which it is drawn. To determine what kind of food stand students prefer, you might consider one of the following probability samples.

Simple Random Sample. The easiest way to select a simple random sample is to use a random number generator program—say, from the university's computer system. The program might select 2,000 students from the 20,000 enrolled. Thus, each student has a 10 percent chance of being selected.

Stratified Random Sample. To select a stratified random sample, you simply divide the population into subgroups and randomly select individuals from each subgroup. Our 20,000 students, might, for example, be divided into their class levels. The random number generator might select 650 names from the 6,500 freshmen, 550 from the 5,500 sophomores, 450 from the 4,500 juniors, and 350 from the 3,500 seniors. Thus, the total sample represents 10 percent of each class. Such samples are particularly useful for comparing responses between subgroups. A stratified sample will be more accurate than a simple random sample.

Cluster Sample. Cluster samples fall into two categories: system clusters and area clusters. In a cluster/system random sample, every *n*th individual is selected. For example, to select a sample of 2,000, the number generator would begin at a random point on the list of 20,000 student names and then select every tenth name. In a cluster/area random sample, the population is divided into subgroups or clusters, often on a geographic basis. For our sample the 20,000 students might be divided into ten home zip code clusters. A number generator randomly selects five zip codes from the ten, and 400 students in each cluster are selected to comprise the sample of 2,000.

NONPROBABILITY SAMPLES. When random samples cost too much or are impossible to obtain, researchers may use nonprobability samples. And the resulting data may be quite useful. But generalizations from such samples are usually not as representative as those from probability samples. That's why ethical researchers always reveal their survey methods. Nonprobability samples include judgment, convenience, and quota samples.

Judgment Sample. A judgment sample consists of nonrandomly selected persons who appear to have the appropriate knowledge related to the survey topic. For example, only students who frequently eat at hamburger stands or health-food bars ("food experts") are surveyed about which eating spot all students would prefer.

Convenience Sample. Sometimes a sample is chosen solely on the basis of its convenience to the researcher. Interviewers might stand outside the campus cafeteria, for example, and question the first 2,000 students who walk by. One form of convenience sample is the *self-selected* sample. MTV, for instance, asks viewers to choose recording artists, such as Madonna or Prince. Since the callers are not randomly selected, their choices may not reflect the feelings of all viewers.

Quota Sample. In a quota sample, individuals are selected from subgroups—but they are not randomly selected. For example, you could question the first 350 seniors you meet, thus filling your 10 percent quota.

Career Track Application

Your class wants to survey 10 percent of the Fortune 500 companies (a list is available at your library). In teams of three or four, select a cluster/system random sample. Discuss how you could develop a stratified random sample and a cluster/area random sample.

tomer telephone wait-time for 60-minute periods at different times throughout a week. Or compare the number of sexual harassment complaints made with the number of investigations undertaken and the resulting action.

Experimentation produces data suggesting causes and effects. Informal experimentation might be as simple as a pretest and posttest in a college course. Did students expand their knowledge as a result of the course? More formal experimentation is undertaken by scientists and professional researchers who control variables to test their effects. Assume, for example, that the Hershey Company wants to test the hypothesis (which is a tentative assumption) that chocolate lifts people out of the doldrums. An experiment testing the hypothesis would separate depressed individuals into two groups: those who ate chocolate (the experimental group) and those who did not (the control group). What effect did chocolate have? Such experiments are not done haphazardly, however. Valid experiments require sophisticated research designs and careful attention to matching the experimental and control groups.

Documenting Data

Documenting data lends credibility, aids the reader, and protects the writer from plagiarism.

Documenting data means revealing and crediting your information sources. Careful documentation in a report serves three purposes:

- **Strengthens your argument.** Including good data from reputable sources will convince readers of your credibility and the logic of your reasoning.
- **Protects you.** Acknowledging your sources keeps you honest. It's unethical and illegal to use others' ideas without proper documentation. The accompanying Ethics box lists specific ways to avoid plagiarism.
- **Instructs the reader.** Citing references enables readers to pursue a topic further and make use of the information themselves.

Three Documentation Formats

Select a suitable format to show textual and bibliographic references for your report sources.

You may choose from traditional or more contemporary formats to document data. Select a format that suits your needs or those of your instructor or organization. Once you begin using a documentation format, stay with that style throughout your report. References are usually cited in two places: (1) a brief citation appears in the text and (2) a complete citation appears in a bibliography at the end of the report. The three most common formats for citations within the text are footnotes, endnotes, and parenthetic notes. Each of these formats has its own textual and bibliographic style, illustrated in Figure 11.9.

Footnotes/Bibliography. Footnoting is a traditional documentation format calling for a superscript (raised) number at the end of a sentence containing a reference. The superscript refers the reader to the foot of the page, where the complete source appears, as shown in Format 1 of Figure 11.9. At the end of the report, a bibliography lists all the references cited in the report (and perhaps all the references consulted). Items in the bibliography are in alphabetical order. This traditional footnote and bibliographic format generally follows the guidelines presented in *The Chicago Manual of Style.*

Endnotes/Bibliography. An alternative to footnotes is endnotes, shown in Format 2 of Figure 11.9. Instead of citing references at the bottom of each page, the writer lists them in "Notes" at the end of the report. This method is certainly easier to prepare than footnotes, and pages are less cluttered. References, however, are less convenient for readers. In addition to the Notes list, the writer may prepare an optional bibliography, like the one shown in Format 1.

ETHICS

AVOIDING PLAGIARISM AND USING QUOTATIONS

Whether you quote directly or paraphrase (put someone else's ideas into your own words), you must acknowledge the source. Using another person's words or ideas without citing the source is plagiarism, a serious offense in the academic world and elsewhere. Students who plagiarize risk a failing grade in a class and even expulsion from school. Businesspeople, professionals, and politicians caught plagiarizing lose not only their credibility but often their jobs. For example, Boston University Dean H. Joachim Maitre lost his job after it was learned that he plagiarized most of a commencement address. And Laura Parker, a newspaper editor in Miami, was fired for pilfering one of her stories from a news service.

Unskilled researchers can unintentionally plagiarize if they're not careful. Here are some suggestions for collecting data that might prevent an embarrassing moment for you.

- **Take excellent notes.** When you find a good data source, write complete notes on cards or separate sheets of paper. Mark the author's ideas and words carefully. Put your own remarks in parentheses or use a different color. Be sure you distinguish your notes and ideas from the author's.
- **Know what should be documented.** Information that is common knowledge requires no documentation. For example, the statement *The Wall Street Journal is a popular business newspaper* would require no footnote or documentation. Statements that are not common knowledge, however, must be documented. For example, *The Wall Street Journal is the largest daily newspaper in the United States* would require a footnote because most people do not know this fact. Also use footnotes to document direct quotations and ideas that you summarize or paraphrase in your own words. Moreover, cite sources for proprietary information such as statistics organized and reported by a newspaper or magazine.
- **Use quotations sparingly.** Wise writers and speakers use direct quotations to (1) provide objective background data and establish the severity of a problem as seen by experts, (2) repeat identical phrasing because of its precision, clarity, or aptness, or (3) duplicate exact wording before criticizing. Avoid the tendency of untrained report writers to overuse quotations. Documents that contain pages of spliced-together quotations carry a hidden message: that these writers have few ideas of their own.
- **Introduce quotations.** When you must use a long quotation, try to summarize and introduce it in your own words. Readers want to know the gist of a quotation before they tackle it. For example, to introduce a quotation discussing the shrinking staffs of large companies, you could precede it with your words: *In predicting employment trends, Charles Waller believes the corporation of the future will depend on a small core of full-time employees.*
- **Cite quotations and sources properly.** Use quotation marks to enclose exact quotations, such as this: "The current image," says Charles Waller, "of a big glass-and-steel corporate headquarters on landscaped grounds directing a worldwide army of tens of thousands of employees may soon be a thing of the past." Select a documentation format, such as superscripts or parenthetic notes, and use it consistently.

Career Track Application

Examine two or more research articles from a professional journal in your career field. How do the writers cite references? Are many quotations used? How are they introduced?

Parenthetic notes/Works cited. The parenthetic method identifies a data source in parentheses close to the textual reference. This identification usually includes the author's name and page cited. If no author is known, a shortened version of the source title is enclosed. At the end of the report appears "Works Cited," an alphabetical list of all references. In many ways this method, recommended by the Modern Language Association (MLA), is more efficient than footnotes or endnotes because only one total list is made. For more instruction on documenting sources, see Appendix C.

FIGURE 11.9 ● Three Reference and Bibliography Formats

Tips for Footnotes

- Use footnotes to place complete references at the bottom of each report page.
- Place a superscript (raised) number at the end of a sentence citing a reference.
- Type the complete reference (author's name, title of publication, date, page) at the bottom of the page where the reference is cited.
- Number footnotes consecutively throughout.
- Separate footnotes from text with a 1½-inch line. Leave one blank line above and below separating line.
- Supply a list of all references, called "BIBLIOGRAPHY," at end of report.

Format 1: Footnotes, Bibliography

Peanut butter was first delivered to the world by a St. Louis physician in 1890, possibly as a protein substitute for elderly patients.[1] However, it was the 1905 Universal Exposition in St. Louis that truly launched peanut butter. Since then, annual peanut butter consumption has zoomed to 3.3 pounds a person in the U.S.[2] America's farmers produce 1.6 million tons of peanuts annually, about half of which is used for oil, nuts, and candy. Lisa Gibbons, executive secretary of the Peanut Advisory Board, says that "peanuts in some form are in four of the top ten candies: Snickers, Reese's Peanut Butter Cups, Peanut M & Ms, and Butterfingers."[3]

---

[1]George T. Rivers and Alison Stuart, Facts at Your Fingertips (Boston: Addison Huntly Publishing Company, 1992), 104.

[2]Elizabeth Ruth Barrons, "USA Goes Completely Nutty Over Peanuts," USA Today, 15 January 1993, C1.

[3]Mark Allen Meadows, "Peanut Crop Is Anything but Peanuts at Home and Overseas," Business Week, 30 September 1994, 31-34.

Tips for Bibliographies

- Make the bibliography the last page of a report.
- Center the heading in all capitals 2 inches from the top of the page.
- Include all the references cited in the report and, optionally, all references consulted in your research.
- Arrange items alphabetically by authors' last names or by the first entry of the reference.
- Single-space within and double-space between references.
- Indent the second and succeeding lines of references.

BIBLIOGRAPHY

Barrons, Elizabeth Ruth. "USA Goes Completely Nutty Over Peanuts." USA Today, 15 January 1993, C1.

Meadows, Mark Allen. "Peanut Crop Is Anything but Peanuts at Home and Overseas." Business Week, 30 September 1994, 31-34.

Rivers, George T., and Alison Stuart. Facts at Your Fingertips (Boston: Addison Huntly Publishing Company, 1992).

Tips for Endnotes

- Place superscript figures in the text after each reference. Do not include the source data on the page where the reference is cited.
- Place the source data for each reference on the last page of the report.
- Entitle the complete list "ENDNOTES" or "NOTES."
- Arrange the source references in the order cited in the report.
- Begin with the author's first name and follow the same format as for footnotes.

Format 2: Endnotes, Works Cited

Peanut butter was first delivered to the world by a St. Louis physician in 1890, possibly as a protein substitute for elderly patients.[1] However, it was the 1905 Universal Exposition in St. Louis that truly launched peanut butter. Since then, annual peanut butter consumption has zoomed to 3.3 pounds a person in the U.S.[2] America's farmers produce 1.6 million tons of peanuts annually, about half of which is used for oil, nuts, and candy. Lisa Gibbons, executive secretary of the Peanut Advisory Board, says that "peanuts in some form are in four of the top ten candies: Snickers, Reese's Peanut Butter Cups, Peanut M & Ms, and Butterfingers."[3]

NOTES

1. George T. Rivers and Alison Stuart, Facts at Your Fingertips (Boston: Addison Huntly Publishing Company, 1992), 104.

2. Elizabeth Ruth Barrons, "USA Goes Completely Nutty Over Peanuts," USA Today, 15 January 1993, C1.

3. Mark Allen Meadows, "Peanut Crop Is Anything but Peanuts at Home and Overseas," Contemporary Agriculture, 30 September 1994, 31-34.

Tips for Parenthetic Notes and Works Cited*

- Before writing, compile a list ot all works to be cited in a report.
- During writing, document each textual reference with a short source description in parentheses.
- Include the last name of the author(s) and the page number cited. Omit a comma, as (Jones 44).
- If no author is known, refer to the title or a shortened version of it, as (Facts at Fingertips 104).
- At the end of the report, present the complete "WORKS CITED" arranged alphabetically. For more information see Appendix C.

Format 3: Parenthetic Notes, Works Cited (MLA Referencing Style)

Peanut butter was first delivered to the world by a St. Louis physician in 1890, possibly as a protein substitute for elderly patients (Rivers and Stuart 104). However, it was the 1905 Universal Exposition in St. Louis that truly launched peanut butter. Since then, annual peanut butter consumption has zoomed to 3.3 pounds a person in the U.S. (Barrons C1). America's farmers produce 1.6 million tons of peanuts annually, about half of which is used for oil, nuts, and candy. Lisa Gibbons, executive secretary of the Peanut Advisory Board, says that "peanuts in some form are in four of the top ten candies: Snickers, Reese's Peanut Butter Cups, Peanut M & Ms, and Butterfingers" (Meadows 32).

WORKS CITED

Barrons, Elizabeth Ruth. "USA Goes Completely Nutty Over Peanuts." USA Today, 16 January 1993: C1.

Meadows, Mark Allen. "Peanut Crop is Anything but Peanuts at Home and Overseas." Business Week, 30 September 1994: 31–34.

Rivers, George T., and Alison Stuart. Facts at Your Fingertips. Boston: Addison Huntly, 1992.

*Referencing style recommended by the Modern Language Association.

c. A recommendation report from a technical specialist to the vice president, Product Development, analyzing ways to prevent piracy of the software company's latest game program. The vice president values straight talk and is familiar with the project.

11.4 Problem and Purpose Statements

The following situations require reports. For each situation write (a) a concise problem question and (b) a simple statement of purpose.

RAND: Career Track Profile

"Regardless of the topic, all good researchers share the same goals: collecting objective data and communicating that data effectively to people who make decisions."

Theodore Downes-Le Guin sits at his desk at RAND in Santa Monica, California, just footsteps from one of the world's most famous beaches. Far from the delights of sand and surf, though, his thoughts are fixed on data he's just collected from a survey of physicians sponsored by the American Medical Association. Theo is operations manager of a research group within RAND, probably the best-known think tank in the country. As a private nonprofit research organization, RAND studies issues affecting national security and public welfare. Its huge staff of researchers works on projects funded by federal, state, and local governments, as well as by foundations and private sector contributions. Because of its prominent reputation, RAND is one of the most-quoted organizations in the news, supplying many experts and "talking heads" for television interviews and news shows.

Theo works on a variety of projects with far-ranging topics but similar goals. For one recent study he collected information to guide government policies supporting AIDS prevention. For another project his group examined public reactions to terrorism, so that decision-makers could better frame and manage policies in this area. Says Theo, "Regardless of the topic, all good researchers share the same goals: collecting objective data and communicating that data effectively to people who make decisions.

"When I start a project," he remarks, "I always try to reduce the purpose of the project to two or three key research questions that need to be answered. This usually means talking with clients and getting them to articulate what they want. People tend to have multiple goals. They give me their 'wish lists,' and then we try to prioritize their wants. My job is to get them to separate what they *need* to know from what they *would like* to know."

After Theo collects the necessary data, he begins the process of interpretation. "You go into analysis with a hypothesis. Good research is driven by an idea about what the data will tell you. You don't just dredge through data indiscriminately. For example, in the terrorism project, we hypothesized that people who were more politically conservative would favor military options in dealing with terrorism." In a market research project, business communicators might hypothesize that people with more education would choose to watch certain TV programs or read certain magazines.

Once the researchers have collected data, they look to see if their hypotheses check out. "Any set of data," observes Theo, "will be packed with possible findings and relationships,

tour operators. You wonder if Magic Mountain in Valencia would also be willing to cooperate with the proposed school. And you remember that Griffith Park is nearby and might make a good tour training spot. Before JAL will settle on Burbank as its choice, it wants to know if access to air travel is adequate. It's also concerned about available school building space. Moreover, JAL wants to know whether city officials in Burbank would be receptive to this tour training school proposal.

encouraging bicycle and moped use, and reducing the number of spaces for visitors. Discuss these solutions and add at least three other possibilities. Then prepare a questionnaire to be distributed on campus. If possible, pilot test the questionnaire before submitting it to your instructor. Be sure to consider how the results will be tabulated and interpreted.

some not applicable to what you want to learn. That's why it's crucial to have a limited set of questions you want to answer. Don't broaden the research so much that every relationship looks interesting." As he points out, keeping the key research questions in mind helps the researcher distinguish the relevant from the irrelevant. It also helps spotlight major points for conclusions.

Shepherding first graders on a field trip requires the attention of both a teacher and a parent volunteer. Such field trip enrichment activities are encouraged in decentralized schools with involved parents. In one of its many studies, RAND, a nonprofit research institution, examined the success of decentralized, site-managed public schools. RAND researchers collected data from urban and suburban schools across the nation. One significant conclusion appearing in RAND's final report indicated that the most successful decentralization programs included considerable parental choice and involvement.

"Moving from the data to the conclusions should not be a big jump," Theo cautions. "Good reports do not leap from findings to 'off-the-wall' conclusions. Although conclusions may be dramatic, they must be founded in the data." In many instances Theo tries to interweave conclusions with his discussion of the findings. "Instead of presenting bare statistics (such as '34 percent of the respondents said that . . .'), I try to offer insights as well. So that readers know I'm making inferences, I use phrases like 'The data suggest that . . .' or 'these data may imply that. . . .' Such warning phrases announce my judgments and allow me to explain what I think is happening."

How much interpreting should be done in a report? "Most people who commission research want more than just the facts," reasons Theo. "What they ultimately expect in a report is for the writer to bring some judgment to bear in drawing conclusions. But they don't want the researcher's personal agenda. They expect objectivity."

To prevent the influence of personal biases, Theo periodically plays devil's advocate, looking at both sides of issues. He also submits his work to peer review, a procedure in which colleagues evaluate report drafts to ensure quality and objectivity. "Peer review is not built into many organizations," he notes. "In some businesses, it's almost a matter of pride to work alone. But, frankly, such isolation is dangerous. All reports benefit from review by someone else, however informal."

In addition to objectivity, report readers seek simplicity and conciseness. "In this information-laden society," Theo observes, "executive summaries are critical. People want the full report as a backup, but they prefer to approach a research question through a summary of the findings. A lot of people won't read a report that's longer than one page."

To novice report writers, Theo offers three specific pointers, gleaned from his experience: (1) find out what's important to the audience by clarifying the purpose of the report; (2) select a few important questions to answer so that you don't overdose on data and get lost in trivia; and (3) get someone with objectivity or distance to review your writing.[1]

Interpreting Data

Interpreting data means sorting, analyzing, combining, and recombining to yield meaningful information.

After collecting information for a report, you must make sense out of it. For informational reports you may organize the facts into a logical sequence, illustrate them, and present a final report. For analytical reports, though, the process is more complex. You'll also interpret the data, draw conclusions, and, if asked, make recommendations.

The data you've collected probably face you in a jumble of note cards, copies of articles, interview notes, questionnaire results, and statistics. You might feel like a contractor who allowed suppliers to dump all the building materials for a new house in a monstrous pile.[2] Like the contractor you must sort the jumble of raw material into meaningful, usable groups. Unprocessed data becomes meaningful information through sorting, analysis, combination, and recombination. You'll be examining each item to see what it means by itself and what it means when connected with other data. You're looking for meanings, relationships, and answers to the research questions posed in your work plan.

Tabulating and Analyzing Responses

Numerical data must be tabulated and analyzed statistically to bring order out of chaos.

If you've collected considerable numerical and other information, you must tabulate and analyze it. Fortunately, several tabulating and statistical techniques can help you create order from the chaos. These techniques simplify, summarize, and classify large amounts of data into meaningful terms. From the condensed data you're more likely to be able to draw valid conclusions and make reasoned recommendations.

Tables permit easy comprehension of quantitative information as well as informed conclusions.

Tables. Numerical data from questionnaires or interviews are usually summarized and simplified in tables. Using systematic columns and rows, tables make quantitative information easier to comprehend. After assembling your data, you'll want to prepare preliminary tables to enable you to see what the information means. Here is a table summarizing the response to one question from a campus survey about student parking:

Question: Should student fees be increased to build parking lots?

	Number	**Percent**	
Strongly agree	76	11.5	*(To simplify the table, combine these items.)*
Agree	255	38.5	
No opinion	22	3.3	
Disagree	107	16.1	*(To simplify the table, combine these items.)*
Strongly disagree	203	30.6	
Total	**663**	**100.0**	

Notice that this preliminary table includes both a total number of responses and a percentage for each response. (To calculate a percentage, divide the figure for each response by the total number of responses.) To simplify the data and provide a broad overview, you can join categories. For example, combining "strongly agree" (11.5 percent) and "agree" (38.5 percent) reveals that 50 percent of the respondents supported the proposal to finance new parking lots with increased student fees.

Analyzing, interpreting, and discussing the responses to a survey are much easier after the raw data have been converted into tables and graphs. Computer software simplifies the task. Once data are arranged logically, researchers are better able to draw valid conclusions and make rational recommendations.

Sometimes data become more meaningful when *cross-tabulated.* This process allows analysis of two or more variables together. By breaking down our student survey data into male/female responses, shown in the following table, we make an interesting discovery.

Cross-tabulating allows the analysis of two or more variables together.

Question: Should student fees be increased to build parking lots?

	Total		Male		Female	
	Number	**Percent**	**Number**	**Percent**	**Number**	**Percent**
Strongly agree	76	11.5	8	2.2	68	22.0
Agree	255	38.5	54	15.3	201	65.0
No opinion	22	3.3	12	3.4	10	3.2
Disagree	107	16.1	89	25.1	18	5.8
Strongly disagree	203	30.6	191	54.0	12	4.0
Total	**663**	**100.0**	**354**	**100.0**	**309**	**100.0**

Although 50 percent of all student respondents supported the proposal, among females the approval rating was much stronger. Notice that 87 percent of female respondents (combining 22 percent "strongly agree" and 65 percent "agree") endorsed the proposal to increase fees for new parking lots. But among male students, *only 17 percent agreed with the proposal.* You naturally wonder why such a disparity exists. Are female students more unhappy than males with the current parking situation? If so, why? Is safety a reason? Are male students more concerned with increased fees than females? By cross-tabulating the findings, you sometimes uncover data that may help answer your problem question or that may prompt you to explore other possibilities. Don't, however, undertake cross-tabulation unless it serves more than mere curiosity.

Tables also help you compare multiple data collected from questionnaires and surveys. Figure 12.1 shows, in raw form, responses to several survey items. To convert these data into a more usable form, you need to calculate percentages for each item. Then you can arrange the responses in some rational sequence, such as largest percentage to smallest.

FIGURE 12.1 ● Converting Survey Data Into Finished Tables

Tips for Converting Raw Data

- Tabulate the responses on a copy of the survey form.
- Calculate percentages (divide the score for an item by the total for all responses to that item; for example, for Item 1, divide 331 by 663).
- Round off figures to one decimal point or to whole numbers.
- Arrange items in a logical order, such as largest to smallest percentage.
- Prepare a table with a title that tells such things as who, what, when, where, and why.
- Include the total number of respondents.

Raw Data from Survey Item

INDICATE YOUR FEELINGS TOWARD THE FOLLOWING PROPOSED SOLUTIONS TO THE STUDENT PARKING PROBLEM ON CAMPUS.

	Agree	No opinion	Disagree
1. Increase student fees to build parking lots	331	22	310
2. Limit student parking to satellite lots, providing shuttle buses to campus	52	31	580
3. Offer incentives to use public transportation	111	29	523
4. Restrict visitor parking	612	15	36

Shows raw figures from which percentages are calculated

Finished Table

REACTIONS OF MIDLAND COLLEGE STUDENTS TO FOUR PROPOSED SOLUTIONS TO CAMPUS PARKING PROBLEM*
Spring, 1994
N = 663 students

	Agree	No opinion	Disagree
Restrict visitor parking	92.3%	2.3%	5.4%
Increase student fees to build parking lots	49.9	3.3	46.8
Offer incentives to use public transportation	16.7	4.4	78.9
Limit student parking to satellite lots, providing shuttle buses to campus	7.8	4.7	87.5

*Figures may not equal 100 percent because of rounding.

Orders items from highest to lowest "Agree" percentages

Uses percent sign only at beginning of column

Avoids cluttering the table with total figures

Once the data are displayed in a table, you can more easily draw conclusions. As Figure 12.1 shows, Midland College students apparently are not interested in public transportation or shuttle buses from satellite lots. They want to park on campus, with restricted visitor parking; and only half are willing to pay for new parking lots.

● **Three statistical concepts—mean, median, and mode—help you describe data.**

The three Ms: mean, median, mode. Tables help you organize data, and the three Ms help you describe it. These statistical terms—mean, median, and mode—are all occasionally used loosely to mean "average." To be safe, though, you should learn to apply these statistical terms precisely.

When people say *average,* they usually intend to indicate the *mean,* or arithmetic average. Let's say that you're studying the estimated starting salaries of graduates from different disciplines, as shown here:

Education	$24,000	
Sociology	25,000	
Humanities	27,000	
Biology	30,000	
Health sciences	31,000	Median (middle point in continuum)
Engineering	33,000	Mode (figure occurring most frequently)
Business	33,000	
Law	35,000	Mean (arithmetic average)
Medicine	77,000	

To find the mean, you simply add up all the salaries and divide by the total number of items ($315,000 ÷ 9 = $35,000). Thus, the mean salary is $35,000. Means are very useful to indicate central tendencies of figures, but they have one major flaw: extremes at either end cause distortion. Notice that the $77,000 figure makes the mean salary of $35,000 deceptively high. It does not represent a valid average for the group. Because means can be misleading, you should use them only when extreme figures do not distort the result.

The *median* represents the midpoint in a group of figures arranged from lowest to highest (or vice versa). In our list of salaries, the median is $31,000 (health sciences). In other words, half the salaries are above this point and half are below it. The median is useful when extreme figures may warp the mean. Whereas salaries for medicine distort the mean, the median, at $31,000, is still a representative figure.

The *mode* is simply the value that occurs most frequently. In our list $33,000 (for engineering and business) represents the mode since it occurs twice. The mode has the advantage of being easily determined—just a quick glance at a list of arranged values reveals it. Although mode is infrequently used by researchers, knowing the mode is useful in some situations. Let's say 7-Eleven sampled its customers to determine what drink size they preferred: 12-ounce, 16-ounce, or Big-Gulp 24-ounce. Finding the mode—the most frequently named figure—makes more sense than calculating the median, which might yield a size that 7-Eleven doesn't even offer. (To remember the meaning of *mode,* think about fashion; the most frequent response, the mode, is the most fashionable.)

The mean is the arithmetic average; the median is the midpoint in a group of figures; the mode is the most frequently occurring figure.

Mean, median, and mode figures are especially helpful when the range of values is also known. *Range* represents the span between the highest and lowest values. To calculate the range, you simply subtract the lowest figure from the highest. In starting salaries for graduates, the range is $53,000 (77,000 − 24,000). Knowing the range enables readers to put mean and median figures into perspective. This knowledge also prompts researchers to wonder why such a range exists, thus stimulating hunches and further investigation to solve problems.

Correlations. In tabulating and analyzing data, you may see relationships among two or more variables that help explain the findings. If your data for graduates' starting salaries also included years of schooling, you would doubtless notice that graduates with more years of education received higher salaries. For example, beginning teachers, with four years of schooling, earn less than beginning physicians, who have completed nine or more years of education. Thus, a correlation may exist between years of education and starting salary.

Correlations between variables suggest possible relationships that will explain research findings.

Intuition suggests correlations that may or may not prove to be accurate. Is there a relationship between studying and good grades? Between new office computers and increased productivity? Between the rise and fall of hemlines and the rise and fall of the stock market (as some newspaper writers have suggested)? If a

FIGURE 12.2 ● Grid to Analyze Complex Verbal Data With Multiple Factors

	Point 1	Point 2	Point 3	Point 4	Overall Reaction
Vice President 1	Disapproves. "Too little, too late."	Strong support. "Best of all points."	Mixed opinion. "Must wait and see market."	Indifferent.	Optimistic, but "hates to delay expansion for 6 months."
Vice President 2	Disapproves. "Creates credit trap."	Approves.	Strong disapproval.	Approves. "Must improve receivable collections."	Mixed support. "Good self-defense plan."
Vice President 3	Strong disapproval.	Approves. "Key to entire plan."	Indifferent.	Approves, but with "caveats."	"Will work only with sale of unproductive fixed assets."
Vice President 4	Disapproves. "Too risky now."	Strong support. "Start immediately."	Approves, "but may damage image."	Approves. "Benefits far outweigh costs."	Supports plan. Suggests focus on Pacific Rim markets.

correlation seems to exist, can we say that one event *caused* the other? Does studying cause good grades? Does more schooling guarantee increased salary? Although one event may not be said to *cause* another, the business researcher who sees a correlation begins to ask why and how the two variables are related. In this way, apparent correlations stimulate investigation and present possible problem solutions to be explored.

In reporting correlations, you should avoid suggesting that a cause-and-effect relationship exists when none can be proved. Only sophisticated research methods can statistically *prove* correlations. Instead, present a correlation as a *possible* relationship (*The data suggest that beginning salaries are related to years of education*). As Theo Downes-Le Guin pointed out, cautious statements followed by explanations gain you credibility and allow readers to make their own decisions.

● **Grids permit analysis of raw verbal data by grouping and classifying.**

Grids. Another technique for analyzing raw data—especially verbal data—is the grid. Let's say you've been asked by the CEO to collect opinions from all vice presidents about the CEO's four-point plan to build cash reserves. The grid shown in Figure 12.2 enables you to summarize the vice presidents' reactions to each point. Notice how this complex verbal information is transformed into concise, manageable data; readers can see immediately which points are supported and opposed. Imagine how long you could have struggled to comprehend the meaning of this verbal information before plotting it on a grid.

Arranging data in a grid also works for projects like feasibility studies that compare many variables. Assume you must recommend a new printer to your manager. To see how four models compare, you could lay out a grid with the names of printer models across the top. Down the left side, you would list such significant variables as price, warranty, service, capacity, compatibility, and specifications. As you fill in the variables for each model, you can see quickly which model has the lowest price, longest warranty, and so forth. *Consumer Reports* often uses grids to show information.

In addition, grids help classify employment data. For example, suppose your boss asked you to recommend one individual from among many job candidates. You could arrange a grid with names across the top and distinguishing characteristics—experience, skills, education, and other employment interests—down the left side. When you had summarized each candidate's points, you'd have a helpful tool for drawing conclusions and writing a report.

Drawing Conclusions in Reports

The most widely read portions of a report are the sections devoted to conclusions and recommendations. Knowledgeable readers go straight to the conclusions to see what the report writer thinks the data mean. Because conclusions summarize and explain the findings, they represent the heart of a report. Your value in an organization rises considerably if you can draw conclusions that analyze information logically and show how the data answer questions and solve problems.

As Theo Downes-Le Guin at RAND noted, any set of data can produce a variety of conclusions. Always bear in mind, though, that the audience for a report wants to know how these data relate to the problem being studied. What do the findings mean in terms of solving the original report problem?

For example, the Marriott Corporation recognized a serious problem among its employees. Conflicting home and work requirements seemed to be causing excessive employee turnover and decreased productivity. To learn the extent of the problem and to consider solutions, Marriott surveyed its staff.[3] It learned, among other things, that nearly 35 percent of its employees had children under age 12, and 15 percent had children under age 5. Other findings, shown in Figure 12.3, indicated that one third of its staff with young children took time off because of child-care difficulties. Moreover, many current employees left previous jobs because of work and family conflicts. The survey also showed that managers did not consider child-care or family problems to be appropriate topics for discussion at work.

A sample of possible conclusions that could be drawn from these findings is shown in Figure 12.3. Notice that each conclusion relates to the initial report problem. Although only a few possible findings and conclusions are shown here, you can see that the conclusions try to explain the causes for the home/work conflict among employees. Many report writers would expand the conclusion section by explaining each item and citing supporting evidence. Even for simplified conclusions, such as those shown in Figure 12.3, you will want to number each item separately and use parallel construction (balanced sentence structure).

Although your goal is to remain objective, drawing conclusions naturally involves a degree of subjectivity. Your goals, background, and frame of reference all color the inferences you make. When Federal Express, for example, tried to expand its next-day delivery service to Europe, it racked up a staggering loss of $1.2 billion in four years of operation.[4] The facts could not be disputed. But what conclusions could be drawn? The CEO might conclude that the competition is greater than anticipated but that FedEx is making inroads; patience is all that is needed. The board of directors and stockholders, however, might conclude that the competition is too well entrenched and that it's time to pull the plug on an ill-fated operation. Findings will be interpreted from the writer's perspective, but they should not be manipulated to achieve a preconceived purpose.

SPOTLIGHT ON COMMUNICATORS

Corporate turnaround artist Mark R. Goldston recommends assesssing a company's potential by analyzing its strengths against the competition. In helping the sluggish Fabergé USA bounce back to record profitability, he drew up a matrix grid. Horizontally he plotted Fabergé's production capabilities, and vertically he listed potential products. His grid, or "opportunity map," enabled managers to draw conclusions and recommend successful new products.

● **Effective report conclusions are objective and bias-free.**

FIGURE 12.3 ● Report Conclusions and Recommendations

Tips for Writing Conclusions

- Interpret and summarize the findings; tell what they mean.
- Relate the conclusions to the report problem.
- Limit the conclusions to the data presented; do not introduce new material.
- Number the conclusions and present them in parallel form.
- Be objective; avoid exaggerating or manipulating the data.
- Use consistent criteria in evaluating options.

REPORT PROBLEM

Marriott Corporation experienced employee turnover and lowered productivity resulting from conflicting home and work requirements. The hotel conducted a massive survey resulting in some of the following findings.

PARTIAL FINDINGS

Condenses significant findings in numbered statements

1. Nearly 35 percent of employees surveyed have children under age twelve.
2. Nearly 15 percent of employees have children under age five.
3. The average employee with children younger than twelve is absent four days a year and tardy five days because of child-related issues.
4. Within a one-year period, nearly 33 percent of employees who have young children take at least two days off because they can't find a replacement when their child-care plans break down.
5. Nearly 20 percent of employees left a previous employer because of work and family concerns.
6. At least 80 percent of female employees and 78 percent of male employees with young children reported job stress as a result of conflicting work and family roles.
7. Managers perceive family matters to be inappropriate issues for them to discuss at work.

From these and other findings, the following conclusions were drawn.

CONCLUSIONS

Uses conclusion to present sensible analysis without exaggerating or manipulating data

Explains what findings mean in terms of report problem

1. Home and family responsibilities directly affect job attendance and performance.
2. Time is the crucial issue to balancing work and family issues.
3. Male and female employees reported in nearly equal numbers the difficulties of managing work and family roles.
4. Problems with child-care arrangements increase the employees' level of stress and limit ability to work certain schedules or overtime.
5. A manager supportive of family and personal concerns is central to a good work environment.

You can make your report conclusions more objective if you use consistent evaluation criteria. Let's say you are comparing computers for an office equipment purchase. If you evaluate each by the same criteria (such as price, specifications, service, and warranty), your conclusions are more likely to be bias-free.

You also need to avoid the temptation to sensationalize or exaggerate your

Tips for Writing Recommendations

- Make specific suggestions for actions to solve the report problem.
- Prepare practical recommendations that will be agreeable to the audience.
- Avoid conditional words like *maybe* and *perhaps*.
- Present each suggestion separately as a command beginning with a verb.
- Number the recommendations for improved readability.
- If requested, describe how the recommendations may be implemented.

RECOMMENDATIONS

1. Develop a child-care resource program to provide parents with professional help in locating affordable child care.
2. Offer a child-care discount program to help parents pay for services.
3. Authorize weekly payroll deductions, using tax-free dollars, to pay for child care.
4. Publish a quarterly employee newsletter devoted to family and child-care issues.
5. Institute a flextime policy that allows employees to adapt their work schedules to home responsibilities.
6. Investigate opening a pilot child development center for preschool children of employees at company headquarters.
7. Provide managers with training in working with personal and family matters.

Tells what actions can solve problems and may include specific ideas for executing recommendations

findings or conclusions. Be careful of words like *many, most,* and *all.* Instead of *many of the respondents felt . . . ,* you might more accurately write *some of the respondents . . .* Examine your motives before drawing conclusions. Don't let preconceptions or wishful thinking color your reasoning.

Writing Report Recommendations

Recommendations, unlike conclusions, make specific suggestions for actions that can solve the report problem. Consider the following examples:

Effective recommendations offer specific suggestions on how to solve a problem.

Conclusion

Our investments are losing value because the stock market continues its decline. The bond market shows strength.

Recommendation

Withdraw at least half of our investment in stocks, and invest it in bonds.

Conclusion

The cost of constructing multilevel parking structures for student on-campus parking is prohibitive.

Recommendation

Explore the possibility of satellite parking lots with frequent shuttle buses to campus.

SPOTLIGHT ON COMMUNICATORS

Outdoorsman, attorney, former state assemblyman, and current president of the National Audubon Society, Peter A. A. Berle turned a nearly insolvent organization into a powerful activist environmental lobby. Among the Audubon Society's greatest successes have been campaigns against acid rain and the loss of ancient forests. Peter Berle encourages broad-based research, collecting vital raw data from citizen scientists. But all the data collected are useless until organized logically and communicated meaningfully to decision-makers in Washington.

Notice that the conclusions explain what the problem is, while the recommendations tell how to solve it. Typically, readers prefer specific recommendations. They want to know exactly how to implement the suggestions. In addition to recommending satellite parking lots for campus parking, for example, the writer could have discussed sites for possible satellite lots and the cost of running shuttle buses.

The specificity of your recommendations depends on your authorization. What are you commissioned to do, and what does the reader expect? In the planning stages of your report project, you anticipate what the reader wants in the report. Your intuition and your knowledge of the audience indicate how far your recommendations should be developed.

In the recommendations section of the Marriott employee survey, shown in Figure 12.3, many of the suggestions are summarized. In the actual report each recommendation could have been backed up with specifics and ideas for implementing them. For example, the child-care resource recommendation would be explained: it provides parents with names of agencies and professionals who specialize in locating child care across the country.

A good report provides practical recommendations that are agreeable to the audience. In the Marriott survey, for example, report researchers knew that the company wanted to help employees cope with conflicts between family and work obligations. Thus, the report's conclusions and recommendations focused on ways to resolve the conflict. If the goal of Marriott had been merely to reduce employee absenteeism and save money, the recommendations could have been quite different.

If possible, make each recommendation a command. Note in Figure 12.3 that each recommendation begins with a verb. This structure sounds forceful and confident and helps the reader comprehend the information quickly. Avoid words like *maybe* and *perhaps;* they suggest conditional statements that reduce the strength of recommendations.

Experienced writers may combine recommendations and conclusions. And in short reports writers may omit conclusions and move straight to recommendations. The important thing about recommendations, though, is that they include practical suggestions for solving the report problem.

Organizing Data

The direct pattern is appropriate for informed or receptive readers; the indirect pattern is appropriate when educating or persuading.

After collecting sets of data, interpreting them, and drawing conclusions, you're ready to organize the parts of the report into a logical framework. Poorly organized reports lead to frustration. Readers will not understand, remember, or be persuaded. Wise writers know that reports rarely "just organize themselves." Instead, organization must be imposed on the data.

Informational reports typically are organized in three parts, as shown in Figure 12.4. Analytical reports typically contain four parts and may be organized directly or indirectly. For readers who know about the project, are supportive, or are eager to learn the results quickly, the direct method is appropriate. Conclusions—and recommendations, if requested—appear up front. For readers who must be educated or persuaded, the indirect method works better. Conclusions/recommendations appear last, after the findings have been presented and analyzed.

Although every report is different (you'll learn specifics for organizing informal and formal reports in Chapters 13 and 14), the overall organizational patterns described here typically hold true. The real challenge, though, lies in (1) organizing the facts/findings and discussion/analysis sections and (2) providing reader cues.

FIGURE 12.4 ● Organizing Informational and Analytical Reports

Informational Reports	Analytical Reports: Direct Pattern	Analytical Reports: Indirect Pattern
I. Introduction/background	I. Introduction/problem	I. Introduction/problem
II. Facts/findings	II. Conclusions/recommendations	II. Facts/findings
III. Summary/conclusion	III. Facts/findings	III. Discussion/analysis
	IV. Discussion/analysis	IV. Conclusions/recommendations

Ordering Information Logically

Whether you're writing informational or analytical reports, the data you've collected must be structured coherently. Five common organizational methods are by time, component, importance, criteria, or convention. Regardless of the method you choose, be sure that it helps the reader understand the data. Reader comprehension, not writer convenience, should govern organization.

● **Organization by time, component, importance, criteria, or convention helps readers comprehend data.**

Time. Ordering data by time means establishing a chronology of events. Agendas, minutes of meetings, progress reports, and procedures are usually organized by time. For example, a report describing an eight-week training program would most likely be organized by weeks. A plan for step-by-step improvement of customer service would be organized by each step. A monthly trip report submitted by a sales rep might describe customers visited Week 1, Week 2, and so on. Beware of overusing time chronologies, however. Although this method is easy and often mirrors the way data are collected, chronologies—like the sales rep's trip report—tend to be boring, repetitious, and lacking in emphasis. Readers can't always pick out what's important.

Component. Especially for informational reports, data may be organized by components such as location, geography, division, product, or part. For instance, a report detailing company expansion might divide the plan into West Coast, East Coast, and Midwest expansion. The report could also be organized by divisions: personal products, consumer electronics, and household goods. A report comparing profits among makers of athletic shoes might group the data by company: Reebok, Nike, L.A. Gear, and so forth. Organization by components works best when the classifications already exist.

Importance. Organization by importance involves beginning with the most important item and proceeding to the least important—or vice versa. For example, a report discussing the reasons for declining product sales would present the most important reason first followed by less important ones. The Marriott report describing work/family conflicts might begin by discussing child care, if the writer considered it the most important issue. Using importance to structure findings involves a value judgment. The writer must decide what is most important, always keeping in mind the readers' priorities and expectations. Busy readers appreciate seeing important points first; they may skim or skip other points. On the other

● **Organizing by level of importance saves the time of busy readers and increases the odds that key information will be retained.**

hand, building to a climax by moving from least important to most important enables the writer to focus attention at the end. Thus, the reader is more likely to remember the most important item. Of course, the writer also risks losing the attention of the reader along the way.

To evaluate choices or plans fairly, apply the same criteria to each.

Criteria. Establishing criteria by which to judge helps writers to treat topics consistently. Let's say your report compares health plans A, B, and C. For each plan you examine the same standards: Criterion 1, cost per employee; Criterion 2, amount of deductible; and Criterion 3, patient benefits. The resulting data could then be organized either by plans or by criteria:

By Plan	By Criteria
Plan A	Criterion 1
Criterion 1	Plan A
Criterion 2	Plan B
Criterion 3	Plan C
Plan B	Criterion 2
Criterion 1	Plan A
Criterion 2	Plan B
Criterion 3	Plan C
Plan C	Criterion 3
Criterion 1	Plan A
Criterion 2	Plan B
Criterion 3	Plan C

Although you might favor organizing the data by plans (because that's the way you collected the data), the better way is by criteria. When you discuss patient benefits, for example, you would examine all three plans' benefits together. Organizing a report around criteria helps readers make comparisons, instead of forcing them to search through the report for similar data.

Organizing by convention simplifies the organizational task and yields easy-to-follow information.

Convention. Many operational and recurring reports are structured according to convention. That is, they follow a prescribed plan that everyone understands. For example, an automotive parts manufacturer might ask all sales reps to prepare a weekly report with these headings: *Competitive observations* (competitors' price changes, discounts, new products, product problems, distributor changes, product promotions), *Product problems* (quality, performance, needs), and *Customer service problems* (delivery, mailings, correspondence). Management gets exactly the information it needs in easy-to-read form.

Like operating reports, proposals are often organized conventionally. They might use such groupings as background, problem, proposed solution, staffing, schedule, costs, and authorization. As you might expect, reports following these conventional, prescribed structures greatly simplify the task of organization.

Providing Reader Cues

When you finish organizing a report, you probably see a neat outline in your mind: major points, supported by subpoints and details. However, readers don't know the material as well as you; they cannot see your outline. To guide them through the data, you need to provide the equivalent of a map and road signs. For both formal and informal reports, devices like introductions, transitions, and headings prevent readers from getting lost.

These well-intentioned officials try to give directions to a lost cyclist. Readers of reports sometimes get lost also. To prevent your readers from wandering astray as they travel through your report, include cues like introductions, transitions, and headings.

Introductions. The best way to point a reader in the right direction is to provide an introduction that does three things:

Good openers tell readers what topics will be covered in what order and why.

- Tells the purpose of the report
- Describes the significance of the topic
- Previews the main points and the order in which they will be developed

The following paragraph includes all three elements in introducing a report on computer security:

> The purpose of this report is to examine the security of our current computer operations and present suggestions for improving security. Lax computer security could mean loss of information, loss of business, and damage to our equipment and systems. Because many former employees, released during recent downsizing efforts, know our systems, major changes must be made. To improve security, I will present three recommendations: (1) begin using *smart cards* that limit access to our computer system, (2) alter sign-on and log-off procedures, (3) move central computer operations to a more secure area.

This opener tells the purpose (examining computer security), describes its significance (loss of information and business, damage to equipment and systems), and outlines how the report is organized (three recommendations). Good openers in effect set up a contract with the reader. The writer promises to cover certain topics in a specified order. Readers expect the writer to fulfill the contract. They want the topics to be developed as promised—using the same wording and presented in the order mentioned. For example, if in your introduction you state that you will discuss the use of *smart cards,* don't change the heading for that section to *access cards.* Remember that the introduction provides a map to a report; switching the names on the map will ensure that readers get lost. To maintain consistency, delay writing the introduction until after you have completed the report. Long, complex reports may require introductions for each section.

Transitions. Expressions like *on the contrary, at the same time,* and *however* show relationships and help reveal the logical flow of ideas in a report. These *transitional expressions* enable writers to tell readers where ideas are headed and how they relate. Notice how abrupt the two following sentences sound without a transition: *American car manufacturers admired Toyota's just-in-time inventory practices. Adopting a JIT system [however] means total restructuring of assembly plants.*

Transitional expressions inform readers where ideas are headed and how they relate.

The following expressions (see Figure 4.7 for a complete list) enable you to show readers how you are developing your ideas.

To Present Additional Thoughts: additionally, again, also, moreover, furthermore

To Suggest Cause and Effect: accordingly, as a result, consequently, therefore

To Contrast Ideas: at the same time, but, however, on the contrary, though, yet

To Show Time and Order: after, before, first, finally, now, previously, then, to conclude

To Clarify Points: for example, for instance, in other words, that is, thus

In using these expressions, recognize that they don't have to sit at the head of a sentence. Listen to the rhythm of the sentence, and place the expression where a natural pause occurs. Used appropriately, logic markers serve readers as guides; misused or overused, they can be as distracting and frustrating as too many road signs on a highway.

Good headings provide organizational cues and spotlight key ideas.

Headings. Good headings are another structural cue that assist readers in comprehending the organization of a report. They highlight major ideas, allowing busy readers to see the big picture in a glance. Moreover, headings provide resting points for the mind and for the eye, breaking up large chunks of text into manageable and inviting segments.

Report writers may use functional or talking heads. *Functional heads* (for example, *Background, Findings, Personnel,* and *Production Costs*) describe functions or general topics. They show the outline of a report but provide little insight for readers. Functional headings are useful for routine reports. They're also appropriate for sensitive topics that might provoke emotional reactions. By keeping the headings general, experienced writers hope to minimize reader opposition or response to controversial subjects. *Talking heads* (for example, *Two Sides to Campus Parking Problem* or *Survey Provides Support for Parking Fees)* provide more information and interest. Unless carefully written, however, talking heads can fail to show readers the organization of a report. With some planning, though, headings can be both functional and talking, such as *Parking Recommendations: Shuttle and New Structures.*

Headings should be brief, parallel, and ordered in a logical hierarchy.

To create the most effective headings, follow a few basic guidelines:

- **Use appropriate heading levels.** The position and format of a heading indicate its level of importance and relationship to other points. Figure 12.5 both illustrates and discusses a commonly used heading format for business reports.
- **Balance headings within levels.** All headings at a given level should be grammatically similar. For example, *Developing Quality Circles* and *Presenting Plan to Management* are balanced, but *Development of Quality Circles* is not parallel with *Presenting Plan to Management.*
- **For short reports use first- or second-level headings.** Many business reports contain only one or two levels of headings. For such reports use first-level headings (centered, underlined) and/or second-level headings (flush left, underlined). See Figure 12.5.
- **Include at least one heading per report page.** Headings increase the readability and attractiveness of report pages. Use at least one per page to break up blocks of text.
- **Keep headings short but clear.** One-word headings are emphatic but not always clear. For example, the heading *Budget* does not adequately describe

FIGURE 12.5 ● Levels of Headings in Reports

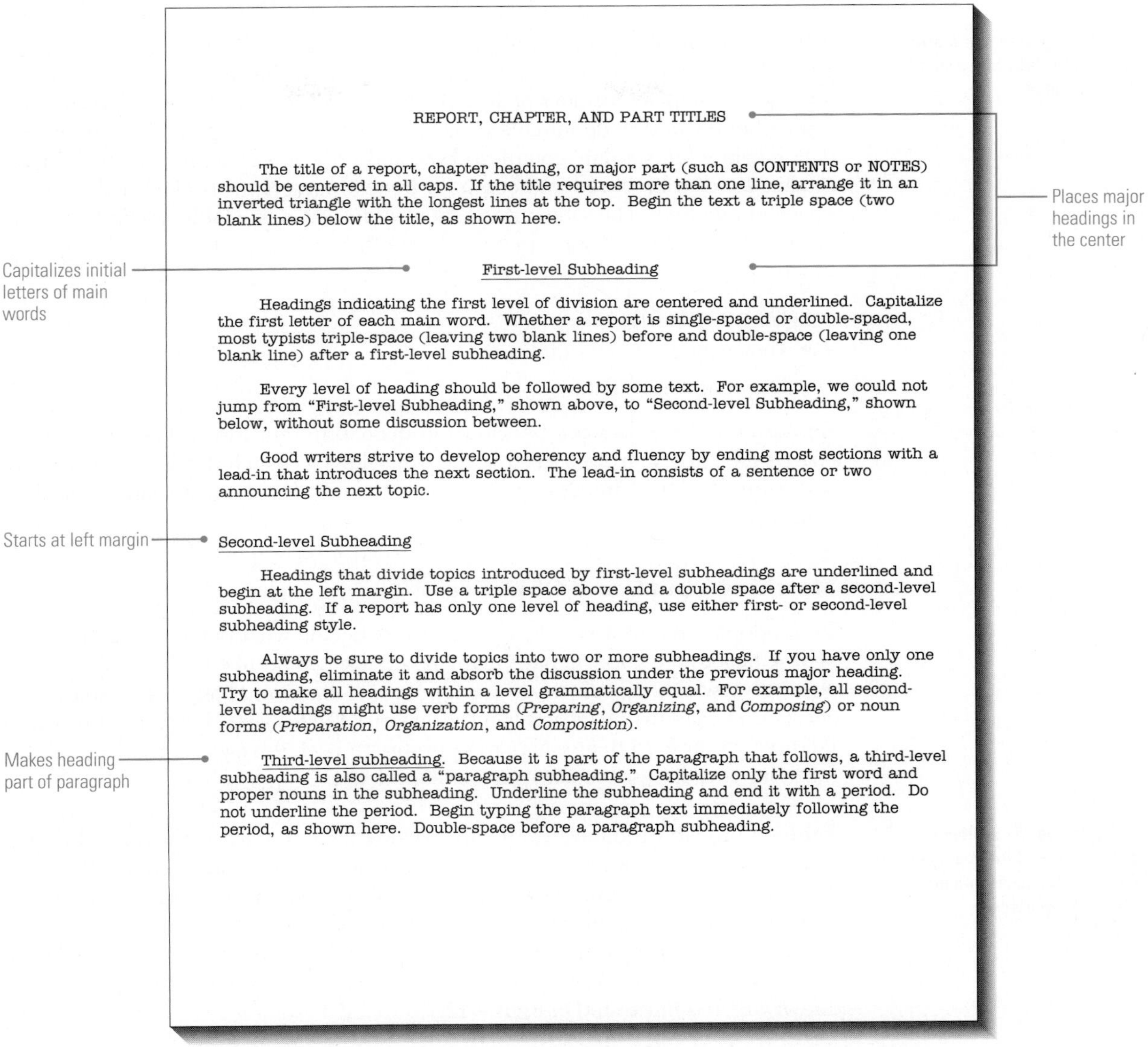

REPORT, CHAPTER, AND PART TITLES

The title of a report, chapter heading, or major part (such as CONTENTS or NOTES) should be centered in all caps. If the title requires more than one line, arrange it in an inverted triangle with the longest lines at the top. Begin the text a triple space (two blank lines) below the title, as shown here.

First-level Subheading

Headings indicating the first level of division are centered and underlined. Capitalize the first letter of each main word. Whether a report is single-spaced or double-spaced, most typists triple-space (leaving two blank lines) before and double-space (leaving one blank line) after a first-level subheading.

Every level of heading should be followed by some text. For example, we could not jump from "First-level Subheading," shown above, to "Second-level Subheading," shown below, without some discussion between.

Good writers strive to develop coherency and fluency by ending most sections with a lead-in that introduces the next section. The lead-in consists of a sentence or two announcing the next topic.

Second-level Subheading

Headings that divide topics introduced by first-level subheadings are underlined and begin at the left margin. Use a triple space above and a double space after a second-level subheading. If a report has only one level of heading, use either first- or second-level subheading style.

Always be sure to divide topics into two or more subheadings. If you have only one subheading, eliminate it and absorb the discussion under the previous major heading. Try to make all headings within a level grammatically equal. For example, all second-level headings might use verb forms (*Preparing*, *Organizing*, and *Composing*) or noun forms (*Preparation*, *Organization*, and *Composition*).

Third-level subheading. Because it is part of the paragraph that follows, a third-level subheading is also called a "paragraph subheading." Capitalize only the first word and proper nouns in the subheading. Underline the subheading and end it with a period. Do not underline the period. Begin typing the paragraph text immediately following the period, as shown here. Double-space before a paragraph subheading.

Places major headings in the center

Capitalizes initial letters of main words

Starts at left margin

Makes heading part of paragraph

figures for a summer project involving student interns for an oil company in Texas. Try to keep your headings brief (no more than eight words), but make sure they are understandable. Experiment with headings that concisely tell who, what, when, where, and why.

- **Integrate headings gracefully.** Try not to repeat the exact wording from the heading in the sentence immediately following. Also avoid using the heading as an antecedent to a pronoun. For example, don't follow the heading *New Office Systems* with *These will be installed . . .*

Illustrating Data

Effective graphics clarify numerical data and simplify complex ideas.

After collecting information and interpreting it, you need to consider how best to present it to your audience. Whether you are delivering your report orally or in writing to company insiders or to outsiders, it will be easier to understand and remember if you include suitable visual aids. Appropriate graphics make numerical data meaningful, simplify complex ideas, and provide visual interest. In contrast, readers tend to be bored and confused by text paragraphs packed with complex data and numbers. The same information summarized in a table or chart becomes clear. Tables, charts, graphs, pictures, and other visuals perform three important functions:

- They clarify data.
- They condense and simplify data.
- They emphasize data.

Because the same data can be shown in many different forms (for example, in a chart, table, or graph), you need to recognize how to match the appropriate visual with your objective. In addition, you need to know how to incorporate visuals in your reports.

Matching Visuals and Objectives

In developing the best visuals, you must first decide what data you want to highlight. Chances are you will have many points you would like to show in a table or chart. But which visuals are most appropriate to your objectives? Tables? Bar charts? Pie charts? Line charts? Surface charts? Flow charts? Organization charts? Pictures? Figure 12.6 summarizes appropriate uses for each type of visual; the following text discusses each visual in more detail.

Tables permit systematic presentation of large amounts of data, while charts enhance visual comparisons.

Tables. Probably the most frequently used visual in reports is the table. Because a table presents quantitative or verbal information in systematic columns and rows, it can clarify large quantities of data in small spaces. You may have made rough tables to help you organize the raw data collected from literature, questionnaires, or interviews. In preparing tables for your readers or listeners, though, you'll need to pay more attention to clarity and emphasis. Here are tips for making good tables, one of which is illustrated in Figure 12.7:

- Provide clear heads for the rows and columns.
- Identify the units in which figures are given (percentages, dollars, units per worker hour, and so forth) in the table title, in the column or row head, with the first item in a column, or in a note at the bottom.
- Arrange items in a logical order (alphabetical, chronological, geographical, highest to lowest) depending on what you need to emphasize.
- Use *N/A* (not available) for missing data.
- Make long tables easier to read by shading alternate lines or by leaving a blank line after groups of five.

FIGURE 12.6 ● Matching Visual Aids to Objectives

Visual Aid		Objective
Table	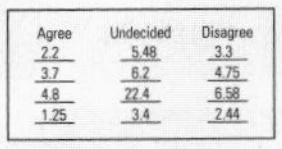	To show exact figures and values
Bar Chart	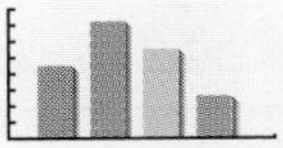	To compare one item with others
Line Chart	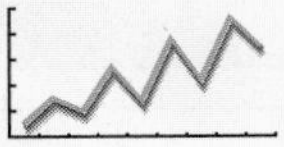	To demonstrate changes in quantitative data over time
Pie Chart	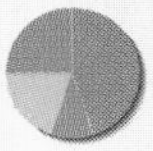	To visualize a whole unit and the proportions of its components
Flow Chart	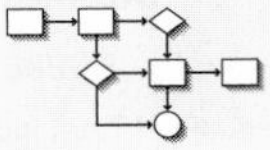	To display a process or procedure
Organization Chart	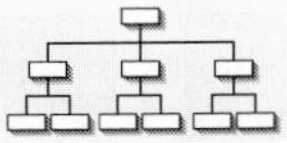	To define a hierarchy of elements
Photograph, Map, Illustration		To create authenticity, to spotlight a location, and to show an item in use

FIGURE 12.7 ● Table Summarizing Precise Data

FIGURE 1
MPM ENTERTAINMENT COMPANY
Income by Division (in millions of dollars)

	Theme Parks	Motion Pictures	Video	Total
1991	$15.8	$39.3	$11.2	$66.3
1992	18.1	17.5	15.3	50.9
1993	23.8	21.1	22.7	67.6
1994	32.2	22.0	24.3	78.5
1995 (projected)	35.1	21.0	26.1	82.2

Source: *Industry Profiles* (New York: DataPro, 1995), 225.

FIGURE 12.8 ● Vertical Bar Chart

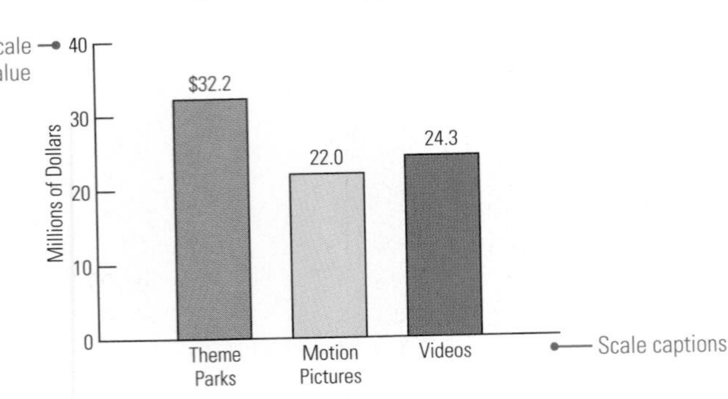

FIGURE 12.9 ● Horizontal Bar Chart

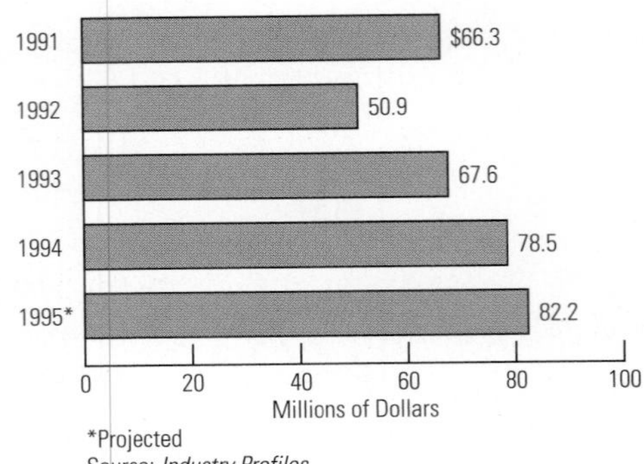

FIGURE 12.10 ● Grouped Bar Chart

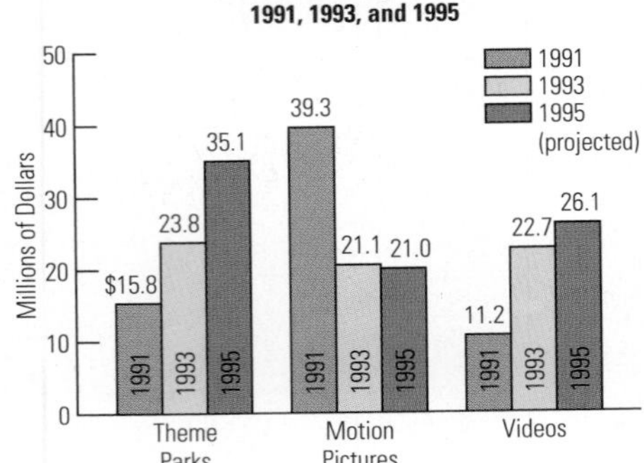

FIGURE 12.11 ● Segmented 100% Bar Chart

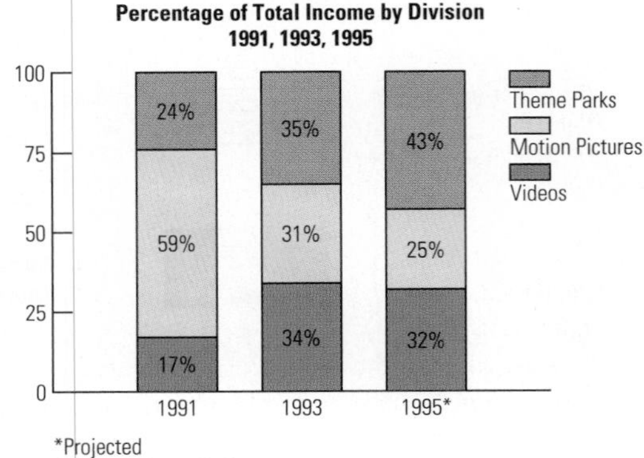

● **Bar charts enable readers to compare related items, see changes over time, and understand how parts relate to a whole.**

Bar charts. Although they lack the precision of tables, bar charts enable you to make emphatic visual comparisons. Bar charts can be used to compare related items, illustrate changes in data over time, and show segments as part of a whole. Figures 12.8 through 12.11 show vertical, horizontal, grouped, and segmented bar charts that highlight some of the data shown in the MPM Entertainment Company table (Figure 12.7). Note how the varied bar charts present information in differing ways.

Many suggestions for tables also hold true for bar charts. Here are a few additional tips:

- Keep the length of each bar and segment proportional.
- Include a total figure in the middle of a bar or at its end if the figure helps the reader and does not clutter the chart.
- Start dollar or percentage amounts at zero.
- Avoid showing too much information, thus producing clutter and confusion.

USING YOUR COMPUTER TO PRODUCE CHARTS

Designing effective bar charts, pie charts, figures, and other images has never been easier than it is now with the use of computer graphics programs.

Spreadsheet programs—such as Lotus 1-2-3, Excel, and QuattroPro—and presentations graphics programs—such as Harvard Graphics, Microsoft PowerPoint, and Lotus Freelance Graphics—allow even nontechnical people to design quality graphics. These graphics can be printed directly on paper for written reports or used for transparency masters and slides for oral presentations. The benefits of preparing visual aids on a computer are near-professional quality, shorter preparation time, and substantial savings in preparation costs.

To prepare a computer graphic, begin by assembling your data, usually in table form. Let's say you work for Dynamo Products, and you prepared the accompanying table showing the number of Dynamo computers sold in each region for each quarter of the fiscal year.

Next, you must decide what type of chart you want: pie chart, grouped bar chart, vertical bar chart, horizontal bar chart, organization chart, or some other graphic. To make a pie chart showing total computers sold by division for the year, key in the data or select the data from an existing file. Add a title for the chart, as well as any necessary labels. For a bar or line chart, indicate the horizontal and vertical axes (reference lines or beginning points). Most programs will automatically generate legends for figures. If you wish, however, you can easily customize titles and legends.

The finished chart can be printed on paper or imported into your word processing document to be printed with your finished report. The pie chart and bar chart shown here were created in a spreadsheet program and then imported into a word processing program.

Another useful feature of most word processing programs involves linking and importing tables. Our table showing the total number of disks sold could be created by importing a Lotus 1-2-3 or QuattroPro worksheet into WordPerfect's table feature. The result is a nicely arranged, easy-to-read table. The table can also be "linked" to the spreadsheet program so that the latest changes made in the worksheet will be automatically reflected in the table as it appears in the word processing document.

Career Track Application

Visit your local software dealer and ask for a demonstration of how to create a pie or bar chart using a computer graphics program. Ask the salesperson to print out a copy of the visual (on a color printer, if available) for you to bring to class for discussion.

TABLE 1

DYNAMO PRODUCTS
Number of Computers Sold

Region	1st Qtr.	2nd Qtr.	3rd Qtr.	4th Qtr.	Yearly Totals
Eastern	13,302	15,003	15,550	16,210	60,065
Northern	12,678	11,836	10,689	14,136	49,339
Southern	9,345	8,921	9,565	10,256	38,087
Western	10,345	11,934	10,899	12,763	45,941
Total	45,670	47,694	46,703	53,365	193,432

Figure 1
Dynamo Products
Yearly Sales

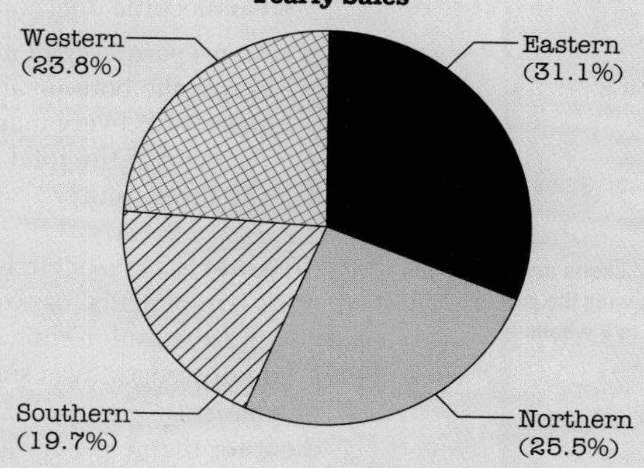

Figure 2
Dynamo Products
1993 Quarterly Sales

Line charts illustrate trends and changes in data over time.

Line charts. The major advantage of line charts is that they show changes over time, thus indicating trends. Figures 12.12 through 12.14 show line charts that reflect income trends for the three divisions of MPM. Notice that line charts do not provide precise data, such as the 1994 MPM Videos income. Instead, they give an overview or impression of the data. Experienced report writers use tables to list exact data; they use line charts or bar charts to spotlight important points or trends.

Simple line charts (Figure 12.12) show just one variable. Multiple line charts combine several variables (Figure 12.13). Segmented line charts (Figure 12.14), also called *surface* charts, illustrate how the components of a whole change over time. Notice how Figure 12.14 helps you visualize the shift in total MPM income from motion pictures to videos and theme parks. By contrast, tables don't permit such visualization.

Here are tips for preparing a line chart:

- Begin with a grid divided into squares.
- Arrange the time component (usually years) horizontally across the bottom; arrange values for the other variable vertically.
- Draw small dots at the intersections to indicate each value at a given year.
- Connect the dots and add color if desired.
- To prepare a segmented (surface) chart, plot the first value (say, video income) across the bottom; add the next item (say, motion picture income) to the first figures for every increment; for the third item (say, theme park income) add its value to the total of the first two items. The top line indicates the total of the three values.

Pie charts are most useful in showing the proportion of parts to a whole.

Pie Charts. Pie, or circle, charts enable readers to see a whole and the proportion of its components, or wedges. Although less flexible than bar or line charts, pie charts are useful in showing percentages, as Figure 12.15 illustrates. Notice that a group of wedges (or a single wedge) can be "exploded" or popped out for special emphasis. In Figure 12.15, which shows MPM 1994 income by division, the segment for theme parks was "exploded" and further divided to show the percentage of total income that each theme park earned.

For the most effective pie charts, follow these suggestions:

- Begin at the 12 o'clock position, drawing the largest wedge first. (Computer software programs don't always observe this advice, but if you're drawing your own charts, you can.)
- Include, if possible, the actual percent or absolute value for each wedge.
- Use four to eight segments for best results; if necessary, group small portions into one wedge called "Other."
- Distinguish wedges with color, shading, or cross-hatching.
- Keep all the labels horizontal.

Many software programs help you prepare professional-looking charts with a minimum of effort. See the accompanying Technology box for more information.

FIGURE 12.12 ● **Simple Line Chart**

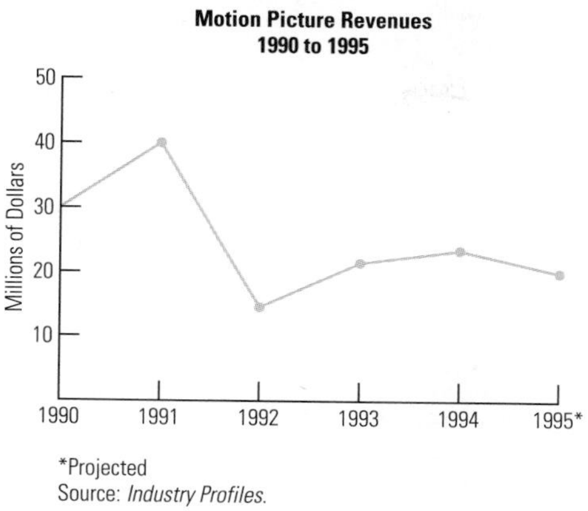

FIGURE 12.13 ● **Multiple Line Chart**

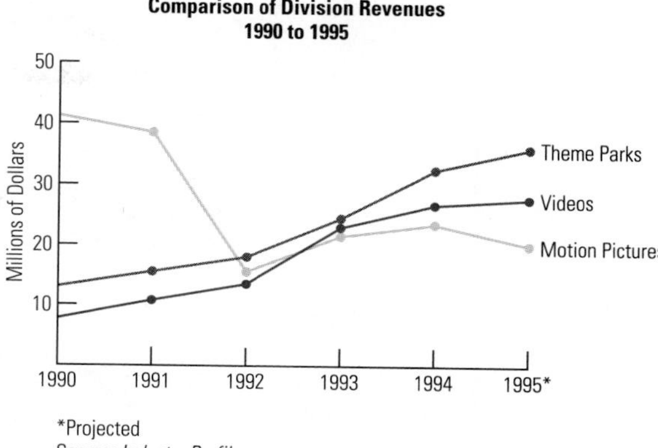

FIGURE 12.14 ● **Segmented Line (Surface) Chart**

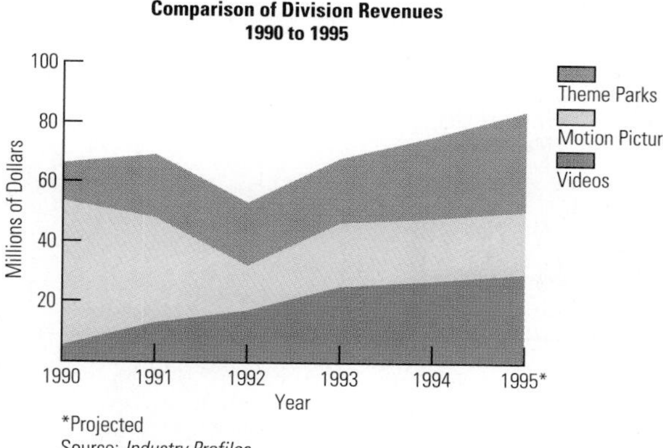

FIGURE 12.15 ● **Pie Chart**

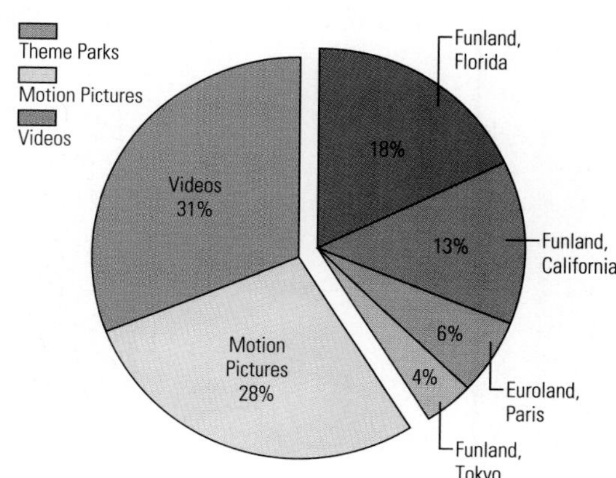

Flow charts. Procedures are simplified and clarified by diagraming them in a flow chart, as shown in Figure 12.16. Whether you need to describe the procedure for handling a customer's purchase order or outline steps in solving a problem, flow charts help the reader visualize the process. Traditional flow charts use the following symbols:

- Ovals to designate the beginning and end of a process
- Diamonds to denote decision points
- Rectangles to represent major activities or steps

FIGURE 12.16 ● **Flow Chart**

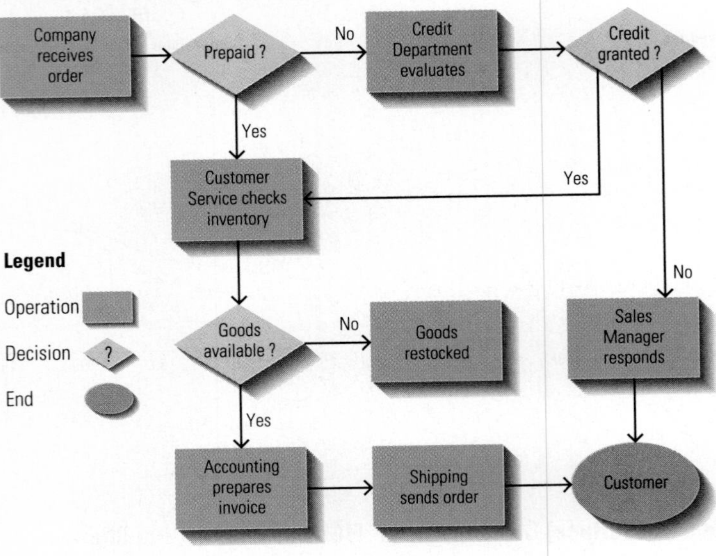

FIGURE 12.17 ● **Organization Chart**

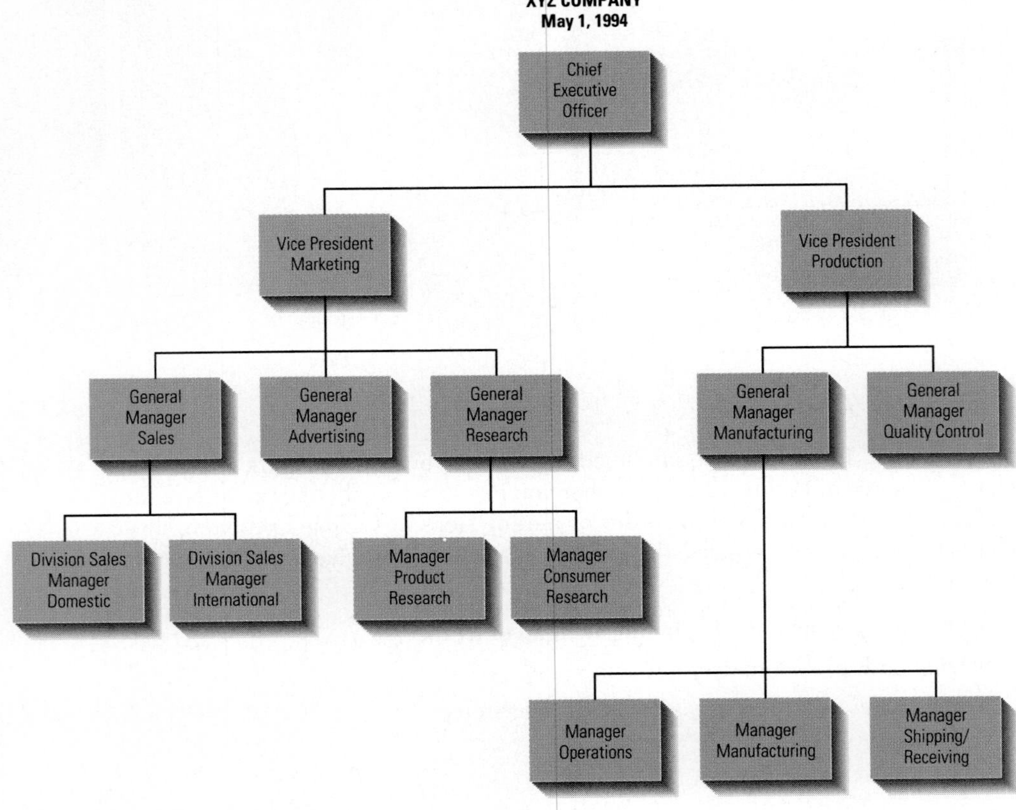

Organization charts. Many large organizations are so complex that they need charts to show the chain of command, from the boss down to line managers and employees. Organization charts like the one in Figure 12.17 provide such information as who reports to whom, how many subordinates work for each manager (the span of control), and what channels of official communication exist. They may also illustrate a company's structure (by function, customer, or product, for example), the work being performed in each job, and the hierarchy of decision making. Organization charts improve reports by helping readers clarify an organization's structure and environment.

● **Organization charts picture the line of command and thus the flow of official communication from management to employees.**

Photographs, maps, and illustrations. Some business reports include photographs, maps, and illustrations to serve specific purposes. Pictures, for example, add authenticity and provide a visual record. Dusty Richter, a location manager for a motion picture company, includes pictures in all his scouting reports; and Eliza Cohn, an environmental engineer, documents hazardous sites with her own photographs. With today's computer technology, photographs and images can be scanned directly into business reports.

● **Computer technology permits photographs, maps, and illustrations to be scanned directly into a report.**

Maps enable report writers to depict activities or concentrations geographically, such as dots indicating sales reps in states across the country. Your reports might show where an organization's new products will be introduced or what states in the country have income taxes. Office supply stores sometimes carry blank state, national, and global maps; and many computer programs provide maps that you can fill in to highlight locations discussed in your reports.

Illustrations and diagrams are useful in indicating how an object looks or operates. A drawing showing the parts of a VCR with labels describing their functions, for example, is more instructive than a photograph or verbal description. Artists can emphasize critical points and delete distracting details.

Incorporating Visuals in Reports

Used appropriately, visuals make reports more interesting and easier to understand. In putting visuals into your reports, follow these suggestions for best effects.

● **Effective visuals are accurate and ethical, avoid overuse of color or decorations, and include titles.**

- **Evaluate the audience.** Size up your readers to determine how many visuals are appropriate. Six charts in an internal report to an executive may seem like overkill; but in a long technical report to outsiders, six may be too few. Evaluate the reader, the content, your schedule, and your budget (graphics take time and money to prepare) in deciding how many visuals to use.
- **Use restraint.** Don't overuse color or decorations. Although color can effectively distinguish bars or segments in charts, too much color can be distracting and confusing. Remember, too, that colors themselves sometimes convey meaning: reds suggest deficits or negative values, blues suggest coolness, and oranges may mean warmth. Also, use decorations (sometimes called "dingbats" or "chartjunk") sparingly, if at all.
- **Be accurate and ethical.** Double-check all visuals for accuracy of figures and calculations. Be certain that your visuals aren't misleading—either accidentally or intentionally. Manipulation of a chart scale can make trends look steeper and more dramatic than they really are. To avoid giving a false picture, experiment with different scales. Then judge whether the resulting trend looks accurate and honest. Also, be sure to cite sources when you use someone else's facts. The accompanying Ethics box discusses in more detail how to make ethical graphs.

MAKING ETHICAL CHARTS AND GRAPHICS

Business communicators must present visual aid data in the same ethical, honest manner required for all other messages. Remember that the information shown in your charts and graphics will be used to inform others or help them make decisions. If this information is not represented accurately, the reader will be incorrectly informed; any decisions based on the data are likely to be faulty. And mistakes in interpreting such information may have serious and long-lasting consequences.

Chart data can be distorted in many ways. Figure 1 shows advertising expenses displayed on an appropriate scale. Figure 2 shows the same information, but the horizontal scale, from 1989 to 1994, has been lengthened. Notice that the data have not changed, but the increases and decreases are smoothed out, so changes in expenses appear to be slight. In Figure 3 the vertical scale is taller and the horizontal scale is shortened, resulting in what appear to be sharp increases and decreases in expenses.

To avoid misrepresenting data, keep the following pointers in mind when designing your visual aids:

- Use an appropriate type of chart or graphic for the message you wish to convey.
- Design the chart so that it focuses on the appropriate information.
- Include all relevant or important data; don't arbitrarily leave out necessary information.
- Don't hide critical information by including too much data in one graphic.
- Use appropriate scales with equal intervals for the data you present.

Career Skill Application

Locate one or two visual aids in a newspaper, magazine article, or annual report. Analyze the strengths and weaknesses of each visual aid. Is the information presented accurately? Select a bar or line chart. Sketch the same chart but change the vertical or horizontal scales on the graphic. How does the message of the chart change?

FIGURE 1
Advertising Expenses

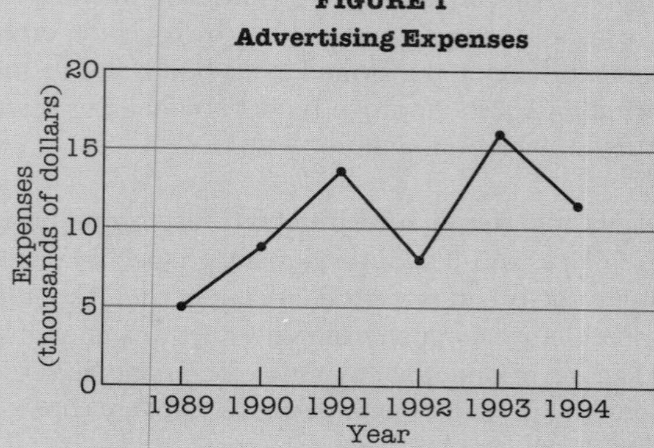

FIGURE 2
Advertising Expenses

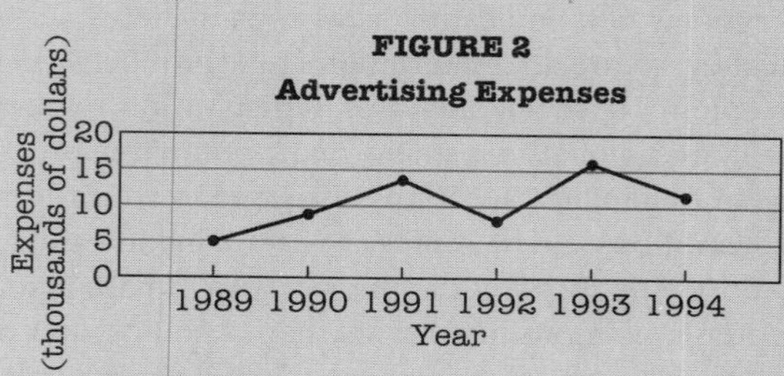

FIGURE 3
Advertising Expenses

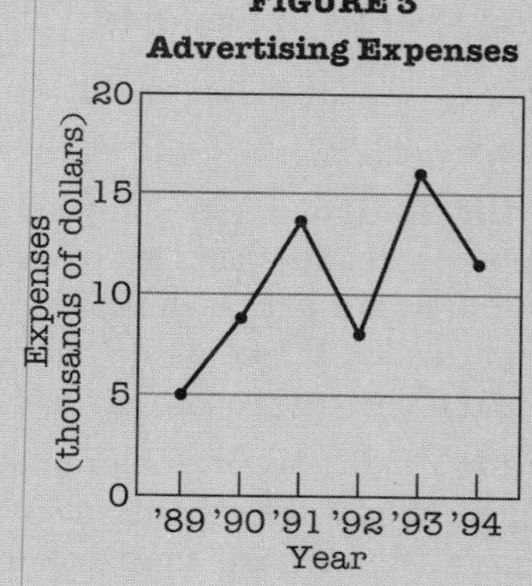

- **Introduce a visual meaningfully.** Refer to every visual in the text, and place the visual close to the point where it is mentioned. Most important, though, help the reader understand the significance of a visual. You can do this by telling the reader what to look for or by summarizing the main point of a visual. Don't assume the reader will automatically draw the same conclusions you reached from a set of data. Instead of *The findings are shown in Figure 3,* tell the reader what to look for: *Two-thirds of the responding employees, as shown in Figure 3, favor a flextime schedule.* The best introductions for visuals interpret them for readers.

- **Choose an appropriate caption or title style.** Like reports, visuals may use "talking" titles or generic, descriptive titles. "Talking" titles are more persuasive; they tell the reader what to think. Descriptive titles describe the facts more objectively.

Talking Title	**Descriptive Title**
Average Annual Health Care Costs per Worker Rise Steeply As Workers Grow Older	Average Annual Health Care Costs per Worker As Shown by Age Groups

Judge the style you should use by your audience and your company's preferences. Regardless of the style, make the titles consistent and specific.

Textual visual aids should be introduced by statements that help readers interpret the aids.

Summary of Learning Goals

1. **Use tabulating and statistical techniques to sort and interpret report data.** Report data becomes more meaningful when sorted into tables or when analyzed by mean (the arithmetic average), median (the midpoint in a group of figures), and mode (the most frequent response). Range represents a span between the highest and lowest figures. Grids help organize complex data into rows and columns.

2. **Draw meaningful conclusions from report data.** Conclusions tell what the survey data mean—especially in relation to the original report problem. They summarize key findings and may attempt to explain what caused the report problem. They are usually enumerated.

3. **Prepare practical report recommendations.** In reports that call for recommendations, writers make specific suggestions for actions that can solve the report problem. Recommendations should be feasible and potentially agreeable to the audience. They should all relate to the initial problem. Recommendations may be combined with conclusions.

4. **Organize report data logically.** Reports may be organized in many ways, including (1) by time (establishing a chronology or history of events), (2) by component (discussing a problem by geography, division, or product), (3) by importance (arranging data from most important to least important, or vice versa), (4) by criteria (comparing items by standards), or (5) by convention (using an already established grouping).

5. **Provide cues to aid report comprehension.** Good communicators help receivers understand a topic's organization by using introductions (to spell out topics), transitional expressions (to indicate where a topic is headed), and headings (to highlight major ideas).

6. **Develop visual aids that create meaning and interest.** Good visual aids improve reports by clarifying, simplifying, and emphasizing data. Tables organize precise data into rows and columns. Bar and line charts enable data to be compared visually. Line charts are especially helpful in showing changes over time. Pie charts show a whole and the proportion of its components. Organization charts, pictures, maps, and illustrations serve specific purposes.
7. **Incorporate visual aids into reports effectively.** In choosing or crafting visuals, smart communicators evaluate their audience, purpose, topic, and budget to determine the number and kind of visuals. These communicators are accurate, ethical, and restrained in developing visuals. And they are consistent in writing "talking" titles (telling readers what to think about the visual) or "descriptive" titles (summarizing the topic objectively).

Chapter Review

1. Forms that use systematic columns and rows to enable you to summarize and simplify numerical data from questionnaires and interviews are called what?

2. What is cross-tabulation? Give an example.

3. Calculate the mean, median, and mode for these figures: 3, 4, 4, 4, 10.

4. How can a grid help classify material?

5. What are the two most widely read sections of a report?

6. How do conclusions differ from recommendations?

7. When reports have multiple recommendations, how should they be presented?

8. Information reports typically are organized into what three parts?

9. Analytical reports may be organized directly or indirectly. How do the organizational patterns differ?

10. Name five methods for organizing report data. Be prepared to discuss each.

11. What three devices can report writers use to prevent readers from getting lost in the text?

12. Briefly compare the advantages and disadvantages of illustrating data with charts (bar and line) versus tables.

13. What is the major advantage of using pie charts to illustrate data?

14. What visual aid is best for illustrating a process or procedure?

15. Describe two kinds of captions or titles for visual aids.

Discussion

1. Why is audience analysis particularly important in making report recommendations?

2. Why is anticipation of the audience's response less important in an information report than in an analytical report?

3. Should all reports be organized so that they follow the sequence of investigation—that is, describing for the reader the initial problem, analysis of issues, data collection, data analysis, and conclusions? Why or why not?

4. Why is it important for reports to contain structural cues clarifying their organization?

5. Ethical Issue: Discuss the ethics of an annual report that disguises a company's net operating loss by using deceptive graphs. The actual figures, as audited by a CPA, show the loss; but they are buried in long tables within the report. By starting with a base figure below 0, the graphics suggested a profit instead of a loss. Graphics are not audited.

Exercises

12.1 Collaborative Tabulation and Interpretation of Survey Results

a. Assume your business communication class at North Shore College was asked by the college bookstore manager, Larry Krause, to conduct a survey (see Figure 11.8). Concerned about the environment, Krause wants to learn students' reactions to eliminating plastic bags, of which 45,000 are given away annually by the bookstore. Students were questioned about a number of proposals, resulting in the following raw data. In groups of four or five, convert the data into a table (see Figure 12.1) with a descriptive title. Arrange the items in a logical sequence.

For major purchases the bookstore should	AGREE	UNDECIDED	DISAGREE
5. Continue to provide plastic bags	132	17	411
6. Provide no bags; encourage students to bring their own bags	414	25	121
7. Provide no bags; offer cloth bags at a reduced price (about $3)	357	19	184
8. Give a cloth bag with each major purchase, the cost to be included in registration fees	63	15	482

b. How could these survey data be cross-tabulated? Would cross-tabulation serve any purpose?

c. Given the conditions of this survey, name at least three conclusions that could be drawn from the data.

d. Prepare three to five recommendations to be submitted to Mr. Krause. How could they be implemented?

12.2 Evaluating Conclusions

Read an in-depth article (800 or more words) in *Business Week, Fortune, Forbes,* or *The Wall Street Journal.* What conclusions does the author draw? Are the conclusions valid, based on the evidence presented? In a memo to your instructor, summarize the main points in the article and analyze the conclusions. What conclusions would you have drawn from the data?

12.3 Distinguishing Between Conclusions and Recommendations

For each of the following statements, indicate whether it could be classified as a conclusion or recommendation.

a. In times of recession, individuals spend less money on meals away from home.

b. Our restaurant should offer a menu featuring a variety of low-priced items in addition to the regular menu.

c. Absenteeism among employees with families decreases when they have adequate child care.

d. Nearly 80 percent of our business comes from only 20 percent of our customers.

e. Datatech Company should concentrate its major sales effort on its largest accounts.

f. The length of vacations for employees across the country is directly correlated with their length of employment.

g. The employee vacation schedule of Datatech Company compares favorably with the averages of other similar U.S. companies.

h. Offering outplacement service (assistance in finding jobs) tends to diffuse the anger that goes with involuntary separation (being released from a job).

12.4 Data Organization

How could the findings in the following reports be best organized? Consider these methods: time, component, importance, criteria, and convention.

a. A report comparing three sites for a company's new production plant. The report presents figures on property costs, construction costs, proximity to raw materials, state taxes, labor availability, and shipping distances.

b. A report describing the history of attempts to standardize computer specifications, starting in 1976 and progressing to the present.

c. An informational brochure for job candidates that describes your company's areas of employment: accounting, finance, information systems, operations management, marketing, production, and computer-aided design.

d. A monthly sales report submitted to the sales manager.

e. A recommendation report, to be submitted to management, presenting four building plans to improve access to your building, in compliance with federal regulations. The plans range considerably in feasibility and cost.

f. A progress report submitted six months into the process of planning the program for your organization's convention.

g. An informational report describing a company's expansion plans in South America, Europe, Australia, and Southeast Asia.

h. An employee performance appraisal submitted annually.

12.5 Evaluating Headings and Titles

Identify the following report headings and titles as "talking" or "functional/descriptive." Discuss the usefulness and effectiveness of each.

a. Problem

b. Need for Tightening Computer ID System

c. Annual Budget

d. How to Implement Quality Circles That Work

e. Case History: Buena Vista Palace Hotel Focuses on Improving Service to Customers

f. Solving Our Records Management Problems

g. Comparing Copier Volume, Ease of Use, and Speed

h. Alternatives

12.6 Selecting Visual Aids

Identify the best kind of visual aid to illustrate the following data.

a. Instructions for workers telling them how to distinguish between worker accidents that must be reported to state and federal agencies and those that need not be reported.

b. Figures showing what proportion of every state tax dollar is spent on education, social services, transportation, debt, and other expenses.

c. Data showing the academic, administrative, and operation divisions of a college, from the president to department chairs and division managers.

d. Figures comparing the sales of VCRs, color TVs, and personal computers over the past ten years.

e. Figures showing the operating profit of a company for the past five years.

f. Data showing areas in the United States most likely to have earthquakes.

g. Percentages showing the causes of forest fires (lightning, 73 percent; arson, 5 percent; campfires, 9 percent; and so on) in the Rocky Mountains.

h. Figures comparing the cost of basic TV cable service in ten areas of the United States for the past ten years (the boss wants to see exact figures).

12.7 Evaluating Visual Aids

Select five visual aids from newspapers or magazines. Look in *The Wall Street Journal, USA Today, Business Week, U.S. News & World Report, Fortune,* or other business news publications. In a memo to your instructor, critique each visual based on what you have learned in this chapter.

12.8 Drawing a Bar Chart

Prepare a bar chart comparing the tax rates of eight industrial countries in the world: Canada, 34 percent; France, 42 percent; Germany, 39 percent; Japan, 26 percent; Netherlands, 48 percent; Sweden, 49 percent; United Kingdom, 37 percent; United States, 28 percent. These figures represent a percentage of the gross domestic product for each country. The sources of the figures are the International Monetary Fund and the Japanese Ministry of Finance. Arrange the entries logically. Write two titles: a talking title and a descriptive title. What conclusion might you draw from these figures? What should be emphasized in the graph and title?

12.9 Drawing a Line Chart

Prepare a line chart showing the sales of Sidekick Athletic Shoes, Inc., for these years: 1994, \$6.7 million; 1993, \$5.4 million; 1992, \$3.2 million; 1991, \$2.1 million; 1990, \$2.6 million; 1989, \$3.6 million. In the chart title highlight the trend you see in the data.

12.10 Studying Visuals in Annual Reports

In a memo to your instructor, evaluate the effectiveness of visual aids in three to five corporation annual reports. Critique their readability, clarity, and success in visualizing data. How were they introduced in the text? What suggestions would you make to improve them?

Typical Business Reports

LEARNING GOALS

After studying this chapter, you should be able to

1. Distinguish between informational and analytical reports
2. Write periodic reports
3. Draft situational reports
4. Prepare investigative and compliance reports
5. Compose direct and indirect justification/recommendation reports
6. Write feasibility reports
7. Draft yardstick reports
8. Discuss research reports

Baltimore Orioles: Career Track Profile

Turning an old train yard into a major-league baseball stadium seems like the ultimate field-of-dreams fairy tale. But the Baltimore Orioles and the Maryland Stadium Authority, with the help of Janet Marie Smith, vice president of new-stadium planning and development, did just that. They succeeded in transforming a derelict area into the popular $105-million Oriole Park at Camden Yards, a new but "old" baseball facility.

"The new park is not a space-age wonderdome or a concrete doughnut," says Janet. "Located in the old Camden Yards, it's an architectural throwback to baseball's glory days before World War II." Janet explains that the owners of the Orioles worked with the state to build a new park close to Baltimore's mass-transit system. Although they wanted all the comforts of a modern facility, the owners dreamed of a stadium that looked as if Babe Ruth had played there.

"I rely heavily on written communication because it provides records and allows me to send the same information to many different people."

For this massive four-year undertaking, Janet functioned as Orioles project supervisor in dealing with the state. "At one time 20 firms and suppliers were working on the project. This meant 20 different deadlines and countless details to manage." To keep everything on track, she developed a flowchart breaking the big project into small steps with "lots of little deadlines."

Trained in architecture at Mississippi State University and in urban planning at City University of New York, Janet was well equipped for the task. She started with eight months of research into stadium design. Visits to other stadiums, including Chicago's Wrigley Field, built in 1914, resulted in stacks of data. "We checked out the players' clubhouses, the hotdog stands, and the line length at the restrooms. We identified a number of architectural elements, seldom used today, that were perfect for our site with the historic warehouse. These included steel trusses in a criss-cross design that supports concrete decks for seats but also lets in light and air through the concourse. And we really admired the slat seats, which are actually more comfortable than the solid plastic ones used in many modern facilities," says Janet.

Much of Janet's research had to be digested and condensed into memos or reports before being sent to the appropriate decision-makers. "I rely heavily on written communication because it provides records and allows me to send the same information to many different people," observes Janet. Her investigative reports did more than merely describe; they also spotlighted applications. She says, for example, "I might report that at Wrigley Field they have food service for fans in restaurant settings along the most active streets. As a result, they can not only provide service for fans during games but can accommodate other groups during nongame times without opening the entire stadium." Converting observations into meaningful applications is an important goal of good reports.

A major priority for Janet was keeping top management up-to-date on the progress of the entire stadium project. "At key times I would write a concise memo of what had been accomplished and what was planned next. I'd accompany this with either an illustration or an example of how it was done elsewhere."

The new Oriole Park at Camden Yards culminated years of preparation and supervision by Janet Marie Smith, vice president of new-stadium planning and development. The key to organizing, she says, is managing the process as well as the project. She prepared a giant flowchart to track each task and then took a "snapshot" every two weeks, sizing up what had and hadn't been done. Keeping everyone informed—management, architects, vendors, staff members—was a terrific communication task, often resulting in presentations, letters, memos, and reports.

In addition to progress reports, Janet often had to submit written recommendations to support the team's choices, such as the decision to go with slat chairs. "I wrote endlessly about them," she confesses. "We looked at them from a number of perspectives. What did the chairs look like in older ballparks, those we wanted to model ourselves after? How durable were the new blow-molded plastic products? What was the extra cost for being innovative? Did the durability and nostalgic appearance of the slat chairs warrant their expense?"

In justifying her recommendations, she wrote letters, memos, and reports. Sometimes she was direct and up front with her requests, and other times—especially when she expected resistance—she used a different approach. If, for example, the Orioles wanted approval to increase the costs in a certain part of the ballpark—say, to build party suites on the club level—she didn't come out bluntly with "We want to spend more money on this." Instead, she would precede or support the Orioles' request to the state with careful reasoning. She would explain the benefits that an upscale enclosed area could offer, such as higher revenues from pregame parties and increased nongame use of the area.

Any request must be supported by relevant details and logical arguments, she notes. "Being armed with the facts is always the best ammunition for successful persuasion. Thinking about the benefits your recommendations will produce now and in the future—this kind of reasoning is far better than recommending something that looks as if it's your personal whimsy."

As Orioles spokesperson for the stadium project, Janet occasionally had to act as umpire. "Every department within the Orioles' organization had a vested interest in how the ballpark would be built. For example, sales wanted as many front-row seats as possible. But baseball operations wanted the dugouts to be long enough to seat more players, thus reducing the number of front-row seats. And public relations wanted to make room for television cameras, potentially eliminating even more seats. Resolving the conflicts meant getting all three groups together and arriving at a compromise. Everyone gave a little, probably because I outlined our common goals at the beginning."

Oriole Park at Camden Yards is now a successful operation, but Janet continues to work toward modifications addressing fans' needs. She's also researching a design for a new Orioles' spring-training facility to be built in Florida or Arizona.[1]

our managers complained that they weren't getting the information they wanted, we sat down together and developed a report form with four categories: (1) activity summary, (2) competition update, (3) product problems and comments, and (4) needs. Then one manager wrote several sample reports that we studied. Now, my reports are shorter and more focused. I try to hit the highlights in covering my daily activities, but I really concentrate on product problems and items that I must have to do a better job. Managers tell us that they need this kind of detailed feedback so that they can respond to the competition and also develop new products that our customers want."

Situational Reports

Situational reports cover nonrecurring events.

Reports covering nonrecurring situations—trips, conventions, conferences, event planning, and progress—are a little more difficult to write than periodic reports. Because samples are generally unavailable to serve as models, you'll probably devote more attention to organizing your material. Like other informational reports, situational reports are generally prepared as memos. The tone of these reports is informal. The length depends on reader expectations and on the actual situation, but shorter is usually better. Before writing, if possible, ask the person who authorized the report how much detail should be included and how long the report should be. You have nothing to lose by clarifying the assignment. Situational reports usually need introductions (to familiarize the reader with the topic) and closings (to give a sense of ending).

Trip, convention, and conference reports should be organized by topic—usually no more than five.

Trip, convention, and conference reports. Employees sent on business trips or to conventions and conferences typically must submit reports when they return. Organizations want to know that their money was well spent in funding the travel. These reports inform management about new procedures, equipment, and laws and supply information affecting products, operations, and service.

The hardest part of writing these reports is selecting the most relevant material and organizing it coherently. Generally, it's best not to use chronological sequencing *(in the morning we did X, at lunch we heard Y, and in the afternoon we did Z).* Instead, you should focus on three to five topics in which your reader will be interested. These items become the body of the report. Then simply add an introduction and closing, and your report is organized. Here is a general outline for trip, conference, and convention reports:

- Begin by identifying the event (exact date, name, and location) and previewing the topics to be discussed.
- Summarize in the body three to five main points that might benefit the reader.
- Itemize your expenses, if requested, on a separate sheet.
- Close by expressing appreciation, suggesting action to be taken, or synthesizing the value of the trip or event.

Jeff Marchant was recently named employment coordinator in the Human Resources Department of an electronics appliance manufacturer headquartered in central Ohio. Recognizing his lack of experience in interviewing job applicants, he asked permission to attend a one-day conference on the topic. His boss, Angela Taylor, encouraged Marchant to attend, saying, "We all need to brush up on our interviewing techniques. Come back and tell us what you learned." When he returned, Marchant wrote the conference report shown in Figure 13.2. Here's how

FIGURE 13.2 ● Conference Report

TO: Angela Taylor **DATE:** April 22, 1994
FROM: Jeff Marchant *JM*
SUBJECT: TRAINING CONFERENCE ON EMPLOYMENT INTERVIEWING

I enjoyed attending the "Interviewing People" training conference sponsored by the National Business Foundation. This one-day meeting, held in Columbus on April 19, provided excellent advice that will help us strengthen our interviewing techniques. Although the conference covered many topics, this report concentrates on three areas: structuring the interview, avoiding common mistakes, and responding to new legislation.

Identifies topic and previews how the report is organized

STRUCTURING THE INTERVIEW

Job interviews usually have three parts. The opening establishes a friendly rapport with introductions, a few polite questions, and an explanation of the purpose for the interview. The body of the interview consists of questions controlled by the interviewer. The interviewer has three goals: (a) educating the applicant about the job, (b) eliciting information about the applicant's suitability for the job, and (c) promoting goodwill about the organization. In closing, the interviewer should encourage the applicant to ask questions, summarize main points, and indicate what actions will follow.

Sets off major topics with centered headings

AVOIDING COMMON MISTAKES

Probably the most interesting and practical part of the conference centered on common mistakes made by interviewers, some of which I summarize here:

1. Not taking notes at each interview. Recording important facts enables you to remember the first candidate as easily as you remember the last—and all those in between.

2. Losing control of the interview. Keep control of the interview by digging into the candidate's answers to questions. Probe for responses of greater depth. Don't move on until a question has been satisfactorily answered.

Covers facts that will most interest and help reader

3. Not testing the candidate's communication skills. To be able to evaluate a candidate's ability to express ideas, ask the individual to explain some technical jargon from his or her current position—preferably, something mentioned during the interview.

4. Having departing employees conduct the interviews for their replacements. Departing employees may be unreliable as interviewers because they tend to hire candidates not quite as strong as they are. Their hidden agenda may be to keep the door open in case the new job fails.

5. Failing to check references. As many as 15 percent of all résumés may contain falsified data. The best way to check references is to network: ask the person whose name has been given to suggest the name of another person.

Angela Taylor April 22, 1994 Page 2

RESPONDING TO NEW LEGISLATION

Recently enacted provisions of the Americans With Disabilities Act prohibit interviewers from asking candidates—or even their references—about candidates' disabilities. A question we frequently asked ("Do you have any physical limitations which would prevent you from performing the job for which you are applying?") would now break the law. Interviewers must also avoid asking about medical history, prescription-drug use, prior workers' compensation claims, work absenteeism due to illness, and past treatment for alcoholism, drug use, or mental illness.

CONCLUSION

This conference provided me with valuable training that I would like to share with other department members at a future staff meeting. Let me know when it can be scheduled.

A volunteer from Xerox works to repair a house as part of the Americares program sponsored by the Xerox Community Involvement Program. Because management must be kept informed, the progress of this and other nonrecurring projects is likely to be described in a report. Progress reports generally describe what has been accomplished, what is being done at present, and what must be completed in future activities.

he describes its preparation: "I know my boss values brevity, so I worked hard to make my report no more than a page and a quarter. The conference saturated me with great ideas, far too many to cover in one brief report. So, I decided to discuss three topics that would be most useful to our staff. Although I had to be brief, I nonetheless wanted to provide as many details—especially about common interviewing mistakes—as possible. By the third draft, I had compressed my ideas into a manageable size without sacrificing any of the meaning."

● **Progress and interim reports describe on-going projects to both internal and external readers.**

Progress and interim reports. Continuing projects often require progress or interim reports to describe their status. These reports may be external (advising customers regarding the headway of their projects) or internal (informing management of the status of activities). Progress reports typically follow this pattern of development:

- Specify in the opening the purpose and nature of the project.
- Provide background information if the audience requires filling in.
- Describe the work completed.
- Explain the work currently in progress, including personnel, activities, methods, and locations.
- Anticipate problems and possible remedies.
- Discuss future activities and provide the expected completion date.

As a location manager in the film industry, Sheila Ryan frequently writes progress reports, such as the one shown in Figure 13.3. Producers want to be informed of what she's doing, and a phone call doesn't provide a permanent record. Here's how she describes her reasoning behind the progress report in Figure 13.3: "I usually include background information in my reports because a director doesn't always know or remember exactly what specifications I was given for a location search. Then I try to hit the high points of what I've completed and what I plan to do next, without getting bogged down in minute details. Although it would be easier to skip them, I've learned to be up front with any problems that I anticipate.

FIGURE 13.3 ● Progress Report

Tips for Writing Progress Reports

- Identify the purpose and the nature of the project immediately.
- Supply background information only if the reader must be educated.
- Describe the work completed.
- Discuss the work in progress, including personnel, activities, methods, and locations.
- Identify problems and possible remedies.
- Consider future activities.
- Close by telling the expected date of completion.

QuaStar Productions

Interoffice Memo

TO: Rick Willens, Executive Producer

DATE: January 7, 1994

FROM: Sheila Ryan, Location Manager SR

SUBJECT: Sites for "Bodega Bay" Telefilm

Identifies project and previews report

This memo describes the progress of my search for an appropriate rustic home, villa, or ranch to be used for the wine country sequences in the telefilm "Bodega Bay." Three sites will be available for you to inspect on January 21, as you requested.

Background: In preparation for this assignment, I consulted Director Dave Durslag, who gave me his preferences for the site. He suggested a picturesque ranch home situated near vineyards, preferably with redwoods in the background. I also consulted Producer Teresa Silva, who told me that the site must accommodate 55 to 70 production crew members for approximately three weeks of filming. Ben Waters, telefilm accountant, requested that the cost of the site not exceed $24,000 for a three-week lease.

Saves space by integrating headings into paragraphs

Work Completed: For the past eight days I have searched the Russian River area in the Northern California wine country. Possible sites include turn-of-the-century estates, Victorian mansions, and rustic farmhouses in the towns of Duncans Mills, Monte Rio, and Guerneville. One exceptional site is the Country Meadow Inn, a 97-year-old farmhouse nestled among vineyards with a breathtaking view of valleys, redwoods, and distant mountains.

Work to Be Completed: In the next five days, I'll search the Sonoma County countryside, including wineries at Korbel, Field Stone, and Napa. Many old wineries contain charming structures that may present exactly the degree of atmosphere and mystery we need. These wineries have the added advantage of easy access. I will also inspect possible structures at the Armstrong Redwoods State Reserve and the Kruse Rhododendron Reserve, both within 100 miles of Guerneville. I've made an appointment with the director of state parks to discuss our project, use of state lands, restrictions, and costs.

Tells the bad news as well as the good

Anticipated Problems: You should be aware of two complications for filming in this area.

1. Property owners seem unfamiliar with the making of films and are suspicious of short-term leases.
2. Many trees won't have leaves again until May. You may wish to change the filming schedule somewhat.

Concludes by giving completion date and describing what follows

By January 14 you'll have my final report describing the three most promising locations. Arrangements will be made for you to visit these sites January 21.

TEN TIPS FOR DESIGNING BETTER DOCUMENTS

Desktop publishing packages, high-level word processing programs, and laser printers now make it possible for you to turn out professional-looking documents. The temptation, though, is to overdo it by incorporating too many features in one document. Here are ten tips for applying good sense and good design principles in "publishing" your documents.

- **Analyze your audience.** Sales brochures and promotional letters can be flashy—with color print, oversized type, and fancy borders—to attract attention. But such effects are out of place for most conservative business documents. Also consider whether your readers will be reading painstakingly or merely browsing. Lists and headings help audiences in a hurry.
- **Choose an appropriate type size.** For most business memos, letters, and reports, the body text should be 10 or 11 points tall (a point is 1/72 of an inch). Larger type looks amateurish, and smaller type is hard to read.
- **Use a consistent type font.** Although your software may provide a variety of fonts, stay with a single family of type within one document—at least until you become more expert. The most popular fonts are Times Roman and Helvetica. For emphasis and contrast, you can vary the font size and weight with **bold,** *italic,* ***bold italic,*** and other selections.
- **Generally, don't justify right margins.** Textbooks, novels, newspapers, magazines, and other long works are usually set with justified (even) right margins. However, for shorter works ragged-right margins are recommended because such margins add white space and help readers locate the beginnings of new lines. Slower readers find ragged-right copy more legible.
- **Separate paragraphs and sentences appropriately.** The first line of a paragraph should be indented or preceded by a blank line. To separate sentences, typists have traditionally left two spaces. This spacing is still acceptable for most business documents. If you are preparing a newsletter or brochure, however, you may wish to adopt printer's standards, leaving one space after end punctuation.
- **Design readable headlines.** Presenting headlines and headings in all caps is generally discouraged because solid blocks of capital letters interfere with recognition of word patterns. To further improve readability, select a sans serif typeface (one without cross strokes or embellishment), such as Helvetica.
- **Strive for an attractive page layout.** In designing title pages or visual aids, provide for a balance between print and white space. Also consider placing the focal point (something that draws the reader's eye) at the optical center of a page—about three lines above the actual center. Moreover, remember that the average reader scans a page from left to right and top to bottom in a Z pattern. Plan your visuals accordingly.
- **Use graphics and clip art with restraint.** Images created with spreadsheet or graphics programs can be imported into documents. Original drawings, photographs, and clip art can also be scanned into documents. Use such images, however, only when they are well drawn, relevant, purposeful, and appropriately sized.
- **Avoid amateurish results.** Many beginning writers, eager to display every graphic device a program offers, produce busy, cluttered documents. Too many typefaces, ruled lines, oversized headlines, and images will overwhelm readers. Strive for simple, clean, and forceful effects.
- **Develop expertise.** Learn to use the desktop publishing features of your current word processing software, or investigate one of the special programs, such as Ventura, PageMaker, Harvard Graphics, Powerpoint, or CorelDraw. Although the learning curve for many of these programs is steep, such effort is well spent if you will be producing newsletters, brochures, announcements, visual aids, and promotional literature.

Career Track Application

Buy a book or two on designing documents, and select ten tips that you could share with the class. In teams of three or four, analyze the design and layout of three or four annual reports. Evaluate the appropriateness of typeface and type size, white space, headings, and graphics.

I don't tell how to solve the problems, but I feel duty-bound to at least mention them."

Investigative Reports

Investigative or information reports deliver data for a specific situation—without offering interpretation or recommendations. These nonrecurring reports are generally arranged in a direct pattern with three segments: introduction, body, and summary. The body—which includes the facts, findings, or discussion—may be organized by time, component, importance, criteria, or convention. What's important is dividing the topic into logical segments, say, three to five areas that are roughly equal and don't overlap.

The subject matter of the report usually suggests the best way to divide and organize it. Beth Givens, an information specialist for a Minneapolis health care consulting firm, was given the task of researching and writing an investigative report for St. John's Hospital. Her assignment: study the award-winning patient-service program at Good Samaritan Hospital, and report how it improved its patient satisfaction rating from 6.2 to 7.8 in just one year. Beth collected data and then organized her findings into four parts: management training, employee training, patient services, and follow-up program. Although we don't show Beth's complete report here, you can see a similar one in Figure 11.2.

Compliance Reports

Government agencies at local, state, and national levels increasingly require organizations to submit reports verifying compliance with laws. Some of these reports—like those covering affirmative action, profit and loss, taxation, and occupational safety—consist primarily of data and figures entered on prepared forms. When you must explain actions and operations without the convenience of printed forms, follow these suggestions:

- Collect and report the specific information requested.
- Ensure the accuracy of the data.
- Provide the desired data in an appropriate format and on time.

Mark Thomas, vice president of Allied Trucking in San Jose, found his company in the unhappy position of responding to an unsatisfactory safety rating from the California Highway Patrol. In preparation for a hearing, Mark wrote a letter report, shown in Figure 13.4, to the city attorney explaining the steps his company was taking to achieve and maintain compliance with the law. In explaining his report, Mark said: "An 'unsatisfactory' safety rating from the state highway patrol is a very serious matter for any trucking company. We immediately shifted into high gear and completely revamped our driver and equipment safety programs. My goal in the report was to show the swift and extensive changes we had made. But I couldn't just talk about the changes. I also had to demonstrate them, so I sent examples of all our new inspection routines, equipment checks, and driver reports. I organized the report around the three main areas of change: education, preventive maintenance, and record keeping."

Mark's compliance report and other informational reports apply most of the suggestions found in the following checklist.

SPOTLIGHT ON COMMUNICATORS

"At the beginning of any project it's more important to know what kinds of questions to raise than how to answer them." So says Eileen Bedell, a managing director of Bankers Trust Company and head of the new Global Settlement Fund. GlobeSet is the world's first mechanism to allow institutional investors to complete commercial transactions in many currencies 24 hours a day. She and her study team began this new business by brainstorming, asking the right questions, investigating options, making recommendations, and, finally, winning financial backing.

FIGURE 13.4 ● Compliance Report

ALLIED TRUCKING, INC.
4920 Mountain View Drive
San Jose, California 94320

October 17, 1994

Mr. John R. Arthur
City Attorney
1330 Courthouse Square
San Jose, CA 94350

Dear Mr. Arthur:

SUBJECT: IMPROVED SAFETY COMPLIANCE PROGRAM

After Allied Trucking received an "unsatisfactory" rating on the California Highway Patrol Safety Compliance Report dated June 15, senior management took immediate action. We initiated systematic procedures to achieve and maintain compliance with state safety regulations. This report describes our three-stage program including (1) education, (2) preventive maintenance, and (3) accurate record keeping. The report is accompanied by numerous examples of records that illustrate our compliance with state and federal safety laws.

STAGE 1: EDUCATION

Our first step in developing an improved safety program was education. We reviewed publications from (1) the California Highway Patrol, (2) the Department of Motor Vehicles, and (3) the California Trucking Association. Several meetings included not only truck drivers and senior management but also middle management, vehicle dispatchers, and mechanics. Then we developed and implemented a safety program with two important components: preventive maintenance and improved record keeping.

STAGE 2: PREVENTIVE MAINTENANCE

Transportation safety depends in large part on precautions taken before vehicles are driven. We have developed a rigorous three-part preventive maintenance program that requires drivers' and mechanics' inspections, as well as careful inspection documentation.

Drivers' Inspections

As required by law, all drivers will submit a documented daily vehicle inspection report before the vehicle is driven on the highway. All reports will be carefully examined, with all defects corrected before the driver leaves for daily deliveries. An example of one of last month's reports is enclosed.

Mechanics' Inspections

In order to ensure the safe operation of our vehicles, Allied mechanics will inspect our trucks and trailers every 30 days (see enclosed schedule). We are aware that the law allows a maximum inspection interval of 90 days; however, we feel that a 30-day interval best suits our current needs.

Provides brief background data because reader is unfamiliar with topic

Previews three major sections of report

Supplies headings that clearly show outline of ideas

Improves readability with ample white space

Checklist for Writing Informational Reports

Introduction

✔ **Begin directly.** Identify the report and its purpose.

✔ **Provide a preview.** If the report is over a page long, give the reader a brief overview of its organization.

✔ **Supply background data selectively.** When readers are unfamiliar with the topic, briefly fill in the necessary details.

Mr. John R. Arthur Page 2 October 17, 1994

Copies of recent mechanics' inspections are enclosed. Please note that all four required systems are being inspected:

a. Brake adjustment
b. Brake system components and leaks
c. Steering and suspension systems
d. Tires and wheels

STAGE 3: RECORD KEEPING AND COMPLIANCE SYSTEMS

To enable Allied Trucking to be certain that it is complying with all local, state, and federal regulations, we have improved our record keeping in three specific areas.

DMV Pull Notices

All Allied drivers are entered and participate in the Department of Motor Vehicles Pull Notice Program. All pull notice reports are now reviewed, signed, and dated before they are filed. In addition, a new computerized monthly review of current drivers allows us to double-check for the enrollment of new or current drivers and/or the deletion of drivers no longer employed. Current pull notice reports are enclosed for review.

Driver Hours of Service

All driver logs and/or time cards are now continually reviewed in an attempt to adhere to federal and state regulations regarding duty time and rest periods. Moreover, all driver logs and time cards are cross-referenced to ensure accurate recording of driving and duty times. Driver and dispatcher education have been very helpful in achieving and maintaining these objectives. A sample of recent logs and time cards is enclosed.

Driving Proficiency Records

We now keep on file all records of the different types and combinations of vehicles each employee is certified to drive. Samples are enclosed.

CONCLUSION

We at Allied Trucking believe that the implementation of this three-stage program has helped us attain our twin goals of driver safety and equipment reliability. Should you have questions about this report, please call me at 383-2290.

Sincerely,

Mark W. Thomas

Mark W. Thomas
Vice President

MWT:eeg
Enclosures

Increases credibility by sending copies of relevant documents

Summarizes report objective and adds concluding thought

Body

- **Divide the topic.** Strive to group the facts or findings into three to five roughly equal segments that do not overlap.
- **Arrange the subtopics logically.** Consider organizing by time, component, importance, criteria, or convention.
- **Use clear headings.** Supply functional or talking heads (at least one per page) that describe each important section.

SPOTLIGHT ON COMMUNICATORS

Start at the library, advises Ruth Owades, who has founded two successful companies, Gardener's Eden and Calyx and Corolla. Whether you're considering the feasibility of an action or an entirely new business, you need facts. Extensive research in the card catalog helped her learn about flowers, florists, marketing, and advertising. She also used books to learn how to write a concise business plan that helped finance her $10 million mail-order flower business with headquarters in San Francisco.

- ✔ **Determine degree of formality.** Use an informal, conversational writing style unless the audience expects a more formal tone.
- ✔ **Enhance readability with graphic highlighting.** Make liberal use of bullets, numbered and lettered lists, headings, underlined items, and white space.

Summary/Conclusion

- ✔ **When necessary, summarize the report.** Briefly review the main points and discuss what action will follow.
- ✔ **Offer a concluding thought.** If relevant, express appreciation or describe your willingness to provide further information.

Analytical Reports

Analytical reports differ significantly from informational reports. Although both seek to collect and present data clearly, analytical reports also analyze the data and typically try to persuade the reader to accept the conclusions and act on the recommendations. Informational reports emphasize facts; analytical reports emphasize reasoning and conclusions.

For some readers analytical reports may be organized directly with the conclusions and recommendations near the beginning. Directness is appropriate when the reader has confidence in the writer, based on either experience or credentials. Front-loading the recommendations also works when the topic is routine or familiar and the reader is supportive.

Directness can backfire, though. If you announce the recommendations too quickly, the reader may immediately object to a single idea, one that you had no suspicion would trigger a negative reaction. Once the reader is opposed, changing an unfavorable mind-set may be difficult or impossible. A reader may also think you have oversimplified or overlooked something significant if you lay out all the recommendations before explaining how you arrived at them. When the reader must be led through the process of discovering the solution or recommendation, use the indirect method: present conclusions and recommendations last.

Most analytical reports answer questions about specific problems. How can we boost sales to baby boomers? Should we close the El Paso plant? Should we buy or lease company cars? How can we improve customer service? Four typical analytical reports answer business questions: justification/recommendation reports, feasibility reports, yardstick reports, and research studies. Because these reports all solve problems, the categories are not mutually exclusive. What distinguishes them is their goals and organization.

Justification/Recommendation Reports

Justification/recommendation reports follow the direct or the indirect pattern depending on the audience and the topic.

Both managers and employees must occasionally write reports that justify or recommend something, such as buying equipment, changing a procedure, hiring an employee, consolidating departments, or investing funds. Large organizations sometimes prescribe how these reports should be organized; they use forms with conventional headings. When you are free to select an organizational plan yourself, however, let your audience and topic determine your choice of direct or indirect structure.

Planning specialists from Bechtel, the giant U.S. engineering company, and representatives from Kuwait spent thousands of hours analyzing how to deal with the destruction caused by Saddam Hussein's occupation. This crew pumps seawater into wells to keep blowouts from recurring, one of the recommendations suggested after experts studied the problem. Analytical reports organized directly identify a problem, announce a recommendation immediately, and then explain the pros and cons of the recommendation.

Direct pattern. For nonsensitive topics and recommendations that will be agreeable to readers, you can organize directly according to the following sequence:

The direct pattern is appropriate for justification/recommendation reports on nonsensitive topics and for receptive audiences.

- Identify the problem or need briefly.
- Announce the recommendation, solution, or action concisely and with action verbs.
- Explain more fully the benefits of the recommendation or steps to be taken to solve the problem.
- Include a discussion of pros, cons, and costs.
- Conclude with a summary specifying the recommendation and action to be taken.

Here's how Justin Brown applied the process in justifying a purchase. Brown is operations manager in charge of a fleet of trucks for a large parcel delivery company in Atlanta. When he heard about a new Goodyear smart tire with an electronic chip, Justin thought his company should give the new tire a try. Because new tires would represent an irregular purchase and because they would require a pilot test, he wrote the justification/recommendation report, shown in Figure 13.5, to his boss. Justin describes his report in this way: "As more and more parcel delivery systems crop up, we have to find ways to cut costs so that we can remain competitive. Although more expensive initially, smart tires may solve a lot of our problems and save us money in the long haul. I knew Bill Montgomery, operations vice president, would be interested in them, particularly if we went slowly and purchased only 24 for a pilot test. Because Bill would be most interested in what they could do for us, I concentrated on benefits. In my first draft the benefits were lost in a couple of long paragraphs. Only after I read what I had written did I see that I was really talking about four separate benefits. Then I looked for words to summarize each one as a heading. So that Bill would know exactly what he should do, I concluded with specifics. All he had to do was say 'Go.'"

Indirect pattern. When a reader may oppose a recommendation or when circumstances suggest caution, don't be in a hurry to reveal your recommendation.

FIGURE 13.5 ● **Justification/Recommendation Report: Direct Pattern**

The Three Phases of the Writing Process

1

Analyze
The purpose of this report is to persuade the manager to authorize the purchase and pilot testing of smart tires.

Anticipate
The audience is a manager who is familiar with operations but not with this product. He will probably be receptive to the recommendation.

Adapt
Present the report data in a direct, straightforward manner.

2

Research
Collect data on how smart tires could benefit operations.

Organize
Discuss the problem briefly. Introduce and justify the recommendation by noting its cost-effectiveness and paperwork benefits. Explain the benefits of smart tires. Describe the action to be taken.

Compose
Write and print first draft.

3

Revise
Revise to break up long paragraphs about benefits. Isolate each benefit in an enumerated list with headings.

Proofread
Double-check all figures. Be sure all headings are parallel.

Evaluate
Does this report make its request concisely but emphatically? Will the reader see immediately what action is required?

TO: Bill Montgomery, Vice President
FROM: Justin Brown, Operations Manager *JB*
SUBJECT: Pilot Testing Smart Tires
DATE: July 19, 1994

Next to fuel, truck tires are our biggest operating cost. Last year we spent $211,000 replacing and retreading tires for 495 trucks. This year the costs will be greater because prices have jumped at least 12 percent and because we've increased our fleet to 550 trucks. Truck tires are an additional burden since they require labor-intensive paperwork to track their warranties, wear, and retread histories. To reduce our long-term costs and to improve our tire tracking system, I recommend that we do the following: *(Introduces problem briefly)*

- Purchase 24 Goodyear smart tires.
- Begin a one-year pilot test on six trucks.

(Presents recommendations immediately)

How Smart Tires Work

Smart tires have an embedded computer chip that monitors wear, performance, and durability. The chip also creates an electronic fingerprint for positive identification of a tire. By passing a hand-held sensor next to the tire, we can learn where and when a tire was made (for warranty and other identification), how much tread it had originally, and its serial number.

How Smart Tires Could Benefit Us

Although smart tires are initially more expensive than other tires, they could help us improve our operations and save us money in four ways:

1. Retreads. Goodyear believes that the wear data is so accurate that we should be able to retread every tire three times, instead of our current two times. If that's true, in one year we could save at least $27,000 in new tire costs.
2. Safety. Accurate and accessible wear data should reduce the danger of blowouts and flat tires. Last year, despite our rigorous maintenance program, drivers reported six blowouts.
3. Record keeping and maintenance. Smart tires could reduce our maintenance costs considerably. Currently, we use an electric branding iron to mark serial numbers on new tires. Our biggest headache is manually reading those serial numbers, decoding them, and maintaining records to meet safety regulations. Reading such data electronically could save us thousands of dollars in labor.
4. Theft protection. The chip can be used to monitor each tire as it leaves or enters the warehouse or yard, thus discouraging theft.

(Justifies recommendation by explaining product and benefits)

Summary and Action

(Explains recommendation in more detail)

Specifically, I recommend that you do the following:

- Authorize the special purchase of 24 Goodyear smart tires at $450 each, plus one electronic sensor at $1,200.
- Approve a one-year pilot test in our Atlanta territory that equips six trucks with smart tires and tracks their performance.

(Specifies action to be taken)

This greenhouse at the famous Keukenhof Gardens in Holland became a key point in the justification report of a tour organizer. In supporting his inclusion of the Keukenhof in a proposed itinerary for an American travel company, the writer argued that tourists can never be rained out. In addition to the 70 acres of outdoor gardens, thousands of flowers bloom under glass. Persuasive justification reports explain fully all the benefits of a recommendation and also anticipate possible reader objections.

Consider using the following sequence for an indirect approach to your recommendations:

The indirect pattern is appropriate for justification/recommendation reports on sensitive topics and for potentially unreceptive audiences.

- Make a general reference to the problem, not to your recommendation, in the subject line.
- Describe the problem or need your recommendation addresses. Use specific examples, supporting statistics, and authoritative quotes to lend credibility to the seriousness of the problem.
- Discuss alternative solutions, beginning with the least likely to succeed.
- Present the most promising alternative (your recommendation) last.
- Show how the advantages of your recommendation outweigh its disadvantages.
- Summarize your recommendation. If appropriate, specify the action it requires.
- Ask for authorization to proceed, if necessary.

Footnoting sources lends added credibility to justification/recommendation reports.

Diane Adams, an executive assistant at a large petroleum and mining company in Grand Prairie, Texas, received a challenging research assignment. Her boss, the director of Human Resources, asked her to investigate ways to persuade employees to quit smoking. Here's how she describes her task: "We banned smoking many years ago inside our buildings, but we never tried very hard to get smokers to actually kick their habits. My job was to gather information about the problem and how other companies have helped workers stop smoking. The report would go to my boss, but I knew he would pass it along to the management council for approval. If the report were just for my boss, I would put my recommendation

FIGURE 13.6 ● Justification/Recommendation Report: Indirect Pattern

TO: Damon Moore, Director, Human Resources **DATE:** October 11, 1994

FROM: Diane Adams, Executive Assistant *DA*

SUBJECT: MEASURES TO HELP EMPLOYEES STOP SMOKING

At your request, I have examined measures that encourage employees to quit smoking. As company records show, approximately 23 percent of our employees still smoke, despite the anti-smoking and clean-air policies we adopted in 1989. To collect data for this report, I studied professional and government publications; I also inquired at companies and clinics about stop-smoking programs. This report presents data describing the significance of the problem, three alternative solutions, and a recommendation based on my investigation.

Significance of Problem: Health Care and Productivity Losses

Employees who smoke are costly to any organization. The following statistics show the effects of smoking for workers and for organizations:

-- Absenteeism is 40 to 50 percent greater among smoking employees.
-- Accidents are two to three times greater among smokers.
-- Bronchitis, lung and heart disease, cancer, and early death are more frequent among smokers.[1]

Although our clean-air policy prohibits smoking in the building, shop, and office, we have done little to encourage employees to stop smoking. Many workers still go outside to smoke at lunch and breaks. Other companies have been far more proactive in their attempts to stop employee smoking. Many companies have found that persuading employees to stop smoking was a decisive factor in reducing their health insurance premiums. Below is a discussion of three common stop-smoking measures tried by other companies, along with a projected cost factor for each.

Alternative 1: Literature and Events

The least expensive and easiest stop-smoking measure involves the distribution of literature, such as "The Ten-Step Plan" from Smokefree Enterprises and government pamphlets citing smoking dangers. Posters are available from the American Lung Association and the American Heart Association. Some companies have also sponsored events such as the Great American Smoke-Out, a one-day occasion intended to develop group spirit in spurring smokers to quit. Studies show, however, that literature and company-sponsored events, operating by themselves, have little permanent effect in helping smokers quit.[2]

Cost: Negligible

---

[1]Kyle Johns, "No Smoking in Your Workplace," HR Focus, May 1993, 14.

[2]Nancy A. Woo, The Last Gasp (New York: Field Publishers, 1992), 145.

Introduces purpose of report, tells method of data collection, and previews organization

Avoids revealing recommendation immediately

Uses headings that combine function and description

Discusses least effective alternative first

Documents data sources for credibility

right up front, because I'm sure he would support it. But the management council is another story. They need persuasion because of the costs involved—and because some of them are smokers. Therefore, I put the alternative I favored last. To gain credibility, I footnoted my sources. I had enough material for a ten-page report, but I kept it to two pages in keeping with our company report policy."

Diane single-spaced her report, as shown in Figure 13.6, because that's her company's preference. Some companies prefer the readability of double spacing, however, so Figure 13.7 shows one page of Diane's report double-spaced. Be sure to check with your organization for its preference before printing out your reports.

Mr. Damon Moore Page 2 October 11, 1994

Alternative 2: Stop-Smoking Programs Outside the Workplace

Local clinics provide treatment programs in classes at their centers. Here in Houston we have Smokers' Treatment Center, ACC Motivation Center, and the New-Choice Program for Stopping Smoking. These behavior-modification stop-smoking programs are acknowledged to be more effective than literature distribution or incentive programs. However, studies of companies using off-workplace programs show that many employees fail to attend regularly and do not complete the programs.

Highlights costs for easy comparison

Cost: $750 per employee, 3-month individual program (New-Choice Program)
$500 per employee, 3-month group sessions

Alternative 3: Stop-Smoking Programs at the Workplace

Arranges alternatives so that most effective is last

Many clinics offer workplace programs with counselors meeting employees in company conference rooms. These programs have the advantage of keeping a firm's employees together so that they develop a group spirit and exert pressure on each other to succeed. The most successful programs are on company premises and also on company time. In other words, more smokers join the program and succeed in quitting when they have twin inducements of (a) a convenient workplace program and (b) release time to attend sessions. Employees participating in such programs had a 72 percent greater success record than employees attending the same stop-smoking program at an outside clinic.[3] A disadvantage of this arrangement, of course, is lost work time—amounting to about two hours a week for three months (using the New-Choice Program).

Cost: $500 per employee, 3-month program
2 hours per week release time for 3 months

Conclusions and Recommendation

Summarizes findings and ends with specific recommendation

Smokers seem to require discipline, counseling, and professional assistance in kicking the nicotine habit. Workplace stop-smoking programs, on company time, are more effective than literature, incentives, and off-workplace programs. If our goal is to reduce our health care costs, increase long-term productivity, and lead our employees to healthful, longer lives, we should invest in a workplace stop-smoking program with release time for smokers. Although the program temporarily reduces productivity, we can expect to recapture that loss in lower health care premiums, better attendance, and healthier employees. Therefore, I recommend that we begin a stop-smoking treatment program on company premises with two hours per week of release time for participants for three months.

Reveals recommendation only after discussing all alternatives

[3]Doug Manley, "Up in Smoke," Management Review, February 1992, 33.

Feasibility Reports

Feasibility reports analyze whether a proposal or plan will work.

Feasibility reports examine the practicality and advisability of following a course of action. They answer this question: Will this plan or proposal work? Feasibility reports typically are internal reports written to advise on matters such as consolidating departments, offering a wellness program to employees, or hiring an outside firm to handle a company's accounting or computing operations. These reports may also be written by consultants called in to investigate a problem. The focus in these reports is on the decision: stopping or proceeding with the proposal. Since your

FIGURE 13.7 ● Double-spaced Report (first page only)

TO: Damon Moore, Director, Human Resources **DATE:** October 11, 1994

FROM: Diane Adams, Executive Assistant DA

SUBJECT: MEASURES TO HELP EMPLOYEES STOP SMOKING

Leave two blank lines after subject

At your request, I have examined measures that encourage employees to quit smoking. As company records show, approximately 23 percent of our employees still smoke, despite the anti-smoking and clean-air policies we adopted in 1989. To collect data for this report, I studied professional and government publications; I also inquired at companies and clinics about stop-smoking programs. This report presents data describing the significance of the problem, three alternative solutions, and a recommendation based on my investigation.

Leave two blank lines above major headings

Significance of Problem: Health Care and Productivity Losses

Employees who smoke are costly to any organization. The following disturbing statistics paint a grim picture of the effects of smoking for workers and for organizations:

-- Absenteeism is 40 to 50 percent greater among smoking employees.

-- Accidents are two to three times greater among smokers.

-- Bronchitis, lung and heart disease, cancer, and early death are more frequent among smokers.[1]

Always indent paragraphs in double-spaced documents

Although our clean-air policy prohibits smoking in the building, shop, and office, we have done little to encourage employees to stop smoking. Many workers still go outside to smoke at lunch and breaks. Other companies have been far more proactive in their attempts to stop employee smoking. Many companies have found that persuading employees to stop smoking was a decisive factor in reducing their health insurance premiums. Following is a discussion of three common stop-smoking

[1]Kyle Johns, No Smoking in Your Workplace, HR Focus, May 1993, 14.

Single-space footnotes with double spacing between notes

role is not to persuade the reader to accept the decision, you'll want to present the decision immediately. In writing feasibility reports, consider these suggestions:

- Announce your decision immediately.
- Provide a description of the background and problem necessitating the proposal.
- Discuss the benefits of the proposal.
- Describe the problems that may result.
- Calculate the costs associated with the proposal, if appropriate.
- Show the time frame necessary for implementation of the proposal.

FIGURE 13.8 ● Feasibility Report

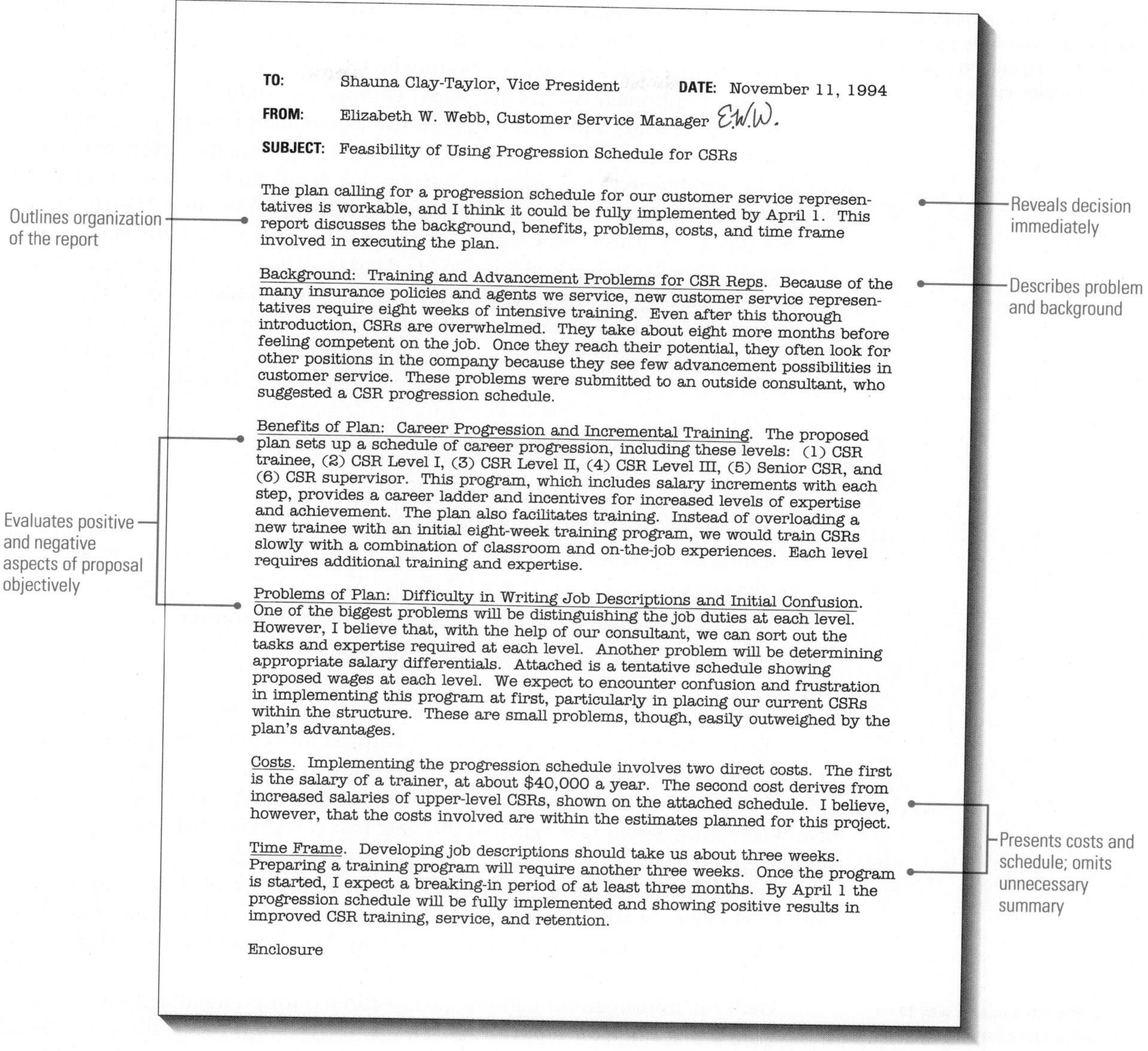

TO: Shauna Clay-Taylor, Vice President **DATE:** November 11, 1994

FROM: Elizabeth W. Webb, Customer Service Manager *E.W.W.*

SUBJECT: Feasibility of Using Progression Schedule for CSRs

The plan calling for a progression schedule for our customer service representatives is workable, and I think it could be fully implemented by April 1. This report discusses the background, benefits, problems, costs, and time frame involved in executing the plan.

Background: Training and Advancement Problems for CSR Reps. Because of the many insurance policies and agents we service, new customer service representatives require eight weeks of intensive training. Even after this thorough introduction, CSRs are overwhelmed. They take about eight more months before feeling competent on the job. Once they reach their potential, they often look for other positions in the company because they see few advancement possibilities in customer service. These problems were submitted to an outside consultant, who suggested a CSR progression schedule.

Benefits of Plan: Career Progression and Incremental Training. The proposed plan sets up a schedule of career progression, including these levels: (1) CSR trainee, (2) CSR Level I, (3) CSR Level II, (4) CSR Level III, (5) Senior CSR, and (6) CSR supervisor. This program, which includes salary increments with each step, provides a career ladder and incentives for increased levels of expertise and achievement. The plan also facilitates training. Instead of overloading a new trainee with an initial eight-week training program, we would train CSRs slowly with a combination of classroom and on-the-job experiences. Each level requires additional training and expertise.

Problems of Plan: Difficulty in Writing Job Descriptions and Initial Confusion. One of the biggest problems will be distinguishing the job duties at each level. However, I believe that, with the help of our consultant, we can sort out the tasks and expertise required at each level. Another problem will be determining appropriate salary differentials. Attached is a tentative schedule showing proposed wages at each level. We expect to encounter confusion and frustration in implementing this program at first, particularly in placing our current CSRs within the structure. These are small problems, though, easily outweighed by the plan's advantages.

Costs. Implementing the progression schedule involves two direct costs. The first is the salary of a trainer, at about $40,000 a year. The second cost derives from increased salaries of upper-level CSRs, shown on the attached schedule. I believe, however, that the costs involved are within the estimates planned for this project.

Time Frame. Developing job descriptions should take us about three weeks. Preparing a training program will require another three weeks. Once the program is started, I expect a breaking-in period of at least three months. By April 1 the progression schedule will be fully implemented and showing positive results in improved CSR training, service, and retention.

Enclosure

Outlines organization of the report
Reveals decision immediately
Describes problem and background
Evaluates positive and negative aspects of proposal objectively
Presents costs and schedule; omits unnecessary summary

Elizabeth Webb, customer service manager for a large insurance company in Omaha, Nebraska, wrote the feasibility report shown in Figure 13.8. She describes the report thus: "We had been losing customer service reps (CSRs) after they were trained and were most valuable to us. When I talked with our vice president about the problem, she didn't want me to take time away from my job to investigate what other companies were doing to retain their CSRs. Instead, we hired a consultant who suggested that we use a CSR career progression schedule. The vice president then wanted to know if the consultant's plan was feasible. Although my report is only one page long, it provides all necessary information: approval, background, benefits, problems, costs, and schedule."

● **A typical feasibility report presents the decision, background information, benefits, problems, costs, and a schedule.**

Yardstick Reports

● **Yardstick reports consider alternative solutions to a problem by establishing criteria against which to weigh options.**

"Yardstick" reports examine problems with two or more solutions. To evaluate the best solution, the writer establishes criteria by which to compare the alternatives. The criteria then act as a yardstick against which all the alternatives are measured. This yardstick approach is effective when companies establish specifications for equipment purchases, and then compare each manufacturer's product with the established specs. The yardstick approach is also effective when exact specifications cannot be established. For example, when the giant aircraft firm McDonnell Douglas considered relocating, it evaluated cities like Mobile, Fort Worth, Houston, Kansas City, Tulsa, Salt Lake City, and Mesa. For each of these sites, McDonnell Douglas compared labor costs, land availability and costs, tax breaks, and housing costs. It also weighed other criteria such as access to markets and transportation costs for raw materials. It did not set up exact specifications for each category; it merely compared each city in these various categories. The real advantage to yardstick reports is that alternatives can be measured consistently using the same criteria.

Reports using a yardstick approach typically are organized this way:

- Begin by describing the problem or need.
- Explain possible solutions and alternatives.
- Establish criteria for comparing the alternatives; tell how they were selected or developed.
- Discuss and evaluate each alternative in terms of the criteria.
- Draw conclusions and make recommendations.

Kelly Lopez, benefits administrator for computer manufacturer CompuTech, was called on to write a report comparing outplacement agencies. These agencies counsel discharged employees and help find new positions; fees are paid by the former employer. Kelly knew that times were bad for CompuTech and that extensive downsizing would take place in the next two years. Her task was to compare outplacement agencies and recommend one to CompuTech.

After collecting information, Kelly's biggest problem was organizing the data and developing a system for making comparisons. All the outplacement agencies she investigated seemed to offer the same basic package of services. Here's how she described her report, shown in Figure 13.9.

● **Grids are a useful way to organize and compare data for a yardstick report.**

"With the information I gathered about three outplacement agencies, I made a big grid listing the names of the agencies across the top. Down the side I listed general categories—such as services, costs, and reputation. Then I filled in the information for each agency. This grid, which began to look like a table, helped me organize all the bits and pieces of information. After studying the grid, I saw that all the information could be grouped into four categories: counseling services, secretarial/research services, reputation, and costs. I made these the criteria I would use to compare agencies. Next, I divided my grid into two parts, which became Table 1 and Table 2. In writing the report, I could have made each agency a separate heading, followed by a discussion of how it measured up to the criteria. Immediately, though, I saw how repetitious that would become. So I used the criteria as headings and discussed how each agency met that criteria—or failed to meet it. Making a recommendation was easy once I had the tables made and could see how the agencies compared."

FIGURE 13.9 ● Yardstick Report

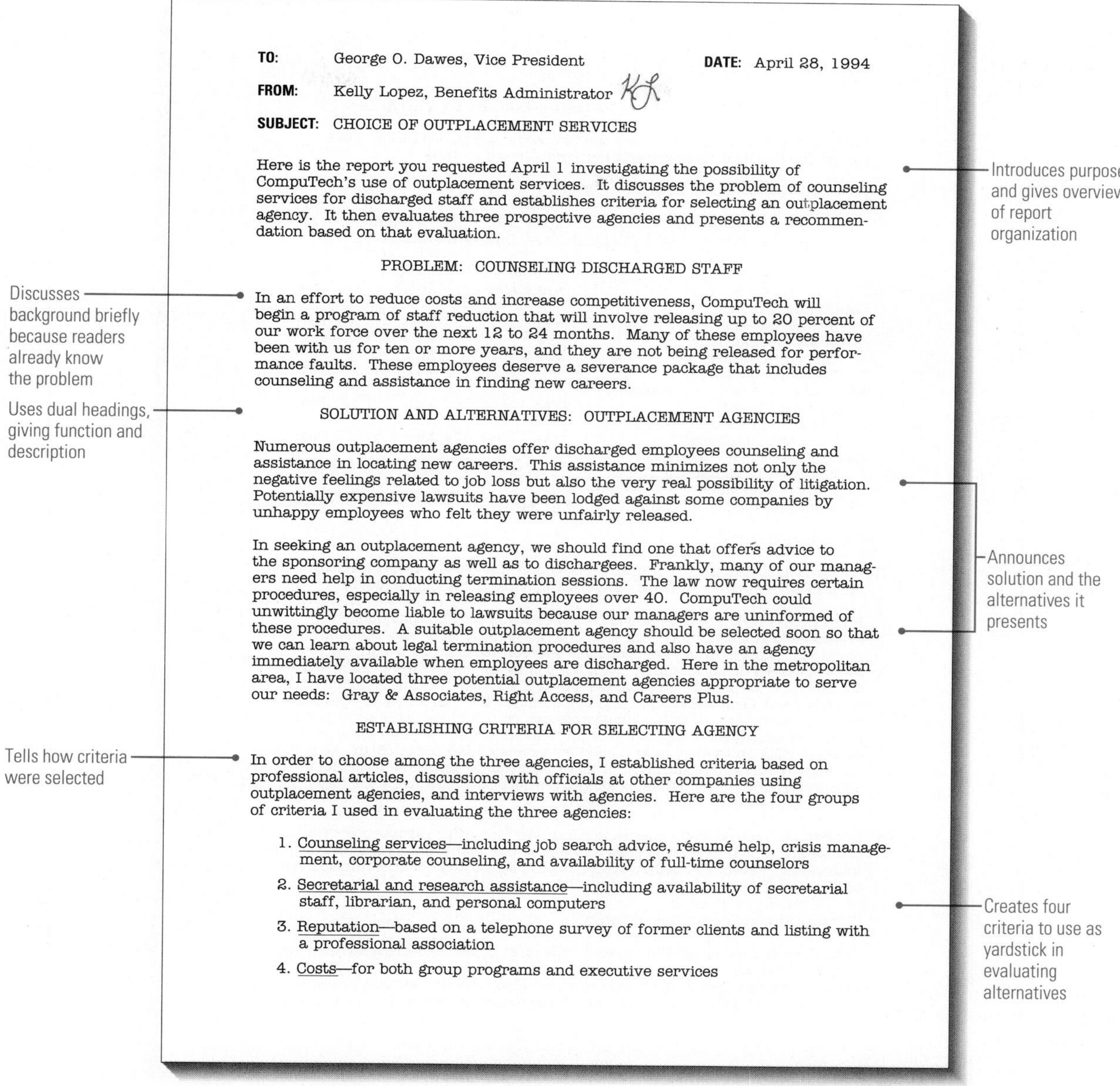

TO: George O. Dawes, Vice President **DATE:** April 28, 1994

FROM: Kelly Lopez, Benefits Administrator *KL*

SUBJECT: CHOICE OF OUTPLACEMENT SERVICES

Here is the report you requested April 1 investigating the possibility of CompuTech's use of outplacement services. It discusses the problem of counseling services for discharged staff and establishes criteria for selecting an outplacement agency. It then evaluates three prospective agencies and presents a recommendation based on that evaluation.

PROBLEM: COUNSELING DISCHARGED STAFF

In an effort to reduce costs and increase competitiveness, CompuTech will begin a program of staff reduction that will involve releasing up to 20 percent of our work force over the next 12 to 24 months. Many of these employees have been with us for ten or more years, and they are not being released for performance faults. These employees deserve a severance package that includes counseling and assistance in finding new careers.

SOLUTION AND ALTERNATIVES: OUTPLACEMENT AGENCIES

Numerous outplacement agencies offer discharged employees counseling and assistance in locating new careers. This assistance minimizes not only the negative feelings related to job loss but also the very real possibility of litigation. Potentially expensive lawsuits have been lodged against some companies by unhappy employees who felt they were unfairly released.

In seeking an outplacement agency, we should find one that offers advice to the sponsoring company as well as to dischargees. Frankly, many of our managers need help in conducting termination sessions. The law now requires certain procedures, especially in releasing employees over 40. CompuTech could unwittingly become liable to lawsuits because our managers are uninformed of these procedures. A suitable outplacement agency should be selected soon so that we can learn about legal termination procedures and also have an agency immediately available when employees are discharged. Here in the metropolitan area, I have located three potential outplacement agencies appropriate to serve our needs: Gray & Associates, Right Access, and Careers Plus.

ESTABLISHING CRITERIA FOR SELECTING AGENCY

In order to choose among the three agencies, I established criteria based on professional articles, discussions with officials at other companies using outplacement agencies, and interviews with agencies. Here are the four groups of criteria I used in evaluating the three agencies:

1. Counseling services—including job search advice, résumé help, crisis management, corporate counseling, and availability of full-time counselors
2. Secretarial and research assistance—including availability of secretarial staff, librarian, and personal computers
3. Reputation—based on a telephone survey of former clients and listing with a professional association
4. Costs—for both group programs and executive services

Introduces purpose and gives overview of report organization
Discusses background briefly because readers already know the problem
Uses dual headings, giving function and description
Announces solution and the alternatives it presents
Tells how criteria were selected
Creates four criteria to use as yardstick in evaluating alternatives

Research Studies

In some business reports the emphasis is on the research. These studies examine a problem, collect data to solve the problem, and reach conclusions growing out of the findings. This scientific approach leads the reader through all the steps to discovering the answer, positive or negative, to a problem. The answer comes as a result of assembling facts and evidence. Throughout the report the emphasis is on educating the reader with objective facts and reasoning.

● **Research studies educate readers through scientific data collection and analysis.**

FIGURE 13.9 (continued)

Vice President Dawes | Page 2 | April 28, 1994

DISCUSSION: EVALUATING AGENCIES BY CRITERIA

Each agency was evaluated using the four criteria just described. Data comparing the first three criteria are summarized in Table 1.

Table 1

A COMPARISON OF SERVICES AND REPUTATIONS FOR THREE LOCAL OUTPLACEMENT AGENCIES

	Gray & Associates	Right Access	Careers Plus
Counseling services			
Résumé advice	Yes	Yes	Yes
Crisis management	Yes	No	Yes
Corporate counseling	Yes	No	No
Full-time counselors	Yes	No	Yes
Secretarial, research assistance			
Secretarial staff	Yes	Yes	Yes
Librarian, research library	Yes	No	Yes
Personal computers	Yes	No	Yes
Listed by National Association of Career Consultants	Yes	No	Yes
Reputation (telephone survey of former clients)	Excellent	Good	Excellent

Places table close to spot where it is first mentioned

Summarizes complex data in table for easy reading and reference

Counseling Services

All three agencies offered similar basic counseling services with job-search and résumé advice. They differed, however, in three significant areas.

Right Access does not offer crisis management, a service that puts the discharged employee in contact with a counselor the same day the employee is released. Experts in the field consider this service especially important to help the discharge begin "bonding" with the counselor immediately. Immediate counseling also helps the discharge through the most traumatic moments of one of life's great disappointments and helps him or her learn how to break the news to family members. Crisis management can be instrumental in reducing lawsuits because discharges immediately begin to focus on career planning instead of concentrating on their pain and need for revenge. Moreover, Right Access does not employ full-time counselors; it hires part-timers according to demand. Industry authorities advise against using agencies whose staff members are inexperienced and employed on an "as-needed" basis.

Highlights the similarities and differences among the alternatives

In addition, neither Right Access nor Careers Plus offer regular corporate counseling, which I feel is critical in training our managers to conduct terminal interviews. Careers Plus, however, suggested that it could schedule special workshops if desired.

Secretarial and Research Assistance

Both Gray & Associates and Careers Plus offer complete secretarial services and personal computers. Dischargees have access to staff and equipment to assist them in their job searches. These agencies also provide research libraries, librarians, and databases of company information to help in securing interviews.

Does not repeat obvious data from table

For example, the cable TV industry hired a research firm to investigate this question: What effect will direct broadcast satellites have on cable TV? Direct broadcast satellite (DBS) systems employ high-power satellites to permit reception by small home-receiving terminals (dishes). Researchers developed three hypotheses. Cable operators would face severe competition if (1) DBS became the first national distributor of high-definition television programs, (2) DBS succeeded in providing low-cost small-antenna home receivers, and (3) DBS was able to offer

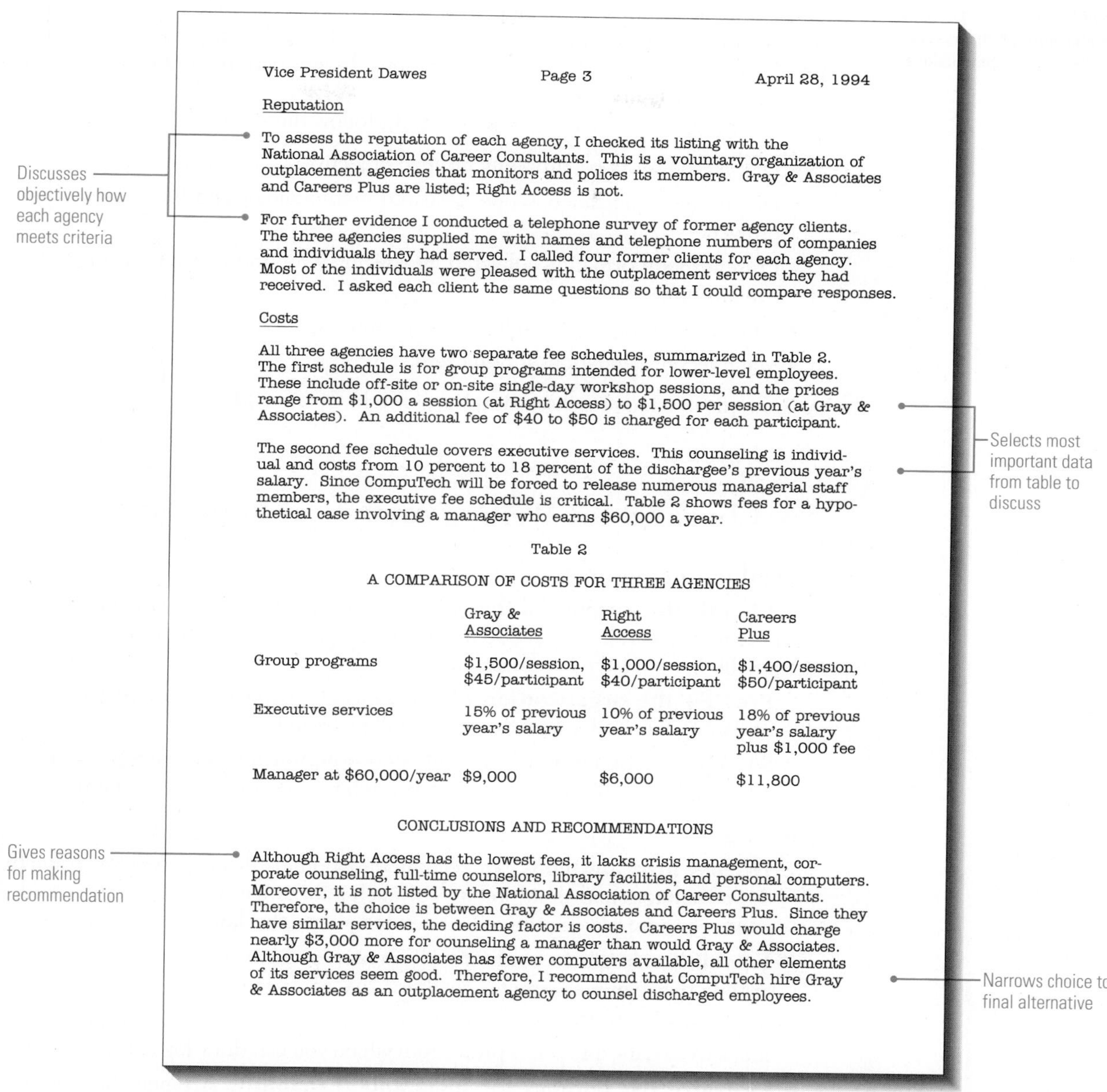

Discusses objectively how each agency meets criteria
Selects most important data from table to discuss
Gives reasons for making recommendation
Narrows choice to final alternative

Vice President Dawes Page 3 April 28, 1994

Reputation

To assess the reputation of each agency, I checked its listing with the National Association of Career Consultants. This is a voluntary organization of outplacement agencies that monitors and polices its members. Gray & Associates and Careers Plus are listed; Right Access is not.

For further evidence I conducted a telephone survey of former agency clients. The three agencies supplied me with names and telephone numbers of companies and individuals they had served. I called four former clients for each agency. Most of the individuals were pleased with the outplacement services they had received. I asked each client the same questions so that I could compare responses.

Costs

All three agencies have two separate fee schedules, summarized in Table 2. The first schedule is for group programs intended for lower-level employees. These include off-site or on-site single-day workshop sessions, and the prices range from $1,000 a session (at Right Access) to $1,500 per session (at Gray & Associates). An additional fee of $40 to $50 is charged for each participant.

The second fee schedule covers executive services. This counseling is individual and costs from 10 percent to 18 percent of the dischargee's previous year's salary. Since CompuTech will be forced to release numerous managerial staff members, the executive fee schedule is critical. Table 2 shows fees for a hypothetical case involving a manager who earns $60,000 a year.

Table 2

A COMPARISON OF COSTS FOR THREE AGENCIES

	Gray & Associates	Right Access	Careers Plus
Group programs	$1,500/session, $45/participant	$1,000/session, $40/participant	$1,400/session, $50/participant
Executive services	15% of previous year's salary	10% of previous year's salary	18% of previous year's salary plus $1,000 fee
Manager at $60,000/year	$9,000	$6,000	$11,800

CONCLUSIONS AND RECOMMENDATIONS

Although Right Access has the lowest fees, it lacks crisis management, corporate counseling, full-time counselors, library facilities, and personal computers. Moreover, it is not listed by the National Association of Career Consultants. Therefore, the choice is between Gray & Associates and Careers Plus. Since they have similar services, the deciding factor is costs. Careers Plus would charge nearly $3,000 more for counseling a manager than would Gray & Associates. Although Gray & Associates has fewer computers available, all other elements of its services seem good. Therefore, I recommend that CompuTech hire Gray & Associates as an outplacement agency to counsel discharged employees.

major network programming. Each of these hypotheses was studied, and data were collected. Researchers described their findings and drew conclusions. One conclusion stated that DBS did, indeed, represent a considerable threat to the cable industry. That cable owners should consider buying into DBS was a natural recommendation following from this conclusion.

In this kind of research study, the reader must be informed and guided through the research so that the conclusions seem rational. Although an executive

Research studies follow the indirect pattern to guide the reader through the research process to the conclusions.

summary may reveal the conclusions and recommendations first, the report itself follows an indirect development pattern so that readers can follow the discovery of the answer. This means that the report begins with discussion of the problem and is followed by exploration of possible solutions. It ends with reasons explaining the selection of one course of action.

In writing the results of a research study, follow this organizational plan:

- Discuss the purpose, problem, or need objectively.
- Define the significance, scope, research methodology, and limitations of the project.
- Present the information collected, organizing it around reasons leading to the conclusions.
- Draw conclusions that result naturally from the findings.
- Make recommendations if requested.

An example of a long research study is shown in Chapter 14.

Checklist for Writing Analytical Reports

Introduction

✔ **Identify the purpose of the report.** Explain why the report is being written. For research studies also include the significance, scope, limitations, and methodology of the investigation.

✔ **Preview the organization of the report.** Especially for long reports, explain to the reader how the report will be organized.

✔ **Summarize the conclusions and recommendations for receptive audiences.** Use the direct pattern only if you have the confidence of the reader.

Findings

✔ **Discuss pros and cons.** In recommendation/justification reports evaluate the advantages and disadvantages of each alternative. For unreceptive audiences consider placing the recommended alternative last.

✔ **Establish criteria to evaluate alternatives.** In "yardstick" studies create criteria to use in measuring each alternative consistently.

✔ **Support the findings with evidence.** Supply facts, statistics, expert opinion, survey data, and other proof from which you can draw logical conclusions.

✔ **Organize the findings for logic and readability.** Arrange the findings around the alternatives or the reasons leading to the conclusion. Use headings, enumerations, lists, tables, and visual aids to focus emphasis.

Conclusions/Recommendations

✔ **Draw reasonable conclusions from the findings.** Develop conclusions that answer the research question. Justify the conclusions with highlights from the findings.

✔ **Make recommendations, if asked.** For multiple recommendations prepare a list. Use action verbs. Explain needed action.

Summary of Learning Goals

1. **Distinguish between informational and analytical reports.** Informational reports provide data and answer questions without offering recommendations or analysis. They may report sales, routine operations, trips, conferences, or compliance. Analytical reports organize data, draw conclusions, and often make recommendations. They may include justification/recommendation, feasibility, yardstick, and research reports.
2. **Write periodic reports.** Periodic reports—such as sales, accounts payable, and personnel reports—generally summarize regular activities occurring during the reporting period. They also describe irregular events demanding attention and highlight special needs and problems.
3. **Draft situational reports.** Trip, convention, and conference reports often specify the event, summarize three to five main points of interest to the reader, itemize expenses, and close with appreciation or a suggestion for action. Progress and interim reports identify a project, provide background data, explain the work currently in progress, anticipate problems and remedies, and discuss future activities. Progress reports should always include an expected completion date.
4. **Prepare investigative and compliance reports.** Investigative reports examine a topic (such as a production problem) but do not draw conclusions or make recommendations. Compliance reports present data in compliance with local, state, and federal laws. These reports should be honest, accurate, and prompt.
5. **Compose direct and indirect justification/recommendation reports.** Justification/recommendation reports organized directly identify a problem, immediately announce a recommendation or solution, explain and discuss its merits, and summarize the action to be taken. Justification/recommendation reports organized indirectly describe a problem, discuss alternative solutions, prove the superiority of one solution, and ask for authorization to proceed with that solution.
6. **Write feasibility reports.** Feasibility reports study the advisability of following a course of action. They generally announce the author's proposal immediately. Then they describe the background, advantages and disadvantages, costs, and schedule for implementing the proposal.
7. **Draft yardstick reports.** "Yardstick" reports compare two or more solutions to a problem by measuring each against a set of established criteria. They usually describe a problem, explain possible solutions, establish criteria for comparing alternatives, evaluate each alternative in terms of the criteria, draw conclusions, and make recommendations. The advantage to yardstick reports is consistency in comparing various alternatives.
8. **Discuss research reports.** Research reports identify a problem, collect data to solve the problem, and reach conclusions drawn from the findings. These scientific reports generally discuss a problem or need objectively; define the significance, scope, methodology, and limitations of the study; gather information; present the data; draw conclusions; and make recommendations, if requested.

Chapter Review

1. Name four categories of informational reports.

2. Describe periodic reports and what they generally contain.

3. Describe situational reports and give two examples.

4. What should a progress report include?

5. How can the body of an investigative or other informational report be organized?

6. What are compliance reports?

7. Informational reports emphasize facts. What do analytical reports emphasize?

8. When should an analytical report be organized directly?

9. How can directness backfire?

10. What sequence should a direct recommendation/justification report follow?

11. What sequence should an indirect recommendation/justification report follow?

12. What is a feasibility report?

13. Are feasibility reports usually intended for internal or external audiences?

14. What is a yardstick report?

15. How do research studies differ from other problem-solving reports?

Discussion

1. Do most reports flow upward or downward? Why?

2. Why are large companies more likely to require reports than smaller ones?

3. If you were doubtful about writing a report directly or indirectly, which pattern would be safer? Why?

4. What are the major differences between informational and analytical reports?

5. **Ethical Issue:** Discuss the ethics of using persuasive tactics to convince a report's readers to accept its conclusions. Is it ethical to be persuasive only when you believe in the soundness and truth of your conclusions?

Exercises

13.1 Periodic Reports

In a business you know, name five situations that would require periodic reports. If you've had little business experience, imagine a large department store. What kinds of periodic reports would management require of department managers, buyers, and operations staff? Describe how one report might be organized.

13.2 Convention, Conference, and Seminar Reports

Select an article from a business publication (such as *The Wall Street Journal, Business Week, Forbes, Fortune,* or *Working Woman*) describing a convention, conference, or seminar. Imagine that you attended that meeting for your company. Outline a report to your boss describing the meeting.

13.3 Situational and Investigative Reports

For each of the following situations, suggest a report type and briefly discuss how the report would be organized.

a. The mail center could save over $10,000 a year if the company would allow it to invest in reusable nylon mail pouches to deliver customer insurance policies to branch offices.

b. The manager wants a quickie overview of quality circles—just to keep her informed. She sees no direct need for the data immediately.

c. Home Depot is considering using shrink wrapping to secure merchandise stored on racks that range from 8 to 16 feet high. Management is concerned about the safety of employees and customers during earthquakes.

d. King Grocery must implement a worker-incentive wage program. This plan would establish standards for warehouse workers and generously reward those who exceed the standard with extra pay and time off. The current wage program pays everyone the same, causing dissension and underachievement. Other wage plans, including a union three-tier system, have drawbacks. Expect management to oppose the worker-incentive plan.

e. Your convention committee has selected a site, set up a tentative program, and is now working on keynote speakers and exhibitors. Report your progress to the organization president.

f. The New Carlisle assembly plant is plagued by high absenteeism and worker turnover. What can be done about eliminating these problems?

13.4 Yardstick Report Criteria

Assume you are a benefits analyst who has been assigned the task of investigating three health care plans for your company. You must recommend a plan that the company can afford and that will satisfy employees. Your company is facing a 45 percent increase in its basic major medical plan. After doing some research, you find two other options: a health maintenance organization and MedicPlus, a plan that offers choice and is somewhat cheaper than your present carrier. You decide to compare the three plans using the "yardstick" approach. What criteria could you use to compare plans? How would you organize the final report?

Problems: Informational Reports

13.5 Periodic Report: Filling in the Boss

Write a report of your month's accomplishments addressed to your boss. For a job that you currently hold or a previous one, describe your regular activities, discuss irregular events that management should be aware of, and highlight any special needs or problems. Use memo format.

13.6 Conference Report: In Your Dreams

From a business periodical select an article describing a conference, seminar, convention, or trip (preferably to an exotic spot) connected with your major area of study. The article must be at least 500 words long. Assume that you attended the meeting or took the trip at the expense of your company. Prepare a memo report to your supervisor.

13.7 Progress Report: Heading Toward That Degree

Assume you have made an agreement with your parents (or spouse, relative, or significant friend) that you would submit a progress report at this time describing headway toward your educational goal (such as employment, degree, or certificate). List your specific achievements, and outline what you have left to complete. Prepare a report in letter format.

13.8 Progress Report: Checking In

If you are preparing a long report (see Chapter 14), write a progress report informing your instructor of your work. Briefly describe the project (its purpose, scope, limitations, and methodology), work you have completed, work yet to be completed, problems encountered, future activities, and expected completion date. Address the memo report to your instructor.

13.9 Investigative Report: All You Ever Wanted to Know

Investigate a Fortune 500 company for whom you might like to work. Describe its major product, service, or emphasis. Find its Fortune 500 ranking, its current stock price (if listed), and its high and low range for the year. Include its profit-to-earnings ratio. Describe its latest marketing plan, promotion, or product. Identify its home office, president's name, and number of employees. Provide a short history of the company. Address a memo report to your professor.

13.10 Investigative Report: Selling Abroad

You have been asked to help prepare the sales section in a training manual for American companies doing business with [select a country, preferably one for which your library has *Culturgram* materials]. Collect data from the Culturgram and from the country's embassy in Washington. Interview an on-campus international student from your assigned country (a list of international students may be available from your campus student affairs office) or a recent business visitor to the country. Collect information about formats for written communication, observance of holidays, customary greetings, business ethics (for example, business bribes), and other topics of interest to businesspeople. Remember that your report should promote business, not tourism. Prepare a memo report addressed to Kelly Johnson, editor.

13.11 Investigative Report: Between the Covers

As a research assistant in an advertising agency, you must maintain data files about various magazines in which your clients may place ads. Select a business-oriented magazine and examine four to six issues. Collect information about articles (length, seriousness of topics, humor), readability (word, sentence, and paragraph length; formal or informal tone), format and design (color, white space, glamor), and pictures and graphics. Examine the ads (advertisers, products and services, appeals). Does the magazine accept tobacco and liquor ads? At what audience is the magazine aimed (sex, education, age, income, interests)? Consider other characteristics in which your clients may be interested. Address a memo report to Judy Gold, print media coordinator.

Problems: Analytical Reports

13.12 Justification/Recommendation Report: We Need It

Identify a piece of equipment that should be purchased or replaced (photocopier, fax, VCR, computer, printer, camera, or the like). Write a memo report addressed to your boss. Assume that you can be direct and straightforward about this request.

13.13 Justification/Recommendation Report: Time for a Change

Identify a problem or a procedure that must be changed at your job (such as poor scheduling of employees, outdated equipment, slow order processing, failure to encourage employees to participate fully, restrictive rules, inadequate training, or disappointed customers). Using an indirect pattern, write a recommendation report suggesting one or more ways to solve the problem. Address the memo report to your boss.

13.14 Collaborative Justification/ Recommendation Report: Solving a Campus Problem

In groups of three to five, investigate a problem on your campus, such as inadequate parking, slow registration, poor class schedules, inefficient bookstore, weak job-placement program, unrealistic degree requirements, or lack of internship programs. Within your group develop a solution to the problem. After reviewing persuasive techniques discussed in Chapter 9, write a group or individual justification/recommendation report(s) addressed to the proper campus official. Decide whether to use direct or indirect patterning based on how you expect the reader to react to your recommendation. With your instructor's approval, send the report.

13.15 Feasibility Report: International Organization

To fulfill a senior project in your department, you have been asked to submit a letter report to the dean evaluating the feasibility of starting an organization of international students on campus. Find out how many international students there are, what nations they represent, how one goes about starting an organization, and whether a faculty sponsor is needed. Assume that you conducted an informal survey of international students. Of the 39 who filled out the survey, 31 said they would be interested in joining.

13.16 Feasibility Report: Improving Employee Fitness

Your company is considering ways to promote employee fitness and morale. Select a possibility that seems reasonable for your company (softball league, bowling teams, basketball league, lunchtime walks, lunchtime fitness speakers and demos, company-sponsored health club memberships, workout room, fitness center, fitness director, and so on). Assume that your boss has tentatively agreed to one of the programs and has asked you to write a memo report investigating its feasibility.

13.17 Feasibility Report: Reducing, Reusing, and Recycling

As a management trainee for a large hotel chain, you have been asked to investigate the feasibility of saving energy and reducing waste within the hotel chain. Your task is to learn how other hotels are improving their environmental record. For example, the Boston Park Plaza eliminated complimentary plastic shower caps and installed thermal windows; the Grand Traverse Resort in Michigan uses a wide array of recycled products and energy-saving utilities; and Days Inn in Fort Myers, Florida, shreds wastepaper for compost mulch. Hotel Inter-Continental, with 100 hotels in 47 countries, has prepared a checklist of 134 actions to help employees "reduce, reuse, and recycle." Your task is not to present specifics on implementing a hotel environmental program, but rather to decide if such a program is feasible. What are the benefits of environmental programs for hotels? You could begin your research by looking at "Saving by Recycling: Greening of the Grand Hotel," *New York Times,* 8 August 1992, Y17. Address your memo report to Leland Jeffrey, Operations.

13.18 Yardstick Report: Evaluating Equipment

You recently complained to your boss that you were unhappy with a piece of equipment that you use (printer, computer, copier, fax, or the like). After some thought, the boss decided you were right and told you to go shopping. Compare at least three different manufacturers' models and recommend one. Since the company will be purchasing ten or more units and since several managers must approve the purchase, write a careful report documenting your findings. Establish at least five criteria for comparing the models. Submit a memo report to your boss.

13.19 Yardstick Report: Measuring the Alternatives

Consider a problem where you work or in an organization you know. Select a problem with several alternative solutions or courses of action (retaining the present status could be one alternative). Develop criteria that could be used to evaluate each alternative. Write a report measuring each alternative by the yardstick you have created. Recommend a course of action to your boss or to the organization head.

Proposals and Formal Reports

LEARNING GOALS

After studying this chapter, you should be able to

1. Discuss the components of informal proposals
2. Discuss the special components in formal proposals
3. Distinguish between proposals and formal reports
4. Identify formal report components that precede its introduction
5. Outline topics that might be covered in the introduction of a formal report
6. Describe the components of a formal report that follow the introduction
7. Specify tips that aid writers of formal reports

Hewlett-Packard: Career Track Profile

"First, you must identify a customer's 'hot buttons.' That's the most important step in putting together any proposal," says Mary Piecewicz.

As a technical editor at the Hewlett-Packard Proposal Center in Burlington, Massachusetts, Mary knows what she's talking about. She has helped write hundreds of successful proposals selling large installations of HP computers to banks, brokerage houses, hotel chains, clothing manufacturers, and insurance companies.

"To conquer writer's block, begin with a bulleted list of what the customer is looking for. This list . . . gets you started and keeps you headed in the right direction."

Pushing customers' "hot buttons" involves finding out exactly what they want in a computer purchase. Often buyers are looking for more than low price and high performance. "Some customers are interested primarily in support. They want to be sure we'll walk them through the whole installation and train their employees. Others want a solid company that promises to stay with them for the long haul. You can't really put a dollar value on these warm and fuzzy things," observes Mary. "But they are critical issues and must be recognized early so that they can be addressed in a proposal."

Like many businesspeople, Mary Piecewicz eventually became an expert in a field that she knew nothing about when she was in college. After graduating from Boston College (with a degree in sociology), she took a job in marketing. Building on a strong foundation of basic language skills, she enrolled in technical writing courses at local universities. Mary also developed on-the-job writing skills at an electronics company, later joining Hewlett-Packard as an editor of proposals.

Proposals (written offers to sell services and equipment) are so important that Hewlett-Packard has a special in-house department devoted wholly to developing them. "Competition today is tough," notes Mary. "Customers are shopping around—especially for big purchases. They want to compare apples to apples, and proposals allow them to do that. Big corporations are now going the proposal route simply because money is tight, and they want to get the most for their dollar. Companies are also trying to protect themselves. Since a proposal is a legally binding document, whatever you put down on paper you have to be able to supply. Proposals allow companies to find the best deal while at the same time giving them protection."

At the HP Proposal Center, all projects are team efforts. "No proposal is ever written in isolation. If you can't work with others or if you have a sensitive ego, you're lost in this field. I've learned to be a kind of Lady Teflon," laughs Mary. A team usually consists of a sales representative familiar with the client, an HP technical consultant who knows the hardware, and support and contracts personnel. The proposal production coordinator and a proposal manager pull the whole project together.

One of the biggest problems for HP sales representatives working on a proposal team is writer's block. Untrained in writing, they often just can't get started. Since they are responsible for preparing the executive summary of the proposal (the most important section), Mary generally offers some coaching. "To conquer writer's block, begin with a bulleted list of what the customer is looking for. This list is like a road map; it gets you started and keeps you headed in the right direction."

This Hewlett-Packard Media Applications Learning Laboratory is one of 50 HP learning centers around the world. The centers emphasize self-paced, interactive training. These research and development laboratories enable HP to study the technology and documentation support materials of its products. HP also uses the labs to formulate and improve curricula for teaching computer studies.

Staying tuned in to the customer's concerns is Mary's number one focus in writing proposals. "Much of the time you think you're focusing on the customer, but you're really just singing your own song. For example, a customer wants a cost-effective solution to a problem, and you try to describe a wonderful solution. But all you talk about is your state-of-the-art technology, performance, and reputation—without mentioning costs. You weren't really listening to what the customer said. It's like writing a college term paper. You've found all this great stuff that you want to use, and whether it's relevant or not, you're going to use it." Ready-made, all-purpose answers are not very persuasive in proposals.

How do you know what customers really want? Mary recalls one proposal written for an international hotel chain that wanted to upgrade its reservations system. But all they sent out was an informal one-page request with few details. Fortunately, HP's sales representative previously had talked extensively with the chain's hotel managers and had a good idea of what they really needed—even though these wants were not spelled out in their vague request. The resulting successful proposal zeroed in on two "hot buttons": corporate reliability and long-term service. "They wanted to know that HP wouldn't leave them high and dry after the equipment was installed."

In organizing proposals, HP always responds to the customer's outline. If the customer doesn't specify a plan, proposals are arranged as follows: Section 1 includes the executive summary and management overview. Section 2 covers specifications and technical descriptions. Section 3 lists costs, terms, conditions. Section 4 presents supplemental literature.

Because of its importance, the executive summary gets special attention. It may open with a brief history of HP, but its primary focus is on the customer's needs. "We address every customer issue and specify our 'differentiators.' What makes HP different from our competitors? What makes us stand out? The executive summary is really the selling tool in our proposals, and we spend the most time on it."[1]

Preparing Formal and Informal Proposals

● **Proposals are persuasive offers to solve problems, provide services, or sell equipment.**

Proposals are written offers to solve problems, provide services, or sell equipment. Although some proposals are internal, often taking the form of justification and recommendation reports, most proposals are external. The external proposals that Mary Piecewicz helps write at Hewlett-Packard are an important means of generating income for the giant computer company.

Because proposals are vital to their success, some businesses hire consultants or maintain specialists, like Mary, who do nothing but write proposals. Such proposals typically tell how a problem can be solved, what procedure will be followed, who will do it, how long it will take, and how much it will cost.

● **Government agencies and large companies use requests for proposals (RFPs) to solicit competitive bids on projects.**

Proposals may be solicited or unsolicited. When firms know exactly what they want, they prepare a request for proposal (RFP) specifying their requirements. Government agencies and large companies are likely to use RFPs to solicit competitive bids on their projects. As Mary noted, companies today want to be able to compare "apples with apples," and they also want the protection offered by proposals, which are legal contracts. Unsolicited proposals are written when an individual or firm sees a problem to be solved and offers a proposal to do so. Clean-Up Technology, an American waste disposal firm, will be submitting several proposals, for example, to government agencies and firms in Mexico. Explaining his bid for Mexican business, the waste disposal company president said, "There's obviously a lot of clean-up work to be done in Mexico, and there's not a lot of expertise in our business."[2] Unsolicited proposals, like those of Clean-Up Technology, seize opportunities and capitalize on potential.

The most important point to remember about proposals—whether solicited or unsolicited—is that they are sales presentations. They must be persuasive, not merely mechanical descriptions of what you can do. Among other things, you may recall, effective persuasive sales messages (1) emphasize benefits for the reader, (2) "toot your horn" by detailing your expertise and accomplishments, and (3) make it easy for the reader to understand and respond.

Proposals may be formal or informal; they differ primarily in length and format. Notice in Figure 14.1 that formal proposals, described shortly, have many more components than informal proposals.

Components of Informal Proposals

● **Informal proposals may contain an introduction, background information, the proposal, staffing requirements, a budget, and authorization.**

Informal proposals may be presented in short (two- to four-page) letters. Sometimes called "letter proposals," they may contain six principal components: introduction, background, proposal, staffing, budget, and authorization. As you can see in Figure 14.1, both formal and informal proposals contain these six basic parts. Figure 14.2, an informal letter proposal to a Cincinnati dentist to improve patient satisfaction, illustrates the six parts of letter proposals.

Introduction. Most proposals begin by briefly explaining the reasons for the proposal and by highlighting the writer's qualifications. To make your introduction more persuasive, you need to provide a "hook" to capture the interest of the reader. One proposal expert suggests these possibilities:[3]

- Hint at extraordinary results with details to be revealed shortly.
- Promise low costs or speedy results.

FIGURE 14.1 ● **Components in Formal and Informal Proposals**

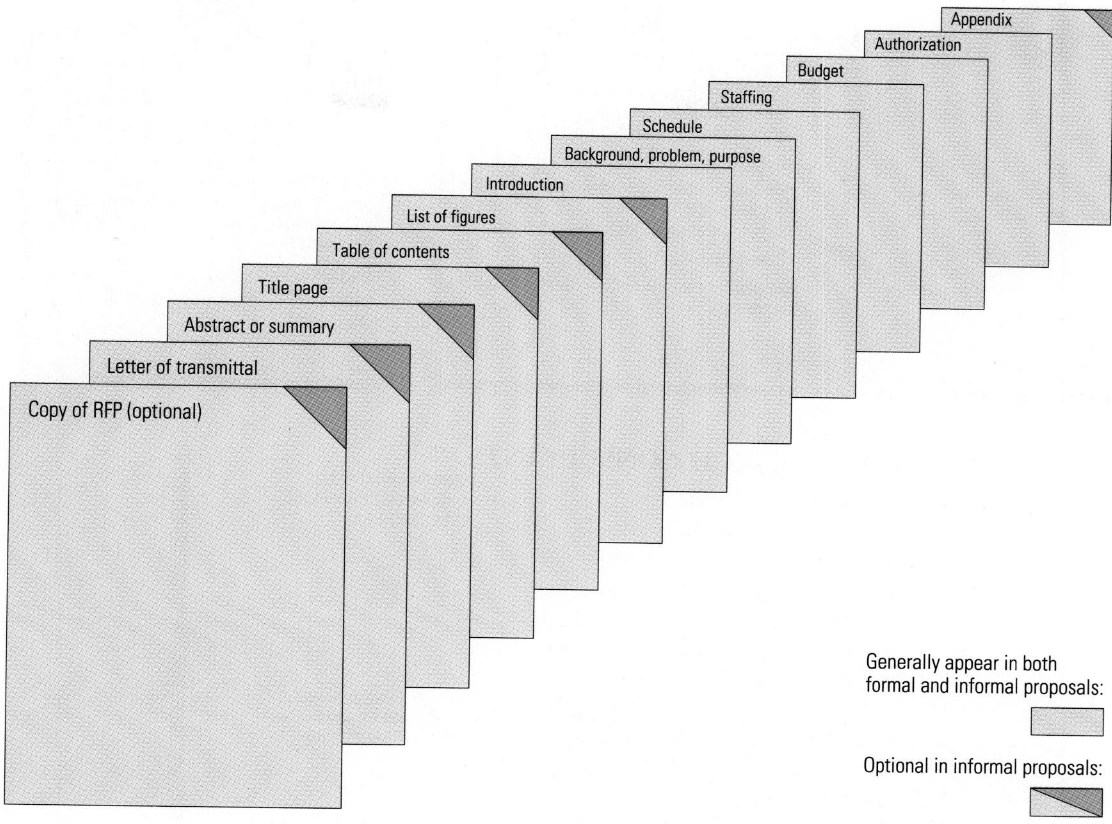

- Mention a remarkable resource (well-known authority, new computer program, well-trained staff) available exclusively to you.
- Identify a serious problem (worry item) and promise a solution, to be explained later.
- Specify a key issue or benefit that you feel is the heart of the proposal.

For example, Jeffrey Myers, in the introduction for his proposal shown in Figure 14.2, focused on a key benefit. In his proposal to conduct a patient satisfaction survey, Jeffrey thought that Dr. Calloway would be most interested in specific recommendations for improving service to his patients. But Jeffrey didn't hit on this hook until he had written a first draft and had come back to it later. Indeed, it's often a good idea to put off writing the proposal introduction until after you have completed other parts. For longer proposals the introduction also describes the scope and limitations of the project, as well as outlining the organization of the material to come.

● **Effective proposal openers "hook" readers by promising extraordinary results or resources or by identifying key benefits, issues, or outcomes.**

Background, problem, purpose. The background section identifies the problem and discusses the goals or purposes of the project. In an unsolicited proposal your goal is to convince the reader that a problem exists. Thus, you must present

FIGURE 14.2 ● Informal Proposal

The Three Phases of the Writing Process

1

Analyze
The purpose is to persuade the reader to accept this proposal.

Anticipate
The reader must be convinced that this survey project is worth its hefty price.

Adapt
Because the reader will be resistant at first, use a persuasive approach that emphasizes benefits.

2

Research
Collect data about the reader's practice and other surveys of patient satisfaction.

Organize
Identify four specific purposes (benefits) of this proposal. Specify the survey plan. Promote the staff, itemize the budget, and ask for approval.

Compose
Prepare for revision by composing at a word processor.

3

Revise
Revise to emphasize benefits. Improve readability with functional headings and lists. Remove jargon and wordiness.

Proofread
Check spelling of client's name. Verify dates and calculation of budget figures. Recheck all punctuation.

Evaluate
Is this proposal convincing enough to sell the client?

MYERS RESEARCH CONSULTANTS
One Riverview Plaza
Cincinnati, Ohio 45268
(513) 356-4300

May 16, 1994

Dr. Matthew M. Calloway
8356 Plainfield Road
Cincinnati, OH 45236

Dear Dr. Calloway:

I enjoyed talking with you several days ago, Dr. Calloway, about your successful general dentistry practice in downtown Cincinnati. Myers Research Consultants is pleased to submit the following proposal outlining our plan to analyze your patients and suggest ways to improve your service to them.

[Uses opening paragraph in place of introduction]

[Grabs attention with "hook" that focuses on key benefit]

Background and Purposes

We understand that you have been incorporating a total quality management system in your practice. Although you have every reason to believe your patients are pleased with the service you provide, you would like to give them an opportunity to discuss what they like and possibly don't like about your service. Specifically, your purposes are to survey your patients to (1) determine the level of their satisfaction with you and your staff, (2) elicit their suggestions for improvement, (3) learn more about how they discovered you, and (4) compare your "preferred" and "standard" patients.

[Identifies four purposes of survey]

[Announces heart of proposal]

Proposed Plan

On the basis of our experience in conducting many local and national customer satisfaction surveys, Myers Research proposes the following plan to you.

[Describes procedure for solving problem or achieving goals]

[Divides total plan into logical segments for easy reading]

Survey. We will develop a short but thorough questionnaire probing the data you desire. Although the survey instrument will include both open-ended and closed questions, it will concentrate on the latter. Closed questions enable respondents to answer easily; they also facilitate systematic data analysis. The questionnaire will measure patient reactions to such elements as courtesy, professionalism, accuracy of billing, friendliness, and waiting time. After you approve it, the questionnaire will be sent to a carefully selected sample of 300 patients whom you have separated into groupings of "preferred" and "standard."

Analysis. Data from the survey will be analyzed by demographic segments, such as patient type, age, and gender. Our experienced team of experts, using state-of-the-art computer systems and advanced statistical measures, will study the (a) degree of patient satisfaction, (b) reasons for satisfaction or dissatisfaction, and (c) relationship between responses of your "preferred" and "standard" patients. Moreover, our team will report to you specific suggestions for making patient visits more pleasant.

Report. You will receive a final report with the key findings clearly spelled out, Dr. Calloway. Our expert staff will also draw conclusions based on these findings. The report will include tables summarizing all responses, broken down into groups of preferred and standard clients.

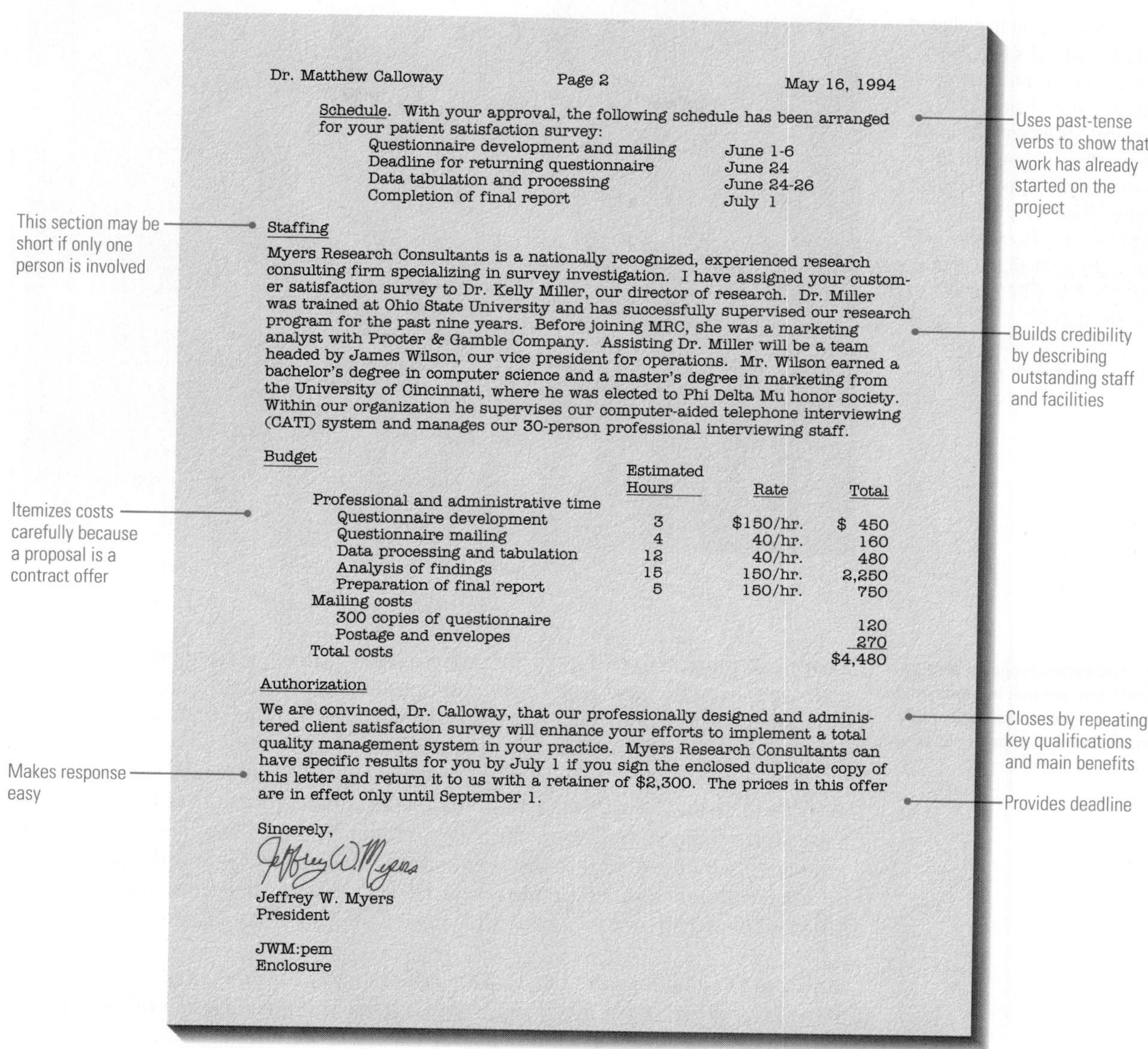

Dr. Matthew Calloway Page 2 May 16, 1994

Schedule. With your approval, the following schedule has been arranged for your patient satisfaction survey:

Questionnaire development and mailing	June 1-6
Deadline for returning questionnaire	June 24
Data tabulation and processing	June 24-26
Completion of final report	July 1

Staffing

Myers Research Consultants is a nationally recognized, experienced research consulting firm specializing in survey investigation. I have assigned your customer satisfaction survey to Dr. Kelly Miller, our director of research. Dr. Miller was trained at Ohio State University and has successfully supervised our research program for the past nine years. Before joining MRC, she was a marketing analyst with Procter & Gamble Company. Assisting Dr. Miller will be a team headed by James Wilson, our vice president for operations. Mr. Wilson earned a bachelor's degree in computer science and a master's degree in marketing from the University of Cincinnati, where he was elected to Phi Delta Mu honor society. Within our organization he supervises our computer-aided telephone interviewing (CATI) system and manages our 30-person professional interviewing staff.

Budget

	Estimated Hours	Rate	Total
Professional and administrative time			
Questionnaire development	3	$150/hr.	$ 450
Questionnaire mailing	4	40/hr.	160
Data processing and tabulation	12	40/hr.	480
Analysis of findings	15	150/hr.	2,250
Preparation of final report	5	150/hr.	750
Mailing costs			
300 copies of questionnaire			120
Postage and envelopes			270
Total costs			$4,480

Authorization

We are convinced, Dr. Calloway, that our professionally designed and administered client satisfaction survey will enhance your efforts to implement a total quality management system in your practice. Myers Research Consultants can have specific results for you by July 1 if you sign the enclosed duplicate copy of this letter and return it to us with a retainer of $2,300. The prices in this offer are in effect only until September 1.

Sincerely,

Jeffrey W. Myers
President

JWM:pem
Enclosure

Uses past-tense verbs to show that work has already started on the project
This section may be short if only one person is involved
Builds credibility by describing outstanding staff and facilities
Itemizes costs carefully because a proposal is a contract offer
Closes by repeating key qualifications and main benefits
Makes response easy
Provides deadline

the problem in detail, discussing such factors as monetary losses, failure to comply with government regulations, or loss of customers. In a solicited proposal your aim is to persuade the reader that you understand the problem completely. Thus, if you are responding to an RFP, this means repeating its language. For example, if the RFP asks for the *design of a maintenance program for high-speed mail-sorting equipment,* you would use the same language in explaining the purpose of your proposal. This section might include segments entitled *Basic Requirements, Most Critical Tasks,* and *Most Important Secondary Problems.*

Many proposals are written by teams who collaborate in developing a plan to sell products and services that solve a client's problem. The most successful teams avoid "canned" solutions. Instead, they gather information to understand a particular client's needs. Then, they work together to customize a "bid package" with all the information necessary to respond to the client's RFP.

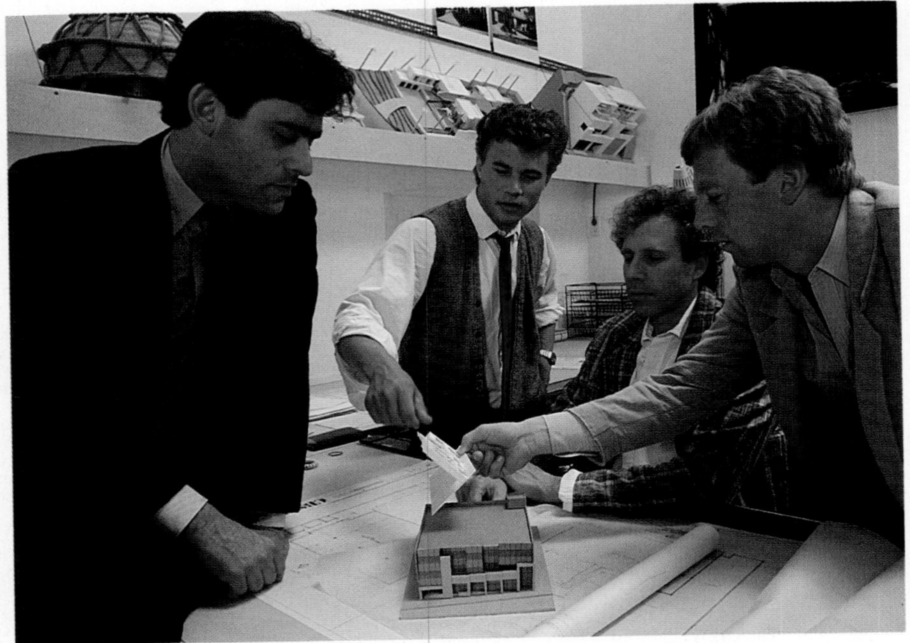

● **The actual proposal section must give enough information to secure the contract but not so much detail that the services are no longer needed.**

Proposal, plan, schedule. In the proposal section itself, you should discuss your plan for solving the problem. In some proposals this is tricky because you want to disclose enough of your plan to secure the contract without giving away so much information that your services are unneeded. Without specifics, though, your proposal has little chance, so you must decide how much to reveal. Tell what you propose to do and how it will benefit the reader. Remember, too, that a proposal is a sales presentation. Sell your methods, product, and "deliverables"—items that will be left with the client. In this section some writers specify how the project will be managed and how its progress will be audited. Most writers also include a schedule of activities or timetable showing when events take place.

Staffing. The staffing section of a proposal describes the credentials and expertise of the project leaders. It may also identify the size and qualifications of the support staff, along with other resources such as computer facilities and special programs for analyzing statistics. In longer proposals, résumés of key people may be provided. The staffing or personnel section is a good place to endorse and promote your staff.

● **Because a proposal is a legal contract, the budget must be carefully researched.**

Budget. A central item in most proposals is the budget, a list of proposed project costs. You need to prepare this section carefully because it represents a contract; you can't raise the price later—even if your costs increase. You can—and should—protect yourself with a deadline for acceptance. In the budget section some writers itemize hours and costs; others present a total sum only. A proposal to install a complex computer system might, for example, contain a detailed line-by-line budget. Similarly, Jeffrey Myers felt that he needed to justify the budget for his firm's patient satisfaction survey, so he itemized the costs, as shown in Figure 14.2. But the budget included for a proposal to conduct a one-day seminar to improve employee communication skills might be a lump sum only. Your analysis of the project will help you decide what kind of budget to prepare.

Authorization. Informal proposals often close with a request for approval or authorization. In addition, the closing should remind the reader of key benefits and motivate action. It might also include a deadline date beyond which the offer is invalid.

Special Components of Formal Proposals

Formal proposals differ from informal proposals not in style but in size and format. Formal proposals respond to big projects and may range from 5 to 200 or more pages. To facilitate comprehension and reference, they are organized into many parts, as shown in Figure 14.1. In addition to the six basic components just described, formal proposals may contain some or all of the following front and end parts.

Formal proposals might also contain a copy of the RFP, a letter of transmittal, an abstract, a title page, a table of contents, a list of figures, and an appendix.

Copy of RFP. A copy of the RFP may be included in the opening parts of a formal proposal. Large organizations may have more than one RFP circulating, and identification is necessary.

Letter of transmittal. A letter of transmittal, usually bound inside formal proposals, addresses the person who is designated to receive the proposal or who will make the final decision. The letter describes how you learned about the problem or confirms that the proposal responds to the enclosed RFP. This persuasive letter briefly presents the major features and benefits of your proposal. Here, you should assure the reader that you are authorized to make the bid, and mention the time limit for which the bid stands. You may also offer to provide additional information, and ask for action, if appropriate.

Abstract or executive summary. An abstract is a brief summary (typically one page) of a proposal's highlights intended for specialists or for technical readers. An executive summary also reviews the proposal's highlights, but it is written for managers and so should be less technically oriented. Formal proposals may contain one or both summaries.

An abstract summarizes a proposal's highlights for specialists; an executive summary does so for managers.

Title page. The title page includes the following items, generally in this order: title of proposal, name of client organization, RFP number or other announcement, date of submission, author's name, and/or his or her organization.

Table of contents. Because most proposals don't contain an index, the table of contents becomes quite important. Tables of contents should include all headings and their beginning page numbers. Items that appear before the contents (copy of RFP, letter of transmittal, abstract, and title page) typically are not listed in the contents. However, any appendixes should be listed.

List of figures. Proposals with many tables and figures often contain a list of figures. This list includes each figure or table title and its page number. If you have just a few figures or tables, however, you may omit this list.

Appendix. Ancillary material of interest to some readers goes in appendixes. Appendix A might include résumés of the principal investigators or letters of testimonial. Appendix B might include examples or a listing of previous projects. Other appendixes could include audit procedures, technical graphics, or professional papers cited in the body of the proposal.

Well-written proposals win contracts and business for companies and individuals. In fact, many companies depend entirely on proposals to generate their income, so proposal writing becomes critical. The following checklist summarizes the primary components of proposals.

Checklist for Writing Proposals

Introduction

- ✔ **Indicate the purpose.** Specify why the proposal is being made.
- ✔ **Develop a persuasive "hook."** Suggest excellent results, low costs, or exclusive resources. Identify a serious problem or name a key issue or benefit.

Background, Problem

- ✔ **Provide necessary background.** Discuss the significance of the proposal and its goals or purposes.
- ✔ **Introduce the problem.** For unsolicited proposals convince the reader that a problem exists. For solicited proposals show that you fully understand the problem and its ramifications.

Proposal, Plan

- ✔ **Explain the proposal.** Present your plan for solving the problem or meeting the need.
- ✔ **Discuss plan management and evaluation.** If appropriate, tell how the plan will be implemented and evaluated.
- ✔ **Outline a timetable.** Furnish a schedule showing what will be done and when.

Staffing

- ✔ **Promote the qualifications of your staff.** Explain the specific credentials and expertise of the key personnel for the project.
- ✔ **Mention special resources or equipment.** Show how your support staff and resources are superior to the competition.

Budget

- ✔ **Show project costs.** For most projects itemize costs. Remember, however, that proposals are contracts.
- ✔ **Include a deadline.** Here or in the conclusion present a date beyond which the bid figures are no longer valid.

Authorization

- ✔ **Ask for approval.** Make it easy for the reader to authorize the project (for example, *Sign and return duplicate copy*).

SPOTLIGHT ON COMMUNICATORS

Consultant Thomas Sant advises proposal writers to (1) state the client's key need or problem, (2) spell out why the need must be addressed, (3) present a solution in concrete terms, and (4) fill in the details. Above all, he says, be sure a proposal is client-focused rather than product-focused. If the price tag is hefty, he suggests highlighting long-term savings and cost effectiveness.

FIGURE 14.3 ● Components in Formal and Informal Reports

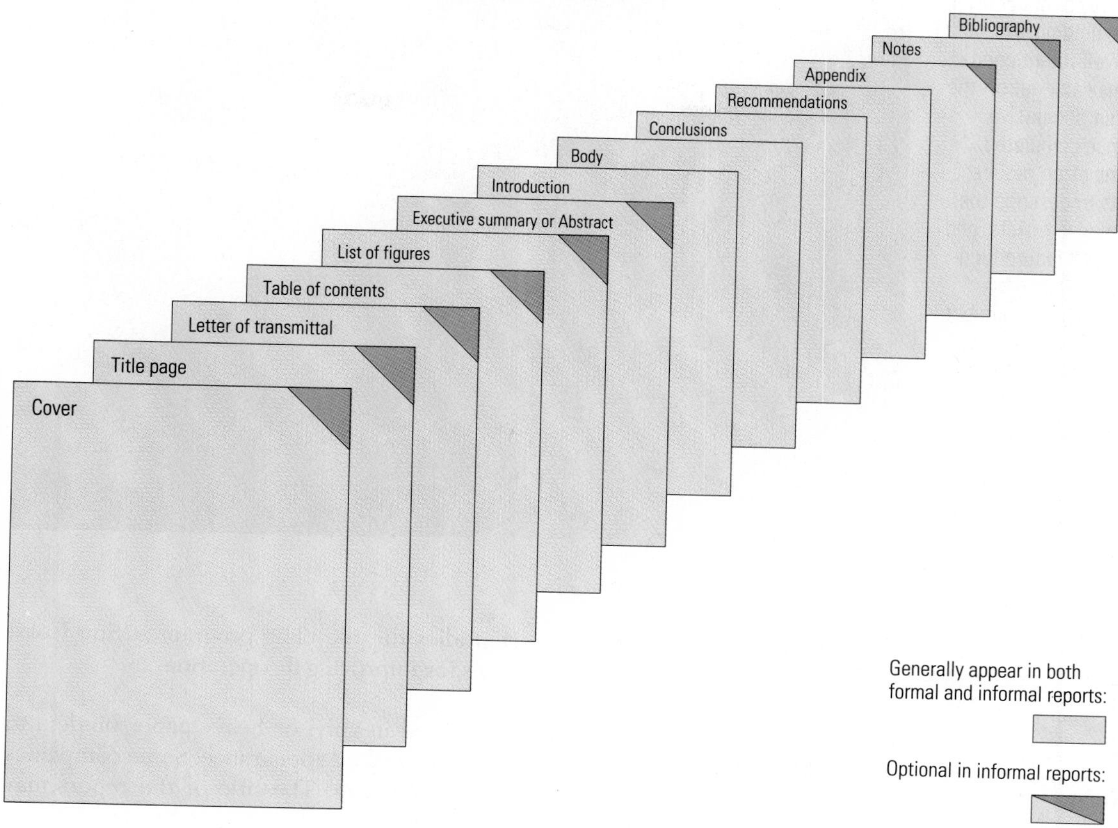

Writing Formal Reports

Formal reports are similar to formal proposals in length, organization, and serious tone. Instead of making an offer, however, formal reports represent the end product of thorough investigation and analysis. They present ordered information to decision-makers in business, industry, government, and education. In many ways formal reports are extended versions of the analytical business reports presented in Chapter 13. Figure 14.3 shows the components of typical formal reports, their normal sequence, and parts that might be omitted in informal reports.

● Formal reports discuss the results of a process of thorough investigation and analysis.

Components of Formal Reports

A number of front and end items lengthen formal reports but enhance their professional tone and serve their multiple audiences. Formal reports may be read by many levels of managers, along with technical specialists and financial consultants. Therefore, breaking a long, formal report into small segments makes its information more accessible and easier to understand for all readers. These segments are discussed here and also illustrated in the model report shown later in the chapter

● Like proposals, formal reports are divided into many segments to make information comprehensible and accessible.

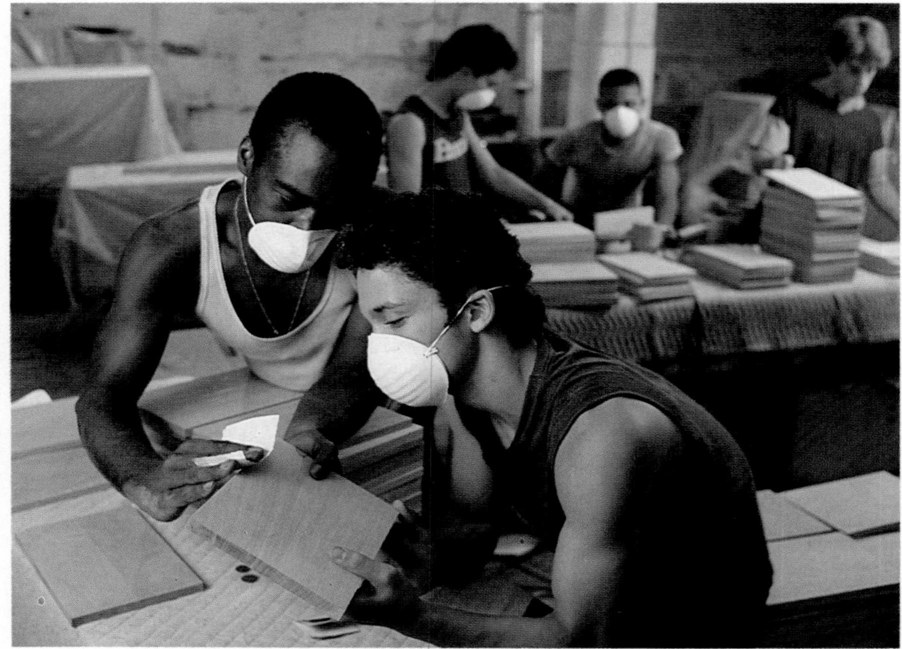

Programs to train minority workers typically begin with proposals for funding. No matter how well-intentioned, such programs can't get off the ground without persuasive proposals. Once completed, such programs often require formal reports to describe the project, summarize results, and evaluate success. Future funding is often determined by the effectiveness of the project, as expressed by the accuracy and thoroughness of the concluding report.

(Figure 14.4). This analytical report studies the recycling program at Sun Coast University and makes recommendations for improving its operation.

Cover. Formal reports are usually enclosed in vinyl or heavy paper binders to protect the pages and to give a professional, finished appearance. Some companies have binders imprinted with their name and logo. The title of the report may appear through a cut-out window or may be applied with an adhesive label. Good stationery and office supply stores usually stock an assortment of report binders and labels.

Title page. A report title page, as illustrated in the Figure 14.4 model report, begins with the name of the report typed in uppercase letters (no underscore and no quotation marks). Next comes *Presented to* (or *Submitted to*) and the name, title, and organization of the individual receiving the report. Lower on the page is *Prepared by* (or *Submitted by*) and the author's name plus any necessary identification. The last item on the title page is the date of submission. All items after the title are typed in a combination of upper- and lowercase letters.

● **A letter of transmittal gives a personalized overview of a formal report.**

Letter of transmittal. Generally written on organization stationery, a letter or memorandum of transmittal introduces a formal report. It follows the direct pattern and is usually less formal than the report itself (for example, the letter may use contractions and the first-person pronouns *I* and *we*). The transmittal letter typically (1) announces the topic of the report and tells how it was authorized; (2) briefly describes the project; (3) highlights the report's findings, conclusions, and recommendations, if the reader is expected to be supportive; and (4) closes with appreciation for the assignment, instruction for the reader's follow-up actions, acknowledgment of help from others, or offers of assistance in answering questions. If a report is going to different readers, a special transmittal letter should be prepared for each, anticipating what each reader needs to know in using the report.

Table of contents. The table of contents shows the headings in a report and their page numbers. It gives an overview of the report topics and helps readers locate them. You should wait to prepare the table of contents until after you've completed the report. For short reports you should include all headings. For longer reports you might want to list only first- and second-level headings. Leaders (spaced or unspaced dots) help guide the eye from the heading to the page number. Items may be indented in outline form or typed flush with the left margin.

List of figures. For reports with several figures or illustrations, you may wish to include a list of figures to help readers locate them. This list may appear on the same page as the table of contents, space permitting. For each figure or illustration, include a title and page number. Some writers distinguish between tables and all other illustrations, which are called figures. If you make this distinction, you should also prepare separate lists of tables and figures. Because the model report in Figure 14.4 has few illustrations, the writer labeled them all "figures," a method that greatly simplifies numbering.

Executive summary or abstract. Executives and other readers appreciate a summary or abstract highlighting report findings, conclusions, and recommendations. As with proposals, report abstracts are aimed at technical experts and may contain specialized language; executive summaries concentrate on what management needs to know, omitting technical jargon. Whether you are writing an abstract or an executive summary, its length and complexity will be determined by the report. For example, a 100-page report might require a 10-page summary. A 10-page report might need only a 1-page summary—or no summary at all. Longer abstracts may include headings and visual aids to adequately highlight main points. Although the executive summary in Figure 14.4 is only one page long, it includes headings to help the reader see the main divisions immediately. Let your organization's practices guide you in determining the length and form of a summary or abstract.

● **The length and complexity of the abstract or executive summary depend on the length of and audience for the report.**

Introduction. Formal reports begin with an introduction that sets the scene and announces the subject. Because they contain many parts serving different purposes, formal reports have a degree of redundancy. The same information may be included in the letter of transmittal, summary, and introduction. To avoid sounding repetitious, try to present the data slightly differently. But don't skip the introduction because you've included some of its information elsewhere. You can't be sure that your reader saw the information earlier. A good report introduction typically covers the following elements, although not necessarily in this order:

- **Background.** Describe events leading up to the problem or need.
- **Problem or purpose.** Explain the report topic and specify the problem or need that motivated the report.
- **Significance.** Tell why the topic is important. You may wish to quote experts or cite newspapers, journals, books, and other secondary sources to establish the importance of the topic.
- **Scope.** Clarify the boundaries of the report, defining what will be included or excluded.
- **Organization.** Launch readers by giving them a road map that previews the structure of the report.

SPOTLIGHT ON COMMUNICATORS

When former Dallas Cowboys quarterback Roger Staubach launched a commercial real estate business, he started with a business plan, which is a long, formal report necessary to attract investors. He then commissioned another long report, a needs survey of more than 200 customers, architects, developers, and others. Listening to customers, as part of his total quality management program, enabled him to analyze data, draw conclusions, and then develop his "Double EE" program centered on ethics and excellence.

Beyond these minimal introductory elements, consider adding any of the following information that is relevant for your readers:

- **Authorization.** Identify who commissioned the report. If no letter of transmittal is included, also tell why, when, by whom, and to whom the report was written.
- **Literature review.** Summarize what other authors and researchers have published on this topic, especially for academic and scientific reports.
- **Sources and methods.** Describe your secondary sources (periodicals, books, databases). Also explain how you collected primary data, including survey size, sample design, and statistical programs used.
- **Definitions of key terms.** Define words that may be unfamiliar to the audience. Also define terms with special meanings, such as *small business* when it specifically means businesses with fewer than 30 employees.

Body. The principal section in a formal report is the body. It discusses, analyzes, interprets, and evaluates the research findings or solution to the initial problem. This is where you show the evidence that justifies your conclusions. Organize the body into main categories following your original outline or using one of the patterns described earlier (such as time, component, importance, criteria, or convention).

Although we refer to this section as the "body," it doesn't carry that heading. Instead, it contains clear headings that explain each major section. Headings may be functional or talking. Functional heads (such as *Results of the Survey, Analysis of Findings,* or *Discussion*) help readers identify the purpose of the section but don't reveal what's in it. Such headings are useful for routine reports or for sensitive topics that may upset readers. Talking heads (for example, *Recycling Habits of Campus Community*) are more informative and interesting, but they don't help readers see the organization of the report. The model report in Figure 14.4 uses functional heads for organizational sections requiring identification ("Introduction," "Conclusions," and "Recommendations") and talking heads to divide the body.

Conclusions. This important section tells what the findings mean, particularly in terms of solving the original problem. Some writers prefer to intermix their conclusions with the analysis of the findings—instead of presenting the conclusions separately. Other writers place the conclusions before the body so that busy readers can examine the significant information immediately. Still others combine the conclusions and recommendations. Most writers, though, present the conclusions after the body because readers expect this structure. In long reports this section may include a summary of the findings. To improve comprehension, you may present the conclusions in a numbered or bulleted list.

The recommendations section of a formal report offers specific suggestions for solving a problem.

Recommendations. When requested, you should submit recommendations that make precise suggestions for actions to solve the report problem. Recommendations are most helpful when they are practical and reasonable. Naturally, they should evolve from the findings and conclusions. Don't introduce new information in the conclusions or recommendations. As with conclusions, the position of recommendations is somewhat flexible. They may be combined with conclusions, or they may be presented before the body, especially when the audience is eager and supportive. Generally, though, in formal reports they come last.

Recommendations require an appropriate introductory sentence, such as *The findings and conclusions in this study support the following recommendations.* When making many recommendations, number them and phrase each as a command, such as *Begin an employee fitness program with a workout room available five days a week.* If appropriate, add information describing how to implement each recommendation. Some reports include a timetable describing the who, what, when, where, and how for putting each recommendation into operation.

Appendix. Incidental or supporting materials belong in appendixes at the end of a formal report. These materials are relevant to some readers but not to all. Appendixes may include survey forms, copies of other reports, tables of data, computer printouts, and related correspondence.

References. Readers look in the reference section to locate the sources of ideas mentioned in a report. Your method of report documentation determines how this section is developed. If you footnoted sources and placed each reference at the bottom of the page where it was cited, you will have no "Endnotes," "Works Cited," or "References" section. If, however, you did not include complete source information within the report, you will need to list the sources in a reference section. You must note the author, title, publication, date of publication, page number, and other significant data for all ideas or quotations used in your report. Consult Chapter 11 and Appendix C to choose an appropriate format for your report.

• The reference and bibliography sections of a formal report identify sources of ideas mentioned in the report.

Bibliography. A bibliography is an alphabetic list of references on a topic. In reports with fewer than ten cited references, a bibliography may be omitted. For reports with many references, the bibliography helps readers locate items because it is arranged alphabetically by author. It may include all the works consulted as well as those actually cited. Unlike footnotes, bibliography entries are arranged in hanging indented form: the second and succeeding lines for each work are indented five spaces from the left margin. Bibliographic entries also differ from footnotes in their arrangement of author and title data. See Appendix C for additional documentation information.

Final Writing Tips

Formal reports are not undertaken lightly. They involve considerable effort in all three phases of writing, beginning with analysis of the problem and anticipation of the audience (as discussed in Chapter 3). Researching the data, organizing it into a logical presentation, and composing the first draft (Chapter 4) make up the second phase of writing. Revising, proofreading, and evaluating (Chapter 5) are the third phase. Although everyone approaches the writing process somewhat differently, the following tips offer advice in problem areas faced by most formal report writers.

• Formal reports require careful attention to all phases of the 3-×-3 writing process.

- **Allow sufficient time.** The main reason given by writers who are disappointed with their reports is "I just ran out of time." Develop a realistic timetable and stick to it.

Smart report writers allow themselves plenty of time, research thoroughly, draw up a useful outline, and work on a computer.

- **Delay writing.** Don't begin writing until you've collected all the data and drawn the primary conclusions. Starting too early often means backtracking. For reports based on survey data, compile the tables and figures first.
- **Work from a good outline.** A big project like a formal report needs the order and direction provided by a clear outline, even if the outline has to be revised as the project unfolds.
- **Provide a proper writing environment.** You'll need a quiet spot where you can spread out your materials and work without interruption. Formal reports demand blocks of concentration time.
- **Use a computer.** Preparing a report on a word processor enables you to keyboard quickly, revise easily, and, with most programs, check spelling and find synonyms readily. A word of warning, though: save your document often and print occasionally so that you have a hard copy. Take these precautions to guard against the grief caused by lost files, power outages, and computer malfunctions.
- **Write rapidly; revise later.** Experts advise writers to record their ideas quickly and save revision until after the first draft is completed. They say that quick writing avoids wasted effort spent in polishing sentences and even sections that may be cut later. Moreover, rapid writing encourages fluency and creativity. However, a quick-and-dirty first draft doesn't work for everyone. Some business writers prefer a more deliberate writing style, so consider this advice selectively.
- **Save hard sections.** If some sections are harder to write than others, save them until you've developed confidence and rhythm working on easier topics.

Effective formal reports maintain parallelism in verb tenses, avoid first-person pronouns, and use the active voice.

- **Be consistent in verb tense.** Use past-tense verbs to describe completed actions (for example, *the respondents said* or *the survey showed*). Use present-tense verbs, however, to explain current actions (*the purpose of the report is, this report examines, the table shows,* and so forth). Don't switch back and forth between present- and past-tense verbs in describing related data.
- **Generally avoid *I* and *we*.** To make formal reports seem as objective and credible as possible, most writers omit first-person pronouns. This formal style sometimes results in the overuse of passive-voice verbs (for example, *periodicals were consulted* and *the study was conducted*). Look for alternative constructions (*periodicals indicated* and *the study revealed*). It's also possible that your organization may allow first-person pronouns, so check before starting your report.
- **Let the first draft sit.** After completing the first version, put it aside for a day or two. Return to it with the expectation of revising and improving it. Don't be afraid to make major changes.
- **Revise for clarity, coherence, and conciseness.** Read a printed copy out loud. Do the sentences make sense? Do the ideas flow together naturally? Can wordiness and flabbiness be cut out? See Chapter 5 for specific revision suggestions.
- **Proofread the final copy three times.** First, read a printed copy slowly for word meanings and content. Then read the copy again for spelling, punctuation, grammar, and other mechanical errors. Finally, scan the entire report to check its formatting and consistency (page numbering, indenting, spacing, headings, and so forth).

Putting It All Together

Formal reports in business generally aim to study problems and recommend solutions. Alan Christopher, business senator to the Office of Associated Students (OAS) at Sun Coast University, was given a campus problem to study, resulting in the formal report shown in Figure 14.4.

The campus recycling program, under the direction of Cheryl Bryant and supported by the OAS, was not attracting the anticipated level of participation. As the campus recycling program began its second year of operation, Cheryl and the OAS wondered if campus community members were sufficiently aware of the program. They also wondered how participation could be increased. Alan volunteered to investigate the problem because of his strong support for environmental causes. He also needed to conduct a research project for one of his business courses, and he had definite ideas for improving the campus OAS recycling program.

Alan's report illustrates many of the points discussed in this chapter. Although it's a good example of typical report format and style, it should not be viewed as the only way to present a report. Wide variation exists in reports.

The following checklist summarizes the report process and report components in one handy list.

Checklist for Preparing Formal Reports

Report Process

- ✔ **Analyze the report problem and purpose.** Develop a problem question *(Is sexual harassment affecting employees at DataTech?)* and a purpose statement *(The purpose of this report is to investigate sexual harassment at DataTech and recommend remedies).*
- ✔ **Anticipate the audience and issues.** Consider primary and secondary audiences. What do they already know? What do they need to know? Divide the major problem into subproblems for investigation.
- ✔ **Prepare a work plan.** Include problem and purpose statements, as well as a description of the sources and methods of collecting data. Prepare a tentative project outline and a work schedule with anticipated dates of completion for all segments of the project.
- ✔ **Collect data.** Begin by searching secondary sources (books, magazines, journals, newspapers, electronic databases) for information on your topic. Then, if necessary, gather primary data by surveying, interviewing, observing, and experimenting.
- ✔ **Document data sources.** Prepare note cards or separate sheets of paper citing all references (author, date, source, page, and quotation). Select a documentation format (Chapter 11) and use it consistently.
- ✔ **Interpret and organize the data.** Arrange the collected information in tables, grids, or outlines to help you visualize relationships and interpret meanings. Organize the data into an outline (Chapter 4).
- ✔ **Prepare visual aids.** Make tables, charts, graphs, and illustrations—but *only* if they serve a function. Use visual aids to help clarify, condense, simplify, or emphasize your data.

- ✔ **Compose the first draft.** At a computer write the first draft from your outline. Use appropriate headings as well as transitional expressions (such as *however, on the contrary,* and *in addition*) to guide the reader through the report.
- ✔ **Revise and proofread.** Revise to eliminate wordiness, ambiguity, and redundancy. Look for ways to improve readability, such as bulleted or numbered lists. Proofread three times for (1) word and content meaning, (2) grammar and mechanical errors, and (3) formatting.
- ✔ **Evaluate the product.** Examine the final report. Will it achieve its purpose? Encourage feedback so that you can learn how to improve future reports.

Report Components

- ✔ **Title page.** Balance the following lines on the title page: (1) name of the report (in all caps); (2) name, title, and organization of the individual receiving the report; (3) author's name, title, and organization; and (4) date submitted.
- ✔ **Letter of transmittal.** Announce the report topic and explain who authorized it. Briefly describe the project and preview the conclusions, if the reader is supportive. Close by expressing appreciation for the assignment, suggesting follow-up actions, acknowledging the help of others, or offering to answer questions.
- ✔ **Table of contents.** Show the beginning page number where each report heading appears in the report. Connect the page numbers and headings with leaders (spaced dots).
- ✔ **List of illustrations.** Include a list of tables, illustrations, or figures showing the title of the item and its page number. If space permits, put these lists on the same page with the table of contents.
- ✔ **Executive summary or abstract.** Summarize the report purpose, findings, conclusions, and recommendations. Gauge the length of the summary by the length of the report and by your organization's practices.
- ✔ **Introduction.** Explain the problem motivating the report; describe its background and significance. Clarify the scope and limitations of the report. Optional items include a review of relevant literature and a description of data sources, methods, and key terms. Close by previewing the report's organization.
- ✔ **Body.** Discuss, analyze, and interpret the research findings or the proposed solution to the problem. Arrange the findings in logical segments following your outline. Use clear, descriptive headings.
- ✔ **Conclusions and recommendations.** Explain what the findings mean in relation to the original problem. If requested, make enumerated recommendations that suggest actions for solving the problem.
- ✔ **Appendix.** Include items of interest to some, but not all, readers, such as a data questionnaire or computer printouts.
- ✔ **References and bibliography.** If footnotes are not provided in the text, list all references in a section called "Endnotes," "Works Cited," or "References." As an option, include a bibliography showing all the works cited (and perhaps all those consulted) arranged alphabetically.

FIGURE 14.4 ● Model Formal Report

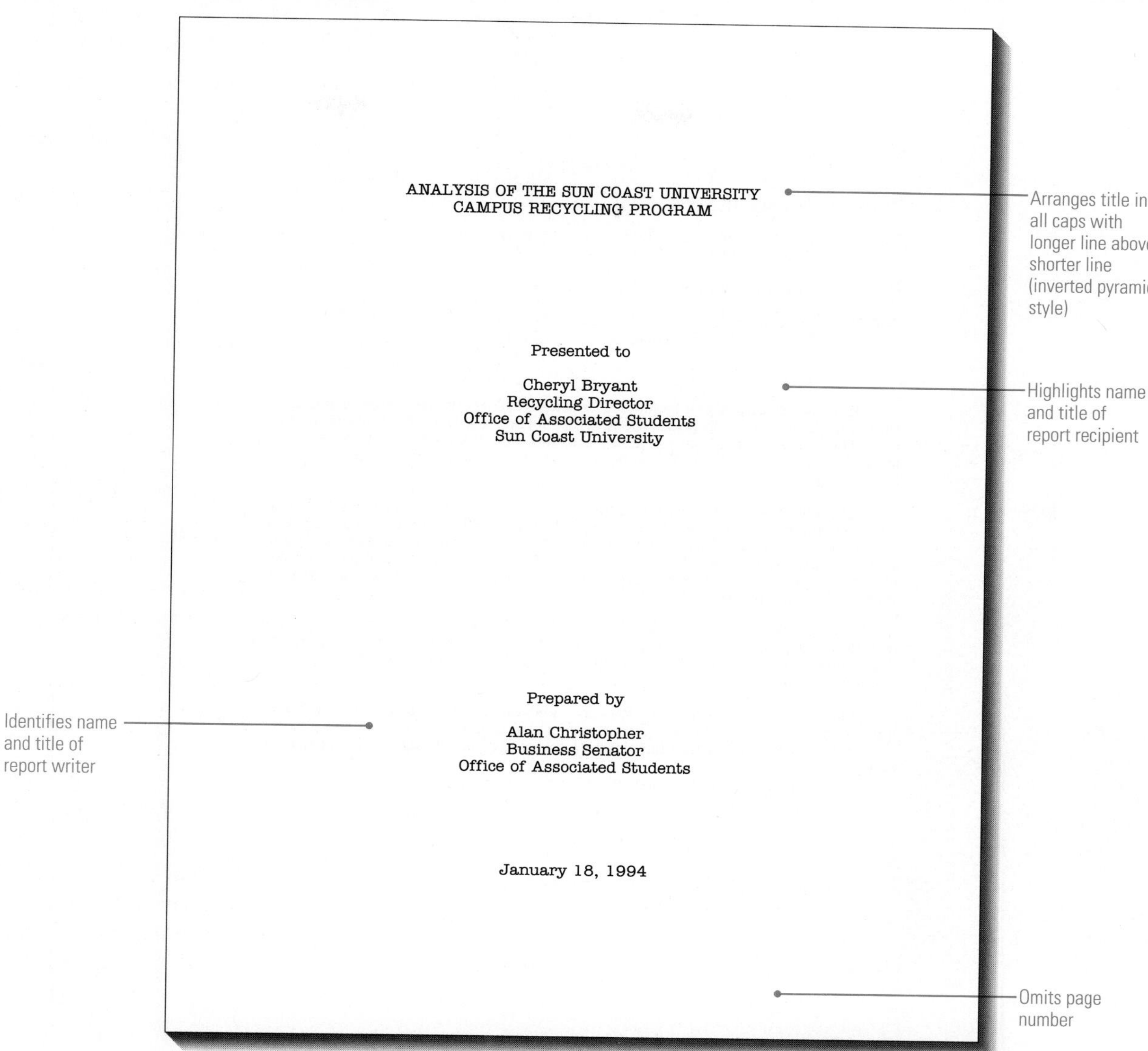

ANALYSIS OF THE SUN COAST UNIVERSITY
CAMPUS RECYCLING PROGRAM
Presented to
Cheryl Bryant
Recycling Director
Office of Associated Students
Sun Coast University
Prepared by
Alan Christopher
Business Senator
Office of Associated Students
January 18, 1994
Arranges title in all caps with longer line above shorter line (inverted pyramid style)
Highlights name and title of report recipient
Identifies name and title of report writer
Omits page number

Alan arranges the title page so that the amount of space above the title is equal to the space below the date. If a report is to be bound on the left, move the left margin and center point 1/4 inch to the right. Notice that no page number appears on the title page, although it is counted as page i.

If you use scalable fonts, word processing capabilities, or a laser printer to enhance your report and title page, be careful to avoid anything unprofessional (such as too many type fonts, oversized print, and inappropriate graphics).

FIGURE 14.4 (continued)

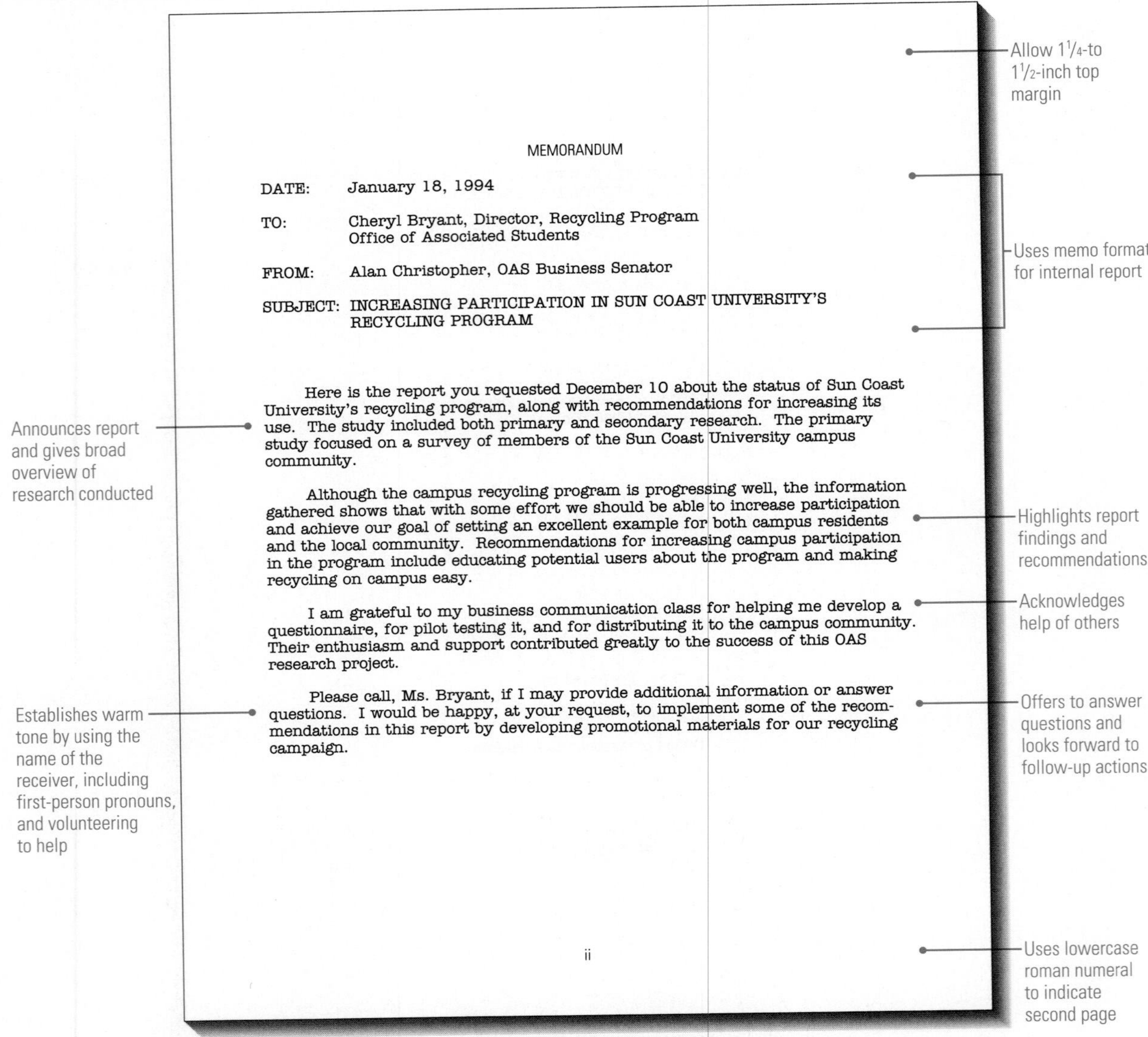
MEMORANDUM

DATE: January 18, 1994

TO: Cheryl Bryant, Director, Recycling Program
Office of Associated Students

FROM: Alan Christopher, OAS Business Senator

SUBJECT: INCREASING PARTICIPATION IN SUN COAST UNIVERSITY'S RECYCLING PROGRAM

Here is the report you requested December 10 about the status of Sun Coast University's recycling program, along with recommendations for increasing its use. The study included both primary and secondary research. The primary study focused on a survey of members of the Sun Coast University campus community.

Although the campus recycling program is progressing well, the information gathered shows that with some effort we should be able to increase participation and achieve our goal of setting an excellent example for both campus residents and the local community. Recommendations for increasing campus participation in the program include educating potential users about the program and making recycling on campus easy.

I am grateful to my business communication class for helping me develop a questionnaire, for pilot testing it, and for distributing it to the campus community. Their enthusiasm and support contributed greatly to the success of this OAS research project.

Please call, Ms. Bryant, if I may provide additional information or answer questions. I would be happy, at your request, to implement some of the recommendations in this report by developing promotional materials for our recycling campaign.

ii

Allow 1¼-to 1½-inch top margin
Uses memo format for internal report
Announces report and gives broad overview of research conducted
Highlights report findings and recommendations
Acknowledges help of others
Establishes warm tone by using the name of the receiver, including first-person pronouns, and volunteering to help
Offers to answer questions and looks forward to follow-up actions
Uses lowercase roman numeral to indicate second page

Because this report is being submitted within his own organization, Alan uses a memorandum of transmittal. Formal organization reports submitted to outsiders would carry a letter of transmittal printed on company stationery.

The margins for the transmittal should be the same as for the report, about 1¼ inches on all sides. If a report is to be bound, add an extra ¼ inch to the left margin.

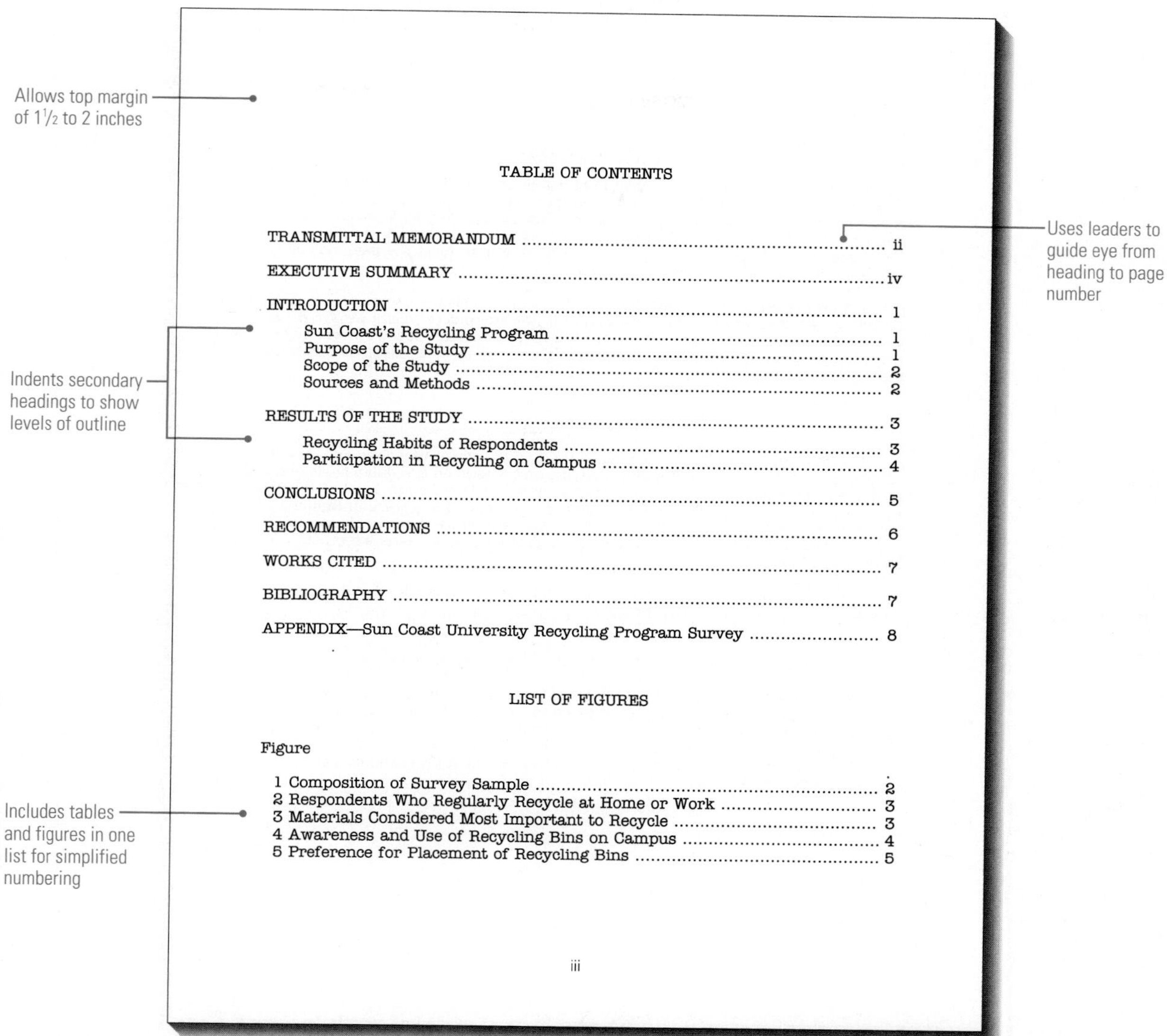

Allows top margin of 1½ to 2 inches
Uses leaders to guide eye from heading to page number
Indents secondary headings to show levels of outline
Includes tables and figures in one list for simplified numbering
TABLE OF CONTENTS
TRANSMITTAL MEMORANDUM ii
EXECUTIVE SUMMARY iv
INTRODUCTION 1
Sun Coast's Recycling Program 1
Purpose of the Study 1
Scope of the Study 2
Sources and Methods 2
RESULTS OF THE STUDY 3
Recycling Habits of Respondents 3
Participation in Recycling on Campus 4
CONCLUSIONS 5
RECOMMENDATIONS 6
WORKS CITED 7
BIBLIOGRAPHY 7
APPENDIX—Sun Coast University Recycling Program Survey 8
LIST OF FIGURES
Figure
1 Composition of Survey Sample 2
2 Respondents Who Regularly Recycle at Home or Work 3
3 Materials Considered Most Important to Recycle 3
4 Awareness and Use of Recycling Bins on Campus 4
5 Preference for Placement of Recycling Bins 5
iii

Because Alan's table of contents and list of figures are small, he combines them on one page. Notice that he uses all caps for the titles of major report parts and a combination of upper- and lowercase letters for first-level headings. This duplicates the style within the report.

Advanced word processing capabilities enable you to generate a contents page automatically, including leaders and accurate page numbering—no matter how many times you revise!

FIGURE 14.4 (continued)

EXECUTIVE SUMMARY

Purpose of the Report

The purposes of this report are (1) to determine the Sun Coast University campus community's awareness of the campus recycling program and (2) to recommend ways to increase participation. Sun Coast's recycling program was intended to respond to the increasing problem of waste disposal, to fulfill its social responsibility as an educational institution, and to meet the demands of legislation requiring individuals and organizations to recycle.

A questionnaire survey was conducted to learn about the campus community's recycling habits and to assess participation in the current recycling program. A total of 220 individuals responded to the survey. Since Sun Coast University's recycling program includes only aluminum, glass, paper, and plastic at this time, these were the only materials considered in this study.

Tells purpose of report and briefly describes survey

Recycling at Sun Coast

Summarizes findings of survey

Most survey respondents recognized the importance of recycling and stated that they do recycle aluminum, glass, paper, and plastic on a regular basis either at home or at work. However, most respondents displayed a low level of awareness and use of the on-campus program. Many of the respondents were unfamiliar with the location of the bins around campus and, therefore, had not participated in the recycling program. Other responses indicated that the bins were not conveniently located.

Draws primary conclusion

The results of this study show that more effort is needed to increase participation in the campus recycling program.

Recommendations for Increasing Recycling Participation

Recommendations for increasing participation in the program include (1) relocating the recycling bins for greater visibility, (2) developing incentive programs to gain the participation of individuals and on-campus student groups, (3) training student volunteers to give on-campus presentations explaining the need for recycling and the benefits of using the recycling program, and (4) increasing advertising about the program.

Concisely enumerates four recommendations using parallel (balanced) phrasing

Numbers pages that precede the body with lowercase roman numerals

iv

For readers who want a quick picture of the report, the executive summary presents its most important elements. Alan has divided the summary into three sections for increased readability.

Executive summaries generally contain little jargon or complex statistics; they condense what management needs to know about a problem and its study. Report abstracts, sometimes written in place of summaries, tend to be more technical and are aimed at specialists rather than management.

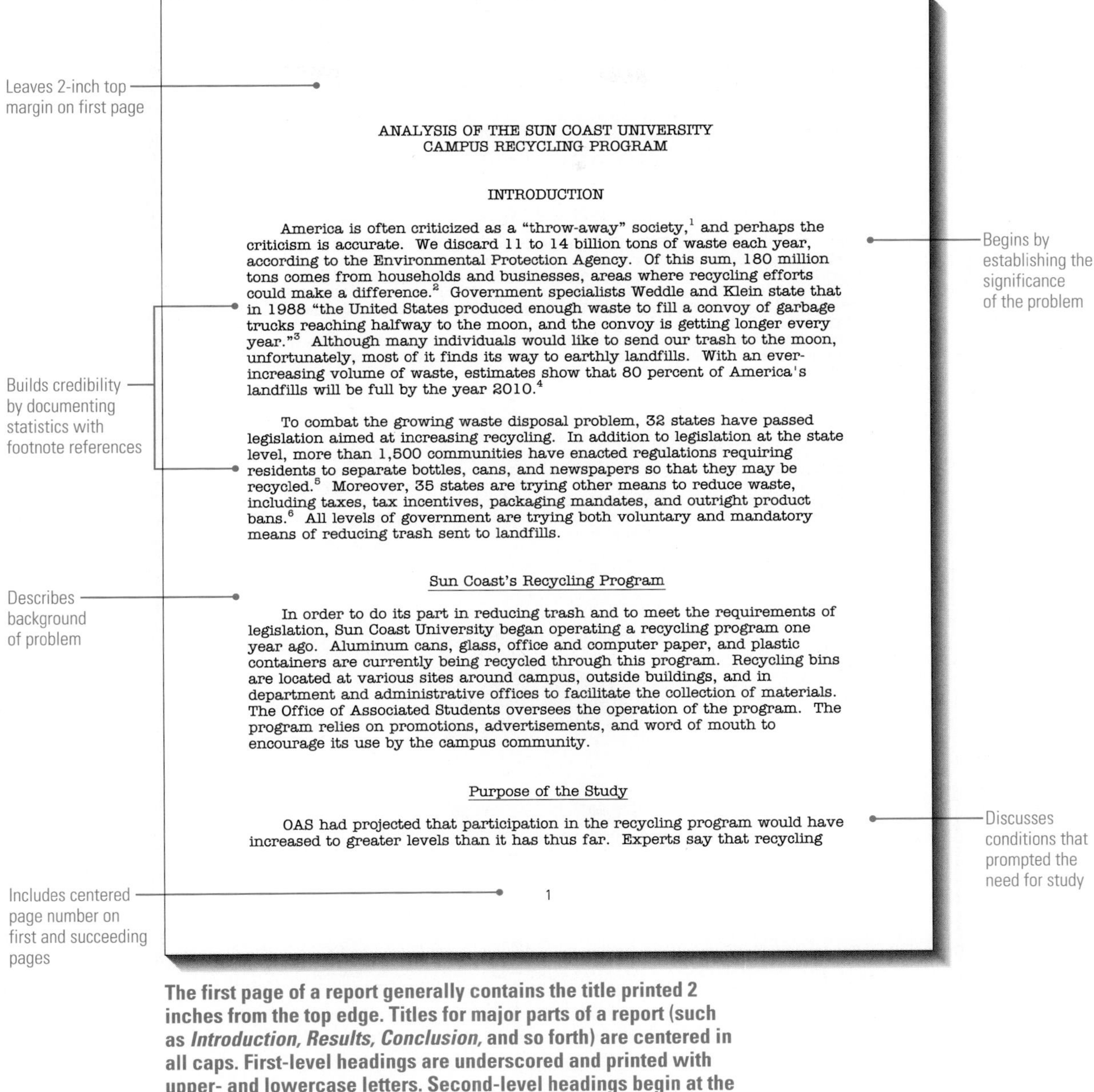
Leaves 2-inch top margin on first page

ANALYSIS OF THE SUN COAST UNIVERSITY
CAMPUS RECYCLING PROGRAM

INTRODUCTION

America is often criticized as a "throw-away" society,[1] and perhaps the criticism is accurate. We discard 11 to 14 billion tons of waste each year, according to the Environmental Protection Agency. Of this sum, 180 million tons comes from households and businesses, areas where recycling efforts could make a difference.[2] Government specialists Weddle and Klein state that in 1988 "the United States produced enough waste to fill a convoy of garbage trucks reaching halfway to the moon, and the convoy is getting longer every year."[3] Although many individuals would like to send our trash to the moon, unfortunately, most of it finds its way to earthly landfills. With an ever-increasing volume of waste, estimates show that 80 percent of America's landfills will be full by the year 2010.[4]

To combat the growing waste disposal problem, 32 states have passed legislation aimed at increasing recycling. In addition to legislation at the state level, more than 1,500 communities have enacted regulations requiring residents to separate bottles, cans, and newspapers so that they may be recycled.[5] Moreover, 35 states are trying other means to reduce waste, including taxes, tax incentives, packaging mandates, and outright product bans.[6] All levels of government are trying both voluntary and mandatory means of reducing trash sent to landfills.

Sun Coast's Recycling Program

In order to do its part in reducing trash and to meet the requirements of legislation, Sun Coast University began operating a recycling program one year ago. Aluminum cans, glass, office and computer paper, and plastic containers are currently being recycled through this program. Recycling bins are located at various sites around campus, outside buildings, and in department and administrative offices to facilitate the collection of materials. The Office of Associated Students oversees the operation of the program. The program relies on promotions, advertisements, and word of mouth to encourage its use by the campus community.

Purpose of the Study

OAS had projected that participation in the recycling program would have increased to greater levels than it has thus far. Experts say that recycling

1

Begins by establishing the significance of the problem
Builds credibility by documenting statistics with footnote references
Describes background of problem
Discusses conditions that prompted the need for study
Includes centered page number on first and succeeding pages

The first page of a report generally contains the title printed 2 inches from the top edge. Titles for major parts of a report (such as *Introduction, Results, Conclusion,* and so forth) are centered in all caps. First-level headings are underscored and printed with upper- and lowercase letters. Second-level headings begin at the side. For illustration of heading formats, see Figure 12.5.

Notice that Alan's report is single-spaced. Many businesses prefer this space-saving format. However, some organizations prefer double-spacing, especially for preliminary drafts. Page numbers may be centered 1 inch from the bottom of the page or placed 1 inch from the upper right corner at the margin.

FIGURE 14.4 (continued)

programs generally must operate at least a year before results become apparent.[7] The OAS program has been in operation one year, yet gains are disappointing. Therefore, OAS authorized this study to determine the campus community's awareness and use of the program. Recommendations for increasing participation in the campus recycling program will be made to the OAS based on the results of this study.

Scope of the Study

Describes what the study includes and excludes

This study investigates potential participants' attitudes toward recycling in general, their awareness of the campus recycling program, their willingness to recycle on campus, and the perceived convenience of the recycling bins. Only aluminum, glass, paper, and plastic are considered in this study, as they are the only materials being recycled on campus at this time. The costs involved in the program were not considered in this study, since a recycling program generally does not begin to pay for itself during the first year. After the first year, the financial benefit is usually realized in reduced disposal costs.[8]

Sources and Methods

Discusses how the study was conducted

Current business periodicals and newspapers were consulted for background information and to learn how other organizations are encouraging use of in-house recycling programs. In addition, a questionnaire survey (shown in the appendix) of administrators, faculty, staff, and students at Sun Coast University campus was conducted to learn about this group's recycling habits. In all, a convenience sample of 220 individuals responded to the self-administered survey. The composition of the sample closely resembles the makeup of the campus population. Figure 1 shows the percentage of students, faculty, staff, and administrators who participated in the survey.

Figure 1

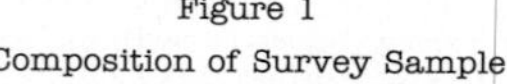
Composition of Survey Sample

Uses computer-generated pie chart to illustrate makeup of survey

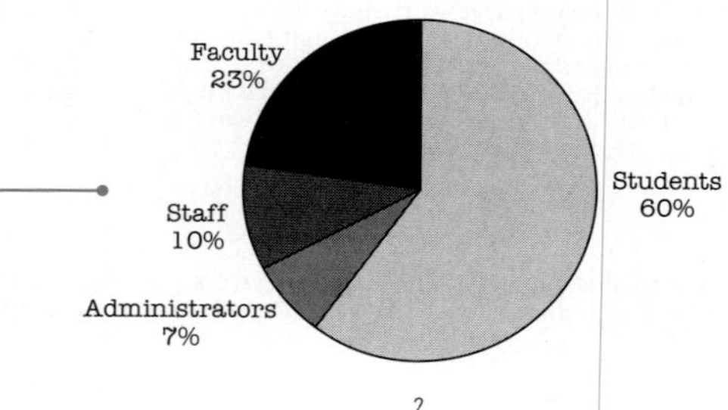

2

Because Alan wants this report to be formal in tone, he avoids "I" and "we." Notice, too, that he uses present-tense verbs to describe his current writing *(this study investigates),* but past-tense verbs to indicate research completed in the past *(newspapers were consulted).*

If you use figures or tables, be sure to introduce them in the text. Although it's not always possible, try to place them close to the spot where they are first mentioned. If necessary to save space, you can print the title of a figure at its side.

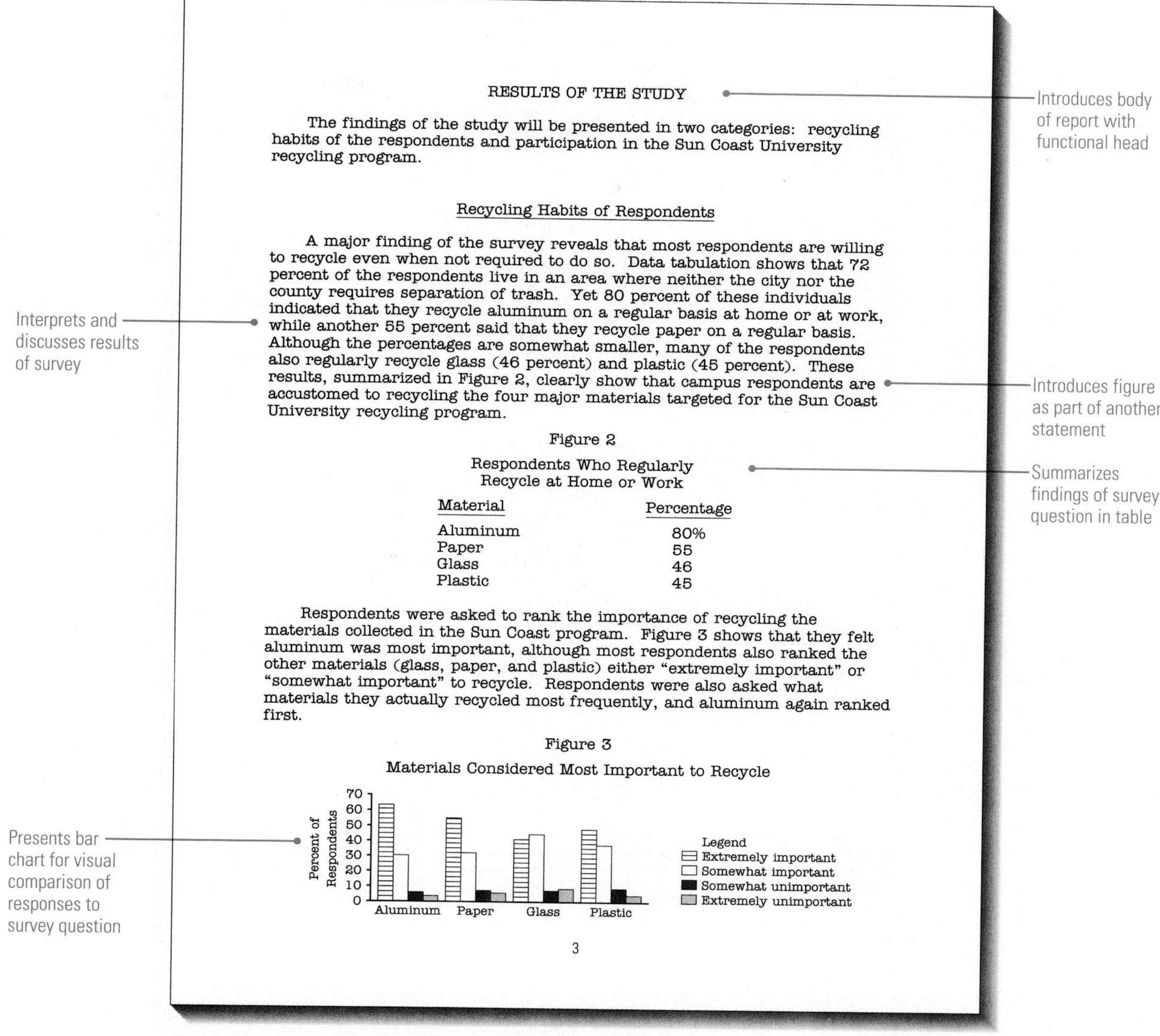

RESULTS OF THE STUDY

The findings of the study will be presented in two categories: recycling habits of the respondents and participation in the Sun Coast University recycling program.

Recycling Habits of Respondents

A major finding of the survey reveals that most respondents are willing to recycle even when not required to do so. Data tabulation shows that 72 percent of the respondents live in an area where neither the city nor the county requires separation of trash. Yet 80 percent of these individuals indicated that they recycle aluminum on a regular basis at home or at work, while another 55 percent said that they recycle paper on a regular basis. Although the percentages are somewhat smaller, many of the respondents also regularly recycle glass (46 percent) and plastic (45 percent). These results, summarized in Figure 2, clearly show that campus respondents are accustomed to recycling the four major materials targeted for the Sun Coast University recycling program.

Figure 2

Respondents Who Regularly Recycle at Home or Work

Material	Percentage
Aluminum	80%
Paper	55
Glass	46
Plastic	45

Respondents were asked to rank the importance of recycling the materials collected in the Sun Coast program. Figure 3 shows that they felt aluminum was most important, although most respondents also ranked the other materials (glass, paper, and plastic) either "extremely important" or "somewhat important" to recycle. Respondents were also asked what materials they actually recycled most frequently, and aluminum again ranked first.

Figure 3

Materials Considered Most Important to Recycle

Percent of Respondents
70
60
50
40
30
20
10
0
Aluminum
Paper
Glass
Plastic
Legend
Extremely important
Somewhat important
Somewhat unimportant
Extremely unimportant

3

Introduces body of report with functional head
Interprets and discusses results of survey
Introduces figure as part of another statement
Summarizes findings of survey question in table
Presents bar chart for visual comparison of responses to survey question

Alan selects the most important survey findings to interpret and discuss for readers. Notice that he continues to use present-tense verbs *(the survey reveals* and *these results clearly show)* to discuss the current report.

Because he has few tables and charts, Alan labels them all as "Figures" and numbers them consecutively. Report writers with a great many tables, charts, and illustrations may prefer to label and number them separately. Tables are labeled as such; everything else is generally called a figure.

FIGURE 14.4 (continued)

Adds personal interpretation

When asked how likely they would be to go out of their way to deposit an item in a recycling bin, 29 percent of the respondents said "very likely," and 55 percent said "somewhat likely." Thus, respondents showed a willingness--at least on paper--to recycle even if it means making a special effort to locate a recycling bin.

Participation in Recycling on Campus

For any recycling program to be successful, participants must be aware of the location of recycling centers and must be trained to use them.[9] Another important ingredient in thriving programs is convenience to users. If recy-cling centers are difficult for users to reach, these centers will be unsuccess-ful. To collect data on these topics, the survey included questions assessing awareness and use of the current bins. The survey also investigated reasons for not participating and the perceived convenience of current bin locations.

Introduces more findings and relates them to the report's purpose.

Student Awareness and Use of Bins

Two of the most significant questions in the survey asked whether respondents were aware of the OAS recycling bins on campus and whether they had used the bins. Responses to both questions were disappointing, as Figure 4 illustrates.

Figure 4

Awareness and Use of Recycling Bins on Campus

Location	Awareness of bins at this location	Use of bins at this location
Social sciences building	38%	21%
Bookstore	29	12
Administration building	28	12
Computer labs	16	11
Library	15	7
Student union	9	5
Engineering building	8	6
Department and administrative offices	6	3
Campus dormitories	5	3
Unaware of any bins; have not used any bins	20	7

Arranges responses from highest to lowest with "unaware" category placed last

Only 38 percent of the respondents, as shown in Figure 4, were aware of the bins located outside the social sciences building. Even fewer were aware of the bins outside the bookstore (29 percent) and outside the administration building (28 percent). Equally dissatisfying, only 21 percent of the respondents had used the most visible recycling bins outside the social sciences

Clarifies and emphasizes meaning of findings

4

In discussing the results of the survey, Alan highlights those that have significance for the purpose of the report.

As you type a report, avoid widows and orphans (ending a page with the first line of a paragraph or carrying a single line of a paragraph to a new page). Strive to start and end pages with at least two lines of a paragraph, even if a slightly larger bottom margin results.

respondents indicated that they had used the recycling bins. Other recycling bin locations were even less familiar to the survey respondents and, of course, were little used. These responses plainly show that the majority of the respondents in the Sun Coast campus community have a low awareness of the recycling program and an even lower record of participation.

Reasons for Not Participating

Respondents offered several reasons for not participating in the campus recycling program. Forty-five percent said that the bins are not convenient to use. Thirty percent said that they did not know where the bins were located. Another 25 percent said that they are not in the habit of recycling. Although many reasons for not participating were listed, the primary one appears to center on convenience of bin locations.

Location of Recycling Bins

When asked specifically how they would rate the location of the bins currently in use, only 13 percent of the respondents felt that the bins were extremely convenient. Another 35 percent rated the locations as somewhat convenient. Over half the respondents felt that the locations of the bins were either somewhat inconvenient or extremely inconvenient. Recycling bins are currently located outside nearly all the major campus buildings, but respondents clearly considered these locations inconvenient or inadequate.

Discusses results of other survey questions not represented in tables or charts

In indicating where they would like recycling bins placed (see Figure 5), 42 percent of the respondents felt that the most convenient locations would be outside each building on campus. Placing recycling bins near the food service facilities on campus seemed most convenient to another 33 percent of those questioned, while 15 percent stated that they would like to see the bins placed near the vending machines. Ten percent of the individuals responding to the survey did not seem to think that the locations of the bins would matter to them.

Clarifies results of another survey question with textual discussion accompanied by table

Figure 5

Preference for Placement of Recycling Bins

Outside each building on campus	42%
Near food service facilities	33
Near vending machines	15
Does not matter	10

CONCLUSIONS

Based on the findings of the recycling survey of members of the Sun Coast University campus community, the following conclusions are drawn:

1. Most members of the campus community are already recycling at home or at work without being required to do so.

5

After completing a discussion of the survey results, Alan articulates what he considers the five most important conclusions to be drawn from this survey. Some writers combine the conclusions and recommendations, particularly when they are interrelated. Alan separated them in his study because the survey findings were quite distinct from the recommendations he would make based on them.

Notice that it is unnecessary to start a new page for the conclusions.

FIGURE 14.4 (continued)

Draws conclusions based on survey findings; summarizes previous discussion

2. Over half of the respondents recycle aluminum and paper on a regular basis; most recycle glass and plastic to some degree.
3. Most of the surveyed individuals expressed a willingness to participate in a recycling program. Many, however, seem unwilling to travel very far to participate; 42 percent would like recycling bins to be located outside every campus building.
4. Awareness and use of the current campus recycling program are low. Only a little over one third of the respondents knew of any recycling bin locations on campus, and only one fifth had actually used them.
5. Respondents considered the locations of the campus bins inconvenient. This perceived inconvenience was given as the principal reason for not participating in the campus recycling program.

RECOMMENDATIONS

Supported by the findings and conclusions of this study, the following recommendations are offered in an effort to improve the operations and success of the Sun Coast recycling program:

Lists specific actions to help solve report problem; suggests practical ways to implement recommendations

1. Increase on-campus awareness and visibility by designing an eye-catching logo that represents the campus recycling program for use in promotions.
2. Enhance comprehension of recycling procedures by training users how to recycle. Use posters to explain the recycling program and to inform users of recycling bin locations. Label each bin clearly as to what materials may be deposited.
3. Add bins in several new locations, particularly in the food service and vending machine areas.
4. Recruit student leaders to promote participation in the recycling program by giving educational talks to classes and other campus groups, informing them of the importance of recycling.
5. Develop an incentive program for student organizations. Offer incentives for meeting recycling goals as determined by OAS. On-campus groups—such as fraternities, sororities, and clubs—could compete in recycling drives designed to raise money for the group, the university, or a charity. Money from the proceeds of the recycling program could be used to fund the incentive program.

6

The most important parts of a report are its conclusions and recommendations. Alan lists five specific and practical actions that can be taken to help solve the original report problem. Each starts with a verb and is stated in command language for emphasis and readability.

Documents references in order of appearance in text

NOTES

1. Vicky Cahan, Waste Not, Want Not? Not Necessarily, Business Week, 17 July 1989, 116.

2. Keith Schneider, As Recycling Becomes a Growth Industry, Its Paradoxes Also Multiply, The New York Times, 20 January 1991, sec. 4, 6.

3. Bruce Weddle and Edward Klein, A Strategy to Control the Garbage Glut, EPA Journal, March/April 1989, 30.

4. Susan de Blanc, Paper Recycling: How to Make It Effective, The Office, December 1991, 32.

5. Keith Schneider, The New York Times, 6.

6. John Holusha, Mixed Benefits From Recycling, The New York Times, 26 July 1991, D2.

7. Susan de Blanc, Paper Recycling, 33.

8. James W. Steelman, Shirley Desmond, and LeGrand Johnson, Facing Global Limitations (New York: Rockford Press, 1992), 145.

9. Susan de Blanc, Paper Recycling, 33.

BIBLIOGRAPHY

May be omitted if few sources are cited

Lists all sources alphabetically for easy reader reference

Cahan, Vicky. Waste Not, Want Not? Not Necessarily. Business Week, 17 July 1989, 116.

de Blanc, Susan. Paper Recycling: How to Make It Effective. The Office, December 1991, 32.

Holusha, John. Mixed Benefits From Recycling. The New York Times, 26 July 1991, D2.

Schneider, Keith. As Recycling Becomes a Growth Industry, Its Paradoxes Also Multiply. The New York Times, 20 January 1991, sec. 4, 6.

Steelman, James W., Shirley Desmond, and LeGrand Johnson. Facing Global Limitations (New York: Rockford Press, 1992), 145.

Weddle, Bruce and Edward Klein. A Strategy to Control the Garbage Glut. EPA Journal, March/April 1989, 30.

7

Alan lists all the references cited within the text on this page. For more information about documentation styles, see Chapter 12 and Appendix C. Notes entries are arranged as they appeared in the text, while bibliography entries are alphabetical. Some authors include all the works they investigated in the bibliography.

Most word processing software today automatically updates footnotes within the text and prints a complete list for you, thus making documentation nearly painless.

FIGURE 14.4 (continued)

Includes copy of survey questionnaire so that report readers can see actual questions

APPENDIX

SUN COAST UNIVERSITY RECYCLING PROGRAM SURVEY

Sun Coast University recently implemented a recycling program on campus. Please take a few minutes to answer the following questions so that we can make this program as convenient and helpful as possible for you to use.

Explains why survey is necessary, emphasizing "you" view

1. Please indicate which items you recycle on a regular basis at home or at work. (Check *all* that apply.)
   - ☐ Aluminum
   - ☐ Glass
   - ☐ Paper
   - ☐ Plastic
2. Do you live in an area where the city/county requires separation of trash?
   ☐ Yes ☐ No
3. How important is it to you to recycle each of the following:

	Extremely Important	Somewhat Important	Somewhat Unimportant	Extremely Unimportant
Aluminum				
Glass				
Paper				
Plastic				

Provides range of answers that will be easy to tabulate

4. How likely would it be for you to go out of your way to put something in a recycling bin?

Very Likely	Somewhat Likely	Somewhat Unlikely	Very Unlikely

5. Which of the following items do you recycle *most* often? (Choose *one* item only.)
   - ☐ Aluminum
   - ☐ Glass
   - ☐ Paper
   - ☐ Plastic
   - ☐ Other
6. The following are locations of the recycling bins on campus. (Check *all* those of which you are aware.)
   - ☐ Administration building
   - ☐ Bookstore
   - ☐ Campus dorms
   - ☐ Computer labs
   - ☐ Engineering building
   - ☐ Library
   - ☐ Social sciences building
   - ☐ Student union
   - ☐ I'm unaware of any of these recycling bins.

8

Alan had space to add the word "Appendix" to the top of the survey questionnaire. If space were not available, he could have typed a separate page with that title on it. If more than one item were included, he would have named them Appendix A, Appendix B, and so on.

Notice that the appendix continues the report pagination.

7. Which of the following recycling bins have you actually used? (Check *all* that you have used.)
- ☐ Administration building
- ☐ Bookstore
- ☐ Campus dorms
- ☐ Computer labs
- ☐ Engineering building
- ☐ Library
- ☐ Social sciences building
- ☐ Student union
- ☐ I've not used any of these recycling bins.

8. If you don't recycle on campus, why don't you participate?
- ☐ I'm not in the habit of recycling.
- ☐ I don't know where the bins are.
- ☐ The bins aren't convenient to me.
- ☐ Other ____________________

9. How do you rate the convenience of the bins' locations?
- ☐ Extremely convenient
- ☐ Somewhat convenient
- ☐ Somewhat inconvenient
- ☐ Extremely inconvenient

10. Which of the following possible recycling bin locations would be most convenient for you to use? (Check *one* only.)
- ☐ Outside each building
- ☐ Near the food service facilities
- ☐ Near the vending machines
- ☐ Does not matter
- ☐ Other ____________________

11. Please indicate:
- ☐ Student
- ☐ Faculty
- ☐ Administrator
- ☐ Staff

COMMENTS:

Thank you for your responses! Please return the questionnaire in the enclosed, stamped envelope to Sun Coast University, School of Business, Rm. 321. If you have any questions, please call (555) 450-2391.

9

Anticipates responses but also supplies "Other" category

Uses scale questions to capture degrees of feeling

Requests little demographic data to keep survey short

Offers comment section for explanations and remarks

Concludes with appreciation and instructions

Summary of Learning Goals

1. **Discuss the components of informal proposals.** Most informal proposals contain (1) a persuasive introduction that explains the purpose of the proposal and qualifies the writer, (2) background material identifying the problem and project goals, (3) a proposal, plan, or schedule outlining the project, (4) a section describing staff qualifications, (5) a budget showing expected costs, and (6) a request for approval or authorization.
2. **Discuss the special components in formal proposals.** Beyond the six components generally contained in informal proposals, formal proposals may include these additional parts: (1) copy of the RFP (request for proposal), (2) letter of transmittal, (3) abstract or executive summary, (4) title page, (5) table of contents, (6) list of illustrations, and (7) appendix.
3. **Distinguish between proposals and formal reports.** Proposals offer to solve problems, provide services, or sell equipment. Formal reports present ordered information to decision-makers in business, industry, government, and education.
4. **Identify formal report components that precede its introduction.** Formal reports may include these beginning components: (1) vinyl or heavy paper cover, (2) title page, (3) letter of transmittal, (4) table of contents, (5) list of illustrations, and (6) executive summary or abstract.
5. **Outline topics that might be covered in the introduction of a formal report.** The introduction to a formal report sets the scene by discussing some or all of the following topics: background material, problem or purpose, significance of the topic, scope and organization of the report, authorization, review of relevant literature, sources and methods, and definitions of key terms.
6. **Describe the components of a formal report that follow the introduction.** The body of a report discusses, analyzes, interprets, and evaluates the research findings or solution to a problem. The conclusion tells what the findings mean and how they relate to the report's purpose. The recommendations tell how to solve the report problem. The last portions of a formal report are the appendix, references, and bibliography.
7. **Specify tips that aid writers of formal reports.** Before writing, develop a realistic timetable and collect all necessary data. During the writing process, work from a good outline, work in a quiet place, and use a computer. Also, try to write rapidly, revising later. While writing, use verb tenses consistently, and avoid *I* and *we*. A few days after completing the first draft, revise to improve clarity, coherence, and conciseness. Proofread the final copy three times.

Chapter Review

1. Proposals are written offers to do what?
2. What is an RFP?
3. What are the six principal parts of a letter proposal?
4. What is a "worry item" in a proposal?
5. Why should a proposal budget be prepared very carefully?

6. What is generally contained in a letter of transmittal accompanying a formal report?

7. What label can a report writer use to describe all illustrations and tables?

8. How is an abstract different from an executive summary?

9. What does "scope" mean in relation to a formal report?

10. Should the body of a report include the heading *Body*?

11. What are the advantages of functional headings? Of talking headings?

12. In a formal report where do most writers place the conclusions?

13. What kind of materials go in an appendix?

14. What kind of environment enhances writing?

15. How should a formal report be proofread?

Discussion

1. Why are proposals important to many businesses?

2. How do formal reports differ from informal reports?

3. Why do some parts of formal reports tend to be redundant?

4. Discuss the three phases of the writing process in relation to formal reports. What activities take place in each phase?

5. Ethical Issue: Is it ethical to have someone else proofread a report that you will be turning in for a grade?

Problems

Consult your instructor to determine the length, format, and emphasis for the following report projects. Some require additional research; others do not.

14.1 Proposal: Outsourcing

Businesses today are doing more "outsourcing" than ever before. This means that they are going outside to find specialists to handle some aspect of their business, such as billing, shipping, or advertising. They're also hiring experts with special training and equipment to solve problems for which they lack the necessary talent and staff. For a business where you have worked or an organization you know, select a problem. Here are some possibilities: poor handling of customer orders, inefficient payroll practices, inadequate computer equipment or software, unsatisfactory inventory control, poor use of sales staff, bad scheduling of employees, poorly trained employees, sexual harassment on the job, and poor telephone techniques. Assume the boss has asked you as a consultant to either solve the problem or study it and tell the organization what to do. Prepare an informal proposal describing your plan to solve the problem or perform a service. Decide how much you will charge and what staff you will need. Send your letter proposal to your boss.

14.2 Proposal: Profiting From Someone Else's Mistakes

"It's amazing," says the owner of one of the country's largest trucking companies. "Companies will require a vice president to sign a check for over $50, but the guy or girl in the back can sign for a half million dollars worth of raw material." Freight transportation experts claim that business owners may be losing millions of dollars a year in their shipping and receiving departments. Poorly trained and paid workers make costly blunders that anger customers and eat away at profits.

Your company, United Traffic Services (UTS), offers solutions, especially for businesses without a transportation specialist on the payroll. UTS audits freight bills and provides consulting services. Specifically, you and your staff of nine check all shipping charges (monthly or quarterly) to ensure that trucking companies are charging the correct rates. You also give advice on how to get the lowest shipping rates. You know that, because of competitiveness in the trucking industry, any company that is not getting at least a 50 percent discount is paying too much. You work with both outbound and inbound shipments. One of your services involves selecting a good carrier. Because of your expertise and research capabilities, you can advise any company about the most financially stable and reliable truckers. You also advise businesses about packing and labeling to avoid problems. You know that 98 percent of actual freight claims start at the point of origin because cartons are marked incorrectly.

In addition to auditing shipments, you file freight claims for your clients as well as fight wrongful claims against them. You have saved companies thousands of dollars. Two years ago, a Rancho Dominguez auto products manufacturer was hit by a claim from a trucking company. "In one fell swoop," said the director of operations, "UTS saved us $29,000. We would have owed twice that amount if we didn't have UTS on our side."

Your fee is one half of whatever you save clients on their shipping transactions. They pay nothing if you don't save them money. Write a letter proposal to Steve Hernandez, President, Club Enterprises, 468 Industry Avenue, Covina, CA 91764, proposing your services. Club Enterprises makes a security device for locking the steering column of a car. Club ships out 2 million pounds of products annually, and it receives 1.5 million pounds of raw materials—most of it by truck. President Hernandez has heard of your service and wants to learn more.[4]

14.3 Proposal: Strangers in a Strange Land

"Probably between $2 billion and $2.5 billion a year is lost from expatriate burnout and failed assignments," said an international personnel expert. Businesses suffer this loss when expatriate employees sent on foreign assignments fail to adjust and pack their bags to come home prematurely. As a result, many cross-cultural training programs are being offered by enterprising consultants. American businesses "are dumb if they don't use cross-cultural training," observed the personnel vice president for overseas branches of Reynolds Metals Company. The expatriate burnout rate for his company dropped to almost zero after it began using cross-cultural training programs.

Global Visions, a consulting firm in Boulder, Colorado, offers a number of training programs for employees being sent to other countries. Global provides previsit orientations, career path counseling, foreign language training, and family cultural immersion programs. Mimi Sams, senior partner in Global Visions, has recently learned that General Motors plans to open a vehicle assembly plant in Kenya. Although the Kenyan government will own 51 percent of the plant and will supply most of the labor force, the plant will be run by GM managers and engineers. Anticipating the need for training the transported staff, Mimi talks to the director of international personnel at GM. He recognizes the benefits of training and would like to consider Global Visions, but he wants a brief written proposal describing the program.

As assistant to Mimi Sams, you have been asked to compose a two-page letter proposal to GM for her approval. Describe your African Total Immersion cross-cultural program. This crash course, conducted at your headquarters in Boulder, includes three full days of intensive training for the employee's entire family. It totally immerses the family, with both group and individual sessions, in African political history, business practices, social customs, and nonverbal communication. The training helps the entire family grasp cultural differences and anticipate culture-shock symptoms such as depression and self-pity.

Because the family's reaction causes more foreign-transfer failure than a manager's work performance, Global Visions focuses on family adjustment. Children and teenagers receive separate training from that of their parents. They sample Indian food, popular in Kenya, and learn how to ride Nairobi public buses and how to speak a little Swahili.

The staff for your African Total Immersion program includes senior trainer Jackson Fox, who was a Peace Corps official in Nigeria for twelve years, responsible for training thousands of new recruits. In addition, you have Idi Midamba, adjunct professor of international relations at Kent State University and son of a Kenyan political leader. Rounding out the staff of African specialists is Innawati Witowalidi, a Kenyan who received an M.S. degree in psychology from the University of Illinois. She specializes in the psychological phases of the process of adjustment. This staff has conducted many successful training sessions for U.S. managers and their families heading for Africa. As part of the program, a former expatriate to Kenya shares his experiences with participants.

Global Visions will tailor a three-day program expressly for the GM managers being sent to Kenya. The sum of $8,000 covers training for four individuals, with $500 for each additional person. The maximum number of trainees for any program is ten. This price includes meals for three days and two nights of lodging at the Grand Peaks Hilton. It also includes a guide book to African social and business customs, along with a Swahili primer. For Mimi Sams's signature write a proposal to Jim Rymers, Director, International Programs, General Motors, Inc., 311 Livonia Place, Bloomfield Hills, MI 48224.[5]

14.4 Proposal: Don't Give Up Your Day Job

As a struggling student, displaced homemaker, or budding entrepreneur, you decide to start your own part-time word processing business in your home. Select a company or professional in your city that might need your services. Often, businesses, medical centers, attorneys, and other professionals have overload transcribing or word processing to farm out to a service. Assess your expertise and equipment. Check out the competition. What do other word processing services offer, and what do they charge? Although many apply a flat hourly rate, you may decide to charge more for items that require heavy editing. Find out what a particular company needs. Prepare a letter proposal addressed to a specific individual outlining your plan to offer your services.

14.5 Proposal: Surf's Up in Kansas!

Amusement parks around the country are constantly searching for sensational new rides to draw crowds. Theme park giants like the Walt Disney Company employ their own staffs to develop hot new rides, but smaller parks can't afford such research. Yet, they need fresh entertainment to attract new thrill-seekers and keep old customers coming back. "The general theory is that you must add a major new ride every two years and a minor one in between," claims one amusement park expert.

Wave Madness, a one-man San Diego company, designs and installs water-related amusement rides. An enormous success for the young company has been Flow Rider, a surfing machine that shoots water against a curved wall creating a wave effect for riders to "surf" down on their stomachs or on boards. At the Schlitterbahn Family Water Park in New Braunsfels, Texas, attendance rose 24 percent, to about 650,000 people, after Flow Rider was installed.

Wave Madness has been approached by the owners of Wichita Fun Park. For next year's summer season, they want a new water ride, similar to the Flow Rider or Waimea Wave, which is popular at the Raging Waters park in Salt Lake City. But they have a limited budget as well as space and energy restrictions. Although water is scarce, they feel that a scaled-down version of Flow Rider or Waimea Wave might be possible. Michael Larson, owner and sole proprietor of Wave Madness, is definitely interested in working with the Wichita people, but he's afraid that he would scare them off if he quoted a price for one of his rides outright. Therefore, he decides to submit a proposal outlining his services as a consultant. At $200 an hour he would be able to talk with them about what they need and how best it can be achieved. If they decide to install one of his rides, his consultation fees would be waived.

In his proposal Larson wants to describe one of his new rides: Master Blaster, a roller coaster using a high-powered stream of water to carry people along. The feeling of being pushed uphill is eerie and exciting, according to users at another park. This new ride is less expensive to install and operate than Flow Rider. On the other hand, he could possibly scale down Flow Rider, which is very popular because of its speed. The surfer moves at only two or three miles an hour down the face of the wall. But the water races past at 20 miles an hour, twice as fast as an ocean wave.

Because the Wichita Fun Park owners want action quickly, Larson develops a tentative schedule. Conferring with the owners would probably take about two days; examining the site and working out the placement of a ride would take about one week; installation of a new ride usually requires thirty working days, weather permitting; testing and adjusting the ride requires two weeks.

Michael Larson comes to you, a writing specialist, to help him with his proposal. His background includes a degree as an attorney and experience as a surfer and real estate developer. When he focused his attention on developing water rides, he obtained technical help at Scripps Institution of Oceanography, a research facility in La Jolla, California. His greatest success thus far has been Flow Rider. He designs and tests every ride himself, never leaving a project until it is installed and working successfully.

Work out a schedule that ensures the ride would be ready for the park's opening May 1. For Michael Larson's signature prepare a proposal addressed to Mr. William Langford, Wichita Entertainment, Inc., 3440 Goddard Avenue, Wichita, KS 67532.[6]

14.6 Research Report: Car Insurance

Costs for car insurance and levels of customer satisfaction vary greatly from one company to another. One of your tasks as a research analyst for Consumers Union is tracking insurance data for state automobile associations. From the most current *Consumer Reports* magazine article on auto insurance, select five representative or well-known insurance carriers that operate within your state. Assume that James Michelin, director of your state automobile association, has asked you to report on these five companies. He's interested in the degree of customer satisfaction, claims problems, nonclaims problems, delayed payments, drop rates, and annual premiums. To investigate and compare premiums, use the figures provided by *Consumer Reports* for typical urban customers. Draw conclusions about these five insurance carriers. Make recommendations to Mr. Michelin, who will be distributing your information to members of the automobile association. Address your report to James Michelin, Director, State Automobile Association in the capital of your state.

14.7 Research Report: Quality Circles

Research shows that 60 percent of Fortune 500 firms either have implemented or are experimenting with different types of employee involvement programs, such as work teams, quality circles, and workplace democracy councils. In large and small firms these programs are thought to reap many benefits—from increasing production to boosting morale. Mike Rivera, vice president of operations at DataTech, which employs about 80 electronics assemblers and 30 supporting employees, wants to learn more about these programs. He asks you, his executive assistant, to prepare a report that investigates how other companies have used them. He's particularly interested in safety applications. Could quality circles or work teams improve DataTech's safety record? How are such programs operated at other companies? Collect secondary data, analyze it, draw conclusions, and make recommendations in a letter report to Mike Rivera.

14.8 Formal Report: Breaking Through the Glass Ceiling

Only 3 to 5 percent of all senior executives in corporate America are women. Some observers suggest that a glass ceiling prevents women from breaking through into upper management. You have been asked by the American Management Association to investigate the success of efforts made in the past decade to train and promote female executives. Does a glass ceiling exist? Discuss some of the programs involving mentoring, coaching, women's councils, and management incentives. Develop recommendations directed toward female college students majoring in business or management. Suggest how they can improve their chances for moving up the career ladder when they enter the work world. Address your report to Barbara M. Loring, Chair, Women's Advisory Council, AMA.[7]

14.9 Formal Report: Entrepreneurial Women

By the year 2000, 40 to 50 percent of all businesses will be owned by women. As an intern at the American Association of Women in Business, you have been asked to collect information for a booklet to be distributed to women who inquire about starting businesses. Specifically, you have been asked to find articles describing three or four women who have started their own businesses. Examine why they started their businesses, how they did it, and how successful they were. In your report draw conclusions about what kinds of women start businesses, why they do it, what kinds of businesses they are likely to start, and what difficulties they face. Speculate on the dramatic increase in the number of female business owners. Make recommendations to women about starting businesses. You may wish to consult the Small Business Administration's Office of Women's Business Ownership, the National Association of Women Business Owners, and the American Women's Economic Development Corporation. Address your report to Rochelle Robinson, Director, American Association of Women in Business.

14.10 Collaborative Formal Report: Lending a Helping Hand to the ASO

Volunteer your class to conduct research aimed at a specific problem facing your campus associated students organization. Ask the president of your campus ASO to visit your class to discuss a problem that requires research. Most ASOs want to learn what students think about their activities, projects, and use of resources. However, ASOs generally lack the expertise and staff needed to gather reliable data. Question the ASO president to isolate the issues to be investigated. For example, the ASO may want students to prioritize activities deserving support. With a limited budget, what activities should the ASO fund: concerts, lectures, intramural sports, movies, a country store, or something else? Other questions may face the leadership: Should the ASO undertake a recycling center? Should it sponsor an adult literacy volunteer program? How should these programs be implemented?

Once a problem for investigation has been selected, divide into groups of three to five to develop a survey questionnaire. Evaluate each group's questionnaire in class, and select the best one. Pilot test the questionnaire. Administer the revised questionnaire to a targeted student group. Tabulate the findings. In teams of three to five or individually, write a report to the ASO president discussing your findings, conclusions, and recommendations.

14.11 Formal Report: Fast-food Checkup

Select a fast-food franchise in your area. Assume that the national franchising headquarters has received complaints about the service, quality, and cleanliness of the unit. You have been sent to inspect and to report on what you see. Visit on two or more occasions. Make notes on how many customers were served, how quickly they received their food, and how courteously they were treated. Observe the number of employees and supervisors working. Note the cleanliness of observable parts of the restaurant. Inspect the restroom as well as the exterior and surrounding grounds. Sample the food. Your boss is a stickler for details; he has no use for general statements like *The restroom was not clean.* Be specific. Draw conclusions. Are the complaints justified? If improvements are necessary, make recommendations. Address your report to Lawrence C. Kelsey, President.

14.12 Formal Report: Readability of Insurance Policies

The 21st Century Insurance Company is concerned about the readability of its policies. State legislators are beginning to investigate complaints of policyholders who say they can't understand their insurance policies. One judge lambasted insurers saying, "The language in these policies is bureaucratic gobbledegook, jargon, double-talk, a form of officialese, federalese, and insurancese that does not qualify as English. The burden upon organizations is to write policies in a manner designed to communicate rather than to obfuscate." Taking the initiative in improving its policies, 21st Century hires you as a consultant to study its standard policy and make recommendations.

Examine a life, fire, or health insurance policy that you own or one from a friend or relative. Select one that is fairly complex. Determine its readability level by calculating its Fog Index (Chapter 5) for several selections. Study the policy for jargon, confusing language, long sentences, and unclear antecedents. Evaluate its format, print size, paper and print quality, amount of white space, and use of headings. Does it have an index or glossary? Are difficult terms defined? How easy is it to find specifics, should a policyholder want to check something?

In addition to the data you collect from your own examination of the policy, 21st Century gives you the data shown in Figure 14.5 from a recent policyholder survey. Prepare a report for Heather Garcia, Vice President, 21st Century Insurance Company, discussing your analysis, conclusions, and recommendations for improving its basic policy.

14.13 Formal Report: Doing Your Own Thing

In a business, organization, or field you know, think about a problem or issue that needs to be investigated. Assume that a(n) president, owner, supervisor, or executive asks you to examine the problem or issue and analyze its causes and ramifications. Consider ways to solve the problem or define the issue. Draw conclusions based on

FIGURE 14.5 ● 21st Century Insurance Company Policyholder Survey

Response to statement "I am able to read and understand the language and provisions of my policy."					
Age Group	**Strongly Agree**	**Agree**	**Undecided**	**Disagree**	**Strongly Disagree**
18–34	2%	9%	34%	41%	14%
35–49	2	17	38	33	10
50–64	1	11	22	35	31
65+	1	2	17	47	33

your analysis. Make specific recommendations for implementing changes necessary to achieve the solution. You may need to design a questionnaire and circulate it. Be sure to narrow the problem sufficiently so that it can be broken into three to five segments or factors.

14.14 Collaborative Formal Report: Intercultural Communication

American businesses are expanding into foreign markets with manufacturing plants, sales offices, and branch offices abroad. Unfortunately, most Americans have little knowledge of or experience with people from other cultures. To prepare for participation in the global marketplace, collect information for a report focused on a Pacific Rim, Latin American, or European country. Before selecting the country, though, consult your campus international student program for volunteers who are willing to be interviewed. Your instructor may make advance arrangements seeking international student volunteers.

In teams of three to five, collect information about your target country from the library and other sources. Then invite an international student representing your target country to be interviewed by your group. In your primary and secondary research, investigate the topics listed in Figure 14.6. Confirm what you learn in your secondary research by talking with your interviewee. When you complete your research, write a report for the CEO of your company (make up a name and company). Assume that your company plans to expand its operations abroad. Your report should advise the company's executives of social customs, family life, attitudes, religions, education, and values in the target country. Remember that your company's interests are business-oriented; don't dwell on tourist information. Write your report individually or in teams.[8]

14.15 Formal Reports Requiring Secondary Research

Select one of the following topics for a report. Discuss with your instructor its purpose, scope, length, format, audience, and data sources. For each topic analyze your findings, draw conclusions, and make logical recommendations. Your instructor may ask teams to complete the secondary research.

a. Are American executives overpaid?

b. How does the compensation of American executives compare with that of Japanese executives?

c. How are corporations managing employee drug and alcohol abuse?

d. Are corporate fitness programs worth their costs?

e. Has the image of women in advertisements today changed from that shown fifteen years ago?

f. How are businesses dealing with computer fraud and malice?

g. Should McDonald's expand its company-owned and franchise restaurants in Latin America and Asia?

h. Should environmentalists engage in junk-mail promotions to advertise their causes?

i. What is the best way for you to invest $100,000?

j. Of three locations, which is the best for a new McDonald's (or Dairy Queen, Subway, or franchise of your choice)?

k. What magazines represent the best advertising choice for Reebok (or a product with which you are familiar)?

l. What effects do aromas have on the senses, and how can aromas be used to advantage in the workplace?

FIGURE 14.6 ● Intercultural Interview Topics and Questions

Social Customs

1. How do people react to strangers? Friendly? Hostile? Reserved?
2. How do people greet each other?
3. What are the appropriate manners when you enter a room? Bow? Nod? Shake hands with everyone?
4. How are names used for introductions? Is it appropriate to inquire about one's occupation or family?
5. What are the attitudes toward touching?
6. How does one express appreciation for an invitation to another's home? Bring a gift? Send flowers? Write a thank-you note? Are any gifts taboo?
7. Are there any customs related to how or where one sits?
8. Are any facial expressions or gestures considered rude?
9. How close do people stand when talking?
10. What is the attitude toward punctuality in social situations? In business situations?
11. What are acceptable eye contact patterns?
12. What gestures indicate agreement? Disagreement?

Family Life

1. What is the basic unit of social organization? Basic family? Extended family?
2. Do women work outside of the home? In what occupations?

Housing, Clothing, and Food

1. Are there differences in the kind of housing used by different social groups? Differences in location? Differences in furnishings?
2. What occasions require special clothing?
3. Are some types of clothing considered taboo?
4. What is appropriate business attire for men? For women?
5. How many times a day do people eat?
6. What types of places, food, and drink are appropriate for business entertainment? Where is the seat of honor at a table?

Class Structure

1. Into what classes is society organized?
2. Do racial, religious, or economic factors determine social status?
3. Are there any minority groups? What is their social standing?

Political Patterns

1. Are there any immediate threats to the political survival of the country?
2. How is political power manifested?
3. What channels are used for expression of popular opinion?
4. What information media are important?
5. Is it appropriate to talk politics in social situations?

Religion and Folk Beliefs

1. To which religious groups do people belong? Is one predominant?
2. Do religious beliefs influence daily activities?
3. Which places have sacred value? Which objects? Which events?
4. How do religious holidays affect business activities?

Economic Institutions

1. What are the country's principal products?
2. Are workers organized in unions?
3. How are businesses owned? By family units? By large public corporations? By the government?
4. What is the standard work schedule?
5. Is it appropriate to do business by telephone?
6. Is participatory management used?
7. Are there any customs related to exchanging business cards?
8. How is status shown in an organization? Private office? Secretary? Furniture?
9. Are businesspersons expected to socialize before conducting business?

Value Systems

1. Is competitiveness or cooperation more prized?
2. Is thrift or enjoyment of the moment more valued?
3. Is politeness more important than factual honesty?
4. What are the attitudes toward education?
5. Do women own or manage businesses? If so, how are they treated?
6. What are your people's perceptions of Americans? Do Americans offend you? What has been hardest for you to adjust to in America? How could Americans make this adjustment easier for you?

14.16 Formal Reports Requiring Primary Research

Select one of the following topics for a report. Discuss with your instructor its purpose, scope, length, format, audience, and data sources. For each topic analyze your findings, draw conclusions, and make logical recommendations. Your instructor may ask teams to complete the primary research.

a. How can your community improve its image and attract new businesses?

b. How can your community improve its recycling efforts?

c. Does your campus need to add or improve a student computer lab?

d. How can the associated student organization (or a club of your choice) increase its membership and support on this campus?

e. Can the registration process at your college or university be improved?

f. Are the requirements for a degree in your major realistic and relevant?

g. How can drug and alcohol abuse be reduced in your community?

h. What is a significant student problem on your campus, and how can it be solved?

i. What does an analysis of local and national newspapers reveal about employment possibilities for college graduates?

FIGURE 14.7 ● AAPA Survey on the Importance of Résumé Items and Formats

	Percentage of respondents who considered résumé items important		
Résumé Item	**1983**	**1988**	**1993**
Name, address, telephone number	100%	100%	100%
Degree	100	100	100
Name of college	100	100	100
Titles of jobs held	99	99	100
Names of previous employers	98	97	100
Special aptitudes, skills	90	91	95
Job, career objective	73	84	92
Awards, scholarships, honors, achievements	88	89	91
Grade point average	85	89	91
Willingness to relocate	74	82	90
Work experience achievements (learning, contributions, accomplishments)	72	81	89
Professional organizations	67	74	84
College activities	85	83	84
References shown on résumé	79	51	32
Note saying that references would be supplied on request	35	21	20
Summary of qualifications	25	42	72
Reasons for leaving jobs	54	37	29
Name of high school	20	14	4
High school grades	18	15	5
High school activities, awards	19	14	5
List of college courses completed	42	34	21
Social security number	32	35	18
Religion, race	10	5	1
Photograph	16	11	2
Marital status	30	19	2
Height/weight	25	11	1
Church involvement	13	8	0
Birthdate	21	17	3
Health	34	19	6
Résumé Format			
Preference for traditional, chronological format	78	81	88
Preference for functional, skills-oriented format	22	19	12

FIGURE 14.8 ● AAPA Survey on Résumé Correctness and Length

Response to statement "The following factor would cause me to lose interest in a candidate."

Factor	Strongly Agree	Agree	Neutral	Disagree	Strongly Disagree	Not Sure
Poor grammar	63%	34%	1%	1%	0%	1%
More than one spelling error	51	42	4	2	0	1
Incorrect word choice	15	51	26	6	0	2
One spelling error	13	37	31	18	1	0
Use of abbreviations	4	18	49	22	4	3
More than one typing error	39	44	10	6	0	1
Poorly reproduced	21	44	25	7	1	2
Poor margins	7	30	42	13	4	4
One typing error	11	27	41	18	2	1
Poor organization	26	52	18	2	1	1
Too long	23	33	30	11	1	2
Too condensed	11	35	35	13	1	5

FIGURE 14.9 ● AAPA Survey on Average Reading Time Per Résumé

Time in Seconds	Percentage of Recruiters
1–29	1%
30–60	26
61–90	15
91–120	16
121–180	28
181+	11
No response	3

j. What demographic characteristics (age, sex, income, major, socioeconomic status, family, employment, interests, and so forth) does the typical student have on your campus?

14.17 Formal Report: The Perfect Résumé

What do personnel administrators and recruiters really want to see in the résumés of job applicants? Assume that the American Association of Personnel Administrators conducts continuing research to answer that very question. Each year this organization samples its members regarding résumé preferences. Some of the data collected for 1983, 1988, and 1993 are shown in Figure 14.7. The AAPA uses a stratified random sample ensuring that an appropriate number of personnel administrators from small, medium, and large businesses are included (small businesses employ fewer than 100 people; medium, 100–999; and large, 1,000 plus). Each year 500 questionnaires are sent; this year 378 usable questionnaires were returned, and this figure is similar to that received in previous surveys.

As a research assistant for the AAPA, analyze the data and prepare a report to be submitted to your boss, Dr. Nancy M. Taylor. Eventually, the report will be distributed to AAPA members, college placement offices, and the news media. The AAPA résumé report has become a popular tool among colleges, who use it to keep their students informed of current résumé practices. Your boss expects you to interpret the findings and speculate about why personnel administrators have responded as they have. Dr. Taylor may add her ideas to the report later, but she wants your analysis first. In addition to the data for 1983, 1988, and 1993, the most recent survey (1993) posed two new questions, shown in Figures 14.8 and 14.9. These questions dealt with correctness and length of résumés as well as the average time each personnel administrator spends reading a résumé.

Draw conclusions and make recommendations for job applicants. Define any terms that college students, a primary audience for the report, may not understand. Write a memo report to Dr. Nancy M. Taylor, director of research.

FIGURE 14.10 ● Survey Results of American Association of CPAs

1. How important are the following communication tasks and skills for "new" accountants?

	Very Important	Somewhat Important	Somewhat Unimportant	Totally Unimportant	Don't Know; No Response
Written Communication					
Audit reports	11%	18%	34%	12%	25%
Articles for publication	9	10	43	21	17
Memos	31	48	11	4	6
Reports	42	38	10	3	7
Letters	28	31	25	6	10
Proposals	16	23	42	13	6
Oral Communication					
Meeting, conference skills	45	33	13	4	5
Interviewing	38	35	16	7	4
Presentations	24	38	21	11	6
Formal speechmaking	7	14	49	23	7

2. Evaluate the level of communication ability of the "new" accountants who have joined your firm.

	Inadequate	Satisfactory	Very Satisfactory	Excellent	Don't Know; No Response
Written Communication					
Reports	79%	10%			11%
Memos	55	31	5%		9
Letters	53	39			8
Proposals	81	7			12
Audit reports	71	18			11
Articles for publication	86	2	2		10
Oral Communication					
Speeches	52	31	5		12
Presentations	39	45	7		9
Meetings/conferences	47	39	5		9
Client interviews	58	34			8

3. Indicate your agreement with the following statement:			
	Agree	Disagree	No Opinion
The primary mission of accounting education should be			
a. preparation for the CPA examination	14%	80%	6%
b. development of well-rounded individuals	91	4	5

4. If you could design a college course or program to develop communication skills, what would it contain?

Representative answers: "More emphasis on writing skills," "extensive case studies requiring brief, concise explanations," "require considerably more nontechnical classes to prepare the accountant for his environment as part of the graduation requirement for a 5-year curriculum," "courses to develop written and oral communication skills in college and continued in training sessions by employers in workshop fashion," "more required written reports in schools to be graded skillfully and critically by competent teachers." The overall emphasis was on "more communication course work."

14.18 Formal Report: Writing Skills for CPAs

For years practitioners from all types and sizes of accounting firms have complained about the weak communication skills of those entering the profession. The American Association of Certified Public Accountants recently conducted a study investigating the communication skills of new accountants. In a survey questionnaire distributed to managing partners of 150 of the largest accounting firms in the United States, 97 partners responded. Some of the results from the study are shown in Figure 14.10.

As a research analyst for the AACPA, interpret the findings and make recommendations to the association. Two issues are particularly important to the AACPA, although these issues were not addressed directly in the survey. The first issue concerns the essay portion of the CPA examination. The exam currently contains essay questions covering auditing theory and business laws, as well as accounting problems for which narrative solutions must be written. Critics want to eliminate all essay questions, contending that the exam is too long, too expensive to administer, and too subjective. A second issue concerns recommendations for colleges offering accounting education. Should the AACPA recommend accounting curricula to colleges and universities that include more or fewer communication courses? In your analysis consider the profession as a whole in addition to the two issues presented here. Address your report to Richard M. Tarsky, Executive Director, American Association of Certified Public Accountants.

Presentation Skills

15 Speaking Skills

16 Employment Messages

CHAPTER 15

Speaking Skills

LEARNING GOALS

After studying this chapter, you should be able to

1. Discuss two important steps in preparing an oral presentation
2. Explain the three parts of an effective oral presentation
3. Plan visual aids and handouts for a presentation
4. Identify delivery techniques for use before, during, and after a presentation
5. Plan, conduct, and participate in effective meetings and conferences
6. Explain videoconferencing and its uses
7. List five techniques for improving your use of the telephone
8. List four techniques for improving your use of voice mail

Walt Disney Imagineering: Career Track Profile

"Before every formal presentation I . . . suffer butterflies. But now I'm able to channel my surging adrenalin . . . it actually helps me perform better."

Jon Georges felt his palms growing sweaty. He surveyed the room packed with fifty Japanese financiers and managers gathered on a sultry, gray morning in Tokyo to hear his presentation. His stomach flip-flopped when he remembered how many employees back in Los Angeles were depending on him and his team to win approval for this project, an extensive addition to Tokyo Disneyland.

The proposal was to add three new attractions based on classic Disney animated films. One of the planned attractions would be a major children's ride similar to the perennial Disneyland favorite, "Dumbo the Flying Elephant." Another would feature an outdoor garden maze, with a network of hedge passageways for children to wander through. For the past year Jon and a Walt Disney Imagineering design team had been working intensively on these ideas.

Preparations and all work would stop, though, without a successful presentation before this group, the owners and operators of Tokyo Disneyland. Jon and the entire team had to convince the assembled Japanese that these new feature attractions, as well as associated merchandise shops and a major restaurant, would be exciting and profitable additions to the existing theme park.

At some point everyone in business has to sell his or her ideas, and such persuasion is usually done in person. Like most of us, Jon does not consider himself a professional speaker. "I was so afraid of public speaking that I totally avoided such classes in high school," he admits. "In college I started a couple of speech courses but always dropped out. Finally, though, I faced the medicine and took a night class. A lot of fear surfaced, but the experience was very helpful." For Jon poise and confidence grew as he found more opportunities to perform while progressing in his career.

Immediately after graduating from UCLA, Jon was hired by Walt Disney Imagineering as an exhibit coordinator. One of his first tasks was working with a pre-Columbian art exhibit for Epcot Center in Florida. Then he was promoted to assistant show producer and finally to show producer. As leader of a creative team, he now develops new ideas for theme park rides and attractions.

In this role Jon makes both formal and informal presentations. He enjoys the informal meetings that require him to describe a current design project to a vice president who may drop in for a quick update. "Ninety percent of our presentations are done informally," observes Jon. "These presentations require little planning because they simply grow out of what we've been doing." Formal presentations, however, are an entirely different story. They require careful preparation, particularly when they are part of a collaborative effort with an important project riding on the outcome.

Understanding the audience and anticipating its reaction are integral parts of Jon's preparations for formal presentations. For the Tokyo Disneyland project Jon and the Disney Imagineering team wanted to present their concepts in broad terms to see if the financiers liked the total idea. But Jon also knew that this audience would be detail-oriented. Therefore, he and the project managers had to be prepared to answer specific questions involving engineering facts, such as the durability of the metal used in the track to make the children's ride. "Even when a project is in the design stages," says Jon, "Japanese businessmen tend to want particulars—like the color of the concrete, the number of restrooms, and the exact location where visitors would exit an attraction."

Few youngsters can forget their adventures on "Dumbo the Flying Elephant" at Disneyland. Jon Georges and the Walt Disney Imagineering team had to convince Japanese financiers that a fairy tale ride designed for the new Child's Land at Tokyo Disneyland could be as attractive and profitable as Dumbo has been in California.

Other adaptations Jon made for the Tokyo presentation involved choice of language and presentation style. Carefully avoiding Disney and design jargon, Jon consciously used common words and simple sentences, which the translator had little trouble converting to Japanese. While the translator delivered a sentence, Jon mentally shaped the next one to eliminate words and phrases that might cause misunderstandings.

In readying his part of the Tokyo presentation, Jon kept in mind these important elements: organization, visuals, and focus. After a year's preparatory work on this project, he had thousands of details he would have been delighted to share with listeners. He also understood, though, the importance of simplicity in his oral presentation. To be effective, his presentation demanded a powerful focus. And that focus wasn't hard to pinpoint. He had to convince his Japanese listeners that this new children's "land" would enhance the value of Tokyo Disneyland and would draw more visitors through the turnstiles. Every aspect of his presentation had to emphasize this benefit for his audience.

Although Jon and his team scored a big triumph in Tokyo, he admits to having felt quite nervous. "Before every formal presentation," he confesses, "I always, always suffer butterflies. But now I'm able to channel my surging adrenalin into an increased level of excitement. It's no longer fear; I look upon it as enthusiasm, and it actually helps me perform better."

Like Jon Georges, many future businesspeople fail to take advantage of opportunities in college to develop speaking skills. Yet, such skills often play an important role in a successful career. This chapter develops skills in making oral presentations, using telephones and voice mail, and participating in meetings and conferences.[1]

Oral Presentations

Effective oral presentations result from thorough preparation, sound organization, sensible use of visual aids, and confident delivery.

"This speech would have been a lot easier if y'all hadn't shown up today," confesses a student as she begins her required classroom presentation.[2] She's certainly not alone in her feelings. Faced with making a speech, most of us feel great stress. The physiological responses that you experience are much like those triggered by a car accident, a mugging, or a narrow escape from a dangerous situation.[3] But giving oral presentations is a common requirement for businesspeople. You might, for example, need to describe your company's expansion plans to your banker or persuade management to support your proposed marketing strategy. You might have to make a sales pitch before customers or speak to a professional gathering.

For any presentation you can reduce your fears and lay the foundation for a professional performance by focusing on four areas: preparation, organization, visual aids, and delivery.[4]

Preparing an Effective Oral Presentation

Getting ready for an oral presentation is similar to the prefatory process for writing a report. That process begins with serious thinking about your purpose and your audience.

Preparing for an oral presentation means identifying the purpose and knowing the audience.

Knowing your purpose. Determining what you want to accomplish in a presentation is the most important part of your preparation. Do you want to persuade management to install networked computers? Do you want to inform customer service reps of three important ways to prevent miscommunication? Whether your goal is to persuade or to inform, you must have a clear idea of where you are going. At the end of your presentation, what do you want your listeners to remember or do?

Eric Evans, a loan officer at First Fidelity Trust, faced such questions as he planned a talk for a class in small business management. Eric's former business professor had asked him to return to campus and give the class advice about borrowing money from banks in order to start new businesses. Because Eric knew so much about this topic, he found it difficult to extract a specific purpose statement for his presentation. After much thought he narrowed his purpose to this: *To inform potential entrepreneurs about three important factors that loan officers consider before granting start-up loans to launch small businesses.* His entire presentation focused on ensuring that the class members understood and remembered three principal ideas.

Audience analysis issues include size, age, gender, experience, attitude, and expectations.

Knowing your audience. A second key element in preparation is analysis of your audience, anticipating its reactions and making appropriate adaptations. Jon Georges adjusted his message and presentation style (using common words and simple sentences, and supplying technical details) in anticipation of the needs of his Japanese audience.

Many factors influence a presentation. A large audience, for example, usually requires a more formal and less personalized approach. Other elements, such as age, gender, education, experience, and attitude toward the subject, will also affect your style and message content. Analyze these factors to determine your strategy, vocabulary, illustrations, and level of detail. Here are specific questions to consider:

- *How will this topic appeal to this audience?*
- *How can I relate this information to their needs?*
- *How can I earn respect so that they accept my message?*
- *Which of the following would be most effective in making my point?* Statistics? Graphic illustrations? Demonstrations? Case histories? Analogies? Cost figures?
- *What measures must I take to ensure that this audience remembers my main points?*

Organizing the Content

Once you have determined your purpose and analyzed the audience, you're ready to collect information and organize it logically. Good organization and conscious repetition are the two most powerful keys to audience comprehension and retention. In fact, many speech experts recommend the following admittedly repetitious, but effective, plan:

- **Step 1:** Tell them what you're going to say.
- **Step 2:** Say it.
- **Step 3:** Tell them what you've just said.

In other words, repeat your main points in the introduction, body, and conclusion of your presentation. Although it sounds deadly, this strategy works surprisingly well. Let's examine how to construct the three parts of a presentation and add appropriate verbal signposts to ensure that listeners understand and remember.

Introduction. The opening of your presentation should strive to accomplish three specific goals:

- Capture listeners' attention and get them involved.
- Identify yourself and establish your credibility.
- Preview your main points.

If you're able to appeal to listeners and involve them in your presentation right from the start, you're more likely to hold their attention until the finish. Consider some of the same techniques that you used to open sales letters: a question, a startling fact, a joke, a story, or a quotation. Some speakers achieve involvement by opening with a question or command that requires audience members to raise their hands or stand up. Additional techniques to gain and keep audience attention are presented in the accompanying Career Skills box.

To establish your credibility, you need to describe your position, knowledge, or experience—whatever qualifies you to speak. Try also to connect with your audience. Listeners are particularly drawn to speakers who reveal something of themselves and identify with them. A consultant addressing office workers might reminisce about how she started as a clerk-typist; a CEO might tell a funny story in which the joke is on himself.

After capturing attention and establishing yourself, you'll want to preview the main points of your topic, perhaps with a visual aid. You may wish to put off actually writing your introduction, however, until after you have organized the rest of the presentation and crystallized your principal ideas.

SPOTLIGHT ON COMMUNICATORS

"Know your audience" is advice frequently given by Les Brown, former Ohio legislator and now a motivational speaker for Fortune 500 companies. Before he addresses a company he reads trade magazines and questions owners and employees to learn what they expect from each other. This "holistic" approach to addressing a group of people enables him to speak their language and relate to their issues.

Attention-grabbing openers include questions, startling facts, jokes, anecdotes, and quotations.

NINE TECHNIQUES FOR GAINING AND KEEPING AUDIENCE ATTENTION

Experienced speakers know how to capture the attention of an audience and how to maintain that attention during a presentation. Here are eight proven techniques.

- **A promise.** Begin with a promise that keeps the audience expectant (for example, "By the end of this presentation I will show you how you can increase your sales by 50 percent").
- **Drama.** Open by telling an emotionally moving story or by describing a serious problem that involves the audience. Throughout your talk include other dramatic elements, such as a long pause after a key statement. Change your vocal tone or pitch. Professionals use high-intensity emotions like anger, joy, sadness, and excitement.
- **Eye contact.** As you begin, command attention by surveying the entire audience to take in all listeners. Take two to five seconds to make eye contact with as many people as possible.
- **Movement.** Leave the lectern area whenever possible. Walk around the conference table or between the aisles of your audience. Try to move toward your audience, especially at the beginning and end of your talk.
- **Questions.** Keep listeners active and involved with rhetorical questions. Ask for a show of hands to get each listener thinking. The response will also give you a quick gauge of audience attention.
- **Demonstrations.** Include a member of the audience in a demonstration (for example, "I'm going to show you exactly how to implement our four-step customer courtesy process, but I need a volunteer from the audience to help me").
- **Samples/gimmicks.** If you're promoting a product, consider using items to toss out to the audience or to award as prizes to volunteer participants. You can also pass around product samples or promotional literature. Be careful, though, to maintain control.
- **Visuals.** Give your audience something to look at besides yourself. Use a variety of visual aids in a single session. Also consider writing the concerns expressed by your listeners on a flipchart or on the board as you go along.
- **Self-interest.** Review your entire presentation to ensure that it meets the critical "What's-in-it-for-me?" audience test. Remember that people are most interested in things that benefit them.

Career Track Application

Watch a lecture series speaker on campus, a department store sales presentation, a TV "infomercial," or some other speaker. Note and analyze specific techniques used to engage and maintain the listener's attention. Which techniques would be most effective in a classroom presentation? Before your boss or work group?

Take a look at Eric Evans' introduction, shown in Figure 15.1, to see how he integrated all the elements necessary for a good opening.

The best oral presentations focus on a few key ideas.

Body. The biggest problem with most oral presentations is a failure to focus on a few principal ideas. Thus, the body of your short presentation (20 or fewer minutes) should include a limited number of main points, say, two to four. Develop each main point with adequate, but not excessive, explanation and details. Too many details can obscure the main message, so keep your presentation simple and logical. Remember, listeners have no pages to leaf back through should they become confused.

When Eric Evans began planning his presentation, he realized immediately that he could talk for hours on his topic. He also knew that listeners are not good at separating major and minor points. Thus, instead of submerging his listeners in a sea of information, he sorted out a few principal ideas. In the mortgage business, loan officers generally ask the following three questions of each applicant for a

FIGURE 15.1 ● Oral Presentation Outline

The Three Phases of the Development Process

1

Analyze
The purpose of this report is to inform listeners of three critical elements in securing business loans.

Anticipate
The audience members are aspiring businesspeople who are probably unfamiliar with loan operations.

Adapt
Because the audience will be receptive but uninformed, explain terms and provide examples. Repeat the main ideas to ensure comprehension.

2

Research
Analyze previous loan applications; interview other loan officers. Gather critical data.

Organize
Group the data into three major categories. Support with statistics, details, and examples. Plan visual aids.

Compose
Prepare a sentence outline. Consider composing a rough draft at a computer.

3

Revise
Develop transitions between topics. Prepare note cards.

Practice
Rehearse the entire talk and time it. Practice enunciating words and projecting your voice. Develop natural hand motions.

Evaluate
Tape record or videotape a practice session to evaluate your movements, voice tone, enunciation, and timing.

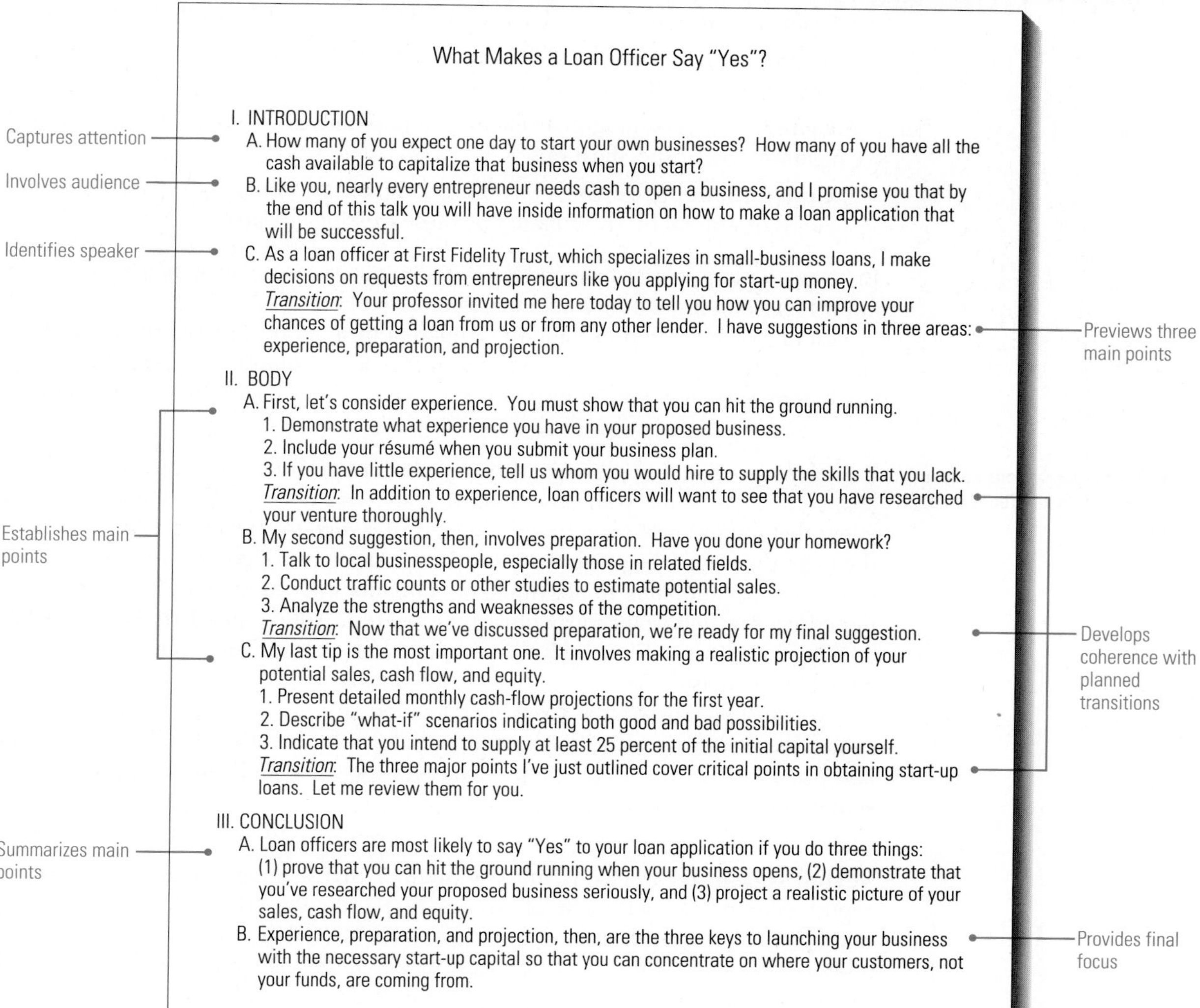

What Makes a Loan Officer Say "Yes"?

I. INTRODUCTION
  A. How many of you expect one day to start your own businesses? How many of you have all the cash available to capitalize that business when you start?
  B. Like you, nearly every entrepreneur needs cash to open a business, and I promise you that by the end of this talk you will have inside information on how to make a loan application that will be successful.
  C. As a loan officer at First Fidelity Trust, which specializes in small-business loans, I make decisions on requests from entrepreneurs like you applying for start-up money.
  Transition: Your professor invited me here today to tell you how you can improve your chances of getting a loan from us or from any other lender. I have suggestions in three areas: experience, preparation, and projection.

II. BODY
  A. First, let's consider experience. You must show that you can hit the ground running.
    1. Demonstrate what experience you have in your proposed business.
    2. Include your résumé when you submit your business plan.
    3. If you have little experience, tell us whom you would hire to supply the skills that you lack.
  Transition: In addition to experience, loan officers will want to see that you have researched your venture thoroughly.
  B. My second suggestion, then, involves preparation. Have you done your homework?
    1. Talk to local businesspeople, especially those in related fields.
    2. Conduct traffic counts or other studies to estimate potential sales.
    3. Analyze the strengths and weaknesses of the competition.
  Transition: Now that we've discussed preparation, we're ready for my final suggestion.
  C. My last tip is the most important one. It involves making a realistic projection of your potential sales, cash flow, and equity.
    1. Present detailed monthly cash-flow projections for the first year.
    2. Describe "what-if" scenarios indicating both good and bad possibilities.
    3. Indicate that you intend to supply at least 25 percent of the initial capital yourself.
  Transition: The three major points I've just outlined cover critical points in obtaining start-up loans. Let me review them for you.

III. CONCLUSION
  A. Loan officers are most likely to say "Yes" to your loan application if you do three things: (1) prove that you can hit the ground running when your business opens, (2) demonstrate that you've researched your proposed business seriously, and (3) project a realistic picture of your sales, cash flow, and equity.
  B. Experience, preparation, and projection, then, are the three keys to launching your business with the necessary start-up capital so that you can concentrate on where your customers, not your funds, are coming from.

small business loan: (1) Are you ready to "hit the ground running" in starting your business? (2) Have you done your homework? and (3) Have you made realistic projections of potential sales, cash flow, and equity investment? These questions would become his main points, but Eric wanted to streamline them further so that his audience would be sure to remember them. He capsulized the questions in three words: *experience, preparation,* and *projection.* As you can see in Figure 15.1, Eric prepared a sentence outline showing these three main ideas. Each is supported by examples and explanations.

Main ideas can be organized according to time, component, importance, criteria, or conventional groupings.

How to organize and sequence main ideas may not be immediately obvious when you begin working on a presentation. Let's review the five organizational methods employed for written reports in Chapter 12, because those methods are equally appropriate for oral presentations. You could structure your ideas by the following elements:

- **Time** (for example, a presentation describing the history of a problem, organized from the first sign of trouble to the present)
- **Component** (a report on sales organized by divisions or products)
- **Importance** (a report describing operating problems arranged from the most important to the least)
- **Criteria** (a presentation evaluating equipment by comparing each model against a set of specifications)
- **Conventional groupings** (a report comparing asset size, fees charged, and yields of mutual funds arranged by these existing categories)

In his presentation Eric arranged the main points by importance, placing the most important point last where it had maximum effect.

In organizing any presentation, prepare a little more material than you think you will actually need. Savvy speakers always have something useful in reserve (such as an extra handout, transparency, or idea)—just in case they finish early.

Effective conclusions summarize main points and focus on a goal.

Conclusion. You should prepare the conclusion carefully because this is your last chance to drive home your main points. Don't end limply with comments like "I guess that's about all I have to say." Skilled speakers use the conclusion to review the main themes of the presentation and focus on a goal. They concentrate on what they want the audience to do, think, or remember. Even though they were mentioned earlier, important ideas must be repeated. Notice how Eric Evans, in the conclusion shown in Figure 15.1, summarized his three main points and provided a final focus to listeners.

When they finish, most speakers encourage questions. If silence ensues, you can prime the pump with "One question that I'm frequently asked is . . ." You can also remark that you will be happy to answer questions individually after the presentation is completed.

Verbal signposts. Speakers must remember that listeners, unlike readers of a report, cannot control the rate of presentation or flip back through pages to review main points. As a result, listeners get lost easily. Knowledgeable speakers help the audience recognize the organization and main points in an oral message with verbal signposts. They keep listeners on track by including helpful previews, summaries, and transitions, such as these:

To Preview

The next segment of my talk presents three reasons for . . .

Let's now consider the causes of . . .

To Summarize

Let me review with you the major problems I've just discussed . . .

You see, then, that the most significant factors are . . .

To Switch Directions

Thus far we've talked solely about . . . ; now let's move to . . .

I've argued that . . . and . . . , but an alternate view holds that . . .

You can further improve any oral presentation by including appropriate transitional expressions such as *first, second, next, then, therefore, moreover, on the other hand, on the contrary,* and *in conclusion.* These expressions lend emphasis and tell listeners where you are headed. Notice in Eric Evans' outline, in Figure 15.1, the specific transitional elements designed to help listeners recognize each new principal point.

Knowledgeable speakers provide verbal signposts to spotlight organization and key ideas.

Planning Visual Aids and Handouts

Before you make a business presentation, consider this wise Chinese proverb: "Tell me, I forget. Show me, I remember. Involve me, I understand." Because your goals as a speaker are to make listeners understand, remember, and act on your ideas, include visual aids to get them interested and involved. Some authorities suggest that we acquire 85 percent of all our knowledge visually. Therefore, an oral presentation that incorporates visual aids is far more likely to be understood and retained than one lacking visual enhancement.

Good visual aids have many purposes. They emphasize and clarify main points, thus improving comprehension and retention. They increase audience interest, and they make the presenter appear more professional, better prepared, and more persuasive. Furthermore, research shows that the use of visual aids actually shortens meetings.[5] Visual aids are particularly helpful for inexperienced speakers because the audience concentrates on the aid rather than on the speaker. Good visuals also serve to jog the memory of a speaker, thus improving self-confidence, poise, and delivery.

Visual aids clarify points, improve comprehension, and aid retention.

Fortunately for today's speakers, many forms of visual media are available to enhance a presentation. Figure 15.2 describes a number of visual aids and compares their cost, degree of formality, and other considerations. Three of the most popular visuals are overhead transparencies, slides, and handouts.

Overhead transparencies. Student and professional speakers alike rely heavily on the overhead projector for many reasons. Most meeting areas are equipped with projectors and screens. Moreover, acetate transparencies for the overhead are cheap, easily prepared on a computer or copier, and simple to use. And, because rooms need not be darkened, a speaker using transparencies can maintain eye contact with the audience. A word of caution, though: stand to the side of the projector so that you don't obstruct the audience's view.

FIGURE 15.2 ● **Presentation Enhancers**

Medium	Cost	Audience Size	Formality Level	Advantages and Disadvantages
Overhead projector	Low	2–200	Formal or informal	Transparencies are easy and inexpensive to produce. Speaker keeps contact with audience.
Flipchart	Low	2–200	Informal	Easels and charts are readily available and portable. Speaker can prepare the display in advance or on the spot.
Write-and-wipe board	Medium	2–200	Informal	Porcelain-on-steel surface replaces messy chalkboard. Speaker can wipe clean with cloth.
Slide projector	Medium	2–500	Formal	Slides provide excellent graphic images. Darkened room may put audience to sleep. Slides demand expertise, time, and equipment to produce.
Video monitor	High	2–100	Formal or informal	A VCR display features motion and sound. Videos require skill, time, and equipment to prepare.
Computer graphics	High	2–200	Formal or informal	Computers generate slides, transparencies, or run-time visuals. Graphics require expertise and equipment to produce.
Handouts	Varies	Unlimited	Formal or informal	Audience appreciates take-home items like outlines, tables, charts, reports, brochures, or summaries. Handouts can divert attention from speaker.

Slides. Slides deliver excellent resolution, create an impression of professionalism, and can be seen by large groups. Yet, their cost, inflexibility, and fairly difficult preparation offset their advantages. Moreover, because they must be projected in a darkened room, a speaker loses eye contact with the audience and runs the risk of putting viewers to sleep. Used carefully, though, slides are very effective. And because today's computer-generated slides are cheaper and easier to produce, they may become increasingly accessible and popular for future business presentations.

Handouts. You can enhance and complement your presentations by distributing pictures, outlines, brochures, articles, charts, summaries, or other supplements. Timing their distribution, though, is tricky. If given out during a presentation, your handouts tend to distract the audience, causing you to lose control. Thus, it's probably best to discuss most handouts during the presentation but delay distributing them until after you finish.

Whenever possible, then, you'll want to incorporate visual aids in a presentation; but keep a few points in mind:

- **Avoid overkill.** Use visual aids only for major points or for information that requires clarification. Excessive or unnecessary visuals dull their effectiveness.
- **Keep all visuals simple.** Spotlight main points. Don't, for example, put the outline for your entire presentation on a transparency.

- **Ensure visibility.** Be sure everyone in your audience can see the visual aids.
- **Enhance comprehension.** Give the audience a moment to study a visual before explaining it. Then, paraphrase it instead of reading it word for word.
- **Practice using them.** Rehearse your talk, perfecting your handling of the visuals. Be sure you talk to the audience and not to the visual.

SPOTLIGHT ON COMMUNICATORS

Novice speakers often speed up their delivery, perhaps out of nervousness or eagerness to sit down. Justice Sandra Day O'Connor, shortly after becoming the first woman on the Supreme Court, revealed a trick she uses when she has important words to speak: "I taught myself early on to speak very slowly—enunciating every word—when I wanted someone's undivided attention."

Polishing Your Delivery

Once you've organized your presentation and prepared visuals, you're ready to practice delivering it. Here are suggestions for selecting a delivery method, along with specific techniques to use before, during, and after your presentation.

Delivery method. Inexperienced speakers often feel that they must memorize an entire presentation to be effective. Unless you're an experienced performer, however, you will sound wooden and unnatural. Moreover, forgetting your place can be disastrous! Therefore, memorizing an entire oral presentation is not recommended. However, memorizing significant parts—the introduction, the conclusion, and perhaps a meaningful quotation—can be dramatic and impressive.

If memorizing won't work, is reading your presentation the best plan? Definitely not! Reading to an audience is boring and ineffective. Because reading suggests that you don't know your topic very well, the audience loses confidence in your expertise. Reading also prevents you from maintaining eye contact. You can't see audience reactions; consequently, you can't benefit from feedback.

Neither the memorizing nor the reading method creates very convincing presentations. The best plan, by far, is a "notes" method. Plan your presentation carefully and talk from note cards or an outline containing key sentences and major ideas. By preparing and then practicing with your notes, you can talk to your audience in a conversational manner. Your notes should be neither entire paragraphs nor single words. Instead, they should contain a complete sentence or two to introduce each major idea. Below the topic sentence(s), outline subpoints and illustrations, as shown in the sample note card in Figure 15.3. Note cards will keep you on track and prompt your memory, but only if you have rehearsed the presentation thoroughly.

Stage fright is both natural and controllable.

Delivery techniques. Nearly everyone experiences some degree of stage fright when speaking before a group. "If you hear someone say he or she isn't nervous before a speech, you're talking either to a liar or a very boring speaker," says corporate speech consultant Dianna Booher.[6] Being afraid is quite natural and results from actual physiological changes occurring in your body. Faced with a frightening situation, your body responds with the fight-or-flight syndrome, discussed more fully in the accompanying Career Skills box. You can learn to control and reduce stage fright, as well as to incorporate techniques for effective speaking, by using the following strategies and techniques before, during, and after your presentation.

Before Your Presentation

Thorough preparation, extensive rehearsal, and stress-reduction techniques can lessen stage fright.

- **Prepare thoroughly.** One of the most effective strategies for reducing stage fright is knowing your subject thoroughly. Research your topic diligently and prepare a careful sentence outline. Those who try to "wing it" usually suffer the worst butterflies—and make the worst presentations.

FIGURE 15.3 ● Note Card for Oral Presentation

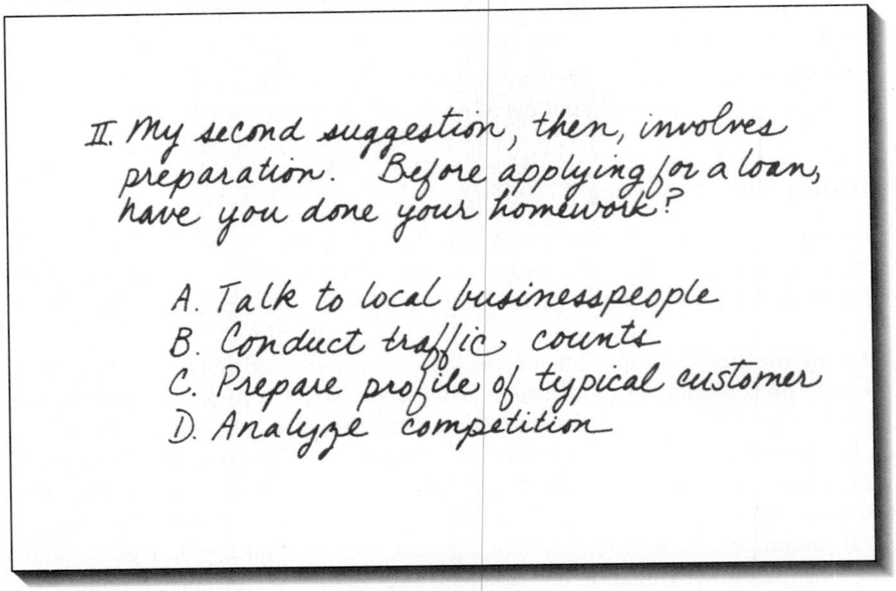

II. My second suggestion, then, involves preparation. Before applying for a loan, have you done your homework?

A. Talk to local businesspeople
B. Conduct traffic counts
C. Prepare profile of typical customer
D. Analyze competition

- **Rehearse repeatedly.** When you rehearse, practice your entire presentation, not just the first half. Place your outline sentences on separate cards. You may also wish to include transitional sentences to help you move to the next topic. Use these cards as you practice, and include your visual aids in your rehearsal. Record your rehearsal on audio- or videotape so that you can evaluate your effectiveness.
- **Time yourself.** Most audiences tend to get restless during longer talks. Thus, try to complete your presentation in no more than 20 minutes. Set a timer during your rehearsal to measure your speaking time.
- **Request a lectern.** Every beginning speaker needs the security of a high desk or lectern from which to deliver a presentation. It serves as a note holder and a convenient place to rest wandering hands and arms.
- **Check the room.** Before you talk, make sure that a lectern has been provided. If you are using sound equipment or a projector, be certain they are operational. Check electrical outlets and the position of the viewing screen. Ensure that the seating arrangement is appropriate to your needs.
- **Practice stress reduction.** If you feel tension and fear while you are waiting your turn to speak, use stress reduction techniques, such as deep breathing. Additional techniques to help you conquer stage fright are presented in the accompanying Career Skills box.

During Your Presentation

- **Begin with a pause.** When you first approach the audience, take a moment to adjust your notes and make yourself comfortable. Establish your control of the situation.

STAGE FRIGHT AND THE FIGHT-OR-FLIGHT RESPONSE

Ever get nervous before giving a speech? Everyone does! And it's not all in your head, either. When you face something threatening or challenging, your body reacts in what psychologists call the *fight-or-flight response.* This response provides your body with increased energy to deal with threatening situations. It also creates those sensations—dry mouth, sweaty hands, increased heartbeat, and stomach butterflies—that we associate with stage fright. The fight-or-flight response arouses your body for action—in this case, giving a speech.

Since everyone feels some form of apprehension before speaking, it's impossible to eliminate the physiological symptoms altogether. But you can help reduce their effects with the following techniques:

- Use deep breathing to ease your fight-or-flight symptoms. Inhale to a count of ten, hold this breath to a count of ten, and exhale to a count of ten. Concentrate on your counting and your breathing; both activities reduce your stress.
- Don't view your sweaty palms and dry mouth as evidence of fear. Interpret them as symptoms of exuberance, excitement, and enthusiasm to share your ideas.
- Feel confident about your topic. Select a topic that you know well and that is relevant to your audience.
- Use positive self-talk. Remind yourself that you know your topic and are prepared. Tell yourself that the audience is on your side—because they are!
- Shift the spotlight to your visuals. At least some of the time the audience will be focusing on your transparencies, handouts, or whatever you have prepared—and not on you.
- Ignore any stumbles. Don't apologize or confess your nervousness. If you keep going, the audience will forget any mistakes quickly.

When you're finished, you'll be surprised at how good you feel. You can take pride in what you've accomplished, and your audience will reward you with applause and congratulations. And, of course, your body will call off the fight-or-flight response and return to normal!

Career Track Application

Interview someone in your field or in another business setting who must make oral presentations. How did he or she develop speaking skills? What advice can this person suggest to reduce stage fright? When you next make a class presentation, try some or all of the techniques described above and note which are most effective for you.

- **Present your first sentence from memory.** By memorizing your opening, you can immediately establish rapport with the audience through eye contact. You'll also sound confident and knowledgeable.
- **Maintain eye contact.** If the size of the audience overwhelms you, pick out two individuals on the right and two on the left. Talk directly to these people.
- **Control your voice and vocabulary.** This means speaking in moderated tones but loudly enough to be heard. Eliminate verbal static, such as *ah, er, you know,* and *um.* Silence is preferable to meaningless fillers when you are thinking of your next idea.
- **Put the brakes on.** Many novice speakers talk too rapidly, displaying their nervousness and making it very difficult for audience members to understand their ideas. Slow down and listen to what you are saying.
- **Move naturally.** You can use the lectern to hold your notes so that you are free to move about casually and naturally. Avoid fidgeting with your notes, your clothing, or items in your pockets. Learn to use your body to express a point.

Eye contact, a moderate tone of voice, and natural movements enhance a presentation.

SPOTLIGHT ON COMMUNICATORS

To give rhythm and punch to your presentations, says corporate speech consultant Dianna Booher, make ample use of these three techniques: *triads* ("we are one nation—black, white, brown; we are Protestants, Jews, and Catholics"; *alliteration* ("we wish you health, happiness, and hope"); and *rhyme* ("American business must automate, emigrate, or evaporate").

- **Use visual aids effectively.** You should discuss and interpret each visual aid for the audience. Move aside as you describe it so that it can be seen fully. Use a pointer if necessary.
- **Avoid digressions.** Stick to your outline and notes. Don't suddenly include clever little anecdotes or digressions that occur to you on the spot. If it's not part of your rehearsed material, leave it out so that you can finish on time. Remember, too, that your audience may not be as enthralled with your topic as you are.
- **Summarize your main points.** Conclude your presentation by reiterating your main points or by emphasizing what you want the audience to think or do. Once you have announced your conclusion, proceed to it directly. Don't irritate the audience by talking for five or ten more minutes.

After Your Presentation

- **Distribute handouts.** If you prepared handouts with data the audience will need, pass them out when you finish.
- **Encourage questions.** If the situation permits a question-and-answer period, announce it at the beginning of your presentation. Then, when you finish, ask for questions. Set a time limit for questions and answers.
- **Repeat questions.** Although the speaker may hear the question, audience members often do not. Begin each answer with a repetition of the question. This also gives you thinking time. Then, direct your answer to the entire audience.
- **Reinforce your main points.** You can use your answers to restate your primary ideas ("I'm glad you brought that up because it gives me a chance to elaborate on . . ."). In answering questions, avoid becoming defensive or debating the questioner.
- **Keep control.** Don't allow one individual to take over. Keep the entire audience involved.
- **End with a summary and appreciation.** To signal the end of the session before you take the last question, say something like "We have time for just one more question." As you answer the last question, try to work it into a summary of your main points. Then, express appreciation to the audience for the opportunity to talk with them.

The time to answer questions, distribute handouts, and reiterate main points is after a presentation.

Preparing and organizing an oral presentation, as summarized in the following checklist, requires attention to content and strategy. Along with the care you devote to developing your talk, consider also its ethics, so that you won't be guilty of committing the "worst deadly sin" spotlighted in the accompanying Ethics box.

Adapting to International and Cross-Cultural Audiences

Every good speaker adapts to the audience, and cross-cultural presentations call for special adjustments and sensitivity. When working with an interpreter or speaking before individuals whose English is limited, you'll need to be very careful about your language. As Jon Georges did in Tokyo, you'll want to speak slowly, use simple English, avoid jargon and clichés, and use short sentences.

Beyond these basic language adaptations, however, more fundamental sensitivity is often necessary. In organizing a presentation for a cross-cultural audience, think twice about delivering your main idea up front. Many people (notably those

THE "WORST DEADLY SIN" IN A PRESENTATION

Audiences appreciate speakers with polished delivery techniques, but they are usually relatively forgiving when mistakes occur. One thing they don't suffer gladly, though, is unethical behavior. Executives in a comprehensive research survey agreed that the "worst deadly sin" a speaker can commit in a presentation is demonstrating a lack of integrity.[7]

What kinds of unethical behavior do audiences reject? They distrust speakers who misrepresent, exaggerate, and lie. They also dislike cover-ups and evasiveness. Everyone expects a speaker who is trying to "sell" a product or idea to emphasize its strong points. Promotion, however, becomes unethical when the speaker intentionally seeks to obscure facts or slant issues to deceive the audience. The following situations clearly signal trouble for speakers because of the unethical actions involved:

- A sales rep, instead of promoting his company's products, suggests that his competitor's business is mismanaged, is losing customers, or offers seriously flawed products.
- A manager distorts a new employee insurance plan, underemphasizing its deficiencies and overemphasizing its strengths.
- An accountant for a charity suggests that management should authorize loose bookkeeping practices in order to mislead the public regarding the use of donors' money.
- A sales rep fabricates an answer to a tough question instead of admitting ignorance.
- A financial planner tries to prove her point by highlighting an irrelevant statistic.
- A real estate broker compares dissimilar properties and locations to inflate the value of some property.
- A speaker deliberately uses excessively technical language to make an idea or proposal seem more important and complex than it is.
- A project manager claims personal credit for a proposal developed largely by consultants.

How can you make certain that your own presentations are ethical? The best strategy, of course, is to present your information honestly, fairly, and without deception. Be aware of your own biases and prejudices so that you don't unconsciously distort data. Remember that the goals of an ethical communicator, discussed in Chapter 3, include telling the truth, labeling opinions so that they can be distinguished from facts, being objective, writing clearly, and giving credit when you use others' ideas or words.

Career Track Application

Watch TV or read news stories about congressional debates. Note how proponents on each side of an issue (usually Democrats and Republicans) present their views in a positive light and cast their opponents' views in a negative light. Make notes of any unethical presentation techniques.

in Japanese, Latin American, and Arabic cultures) consider such directness to be brash and inappropriate. Remember that others may not share our cultural emphasis on straightforwardness.

Addressing cross-cultural audiences requires a speaker to consider audience expectations and cultural conventions.

Also consider breaking your presentation into short, discrete segments. In Japan, Jon divided his talk into three distinct topics: theme park attractions, merchandise shops, and food services. He developed each topic separately, encouraging discussion periods after each. Such organization enables participants to ask questions and digest what has been presented. This technique is especially effective in cultures where people communicate in "loops." In the Middle East, for example, Arab speakers "mix circuitous, irrelevant (by American standards) conversations with short dashes of information that go directly to the point." Presenters who are patient, tolerant, and "mature" (in the eyes of the audience) will make the sale or win the contract.[8]

Remember, too, that some cultures prefer greater formality than Americans exercise. Writing on a flipchart or transparency seems natural and spontaneous in this country. Abroad, though, such informal techniques may suggest that the speaker does not value the audience enough to prepare proper visual aids in advance.[9]

This caution aside, you'll still want to use visual aids to communicate your message. These visuals should be written in both languages, so that you and your audience understand them. Never use numbers without writing them out for all to see. If possible, say numbers in both languages. Distribute translated handouts, summarizing your important information, when you finish. Finally, be careful of your body language. Looking people in the eye suggests intimacy and self-confidence in this country, but in other cultures such eye contact may be considered disrespectful.

Checklist for Preparing and Organizing Oral Presentations

Getting Ready to Speak

✔ **Identify your purpose.** Decide what you want your audience to believe, remember, or do when you finish. Aim all parts of your talk toward this purpose.

✔ **Analyze the audience.** Consider how to adapt your message (its organization, appeals, and examples) to your audience's knowledge and needs.

Organizing the Introduction

✔ **Get the audience involved.** Capture the audience's attention by opening with a promise, story, startling fact, question, quote, relevant problem, or self-effacing joke.

✔ **Establish yourself.** Demonstrate your credibility by identifying your position, expertise, knowledge, or qualifications.

✔ **Preview your main points.** Introduce your topic and summarize its principal parts.

Organizing the Body

✔ **Develop two to four main points.** Streamline your topic so that you can concentrate on its major issues.

✔ **Arrange the points logically.** Sequence your points chronologically, from most important to least important, by comparison and contrast, or by some other strategy.

✔ **Prepare transitions.** Between each major point write "bridge" statements that connect the previous item to the next one. Use transitional expressions as verbal signposts (*first, second, then, however, consequently, on the contrary,* and so forth).

✔ **Have extra material ready.** Be prepared with more information and visuals in case you have additional time to fill.

Organizing the Conclusion

✔ **Review your main points.** Emphasize your main ideas in your closing so that your audience will remember them.

- ✔ **Provide a final focus.** Tell how your listeners can use this information, why you have spoken, or what you want them to do.

Designing Visual Aids

- ✔ **Select your medium carefully.** Consider the size of your audience, degree of formality desired, cost and ease of preparation, and potential effectiveness.
- ✔ **Highlight main ideas.** Use visual aids to illustrate major concepts only. Keep them brief and simple.
- ✔ **Use aids skillfully.** Talk to the audience, not to the visuals. Paraphrase their contents. Remove each visual as soon as you finish with it.

Meetings and Conferences

Whether you like attending them or not, meetings and conferences are becoming increasingly important in business today. Many organizations are progressing toward team-oriented management; they're reorganizing the rank and file along team lines. Much of this shift toward employee empowerment has resulted from the "total quality" movement. Facing stiff global competition, companies realized that they had to provide both quality products and service. But quality goals in any organization can't be achieved without a key ingredient: involved employees with a commitment toward the organization's goals. Three central strategies have emerged from the total quality movement: (1) worker teams (with control of their projects), (2) benchmarking (studying and emulating the best ideas of top companies), and (3) employee empowerment (authority to resolve customer problems). Such trends toward greater employee involvement and team decisions suggest that you'll probably be attending more meetings and conferences than ever before.

The trend toward worker teams, benchmarking, and employee empowerment means employees will spend more time in meetings.

Meetings differ from conferences in that they are smaller and less formal. We'll concentrate on meetings in this discussion, although most of the advice holds for conferences as well.

Meetings consist of three or more individuals who gather to pool information, clarify policy, seek consensus, and solve problems. It's important to note that meetings also differ from speeches, where one person talks *at* an audience. In meetings people are expected to *exchange* ideas; emphasis should be on interaction.

From an organization's view meetings are occasions for a productive exchange of information. From your own personal view, though, meetings should represent opportunities. At meetings judgments are formed and careers are made. Therefore, instead of treating them as thieves of your valuable time, see them as golden opportunities to demonstrate your leadership and communication skills. Jon Georges, at Walt Disney Imagineering, wisely recognized presentations and meetings as chances to impress management. So that you, too, can make the most of these opportunities, here are techniques for planning, conducting, and participating in successful meetings.

Planning Meetings

Successful meetings begin with planning. This means deciding on a goal or an objective, and then determining whether a meeting is the best way to achieve that goal. If, for example, the goal is to announce a new policy regarding flexible work schedules, a meeting may be unnecessary. Perhaps a memo or electronic mail message would be better. Or if the goal is to inform management of department or

Successful meetings result from a planned agenda and a tight focus.

Videoconferences allow groups in distant locations to see each other and exchange ideas without the fatigue and disruption of travel. As equipment costs decline, companies are increasingly using videoconferences to replace face-to-face meetings.

Syntec Corporation, a large multinational pharmaceutical company, figures that it saves $1,700 in travel expenses each time an employee attends a video meeting instead of making a business trip. The real savings, though, are in travel time and fatigue. "We are a research-oriented company operating in every continent except Africa with a very high percentage of professionals," says the CEO. "The time of our people is worth a lot more than saving $1,700 a day in travel costs. Our primary goal is to avoid travel."[13]

Videoconferencing has other benefits. Because the transmission format creates a slight delay, conferees can't interrupt one another. As a result, says one expert, "It's back to Robert's Rules of Order. People actually have to listen to each other now."[14]

Telephones and Voice Mail

Telephones and voice mail should promote goodwill and increase productivity.

The telephone is the most universal—and, some would say, the most important—piece of equipment in offices today.[15] The telephone has spawned an entire new industry—voice mail systems, which are rapidly replacing switchboards and receptionists. These computerized message systems save labor costs and provide sophisticated capabilities and flexibility unavailable in the past. Regardless of their advanced technology, though, telephones and voice mail are valuable business tools *only* when they generate goodwill and increase productivity. Poor communication techniques can easily offset any benefits arising from improved equipment. What good is an extensive voice mail system if callers hang up in frustration after waiting through a long list of menu options without learning what they need? Here are suggestions aimed at helping business communicators make the best use of telephone and voice mail equipment.

Making Productive Telephone Calls

Before making a telephone call, decide whether the intended call is really necessary. Could you find the information yourself? If you wait a while, would the problem resolve itself? Perhaps your message could be delivered more efficiently by some other means. One West Coast company found that telephone interruptions consumed about 18 percent of staff members' workdays. Another study found that two thirds of all calls were less important than the work they interrupted.[16] Alternatives to telephone calls include electronic mail (E-mail) messages, memos, or calls to voice mail systems. If a telephone call must be made, consider using the following suggestions to make it fully productive.

Making productive telephone calls means planning an agenda, identifying the purpose, being courteous and cheerful, and avoiding rambling.

- **Plan a mini agenda.** Have you ever been embarrassed when you had to make a second telephone call because you forgot an important item the first time? Before placing a call, jot down notes regarding all the topics you need to discuss. Following an agenda guarantees not only a complete call but also a quick one. You'll be less likely to wander from the business at hand while rummaging through your mind trying to remember everything.
- **Use a three-point introduction.** When placing a call, immediately give (1) your name, (2) your affiliation, and (3) a brief explanation of your reason for calling. For example: "May I speak to Larry Lopez? This is Hillary Dahl of Sebastian Enterprises, and I'm seeking information about a software program called 'Power Presentations.' " This kind of introduction enables the receiving individual to respond immediately without asking further questions.
- **Be cheerful and accurate.** Let your voice show the same kind of animation that you radiate when you greet people in person. In your mind try to envision the individual answering the telephone. A smile can certainly affect the tone of your voice, so smile at that person. Moreover, be accurate about what you say. "Hang on a second; I'll be right back" rarely is true. Better to say, "It may take me two or three minutes to get that information. Would you prefer to hold or have me call you back?"
- **Bring it to a close.** The responsibility for ending a call lies with the caller. This is sometimes difficult to do if the other person rambles on. You may need to use suggestive closing language, such as "I've certainly enjoyed talking with you," "I've learned what I needed to know, and now I can proceed with my work," "Thanks for your help," or "I must go now, but may I call you again in the future if I need . . . ?"
- **Avoid telephone tag.** If you call someone who's not in, ask when it would be best for you to call again. State that you will call at a specific time—and do it. If you ask a person to call you, give a time when you can be reached—and then be sure you are in at that time.
- **Leave complete voice mail messages.** Remember that there's no rush when you leave a voice mail message. Always enunciate clearly. And be sure to provide a complete message, including your name, telephone number, and the time and date of your call. Explain your purpose so that the receiver can be ready with the required information when returning your call.

Receiving Productive Telephone Calls

Receiving productive telephone calls means identifying oneself, being responsive and helpful, and taking accurate messages.

With a little forethought you can make your telephone a productive, efficient work tool. Developing good telephone manners also reflects well on you and on your organization.

- **Identify yourself immediately.** In answering your telephone or someone else's, provide your name, title or affiliation, and, possibly, a greeting. For example, "Larry Lopez, Proteus Software. How may I help you?" Force yourself to speak clearly and slowly. Remember that the caller may be unfamiliar with what you are saying and fail to recognize slurred syllables.
- **Be responsive and helpful.** If you are in a support role, be sympathetic to callers' needs. Instead of "I don't know," try "That's a good question; let me investigate." Instead of "We can't do that," try "That's a tough one; let's see what we can do." Avoid "No" at the beginning of a sentence. It sounds especially abrasive and displeasing because it suggests total rejection.
- **Be cautious when answering calls for others.** Be courteous and helpful, but don't give out confidential information. Better to say, "She's away from her desk" or "He's out of the office" than to report a colleague's exact whereabouts.
- **Take messages carefully.** Few things are as frustrating as receiving a potentially important phone message that is illegible. Repeat the spelling of names and verify telephone numbers. Write messages legibly and record their time and date. Promise to give the messages to intended recipients, but don't guarantee return calls.
- **Explain what you're doing when transferring calls.** Give a reason for transferring, and identify the extension to which you are directing the call in case the caller is disconnected.

Making the Best Use of Voice Mail

Voice mail eliminates telephone tag, inaccurate message-taking, and time-zone barriers; it also allows communicators to focus on essentials.

Voice mail links a telephone system to a computer that digitizes and stores incoming messages. Some systems also provide functions like automated attendant menus, allowing callers to reach any associated extension by pushing specific buttons on a touch-tone telephone. Interactive systems allow callers to receive verbal information from a computer database. For example, a ski resort in Colorado uses voice mail to answer routine questions that once were routed through an operator: "Welcome to Snow Paradise. For information on accommodations, touch 1; for snow conditions, touch 2; for ski equipment rental, touch 3," and so forth.

Voice mail serves many functions, but the most important is message storage. Because half of all business calls require no discussion or feedback (according to AT&T estimates), the messaging capabilities of voice mail can mean huge savings for businesses. Incoming information is delivered without interrupting potential receivers and without all the niceties that most two-way conversations require. Stripped of superfluous chit-chat, voice mail messages allow communicators to focus on essentials. Voice mail also eliminates telephone tag, inaccurate message-taking, and time-zone barriers. Critics complain, nevertheless, that automated systems seem cold and impersonal and are sometimes confusing and irritating.

In any event, here are some ways that you can make voice mail work more effectively for you.

- **Announce your voice mail.** If you rely principally on a voice mail message system, identify it on your business stationery and cards. Then, when people call, they will be ready to leave a message.
- **Prepare a warm and informative greeting.** Make your mechanical greeting sound warm and inviting, both in tone and content. Identify yourself and your organization so that callers know they have reached the right number. Thank the caller and briefly explain that you are unavailable. Invite the caller to leave a message or, if appropriate, call back. Here's a typical voice mail greeting: "Hi! This is Larry Lopez of Proteus Software, and I appreciate your call. You've reached my voice mailbox because I'm either working with customers or talking on another line at the moment. Please leave your name, number, and reason for calling so that I can be prepared when I return your call." Give callers an idea of when you will be available, such as "I'll be back at 2:30" or "I'll be out of my office until Wednesday, May 20." If you screen your calls as a time-management technique, try this message: "I'm not near my phone right now, but I should be able to return calls after 3:30."
- **Test your message.** Call your number and assess your message. Does it sound inviting? Sincere? Understandable? Are you pleased with your tone? If not, says one consultant, have someone else, perhaps a professional, record a message for you.

Summary of Learning Goals

1. **Discuss two important steps in preparing an effective oral presentation.** First, identify what your purpose is and what you want the audience to believe or do so that you can aim the entire presentation toward your goal. Second, know your audience so that you can adjust your message and style to its knowledge and needs.
2. **Explain the three parts of an effective oral presentation.** The introduction of a good presentation should capture the listener's attention, identify the speaker, establish credibility, and preview the main points. The body should discuss two to four main points, with appropriate explanations, details, and verbal signposts to guide listeners. The conclusion should review the main points and provide a final focus.
3. **Plan visual aids and handouts for a presentation.** Use simple, easily understood visual aids to emphasize and clarify main points. Choose transparencies, flipcharts, slides, or other visuals depending on audience size, degree of formality desired, and budget. Generally, it's best to distribute handouts after a presentation.
4. **Identify delivery techniques for use before, during, and after a presentation.** Before your talk prepare a sentence outline on note cards and rehearse repeatedly. Check the room, lectern, and equipment. During the presentation consider beginning with a pause and presenting your first sentence from memory. Make eye contact, control your voice, speak and move naturally, and avoid digressions. After your talk distribute handouts and answer questions. End gracefully and express appreciation.

5. **Plan, conduct, and participate in effective meetings and conferences.** In planning a successful meeting or conference, determine a goal, prepare an agenda with a limited number of items, and allocate time for each item to be discussed. In conducting a meeting, start on time, introduce the goal of the meeting, assign a note taker, and encourage a balanced discussion. Follow the agenda and stop on time. As a participant at meetings, do research to prepare for the topic, arrive on time, and consider the best strategy for introducing your ideas.
6. **Explain videoconferencing and its uses.** Videoconferences use fiber-optic networks and video screens to enable people to meet electronically instead of in person. They greatly reduce costs, fatigue, and time lost in traveling to meetings.
7. **List five techniques for improving your use of the telephone.** You can improve your telephone calls by planning a mini-agenda and using a three-point introduction (name, affiliation, and purpose). Be cheerful and responsive, and use closing language to end a conversation. Avoid telephone tag by leaving complete messages. In answering calls, identify yourself immediately, avoid giving out confidential information when answering for others, and take careful messages.
8. **List four techniques for improving your use of voice mail.** In setting up an automated-attendance voice mail menu, limit the number of choices. For your own message prepare a warm and informative greeting. Tell when you will be available. Evaluate your message by calling it yourself.

Chapter Review

1. The planning of an oral presentation should begin with serious thinking about what two factors?

2. Name three goals to be achieved in the introduction of an oral presentation.

3. For a 30-minute presentation, how many main points should be developed?

4. What should the conclusion to an oral presentation include?

5. Why are visual aids particularly useful to inexperienced speakers?

6. Why are transparencies a favorite visual aid?

7. What delivery method is most effective for speakers?

8. Why should speakers deliver the first sentence from memory?

9. When should handouts be distributed?

10. How do meetings differ from speeches?

11. What items should the agenda of a meeting include?

12. How should the leader of a meeting begin?

13. Why are businesses increasingly using video conferences for meetings between distant groups?

14. What is a three-point introduction for a telephone call?

15. What is voice mail?

Discussion

1. Why is it necessary to repeat key points in an oral presentation?

2. How can a speaker make the most effective use of visual aids?

3. Discuss effective techniques for reducing stage fright.

4. How are meetings important to a person's career advancement?

5. Ethical Issue: How can business communicators ensure that their oral presentations are ethical?

Activities

15.1 Critiquing a Speech

Visit your library and select a speech from *Vital Speeches of Our Day*. Write a memo report to your instructor critiquing the speech in terms of the following:

a. Effectiveness of the introduction, body, and conclusion

b. Evidence of effective overall organization

c. Use of verbal signposts to create coherence

d. Emphasis of two to four main points

e. Effectiveness of supporting facts (use of examples, statistics, quotations, and so forth)

15.2 Preparing an Oral Presentation from an Article

Select a newspaper or magazine article and prepare an oral report based on it. Submit your outline, introduction, and conclusion to your instructor, or present the report to your class.

15.3 Describing Stage Fright

Write a memo to your instructor describing the fears or anxieties that you have experienced when speaking before a group. Suggest ways to reduce your fears.

15.4 Investigating Oral Communication in Your Field

Interview one or two individuals in your professional field. How is oral communication important in this profession? Does the need for oral skills change as one advances? What suggestions can these people make to newcomers to the field for developing proficient oral communication skills? Discuss your findings with your class.

15.5 Outlining an Oral Presentation

One of the hardest parts of preparing an oral presentation is developing the outline. Select an oral presentation topic from the list in Activity 15.6 or suggest an original topic. Prepare an outline for your presentation using the following format.

Title	
Purpose	
	I. INTRODUCTION
Gain attention of audience	A.
Involve audience	B.
Establish credibility	C.
Preview main points	D.
Transition	
	II. BODY
Main point	A.
Illustrate, clarify, contrast	1.
	2.
	3.
Transition	
Main point	B.
Illustrate, clarify, contrast	1.
	2.
	3.
Transition	
Main point	C.
Illustrate, clarify, contrast	1.
	2.
	3.
Transition	
	III. CONCLUSION
Summarize main points	A.
Provide final focus	B.
Encourage questions	C.

15.6 Choosing a Topic for an Oral Presentation

Select a topic from the list below or from the report topics in Exercise 14.15 for a five- to ten-minute oral presentation. Consider yourself an expert who has been called in to explain some aspect of the topic before a group of interested people. Since your time is limited, prepare a concise yet forceful presentation with effective visual aids.

a. What kinds of employment advertisements are legal, and what kinds are potentially illegal?

b. What aspects of Japanese management techniques might work in this country?

c. What graphics package should your fellow students use to prepare visual aids for reports?

d. What is the employment outlook in three career areas of interest to you?

e. What is telecommuting, and for what kind of workers is it an appropriate work alternative?

f. How much choice should parents have in selecting schools for their young children (within their district, interdistrict, or parochial/private)?

g. What travel location would you recommend for college students at Christmas (or another holiday or in summer)?

h. What is the economic outlook for a given product (such as domestic cars, laptop computers, economy cameras, fitness equipment, or a product of your choice)?

i. How can your institution (or company) improve its image?

j. Why should people invest in a company or scheme of your choice?

k. What brand and model of computer and printer represent the best buy for college students today?

l. What franchise would offer the best investment opportunity for an entrepreneur in your area?

m. How should a job candidate dress for an interview?

n. Why should you be hired for a position for which you have applied?

o. How do the accounting cycles in manual and computerized systems compare?

p. How is an administrative assistant different from a secretary?

q. Where should your organization hold its next convention?

r. What is your opinion of the statement "Advertising steals our time, defaces the landscape, and degrades the dignity of public institutions"?[17]

s. How can individuals reduce their income tax responsibilities?

t. What is the outlook for real estate (commercial or residential) investment in your area?

u. What are the pros and cons of videoconferencing for [name an organization]?

15.7 Planning a Meeting

Assume that the next meeting of your associated students organization will discuss preparations for a careers day in the spring. The group will hear reports from committees working on speakers, business recruiters, publicity, reservations of campus space, setup of booths, and any other matters you can think of. As president of your ASO, prepare an agenda for the meeting. Compose your introductory remarks to open the meeting. Your instructor may ask you to submit these two documents or use them in staging an actual meeting in class.

15.8 Analyzing a Meeting

Attend a structured meeting of a college, social, business, or other organization. Compare the conduct within the meeting with the suggestions presented in this chapter. Why did the meeting succeed or fail? Prepare a memo for your instructor or be ready to discuss your findings in class.

15.9 Improving Telephone Skills by Role Playing

Your instructor will divide the class into pairs. For each scenario take a moment to read and rehearse your role silently. Then play the role with your partner. If time permits, repeat the scenarios, changing roles.

	Partner 1	Partner 2
A.	You are the personnel manager of Datatronics, Inc. Call Elizabeth Franklin, office manager at Computers Plus. Inquire about a job applicant, Chelsea Chavez, who listed Ms. Franklin as a reference. Place the call.	You are the receptionist for Computers Plus. The caller asks for Elizabeth Franklin, who is home sick today. You don't know when she will be able to return. Answer the call appropriately.
B.	Call Ms. Franklin again the following day to inquire about the same job applicant, Chelsea Chavez. Ms. Franklin answers today, but she talks on and on, describing the applicant in great detail. Tactfully close the conversation.	You are now Ms. Franklin, office manager. Describe Chelsea Chavez, an imaginary employee. Think of someone with whom you've worked. Include many details, such as her ability to work with others, her appearance, her skills at computing, her schooling, her ambition, and so forth.
C.	You are now the receptionist for Tom Wing, of Wing Imports. Answer a call for Mr. Wing, who is working in another office, at ext. 134, where he will accept calls.	You are now an administrative assistant for attorney Michael Murphy. Call Tom Wing to verify a meeting date Mr. Murphy has with Mr. Wing. Use your own name in identifying yourself.
D.	You are now Tom Wing, owner of Wing Imports. Call your attorney, Michael Murphy, about a legal problem. Leave a brief, incomplete message.	You are now the receptionist for attorney Michael Murphy. Mr. Murphy is skiing in Aspen and will return in two days, but he doesn't want his clients to know where he is. Take a message.
E.	Call Mr. Murphy again. Leave a message that will prevent telephone tag.	Take a message again.

Employment Messages

LEARNING GOALS

After studying this chapter, you should be able to

1. Evaluate your assets, career paths, and the job market in preparation for employment
2. Compare and contrast chronological, functional, and combination résumés
3. Organize, format, and produce a persuasive résumé
4. Avoid pitfalls that lead to an unethical résumé
5. Write a persuasive letter of application to accompany your résumé
6. Write effective employment follow-up letters and other messages
7. Evaluate successful job interview strategies

Residence Inn® by Marriott: Career Track Profile

"The best résumés are straightforward and honest."

"The résumés that really catch our attention," admits Tania Romero, "are those that have been tailored to our company. You can spot them immediately."

Tania works with the director of employment for Residence Inn, a division of Marriott Corporation, one of the nation's largest employers. Hundreds of unsolicited résumés reach her desk each year in Washington, DC, the location of Marriott's headquarters.

Tania and her boss review all résumés submitted to determine an appropriate response. "Some résumés make a bad impression right off," she observes. "They have pencil marks, scribbles, or typos. Some writers even misspell *Marriott,* making us wonder how interested they can be in our company. We would hope that they have done some research, and certainly getting our name right is a critical first step." Tania's initial focus is also on the length of a résumé. "One-page résumés are best because you can keep everything in view as you weigh the candidate's assets. We expect recent college graduates to have one-page résumés. Applicants, however, who have been in their professions for ten or more years generally submit two-page résumés."

After a quick overall appraisal, Tania examines a résumé to see how advanced the candidate is in her or his career. For recent graduates Tania notes the applicant's school, date of graduation, and major studies. Even more important is experience. "We look to see if an applicant's experience correlates with the area of application. It doesn't help a lot if a person sold shoes in the summer and then applies for a job in computing. We're looking for a match between a person's background and a division within our organization. Where will an applicant best fit?

"We pay careful attention to descriptions of accomplishments. Some applicants just list the duties they had on a job, using phrases like 'performed sales calls.' This is too vague. We want more information. What kind of 'sales calls'? How many? In what kind of market? With what success? If a candidate claims to have 'increased sales,' we would ask, by how much? How was it done? What was the strategy, and who developed it? Applicants can really sell themselves by giving specifics about their accomplishments."

Extracurricular activities make a difference, too. "We're interested in participation in sales and marketing clubs or hotel management associations. These activities suggest a well-rounded individual."

Regarding the structure of a résumé, Tania notes that a chronological format is preferable to a functional format. That is, she favors résumés organized by jobs (listed sequentially) instead of résumés focused on skills only. "We want to see how long applicants have been in each position, where they started, and how they moved up. Chronological résumés can do that for us; functional résumés do not. We're interested in signs of stability."

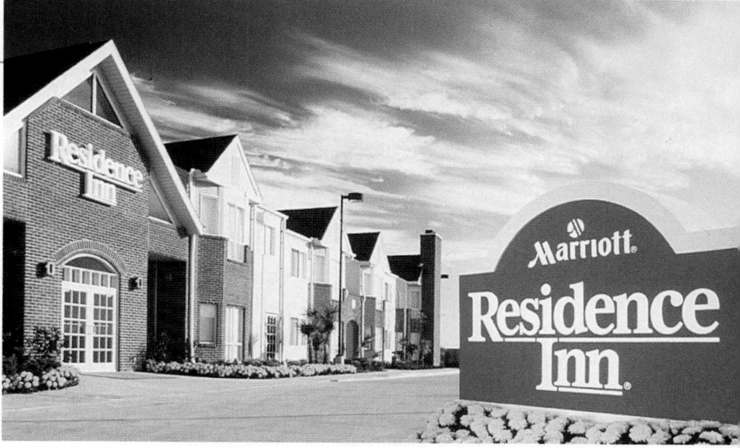

Residence Inn by Marriott encourages college students majoring in hotel management and allied fields to try out their career choices in internship positions. Such experiences not only enhance a résumé but also develop networking connections and help refine a candidate's career decisions.

In reading some résumés, Tania gets an impression that job-seekers are "puffing up" their qualifications. "Sometimes the responsibilities sound inappropriate for the title. Applicants may talk unconvincingly about experience in budgeting, or managing many people, or using some total quality management technique that sounds doubtful. Or someone takes full credit for a big project that probably required assistance. From that point on I begin to question everything I read. The best résumés are straightforward and honest."

In addition to résumés, cover letters are very important to Tania. "When résumés arrive without cover letters, we don't take them seriously. It looks as if the applicant doesn't know how to write a cover letter or is too lazy to make the effort. Either way, we're not impressed. We like letters that briefly introduce the candidates by describing their areas of interest, where they would like to be located geographically, why they are qualified, and what they can do for us. A cover letter shouldn't be too long—two or three paragraphs at most." Tania notes that the best cover letters are concise but personalized. They don't refer to "your company," a dead giveaway that this is a form letter sent to many companies. Good cover letters show that writers know something about the target company and have ideas about what they can contribute to it.

Tania advises all college students to find a way to get experience in their intended fields. In her last semester at the University of Maryland, she worked three days a week as a temporary secretary/administrative assistant at Marriott. After graduation she was ready when a permanent position opened up at the firm. Another way to get experience is through an internship. Like many large organizations Marriott offers an extensive program of internships so that prospective employees can become familiar with the organization while at the same time discovering their own talents and interests. A Residence Inn internship usually lasts three months. Trainees alternate their work experiences in various areas of hotel management: front office, maintenance, sales, housekeeping, and so forth. "You must gain experience," says Tania, "because you need evidence of relevant accomplishments to impress recruiters. You want to be able to say convincingly, 'I really enjoy working in the front office or in sales, and I can be an asset to your company.' "[1]

Preparing for Employment

● **Finding a satisfying career means learning about oneself, the job market, and the employment process.**

Learning how to evaluate your assets and how to manage the entire employment process demands preparation. Whether you are looking for an internship, applying for a permanent position, competing for a promotion, or changing careers, you must invest time and effort preparing yourself. You can't hope to find the position of your dreams without first (1) knowing yourself, (2) knowing the job market, and (3) knowing the employment process. Learning about yourself involves identifying your interests, preferences, and goals so that you choose a satisfying career. Your self-evaluation should also include assessing your qualifications and skills. In addition, you must obtain career information and choose a specific job objective. At the same time, you should be studying the job market. Finally, you'll need to design a persuasive résumé and letter of application. Following these steps, summarized in Figure 16.1 and described in this chapter, gives you a master plan for getting the job you want.[2]

Identifying Your Interests

● **Answer specific questions to help yourself choose a career.**

The employment process begins with introspection. This means looking inside yourself to analyze what you like and dislike so that you can make good employment choices. Career counselors charge large sums for helping individuals learn about themselves. You can do the same kind of self-examination—without spending a dime. For guidance in choosing a field that eventually proves to be satisfying, answer the following questions. If you have already chosen a field, think carefully about how your answers relate to that choice.

- *Do you enjoy working with people, data, or things?*
- *How important is it to be your own boss?*
- *How important are salary, benefits, and job stability?*
- *How important are working environment, colleagues, and job stimulation?*
- *Would you rather work for a large or small company?*
- *Must you work in a specific city, geographical area, or climate?*
- *Are you looking for security, travel opportunities, money, power, or prestige?*
- *How would you describe the perfect job, boss, and coworkers?*

Evaluating Your Qualifications

In addition to your interests, assess your qualifications. As Tania Romero at Marriott pointed out, employers want to know what assets you have to offer them. Your responses to the following questions will target your thinking as well as prepare a foundation for your résumé. Remember, though, that employers seek more than empty assurances; they will want proof of your qualifications.

- *What skills have you acquired in school, on the job, or through other activities?* Employers are especially interested in communication and computer skills.
- *Do you work well with people?* What proof can you offer? Consider extracurricular activities, clubs, and jobs.
- *Are you a leader, self-starter, or manager?* What evidence can you offer?
- *Do you speak, write, or understand another language?*

FIGURE 16.1 ● The Employment Search

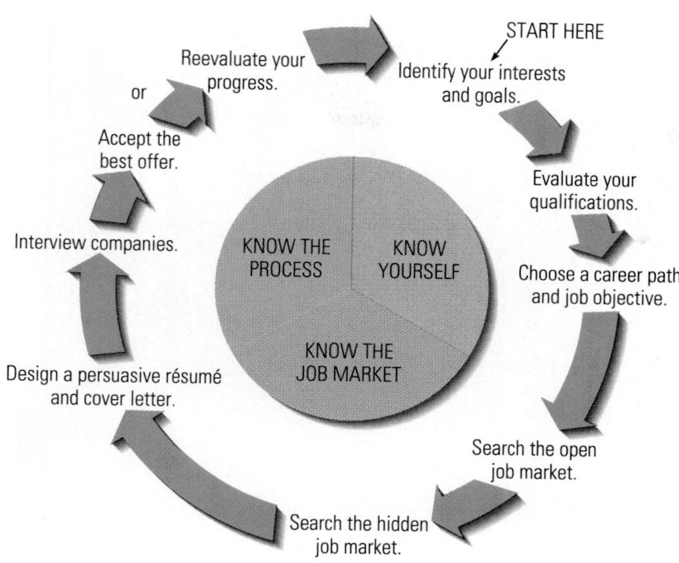
START HERE
Identify your interests and goals.
Evaluate your qualifications.
Choose a career path and job objective.
Search the open job market.
Search the hidden job market.
Design a persuasive résumé and cover letter.
Interview companies.
Accept the best offer.
or
Reevaluate your progress.
KNOW THE PROCESS
KNOW YOURSELF
KNOW THE JOB MARKET

- *Do you learn quickly? Are you creative?* How can you demonstrate these characteristics?
- *Do you communicate well in speech and in writing?* How can you verify these talents?

Choosing a Career Path

As a result of job trends and personal choices, the average American changes careers at least three times in a lifetime. Some of you probably have not settled on your first career choice yet; others are returning to college to retrain for a new career. You'll make the best career decisions when you can match your interests and qualifications with the requirements and rewards in specific careers. But where can you get specific career data? Here are some suggestions:

● Career information can be obtained at campus career centers and libraries, in classified ads, and from professional organizations.

- **Visit your campus career center.** Most have literature, inventories, and software programs that allow you to investigate such fields as accounting, finance, office administration, hotel management, and so forth.
- **Use your library.** Several publications are especially helpful. Consult the latest edition of the *Dictionary of Occupational Titles, Occupational Outlook Handbook,* and *The Jobs Rated Almanac* for information about career duties, qualifications, salaries, and employment trends.
- **Take a summer job, internship, or part-time position in your field.** As Tania Romero pointed out, nothing is better than trying out a career by actually working in it or an allied area. Many companies offer internships and temporary jobs to begin training college students and to develop relationships with them. These relationships sometimes blossom into permanent positions. Jon Georges, profiled in Chapter 15, commuted 90 minutes each way to work at Disneyland while in high school and college. That tenacity undoubtedly

● Summer and part-time jobs and internships are good opportunities to learn about different careers.

Preparing for a career begins long before you search the classified ads and write your résumé. Some of the best ways to learn about career paths involve taking a summer job, internship, or part-time position in the area of your interest. Most often these positions don't just fall in your lap. They require determination and effort.

helped his résumé stand out from the hundreds Disney Imagineering received.

- **Interview someone in your chosen field.** People are usually flattered when asked to describe their careers. Inquire about needed skills, required courses, financial and other rewards, benefits, working conditions, future trends, and entry requirements.
- **Monitor the classified ads.** Early in your college career, begin scanning want ads in your career area. Check job availability, qualifications sought, duties, and salary range. Don't wait until you're about to graduate to see how the job market looks.
- **Join professional organizations in your field.** Frequently, they offer student membership status and reduced rates. You'll get an inside track on issues, career news, and possibly jobs.

Searching the Job Market

● A job-search campaign might include checking classified ads and announcements in professional publications, contacting companies, and developing a network of contacts.

Finding the perfect job, even when the economy is flourishing, requires an early start and a determined effort. Some universities now require first- and second-year students to take an employment seminar called "Reality 101." Students are told early on that a college degree alone doesn't guarantee a job. They are cautioned that grade-point averages make a difference to employers. And they are advised of the importance of experience and an aggressive job search campaign, including some or all of the following steps:

- **Check classified ads in local and national newspapers.** Be aware, though, that classified ads are only one small source of jobs, as discussed in the accompanying Career Skills box.
- **Check announcements in publications of professional organizations.** If you do not have a student membership, ask your professors to share current copies of professional journals, newsletters, and so on. Your college library is another good source.

CAREER SKILLS

NETWORKING TO EXPLORE THE HIDDEN JOB MARKET

When you look in the classified ads, you see only a fraction of the jobs that really exist. Amazingly, the "hidden" job market—those positions never advertised or announced publicly—accounts for two thirds to three fourths of all positions available!

Employers don't advertise job openings for many reasons. For one thing, such advertisements are expensive and time-consuming. One employer, for example, advertised for a receptionist and had 80 applicants, tying up phone lines and disrupting normal business considerably.[3] Moreover, employers dislike hiring "strangers." One personnel specialist explains, "If I'm in a hiring position, I'm first going to look around among my friends and acquaintances. If I can't find anybody, I'll look around for their friends and acquaintances. Only if I can't find anybody will I advertise."[4] Employers are much more comfortable hiring a person they know.

The real key to finding a good job, then, is converting yourself from a "stranger" into a known quantity. You can become a known quantity and cultivate your own personal network with a three-step plan.

STEP 1: DEVELOP A LIST. Make a list of anyone who would be willing to talk with you about finding a job. These people do not have to be in your career area. In fact, most won't be. List your friends, relatives, former employers, former coworkers, classmates from grade school and high school, college friends, members of your church, people in social and athletic clubs, present and former teachers, neighbors, and people who sell you things (such as services, insurance, and supplies). And don't overlook your parents—you often find a rich source of possibilities among their friends, colleagues, and so on.

STEP 2: MAKE CONTACTS. Call the people on your list or, even better, try to meet with them in person. A personal visit makes a much greater impression than a telephone call. To set up a meeting, you might say something like, "Hi, Aunt Jenny! I'm looking for a job and I wonder if you could help me out. When could I come over to talk about it?" During your visit be friendly, well organized, polite, and interested in what your contact has to say. Provide a copy of your résumé, and try to keep the conversation centered on your job search area. Your goal is to get two or more referrals. In pinpointing your request, ask three questions. "Do you know of anyone who might have an opening for a person with my skills?" If not, "Do you know of anyone else who might know of someone who would?" If not, "Do you know someone who knows lots of people?"

STEP 3: FOLLOW UP ON YOUR REFERRALS. Call the people whose names are on your referral list. You might say something like, "Hello. I'm Carlos Ramos, a friend of Connie Cole. She suggested that I call and ask you for help. I'm looking for a position as a marketing trainee, and she thought you might be willing to see me and give me a few ideas." Don't ask for a job. Most of the people you meet this way will not be in a position to offer a job, but they may know other people and be willing to refer you to them.

During your referral interview ask how the individual got started in this line of work, what he or she likes best (or least) about the work, what career paths exist in the field, and what problems must be overcome by a newcomer. Most importantly, ask how a person with your background and skills might get started in the field.

Send an informal thank-you note to anyone who helps you in your job search, and stay in touch with the most promising contacts. Ask if you may call every three weeks or so during your job search.

Career Track Application

Begin developing your network. Conduct at least one referral interview. Take notes, and report your reactions and findings to your class.

- **Contact companies in which you're interested, even if you know of no current opening.** Write an unsolicited letter and include your résumé. Follow up with a telephone call.
- **Sign up for campus interviews with visiting company representatives.** Campus recruiters may open your eyes to exciting jobs and locations.
- **Ask for advice from your professors.** They often have contacts and ideas for expanding your job search.

SPOTLIGHT ON COMMUNICATORS

Michael Saafir tried everything to land a job, including wearing a sandwich board and passing out résumés to passing motorists. What eventually worked for him, though, was networking. A cousin had heard of job openings at a bank and suggested that Michael apply. He got the job. Developing an extensive personal network is one of the most effective job search tactics for any candidate.

- **Develop your own network of contacts.** Networking accounts for nearly two thirds of the jobs found by candidates.[5] Therefore, plan to spend the majority of your job search time developing a personal network. The Career Skills box gives you step-by-step instructions in cultivating a network and following through with referral interviews.

Above all, be persistent in your job search. Karen Peterson, a former Orange County school district food services manager, sent over 300 letters, made nearly 800 phone calls, and spent five months finding a new career. But her determination paid off; she's now happily entrenched in her new position as an account executive at Pizza Hut's Western Division.[6]

The Persuasive Résumé

After learning about the employment market and developing job leads, your next step is writing a persuasive résumé. Such a résumé does more than merely list your qualifications. It packages your assets into a convincing advertisement that sells you for a specific job. The goal of a persuasive résumé is winning an interview. Even if you are not in the job market at this moment, preparing a résumé now has advantages. Having a current résumé makes you look well organized and professional should an unexpected employment opportunity arise. Moreover, preparing a résumé early helps you recognize weak qualifications and gives you two or three years in which to bolster them.

Choosing a Résumé Style

Your qualifications and career goal will help you choose from among three résumé styles: chronological, functional, and combination.

Chronological. Most popular with recruiters is the chronological résumé, shown in Figure 16.2. It lists work history job by job, starting with the most recent position. As Tania Romero at Marriott pointed out, recruiters favor the chronological style because such résumés quickly reveal a candidate's work stability and promotion record. Another corporate recruiter said, "I'm looking for applicable experience; chronological résumés are the easiest to assess."[7] The chronological style works well for candidates who have experience in their field of employment and for those who show steady career growth.

Chronological résumés focus on past employment; functional résumés focus on skills.

Functional. The functional résumé, shown in Figure 16.3, focuses attention on a candidate's skills rather than on past employment. Like a chronological résumé the functional résumé begins with the candidate's name, address, telephone number, job objective, and education. Instead of listing jobs, though, the functional résumé groups skills and accomplishments in special categories, such as *Supervisory and Management Skills* or *Retailing and Marketing Experience.* This résumé style highlights accomplishments and can deemphasize a negative employment history. People who have changed jobs frequently or who have gaps in their employment records may prefer the functional résumé. Recent graduates with little employment experience may also find the functional résumé useful. Outweighing its advantages, however, is the fact that some recruiters immediately assume that a functional résumé is hiding something. Remember how Tania Romero looked for a clear, concise record of employment? Functional résumés do not generally provide such a record.

FIGURE 16.2 ● Chronological Résumé

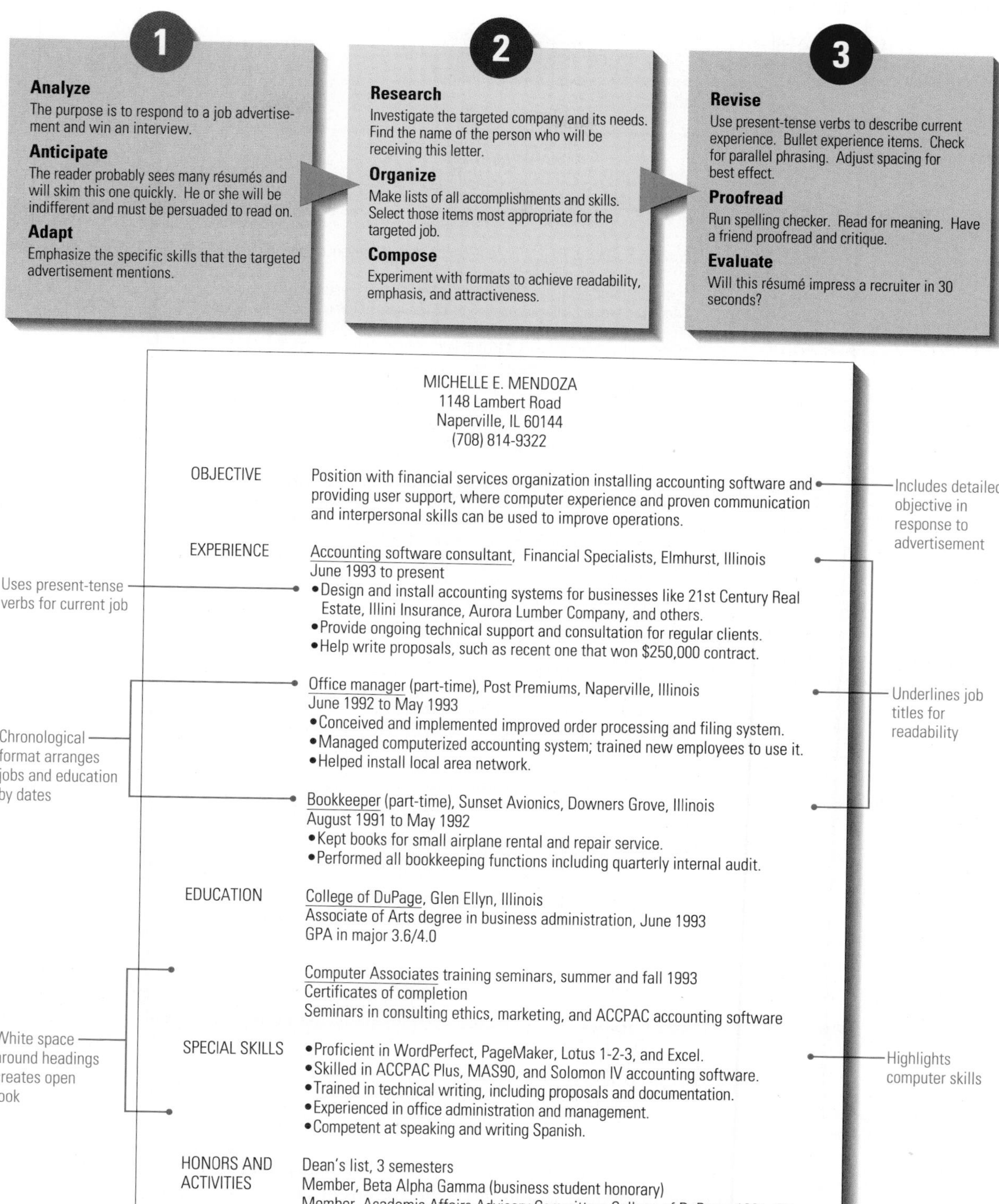

The Three Phases of the Writing Process
1
Analyze
The purpose is to respond to a job advertisement and win an interview.
Anticipate
The reader probably sees many résumés and will skim this one quickly. He or she will be indifferent and must be persuaded to read on.
Adapt
Emphasize the specific skills that the targeted advertisement mentions.
2
Research
Investigate the targeted company and its needs. Find the name of the person who will be receiving this letter.
Organize
Make lists of all accomplishments and skills. Select those items most appropriate for the targeted job.
Compose
Experiment with formats to achieve readability, emphasis, and attractiveness.
3
Revise
Use present-tense verbs to describe current experience. Bullet experience items. Check for parallel phrasing. Adjust spacing for best effect.
Proofread
Run spelling checker. Read for meaning. Have a friend proofread and critique.
Evaluate
Will this résumé impress a recruiter in 30 seconds?
Includes detailed objective in response to advertisement
Uses present-tense verbs for current job
Underlines job titles for readability
Chronological format arranges jobs and education by dates
White space around headings creates open look
Highlights computer skills

MICHELLE E. MENDOZA
1148 Lambert Road
Naperville, IL 60144
(708) 814-9322

OBJECTIVE

Position with financial services organization installing accounting software and providing user support, where computer experience and proven communication and interpersonal skills can be used to improve operations.

EXPERIENCE

Accounting software consultant, Financial Specialists, Elmhurst, Illinois
June 1993 to present
- Design and install accounting systems for businesses like 21st Century Real Estate, Illini Insurance, Aurora Lumber Company, and others.
- Provide ongoing technical support and consultation for regular clients.
- Help write proposals, such as recent one that won $250,000 contract.

Office manager (part-time), Post Premiums, Naperville, Illinois
June 1992 to May 1993
- Conceived and implemented improved order processing and filing system.
- Managed computerized accounting system; trained new employees to use it.
- Helped install local area network.

Bookkeeper (part-time), Sunset Avionics, Downers Grove, Illinois
August 1991 to May 1992
- Kept books for small airplane rental and repair service.
- Performed all bookkeeping functions including quarterly internal audit.

EDUCATION

College of DuPage, Glen Ellyn, Illinois
Associate of Arts degree in business administration, June 1993
GPA in major 3.6/4.0

Computer Associates training seminars, summer and fall 1993
Certificates of completion
Seminars in consulting ethics, marketing, and ACCPAC accounting software

SPECIAL SKILLS

- Proficient in WordPerfect, PageMaker, Lotus 1-2-3, and Excel.
- Skilled in ACCPAC Plus, MAS90, and Solomon IV accounting software.
- Trained in technical writing, including proposals and documentation.
- Experienced in office administration and management.
- Competent at speaking and writing Spanish.

HONORS AND ACTIVITIES

Dean's list, 3 semesters
Member, Beta Alpha Gamma (business student honorary)
Member, Academic Affairs Advisory Committee, College of DuPage, 1991–93

FIGURE 16.3 ● **Functional Résumé**

Donald, a recent graduate, chose this functional format to de-emphasize his meager work experience and emphasize his potential in sales and marketing. He included an employment section to satisfy recruiters.

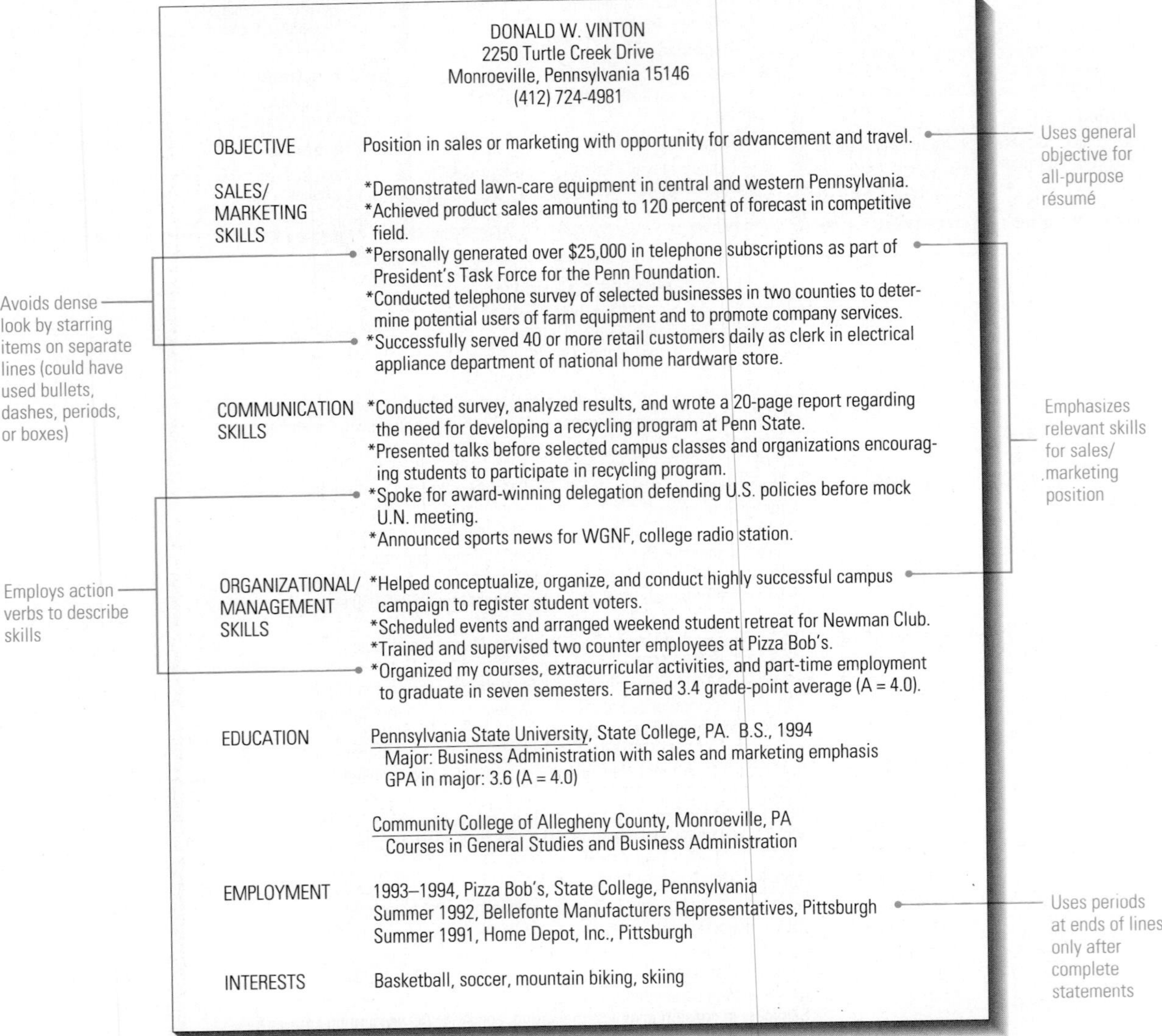
DONALD W. VINTON
2250 Turtle Creek Drive
Monroeville, Pennsylvania 15146
(412) 724-4981

OBJECTIVE	Position in sales or marketing with opportunity for advancement and travel.
SALES/ MARKETING SKILLS	*Demonstrated lawn-care equipment in central and western Pennsylvania. *Achieved product sales amounting to 120 percent of forecast in competitive field. *Personally generated over $25,000 in telephone subscriptions as part of President's Task Force for the Penn Foundation. *Conducted telephone survey of selected businesses in two counties to determine potential users of farm equipment and to promote company services. *Successfully served 40 or more retail customers daily as clerk in electrical appliance department of national home hardware store.
COMMUNICATION SKILLS	*Conducted survey, analyzed results, and wrote a 20-page report regarding the need for developing a recycling program at Penn State. *Presented talks before selected campus classes and organizations encouraging students to participate in recycling program. *Spoke for award-winning delegation defending U.S. policies before mock U.N. meeting. *Announced sports news for WGNF, college radio station.
ORGANIZATIONAL/ MANAGEMENT SKILLS	*Helped conceptualize, organize, and conduct highly successful campus campaign to register student voters. *Scheduled events and arranged weekend student retreat for Newman Club. *Trained and supervised two counter employees at Pizza Bob's. *Organized my courses, extracurricular activities, and part-time employment to graduate in seven semesters. Earned 3.4 grade-point average (A = 4.0).
EDUCATION	Pennsylvania State University, State College, PA. B.S., 1994 Major: Business Administration with sales and marketing emphasis GPA in major: 3.6 (A = 4.0) Community College of Allegheny County, Monroeville, PA Courses in General Studies and Business Administration
EMPLOYMENT	1993–1994, Pizza Bob's, State College, Pennsylvania Summer 1992, Bellefonte Manufacturers Representatives, Pittsburgh Summer 1991, Home Depot, Inc., Pittsburgh
INTERESTS	Basketball, soccer, mountain biking, skiing

Uses general objective for all-purpose résumé
Avoids dense look by starring items on separate lines (could have used bullets, dashes, periods, or boxes)
Emphasizes relevant skills for sales/ marketing position
Employs action verbs to describe skills
Uses periods at ends of lines only after complete statements

Functional résumés are also called "skill" résumés. Although the functional résumé of Donald Vinton shown here concentrates on skills, it does include a short employment section because recruiters expect it. Notice that Donald breaks his skills into three categories. An alternative—and easier—method is to make one large list, perhaps with a title such as *Areas of Accomplishment, Summary of Qualifications*, or *Areas of Expertise and Ability*.

FIGURE 16.4 ● Combination Résumé

Because Susan wanted to highlight her skills and capabilities along with her experience, she combined the best features of functional and traditional résumés. This résumé style is becoming increasingly popular. Although it's not standard practice, Susan included references because employers in her area expected them.

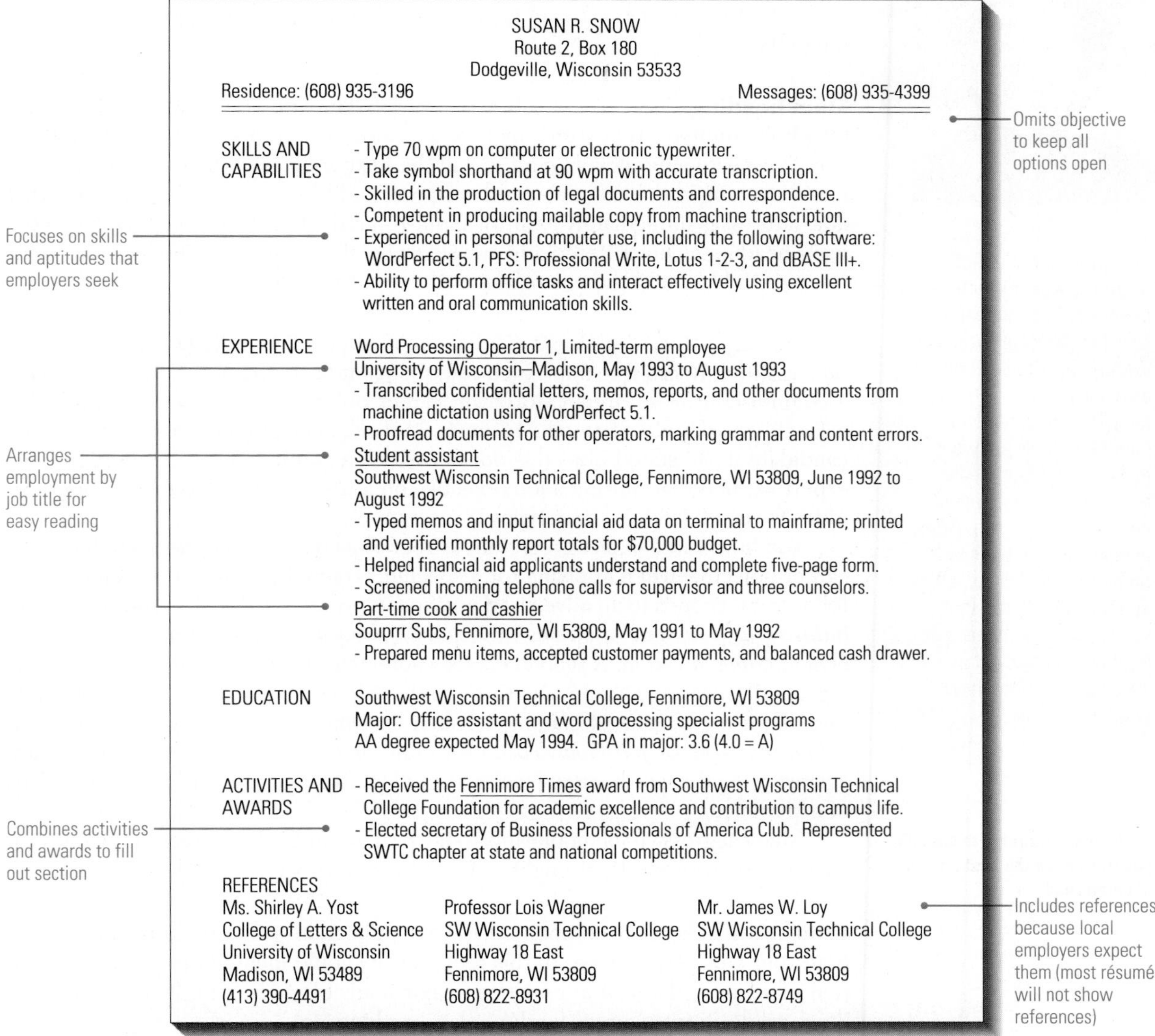

SUSAN R. SNOW
Route 2, Box 180
Dodgeville, Wisconsin 53533
Residence: (608) 935-3196 Messages: (608) 935-4399

SKILLS AND CAPABILITIES
- Type 70 wpm on computer or electronic typewriter.
- Take symbol shorthand at 90 wpm with accurate transcription.
- Skilled in the production of legal documents and correspondence.
- Competent in producing mailable copy from machine transcription.
- Experienced in personal computer use, including the following software: WordPerfect 5.1, PFS: Professional Write, Lotus 1-2-3, and dBASE III+.
- Ability to perform office tasks and interact effectively using excellent written and oral communication skills.

EXPERIENCE
Word Processing Operator 1, Limited-term employee
University of Wisconsin–Madison, May 1993 to August 1993
- Transcribed confidential letters, memos, reports, and other documents from machine dictation using WordPerfect 5.1.
- Proofread documents for other operators, marking grammar and content errors.

Student assistant
Southwest Wisconsin Technical College, Fennimore, WI 53809, June 1992 to August 1992
- Typed memos and input financial aid data on terminal to mainframe; printed and verified monthly report totals for $70,000 budget.
- Helped financial aid applicants understand and complete five-page form.
- Screened incoming telephone calls for supervisor and three counselors.

Part-time cook and cashier
Souprrr Subs, Fennimore, WI 53809, May 1991 to May 1992
- Prepared menu items, accepted customer payments, and balanced cash drawer.

EDUCATION
Southwest Wisconsin Technical College, Fennimore, WI 53809
Major: Office assistant and word processing specialist programs
AA degree expected May 1994. GPA in major: 3.6 (4.0 = A)

ACTIVITIES AND AWARDS
- Received the Fennimore Times award from Southwest Wisconsin Technical College Foundation for academic excellence and contribution to campus life.
- Elected secretary of Business Professionals of America Club. Represented SWTC chapter at state and national competitions.

REFERENCES

Ms. Shirley A. Yost	Professor Lois Wagner	Mr. James W. Loy
College of Letters & Science	SW Wisconsin Technical College	SW Wisconsin Technical College
University of Wisconsin	Highway 18 East	Highway 18 East
Madison, WI 53489	Fennimore, WI 53809	Fennimore, WI 53809
(413) 390-4491	(608) 822-8931	(608) 822-8749

Omits objective to keep all options open
Focuses on skills and aptitudes that employers seek
Arranges employment by job title for easy reading
Combines activities and awards to fill out section
Includes references because local employers expect them (most résumés will not show references)

Combination. The combination résumé style, shown in Figure 16.4, draws on the best features of the chronological and functional résumés. It emphasizes a candidate's capabilities while also including a complete job history. For recent graduates the combination résumé is a good choice because it enables them to profile what they can do for a prospective employer. If the writer has a specific job in mind, the items can be targeted to that job description.

SPOTLIGHT ON COMMUNICATORS

Being persistent about acquiring work experience in your field is crucial, says Los Angeles TV anchor Wendy Tokuda. She started as a secretary at Seattle's King TV. But she forced herself to dress up, wear makeup, and repeatedly ask an intimidating news director for a chance. After being turned down six times, she finally won an audition. She thinks that having the "persistence of a pit bull" can result in an opportunity to show what you can do.

Arranging the Parts

Although résumés have standard parts, their arrangement and content should be strategically planned. The most persuasive résumés emphasize skills and achievements aimed at a particular job or company. They show a candidate's most important qualifications first, and they deemphasize any weaknesses. In arranging the parts, try to create as few headings as possible; more than six generally looks cluttered. No two résumés are ever exactly alike, but most writers consider the following parts.

Main heading. Your résumé should always begin with your name, address, and telephone number. If possible, include a number where messages may be left for you. Prospective employers tend to call the next applicant when no one answers. Avoid showing both permanent and temporary addresses; some specialists say that dual addresses immediately identify about-to-graduate college students. Keep the main heading as uncluttered and simple as possible. And don't include the word *résumé;* it's like putting the word *letter* above correspondence.

Career objective. Opinion is divided on the effect of including a career objective on a résumé. Recruiters think such statements indicate that a candidate has made a commitment to a career. Moreover, career objectives make the recruiter's life easier by quickly classifying the résumé. But such declarations can also disqualify a candidate if the stated objective doesn't match a company's job description. One expert warned that putting a job objective on a résumé has "killed more opportunities for candidates . . . than typos."[8]

You have three choices regarding career objectives. One option is to include a career objective when applying for a specific, targeted position. For example, the following responds to an advertised position: *Objective: To work in the health care industry as a human resources trainee with exposure to recruiting, training, and benefit administration.* A second choice—one that makes sense if you are preparing an all-purpose résumé—is to omit the career objective. A third possibility involves using a general statement, such as *Objective: Challenging position in urban planning* or *Job Goal: Position in sales/marketing.* Some consultants warn against using the words *entry-level* in your objective, as such words emphasize lack of experience.

● **Résumés targeted to specific positions have the best chance of being read.**

Many aggressive job applicants today prepare individual targeted résumés for each company or position sought. Thanks to word processing, the task is easy.

Education. The next component is your education—if it is more noteworthy than your work experience. In this section you should include the name and location of schools, dates of attendance, major fields of study, and degrees received. Your grade-point average and/or class ranking are important to prospective employers. One way to enhance your GPA is to calculate it in your major courses only (for example, *3.6/4.0 in major*). A list of completed courses makes dull reading; refer to courses only if you can relate them to the position sought. When relevant, include certificates earned, seminars attended, and workshops completed. Because employers are interested in your degree of self-sufficiency, you might wish to indicate the percentage of your education for which you paid. If your education is incomplete, include such statements as *B.S. degree expected 6/96* or *80 units completed in 120-unit program.* Entitle this section *Education, Academic Preparation,* or *Professional Training.*

Work experience. If your work experience is significant and relevant to the position sought, this information should appear before education. List your most recent employment first and work backwards, including only those jobs that you think will help you win the targeted position. A job application form may demand a full employment history, but your résumé may be selective. (Be aware, though, that time gaps in your employment history will probably be questioned in the interview.) For each position show the following:

Educational achievements should precede employment history on a résumé only when they are more noteworthy.

- Employer's name, city, and state
- Dates of employment, including month and year
- Most important job title
- Significant duties, activities, accomplishments, and promotions

Describe your employment achievements concisely but concretely. Avoid generalities like *Worked with customers.* Be more specific, with statements such as *Served 40 or more retail customers a day, Successfully resolved problems about custom stationery orders,* or *Acted as intermediary between customers, printers, and suppliers.* If possible, quantify your accomplishments, such as *Conducted study of equipment needs of 100 small businesses in Phoenix, Personally generated orders for sales of $90,000 annually, Keyboarded all the production models for a 250-page employee procedures manual,* or *Assisted editor in layout, design, and news writing for 12 issues of division newsletter.*

The work experience section of a résumé should list specifics and quantify achievements.

In addition to technical skills, employers seek individuals with communication, management, and interpersonal capabilities. This means you'll want to select work experiences and achievements that illustrate your initiative, dependability, responsibility, resourcefulness, and leadership. Employers also want people who can work together in teams. Thus, include statements like *Collaborated with interdepartmental task force in developing 10-page handbook for temporary workers* and *Headed student government team that conducted most successful voter registration in campus history.*

Statements describing your work experience can be made forceful and persuasive by using action verbs, such as those listed in Figure 16.5 and demonstrated in Figure 16.6.

Capabilities and skills. Recruiters want to know specifically what you can do for their companies. Therefore, list your special skills, such as *Proficient in preparing correspondence and reports using WordPerfect 5.1.* Include your ability to use computer programs, office equipment, foreign languages, or sign language. Describe proficiencies you have acquired through training and experience, such as *Trained in computer accounting, including general ledger, accounts receivable, accounts payable, and payroll.* Use expressions like *competent in, skilled in, proficient with, experienced in* and *ability to;* for example, *Competent in typing, editing, and/or proofreading reports, tables, letters, memos, manuscripts, and business forms.*

Emphasize the skills and aptitudes that recommend you for a specific position.

You'll also want to highlight exceptional aptitudes, such as working well under stress and learning computer programs quickly. If possible, provide details and evidence that back up your assertions; for example, *Mastered the Barrister computer program in 25 hours with little instruction.* Search for examples of your writing, speaking, management, organizational, and interpersonal skills—particularly those talents that are relevant to your targeted job.

FIGURE 16.5 ● Action Verbs for Persuasive Résumés*

Management Skills	Communication Skills	Research Skills	Technical Skills	Teaching Skills
administered	addressed	clarified	assembled	adapted
analyzed	arbitrated	collected	built	advised
consolidated	arranged	critiqued	calculated	clarified
coordinated	collaborated	diagnosed	computed	coached
delegated	convinced	evaluated	designed	communicated
developed	developed	examined	devised	coordinated
directed	drafted	extracted	engineered	developed
evaluated	edited	identified	executed	enabled
improved	explained	inspected	fabricated	encouraged
increased	formulated	interpreted	maintained	evaluated
organized	interpreted	interviewed	operated	explained
oversaw	negotiated	investigated	overhauled	facilitated
planned	persuaded	organized	programmed	guided
prioritized	promoted	summarized	remodeled	informed
recommended	publicized	surveyed	repaired	instructed
scheduled	recruited	systematized	solved	persuaded
strengthened	translated		upgraded	set goals
supervised	wrote			trained

*The **underlined** words are especially good for pointing out **accomplishments.**

For recent graduates, this section can be used to give recruiters evidence of your potential. Instead of *Capabilities,* the section might be called *Skills and Abilities.*

● **Awards, honors, and activities are appropriate for résumés; most personal data are not.**

Awards, honors, and activities. If you have three or more awards or honors, highlight them by listing them under a separate heading. If not, put them with activities. Include awards, scholarships (financial and other), fellowships, honors, recognition, commendations, and certificates. Be sure to identify items clearly. Your reader may be unfamiliar, for example, with Greek organizations, honoraries, and awards; tell what they mean. Instead of saying *Recipient of Star award,* give more details: *Recipient of Star award given by Pepperdine University to outstanding graduates who combined academic excellence and extracurricular activities.*

It's also appropriate to include school, community, and professional activities. Employers are interested in evidence that you are a well-rounded person. This section also provides an opportunity to demonstrate leadership and interpersonal skills. Strive to use action statements. For example, instead of saying *Treasurer of business club,* explain more fully: *Collected dues, kept financial records, and paid bills while serving as treasurer of 35-member business management club.*

Financial Skills	Creative Skills	Helping Skills	Clerical or Detail Skills	More Verbs for Accomplishments
administered	acted	assessed	approved	achieved
allocated	conceptualized	assisted	catalogued	expanded
analyzed	created	clarified	classified	improved
appraised	customized	coached	collected	pioneered
audited	designed	counseled	compiled	reduced (losses)
balanced	developed	demonstrated	generated	resolved (problems)
budgeted	directed	diagnosed	inspected	restored
calculated	established	educated	monitored	spearheaded
computed	founded	expedited	operated	transformed
developed	illustrated	facilitated	organized	
forecasted	initiated	familiarized	prepared	
managed	instituted	guided	processed	
marketed	introduced	motivated	purchased	
planned	invented	referred	recorded	
projected	originated	represented	screened	
researched	performed		specified	
	planned		systematized	
	revitalized		tabulated	

Source: Adapted from Yana Parker, *The Damn Good Résumé Guide* (Berkeley, CA: Ten Speed Press, 1989).

FIGURE 16.6 ● Using Action Verbs to Strengthen Your Résumé

Identified weaknesses in internship program and **researched** five alternate programs.
Reduced delivery delays by an average of three days per order.
Streamlined filing system, thus reducing 400-item backlog to 0.
Organized holiday awards program for 1200 attendees and 140 awardees.
Created a 12-point checklist for managers to use when requesting temporary workers.
Designed five posters announcing new employee suggestion program.
Calculated shipping charges for overseas deliveries and **recommended** most economical rates.
Managed 24-station computer network linking data and employees in three departments.
Distributed and **explained** over 500 voter registration forms to prospective student voters.

SPOTLIGHT ON COMMUNICATORS

CEO Wayne Calloway looks at the total picture when he interviews or evaluates employees at PepsiCo. An accounting major and basketball player in college, he values well-rounded individuals. But his real goal is finding and promoting people who will be so involved that they act like company owners. In interviews he discusses topics that allow him to evaluate a candidate's qualifications and values.

Personal data. The trend in résumés today is to omit personal data, such as birth date, marital status, height, weight, and religious affiliation. Such information doesn't relate to genuine occupational qualifications, and recruiters are legally barred from asking for such information. Some job seekers do, however, include hobbies or interests (such as skiing or photography) that might grab the recruiter's attention or serve as conversation starters. Naturally, you wouldn't mention dangerous pastimes (such as bungee jumping or sports car racing) or time-consuming interests. But you should indicate your willingness to travel or to relocate, since many companies will be interested.

References. Listing references on a résumé is favored by some recruiters and opposed by others. Such a list takes up valuable space. Moreover, it is not normally instrumental in securing an interview—few companies check references before the interview. Instead, they prefer that a candidate bring to the interview a list of individuals willing to discuss her or his qualifications. If you do list them, use parallel form. For example, if you show a title for one person *(Professor, Dr., Mrs.)*, show titles for all. Include addresses and telephone numbers.

Whether or not you include references on your résumé, you should have their names available when you begin your job search. Ask three to five instructors or previous employers whether they will be willing to answer inquiries regarding your qualifications for employment. Be sure, however, to provide them with an opportunity to refuse. No reference is better than a negative one. Do not include personal or character references, such as friends or neighbors, because recruiters rarely consult them. Companies are more interested in the opinions of objective individuals.

One final note: personnel officers see little reason for including the statement *References furnished upon request.* "It's like saying the sun comes up every morning," remarked one human resources professional.[9]

Applying the Final Touches

● **In addition to being well written, a résumé must be carefully formatted and meticulously proofread.**

Because your résumé is probably the most important message you will ever write, you'll revise it many times. With so much information in concentrated form and with so much riding on its outcome, your résumé demands careful polishing, proofreading, and critiquing.

As you revise, be certain to verify all the facts, particularly those involving your previous employment and education. Don't be caught in a mistake, or worse, distortion of previous jobs and dates of employment. These items likely will be checked. And the consequences of puffing up a résumé with deception or flat-out lies are simply not worth the risk. Other ethical traps you'll want to avoid are described in the accompanying Ethics box.

As you continue revising, look for other ways to improve your résumé. For example, consider consolidating headings. By condensing your information into as few headings as possible, you'll produce a clean, professional-looking document. Study other résumés for valuable formatting ideas. Ask yourself what graphics highlighting techniques you can use to improve readability: capitalization, underlining, indenting, and bulleting. Experiment with headings and styles to achieve a pleasing, easy-to-read message. Moreover, look for ways to eliminate wordiness. For example, instead of *Supervised two employees who worked at the counter,* try *Supervised two counter employees.* Review Chapter 5 for more tips.

Above all, make your résumé look professional. Avoid anything humorous or "cute," such as a help-wanted poster with your name or picture inside. Eliminate

AVOIDING WRITING AN UNETHICAL RÉSUMÉ

A résumé is expected to showcase a candidate's strengths and minimize weaknesses. Recruiters expect a certain degree of self-promotion. But some résumé writers step over the line that separates honest self-marketing from deceptive half-truths and flat-out lies. Distorting facts on a résumé is unethical; lying is illegal. And either practice can destroy a career.

Although recruiters can't check everything, most will verify previous employment and education before hiring candidates. Over half will require official transcripts.[10] And after hiring, the checking process may continue. At one of the nation's top accounting firms, the human resources director described their posthiring routine: "If we find a discrepancy in GPA or prior experience due to an honest mistake, we meet with the new hire to hear an explanation. But if it wasn't a mistake, we terminate the person immediately. Unfortunately, we've had to do that too often."[11]

No job seeker wants to be in the unhappy position of explaining résumé errors or defending misrepresentation. Avoiding the following common problems can keep you off the hot seat:

- **Inflated education, grades, or honors.** Some job candidates claim degrees from colleges or universities when in fact they merely attended classes. Others increase their grade-point averages or claim fictitious honors. Any such dishonest reporting is grounds for dismissal when discovered.
- **Enhanced job titles.** Wishing to elevate their status, some applicants misrepresent their titles. For example, one technician called himself a "programmer" when he had actually programmed only one project for his boss. A mail clerk who assumed added responsibilities conferred upon herself the title of "supervisor." Even when the description seems accurate, it's unethical to list any title not officially granted.
- **Puffed-up accomplishments.** Some job seekers inflate their employment experience or achievements. One clerk, eager to make her photocopying duties sound more important, said that she *assisted the vice president in communicating and distributing employee directives.* An Ivy League graduate who spent the better part of six months watching rented videos on his VCR described the activity as *Independent Film Study.* The latter statement may have helped win an interview, but it lost him the job.[12] In addition to avoiding puffery, guard against taking sole credit for achievements that required many people. When recruiters suspect dubious claims on résumés, they nail applicants with specific—and often embarrassing—questions during their interviews.[13]
- **Altered employment dates.** Some candidates extend the dates of employment to hide unimpressive jobs or to cover up periods of unemployment and illness. Let's say that several years ago Cindy was unemployed for fourteen months between working for Company A and being hired by Company B. To make her employment history look better, she adds seven months to her tenure with Company A and seven months to Company B. Now her employment history has no gaps, but her résumé is dishonest and represents a potential booby trap for her.

The employment process can easily lure you into ethical traps, such as those described in Chapter 3. Beware of these specific temptations:

- **The relative-filth trap:** "A little fudging on my GPA is nothing compared with the degrees that some people buy in degree mills."
- **The rationalization trap:** "I deserve to call myself 'manager' because that's what I really did."
- **The self-deception trap:** "Giving myself a certificate from the institute is OK because I really intended to finish the program, but I got sick."

Falling into these ethical traps risks your entire employment future. If your honest qualifications aren't good enough to get you the job you want, start working now to improve them.

Career Track Application

As a class, discuss the ethics of writing résumés. What's the difference between honest self-marketing and deception? What are some examples from your experience? Where could college students go wrong in preparing their résumés? Is a new employee "home free" if an inflated résumé is not detected in the hiring process? Are job candidates obligated to describe every previous job on a résumé? How can candidates improve an unimpressive résumé without resorting to "puffing it up"?

FIGURE 16.7 ● Chronological Résumé

Although Jeffrey had little paid work experience off campus, his résumé looks impressive because of his relevant summer, campus, and extern experiences. He describes specific achievements related to finance, his career goal.

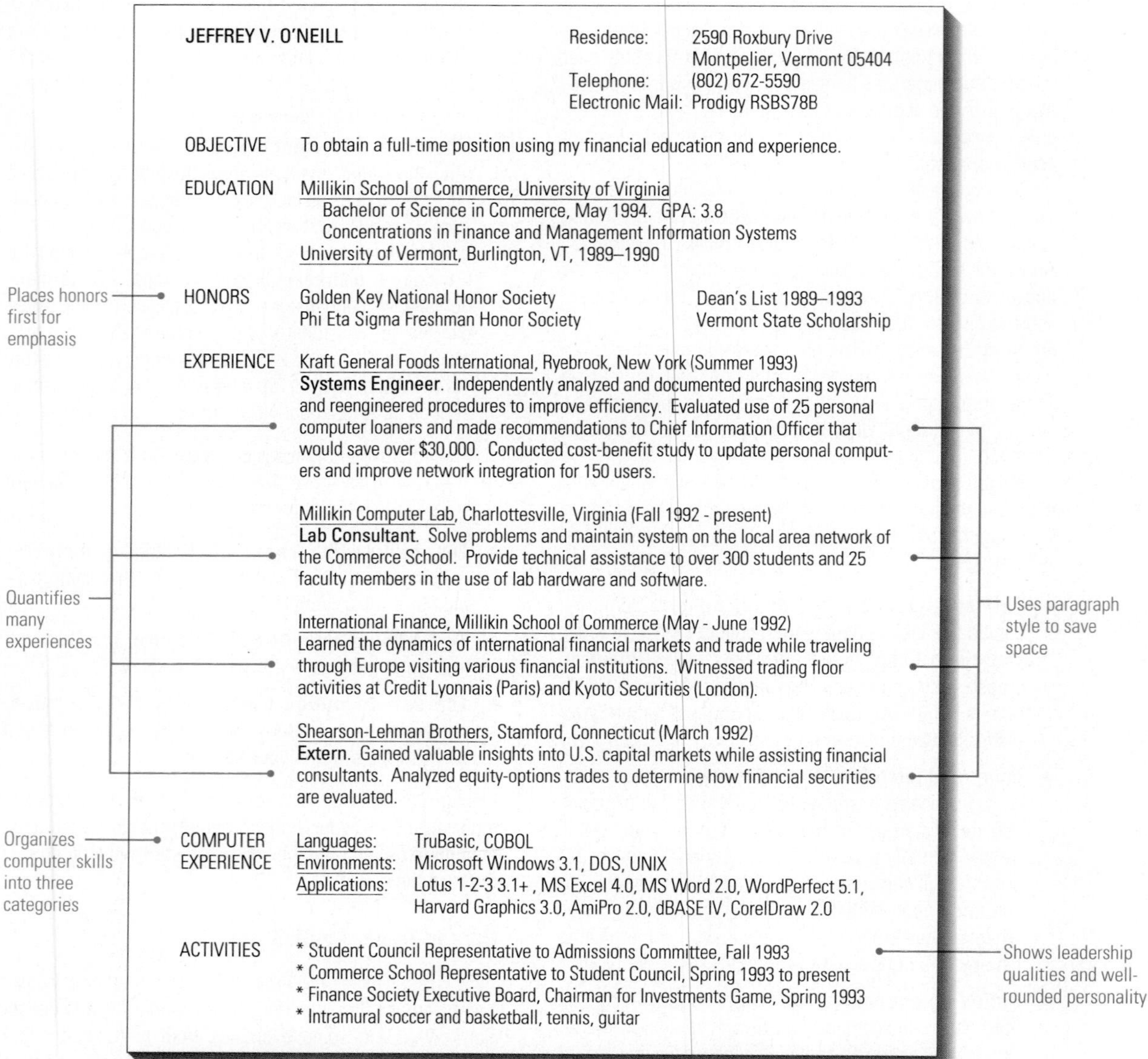

JEFFREY V. O'NEILL

Residence: 2590 Roxbury Drive
Montpelier, Vermont 05404
Telephone: (802) 672-5590
Electronic Mail: Prodigy RSBS78B

OBJECTIVE — To obtain a full-time position using my financial education and experience.

EDUCATION — Millikin School of Commerce, University of Virginia
Bachelor of Science in Commerce, May 1994. GPA: 3.8
Concentrations in Finance and Management Information Systems
University of Vermont, Burlington, VT, 1989–1990

HONORS — Golden Key National Honor Society; Phi Eta Sigma Freshman Honor Society; Dean's List 1989–1993; Vermont State Scholarship

EXPERIENCE — Kraft General Foods International, Ryebrook, New York (Summer 1993)
Systems Engineer. Independently analyzed and documented purchasing system and reengineered procedures to improve efficiency. Evaluated use of 25 personal computer loaners and made recommendations to Chief Information Officer that would save over $30,000. Conducted cost-benefit study to update personal computers and improve network integration for 150 users.

Millikin Computer Lab, Charlottesville, Virginia (Fall 1992 - present)
Lab Consultant. Solve problems and maintain system on the local area network of the Commerce School. Provide technical assistance to over 300 students and 25 faculty members in the use of lab hardware and software.

International Finance, Millikin School of Commerce (May - June 1992)
Learned the dynamics of international financial markets and trade while traveling through Europe visiting various financial institutions. Witnessed trading floor activities at Credit Lyonnais (Paris) and Kyoto Securities (London).

Shearson-Lehman Brothers, Stamford, Connecticut (March 1992)
Extern. Gained valuable insights into U.S. capital markets while assisting financial consultants. Analyzed equity-options trades to determine how financial securities are evaluated.

COMPUTER EXPERIENCE —
Languages: TruBasic, COBOL
Environments: Microsoft Windows 3.1, DOS, UNIX
Applications: Lotus 1-2-3 3.1+ , MS Excel 4.0, MS Word 2.0, WordPerfect 5.1, Harvard Graphics 3.0, AmiPro 2.0, dBASE IV, CorelDraw 2.0

ACTIVITIES —
* Student Council Representative to Admissions Committee, Fall 1993
* Commerce School Representative to Student Council, Spring 1993 to present
* Finance Society Executive Board, Chairman for Investments Game, Spring 1993
* Intramural soccer and basketball, tennis, guitar

Places honors first for emphasis
Quantifies many experiences
Organizes computer skills into three categories
Uses paragraph style to save space
Shows leadership qualities and well-rounded personality

the personal pronoun *I*. The abbreviated, objective style of a résumé precludes the use of personal pronouns. Use white, off-white, or buff-colored heavy bond paper (24-pound) and a first-rate printer.

After revising, proofread, proofread, and proofread again: for spelling and mechanics, for content, and for format. Then, have a knowledgeable friend or relative proofread it again. This is one document that must be perfect.

FIGURE 16.8 ● Combination Résumé

Rick's résumé responds to an advertisement specifying skills for a staff accountant. He uses the combination format to allow him to highlight the skills his education and limited experience have provided. To make the résumé look professional, he uses the italics, bold, and scalable font features of his word processing program.

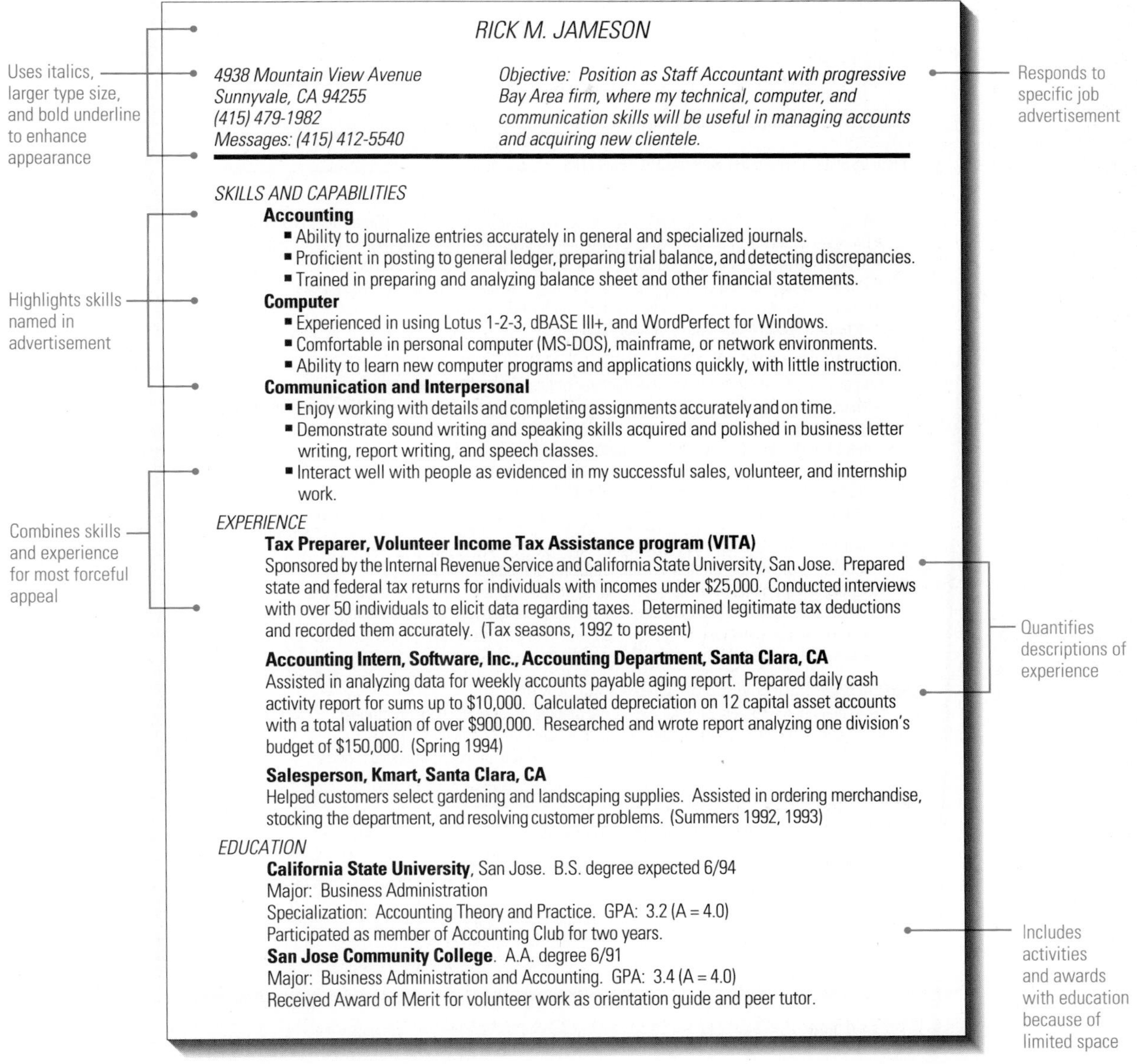

RICK M. JAMESON

4938 Mountain View Avenue
Sunnyvale, CA 94255
(415) 479-1982
Messages: (415) 412-5540

Objective: Position as Staff Accountant with progressive Bay Area firm, where my technical, computer, and communication skills will be useful in managing accounts and acquiring new clientele.

SKILLS AND CAPABILITIES

Accounting

- Ability to journalize entries accurately in general and specialized journals.
- Proficient in posting to general ledger, preparing trial balance, and detecting discrepancies.
- Trained in preparing and analyzing balance sheet and other financial statements.

Computer

- Experienced in using Lotus 1-2-3, dBASE III+, and WordPerfect for Windows.
- Comfortable in personal computer (MS-DOS), mainframe, or network environments.
- Ability to learn new computer programs and applications quickly, with little instruction.

Communication and Interpersonal

- Enjoy working with details and completing assignments accurately and on time.
- Demonstrate sound writing and speaking skills acquired and polished in business letter writing, report writing, and speech classes.
- Interact well with people as evidenced in my successful sales, volunteer, and internship work.

EXPERIENCE

Tax Preparer, Volunteer Income Tax Assistance program (VITA)
Sponsored by the Internal Revenue Service and California State University, San Jose. Prepared state and federal tax returns for individuals with incomes under $25,000. Conducted interviews with over 50 individuals to elicit data regarding taxes. Determined legitimate tax deductions and recorded them accurately. (Tax seasons, 1992 to present)

Accounting Intern, Software, Inc., Accounting Department, Santa Clara, CA
Assisted in analyzing data for weekly accounts payable aging report. Prepared daily cash activity report for sums up to $10,000. Calculated depreciation on 12 capital asset accounts with a total valuation of over $900,000. Researched and wrote report analyzing one division's budget of $150,000. (Spring 1994)

Salesperson, Kmart, Santa Clara, CA
Helped customers select gardening and landscaping supplies. Assisted in ordering merchandise, stocking the department, and resolving customer problems. (Summers 1992, 1993)

EDUCATION

California State University, San Jose. B.S. degree expected 6/94
Major: Business Administration
Specialization: Accounting Theory and Practice. GPA: 3.2 (A = 4.0)
Participated as member of Accounting Club for two years.
San Jose Community College. A.A. degree 6/91
Major: Business Administration and Accounting. GPA: 3.4 (A = 4.0)
Received Award of Merit for volunteer work as orientation guide and peer tutor.

Uses italics, larger type size, and bold underline to enhance appearance
Highlights skills named in advertisement
Combines skills and experience for most forceful appeal
Responds to specific job advertisement
Quantifies descriptions of experience
Includes activities and awards with education because of limited space

Finally, be sure to write your résumé yourself because no one knows you as well as you. Don't delegate the task to a résumé-writing service. Such services tend to produce eye-catching, elaborate documents with lofty language, fancy borders, and fuzzy thinking. Here's an example: "Seeking a position which will utilize academic achievements and hands-on experience while providing for career-development opportunities."[14] Save your money and buy a good interview suit instead.

FIGURE 16.9 ● Chronologial Résumé

Because Rachel has many years of experience and seeks high-level employment, she focuses on her experience. Notice how she includes specific achievements and quantifies them whenever possible.

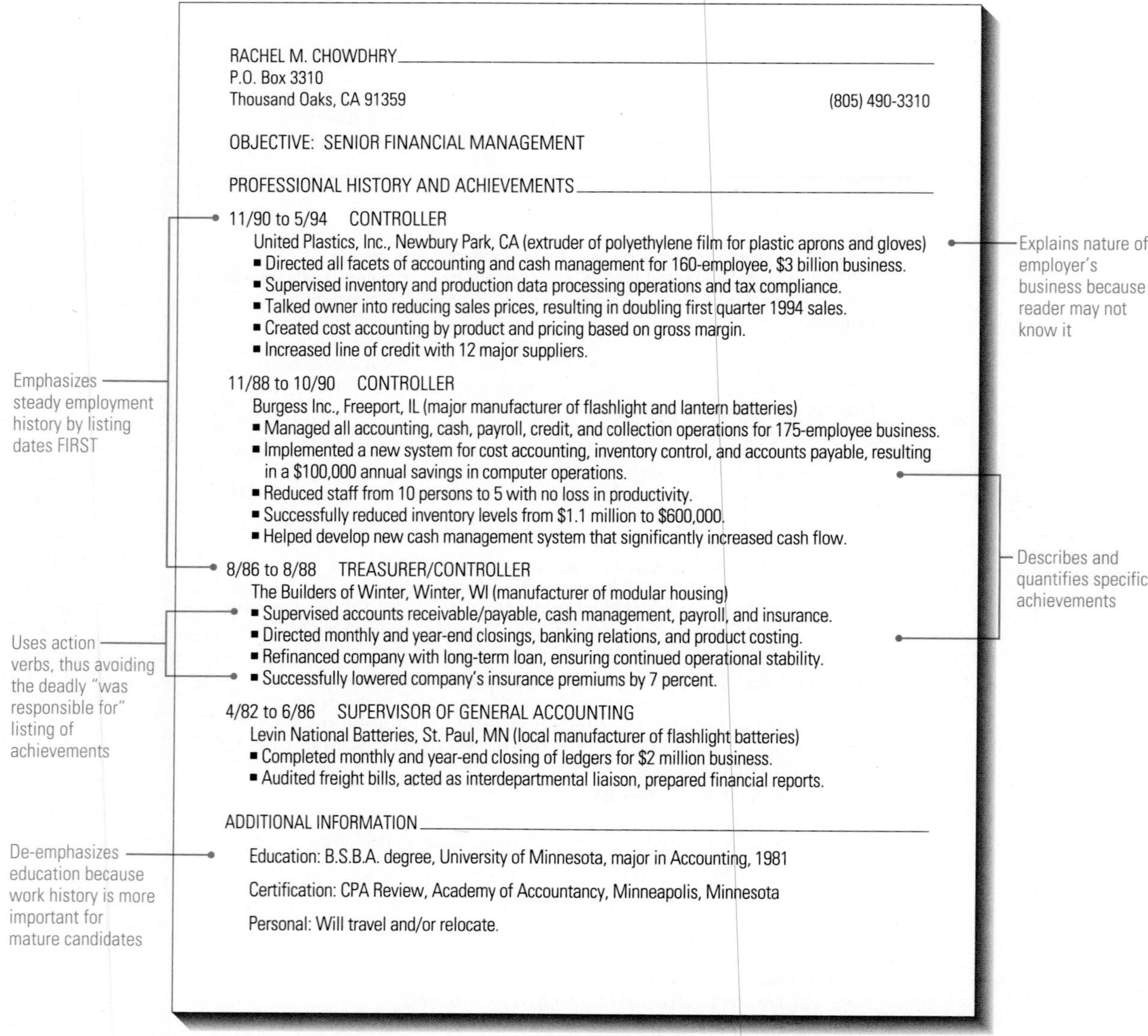
RACHEL M. CHOWDHRY
P.O. Box 3310
Thousand Oaks, CA 91359
(805) 490-3310

OBJECTIVE: SENIOR FINANCIAL MANAGEMENT

PROFESSIONAL HISTORY AND ACHIEVEMENTS

11/90 to 5/94 CONTROLLER
United Plastics, Inc., Newbury Park, CA (extruder of polyethylene film for plastic aprons and gloves)
- Directed all facets of accounting and cash management for 160-employee, $3 billion business.
- Supervised inventory and production data processing operations and tax compliance.
- Talked owner into reducing sales prices, resulting in doubling first quarter 1994 sales.
- Created cost accounting by product and pricing based on gross margin.
- Increased line of credit with 12 major suppliers.

11/88 to 10/90 CONTROLLER
Burgess Inc., Freeport, IL (major manufacturer of flashlight and lantern batteries)
- Managed all accounting, cash, payroll, credit, and collection operations for 175-employee business.
- Implemented a new system for cost accounting, inventory control, and accounts payable, resulting in a $100,000 annual savings in computer operations.
- Reduced staff from 10 persons to 5 with no loss in productivity.
- Successfully reduced inventory levels from $1.1 million to $600,000.
- Helped develop new cash management system that significantly increased cash flow.

8/86 to 8/88 TREASURER/CONTROLLER
The Builders of Winter, Winter, WI (manufacturer of modular housing)
- Supervised accounts receivable/payable, cash management, payroll, and insurance.
- Directed monthly and year-end closings, banking relations, and product costing.
- Refinanced company with long-term loan, ensuring continued operational stability.
- Successfully lowered company's insurance premiums by 7 percent.

4/82 to 6/86 SUPERVISOR OF GENERAL ACCOUNTING
Levin National Batteries, St. Paul, MN (local manufacturer of flashlight batteries)
- Completed monthly and year-end closing of ledgers for $2 million business.
- Audited freight bills, acted as interdepartmental liaison, prepared financial reports.

ADDITIONAL INFORMATION

Education: B.S.B.A. degree, University of Minnesota, major in Accounting, 1981

Certification: CPA Review, Academy of Accountancy, Minneapolis, Minnesota

Personal: Will travel and/or relocate.

Emphasizes steady employment history by listing dates FIRST
Uses action verbs, thus avoiding the deadly "was responsible for" listing of achievements
De-emphasizes education because work history is more important for mature candidates
Explains nature of employer's business because reader may not know it
Describes and quantifies specific achievements

Nearly everyone writes a résumé by adapting a model, such as those in Figures 16.2 through 16.4 and 16.7 through 16.9. The chronological résumé for Rachel shown on this page is typical of candidates with considerable working experience. Although she describes four positions that span a 14-year period, she manages to fit her résumé on one page. However, two-page résumés are justified for people with long work histories.

As you prepare to write your current résumé, consult the following checklist to review the job search process and important résumé-writing techniques.

Checklist for Writing a Persuasive Résumé

Preparation

- ✔ **Research the job market.** Learn about available jobs, common qualifications, and potential employers. The best résumés are targeted for specific jobs with specific companies.
- ✔ **Analyze your strengths.** Determine what aspects of your education, experience, and personal characteristics will be assets to prospective employers.
- ✔ **Study models.** Look at other résumés for formatting and element placement ideas. Experiment with headings and styles to achieve an artistic, readable product.

Heading and Objective

- ✔ **Identify yourself.** List your name, address, and telephone number. Skip the word *résumé.*
- ✔ **Include a career objective for a targeted job.** If this résumé is intended for a specific job, include a statement tailored to it *(Objective: Cost accounting position in the petroleum industry).*

Education

- ✔ **Name your degree, date of graduation, and institution.** Emphasize your education if your experience is limited.
- ✔ **List your major and GPA.** Give information about your studies, but don't inventory all your courses.

Work Experience

- ✔ **Itemize your jobs.** Start with your most recent job. Give the employer's name and city, dates of employment (month, year), and most significant job title.
- ✔ **Describe your experience.** Use action verbs to summarize achievements and skills relevant to your targeted job.
- ✔ **Present nontechnical skills.** Give evidence of communication, management, and interpersonal talents. Employers want more than empty assurances; try to quantify your skills and accomplishments *(Collaborated with six-member task force in producing 20-page mission statement).*

Special Skills, Achievements, and Awards

- ✔ **Highlight computer skills.** Remember that nearly all employers seek employees who are proficient with word processing, databases, and spreadsheets.
- ✔ **Show that you are a well-rounded individual.** List awards, experiences, and extracurricular activities—particularly if they demonstrate leadership, teamwork, reliability, loyalty, industry, initiative, efficiency, and self-sufficiency.

Final Tips

- ✔ **Consider omitting references.** Have a list of references available for the interview, but don't include them or refer to them unless you have a specific reason to do so.

SPOTLIGHT ON COMMUNICATORS

Lee Morrison of Oklahoma City, Kathleen Korzan of North Haven, Connecticut, and Gary Hernandez of Bloomfield, New Jersey, all found jobs in Las Vegas through a computer. For a $49 fee, Skillsearch of Nashville will offer a computerized version of your résumé to corporate clients. Employers can search efficiently for people who meet their exact requirements. In this case the three new hires listed their résumés with Skillsearch to advance their careers. Some universities run similar job banks, so check with your campus placement office.

- ✔ **Look for ways to condense your data.** Omit all street addresses except your own. Consolidate your headings. Study models and experiment with formats to find the most readable and efficient groupings.
- ✔ **Double-check for parallel phrasing.** Be sure that all entries have balanced construction, such as similar verb forms *(Organized files, trained assistants, scheduled events).*
- ✔ **Project professionalism and quality.** Avoid personal pronouns and humor. Use 24-pound bond paper and a high-quality printer.
- ✔ **Proofread, proofread, proofread.** Make this document perfect by proofreading at least three times.

The Persuasive Letter of Application

Letters of application introduce résumés, relate writer strengths to reader benefits, and seek an interview.

To accompany your résumé, you'll need a persuasive letter of application (also called a *cover letter*). The letter of application has three purposes: (1) introducing the résumé, (2) highlighting your strengths in terms of benefits to the reader, and (3) gaining an interview. In many ways your letter of application is a sales letter; it sells your talents and tries to beat the competition. It will, accordingly, include many of the techniques you learned for sales presentations (Chapter 9).

Personnel professionals disagree on how long to make the letter of application. Many prefer short letters with no more than four paragraphs; instead of concentrating on the letter, these readers focus on the résumé. Others desire longer letters that supply more information, thus giving them a better opportunity to evaluate a candidate's qualifications. The latter personnel professionals argue that hiring and training new employees is expensive and time-consuming; therefore, they welcome extra data to guide them in making the best choice the first time. Follow your judgment whether to write a brief or a lengthier letter of application. If you feel, for example, that you need space to explain in more detail what you can do for a prospective employer, do so.

Regardless of its length, a letter of application should have three primary parts: (1) an opening that gains attention, (2) a body that builds interest and reduces resistance, and (3) a closing that motivates action.

Gaining Attention in the Opening

The opener in a letter of application gains attention by addressing the receiver by name.

The first step in gaining the interest of your reader is addressing that individual by name. Rather than sending your letter to the "Personnel Manager" or "Human Resources Department," make an effort to identify the name of the appropriate individual. Make it a rule to call the organization for the correct spelling and the complete address. This personal touch distinguishes your letter and demonstrates your serious interest.

How you open your letter of application depends largely on whether the application is solicited or unsolicited. If an employment position has been announced and applicants are being solicited, you can use a direct approach. If you do not know whether a position is open and you are prospecting for a job, use an indirect approach. Whether direct or indirect, the opening should attract the attention of the reader. Strive for openings that are more imaginative than *Please consider this letter an application for the position of . . .* or *I would like to apply for . . .*

Openings for solicited jobs. Here are some of the best techniques to open a letter of application for a job that has been announced:

Openers for solicited jobs refer to the source of the information, the job title, and qualifications for the position.

- **Refer to the name of an employee in the company.** Remember that employers always hope to hire known quantities rather than complete strangers:

  Mitchell Sims, a member of your Customer Service Department, told me that DataTech is seeking an experienced customer service representative. The attached summary of my qualifications demonstrates my preparation for this position.

  At the suggestion of Ms. Jennifer Larson of your Human Resources Department, I submit my qualifications for the position of personnel assistant.

- **Refer to the source of your information precisely.** If you are answering an advertisement, include the exact position advertised and the name and date of the publication. For large organizations it's also wise to mention the section of the newspaper where the ad appeared:

  Your advertisement in Section C-3 of the June 1 *Daily News* for a junior accountant greatly appeals to me. With my accounting training and computer experience, I believe I could serve DataTech well.

  The September 10 issue of the *Washington Post* reports that you are seeking a mature, organized, and reliable administrative assistant with excellent communication skills.

  Susan Butler, placement director at Sierra University, told me that DataTech has an opening for a technical writer with knowledge of desktop publishing techniques.

- **Refer to the job title and describe how your qualifications fit the requirements.** Personnel directors are looking for a match between an applicant's credentials and the job needs:

  Will an honors graduate with a degree in recreation and two years of part-time experience organizing social activities for a convalescent hospital qualify for your position of activity director?

  Because of my specialized training in computerized accounting at Nicholls State University, I feel confident that I have the qualifications you described in your advertisement for a cost accountant trainee.

Openings for unsolicited jobs. If you are unsure whether a position actually exists, you may wish to use a more persuasive opening. Since your goal is to convince this person to read on, try one of the following techniques:

Openers for unsolicited jobs show interest in and knowledge of the company, as well as spotlighting reader benefits.

- **Demonstrate interest in and knowledge of the reader's business.** Show the personnel director that you have done your research and that this organization is more than a mere name to you:

  Since Signa HealthNet, Inc., is organizing a new information management team for its recently established group insurance division, could you use the services of a well-trained business administration graduate who seeks to become a data processing professional?

- **Show how your special talents and background will benefit the company.** Personnel directors need to be convinced that you can do something for them:

  Could your rapidly expanding editorial division use the services of an editorial assistant who offers exceptional language skills, an honors degree from the University of Maine, and two years' experience in producing a campus literary publication?

FIGURE 16.10 ● Solicited Letter of Application

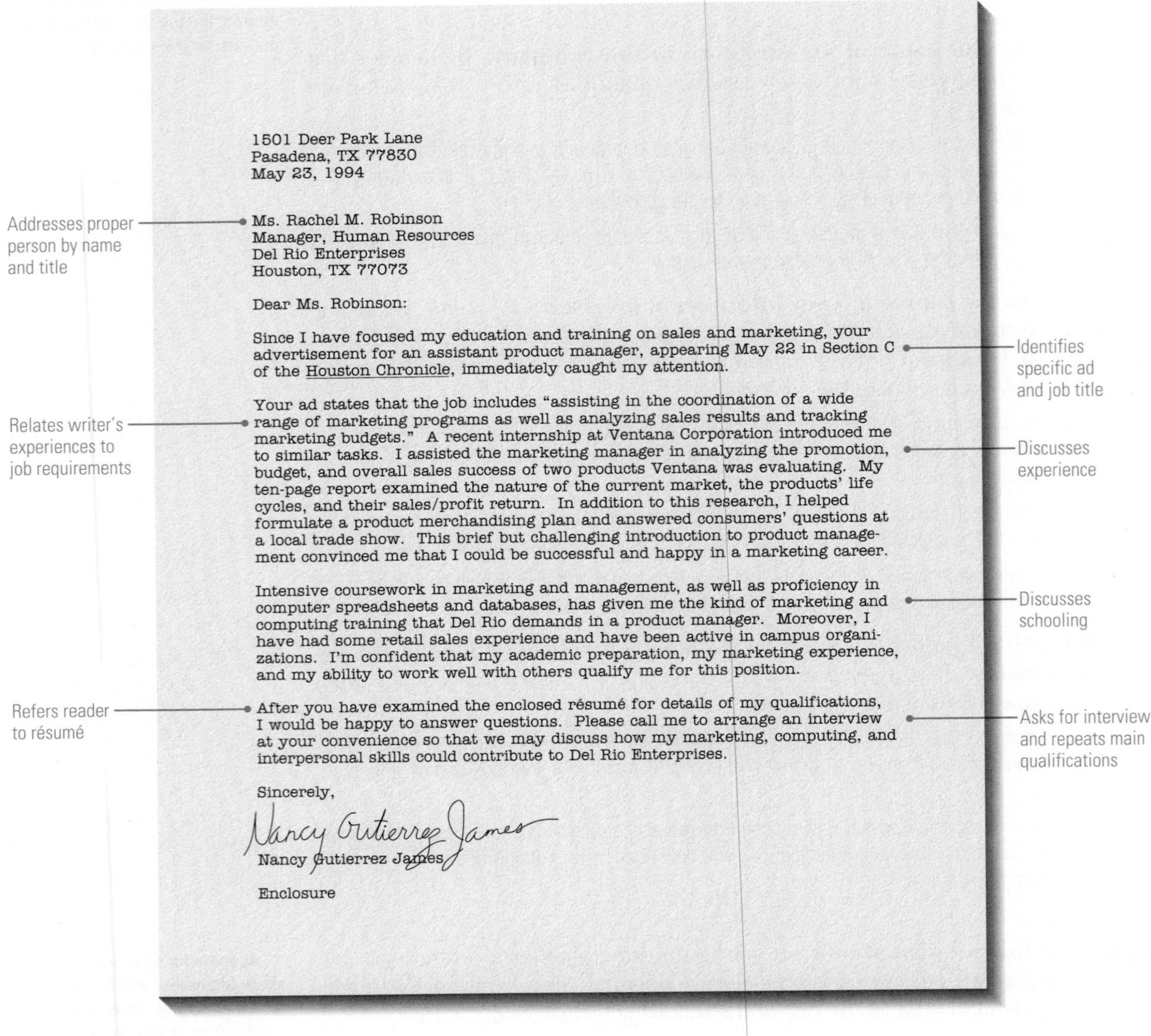

1501 Deer Park Lane
Pasadena, TX 77830
May 23, 1994

Ms. Rachel M. Robinson
Manager, Human Resources
Del Rio Enterprises
Houston, TX 77073

Dear Ms. Robinson:

Since I have focused my education and training on sales and marketing, your advertisement for an assistant product manager, appearing May 22 in Section C of the Houston Chronicle, immediately caught my attention.

Your ad states that the job includes "assisting in the coordination of a wide range of marketing programs as well as analyzing sales results and tracking marketing budgets." A recent internship at Ventana Corporation introduced me to similar tasks. I assisted the marketing manager in analyzing the promotion, budget, and overall sales success of two products Ventana was evaluating. My ten-page report examined the nature of the current market, the products' life cycles, and their sales/profit return. In addition to this research, I helped formulate a product merchandising plan and answered consumers' questions at a local trade show. This brief but challenging introduction to product management convinced me that I could be successful and happy in a marketing career.

Intensive coursework in marketing and management, as well as proficiency in computer spreadsheets and databases, has given me the kind of marketing and computing training that Del Rio demands in a product manager. Moreover, I have had some retail sales experience and have been active in campus organizations. I'm confident that my academic preparation, my marketing experience, and my ability to work well with others qualify me for this position.

After you have examined the enclosed résumé for details of my qualifications, I would be happy to answer questions. Please call me to arrange an interview at your convenience so that we may discuss how my marketing, computing, and interpersonal skills could contribute to Del Rio Enterprises.

Sincerely,

Nancy Gutierrez James

Nancy Gutierrez James

Enclosure

Addresses proper person by name and title
Relates writer's experiences to job requirements
Refers reader to résumé
Identifies specific ad and job title
Discusses experience
Discusses schooling
Asks for interview and repeats main qualifications

In applying for an advertised job, Nancy Gutierrez James wrote the solicited letter of application shown above. Notice that her opening identifies the position and the newspaper completely so that the reader knows exactly what advertisement Nancy means. More challenging are unsolicited letters of application, such as Donald Vinton's shown in Figure 16.11. Because he hopes to discover or create a job, his opening must grab the reader's attention immediately. To do that, he capitalizes on company information appearing in the newspaper. Notice, too, that Donald purposely kept his cover letter short and to the point because he anticipated that a busy executive would be unwilling to read a long, detailed letter.

FIGURE 16.11 ● **Unsolicited Letter of Application**

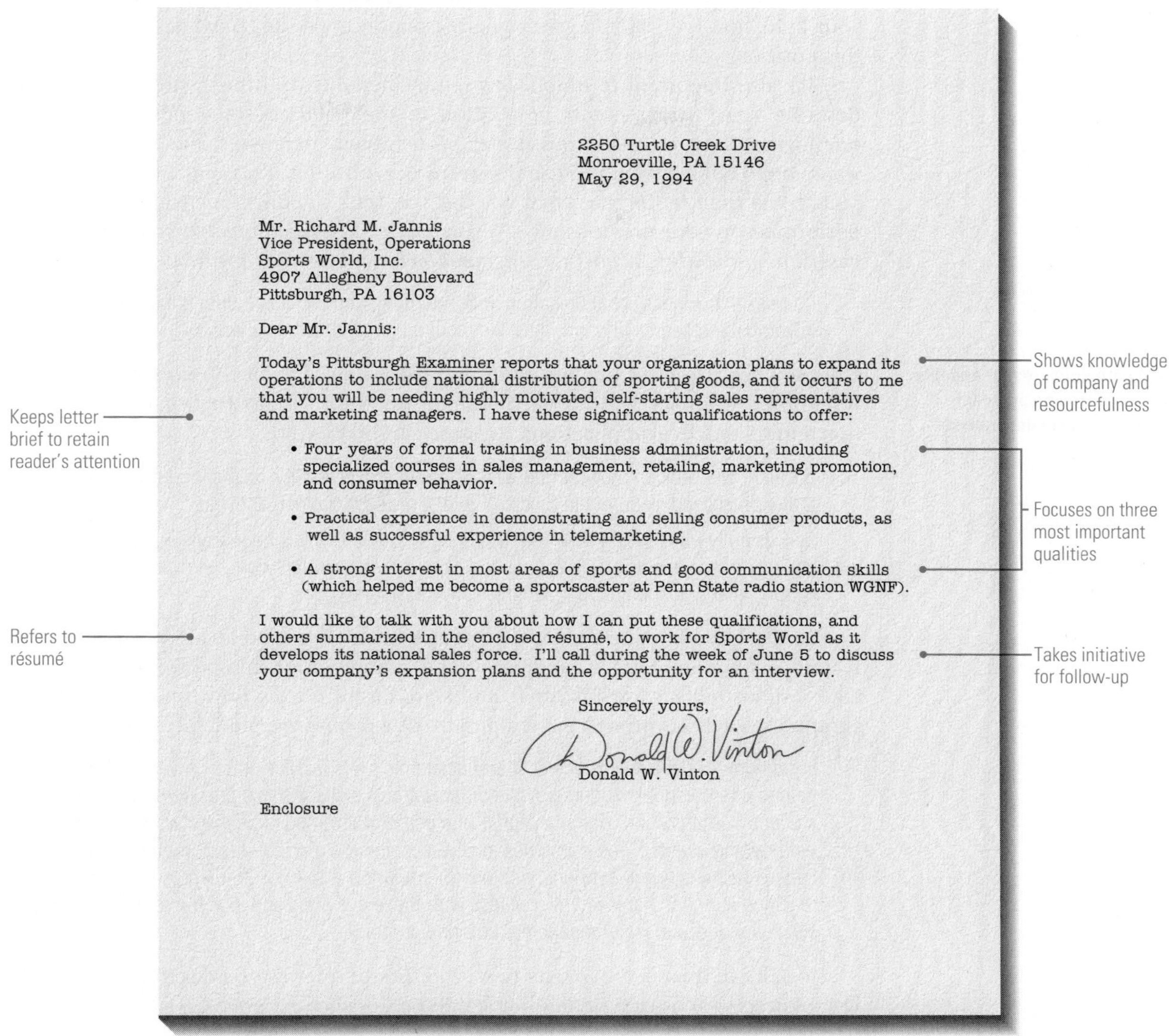
2250 Turtle Creek Drive
Monroeville, PA 15146
May 29, 1994

Mr. Richard M. Jannis
Vice President, Operations
Sports World, Inc.
4907 Allegheny Boulevard
Pittsburgh, PA 16103

Dear Mr. Jannis:

Today's Pittsburgh Examiner reports that your organization plans to expand its operations to include national distribution of sporting goods, and it occurs to me that you will be needing highly motivated, self-starting sales representatives and marketing managers. I have these significant qualifications to offer:

- Four years of formal training in business administration, including specialized courses in sales management, retailing, marketing promotion, and consumer behavior.
- Practical experience in demonstrating and selling consumer products, as well as successful experience in telemarketing.
- A strong interest in most areas of sports and good communication skills (which helped me become a sportscaster at Penn State radio station WGNF).

I would like to talk with you about how I can put these qualifications, and others summarized in the enclosed résumé, to work for Sports World as it develops its national sales force. I'll call during the week of June 5 to discuss your company's expansion plans and the opportunity for an interview.

Sincerely yours,

Donald W. Vinton

Enclosure

Keeps letter brief to retain reader's attention
Refers to résumé
Shows knowledge of company and resourcefulness
Focuses on three most important qualities
Takes initiative for follow-up

Donald's unsolicited letter, shown above, "prospects" for a job. Some job candidates feel that such letters may be even more productive than efforts to secure advertised jobs, since "prospecting" candidates face less competition.

Building Interest in the Body

● **The body of a letter of application should build interest, reduce resistance, and discuss relevant personal traits.**

Once you have captured the attention of the reader, you can use the body of the letter to build interest and reduce resistance. Keep in mind that your résumé emphasizes what you have *done;* your application letter stresses what you *can do* for the employer.

Your first goal is to relate your remarks to a specific position. If you are responding to an advertisement, you'll want to explain how your preparation and experience fill the stated requirements. If you are prospecting for a job, you may not know the exact requirements. Your employment research and knowledge of your field, however, should give you a reasonably good idea of what is expected for this position.

It's also important to emphasize reader benefits. In other words, you should describe your strong points in relation to the needs of the employer. In one employment survey many personnel professionals expressed the same view: "I want you to tell me what you can do for my organization. This is much more important to me than telling me what courses you took in college or what 'duties' you performed on your previous jobs."[15] Instead of *I have completed courses in business communication, report writing, and technical writing,* try this:

> Courses in business communication, report writing, and technical writing have helped me develop the research and writing skills required of your technical writers.

Spotlighting reader benefits means matching personal strengths to employer needs.

Choose your strongest qualifications and show how they fit the targeted job. And remember, students with little experience are better off spotlighting their education and its practical applications, as these candidates did:

> Because you seek an architect's apprentice with proven ability, I submit a drawing of mine that won second place in the Sinclair College drafting contest last year.

> Successfully transcribing over 100 letters and memos in my college transcription class gave me experience in converting the spoken word into the written word, an exacting communication skill demanded of your administrative assistants.

In the body of your letter, you'll also want to discuss relevant personal traits. Employers are looking for candidates who, among other things, are team players, take responsibility, show initiative, and learn easily. Notice how the following paragraph uses action verbs to paint a picture of a promising candidate:

> In addition to developing technical and academic skills at Mid-State University, I have gained interpersonal, leadership, and organizational skills. As vice president of the business students' organization, Gamma Alpha, I helped organize and supervise two successful fund-raising events. These activities involved conceptualizing the tasks, motivating others to help, scheduling work sessions, and coordinating the efforts of 35 diverse students in reaching our goal. I enjoyed my success with these activities and look forward to applying such experience in your management trainee program.

Finally, in this section or the next, you should refer the reader to your résumé. Do so directly or as part of another statement, as shown here:

> Please refer to the attached résumé for additional information regarding my education, experience, and references.

> As you will notice from my résumé, I will graduate in June with a bachelor's degree in business administration.

Motivating Action in the Closing

The closing of a letter of application should include a request for an interview.

After presenting your case, you should conclude with a spur to action. This is where you ask for an interview. If you live in a distant city, you may request an employment application or an opportunity to be interviewed by the organization's nearest representative. However, never ask for the job. To do so would be presumptuous and naive. In requesting an interview, suggest reader benefits or review your strongest points. Sound sincere and appreciative. Remember to make it easy for the reader to agree by supplying your telephone number and best times to call you. And keep in mind that some personnel directors prefer that you take the initiative to call them. Here are possible endings:

> I hope this brief description of my qualifications and the additional information on my résumé indicate to you my genuine desire to put my skills in accounting to work for you. Please call me at (405) 488-2291 before 10 a.m. or after 3 p.m. to arrange an interview.
>
> To add to your staff an industrious, well-trained word processing specialist with proven communication skills, call me at (350) 492-1433 to arrange an interview. I can meet with you at any time convenient to your schedule.
>
> Next week, after you have examined the attached résumé, I will call you to discuss the possibility of arranging an interview.

Final Tips

As you revise your letter of application, notice how many sentences begin with *I*. Although it's impossible to talk about yourself without using *I*, you can reduce "I" domination with this writing technique. Make activities and outcomes, and not yourself, the subjects of sentences. For example, rather than *I took classes in word processing and desktop publishing,* say *Classes in word processing and desktop publishing prepared me to . . .* Instead of *I enjoyed helping customers,* say *Helping customers was a real pleasure.*

A letter of application should look professional and suggest quality.

Like the résumé your letter of application must look professional and suggest quality. This means using a traditional letter style, such as block or modified block. Also, be sure to print it on the same bond paper as your résumé. And, as with your résumé, proofread it several times yourself; then, have a friend read it for content and mechanics. The following checklist provides a quick summary of suggestions to review when you compose and proofread your cover letter.

Checklist for Writing a Persuasive Letter of Application

Opening

- ✔ **Use the receiver's name.** Whenever possible, address the proper individual by name.
- ✔ **Identify your information source, if appropriate.** In responding to an advertisement, specify the position advertised as well as the date and publication name. If someone referred you, name that person.
- ✔ **Gain the reader's attention.** Use one of these techniques: (1) tell how your qualifications fit the job specifications, (2) show knowledge of the reader's business, (3) describe how your special talents will be assets to the company, or (4) use an original and relevant expression.

Body

- ✔ **Describe what you can do for the reader.** Demonstrate how your background and training fill the job requirements.
- ✔ **Highlight your strengths.** Summarize your principal assets from education, experience, and special skills. Avoid repeating specific data from your résumé.

✔ **Refer to your résumé.** In this section or the closing, direct the reader to the attached résumé. Do so directly or incidentally as part of another statement.

Closing

✔ **Ask for an interview.** Also consider reviewing your strongest points or suggesting how your assets will benefit the company.

✔ **Make it easy to respond.** Tell when you can be reached during office hours or announce when you will call the reader. Note that some personnel officers prefer that you call them.

Follow-up Letters and Other Employment Documents

Although the résumé and letter of application are your major tasks here, other important letters and documents are often required during the employment process. You may need to make requests, write follow-up letters, or fill out employment applications. Because each of these tasks reveals something about you and your communication skills, you'll want to put your best foot forward. These documents often subtly influence company officials to extend an interview or offer a job.

Reference Request

To get good letters of recommendation, find willing people and provide ample data about yourself.

Most employers expect job candidates at some point to submit names of individuals who are willing to discuss the candidates' qualifications. Before you list anyone as a reference, however, be sure to ask permission. Try to do this in person. Ask an instructor, for example, if he or she would be willing and has the time to act as your recommender. If you detect any sign of reluctance, don't force the issue. Your goal is to find willing individuals who think well of you.

What your recommenders need most is information about you. What should they stress to prospective employers? Let's say you're applying for a specific job that requires a letter of recommendation. Professor Smith has already agreed to be a reference for you. To get the best letter of recommendation from Professor Smith, help her out. Write a letter telling her about the position, its requirements, and the recommendation deadline. Include a copy of your résumé. You might remind her of a positive experience with you *(You said my report was well organized)* that she could use in the recommendation. Remember that recommenders need evidence to support generalizations. Give them appropriate ammunition, as the student has done in the following request:

Dear Professor Smith:

Identify the target position and company. Tell immediately why you are writing.

Recently I applied for the position of administrative assistant in the Human Resources Department of Host International. Because you kindly agreed to help me, I am now asking you to write a letter of recommendation to Host.

Specify the job requirements so that the recommender knows what to stress in the letter. Also, supply data to jog the memory of the writer.

The position calls for good organizational, interpersonal, and writing skills, as well as computer experience. To help you review my skills and training, I enclose my résumé. As you may recall, I earned an A in your business communication class; and you commended my long report for its clarity and organization.

Provide a stamped, addressed envelope.

Please send your letter before July 1 in the enclosed stamped, addressed envelope. I'm grateful for your support, and I promise to let you know the results of my job search.

Application Request Letter

Some organizations consider candidates only when they submit a completed application form. To secure a form, write a routine letter of request. But provide enough information about yourself, as shown in the following example, to assure the reader that you are a serious applicant:

> Dear Mr. Adams:
>
> Please send me an application form for work in your Human Resources Department. In June I will be completing my studies in psychology and communications at Northwestern University in Evanston, Illinois. My program included courses in public relations, psychology, and communications.
>
> Please send this application by May 15 so that I may complete it before making a visit to your city in June. I'm looking forward to beginning a career in personnel management.

Because you expect a positive response, announce your request immediately.

Supply an end date, if it seems appropriate. End on a forward-looking note.

Application or Résumé Follow-up Letter

If your letter or application generates no response within a reasonable time, you may decide to send a short follow-up letter like the one below. Doing so (1) jogs the memory of the personnel officer, (2) demonstrates your serious interest, and (3) allows you to emphasize your qualifications or to add new information.

> Dear Ms. Lopez:
>
> Please be assured that I am still interested in becoming an administrative assistant with DataTech, Inc.
>
> Since I submitted an application in May, I have completed my schooling and have been employed as a summer replacement for office workers in several downtown offices. This experience has honed my word processing and communication skills. It has also introduced me to a wide range of office procedures.
>
> Please keep my application in your active file and let me know when I may put my formal training, technical skills, and practical experience to work for you.

Open by reminding the reader of your interest.

Substitute *letter* or *résumé* if appropriate. Use this opportunity to review your strengths or to add new qualifications.

Close by looking forward positively; avoid accusations that make the reader defensive.

Interview Follow-up Letter

After a job interview you should always send a brief letter of thanks. This courtesy sets you apart from other applicants (most of whom will not bother). Your letter also reminds the interviewer of your visit as well as suggesting your good manners and genuine enthusiasm for the job.

Follow-up letters are most effective if sent immediately after the interview.[16] In your letter refer to the date of the interview, the exact job title for which you were interviewed, and specific topics discussed. Avoid worn-out phrases, such as *Thank you for taking the time to interview me.* Be careful, too, about overusing *I*, especially to begin sentences. Most importantly, show that you really want the job and that you are qualified for it. Notice how the following letter conveys enthusiasm and confidence:

> Dear Ms. Cogan:
>
> Talking with you Thursday, May 23, about the graphic designer position was both informative and interesting.
>
> Thanks for describing the position in such detail and for introducing me to Ms. Thomas, the senior designer. Her current project designing the annual report in four colors on a Macintosh sounds fascinating as well as quite challenging.

Mention the interview date and specific position.

Show appreciation, good manners, and perseverance—traits that recruiters value.

Personalize your letter by mentioning topics discussed in the interview. Highlight a specific skill you have for the job.

Now that I've learned in greater detail the specific tasks of your graphic designers, I'm more than ever convinced that my computer and creative skills can make a genuine contribution to your graphic productions. My training in Macintosh design and layout ensures that I could be immediately productive on your staff.

Remind the reader of your interpersonal skills as well as your enthusiasm and eagerness for this job.

In addition to my technical skills, you will find me an enthusiastic and hard-working member of any team effort. I'm eager to join the graphics staff at your Santa Barbara headquarters, and I look forward to hearing from you soon.

Rejection Follow-up Letter

If you didn't get the job and you think it was perfect for you, don't give up. Employment consultant Patricia Windelspecht advises, "You should always respond to a rejection letter. . . . I've had four clients get jobs that way." In a rejection follow-up letter, it's okay to admit you're disappointed. Be sure to add, however, that you're still interested and will contact them again in a month in case a job opens up. Then follow through for a couple of months—but don't overdo it. "There's a fine line between being professional and persistent and being a pest," adds consultant Windelspecht.[17] Here's an example of an effective rejection follow-up letter:

Dear Mr. Crenshaw:

Subordinate your disappointment to your appreciation at being notified promptly and courteously.

Although I'm disappointed that someone else was selected for your accounting position, I appreciate your promptness and courtesy in notifying me.

Emphasize your continuing interest. Express confidence in meeting the job requirements.

Because I firmly believe that I have the technical and interpersonal skills needed to work in your fast-paced environment, I hope you will keep my résumé in your active file. My desire to become a productive member of your Transamerica staff remains strong.

Refer to specifics of your interview. If possible, tell how you are improving your skills.

I enjoyed our interview, and I especially appreciate the time you and Mr. Samson spent describing your company's expansion into international markets. To enhance my qualifications, I've enrolled in a course in International Accounting at CSU.

Take the initiative; tell when you will call for an update.

Should you have an opening for which I am qualified, you may reach me at (818) 719-3901. In the meantime, I will call you in a month to discuss employment possibilities.

Application Form

Some organizations require job candidates to fill out job application forms instead of submitting résumés. This practice permits them to gather and store standardized data about each applicant. Here are some tips for filling out such forms:

- Carry a card summarizing those vital statistics not included on your résumé. If you are asked to fill out an application form in an employer's office, you will need a handy reference to the following data: social security number, graduation dates, beginning and ending dates of all employment; salary history; full names, titles, and present work addresses of former supervisors; and full names, occupational titles, occupational addresses, and telephone numbers of persons who have agreed to serve as references.
- Look over all the questions before starting. Fill out the form neatly, printing if your handwriting is poor.
- Answer all questions. Write *Not applicable* if appropriate.
- Be prepared for a salary question. Unless you know what comparable employees are earning in the company, the best strategy is to suggest a salary range or to write in *Negotiable* or *Open*.
- Ask if you may submit your résumé in addition to the application form.

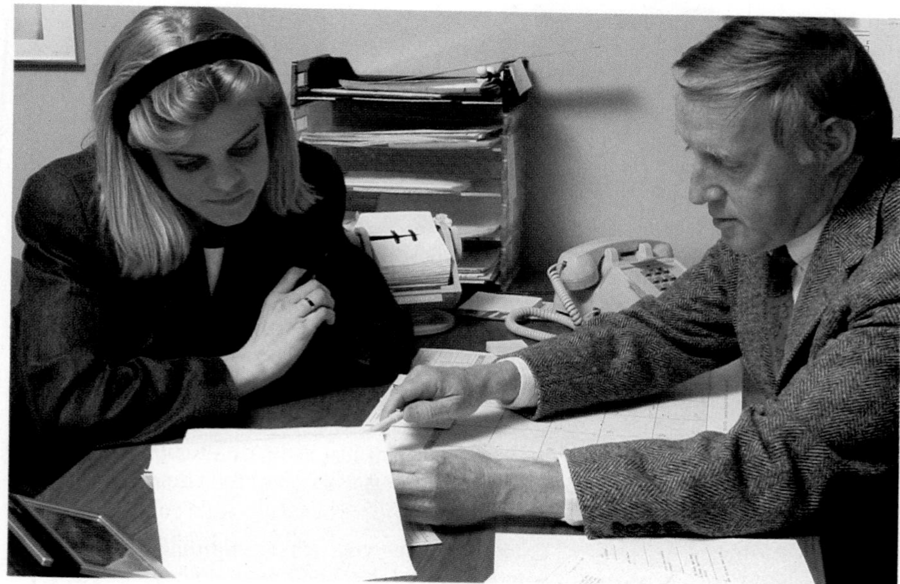

A job interview gives you a chance to explain your résumé and sell your technical expertise as well as your communication and interpersonal skills. But the interview also allows the recruiter to promote his company and explain the duties of the position. Be prepared to ask meaningful questions.

Interviewing for Employment

Job interviews, for most of us, are intimidating; no one enjoys being judged and, possibly, rejected. You can overcome your fear of the interview process by knowing how it works and how to prepare for it.

Trained recruiters generally structure the interview in three separate activities: (1) establishing a cordial relationship, (2) eliciting information about the candidate, and (3) giving information about the job and company. During the interview its participants have opposing goals. The interviewer tries to uncover any negative information that would eliminate a candidate. The candidate, of course, tries to minimize faults and emphasize strengths to avoid being eliminated.

You can become a more skillful player in the interview game if you know what to do before, during, and after the interview.

Before the Interview

Prior to an interview, applicants should research the organization and plan answers to potential questions.

- **Research the organization.** Never enter an interview cold. Visit the library to search for information about the target company or its field, service, or product. Call the company to request annual reports, catalogs, or brochures. Ask about the organization and possibly the interviewer. Learn something about the company's size, number of employees, competitors, reputation, and strengths and weaknesses.
- **Learn about the position.** Obtain as much specific information as possible. What are the functions of an individual in this position? What is the typical salary range? What career paths are generally open to this individual? What did the last person in this position do right or wrong?
- **Plan to sell yourself.** Identify three to five of your major selling points regarding skills, training, personal characteristics, and specialized experience. Memorize them; then in the interview be certain to find a place to insert them.
- **Prepare answers to possible questions.** Imagine the kinds of questions you may be asked and work out sample answers. Although you can't anticipate

ANSWERING TEN FREQUENTLY ASKED INTERVIEW QUESTIONS

Interviewers want to learn about your job experiences and education so that they can evaluate who you are and predict how you might perform on the job. Study each of the following frequently asked interview questions and the strategies for answering them successfully.

- **Why do you want to work for us?** Questions like this illustrate the need for you to research an organization thoroughly before the interview. Do library research, ask friends, and read the company's advertisements and other printed materials to gather data. Describe your desire to work for them not only from your perspective but also from their point of view. What have you to offer them?
- **Why should we hire you?** Here is an opportunity for you to sell your strong points in relation to this specific position. Describe your skills, academic preparation, and relevant experience. If you have little experience, don't apologize—the interviewer has read your résumé. Emphasize strengths as demonstrated in your education, such as initiative and persistence in completing assignments, ability to learn quickly, self-sufficiency, and excellent attendance.
- **What can you tell me about yourself?** Use this chance to promote yourself. Stick to professional or business-related strengths; avoid personal or humorous references. Be ready with at least three success stories illustrating characteristics important to this job. Demonstrate responsibility you have been given; describe how you contributed as a team player.
- **What are your strongest (or weakest) personal qualities?** Stress your strengths, such as "I believe I am conscientious, reliable, tolerant, patient, and thorough." Add examples that illustrate these qualities: "My supervisor said that my research was exceptionally thorough." If pressed for a weakness, give a strength disguised as a weakness: "Perhaps my greatest fault is being too painstaking with details." Or, "I am impatient when tasks are not completed on time." Don't admit weaknesses, not even to sound human. You'll be hired for your strengths, not your weaknesses.
- **What do you expect to be doing ten years from now?** Formulate a realistic plan with respect to your present age and situation. The important thing is to be prepared for this question.
- **Do you prefer working with others or by yourself?** This question can be tricky. Provide a middle-of-the-road answer that not only suggests your interpersonal qualities but also reflects an ability to make independent decisions and work without supervision.
- **Have you ever changed your major during your education? Why?** Another tricky question. Don't admit weaknesses or failures. In explaining changes, suggest career potential and new aspirations awakened by your expanding education, experience, or maturity.
- **What have been your most rewarding or disappointing work (or school) experiences?** If possible, concentrate on positive experiences such as technical and interpersonal skills you acquired. Avoid dwelling on negative or unhappy topics. Never criticize former employers. If you worked for an ungrateful, penny-pinching slave driver in a dead-end position, say that you learned all you could from that job. Move the conversation to the prospective position and what attracts you to it.
- **Have you established any new goals lately?** Watch out here. If you reveal new goals, you may inadvertently admit deficiencies. Instead of "I've resolved to finally learn how to operate a computer," try "Although I'm familiar with basic computer applications, I'm now reading and studying more about computer applications in . . ."
- **What are your long- and short-term goals?** Suggest realistic goals that you have consciously worked out before the interview. Know what you want to do with your future. To admit to an interviewer that you're not sure what you want to do is a sign of immaturity, weakness, and indecision.

Career Track Application

In teams of two to four, role-play an employment interview. Take turns playing interviewer and interviewee. Each student should answer four to five questions. Imagine a company where you'd like to work and answer accordingly.

precise questions, you can expect to be asked about your education, skills, experience, and availability. The accompanying Career Skills box shows ten of the most common questions and suggests responses.

- **Prepare success stories.** Rehearse two or three incidents that you can relate about your accomplishments. These may focus on problems you have solved, promotions you have earned, or recognition or praise you have received.
- **Arrive early.** Get to the interview five or ten minutes early. If you are unfamiliar with the area where the interview is to be held, you might visit it before the scheduled day. Locate the building, parking facilities, and office. Time yourself.
- **Dress appropriately.** Heed the advice of one expert: "Dress and groom like the interviewer is likely to dress—but cleaner."[18] Don't overdo perfume, jewelry, or after-shave lotion. Avoid loud colors; strive for a coordinated, natural appearance. Favorite "power" colors for interviews are gray and dark blue. It's not a bad idea to check your appearance in a restroom before entering the office.

During the Interview

- **Establish the relationship.** Shake hands firmly. Don't be afraid to offer your hand first. Address the interviewer formally ("Hello, Mrs. Jones"). Allow the interviewer to put you at ease with small talk.
- **Act confident but natural.** Establish and maintain eye contact, but don't get into a staring contest. Sit up straight, facing the interviewer. Don't cross your arms and legs at the same time (review body language cues in Chapter 2). Don't manipulate objects, like a pencil or keys, during the interview. Try to remain natural and at ease.
- **Don't criticize.** Avoid making negative comments about previous employers, instructors, or others. Such criticism may be taken to indicate a negative personality. Employers are not eager to hire complainers. Moreover, such criticism may suggest that you would do the same to this organization.

During an interview, applicants should act confident, focus on their strengths, and sell themselves.

- **Stay focused on your strengths.** If the interviewer asks a question that does not help you promote your strongest qualifications, answer briefly. Alternatively, try to turn your response into a positive selling point, such as this: "I have not had extensive paid training in that area, but I have completed a 50-hour training program that provided hands-on experience using the latest technology and methods. My recent training taught me to be open to new ideas and showed me how I can continue learning on my own. I was commended for being a quick learner."
- **Find out about the job early.** Because your time will be short, try to learn all you can about the target job early in the interview. Ask about its responsibilities and the kinds of people who have done well in the position before. Knowing this information early will enable you to shape your responses to the job requirements.
- **Prepare for salary questions.** Remember that nearly all salaries are negotiable, depending on your qualifications. Knowing the typical salary range for the target position helps. The recruiter can tell you the salary ranges—but you will have to ask. If you've had little experience, you will probably be offered a salary somewhere between the low point and the midpoint in the range. With more experience you can negotiate for a higher figure. A word of caution,

though. One personnel manager warns that candidates who emphasize money are suspect because they may leave if offered a few thousand dollars more elsewhere.

- **Be ready for inappropriate questions.** If you are asked a question that you think is illegal, politely ask the interviewer how that question is related to this job. Ask the purpose of the question. Perhaps valid reasons exist that are not obvious.
- **Ask your own questions.** Often, the interviewer concludes an interview with "Do you have any questions about the position?" Inquire about career paths, orientation or training for new employees, or the company's promotion policies. Have a list of relevant questions prepared. If the interview has gone well, ask the recruiter about his or her career in the company.
- **Conclude positively.** Summarize your strongest qualifications, show your enthusiasm for obtaining this position, and thank the interviewer for a constructive interview. Be sure you understand the next step in the employment process.

After the Interview

- **Make notes on the interview.** While the events are fresh in your mind, jot down the key points—good and bad.
- **Write a thank-you letter.** Immediately write a letter thanking the interviewer for a pleasant and enlightening discussion. Be sure to spell his or her name correctly.

Summary of Learning Goals

1. **Evaluate your assets, career paths, and the job market in preparation for employment.** The employment process begins with an analysis of your likes and your qualifications. Learn about career opportunities through your school, want ads, part-time employment, internships, professional organizations, and interviews. Develop a personal network by asking for referrals from friends and relatives.
2. **Compare and contrast chronological, functional, and combination résumés.** Chronological résumés, listing work and education by dates, rank highest with recruiters. Functional résumés, highlighting skills instead of jobs, appeal to people changing careers or those having negative employment histories. Combination résumés, including a complete job history along with skill areas, are increasingly popular.
3. **Organize, format, and produce a persuasive résumé.** Target your résumé for a specific job. Study models to arrange most effectively your main heading, career objective (optional), education, work experience, capabilities, awards and activities, personal data, and references (optional). Use action verbs to show how your assets will help the target organization.
4. **Avoid pitfalls that lead to an unethical résumé.** Beware of inflating your education, grades, or honors. Avoid misrepresenting job titles, puffing up accomplishments, and altering employment dates.
5. **Write a persuasive letter of application to accompany your résumé.** Gain attention in the opening by mentioning the job or a person who referred

you. Build interest in the body by stressing what you can do for the targeted company. Refer to your résumé, request an interview, and motivate action in the closing.

6. **Write effective employment follow-up letters and other messages.** Follow up all your employment activities with appropriate messages. After submitting your résumé, after an interview—even after being rejected—follow up with letters that express your appreciation and continuing interest.
7. **Evaluate successful job interview strategies.** Learn about the job and the organization. Prepare answers to possible questions and be ready with success stories. Act confident and natural. Be prepared to ask or answer salary questions. Have a list of your own questions, summarize your key strengths, and stay focused on your strong points. Afterwards, send a thank-you letter.

Chapter Review

1. Before beginning an employment search, you should prepare by gathering information and insights in what three areas?

2. List five sources of career information.

3. How are most jobs likely to be found? Through classified ads? Employment agencies? Networking?

4. What is the goal of your résumé?

5. Describe a chronological résumé and discuss its advantages.

6. Describe a functional résumé and discuss its advantages.

7. What are the disadvantages of a functional résumé?

8. When does it make sense to include a career objective on your résumé?

9. On a chronological résumé what information should you include for the jobs you list?

10. In addition to technical skills, what traits and characteristics do employers seek?

11. Name graphics highlighting techniques that can improve the appearance and readability of a résumé.

12. What are the three purposes of a letter of application?

13. How can you make it easy for a personnel director to reach you?

14. Other than a letter of application, name five kinds of letters you might need to write in the employment process.

15. On a company job application form, how should you respond to questions regarding salary?

Discussion

1. What kinds of questions should you ask yourself to identify your employment interests?

2. How is a résumé different from a company employment application?

3. Some job candidates think that applying for unsolicited jobs can be more fruitful than applying for advertised openings. Discuss the advantages and disadvantages of letters that "prospect" for jobs.

4. How do the interviewer and interviewee play opposing roles during job interviews? What strategies should the interviewee prepare in advance?

5. Ethical Issue: Job candidate Karen accepts a position with Company A. One week later she receives a better offer from Company B. She wants very much to accept it. What should she do?

Activities

16.1 Identifying Your Employment Interests

In a memo addressed to your instructor, answer the questions in the section "Identifying Your Interests" at the beginning of the chapter. Draw a conclusion from your answers. What kind of career, company, position, and location seem to fit your self-analysis?

16.2 Evaluating Your Qualifications

Prepare four worksheets that inventory your qualifications in these areas: employment, education, capabilities and skills, and honors and activities. Use active verbs when appropriate.

a. *Employment.* Begin with your most recent job or internship. For each position list the following information: employer, job title, dates of employment, and three to five duties, activities, or accomplishments. Emphasize activities related to your job goal. Strive to quantify your achievements.

b. *Education.* List degrees, certificates, and training accomplishments. Include courses, seminars, or skills that are relevant to your job goal. Calculate your grade-point average in your major.

c. *Capabilities and skills.* List all capabilities and skills that recommend you for the job you seek. Use words like *skilled, competent, trained, experienced* and *ability to.* Also list five or more qualities or interpersonal skills necessary for a successful individual in your chosen field. Write action statements demonstrating that you possess some of these qualities. Empty assurances aren't good enough; try to show evidence *(Developed teamwork skills by working with a committee of eight to produce a . . .).*

d. *Awards, honors, and activities.* Explain any awards so that the reader will understand them. List campus, community, and professional activities that suggest you are a well-rounded individual or possess traits relevant to your target job.

16.3 Choosing a Career Path

Visit your college or local library. Photocopy a page from the *Dictionary of Occupational Titles* that describes a position for which you could apply in two to five years. Photocopy pages from the *Occupational Outlook Handbook* that describe employment in the area in which you are interested. If your instructor directs, attach these copies to the letter of application you will write in Problem 16.8.

16.4 Searching the Job Market

Clip a job advertisement from the classified section of a local or national newspaper. Select an ad describing the kind of employment you are seeking now or plan to seek when you graduate. Save this advertisement to attach to the résumé you will write in Problem 16.7.

16.5 Draft Document: Résumé

Analyze the following résumé. Discuss its strengths and weaknesses. Your instructor may ask you to revise sections of this résumé before showing you an improved version.

Deborah M. Duchane
2190 14th Street
Platteville, WI 53818
(608) 347-2290

EDUCATION
Western Wisconsin College, Fennimore, WI 53809.
Major: Office Technology. A.A. degree expected 5/94
Platteville High School, Platteville, WI 53818.
Graduation 6/67 Major: General studies.

EXPERIENCE
- Clerk-typist, USASAC, Boulder, Colorado (1975–1977)
- USASAC, Boulder, Colorado. Worked as Management Analyst Technician. 1977–1980. Duties: Assisted in development of manpower staffing standards, statistical data gathered by on-site surveys, and analyzed data for accuracy.
- Employed two peak seasons for Lands' End, Dodgeville, WI. Duties: Input phone orders on CRT. 1989 and 1990.
- Financial Aid Office, WWC, 1993–present. Duties: input data on computer, budget reconciliation, filing, letters and memos from oral dictation. Handle mail, telephone. Title: Office clerk.

CAPABILITIES
- Know PFS: Professional File, PFS: Professional Write, WordPerfect. 5.1, and Lotus 1-2-3.
- Can function in IBM MS/DOS environment or with mainframe terminals.
- Competent in typing, editing, and/or proofreading reports, tables, letters, memos, manuscripts, and business forms. Type: 60 wpm.
- Have completed courses in accounting, business math, and word processing.
- Possess sound written and oral communication skills.

AWARDS, ACTIVITIES
- WWC President's Award, 1993
- I served as officer (historian) for Business Professionals of America.
- Keep books and records for my family's registered dairy and beef business.

16.6 Draft Document: Letter of Application

Analyze each section of the following letter of application written by an accounting major about to graduate.

> Dear Human Resources Director:
>
> Please consider this letter as an application for the position of staff accountant that I saw advertised in the *Houston Post.* Although I have had no paid work experience in this field, accounting has been my major in college and I'm sure I could be an asset to your company.
>
> For four years I have studied accounting, and I am fully trained for full-charge bookkeeping as well as computer accounting. I have taken 36 units of college accounting and courses in business law, economics, statistics, finance, management, and marketing.
>
> In addition to my course work, during the tax season I have been a student volunteer for VITA. This is a project to help individuals in the community prepare their income tax returns, and I learned a lot from this experience. I have also received some experience in office work and working with figures when I was employed as an office assistant for Copy Quick, Inc.
>
> I am a competent and responsible person who gets along pretty well with others. I have been a member of some college and social organizations and have even held elective office.
>
> I feel that I have a strong foundation in accounting as a result of my course work and my experience. Along with my personal qualities and my desire to succeed, I hope that you will agree that I qualify for the position of staff accountant with your company.
>
> Sincerely,

Problems

16.7 Résumé

Using the data you developed in Activity 16.2, write your résumé. Aim it at a full-time job, part-time position, or internship. Attach a clipping if possible (from Activity 16.4). Use a word processor. Revise your résumé until it is perfect.

16.8 Letter of Application

Write a cover letter introducing your résumé. Again, use a word processor. Revise your cover letter until it is perfect.

16.9 Interview Follow-up Letter

Assume you were interviewed for the position you seek. Write a follow-up thank-you letter.

16.10 Reference Request

Assume that your favorite professor has agreed to recommend you. Write to the professor and request that he or she send a letter of recommendation to a company where you are applying for a job. Provide data about the job description and about yourself so that the professor can target its content.

16.11 Résumé Follow-up Letter

A month has passed since you sent your résumé and letter of application in response to a job advertisement. Write a follow-up letter that doesn't offend the reader or damage your chances of employment.

16.12 Application Request

Select a company for which you'd like to work. Write a letter requesting an employment application, which they require for all job seekers.

16.13 Rejection Follow-up Letter

Assume you didn't get the job. Although someone else was selected, you hope that other jobs may become available. Write a follow-up letter that keeps the door open.

Competent Language Usage Essentials: A Business Communicator's Guide

In the business world, people are often judged by the way they speak and write. Using the language competently can mean the difference between individual success and failure. Often a speaker sounds accomplished; but when that same individual puts ideas on paper, errors in language usage destroy his or her credibility. One student observed, "When I talk, I get by on my personality; but when I write, the flaws in my communication show through. That's why I'm in this class."

 What C.L.U.E. Is

This appendix provides a condensed guide to competency in language usage essentials (C.L.U.E.). Fifty guidelines review sentence structure, grammar, usage, punctuation, capitalization, and number style. These guidelines focus on the most frequently used—and abused—language elements. Presented from a business communicator's perspective, the guidelines also include realistic tips for application. And frequent checkpoint exercises enable you to try out your skills immediately. In addition to the 50 language guides in this appendix, you'll find a list of 150 frequently misspelled words plus a quick review of selected confusing words.

The concentrated materials in this guide will help novice business communicators focus on the major areas of language use. The guide is not meant to teach or review *all* the principles of English grammar and punctuation. It focuses on a limited number of language guidelines and troublesome words. Your objective should be mastery of these language principles and words, which represent a majority of the problems typically encountered by business writers.

For a more comprehensive treatment of grammar and punctuation correctness, consult a good reference book, such as Clark and Clark's *HOW: Handbook for Office Workers* or a business English textbook, such as Guffey's *Business English.*

How to Use C.L.U.E.

Your instructor may give you a language diagnostic test to help you assess your competency. After taking this test, read and work your way through the 50 guidelines. Concentrate on areas where you are weak. Memorize the spelling list and definitions for the confusing words.

Two kinds of exercises are available for your practice. (1) *Checkpoints*, located in this appendix, focus on a small group of language guidelines. Use them to test your comprehension as you complete each section. (2) *Review exercises*, located in Chapters 1 through 10, cover all guidelines, spelling words, and confusing words. Use the review exercises to reinforce your language skills at the same time you are learning about the processes and products of business communication. The student Study Guide includes additional C.L.U.E. review exercises. In marking your revisions, you may wish to use the standard proofreading marks shown in Chapter 5 (see page 127).

Guidelines: Competent Language Usage Essentials

Sentence Structure

GUIDE 1: Express ideas in complete sentences. You can recognize a complete sentence because it (a) includes a subject (a noun or pronoun that interacts with a verb), (b) includes a verb (a word expressing action or describing a condition), and (c) makes sense (comes to a closure). A complete sentence is an independent clause. One of the most serious errors a writer can make is punctuating a fragment as if it were a complete sentence. A fragment is a broken-off part of a sentence.

Fragment	**Improved**
Because 90 percent of all business transactions involve written correspondence. Good writing skills are critical.	Because 90 percent of all business transactions involve written correspondence, good writing skills are critical.
The personnel director requested a writing sample. Even though the candidate seemed to communicate well.	The personnel director requested a writing sample, even though the candidate seemed to communicate well.

Tip. Fragments often can be identified by the words that introduce them—words like *although, as, because, even, except, for example, if, instead of, since, so, such as, that, which,* and *when.* These words introduce dependent clauses. Make sure such clauses are always connected to independent clauses.

DEPENDENT CLAUSE: Since she became supervisor, | INDEPENDENT CLAUSE: she had to write more memos and reports.

Since she became supervisor, she had to write more memos and reports.

GUIDE 2: Avoid run-on (fused) sentences. A sentence with two independent clauses must be joined by a coordinating conjunction (*and, or, nor, but*) or by a semicolon (;). Without a conjunction or a semicolon, a run-on sentence results.

Run-on	Improved
Robin visited resorts of the rich and the famous he also dropped in on luxury spas.	Robin visited resorts of the rich and famous, and he also dropped in on luxury spas.
	Robin visited resorts of the rich and famous; he also dropped in on luxury spas.

GUIDE 3: Avoid comma-splice sentences. A comma splice results when a writer joins (splices together) two independent clauses—without using a coordinating conjunction (*and, or, nor, but*).

Comma Splice	Improved
Disney World operates in Orlando, EuroDisney serves Paris.	Disney World operates in Orlando; EuroDisney serves Paris.
	Disney World operates in Orlando, and EuroDisney serves Paris.
Visitors wanted a resort vacation, however they were disappointed.	Visitors wanted a resort vacation; however, they were disappointed.

Tip. In joining independent clauses, beware of using a comma and words like *consequently, furthermore, however, therefore, then, thus,* and so on. These conjunctive adverbs require semicolons.

✔ Checkpoint

Revise the following to rectify sentence fragments, comma splices, and run-ons.

1. When McDonald's tested pizza, Pizza Hut fought back. With aggressive ads ridiculing McPizza.

2. Aggressive ads can backfire, consequently, marketing directors consider them carefully.

3. Corporations study the legality of attack advertisements they also retaliate with counterattacks.

4. Although Pizza Hut is the country's No. 1 pizza chain. Domino's Pizza leads in deliveries.

5. About half of the 6,600 outlets make deliveries, the others concentrate on walk-in customers.

For all the Checkpoint sentences, compare your responses with the answers at the end of Appendix A (page 506).

Grammar

Verb Tense

GUIDE 4: Use present tense, past tense, and past participle verb forms correctly.

Present Tense	**Past Tense**	**Past Participle**
Today I ______	Yesterday I ______	I have ______
am	was	been
begin	began	begun
break	broke	broken
bring	brought	brought
choose	chose	chosen
come	came	come
do	did	done
give	gave	given
go	went	gone
know	knew	known
pay	paid	paid
see	saw	seen
steal	stole	stolen
take	took	taken
write	wrote	written

The package *came* yesterday, and they *knew* what to do with it.

If I *had seen* the shipper's bill, I *would have paid* it immediately.

I *know* the answer now; I wish I *had known* it yesterday.

Tip: Probably the most frequent mistake in tenses results from substituting the past participle form for the past tense. Notice that the past participle tense requires auxiliary verbs such as *has, had, have, would have,* and *could have.*

Faulty	**Correct**
When he *come* over last night, he *brung* pizza.	When he *came* over last night, he *brought* pizza.
If he *had came* earlier, we *could have saw* the video.	If he *had come* earlier, we *could have seen* the video.

Verb Mood

GUIDE 5: Use the subjunctive mood to express hypothetical (untrue) ideas. The most frequent use of the subjunctive mood involves the use of *was* instead of *were* in clauses introduced by *if* and *as though* or containing *wish.*

If I *were* (not *was*) you, I would take a business writing course.

Sometimes I wish I *were* (not *was*) the manager of this department.

He acts as though he *were* (not *was*) in charge of this department.

Tip. If the statement could possibly be true, use *was.*

If I *was* to blame, I accept the consequences.

✔ Checkpoint

Correct faults in verb tenses and mood.

6. If I was in your position, I would have wrote the manager a letter.

7. You could have wrote a better résumé if you have read the chapter first.

8. When Trevor seen the want ad, he immediately contacted the company.

9. I wish I was able to operate a computer so that I could have went to work there.

10. Because she had took many computer courses, Maria was able to chose a good job.

Verb Agreement

GUIDE 6: Make subjects agree with verbs despite intervening phrases and clauses. Become a detective in locating *true* subjects. Don't be deceived by prepositional phrases and parenthetic words that often disguise the true subject.

> Our study of annual budgets, five-year plans, and sales proposals *is* (not *are*) progressing on schedule. (The true subject is *study.*)
>
> The budgeted item, despite additions proposed yesterday, *remains* (not *remain*) as submitted. (The true subject is *item.*)
>
> A salesperson's evaluation of the prospects for a sale, together with plans for follow-up action, *is* (not *are*) what we need. (The true subject is *evaluation.*)

Tip. Subjects are nouns or pronouns that control verbs. To find subjects, cross out prepositional phrases beginning with words like *about, at, by, for, from, of,* and *to.* Subjects of verbs are not found in prepositional phrases. Also, don't be tricked by expressions introduced by *together with, in addition to,* and *along with.*

GUIDE 7: Subjects joined by *and* require plural verbs. Watch for true subjects joined by the conjunction *and.* They require plural verbs.

> The CEO and one of his assistants *have* (not *has*) ordered a limo.
>
> Kentucky Fried Chicken and Pizza Hut, although individual franchisees operate each unit, *are* (not *is*) owned by PepsiCo.
>
> Exercising in the gym and jogging every day *are* (not *is*) how he keeps fit.

GUIDE 8: Subjects joined by *or* or *nor* may require singular or plural verbs. The verb should agree with the closest subject.

> Either the software or the printer *is* (not *are*) causing the glitch. (The verb is controlled by closer subject, *printer.*)
>
> Neither St. Louis nor Chicago *has* (not *have*) a chance of winning. (The verb is controlled by *Chicago.*)

Tip. In joining singular and plural subjects with *or* or *nor,* place the plural subject closer to the verb. Then, the plural verb sounds natural. For example, *Either the manufacturer or the distributors are responsible.*

GUIDE 9: Use singular verbs for most indefinite pronouns. For example: *anyone, anybody, anything, each, either, every, everyone, everybody, everything, neither, nobody, nothing, someone, somebody,* and *something* all take singular verbs.

> Everyone in both offices *was* (not *were*) given a bonus.
>
> Each of the employees *is* (not *are*) being interviewed.

GUIDE 10: Use singular or plural verbs for collective nouns, depending on whether the members of the group are operating as a unit or individually. Words like *faculty, administration, class, crowd,* and *committee* are considered *col-*

lective nouns. If the members of the collective are acting as a unit, treat them as singular subjects. If they are acting individually, it's usually better to add the word *members* and use a plural verb.

Correct

The Finance Committee *is* working harmoniously. (*Committee* is singular because its action is unified.)

The Planning Committee *are* having difficulty agreeing. (*Committee* is plural because its members are acting individually.)

Improved

The Planning Committee members *are* having difficulty agreeing. (Add the word *members* if a plural meaning is intended.)

Tip. In America collective nouns are generally considered singular. In Britain these collective nouns are generally considered plural.

✔ Checkpoint

Correct the errors in subject-verb agreement.

11. A manager's time and energy has to be focused on important issues.

12. Promotion of women, despite managerial training programs and networking efforts, are disappointingly small.

13. We're not sure whether Mr. Murphy or Ms. Wagner are in charge of the program.

14. Each of the Fortune 500 companies are being sent a survey regarding women in management.

15. Our CEO, like other good executives, know how to be totally informed without being totally involved.

Pronoun Case

GUIDE 11: Learn the three cases of pronouns and how each is used. Pronouns are substitutes for nouns. Every business writer must know the following pronoun cases.

Nominative or Subjective Case	**Objective Case**	**Possessive Case**
Used for subjects of verbs and subject complements	Used for objects of prepositions and objects of verbs	Used to show possession
I	me	my, mine
we	us	our, ours
you	you	you, yours
he	him	his
she	her	her, hers
it	it	its
they	them	their, theirs
who, whoever	whom, whomever	whose

GUIDE 12: Use nominative case pronouns as subjects of verbs and as complements. Complements are words that follow linking verbs (such as *am, is, are, was, were, be, being,* and *been*) and rename the words to which they refer.

She and *I* (not *her* and *me*) prefer easy-riding mountain bikes. (Use nominative case pronouns as the subjects of the verb *prefer.*)

We think that *she* and *he* (not *her* and *him*) will win the race. (Use nominative case pronouns as the subjects of the verb *will win.*)

It must have been *she* (not *her*) who called last night. (Use a nominative case pronoun as a subject complement.)

Tip. If you feel awkward using nominative pronouns after linking verbs, rephrase the sentence to avoid the dilemma. Instead of *It is she who is the boss*, say *She is the boss.*

GUIDE 13: Use objective case pronouns as objects of prepositions and verbs.

Please order stationery for *her* and *me* (not *she* and *I*). (The pronouns *her* and *me* are objects of the preposition *for.*)

The CEO appointed *him* (not *he*) to the position. (The pronoun *him* is the object of the verb *appointed.*)

Tip. When a pronoun appears in combination with a noun or another pronoun, ignore the extra noun or pronoun and its conjunction. Then, the case of the pronoun becomes more obvious.

Jason asked Jennifer and *me* (not *I*) to lunch. (Ignore *Jennifer and.*)

The waiter didn't know whether to give the bill to Jason or *her* (not *she*). (Ignore *Jason or.*)

Tip. Be especially alert to the following prepositions: *except, between, but,* and *like.* Be sure to use objective pronouns as their objects.

Just between you and *me* (not *I*), their mineral water comes from the tap.

Computer grammar checkers work well for writers like Lee and *him* (not *he*).

GUIDE 14: Use possessive case pronouns to show ownership. Possessive pronouns (such as *hers, yours, whose, ours, theirs,* and *its*) require no apostrophes.

All reports except *yours* (not *your's*) have to be rewritten.

The printer and *its* (not *it's*) fonts produce exceptional copy.

Tip. Don't confuse possessive pronouns and contractions. Contractions are shortened forms of subject-verb phrases (such as *it's* for *it is, there's* for *there is, who's* for *who is,* and *they're* for *they are*).

✔ Checkpoint

Correct errors in pronoun case.

16. Although my friend and myself are interested in this computer, it's price seems high.

17. Letters addressed to he and I were delivered to you and Ann in error.

18. Just between you and I, the mail room and its procedures need improvement.

19. Several applications were lost; your's and her's were the only ones delivered.

20. It could have been her who sent the program update to you and I.

GUIDE 15: Use *self*-ending pronouns only when they refer to previously mentioned nouns or pronouns.

The president *himself* ate all the M & Ms.

Send the package to Marcus or *me* (not *myself*).

Tip. Trying to sound less egocentric, some radio and TV announcers incorrectly substitute *myself* when they should use *I*. For example, "Jerry and *myself* (should be *I*) are cohosting the telethon."

GUIDE 16: Use *who* or *whoever* for nominative case constructions and *whom* or *whomever* for objective case constructions. In determining the correct choice, it's helpful to substitute *he* for *who* or *whoever* and *him* for *whom* or *whomever*.

For *whom* was this software ordered? (The software was ordered for *him*.)

Who did you say called? (You did say *he* called?)

Give the supplies to *whoever* asked for them. (In this sentence the clause *whoever asked for them* functions as the object of the preposition *to*. Within the clause *whoever* is the subject of the verb *asked*. Again, try substituting *he*: *he asked for them*.)

✔ Checkpoint

Correct any errors in the use of *self*-ending pronouns and *who/whom*.

21. The boss herself is willing to call whoever we nominate for the position.

22. Who would you like to see nominated?

23. These supplies are for whomever ordered them.

24. The meeting is set for Tuesday; however, Jeff and myself cannot attend.

25. Incident reports are to be written by whomever experiences a sales problem.

Pronoun Reference

GUIDE 17: Make pronouns agree in number and gender with the words to which they refer (their antecedents). When the gender of the antecedent is obvious, pronoun references are simple.

One of the boys lost *his* (not *their*) pump-up tennis shoes. (The singular pronoun *his* refers to the singular *One*.)

Each of the female nurses was escorted to *her car* (not *their cars*). (The singular pronoun *her* and singular noun *car* are necessary because they refer to the singular subject *Each*.)

Somebody on the girls' team left *her* (not *their*) headlights on.

When the gender of the antecedent could be male or female, sensitive writers today have a number of options.

Faulty	Improved
Every employee should receive *their* check Friday. (The plural pronoun *their* does not agree with its singular antecedent *employee*.)	All employees should receive *their* checks Friday. (Make the subject plural so that the plural pronoun *their* is acceptable. This option is preferred by many writers today.)

Faulty	Improved
Every employee should receive *their* check Friday.	All employees should receive checks Friday. (Omit the possessive pronoun entirely.)
	Every employee should receive *a* check Friday. (Substitute *a* for a pronoun.)
	Every employee should receive *his or her* check Friday. (Use the combination *his or her*. However, this option is wordy and should be avoided.)

GUIDE 18: Be sure that pronouns like *it, which, this,* and *that* refer to clear antecedents. Vague pronouns confuse the reader because they have no clear single antecedent. The most troublesome are *it, which, this,* and *that.* Replace vague pronouns with concrete nouns, or provide these pronouns with clear antecedents.

Faulty	Improved
Our office recycles as much paper as possible because *it* helps the environment. (Does *it* refer to *paper, recycling,* or *office?*)	Our office recycles as much paper as possible because *such efforts* help the environment. (Replace *it* with *such efforts.*)
The disadvantages of local area networks can offset their advantages, *which* merits further evaluation. (What merits evaluation: advantages, disadvantages, or offsetting of one by the other?)	The disadvantages of local area networks can offset their advantages, a *fact* which merits further evaluation. (*Fact* supplies a clear antecedent for *which.*)
Negotiators announced an expanded health care plan, reductions in dental coverage, and a proposal of on-site child care facilities. *This* caused employee protests. (What exactly caused employee protests?)	Negotiators announced an expanded health care plan, reductions in dental coverage, and a proposal of on-site child care facilities. *This announcement* caused employee protests. (The pronoun *This* now clearly refers to *announcement.*)

Tip. Whenever you use the words *this, that, these,* and *those* by themselves, a red flag should pop up. These words are dangerous when they stand alone. Inexperienced writers often use them to refer to an entire previous idea, rather than to a specific antecedent, as shown in the preceding example. You can often solve the problem by adding another idea to the pronoun (as *this announcement*).

✔ Checkpoint

Correct the faulty and vague pronoun references in the following sentences. Numerous remedies exist.

26. Every employee is entitled to have their tuition reimbursed.

27. Flexible working hours may mean slower career advancement, but it appeals to me anyway.

28. Any subscriber may cancel their subscription at any time.

29. Every voter must have their name and address verified at the polling place.

30. Obtaining agreement on job standards, listening to coworkers, and encouraging employee suggestions all helped to open lines of communication. This is particularly important in team projects.

Adjectives and Adverbs

GUIDE 19: Use adverbs, not adjectives, to describe or limit the action of verbs.

Andrew said he did *well* (not *good*) on the exam.

After its tune-up, the engine is running *smoothly* (not *smooth*).

Don't take the manager's criticism *personally* (not *personal*).

GUIDE 20: Hyphenate two or more adjectives that are joined to create a compound modifier before a noun.

Follow the *step-by-step* instructions to construct the *low-cost* bookshelves.

A *well-designed* keyboard is part of their *state-of-the-art* equipment.

Tip. Don't confuse adverbs ending in *-ly* with compound adjectives: *newly enacted* law and *highly regarded* CEO would not be hyphenated.

✔ Checkpoint

Correct any problems in the use of pronouns, adjectives, and adverbs.

31. My manager and myself prepared a point by point analysis of the proposal.

32. Because we completed the work so quick, we were able to visit the recently-opened snack bar.

33. If I do good on the placement exam, I qualify for many part time jobs and a few full time positions.

34. The vice president told him and I not to take the announcement personal.

35. In the not too distant future, we may enjoy interactive television.

PUNCTUATION

GUIDE 21: Use commas to separate three or more items (words, phrases, or short clauses) in a series.

Downward communication delivers job instructions, procedures, and appraisals.

In preparing your résumé, try to keep it brief, make it easy to read, and include only job-related information.

The new ice cream flavors include cookie dough, chocolate raspberry truffle, cappuccino, and almond amaretto.

Tip. Some professional writers omit the comma before *and.* However, most business writers prefer to retain that comma because it prevents misreading the last two items as one item. Notice in the previous example how the final two ice cream flavors could have been misread if the comma had been omitted.

GUIDE 22: Use commas to separate introductory clauses and certain phrases from independent clauses. This guideline describes the comma most often omitted by business writers. Sentences that open with dependent clauses (often introduced by words like *since, when, if, as, although,* and *because*) require commas to separate them from the main idea. The comma helps readers recognize where the introduction ends and the big idea begins. Introductory phrases of more than five words or phrases containing verbal elements also require commas.

> If you recognize introductory clauses, you will have no trouble placing the comma. (Comma separates introductory dependent clause from main clause.)
>
> When you have mastered this rule, half the battle with commas will be won.
>
> As expected, additional explanations are necessary. (Use a comma even if the introductory clause omits the understood subject: *As we expected*.)
>
> In the spring of last year, we opened our franchise. (Use a comma after a phrase containing five or more words.)
>
> Having considered several alternatives, we decided to invest. (Use a comma after an introductory verbal phrase.)
>
> To invest, we needed $100,000. (Use a comma after an introductory verbal phrase, regardless of its length.)

Tip. Short introductory prepositional phrases (four or fewer words) require no commas. Don't clutter your writing with unnecessary commas after introductory phrases such as *by 1995, in the fall,* or *at this time.*

GUIDE 23: Use a comma before the coordinating conjunction in a compound sentence. The most common coordinating conjunctions are *and, or, nor,* and *but.* Occasionally, *for* and *so* may also function as coordinating conjunctions. When coordinating conjunctions join two independent clauses, commas are needed.

> The investment sounded too good to be true, *and* many investors were dubious. (Use a comma before the coordinating conjunction *and* in a compound sentence.)
>
> Southern California is the financial fraud capital of the world, *but* some investors refuse to heed warning signs.

Tip. Before inserting a comma, test the two clauses. Can each of them stand alone as a complete sentence? If either is incomplete, skip the comma.

> Promoters said the investment offer was for a limited time and couldn't be extended even one day. (Omit a comma before *and* because the second part of the sentence is not a complete independent clause.)
>
> Home is a place you grow up wanting to leave but grow old wanting to return to. (Omit a comma before *but* because the second half of the sentence is not a complete clause.)

✔ Checkpoint

Add appropriate commas.

36. Before he entered this class Jeff used to sprinkle his writing with commas semicolons and dashes.

37. After studying punctuation he learned to use commas more carefully and to reduce his reliance on dashes.

38. At this time Jeff is engaged in a strenuous body-building program but he also finds time to enlighten his mind.

39. Next spring Jeff may enroll in accounting and business law or he may work for a semester to earn money.

40. When he completes his degree he plans to apply for employment in San Diego Orlando or Seattle.

GUIDE 24: Use commas appropriately in dates, addresses, geographical names, degrees, and long numbers.

September 30, 1963, is her birthday. (For dates use commas before and after the year.)

Send the application to James Kirby, 20045 45th Avenue, Lynnwood, WA 98036, as soon as possible. (For addresses use commas to separate all units except the two-letter state abbreviation and the zip code.)

She expects to move from Cupertino, California, to Sonoma, Arizona, next fall. (For geographical areas use commas to enclose the second element.)

Karen Munson, CPA, and Richard B. Larsen, Ph.D., were the speakers. (For professional designations and academic degrees following names, use commas to enclose each item.)

The latest census figures show the city's population to be 342,000. (In figures use commas to separate every three digits, counting from the right.)

GUIDE 25: Use commas to set off internal sentence interrupters. Sentence interrupters may be verbal phrases, dependent clauses, contrasting elements, or parenthetical expressions (also called transitional phrases). These interrupters often provide information that is not grammatically essential.

Harvard researchers, working steadily for 18 months, developed a new cancer therapy. (Use commas to set off an interrupting verbal phrase.)

The new therapy, which applies a genetically engineered virus, raises hopes among cancer specialists. (Use commas to set off nonessential dependent *clauses.*)

Dr. James C. Morrison, who is one of the researchers, made the announcement. (Use commas to set off nonessential dependent clauses.)

It was Dr. Morrison, not Dr. Arturo, who led the team effort. (Use commas to set off a contrasting element.)

This new therapy, by the way, was developed from a herpes virus. (Use commas to set off a parenthetical expression.)

Tip. Parenthetical (transitional) expressions are helpful words that guide the reader from one thought to the next. Here are representative parenthetical expressions that require commas:

as a matter of fact	in the meantime
as a result	nevertheless
consequently	of course
for example	on the other hand
in addition	therefore

Tip. Always use *two* commas to set off an interrupter, unless it begins or ends a sentence.

✔ Checkpoint

Insert necessary commas.

41. Sue listed 222 Georgetown Road Jacksonville NC 28540 as her forwarding address.

42. The personnel director felt nevertheless that the applicant should be given an interview.

43. Employment of paralegals which is expected to increase 32 percent next year is growing rapidly because of the expanding legal services industry.

44. The contract was signed April 1 1993 and remains in effect until January 1 1996.

45. As a matter of fact the average American drinks enough coffee to require 12 pounds of coffee beans annually.

GUIDE 26: Avoid unnecessary commas. Do not use commas between sentence elements that belong together. Don't automatically insert commas before every *and* or at points where your voice might drop if you were saying the sentence out loud.

Faulty

Growth will be spurred by the increasing complexity of business operations, and by large employment gains in trade and services. (A comma unnecessarily precedes *and.*)

All students with high grades, are eligible for the honor society. (A comma unnecessarily separates the subject and verb.)

One of the reasons for the success of the business honor society is, that it is very active. (A comma unnecessarily separates the verb and its complement.)

Our honor society has, at this time, over 50 members. (Commas unnecessarily separate a prepositional phrase from the sentence.)

✔ Checkpoint

Remove unnecessary commas. Add necessary ones.

46. Businesspeople from all over the world, gathered in Las Vegas for the meeting.

47. When shopping for computer equipment consider buying products that have been on the market for at least a year.

48. The trouble with talking fast is, that you sometimes say something before you've thought of it.

49. We think on the other hand, that we must develop management talent pools with the aim of promoting women minorities and people with disabilities.

50. A powerful reason for mail-order purchasing is, that customers make big savings.

Semicolons, Colons

GUIDE 27: Use a semicolon to join closely related independent clauses. Mature writers use semicolons to show readers that two thoughts are closely associated. If the ideas are not related, they should be expressed as separate sentences. Often, but not always, the second independent clause contains a conjunctive adverb (such as *however, consequently, therefore,* or *furthermore*) to show the relation between the two clauses.

Learning history is easy; learning its lessons is almost impossible.

He was determined to complete his degree; consequently, he studied diligently.

Most people want to be delivered from temptation; they would like, however, to keep in touch.

Tip. Don't use a semicolon unless each clause is truly independent. Try the sentence test. Omit the semicolon if each clause could not stand alone as a complete sentence.

Faulty	**Improved**
There's no point in speaking; unless you can improve on silence. (The second half of the sentence is a dependent clause. It could not stand alone as a sentence.)	There's no point in speaking unless you can improve on silence.

Faulty	Improved
Although I cannot change the direction of the wind; I can adjust my sails to reach my destination. (The first clause could not stand alone.)	Although I cannot change the direction of the wind, I can adjust my sails to reach my destination.

GUIDE 28: Use a semicolon to separate items in a series when one or more of the items contains internal commas.

Representatives from as far away as Blue Bell, Pennsylvania; Bowling Green, Ohio; and Phoenix, Arizona, attended the conference.

Stories circulated about Henry Ford, founder, Ford Motor Company; Lee Iacocca, CEO, Chrysler Motor Company; and Shoichiro Toyoda, chief, Toyota Motor Company.

GUIDE 29: Use a colon after a complete thought that introduces a list of items. Words such as *these, the following,* and *as follows* may introduce the list or they may be implied.

The following cities are on the tour: Louisville, Memphis, and New Orleans.

An alternate tour includes several western cities: Seattle, San Francisco, and San Diego.

Tip. Be sure that the statement before a colon is grammatically complete. An introductory statement that ends with a preposition (such as *by, for, at,* and *to*) or a verb (such as *is, are,* or *were*) is incomplete. The list following a preposition or a verb actually functions as an object or as a complement to finish the sentence.

Faulty	Improved
Three Big Macs were ordered by: Pam, Jim, and Lee. (Do not use a colon after an incomplete statement.)	Three Big Macs were ordered by Pam, Jim, and Lee.
Other items that they ordered were: fries, Cokes, and salads. (Do not use a colon after an incomplete statement.)	Other items that they ordered were fries, Cokes, and salads.

GUIDE 30: Use a colon after business letter salutations and to introduce long quotations.

Gentlemen: Dear Mr. Wang: Dear Lisa:

The Asian consultant bluntly said: "Americans tend to be too blabby, too impatient, and too informal for Asian tastes. To succeed in trade with Pacific Rim countries, Americans must become more willing to observe native cultures."

Tip. Use a comma to introduce short quotations. Use a colon to introduce long one-sentence quotations and quotations of two or more sentences.

✔ Checkpoint

Add appropriate semicolons and colons.

51. My short-time goal is an entry-level job my long-term goal however is a management position.

52. Reebok interviewed the following candidates Joni Sims Auburn University James Jones University of Georgia and Madonna Farr Louisiana Tech.

53. The recruiter was looking for three qualities initiative versatility and enthusiasm.

54. Reebok seeks experienced individuals however it will hire recent graduates who have excellent records.

55. Portland is an expanding area therefore many business opportunities are available.

Apostrophe

GUIDE 31: Add an apostrophe plus *s* to an ownership word that does not end in an *s*.

We hope to show a profit in one year's time. (Add *'s* because the ownership word *year* does not end in an *s*.)

The company's assets rose in value. (Add *'s* because the ownership word *company* does not end in *s*.)

All the women's votes were counted. (Add *'s* because the ownership word *women* does not end in *s*.)

GUIDE 32: Add only an apostrophe to an ownership word that ends in an *s*—unless an extra syllable can be pronounced easily.

Some workers' benefits will be increased. (Add only an apostrophe because the ownership word *workers* ends in an *s*.)

Several months' rent were paid in advance. (Add only an apostrophe because the ownership word *months* ends in an *s*.)

The boss's son got the job. (Add *'s* because an extra syllable can be pronounced easily.)

Tip. To determine whether an ownership word ends in an *s*, use it in an *of* phrase. For example, *one month's salary* becomes *the salary of one month*. By isolating the ownership word without its apostrophe, you can decide if it ends in an *s*.

GUIDE 33: Use 's to make a noun possessive when it precedes a gerund, a verb form used as a noun.

We all protested *Laura's* (not *Laura*) smoking.

His (not *Him*) talking interfered with the video.

I appreciate *your* (not *you*) answering the telephone while I was gone.

✔ Checkpoint

Correct erroneous possessives.

56. Both companies presidents received huge salaries, even when profits were falling.

57. Within one months time we were able to verify all members names and addresses.

58. Bryans supporters worry that there's little chance of him being elected.

59. The position requires five years experience in waste management.

60. Ms. Jackson car is serviced every six months.

GUIDE 34: Use a period to end a statement, command, indirect question, or polite request.

Everyone must row with the oars that he or she has. (Statement)

Send the completed report to me by June 1. (Command)

Stacy asked if she could use the car next weekend. (Indirect question)

Will you please send me an employment application. (Polite request)

Tip. Polite requests often sound like questions. To determine the punctuation, apply the action test. If the request prompts an action, use a period. If it prompts a verbal response, use a question mark.

Faulty	**Improved**
Could you please correct the balance on my next statement? (This polite request prompts an action rather than a verbal response.)	Could you please correct the balance on my next statement.

GUIDE 35: Use a question mark after a direct question and after statements with questions appended.

Is it illegal to duplicate training videotapes?

Most of their training is in-house, isn't it?

GUIDE 36: Use a dash to (a) set off parenthetical elements containing internal commas, (b) emphasize a sentence interruption, or (c) separate an introductory list from a summarizing statement. The dash has legitimate uses. However, some writers use it whenever they know that punctuation is necessary, but they're not sure exactly what. The dash can be very effective, if not misused.

Three top students—Gene Engle, Donna Hersh, and Mika Sato—won awards. (Use dashes to set off elements with internal commas.)

Executives at IBM—despite rampant rumors in the stock market—remained quiet regarding dividend earnings. (Use dashes to emphasize a sentence interruption.)

IBM, Compaq, and Apple—these were the three leading computer manufacturers. (Use a dash to separate an introductory list from a summarizing statement.)

GUIDE 37: Use parentheses to set off nonessential sentence elements, such as explanations, directions, questions, or references.

Researchers find that the office grapevine (see Chapter 1 for more discussion) carries surprisingly accurate information.

Only two dates (February 15 and March 1) are suitable for the meeting.

Tip. Careful writers use parentheses to deemphasize and the dash to emphasize parenthetical information. One expert said, "Dashes shout the news; parentheses whisper it."

GUIDE 38: Use quotation marks to (a) enclose the exact words of a speaker or writer, (b) distinguish words used in a special sense, such as slang, or (c) enclose titles of articles, chapters, or other short works.

"If you make your job important," said the consultant, "it's quite likely to return the favor."

The personnel director said that she was looking for candidates with good communication skills. (Omit quotation marks because the exact words of the speaker are not quoted.)

This office discourages "rad" hair styles and clothing. (Use quotes for slang.)

In Business Week I saw an article entitled "Communication for Global Markets." (Use quotation marks around the title of an article; use all caps, underlines, or italics for the name of the publication.)

Tip. Never use quotation marks arbitrarily, as in *Our "spring" sale starts April 1.*

 Checkpoint

Add appropriate punctuation.

61. Will you please send me your latest catalog as soon as possible

62. (Direct quote) The only thing you get in a hurry said the professor is trouble

63. (Deemphasize) Two kinds of batteries see page 16 of the instruction booklet may be used in this camera.

64. (Emphasize) The first three colors that we tested red, yellow, and orange were selected.

65. All letters with erroneous addresses were reprinted weren't they

CAPITALIZATION

GUIDE 39: Capitalize proper nouns and proper adjectives. Capitalize the *specific* names of persons, places, institutions, buildings, religions, holidays, months, organizations, laws, races, languages, and so forth. Don't capitalize common nouns that make *general* references.

Proper Nouns	**Common Nouns**
Michelle DeLuca	the manufacturer's rep
Everglades National Park	the wilderness park
College of the Redwoods	the community college
Empire State Building	the downtown building
Environmental Protection Agency	the federal agency
Persian, Armenian, Hindi	modern foreign languages

Proper Adjectives

Hispanic markets	Italian dressing
Xerox copy	Japanese executives
Swiss chocolates	Reagan economics

GUIDE 40: Capitalize only specific academic courses and degrees.

Professor Jane Mangrum, Ph.D., will teach Accounting 121 next spring.

James Barker, who holds bachelor's and master's degrees, teaches business communications and marketing.

Jessica enrolled in classes in management, English, and business law.

GUIDE 41: Capitalize personal and business titles when they (a) precede names, (b) appear in addresses, salutations, and closing lines, and (c) represent high governmental rank or religious office.

Vice President Garcia	Aunt Edna
Board Chairman Ames	Dr. Johnson

Governor James Wilson
the President of the United States
the Governor of Arizona
Supervisor Vallone
the Pope
the Senator from Michigan

Do not capitalize business titles appearing alone or those following names, unless they represent addresses.

The president met with our office manager and the supervisor today.

Charles B. Fruit, former vice president with Anheuser-Busch, became the new marketing manager at Coca-Cola Company.

Send the package to Amanda Haar, Advertising Manager, Kent Publishing Company, 20 Park Plaza, Boston, MA.

GUIDE 42: Capitalize the principal words in the titles of books, magazines, newspapers, articles, movies, plays, songs, poems, and reports. Do *not* capitalize articles (*a, an, the*) and prepositions of fewer than four letters (*in, to, by, for*) unless they begin or end the title.

I enjoyed the book A Customer Is More Than a Name.

Did you read the article entitled "Companies in Europe Seeking Executives With Multinational Skills"?

We liked the article entitled "Advice From a Pro: How to Say It With Pictures."

(Note that the titles of books are underlined or italicized while the titles of articles are enclosed in quotation marks.)

GUIDE 43: Capitalize *north, south, east, west* and their derivatives only when they represent specific geographical regions.

from the Pacific Northwest
living in the East
Midwesterners, Southerners
heading northwest on the highway
east of the city
western Oregon, southern Ohio

GUIDE 44: Capitalize the names of departments, divisions, or committees within your own organization. Outside your organization capitalize only *specific* department, division, or committee names.

Attorneys in our Legal Assistance Department handle numerous cases.

Samsung offers TVs in its Consumer Electronics Division.

We volunteered for the Employee Social Responsibility Committee.

You might send an application to their personnel department.

GUIDE 45: Capitalize product names only when they refer to trademarked items. Don't capitalize the common names following manufacturers' names.

Pitney Bowes Dictaphone
Eveready Energizer
Coca-Cola
Skippy peanut butter
Norelco razor
Apple computer
NordicTrack
Kodak color copier
Big Mac

GUIDE 46: Capitalize most nouns followed by numbers or letters (except in page, paragraph, line, and verse references).

Chapter 9
Figure 2.1
Exhibit A
Plan No. 1
Flight 12, Gate 43
Model Z2010

✔ Checkpoint

Capitalize all appropriate words.

66. vice president ellis bought a toshiba computer for use on her trips to europe.

67. our director of research brought plan no. 1 with him to the meeting in our engineering research department.

68. proceed west on highway 10 until you reach the mt. vernon exit.

69. you are booked on american airlines flight 164 leaving from gate 5 at stapleton international airport.

70. to improve their english, many hispanics purchased the book entitled the power of language is yours.

Number Usage

GUIDE 47: Use word form to express (a) numbers *ten* and under and (b) numbers beginning sentences. General references to numbers *ten* and under should be expressed in word form. Also use word form for numbers that begin sentences. If the resulting number involves more than two words, however, the sentence should be recast so that the number does not fall at the beginning.

We answered *six* telephone calls for the *four* sales reps.

Fifteen customers responded to the *three* advertisements today.

A total of 155 cameras were awarded as prizes. (Avoid beginning the sentence with a long number such as *one hundred fifty-five.*)

GUIDE 48: Use words to express general references to ages, small fractions, and periods of time.

When she reached *twenty-one*, she received *one half* of the estate.

James owns a *one-third* interest in the electronics business. (Note that fractions are hyphenated only when they function as adjectives.)

That business was founded *thirty-five* years ago.

Tip. Exact ages and specific business terms may be expressed in figures.

Both Meredith Jones, 55, and Jack Jones, 57, appeared in the article.

The note is payable in 60 days.

GUIDE 49: Use figures to express most references to numbers *11* and over.

Over *150* people from *53* companies attended the two-day workshop.

A four-ounce serving of Haagen-Dazs toffee crunch ice cream contains *300* calories and *19* grams of fat.

GUIDE 50: Use figures to express money, dates, clock time, decimals, and percents. Use a combination of words and figures to express sums of 1 million and over.

One item cost only *$1.95*; most, however, were priced between *$10* and *$35*. (Omit the decimals and zeros in even sums of money.)

A total of *3,700* employees approved the contract *May 12* at *3 p.m.*

When U.S. sales dropped *4.7* percent, net income fell *9.8* percent. (Use the word *percent* instead of the *%* symbol.)

Orion lost *$62.9 million* in the latest fiscal year on revenues of *$584 million.* (Use a combination of words and figures for sums 1 million and over.)

Tip. To ease your memory load, concentrate on the numbers normally expressed in words: numbers *ten* and under, numbers at the beginning of a sentence, and small fractions. Nearly everything else in business is generally written with figures.

✔ Checkpoint

Correct any inappropriate expression of numbers.

71. McDonald's new McLean Deluxe, priced at one dollar and fifty-nine cents, has only three hundred ten calories and nine percent fat.

72. 175 employees will attend the meeting January tenth at one p.m.

73. The Nordstrom family, which owns forty percent of the company's stock, recently added four co-presidents.

74. Our three branch offices, with a total of ninety-six workers, needs to add six computers and nine printers.

75. On March eighth we paid thirty-two dollars a share to acquire one third of the stocks.

Key to C.L.U.E. Checkpoint Exercises in Appendix A

This key shows all corrections. If you marked anything else, double-check the appropriate guideline.

1. Pizza Hut fought back with
2. backfire; consequently,
3. advertisements; they
4. chain, Domino's
5. deliveries; the

6. If I *were* . . . I would have *written*
7. could have *written* . . . if you *had* read
8. When Trevor *saw*
9. I wish I *were* . . . could have *gone*
10. she had *taken* . . . able to *choose*

11. energy *have*
12. efforts, *is* disappointingly
13. Ms. Wagner *is* in charge
14. companies *is* being
15. *knows* how

16. my friend and *I* . . . *its* price
17. to *him* and *me*
18. between you and *me*
19. *yours* and *hers*
20. could have been *she* . . . to you and *me*
21. *whomever* we nominate
22. *Whom* would you
23. *whoever* ordered
24. Jeff and *I*
25. by *whoever* experiences
26. to have *his or her* tuition; to have *the* tuition; *all employees are entitled to have their tuition reimbursed*
27. but *this advancement plan* appeals (*Revise to avoid vague pronoun* it.)
28. may cancel *his or her* subscription; may cancel *the* subscription; *subscribers* may cancel *their* subscriptions
29. *his or her* name and address; *all voters must have their names and addresses*
30. *These activities are* particularly important (*Revise to avoid the vague pronoun* this.)
31. my manager and *I* . . . point-by-point
32. completed the work so *quickly* . . . recently opened (*Omit hyphen.*)
33. If I do *well* . . . part-time . . . full-time
34. told him and *me* . . . *personally*
35. *not-too-distant* future
36. class, Jeff . . . commas, semicolons, and
37. punctuation, (*No comma before* and!)
38. program, but
39. business law, or
40. degree, he . . . San Diego, Orlando, or
41. 222 Georgetown Road, Jacksonville, NC 28540, as her
42. felt, nevertheless,
43. paralegals, which . . . year,
44. April 1, 1993, . . . January 1, 1996.
45. As a matter of fact,
46. (*Remove comma.*)
47. equipment,
48. (*Remove comma.*)
49. think, on the other hand, . . . women, minorities, and
50. (*Remove comma.*)

51. entry-level job; my . . . goal, however,

52. candidates: Joni Sims, Auburn University; James Jones, University of Georgia; and Madonna Farr, Louisiana Tech.

53. qualities: initiative, versatility, and

54. individuals; however,

55. area; therefore,

56. companies'

57. one month's time . . . members'

58. Bryan's . . . *his* being elected

59. years' experience

60. Jackson's car

61. possible.

62. "The only thing you get in a hurry," said the professor, "is trouble."

63. batteries (see page 16 of the instruction booklet) may be

64. tested—red, yellow, and orange—were selected.

65. reprinted, weren't they?

66. Vice President Ellis . . . Toshiba computer . . . Europe

67. Our . . . Plan No. 1 . . . Engineering Research Department

68. Proceed . . . Highway 10 . . . Mt. Vernon exit.

69. You . . . American Airlines Flight 164 . . . Gate 5 at Stapleton International Airport.

70. To improve their English, many Hispanics . . . The Power of Language Is Yours.

71. priced at $1.59, has only 310 calories and 9 percent fat.

72. A total of 175 employees . . . January 10 at 1 p.m.

73. 40 percent

74. 96 workers

75. March 8 . . . $32

Guide to Document Formats

Business documents carry two kinds of messages. Verbal messages are conveyed by the words chosen to express the writer's ideas. Nonverbal messages are conveyed largely by the appearance of a document. If you compare an assortment of letters and memos from various organizations, you will notice immediately that some look more attractive and more professional than others. The nonverbal message of the professional-looking documents suggests that they were sent by people who are careful, informed, intelligent, and successful. Understandably, you're more likely to take seriously documents that use attractive stationery and professional formatting techniques.

Over the years certain practices and conventions have arisen regarding the appearance and formatting of business documents. Although these conventions offer some choices (such as letter and punctuation styles), most business letters follow standardized formats. To ensure that your documents carry favorable nonverbal messages about you and your organization, you'll want to give special attention to the appearance and formatting of your letters, envelopes, memos, and fax cover sheets.

 Appearance

To ensure that a message is read and valued, you need to give it a professional appearance. Two important elements here are type of stationery and placement of the message on the page.

Stationery. Most organizations use high-quality stationery for business documents. This stationery is printed on select paper that meets two qualifications: weight and cotton-fiber content.

Paper is measured by weight and may range from 9 pounds (thin onionskin paper) to 32 pounds (thick card and cover stock). Most office stationery is in the 16- to 24-pound range. Lighter 16-pound paper is generally sufficient for internal documents including memos. Heavier 20- to 24-pound paper is used for printed letterhead stationery.

Paper is also judged by its cotton-fiber content. Cotton fiber makes paper stronger, softer in texture, and less likely to yellow. Good-quality stationery contains 25 percent or more cotton fiber.

Spacing. In preparing business documents on a typewriter or word processor, follow accepted spacing conventions. These conventions include double-spacing after all end punctuation marks (period, question mark, and exclamation point). Business typists also leave two spaces after a colon, except in the expression of time, as shown here:

Ann called at 3:15 yesterday. She wants to ask . . .
It comes in three colors: amber, rust, and wheat.

Professional typographers leave only one space after all punctuation marks, as you will notice in books, magazines, and newspapers. Business writers, however, are not working within such tight space constraints. Leaving two spaces after end punctuation and colons helps readers separate ideas.

Justification. Many word processing programs automatically justify right margins, a print feature you'll want to avoid for letters and memos. Justification adds extra space between words to make all lines of text end evenly (as here). If you have a printer with proportional spacing, these extra spaces are distributed evenly. But many printers lack this capacity, thus resulting in awkward spacing gaps. Moreover, experts tell us that justified right margins make documents more difficult to read, since the eye cannot easily see where individual lines end. Natural resting points for the eye are removed. And justified business letters look computer-generated and thus less personal. This is why smart communicators use ragged, unjustified right margins for business letters and memos.

Justified right margins, however, are appropriate for special documents, such as formal reports, brochures, newsletters, and announcements. Writers with laser printers and scalable fonts (which permit a variety of type faces and sizes) include justification as one of many techniques to create print-quality output.

Letter Placement

Business letters should be typed so that they are framed by white space. By setting proper margins and by controlling the amount of space between the date and the inside address, you can balance a letter attractively on a page.

The chart below shows margins for short, medium, and long letters. To use the chart, first estimate the number of words in the body of your letter (excluding the inside address and closing lines). Then set the appropriate margins. Notice that a short letter (under 100 words) requires 2-inch margins while a long letter (over 200 words) uses margins of 1 to 1¼ inches. Your goal is to place your message in the middle of a page surrounded by a balanced frame of white space.

Letter Length	Words in Body	Side Margins	Blank Lines After Date
Short	Under 100	2 inches	7 to 11 (12 pitch) 6 to 8 (10 pitch)
Medium	100 to 200	1½ inches	2 to 8 (12 pitch) 2 to 3 (10 pitch)
Long	Over 200	1 to 1¼ inches	2 to 8 (12 pitch) 2 to 3 (10 pitch)

Some companies prescribe standard margins, usually 1 to 1¼ inches. This practice improves efficiency because margins are never changed; however, standard margins often result in unbalanced documents, particularly for short messages. Adjusting the number of blank lines between the date and the inside address helps balance a letter on the page. Another aid, available in some word processing programs, is a command that automatically centers a document on the page. Word processing programs also improve efficiency by storing preset margins for different documents. Learning to use the special features of your word processing program can save time in the long run and improve the appearance of your documents.

Letter Parts

Professional-looking business letters are arranged in a conventional sequence with standard parts. Following is a discussion of how to use these letter parts properly. Figure B.1 illustrates the parts in a block-style letter. (See Chapter 6 for additional discussion of letters and their parts.)

Letterhead. Most business organizations use 8½- by 11-inch paper printed with a letterhead displaying their official name, address, and telephone and fax numbers. The letterhead may also include a logo and an advertising message such as *Great Western Banking: A new brand of banking.*

Dateline. On letterhead paper you should place the date two lines below the last line of the letterhead or 2 inches from the top edge of the paper (line 13). On plain paper place the date immediately below your return address. Since the date goes on line 13, start the return address an appropriate number of lines above it. The most common dateline format is as follows: *June 9, 1995.* Don't use *th* (or *rd*) when the date is written this way. For European or military correspondence, use the following dateline format: *9 June 1995.* Notice that no commas are used.

Addressee and delivery notations. Delivery notations such as *FAX TRANSMISSION, OVERNIGHT DELIVERY, CONFIDENTIAL,* or *CERTIFIED MAIL* are typed in all capital letters two line spaces above the inside address.

Inside address. Type the inside address—that is, the address of the organization or person receiving the letter—single-spaced, starting at the left margin. The number of lines between the dateline and the inside address depends on the size of the letter body, the type size (point or pitch size), and the length of the typing lines. Generally, two to ten lines are appropriate.

Be careful to duplicate the exact wording and spelling of the recipient's name and address on your documents. Usually, you can copy this information from the letterhead of the correspondence you are answering. If, for example, you are responding to *Jackson & Perkins Company,* don't address your letter to *Jackson and Perkins Corp.*

Always be sure to include a courtesy title such as *Mr., Ms., Mrs., Dr.,* or *Professor* before a person's name in the inside address—for both the letter and the envelope. Although many women in business today favor *Ms.,* you'll want to use whatever title the addressee prefers.

Remember that the inside address is not included for readers who already know who and where they are. It's there to help writers accurately file a copy of the message.

In general, avoid abbreviations (such as *Ave.* or *Co.*) unless they appear in the printed letterhead of the document being answered.

FIGURE B.1 ● Block and Modified Block Letter Styles

Block style
Open punctuation

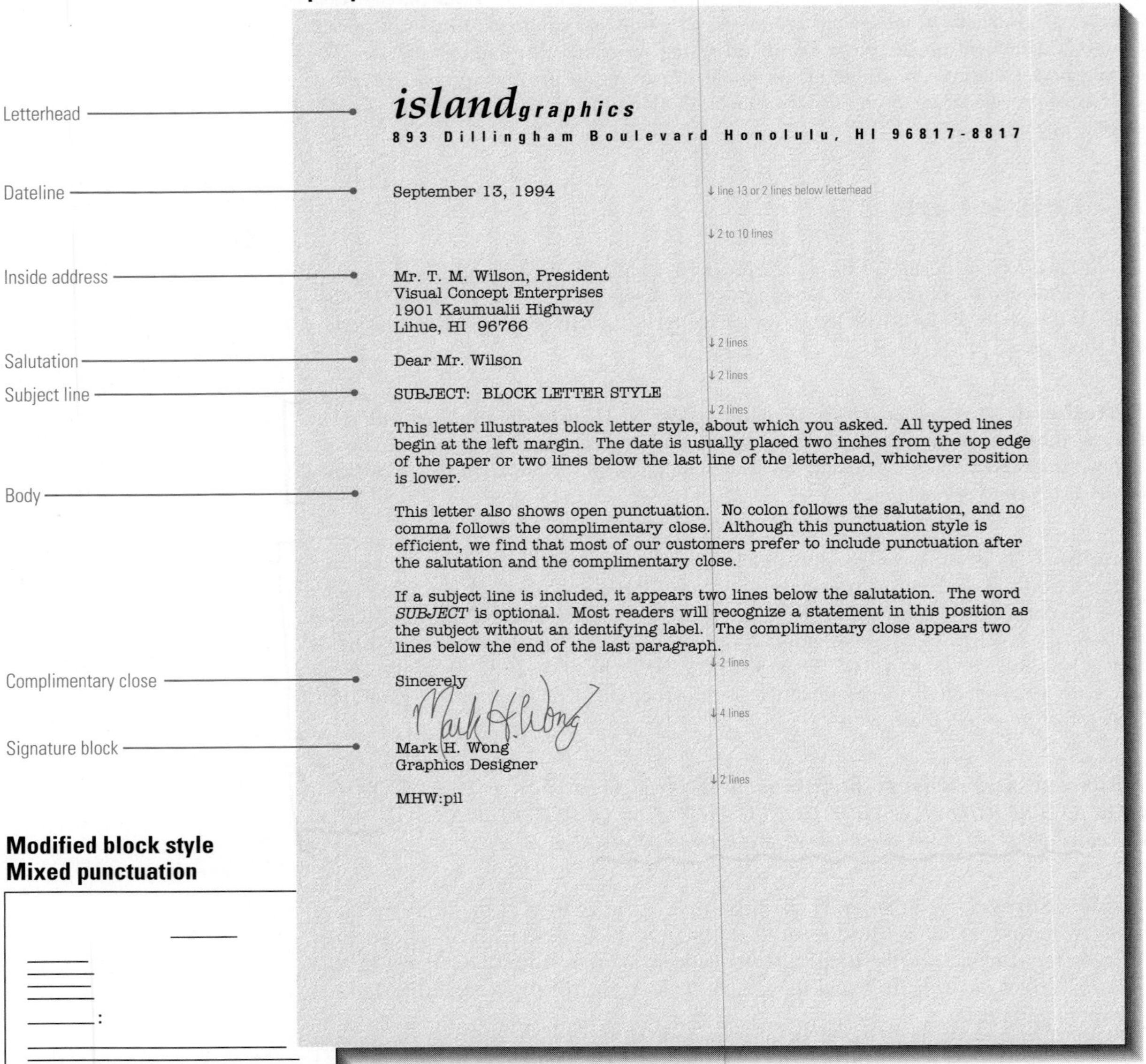

*island*graphics
893 Dillingham Boulevard Honolulu, HI 96817-8817

September 13, 1994 ↓ line 13 or 2 lines below letterhead

↓ 2 to 10 lines

Mr. T. M. Wilson, President
Visual Concept Enterprises
1901 Kaumualii Highway
Lihue, HI 96766

↓ 2 lines

Dear Mr. Wilson

↓ 2 lines

SUBJECT: BLOCK LETTER STYLE

↓ 2 lines

This letter illustrates block letter style, about which you asked. All typed lines begin at the left margin. The date is usually placed two inches from the top edge of the paper or two lines below the last line of the letterhead, whichever position is lower.

This letter also shows open punctuation. No colon follows the salutation, and no comma follows the complimentary close. Although this punctuation style is efficient, we find that most of our customers prefer to include punctuation after the salutation and the complimentary close.

If a subject line is included, it appears two lines below the salutation. The word *SUBJECT* is optional. Most readers will recognize a statement in this position as the subject without an identifying label. The complimentary close appears two lines below the end of the last paragraph.

↓ 2 lines

Sincerely

↓ 4 lines

Mark H. Wong
Graphics Designer

↓ 2 lines

MHW:pil

Modified block style
Mixed punctuation

In the modified block-style letter shown at the left, the date is centered or aligned with the complimentary close and signature block, which start at the center. Paragraphs may be blocked or indented. Mixed punctuation includes a colon after the salutation and a comma after the complimentary close.

Attention line. An attention line allows you to send your message officially to an organization but to direct it to a specific individual, officer, or department. However, if you know an individual's complete name, it's always better to use it as the first line of the inside address and avoid an attention line. Here are two common formats for attention lines:

MultiMedia Enterprises 931 Calkins Road Rochester, NY 14301 ATTENTION MARKETING DIRECTOR	MultiMedia Enterprises Attention: Marketing Director 931 Calkins Road Rochester, NY 14301

Attention lines may be typed in all caps or with upper- and lowercase letters. The colon following *Attention* is optional. Notice that an attention line may be placed two lines below the address block or printed as the second line of the inside address. You'll want to use the latter format if you're composing on a word processor because the address block may be copied to the envelope and the attention line will not interfere with the last-line placement of the zip code. (Mail can be sorted more easily if the zip code appears in the last line of a typed address.)

Whenever possible, use a person's name as the first line of an address instead of putting that name in an attention line. Some writers use an attention line because they fear that letters addressed to individuals at companies may be considered private. They worry that if the addressee is no longer with the company, the letter may be forwarded or not opened. Actually, unless a letter is marked "Personal" or "Confidential," it will very likely be opened as business mail. Figure B.2 shows more examples of attention lines.

Salutation. For most letter styles place the letter greeting, or salutation, two lines below the last line of the inside address or the attention line (if used). If the letter is addressed to an individual, use that person's courtesy title and last name (*Dear Mr. Lanham*). Even if you are on a first-name basis (*Dear Leslie*), be sure to add a colon (not a comma or a semicolon) after the salutation. Do not use an individual's full name in the salutation (not *Dear Mr. Leslie Lanham*) unless you are unsure of gender (*Dear Leslie Lanham*).

For letters with attention lines or those addressed to organizations, the selection of an appropriate salutation has become more difficult. Formerly, *Gentlemen* was used generically for all organizations. With increasing numbers of women in business management today, however, *Gentlemen* is less accurate. Because no universally acceptable salutation has emerged as yet, you'll probably be safest with *Ladies and Gentlemen* or *Gentlemen and Ladies.*

One way to avoid the salutation dilemma is to address a document to a specific person. Another alternative is to use the simplified letter style, which conveniently omits the salutation (and the complimentary close). Figure B.2 discusses and illustrates letter addresses and appropriate salutations.

Subject and reference lines. Although experts suggest placing the subject line two lines below the salutation, many businesses actually place it above the salutation. Use whatever style your organization prefers. Reference lines often show policy or file numbers; they generally appear two lines above the salutation.

Body. Most business letters and memorandums are single-spaced, with double line spacing between paragraphs. Very short messages may be double-spaced with indented paragraphs.

Complimentary close. Typed two lines below the last line of the letter, the complimentary close may be formal (*Very truly yours*) or informal (*Sincerely yours* or *Cordially*). The simplified letter style omits a complimentary close.

FIGURE B.2 ● Letter Addressees and Salutations

Addressee	Salutation	Explanation
Individual		
Mr. Leslie Lanham, CEO Atlantic Associates, Inc. 2320 Park Avenue Boston, MA 02115-2320	Dear Mr. Lanham: Dear Leslie:	For specific individuals use a courtesy title (such as *Mr.* or *Ms.*) and the person's last name. For friends use a first-name greeting. When you are unsure of an addressee's gender, include the full name (*Dear Leslie Lanham*). A helpful alternative is the simplified letter style, which omits a salutation.
Organization		
Pacific Builders Association Sequoia Building, Suite 303 105 Redwood Boulevard Seattle, WA 98104-1105	Ladies and Gentlemen: Gentlemen: Ladies:	When females are part of management or if you are unsure, use *Ladies and Gentlemen.* If you know a company has only male managers, use *Gentlemen.* For a company with only female managers, use *Ladies.* An alternative that avoids this dilemma is the simplified letter style, which omits a salutation.
Individual Within Organization		
Michigan Fabricators, Inc. Attention: Ms. Lisa Jonas, Sales 3088 North Jennings Flint, MI 48433-3088	Ladies and Gentlemen:	Although an attention line is included here, the message is addressed to the organization—hence the salutation *Ladies and Gentlemen.* However, when you know an individual's name, as in this case, it's better to use that name on the first line of the address without *Attention.* Then the salutation would be *Dear Ms. Jonas.*
Position or Department Within Organization		
Magnaflex Enterprises, Inc. Attention: Marketing Manager 200 Main Street Fort Morgan, CO 80701-2200	Ladies and Gentlemen:	When a letter is addressed to an organization for the attention of an individual in a specific position, the salutation should address the organization. If this salutation sounds awkward, use the simplified letter style and avoid a salutation.
Group of People		
Customers or individuals from a large database.	Dear Customer: Dear Policyholder:	When you are sending form letters to a large group and cannot use individual salutations, use an appropriate general salutation.

Signature block. In most letter styles the writer's typed name and optional identification appear three to four lines below the complimentary close. The combination of name, title, and organization information should be arranged to achieve a balanced look. The name and title may appear on the same line or on separate lines, depending on the length of each. Use commas to separate categories within the same line, but not to conclude a line. Women may choose to include *Ms., Mrs.,* or *Miss* before their names. Parentheses are optional. Men do not use *Mr.* before their names.

Sincerely yours,	Cordially yours,
Jeremy M. Wood, Manager Technical Sales and Services	Casandra Baker-Murillo Executive Vice President

Some organizations include their names in the signature block. In such cases the organization name appears in all caps two lines below the complimentary close, as shown below.

Cordially,

LITTON COMPUTER SERVICES

Ms. Shelina A. Simpson
Executive Assistant

Reference initials. If used, the initials of the typist and writer are typed two lines below the writer's name and title. Generally, the writer's initials are capitalized and the typist's are lowercased, but this format varies.

Enclosure notation. When an enclosure or attachment accompanies a document, a notation to that effect appears two lines below the reference initials. This notation reminds the typist to insert the enclosure in the envelope, and it reminds the recipient to look for the enclosure or attachment. The notation may be spelled out (*Enclosure, Attachment*), or it may be abbreviated (*Enc., Att.*). It may indicate the number of enclosures or attachments, and it may also identify a specific enclosure (*Enclosure: Form 1099*).

Copy notation. If you make copies of correspondence for other individuals, you may use *cc* to indicate carbon copy, *pc* to indicate photocopy, or merely *c* for any kind of copy. A colon following the initial(s) is optional.

Second-page heading. When a letter extends beyond one page, use plain paper of the same quality and color as the first page. Identify the second and succeeding pages with a heading consisting of the name of the addressee, the page number, and the date. Use either of the following two formats:

Ms. Rachel Ruiz 2 May 3, 1994

Ms. Rachel Ruiz
Page 2
May 3, 1994

Both headings appear on line 7 followed by two blank lines to separate them from the continuing text. Avoid using a second page if you have only one line or the complimentary close and signature block to fill that page.

Plain-paper return address. If you prepare a personal or business letter on plain paper, place your address immediately above the date. Do not include your name; you will type (and sign) your name at the end of your letter. If your return address contains two lines, begin typing it on line 11 so that the date appears on line 13. Avoid abbreviations except for a two-letter state abbreviation.

580 East Leffels Street
Springfield, OH 45501
December 14, 1994

Ms. Ellen Siemens
Escrow Department
TransOhio First Federal
1220 Wooster Boulevard
Columbus, OH 43218-2900

Dear Ms. Siemens:

For letters prepared in the block style, type the return address at the left margin. For modified block-style letters, start the return address at the center to align with the complimentary close.

 Letter Styles

Business letters are generally prepared in one of three formats. The most popular is the block style, but the simplified style has much to recommend it.

Block style. In the block style, shown earlier in Figure B.1, all lines begin at the left margin. This style is a favorite because it is easy to format.

Modified block style. The modified block style differs from block style in that the date and closing lines appear in the center, as shown at the bottom of Figure B.1. The date may be (1) centered, (2) begun at the center of the page (to align with the closing lines), or (3) backspaced from the right margin. The signature block—including the complimentary close, writer's name and title, or organization identification—begins at the center. The first line of each paragraph may begin at the left margin or may be indented five or ten spaces. All other lines begin at the left margin.

Simplified style. Introduced by the Administrative Management Society a number of years ago, the simplified letter style, shown in Figure B.3, requires little formatting. Like the block style, all lines begin at the left margin. A subject line appears in all caps three lines below the inside address and three lines above the first paragraph. The salutation and complimentary close are omitted. The signer's name and identification appear in all caps five lines below the last paragraph. This letter style is efficient and avoids the problem of appropriate salutations and courtesy titles.

 Punctuation Styles

Two punctuation styles are commonly used for letters. *Open* punctuation, shown with the block-style letter in Figure B.1, contains no punctuation after the salutation or complimentary close. *Mixed* punctuation, shown with the modified block-style letter in Figure B.1, requires a colon after the salutation and a comma after the complimentary close. Many business organizations prefer mixed punctuation, even in a block-style letter.

If you choose mixed punctuation, be sure to use a colon—not a comma or semicolon—after the salutation. Even when the salutation is a first name, the colon is appropriate.

 Envelopes

An envelope should be printed on the same quality and color of stationery as the letter it carries. Because the envelope introduces your message and makes the first impression, you need to be especially careful in addressing it. Moreover, how you fold the letter is important.

Return address. The return address is usually printed in the upper left corner of an envelope, as shown in Figure B.4. In large companies some form of identification (the writer's initials, name, or location) may be typed above the company name and return address. This identification helps return the letter to the sender in case of nondelivery.

FIGURE B.3 ● Simplified Letter Style

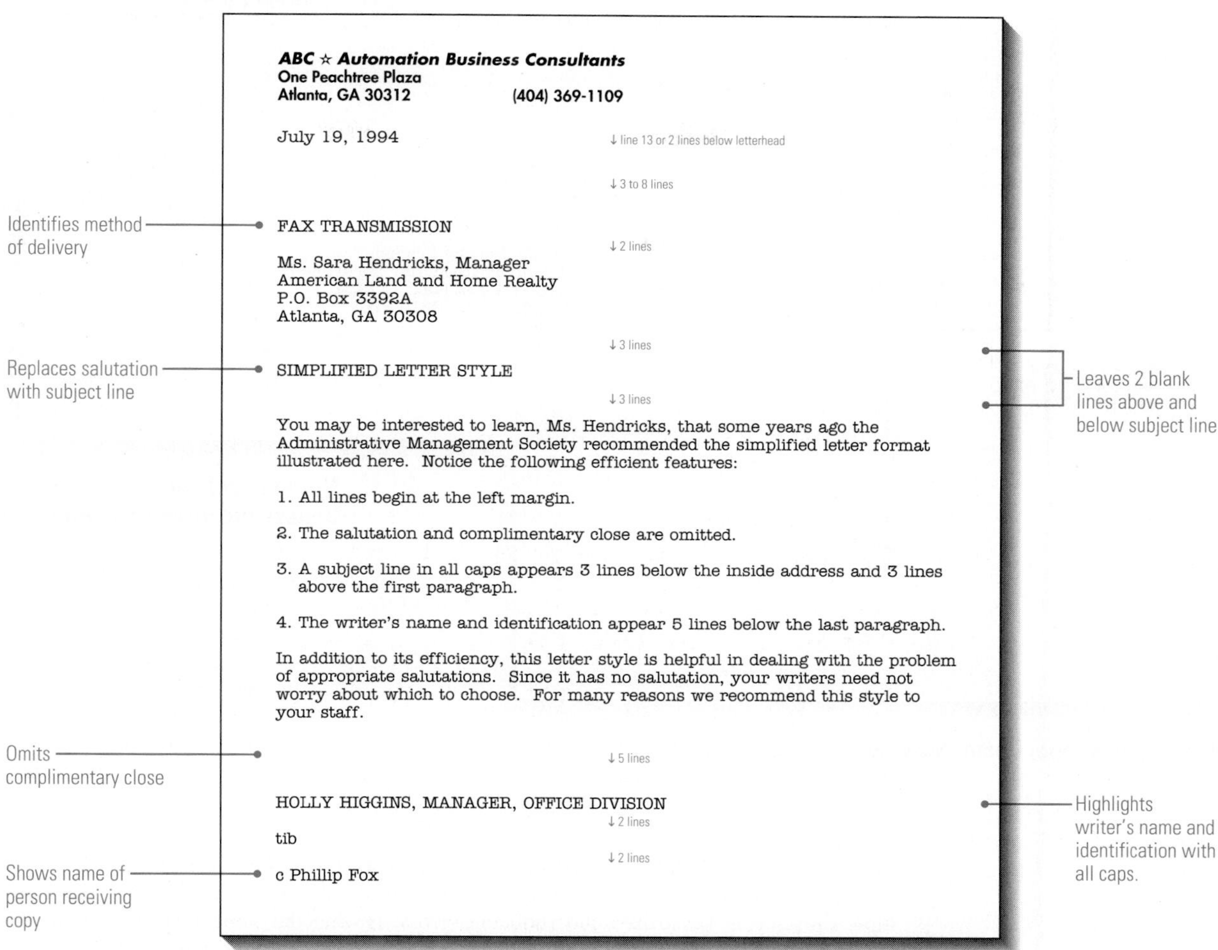
ABC ⋆ Automation Business Consultants
One Peachtree Plaza
Atlanta, GA 30312 (404) 369-1109

July 19, 1994

FAX TRANSMISSION

Ms. Sara Hendricks, Manager
American Land and Home Realty
P.O. Box 3392A
Atlanta, GA 30308

SIMPLIFIED LETTER STYLE

You may be interested to learn, Ms. Hendricks, that some years ago the Administrative Management Society recommended the simplified letter format illustrated here. Notice the following efficient features:

1. All lines begin at the left margin.

2. The salutation and complimentary close are omitted.

3. A subject line in all caps appears 3 lines below the inside address and 3 lines above the first paragraph.

4. The writer's name and identification appear 5 lines below the last paragraph.

In addition to its efficiency, this letter style is helpful in dealing with the problem of appropriate salutations. Since it has no salutation, your writers need not worry about which to choose. For many reasons we recommend this style to your staff.

HOLLY HIGGINS, MANAGER, OFFICE DIVISION

tib

c Phillip Fox

On an envelope without a printed return address, single-space the return address in the upper-left corner. Beginning on line 3 on the fourth space (½ inch) from the left edge, type the writer's name, title, company, and mailing address.

Mailing address. On legal-sized No. 10 envelopes (4⅛ by 9½ inches), begin the address on line 13 about 4¼ inches from the left edge, as shown in Figure B.4. For small envelopes (3⅝ by 6½ inches), begin typing on line 12 about 2½ inches from the left edge.

The U.S. Postal Service recommends that addresses be typed in all caps without any punctuation. This Postal Service style, shown in the small envelope in Figure B.4, was originally developed to facilitate scanning by optical character readers. Today's OCR readers, however, are so sophisticated that they scan upper- and lowercase letters easily. Many companies today do not follow the Postal Service format because they prefer to use the

FIGURE B.4 ● Envelope Formats

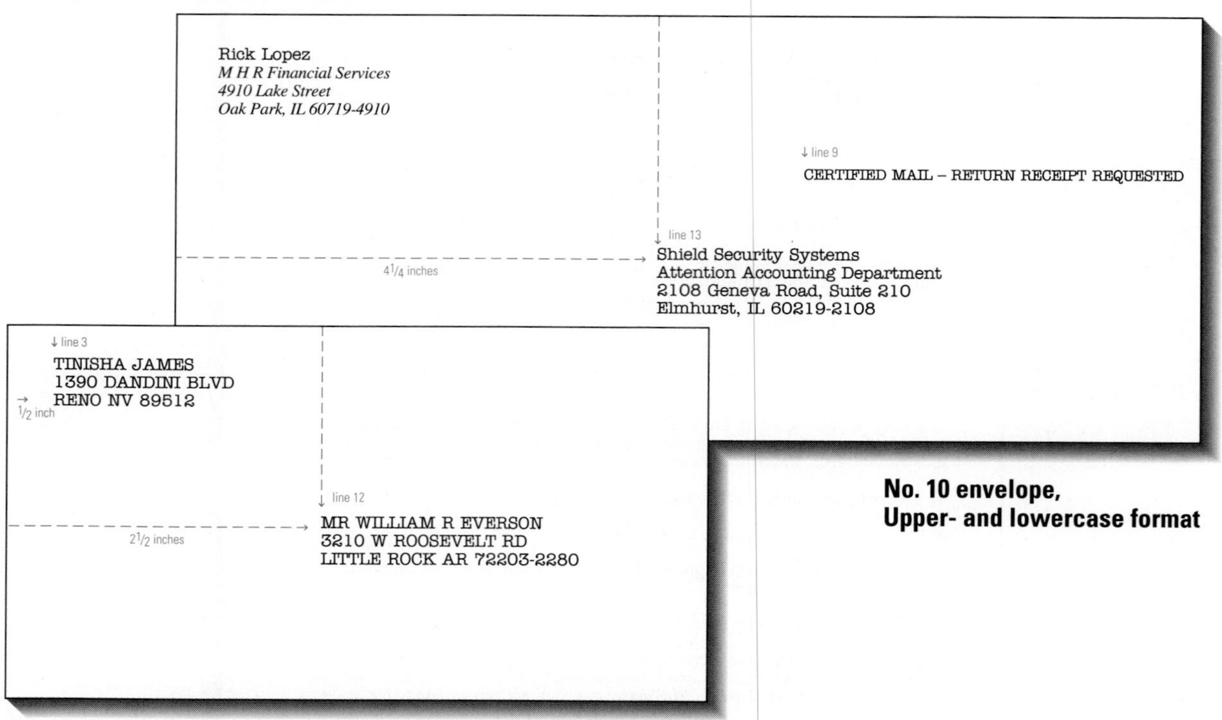

Rick Lopez
M H R Financial Services
4910 Lake Street
Oak Park, IL 60719-4910
line 9
CERTIFIED MAIL – RETURN RECEIPT REQUESTED
line 13
4¼ inches
Shield Security Systems
Attention Accounting Department
2108 Geneva Road, Suite 210
Elmhurst, IL 60219-2108
line 3
TINISHA JAMES
1390 DANDINI BLVD
RENO NV 89512
½ inch
line 12
2½ inches
MR WILLIAM R EVERSON
3210 W ROOSEVELT RD
LITTLE ROCK AR 72203-2280
No. 10 envelope,
Upper- and lowercase format

No. 6¾ envelope, Postal Service uppercase format

same format on the envelope as for the inside address. If the same format is used, writers can take advantage of word processing programs to "copy" the inside address to the envelope, thus saving keystrokes and reducing errors. Having the same format on both the inside address and the envelope also looks more professional and consistent. For these reasons you may choose to use the familiar upper- and lowercase combination format. But you will want to check with your organization to learn its preference.

In addressing your envelopes for delivery in this country or in Canada, use the two-letter state and province abbreviations shown in Figure B.5. Notice that these abbreviations are in capital letters without periods.

Folding. The way a letter is folded and inserted into an envelope sends additional nonverbal messages about a writer's professionalism and carefulness. Most businesspeople follow the procedures shown here, which produce the least number of creases to distract readers.

For large No. 10 envelopes, begin with the letter face up. Fold slightly less than one third of the sheet toward the top, as shown below. Then fold down the top third to within ⅓ inch of the bottom fold. Insert the letter into the envelope with the last fold toward the bottom of the envelope.

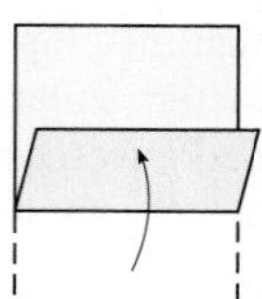
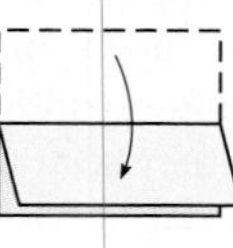
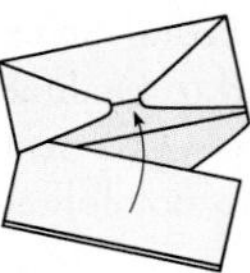

FIGURE B.5 ● **Abbreviations of States, Territories, and Provinces**

State or Territory	Two-Letter Abbreviation
Alabama	AL
Alaska	AK
Arizona	AZ
Arkansas	AR
California	CA
Canal Zone	CZ
Colorado	CO
Connecticut	CT
Delaware	DE
District of Columbia	DC
Florida	FL
Georgia	GA
Guam	GU
Hawaii	HI
Idaho	ID
Illinois	IL
Indiana	IN
Iowa	IA
Kansas	KS
Kentucky	KY
Louisiana	LA
Maine	ME
Maryland	MD
Massachusetts	MA
Michigan	MI
Minnesota	MN
Mississippi	MS
Missouri	MO
Montana	MT
Nebraska	NE
Nevada	NV
New Hampshire	NH
New Jersey	NJ
New Mexico	NM
New York	NY
North Carolina	NC

State or Territory	Two-Letter Abbreviation
North Dakota	ND
Ohio	OH
Oklahoma	OK
Oregon	OR
Pennsylvania	PA
Puerto Rico	PR
Rhode Island	RI
South Carolina	SC
South Dakota	SD
Tennessee	TN
Texas	TX
Utah	UT
Vermont	VT
Virgin Islands	VI
Virginia	VA
Washington	WA
West Virginia	WV
Wisconsin	WI
Wyoming	WY

Canadian Province	Two-Letter Abbreviation
Alberta	AB
British Columbia	BC
Labrador	LB
Manitoba	MB
New Brunswick	NB
Newfoundland	NF
Northwest Territories	NT
Nova Scotia	NS
Ontario	ON
Prince Edward Island	PE
Quebec	PQ
Saskatchewan	SK
Yukon Territory	YT

For small No. 6¾ envelopes, begin by folding the bottom up to within ⅓ inch from the top edge. Then fold the right third over to the left. Fold the left third to within ⅓ inch from the last fold. Insert the last fold into the envelope first.

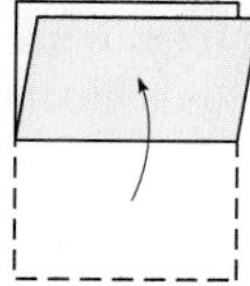
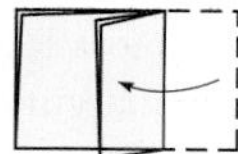
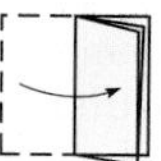
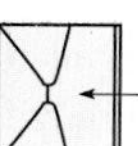

FIGURE B.6 ● Printed Memo Forms

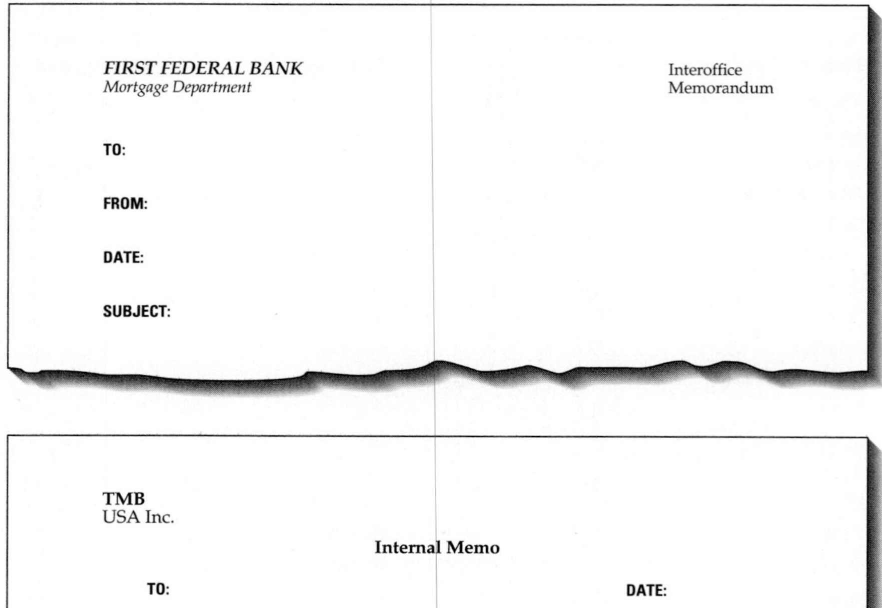

FIRST FEDERAL BANK
Mortgage Department

Interoffice
Memorandum

TO:

FROM:

DATE:

SUBJECT:

TMB
USA Inc.

Internal Memo

TO: **DATE:**

FROM: **FILE:**

SUBJECT:

Memorandums

As discussed in Chapter 7, memorandums deliver messages within organizations. Many offices use memo forms imprinted with the organization name and, optionally, the department or division names, as shown in Figure B.6. Although the design and arrangement of memo forms vary, they usually include the basic elements of TO, FROM, DATE, and SUBJECT. Large organizations may include other identifying headings, such as FILE NUMBER, FLOOR, EXTENSION, LOCATION, and DISTRIBUTION.

Because of the difficulty of aligning computer printers with preprinted forms, many business writers store memo formats in their computers and call them up when preparing memos. The guide words are then printed with the message, thus eliminating alignment problems.

If no printed or stored computer forms are available, memos may be typed on company letterhead or plain paper, as shown in Figure B.7. On a full sheet of paper, start on line 13; on a half sheet, start on line 7. Double-space and type in all caps the guide words: TO:, FROM:, DATE:, SUBJECT:. Align all the fill-in information two spaces after the longest guide word (SUBJECT:). Leave three lines after the last line of the heading and begin typing the body of the memo. Like business letters, memos are single-spaced.

Memos are generally formatted with side margins of 1¼ inches, or they may conform to the printed memo form. (For more information about memos, see Chapter 7.)

FIGURE B.7 ● Memo on Plain Paper

line 10

MEMO

1 1/4 inches

TO: Dawn Stewart, Manager
Sales and Marketing

DATE: February 3, 1994

FROM: Jay Murray, Vice President
Operations

SUBJECT: TELEPHONE SERVICE REQUEST FORMS

3 lines

To speed telephone installation and improve service within the Bremerton facility, we are starting a new application procedure.

Service request forms will be available at various locations within the three buildings. When you require telephone service, obtain a request form at one of the locations that is convenient for you. Fill in the pertinent facts, obtain approval from your division head, and send the form to Brent White. Request forms are available at the following locations:

FIGURE B.8 ● Fax Cover Sheet

FAX TRANSMISSION

DATE: ______________________

TO: ______________________ **FAX NUMBER:** ______________________

____

____

FROM: ______________________ **FAX NUMBER:** ______________________

____

____

NUMBER OF PAGES TRANSMITTED INCLUDING THIS COVER SHEET: ______________________

MESSAGE:

If any part of this fax transmission is missing or not clearly received, please call:

NAME: ______________________

PHONE: ______________________

Fax Cover Sheet

Documents transmitted by fax are usually introduced by a cover sheet, such as that shown in Figure B.8. As with memos, the format varies considerably. Important items to include are (1) the name and fax number of the receiver, (2) the name and fax number of the sender, (3) the number of pages being sent, and (4) the name and telephone number of the person to notify in case of unsatisfactory transmission.

When the document being transmitted requires little explanation, you may prefer to attach an adhesive note (such as a Post-it™ fax transmittal form) instead of a full cover sheet. These notes carry essentially the same information as shown in our printed fax cover sheet. They are perfectly acceptable in most business organizations and can save considerable paper and transmission costs.

Documentation Formats

Not many writers enjoy the task, but most take pains to properly document report data—for many reasons. Citing sources strengthens a writer's argument, as you learned in Chapter 11. Acknowledging sources also shields writers from charges of plagiarism. Moreover, good references help your readers pursue further research. Fortunately, word processing programs have taken much of the pain out of documenting data, so the task is no longer so tedious.

The task is further eased by recognizing the difference between *source* notes and *content* notes. Source notes identify quotations, paraphrased passages, and author references. They lead readers to the sources of cited information, and they must follow a consistent format. Content notes, on the other hand, enable writers to add comments, explain information not directly related to the text, or refer readers to other sections of a report. Because content notes are generally infrequent, most writers identify them in the text with a raised asterisk (*). At the bottom of the page, the asterisk is repeated with the content note following. If two content notes appear on one page, a double asterisk identifies the second reference.

Your real concern will be with source notes. These identify quotations or paraphrased ideas in the text, and they direct readers to the complete list (bibliography) of references at the end of your report.

 Source Notes

Source notes tell where ideas and information in the text originated. Researchers have struggled for years to develop the perfect documentation system, one that is efficient for the writer and crystal clear to the reader. As a result, many systems exist, each with its advantages. The important thing for you is to adopt one system and use it consistently. Naturally, you'll check with your organization to learn its preferences. To simplify matters in our discussion, we'll concentrate on the three most common source note formats: footnotes, endnotes, and parenthetic notes. Figure 11.9 in Chapter 11 illustrates these three formats and compares them briefly. The following expanded discussion focuses on note placement and format.

Footnotes

A traditional method for citing sources is footnoting. As the name suggests, references appear at the foot or bottom of each page. Footnotes position the references where readers can see them easily. Although manual placement of notes at the bottom of pages is admittedly difficult, today's word processing software greatly simplifies the process. At a command your software inserts a superscript (raised) number in the text and allows you to key in the footnote information. The program then stores this information. At print time it automatically calculates the number of lines required to position the text and footnotes on each page. Best of all, it renumbers all footnotes after any additions or deletions so that the list is always consecutive and current.

Placement. Generally, you'll try to place a source note reference, as shown in the following example, at the *end* of a sentence containing information to be acknowledged. If, however, the sentence is long and the reader might confuse the reference, place the reference number closer to the quoted or paraphrased information, as shown in the following example. Notice, too, that you need not repeat an author's name in the footnote if it is mentioned in the text.

> People who do well internationally are flexible, patient, and willing to invest in relationships. No one flies into Beijing or Cairo or Rome one day, works out a deal the next day, and returns home on the third day with the job complete.[1] Peters reports that it took Arco three and a half years to negotiate an off-shore drilling contract with China,[2] and other experts also stress the need to establish relationships before conducting business.
>
> ---
>
> [1]Leonard A. Cohen and Cordeleeza Love, "Investing in International Relationships," Forbes, 20 August 1993, 39.
>
> [2]Thriving on Chaos (New York: Alfred A. Knopf, 1991), 256.

Footnotes appear at the bottom of the page, separated from the text by a 1½-inch line. This separating line has a single blank line above and below it. Entries are single-spaced with a double space between them.

Format. Because consistency is important in source note formatting, you'll want to study the sequence, capitalization, and punctuation of the model formats shown in the list on pages 527–528. If you aren't sure how much information to include in your notes, put yourself in the position of the reader trying to track down your citation. And remember, it's always better to include too much information than too little.

Our examples show small superscript figures with each note at the bottom of the page. Your word processing program, however, may print full-sized figures that are not raised—and that format is certainly acceptable.

Endnotes

A second alternative for documenting references is the endnote method. Like footnotes, endnotes use superscript numerals within the text to identify cited data. Instead of appearing at the bottom of each page, however, all source notes are located at the end of the report on a separate page, generally called Notes. This method is easier for the writer but not quite so convenient for the reader, who must flip to the end of a report to find its references. Most word processing programs offer a choice of footnote or endnote placement.

Endnotes are listed in the order cited in the text, and they are numbered consecutively, as shown in the brief sample here.

Notes

1. Laurie M. Grossman, "From Sharks to Hornets, Team Logos Help Sports Apparel Score," The Wall Street Journal, 3 January 1994, B1.

2. Dean Peebles and John Ryans, Management of International Advertising, 2nd ed. (Chicago: Intercultural Press, 1992), 304.

3. Katherine J. Klein, "The 100 Best Companies to Work for in America," Los Angeles Times, 12 February 1994, C1, C5.

To review a complete list of endnotes, see Figure 14.4. Because the formats for footnotes and endnotes are identical, the models shown in the list on pages 525–526 are appropriate for both.

Parenthetic Notes

A third documentation method uses parenthetical data within the text to cite and identify references. The two best-known parenthetic methods are the MLA system and the APA system.

MLA System. The Modern Language Association recommends that writers cite references with a brief note within the text, such as *(Peters 214)*. This parenthetical comment usually consists of the author's last name and the page on which the reference is found. If no author name is available, as sometimes is the case in newspaper and magazine articles, an abbreviated title is used to identify the reference. The following excerpt illustrates the MLA documentation method:

> In many countries business card etiquette is no mere ritual. In places such as Japan, a business card is both a mini-résumé and a ticket to the game of business (Copeland and Griggs 161). In emphasizing the importance of business cards, experts say that the first rule is never to be without an ample supply ("Business Without Boundaries" 32). Author Roger Axtell notes that Americans must learn to treat business cards with reverence (158).

The main purpose of the parenthetical reference is to point the reader to a list of complete references in the Bibliography or Works Cited. For more information about the MLA referencing style, see the *MLA Handbook for Writers of Research Papers,* 3rd ed., by Joseph Gibaldi and Walter S. Achtert (New York: The Modern Language Association, 1988).

APA System. Another referencing system that uses parenthetic citations is the APA style, recommended by the American Psychological Association. In this style the author's last name, the year of publication, and pertinent page number(s) appear in parentheses after the information cited, such as *(Smith, 1990, p. 4)*. For a more thorough discussion of the APA system, consult the *Publication Manual of the American Psychological Association*, 3rd ed. (Washington, D.C.: American Psychological Association, 1983).

Bibliographies

A bibliography is a complete list of all references cited in a report. It may also include all references consulted by the researcher, particularly for more formal reports. For less formal reports and those with fewer than ten footnotes or endnotes, a bibliography may be omitted. For reports with many references, though, a bibliography is necessary because its alphabetical arrangement helps readers locate items quickly. If a bibliography has a great many entries, it may be divided into sections, such as books, periodicals, and professional journals.

Like source notes, bibliographies have different styles. For our purposes we'll show only two styles: the traditional bibliography and the MLA Works Cited style.

Traditional Bibliography

In the traditional bibliography, entries are listed by the author's last name or by the first word of an entry. The format of each entry, as shown in the list on pages 526–527, is similar to that of a source note. The primary differences are in punctuation and indentations.

Notice that each segment of the entry ends with a period instead of a comma. The author's full name is followed by a period, the title is followed by a period, and so on. Note, too, that entries are typed in hanging indented form, with the second and succeeding lines indented five spaces from the first line. This placement highlights the first word of each entry, thus enabling readers to locate specific entries quickly. Entries are single-spaced with double spacing between them. If the bibliography appears on a page by itself, the title is centered on line 13. To review an example of a complete bibliography, see the model report in Figure 14.4.

BIBLIOGRAPHY

Bonoma, Elizabeth. "Gone Are the Cash Cows of Yesteryear." U.S. News and World Report, 19 May 1993, 58–61.

Kaplan, Robert S. Relevance Lost: The Rise and Fall of Management Accounting. Paper presented at the annual meeting of the American Association of Accountancy, Boston, April 1992.

Peters, Tom. Thriving on Chaos. New York: Alfred A. Knopf, 1991.

Works Cited Bibliography

Reports prepared according to the MLA (Modern Language Association) style include parenthetic source notes, discussed earlier, along with a Works Cited bibliography. Writers are advised to prepare a complete list of all works planned as references for the report *before* composing the report. From this list, writers know what information to present in parenthetic source notes within the text. A citation such as *(Peters 59–61)*, for example, directs readers to the complete reference in the Works Cited.

Bibliographic entries in a Works Cited list are formatted similarly to those in traditional bibliographies. Notice in the following example that references are listed alphabetically in the hanging indented style. However, they are double-spaced. Moreover, in a reference for a newspaper, magazine, or other periodical, dates are separated from page numbers by colons. Months are abbreviated.

Works Cited

Chang, Alicia. "America's New-Wave Chip Firms." The Wall Street Journal 20 Jan. 1994: B1, B5.

Dreyfuss, Joel. The Leadership Challenge: Shaping and Managing Shared Values. Homewood, Illinois: Dow Jones–Irwin, 1992.

Levitt, Theodore. "Marketing Success Through Differentiation—of Anything." Harvard Business Review 46 (Jan/Feb 1993): 324–331. *["46" refers to vol. 46]*

Walton, Mary A., and Steven M. Gilbert. "The Riches in Market Niches." Entrepreneur Feb 1992: 45.

If you prepare a research report using the parenthetic source note method, along with a Works Cited bibliography, you'll want to refer to the *MLA Handbook for Writers of Research Papers.*

Source Note Formats for Endnotes and Footnotes*

Book, one author

[1] Jane Bryant Quinn, Making the Most of Your Money (New York: Simon & Schuster), 359.

Book, two authors, edition

[2] Dean Peebles and John Ryans, Management of International Advertising, 2nd ed. (Chicago: Intercultural Press, 1992), 304.

Book, edited

[3] Glen Fisher, ed., International Negotiation: A Cross-Cultural Perspective (Rockleigh, NJ: Allyn and Bacon, 1993), 155.

Book, chapter or section

[4] John L. Waltman, "Evaluating Technical Reports," in The Handbook of Executive Communication, ed. John Louis Digaetani (Homewood, Illinois: Dow Jones–Irwin, 1986), 436.

Annual report, pamphlet, or other publication from private organization

[5] Federal Express Corporation, 1993 Annual Report (Memphis: Federal Express, 1993), 2–3.

[6] Pinkerton Investigation Services, The Employers' Guide to Investigation Services (Atlanta: Pinkerton Information Center, 1994), 5, 15–16.

Government publication

[7] U.S. Small Business Administration, Business Plan for Small Manufacturers (Washington: U.S. Government Printing Office, 1992), 11.

Magazine article, one author

[8] Peter Coy, "Cheers for Corporate Collaboration," Business Week, 3 May 1994, 39. [Note that popular magazines do not require volume and part numbers.]

Magazine article, no author

[9] "Inc. 100: The Hottest Small Public Companies," Inc., May 1993, 42.

Newspaper article, one author

[10] Laurie M. Grossman, "From Sharks to Hornets, Team Logos Help Sports Apparel Score," The Wall Street Journal, 3 January 1994, B1.

*The formats shown are based on traditional format alternatives contained in *The Chicago Manual of Style,* 13th ed. (Chicago and London: University of Chicago Press, 1982), pp. 399–420, 485–510. The fourteen edition, not available in time for this publication, will be released in September 1993.

Newspaper article, no author

[11] "Executives, Take Your Risks," The New York Times, 27 March 1993, C1.

Professional journal with volume and part numbers

[12] Nancy M. Burson, John A. Walker, and Jill I. Wiley, "Tensions in Conflict Situations as Revealed by Metaphoric Analysis," Journal of Management Communication 6, no. 2 (November 1993): 116. [An alternate but acceptable form identifies the volume and part numbers more clearly: Journal of Management Communication, vol. 6, no. 2, November 1993, 116.]

Interviews and unpublished materials

[13] John F. Welch, Jr., interview with author, Fairfield, Connecticut, 2 April 1993.

[14] Dr. Marie Meir-Lansky, letter to Richard M. Law, 4 June 1992.

[15] Chan Su Park, "Estimation and Prediction of Brand Equities Through Survey Measurement of Consumer Preference Structures" (Ph.D. diss., Stanford University, 1993), 259.

Second references

[16] Peebles and Ryans, 307. [Include only last names and page numbers.]

[17] Waltman, Handbook of Executive Communication, 483. [Add a shortened title if the author has more than one title listed.]

Bibliographic Formats for Endnotes and Footnotes

Book, one author

Peters, Tom. Thriving on Chaos. New York: Alfred A. Knopf, 1991.

Book, two authors, edition

Peebles, Dean, and John Ryans. Management of International Advertising. 2nd. ed. Chicago: Intercultural Press, 1992.

Book, edited

Mendoza, Jeremy, ed. Quest for Quality. Minneapolis: Franklin Press, 1990.

Book, chapter or section

Waltman, John L. "Evaluating Technical Reports." In The Handbook of Executive Communication, edited by John Louis Digaetani. Homewood, Illinois: Dow Jones–Irwin, 1986.

Annual report, pamphlet, or other publication from private organization

AMR Corporation. 1993 Annual Report. Fort Worth: American Airlines, 1993.

Pinkerton Investigation Services. The Employer's Guide to Investigation Services. Atlanta: Pinkerton Information Center, 1994.

Government publication

Statistical Abstract of the United States. U.S. Bureau of the Census. Washington, D.C.: Government Printing Office, 1993.

Magazine article, one author

Bonoma, Elizabeth. "Gone Are the Cash Cows of Yesteryear." U.S. News and World Report, 19 May 1993, 58–61.

Magazine article, no author

"America Must Compete on Value, Not Price," Industry Week, 29 June 1993, 34–37.

Newspaper article, one author

Klein, Katherine J. "The 100 Best Companies to Work for in America," Los Angeles Times. 12 February 1994, C1, C5.

Newspaper article, no author

"The Winning Edge." Kansas City Star, 3 January 1994. Sports sec., 2.

Professional journal with volume and part numbers

Phillips, Ramon D., Jr. "Exploring Determinants of Success in Corporate Ventures." Journal of Business Venturing, 22, no. 3 (Winter 1993):254–73. [Alternate form: Journal of Business Venturing, vol. 22, no. 3 (Winter 1993), 254–73.]

Interviews and unpublished materials

Tully, Susanne. Telephone interview with author. 14 March 1993.

Kaplan, Robert S. Relevance Lost: The Rise and Fall of Management Accounting. Paper presented at the annual meeting of the American Association of Accountancy, Boston, April 1992.

Correction Symbols

In marking your papers, your instructor may use the following symbols or abbreviations to indicate writing weaknesses. You'll find that studying these symbols and suggestions will help you understand your instructor's remarks. Knowing this information can also help you evaluate and improve your own letters, memos, reports, and other writing. For specific writing guidelines and self-help exercises, see Appendix A, Competent Language Usage Essentials (C.L.U.E.).

Strategy and Organization

Coh Develop coherence between ideas. Repeat key idea or add transitional expression.
DS Use direct strategy. Start with main idea or good news.
IS Use indirect strategy. Explain before introducing main idea.
Org Improve organization. Keep similar topics together.
Plan Apply appropriate plan for message.
Trans Include transition to join ideas.

Content and Style

Acc Verify accuracy of names, places, amounts, and other data.
AE Use action ending that tells reader what to do.
ACE Avoid copying examples.
ACP Avoid copying case problems.
Act Use active voice.
Awk Rephrase to avoid awkward or unidiomatic expression.
Asn Check assignment for instructions or facts.
Chop Use longer sentences to avoid choppiness. Vary sentence patterns.
Cl Improve clarity of ideas or expression.
Con Condense into shorter form.
Emp Emphasize this idea.
Eth Use language that projects honest, ethical business practices.
Exp Explain more fully or clearly.

Inc Expand an incomplete idea.
Jar Avoid jargon or specialized language that reader may not know.
Log Remedy faulty logic.
Neg Revise negative expression with more positive view.
Obv Avoid saying what is obvious.
Par Use parallel (balanced) expression.
PV Express idea from reader's point of view.
RB Show reader benefits. What's in it for reader?
Rdn Revise to eliminate redundant idea or expression.
Rep Avoid unintentional repetition of word, idea, or sound.
Sin Use language that sounds sincere.
Spec Develop idea with specific details.
Sub Subordinate this point to lessen its impact.
SX Avoid sexist language.
Tone Use more conversational or positive tone.
You Emphasize *you*-view.
Var Vary sentences with different patterns.
Vag Avoid vague pronoun. Don't use *they, that, this, which, it,* or other pronouns unless their references are clear.
Vb Use correct verb tense. Avoid verb shift.
W Condense to avoid wordiness.
WC Improve word choice. Find a more precise word.

Grammar and Mechanics

Abv Avoid most abbreviations in text. Use correct abbreviation if necessary.
Agr Make each subject and verb or pronoun and noun agree.
Apos Use an apostrophe to show possession or contraction.
Art Choose a correct article (*a, an,* or *the*).
Cap Capitalize appropriately.
Cm Use a comma.
CmConj Use a comma preceding coordinating conjunction (*and, or, nor, but*) that joins independent clauses.
CmIntro Use a comma following introductory dependent clause or long phrase.
CmSer Use commas to separate items in a series.
CS Rectify a comma splice by separating independent clauses with a period or a semicolon.
Div Improve word division by hyphenating between syllables.
DM Rectify a dangling modifier by supplying a clear subject for modifying element.
Exp Avoid expletives such as *there is, there are,* and *it is.*
Frag Revise fragment to form complete sentence.
Gram Use correct grammar.
Hyp Hyphenate a compound adjective.
lc Use lower case instead of capital.
MM Correct misplaced modifier by moving modifier closer to word it describes or limits.
Num Express numbers in correct word or figure form.
Pn Use correct punctuation.
Prep Correct use of preposition.
RO Rectify run-on sentence with comma or semicolon to separate independent clauses.
Sem Use semicolon to join related independent clauses.
Sp Check spelling.
SS Shorten sentences.
UnCm Avoid unnecessary comma.

Format

Cen Center a document appropriately on the page.
DSp Insert a double space, or double-space throughout.
F Choose appropriate format for this item or message.
GH Use graphic highlighting (bullets, lists, indentions, and headings) to improve readability.
Mar Improve margins to frame a document on the page.
SSp Insert a single space, or single-space throughout.
TSp Insert a triple space.

PROOFREADING MARKS

Proofreading Mark	Draft Copy	Final Copy
Align horizontally	TO: Rick Munoz	TO: Rick Munoz
Align vertically	166.32 132.45	166.32 132.45
Capitalize	Coca-cola runs on ms-dos	Coca-Cola runs on MS-DOS
Close up space	meeting at 3 p. m.	meeting at 3 p.m.
Center	Recommendations	Recommendations
Delete	in my final judgement	in my judgment
Insert apostrophe	our companys product	our company's product
Insert comma	you will of course	you will, of course,
Insert hyphen	tax free income	tax-free income
Insert period	Ms Holly Hines	Ms. Holly Hines
Insert quotation mark	shareholders receive a bonus.	shareholders receive a "bonus."
Insert space	wordprocessing program	word processing program
Lowercase (remove capitals)	the Vice President HUMAN RESOURCES	the vice president Human Resources
Move to left	I. Labor costs	I. Labor costs
Move to right	A. Findings of study	A. Findings of study
Spell out	aimed at 2 depts	aimed at two departments
Start new paragraph	Keep the screen height of your computer at eye level.	Keep the screen height of your computer at eye level.
Stet (don't delete)	officials talked openly	officials talked openly
Transpose	accounts recievable	accounts receivable
Use boldface	Conclusions	**Conclusions**
Use italics	The Perfect Résumé	*The Perfect Résumé*

Key to C.L.U.E. Exercises

Revised words and punctuation are shown in bold type.

Chapter 1

1. After he checked many statements, our **accountant** found the error in **Column** 2 of the balance sheet.

2. Because Mr. **Lockwood's** business owned considerable property, we were **surprised** by **its** lack of liquid assets.

3. The mortgage company checked all property titles **separately;** however, it found no discrepancies.

4. When Ms. Diaz finished the audit, she wrote **three** letters **to apprise** the owners of her findings.

5. Just between you and **me, who** do you think could have ordered all this **stationery?**

6. Assets and liabilities **are** what the **four** buyers want to see; consequently, we are preparing this **year's** statements.

7. Next spring my brother and **I** plan to enroll in the following courses: marketing, **English,** and history.

8. Dan felt that he had done **well** on the exam, but he wants to do even better when it's given again next **fall.**

9. Our records show that your **end-of-the-month** balance was **$96.30.**

10. When the **principal** in the account grows **too** large, we must make annual withdrawals.

Chapter 2

1. To avoid **embarrassing** any employee, the **personnel** manager and **I have** decided to talk **personally** to each individual.

2. **Three** assistants were sent on a **search-and-destroy** mission in a conscious effort to remove at least **15,000** old documents from the files.

3. Electronic mail, now used by **three fourths** [or **three quarters**] of **America's** largest **companies,** will transmit messages instantly.

4. An article entitled **"What's New With Managers"** appeared in **Reader's Digest,** which is read by **60 million Americans.**

5. Your account is now **60** days overdue; consequently, we have only **one** alternative left.

6. The marketing **manager's itinerary** listed the following three destinations: **Seattle, Portland,** and **Eugene.**

7. Each of the **beautifully printed** [delete hyphen] books available at **Pickwick Book Company has** been reduced to **$30.**

8. We **recommend, therefore,** that a committee study our mail procedures for a **three-week** period and submit a report of **its** findings.

9. **They're** going to visit **their** relatives in **Columbus, Ohio,** over the **Memorial Day** holiday.

10. The hotel can **accommodate 300** convention guests, but it has parking facilities for only **100** cars.

Chapter 3

1. If I **were** you, I would schedule the conference for one of these cities: Atlanta, Memphis, or Nashville.

2. The **committee's** next meeting is scheduled for May **5** at **3** p.m. [omit comma] and should last about two hours.

3. **We're** not asking you to **alter** the figures; we are asking you to check **their** accuracy. [or start a new sentence with "We are."]

4. Will you please fax me a list of our **independent contractors'** names and addresses.

5. The vacation **calendar** fills up **quickly** for the **summer** months; therefore, you should make your plans early.

6. After the inspector issues the **waiver,** we will be able to **proceed** with the **architect's** plan.

7. If we can't give out **necessary information,** what is the point in **our** answering the telephone?

8. New **employees** will receive their orientation packets [omit comma] and be told about parking **privileges.** [Or Every new employee will receive **an** orientation packet and be told about parking **privileges.** Or Every new employee will receive **his or her** orientation packet and be told about **his or her** parking **privileges.**]

9. About **85** percent of all new entrants into the workforce in the 1990s **are** expected to be [omit colon] women, minorities, and immigrants.

10. Our **vice president** in the Human Resources Development Department asked the **manager** and **me** to come to her office at **3:30** p.m.

Chapter 4

1. Although [omit comma] we **formerly** used a neighborhood printer for all our print jobs, we are now saving almost **$500** a month by using desktop publishing.

2. Powerful **software**, however, cannot **guarantee** a good final product.

3. To develop a better sense of design, we collected **desirable** samples from [omit colon] books, magazines, brochures, and newsletters.

4. We wanted that [omit comma] poorly [omit hyphen] designed projects often **were** filled with cluttered layouts, incompatible typefaces, and **too** many typefaces.

5. Our layout design **is** usually formal, but **occasionally** we use an informal layout design, which is shown in **Figure 6**.

6. We **usually** prefer a **black-and-white** design [omit semicolon] because color printing is much more costly.

7. Expensive color printing jobs are sent to foreign countries; for example, **China, Italy,** and **Japan.**

8. Jeffrey's article, which he entitled "The Shaping of a **Corporate Image,** was **accepted** for publication in **The Journal of Communication.**

9. Every employee will **personally receive** a copy of **his or her performance evaluation,** which the **president** said will be the **principal** basis for promotion. [Or **All employees** will **personally receive** copies of their **performance evaluations**. . . .]

10. We will print **350** copies of the newsletter [omit comma] to be sent to **whoever** is currently listed in our database.

Chapter 5

1. Business documents must be written **clearly** to **ensure** that readers comprehend the message **quickly**.

2. We expect Mayor Wilson to visit the **governor** in an attempt to increase the **city's** share of **state** funding.

3. The caller could have been **he,** but we don't know for sure [optional comma] since he didn't leave his name.

4. The survey was **cited** in an article entitled **"What's New in Software";** however, I can't locate it now.

5. All three of our **company's** auditors—Jim Lucus, Doreen Delgado, and Brad Kirby—**criticized their** accounting procedures.

6. Any one of the auditors **is** authorized to **proceed** with an **independent** action; however, only a member of the management **council** can alter policy.

7. Because our printer has been **broken every day** this week, **we're** looking at new models.

8. Have you **already** ordered the following**:** a dictionary, a reference manual, and a style book**?**

9. In the morning **Mrs.** Williams **ordinarily** opens the office; in the evening **Mr.** Williams **usually** closes it.

10. When you travel in **England** and **Ireland,** I **advise** you to charge purchases to your **Visa** [or **VISA**] credit card.

Chapter 6

1. The **extraordinary** increase in sales is related to **our** placing the staff on a commission basis, and the increase also **affected** our stock value.

2. She acts as if she **were** the only person who ever received a **compliment** about **his or her** business **writing.** [Or omit **his or her**]

3. Karen is interested in working for the U.S. **Foreign Service,** [optional comma] since she is **hoping** to travel.

4. Major Hawkins, **who** I think will be elected, has **already** served three **consecutive** terms as a member of the **Gulfport City Council**.

5. After Mr. Freeman and **he** returned from lunch, the **customers** were handled more **quickly.**

6. Our new **employees'** cafeteria, which opened six months ago, has a salad bar that everyone **definitely** likes. [Or Our new **employee** cafeteria, . . .]

7. On Tuesday **Ms.** Adams can see you at **2** p.m.; on Wednesday she has a full **schedule**.

8. His determination, courage, and sincerity could not be denied; however, his methods were often questioned.

9. After you have checked the matter **further**, report to the CEO and **me.**

10. Mr. Garcia and **she** advised me not to **desert** my employer at this time, although they were quite sympathetic to my **personal** problems.

Chapter 7

1. Mr. Krikorian always tries, however, to wear a tie and shirt that **have complementary** colors.

2. The **Federal Trade Commission is** holding hearings to **elicit** information about **IBM's** request to expand marketing in **21 cities**.

3. Consumer buying and spending for the past five years [omit comma] **are** being studied by a **federal** team of analysts.

4. Because we recommmend that students bring **their** own supplies, the total expense for the trip should be a **minor** amount.

5. Wasn't it **Mr.** Cohen, not **Ms.** Lyons, who asked for a tuition **waiver?**

6. As soon as we can verify the figures, either my sales manager or **I** will call you; nevertheless, you must continue to **disburse** payroll funds.

7. Our **Human Resources Department**, which was **formerly** in **Room** 35, has moved **its** offices to **Room** 5.

8. We have arranged interviews on the following dates: Wednesday at **3:30 p.m.**, Thursday at **10:30 a.m.**, and Friday at **4:15 p.m.**

9. The <u>**Post Dispatch**</u>, our local newspaper, featured as its **principal** article, a story entitled [omit comma] "**Smarter** E-Mail **Is Here.**"

10. Everyone on the payroll, which includes all dispatchers and **supervisors, was** cautioned to maintain careful records **every day**.

Chapter 8

1. Your advertisement in the **June 2** edition of the <u>**Boston Globe**</u> [omit comma] caught my attention [omit semicolon] because my training and experience **match** your requirements.

2. Undoubtedly, the bank is closed at this hour, but **its** ATM will enable you to **receive** the cash you need.

3. A flow chart detailing all **sales** procedures in **four** divisions **was** prepared by our **vice president**.

4. The computer and printer **were** working **well** yesterday [omit comma] and appeared to be **all right** this morning [omit semicolon] when I used **them** for my report.

5. If I **were** you, I would be more concerned with **long-term**, not **short-term**, returns on the invested **capital**.

6. We make a **conscious** effort, by the way, to find **highly qualified** individuals with **up-to-date** computer skills.

7. If your résumé had **come** earlier, I could have **shown** it to Mr. Sutton and **her** before your interview.

8. Deborah's report summary is [omit **more**] easier to read **than David's** because she used **consistent** headings and efficient writing techniques.

9. At McDonald's we ordered **four Big Macs, three** orders of french fries, and **five Coca-Colas** for lunch.

10. Because the budget cuts will severely **affect** all programs, the faculty **has** unanimously opposed **them**.

Chapter 9

1. Two loans made to Consumer **Products Corporation** must be repaid within 90 days, **or** the owners will be in default.

2. One loan was for property **appraised** at **$40,000;** the other was for property estimated to be worth **$10,000**.

3. Our **senior marketing director** and the sales manager are quite **knowledgeable** about communications hardware; therefore, they are traveling to the **computer** show in northern California.

4. We **congratulate** you on winning the award [omit comma] and hope that you will continue to experience **similar** success [omit comma] in the future.

5. Mr. Salazar left **$3 million** to be divided among **four** heirs, one of whom is a successful **manufacturer**.

6. If the CEO and **he** had behaved more **professionally**, the chances of a **practical** settlement would be considerably greater.

7. Just inside the entrance [omit comma] **are** the desk of the receptionist and a complete directory of all **departments.**

8. All new **employees** must **receive** their **permits** to park in **Lot** 5-A, or **their cars** will be **cited**. [Or **Every** new **employee** must **receive a** permit to park in **Lot** 5-A, or **his or her** car will be **cited**.]

9. When we open our office in Montreal, we will need at least **three** people **who** are fluent in **French** and **English**.

10. Most **companies** can boost profits almost **100** percent by retaining just 5 **percent** more of **their permanent** customers.

Chapter 10

1. U.S. exports **have** increased by **76** percent in the past five years, and our trade deficit has **fallen** to **its** lowest level since 1974.

2. After years of downsizing and restructuring, the U.S. has now become one of the **world's** most competitive producers in many **industries.**

3. However, many **companies'** products still sell better at home **than** abroad [omit semicolon] because these **companies** lack overseas experience.

4. Companies like Amway [omit comma] discovered that **their** unique **door-to-door** selling method was very successful in **Japan**.

5. The U.S. **Commerce Department** asked Mr. Sato and **me** to describe the marketing of [omit colon] aircraft, high-tech products, and biomedical technology.

6. Some of the products most likely to **succeed** abroad are [omit colon] blue jeans, **Coke,** home appliances, and prepared foods.

7. As **American companies** learn to **accommodate** global tastes, they will be expanding into vast new markets in **China, South America,** and **Europe**.

8. The seminar **emphasizing** exporting will cost **$300,** which seems expensive for a **newly formed** company.

9. The manager thinks that **your** attending the **three-day** seminar is a good idea; however, we must still check your work **calendar.**

10. Exports from small companies **have** increased, thereby **affecting** this **country's** trade balance positively.

Notes

Chapter 1

1. Lois Therrien, "This Marketing Effort Has L'eggs," *Business Week,* 23 December 1991, 50.

2. John H. Bryan, speech before the Corporate Affairs Communications Conference, 21 May 1990, Chicago.

3. *Leeway* magazine, Sara Lee Corporation, March 1992.

4. Renee A. G. Rodriguez, interview with Mary Ellen Guffey, 4 June 1992.

5. Alvin Toffler, *PowerShift* (New York: Bantam Books, 1990), 238.

6. Peter Drucker, "New Realities, New Ways of Managing," *Business Month,* May 1989, 50–51.

7. See, for example, "Employers Rate Enthusiasm and Communication as Top Job Skills," *Marketing News,* 27 March 1989; James C. Bennett and Robert J. Olney, "Executive Priorities for Effective Communication in an Information Society," *The Journal of Business Communication,* Spring 1986, 13–22; Frances W. Weeks, "Communication Competencies Listed in Job Descriptions," *The Bulletin of the American Business Communication Association,* September 1971, 18–37, and December 1974, 22–34; Marie E. Flatley, "Comparative Analysis of the Written Communication of Managers at Various Organizational Levels in the Private Business Sector," *The Journal of Business Communication,* Summer 1982, 35–49.

8. Mona J. Casady and F. Stanford Wayne, "Communication Skills in Employment Ads of Major United States Newspapers," *The Delta Pi Epsilon Journal,* Spring, 1992.

9. Arthur Andersen & Co.; Arthur Young; Coopers & Lybrand; Deloitte, Haskins, & Sells; Ernst & Whitney; Peat, Marwick, & Co.; Price Waterhouse; & Touche Ross, *Perspectives on Education: Capabilities for Success in the Accounting Profession* (New York, 1989). See also A. R. Pustorino, "CPAs Need Better Communication Skills," *The CPA Journal,* June 1989, 6, 10.

10. "Modern Office Machines Defray Rising Business-Letter Costs," Dartnell Target Study (Chicago: Dartnell, 1992), 4.

11. Barrett J. Mandel and Judith Yellen, "Mastering the Memo," *Working Woman,* September 1989, 135.

12. Barbara DePompa, "Start Your Engines," *Success,* December 1990, 24.

13. Lester Faigley and Thomas P. Miller, "What We Learn From Writing on the Job," *College English,* vol. 44 (1982): 557–69.

14. Cheryl Hamilton with Cordell Parker, *Communicating for Results* (Belmont, CA: Wadsworth, 1990), 8.

15. Jerry Sullivan, Naoki Karmeda, and Tatsuo Nobu, "Bypassing in Managerial Communication," *Business Horizons,* January/February 1991, 72.

16. Warren R. Plunkett and Raymond F. Attner, *Introduction to Management* (Boston: PWS/Kent, 1988), 84.

17. Peter Drucker, *Managing the Non-Profit Organization: Practices and Principles* (New York: HarperCollins, 1990), 46.

18. Interview With Susan Rebell, as reported in "New Key Steps to Take in Global Marketing," *Boardroom Reports,* 1 February 1991, 4.

19. "The Written Word," *Success,* December 1990, 24.

20. Ray Killian, *Managing by Design . . . for Executive Effectiveness* (New York: American Management Association, 1968), 255.

21. Peter Blau, *On the Nature of Organizations* (New York: Wiley, 1974), 7.

22. "Who Told You That?" *The Wall Street Journal,* 23 May 1985, 33.

23. Eugene Walton, "How Effective Is the Grapevine?" *Personnel 28* (1961): 45–49; and Keith Davis, *Human Behavior at Work,* 5th ed. (New York: McGraw-Hill, 1977), 277–286.

24. Eugene Walton, "Communicating Down the Line: How They Really Get the Word," *Personnel 28* (1961): 22–24.

25. Hamilton, *Communicating for Results,* 12–13.

26. Faye Rice, "Champions of Communication," *Fortune,* 3 June 1991, 111.

27. Paul Ingrassia and Bradley A. Stertz, "With Chrysler Ailing, Lee Iacocca Concedes Mistakes in Managing," *The Wall Street Journal,* 17 September 1990, A9.

28. Rice, "Champions of Communication," 111.

29. Patricia Wells, "Large Corporate Communication," in *The Handbook of Executive Communication,* John L. DiGaetani (Homewood, IL: Dow Jones/Irwin, 1986), 81–82.

30. Rice, "Champions of Communication," 112.

31. Andrew S. Grove, "Managing for 'Just-in-Time Business,'" *Newsweek,* 11 May 1991, Management Digest sec.

32. Gerald M. Goldhaber, *Organizational Communication,* 5th ed. (Dubuque, IA: William C. Brown, 1990), 5.

33. Matt Miller, "Psssst . . . Have You Heard the Latest?" *Fortune,* May 1984, 2.

34. "New Worker-Survey Findings," *The Fact Finder,* March 1991, 4, reports study of Evan G. Bane, "1990 Deluxe Data

Systems Employee Communications Survey."
35. John H. Bryan, speech before the Corporate Affairs Communications Conference, 21 May 1990, Chicago.

Chapter 2

1. Andrea Ciriello, interview with Mary Ellen Guffey, 26 June 1992. Other information from The Travelers Corporation, *1991 Annual Report* (Hartford, CT: The Travelers Corporation, 1992), 1–12; and *Protection* (Hartford, CT: The Travelers Printing Center, 1992).
2. Tom W. Harris, "Listen Carefully," *Nation's Business*, June 1989, 78.
3. Harris, "Listen Carefully," 78.
4. L. K. Steil, L. L. Barker, and K. W. Watson, *Effective Listening: Key to Your Success* (Reading, MA: Addison-Wesley, 1983).
5. Interview with John Sculley, "Pinnacle," Cable News Network, New York, 12 December 1987.
6. Eric H. Nelson and Jan Gypen, "The Subordinate's Predicament," *Harvard Business Review*, September/October, 1979, 133.
7. Stephen Golen, "A Factor Analysis of Barriers to Effective Listening" *The Journal of Business Communication*, Winter 1990, 25–37.
8. Albert Mehrabian, *Silent Messages* (Belmont, CA: Wadsworth, 1971), 44.
9. J. Burgoon, D. Coker, and R. Coker, "Communicative Explanations," *Human Communication Research*, 12 (1986): 463–494.
10. Julius Fast, *Subtext: Making Body Language Work in the Workplace* (New York: Viking, 1991), 129.
11. Ray Birdwhistel, *Kinesics and Context* (Philadelphia: University of Pennsylvania Press, 1970).
12. "In Athens, It's Palms In," *Newsweek*, 10 December 1990, 79Q.
13. Anne Russell, "Fine-Tuning Your Corporate Image," *Black Enterprise*, May 1992, 74.
14. Russell, "Fine-Tuning Your Corporate Image," 80.
15. Cheryl Hamilton with Cordell Parker, *Communicating for Results* (Belmont, CA: Wadsworth, 1990), 127.
16. David L. James, "The Art of the Deal (Japan-Style)," *Business Month*, November 1989, 93.
17. Murray Weidenbaum, "Success Isn't Guaranteed in the Global Marketplace," *Los Angeles Times*, 5 May 1991, D2.
18. Endel-Jakob Kolde, *Environment of International Business*, 2nd ed. (Boston: PWS/Kent, 1985), 420–424.
19. Kathleen K. Reardon, *Where Minds Meet* (Belmont, CA: Wadsworth, 1987), 199.
20. Vivienne Luk, Mumtaz Patel, and Kathryn White, "Personal Attributes of American and Chinese Business Associates," *The Bulletin of the Association for Business Communication*, December 1990, 67.
21. Susan S. Jarvis, "Preparing Employees to Work South of the Border," *Personnel*, June 1990, 63.
22. Lennie Copeland and Lewis Griggs, *Going International* (New York: Penguin Books, 1985), 12.
23. Copeland and Griggs, *Going International*, 108.
24. Shari Caudron, "Training Ensures Success Overseas," *Personnel Journal*, December 1991, 29.
25. Robert McGarvey, "Foreign Exchange," *USAir Magazine*, June 1992, 61.
26. Jeff Copeland, "Stare Less, Listen More," *American Way*, American Air Lines, 15 December 1990.
27. Ted Holden and Jennifer Wiener, "Revenge of the 'Office Ladies,'" *Business Week*, 13 July 1992, 42–43.
28. Nancy Rivera Brooks, "Exports Boom Softens Blow of Recession," *Los Angeles Times*, 29 May 1991, D1.
29. Roger Axtell, *Do's and Taboos Around the World*, 2nd ed. (New York: Wiley, 1990), 171.
30. Bob Weinstein, "When in Rome," *Entrepreneur*, March 1991, 70.
31. Robert McGarvey, "Foreign Exchange," *USAir Magazine*, June 1992, 64.

Chapter 3

1. Brian Finnegan, interview with Mary Ellen Guffey, June 1992. Additional information from Lands' End, *1992 Annual Report* (Dodgeville, WI: Lands' End, 1993), 3–7; Kate Fitzgerald, "Lands' End to Fashion New Look," *Advertising Age*, 30 April 1990, 25; Ronit Addis, "Big Picture Strategy," *Forbes*, 9 January 1989, 70; Patricia Sellers, "Getting Customers to Love You," *Fortune*, 13 March 1989, 38; Eric N. Berg, "Standout in the Land of Catalogues," *The New York Times*, 8 December 1988, D1; and Brian Bremner and Keith H. Hammonds, "Lands' End Looks a Bit Frayed at the Edges," *Business Week*, 19 March 1990, 42.
2. Julia Lawler, "Akers, Gates Find Loaded Memos Can Backfire," *USA Today*, 20 June 1991, B1.
3. Elizabeth Fisher, "Campaigners in the Communications War," *Accountancy*, December 1989, 98.
4. Earl N. Harbert, "Knowing Your Audience," in *The Handbook of Executive Communication*, ed. John L. DiGaetani (Homewood, IL: Dow Jones/Irwin, 1986), 3.
5. Vanessa Dean Arnold, "Benjamin Franklin on Writing Well," *Personnel Journal*, August 1986, 17.
6. Mark Bacon, quoted in "Business Writing: One-on-One Speaks Best to the Masses," *Training*, April 1988, 95.
7. Claudia H. Deutsch, "Mastering the Language of Disability," *The New York Times*, 10 February 1991, F25.
8. Leslie Matthies, quoted in Carl Heyel, "Policy and Procedure Manuals," *The Handbook of Executive Communication*, 212.
9. Robert McGarvey, "Do the Right Thing," *Entrepreneur*, October 1992, 140.
10. Max M. Thomas, "Classroom Conundrum: Profits + Ethics = ?" *Business Month*, February 1990, 6.
11. Robert C. Solomon and Kristine Hanson, *It's Good Business* (New York: Atheneum, 1985).
12. Mary E. Guy, *Ethical Decision Making in Everyday Work Situations* (New York: Quorum Books, 1990), 3.
13. Guy, *Ethical Decision Making*, 4.
14. Alison Bell, "What Price Ethics?" *Entrepreneurial Woman*, January/February 1991, 68.
15. Based on Michael Josephson's remarks reported in Bell, "What Price Ethics?" *Entrepreneurial Woman*, 68.
16. Diane Cole, "Ethics: Companies Crack Down on Dishonesty," *The Wall Street Journal*, Spring 1991, Managing Your Career, sec. 8.
17. Joanne Lipman, "FTC Puts Advertisers on Notice of Crackdown on Misleading Ads," *The Wall Street Journal*, 4 February 1991, B6.
18. Jane Applegate, "Women Starting Small Businesses Twice as Fast as Men," *The Washington Post*, 2 September 1991, WB10.

19. Parts of this section are based on Kristin R. Woolever's "Corporate Language and the Law: Avoiding Liability in Corporate Communications," *IEE Transactions on Professional Communication,* 2 June 1990, 94–98.
20. Woolever, *IEE Transactions,* 96.
21. Woolever, *IEE Transactions,* 97.
22. Judy E. Pickens, "Communication: Terms of Equality: A Guide to Bias-Free Language," *Personnel Journal,* August 1985, 24.
23. "Faxpoll," *Business Month,* December 1989, 7.

Chapter 4

1. Susanne Tully, interview with Mary Ellen Guffey, 7 July and 23 July 1992; *We're Hanging Our Hopes on You,* (North Bergen, NJ: Liz Claiborne, Inc., 1991), 1–18; Nancy Marx Better, "The Secret of Liz Claiborne's Success," *Working Woman,* April 1992, 68–71; "Fashionable Cash," *Forbes,* 2 September 1991, 332; and Nina Darnton, "The Joy of Polyester," *Newsweek,* 3 August 1992, 61.
2. Andrew Fluegelman and Jeremy Joan Hewes, "The Word Processor and the Writing Process," in *Strategies for Business and Technical Writing,* ed. Kevin J. Harty (San Diego: Harcourt Brace Jovanovich, 1989), 43.
3. Michael Granberry, "Lingerie Chain Fined $100,000 for Gift Certificates," *Los Angeles Times,* 14 November 1992, D3.
4. Advertisement appearing in *The New York Times,* 12 December 1992, 7.
5. Kim Foltz, "Scali Quits Volvo Account, Citing Faked Commercial," *The New York Times,* 14 November 1990, C1; and Stuart Elliott, "Volvo Says It's Crushed Over Misleading Ads," *USA Today,* 6 November 1990, B1.
6. Bruce Horovitz, "Ad Nauseam," *Los Angeles Times,* 10 December 1992, D1.
7. Horovitz, "Ad Nauseam," D1.
8. Robert W. Goddard, "Communication: Use Language Effectively," *Personnel Journal,* April 1989, 32.
9. Frederick Crews, *The Random House Handbook,* 5th ed. (New York: Random House, 1987), 152.
10. Lisa S. Ede and Andrea A. Lunsford, "Collaborative Learning: Lessons from the World of Work," *WPA: Writing Program Administration,* Spring 1986, 17–26.
11. Lester Faigley and Thomas P. Miller, "What We Learn From Writing on the Job," *College English 44* (1982): 557–569; Barbara Couture and Jone Rymer, "Interactive Writing on the Job: Definitions and Implications of 'Collaboration,' " in *Writing in the Business Professions,* ed. Myra Kogen (Urbana, IL: National Council of Teachers of English, 1989), 74.
12. Based on Ruth G. Newman, "Collaborative Writing With Purpose and Style," *Personnel Journal,* April 1988, 37.

Chapter 5

1. Louise Lague, interview with Mary Ellen Guffey, 5 February 1992. Other information from "News About *People:* The Personality Journalism Phenomenon," (news release, *People* magazine); and "As 'People' Goes, So . . ." *Advertising Age,* 24 October 1988, S30.
2. Peter Elbow, *Writing With Power: Techniques for Mastering the Writing Process* (Oxford: Oxford University Press, 1981); Michael E. Adelstein, *Contemporary Business Writing* (New York: Random House, 1971).
3. John S. Fielden, "What Do You Mean You Don't Like My Style?" *Harvard Business Review,* May/June 1982, 138.
4. Thomas J. Peters and Robert H. Waterman, Jr., *In Search of Excellence* (New York: Warner Books, 1982), 65.
5. Claire K. Cook, *Line by Line* (Boston: Houghton Mifflin, 1985), 17.
6. William Power and Michael Siconolfi, "Memo to: Mr. Ball, RE: Your Messages, Sir: They're Weird," *The Wall Street Journal,* 30 November 1990, 1.
7. Al Neuharth, "Why Washington Is Lost in the Fog," *USA Today,* 12 October 1990, A13.
8. Berle Haggblade, "Has Technology Solved the Spelling Problem?" *The Bulletin of the Association for Business Communication,"* March 1988, 23.
9. Spell checker poem attributed to John Placona and acquired from Dr. Brian G. Wilson, College of Marin, Marin, California.
10. Lague, interview.
11. Malcolm Forbes, "How to Write a Business Letter," International Paper Company, reprinted in *Strategies for Business and Technical Writing,* ed. Kevin J. Harty (San Diego: Harcourt Brace Jovanovich, 1989), 115.

Chapter 6

1. Alice Blachly, interview with Mary Ellen Guffey, 12 January 1993. Other information from Jennifer J. Laabs, "Unmarried . . . With Benefits," *Personnel Journal,* December 1991, 62; Ellie Winninghoff, "Citizen Cohen," *Mother Jones,* January 1990, 12; Kim Hubbard and Tony Kahn, "For New Age Ice-Cream Moguls Ben and Jerry, Making 'Cherry Garcia' and 'Chunky Monkey' Is a Labor of Love," *People,* 10 September 1990; Joe Queenan, "Purveying Yuppie Porn," *Forbes,* 13 November 1989, 60; and Erik Larson, "I Scream, You Scream . . . ," *Utne Reader,* January/February 1989, 64.
2. Malcolm Forbes, "How to Write a Business Letter," International Paper Company, reprinted in *Strategies for Business and Technical Writing,* 3rd ed., ed. Kevin Harty (San Diego: Harcourt Brace Jovanovich, 1989), 115.
3. Sylvia Porter, "Dear Boss: Just What Was Your Memo Trying to Say?" *Los Angeles Daily News,* 28 April 1986.
4. *Business Week,* 6 July 1981, 107.
5. "The Quality Imperative," *Business Week,* 25 October 1991, 7–16.
6. "Nixdorf Computer Corporation," *Excellence Achieved* (New York: Bureau of Business Practice, 1991), 141.
7. Robert J. Aalberts and Lorraine A. Krajewski, "Claim and Adjustment Letters: Theory Versus Practice and Legal Implications," *The Bulletin of the Association for Business Communication,* September 1987, 5.
8. "Reader's Digest," *Excellence Achieved* (Waterford, CT: Bureau of Business Practice/Prentice Hall, 1990), 54.
9. "L. L. Bean," *Excellence Achieved* (Waterford, CT: Bureau of Business Practice/Prentice Hall, 1990), 37.
10. Aalberts and Krajewski, "Claim and Adjustment Letters," 2.
11. Saburo Haneda and Hirosuke Shima, "Japanese Communication Behavior as Reflected in Letter Writing," *The Journal of Business Communication, 1* (1982): 29.
12. Wolfgang Manekeller, as cited in Iris I. Varner, "Internationalizing Business Communication Courses," *The Bulletin of the Association for Business Communication,* December 1987, 10.
13. Dr. Annette Luciani-Samec, French instructor, and Dr. Pierre Samec, French businessman, interviews with author,

Palo Alto, California, November and December 1991.
14. Retha H. Kilpatrick, "International Business Communication Practices," *The Journal of Business Communication,* Fall 1984, 42–43.
15. Leonard Silk, "The New (Improved) Creed of Social Responsibility," *Business Month,* November 1988, 109.
16. Larry Stevens, "Automating the Selection Process," *Personnel Journal,* November 1991, 59–60.
17. Based on articles by Frank Edward Allen, "McDonald's to Reduce Waste in Plan Developed With Environmental Group," *Wall Street Journal,* 17 April 1991, B1; Martha T. Moore, "McDonald's Trashes Sandwich Boxes," *USA Today,* 2 November 1990, 9B; and Michael Parrish, "McDonald's To Do Away With Foam Packages," *Los Angeles Times,* 2 November 1990, 1.
18. Based on the case of First Union National Bank of Charlotte, North Carolina, described in James L. Heskett, *Service Breakthroughs* (New York: Free Press), as reported in "How to Correct Service Mistakes Without Losing Customers," *Boardroom Reports,* 15 March 1990, 2.

Chapter 7

1. Kenneth H. Kim, interview with Mary Ellen Guffey, 1 February 1993. Other information from "Behemoths of Banking," *U.S. News & World Report,* 26 August 1991, 18; Russell Mitchell and Joan Hamilton, "Bank of America's Big Bang," *Business Week,* 26 August 1991, 24; Catherine Yang, "Greasing the Rails for the Bank-Merger Express, *Business Week,* 26 August 1991, 25; "How to Revive a Dying Bank," *U.S. News & World Report,* 1 October 1990, 52; and Jonathan B. Levine, "Watch Out: Here Comes Bank of America Again," *Business Week,* 20 February 1989, 129.
2. See Anita S. Bednar and Robert J. Olney, "Communication Needs of Recent Graduates," *The Bulletin of the Association for Business Communication,* December 1987, 22; see also Mary K. Kirtz and Diana C. Reep, "A Survey of the Frequency, Types and Importance of Writing Tasks in Four Career Areas," *The Bulletin of the Association for Business Communication,* December 1990, 3.
3. Revealed by Robert Half International, as cited in Cynthia A. Barnes, *Model Memos* (Englewood Cliffs, NJ: Prentice-Hall, 1990), 4.
4. Bednard and Olney, "Communication Needs of Recent Graduates," 22.
5. Richard H. Needham, "First Job Survival Guide," *Managing Your Career, The Wall Street Journal,* Spring 1991, 7.
6. Rosalind Gold, " 'Reader-Friendly' Writing," *Supervisory Management,* January 1989, 40.
7. Marya W. Holcombe, "Wisdom or Information? Managerial Writing in the Office of the Future," in *The Handbook of Executive Communication,* ed. John L. DiGaetani (New York: Dow Jones/Irwin, 1986), 261.
8. Robert H. Anderson, "Toward an Ethic and Etiquette for Electronic Mail" (Santa Monica, CA: Rand Corporation, 1985).
9. Amy Kuebelbeck, "Getting the Message," *Los Angeles Times,* 4 September 1992, E1.
10. Tekla S. Perry, "E-Mail: Pervasive and Persuasive," Institute of Electrical and Electronic Engineers, *IEEE Spectrum,* October 1992, 23.
11. John Fielden, "Clear Writing Is Not Enough," *Management Review,* April 1989, 51.
12. Based on Leslie Lamkin and Emily W. Carmain "Crisis Communication at Georgia Power," *Personnel Journal,* January 1991, 35–37.

Chapter 8

1. Darin Richins, interview with Mary Ellen Guffey, 27 May 1992. Other information from "Listening to Customers Pays Off Big," *Boardroom Reports,* 15 June 1990; "Thriving on Crisis," *Success,* April 1990, 16; "WordPerfect Sets a Lofty (and Costly) Standard for Service," *PC World,* October 1990, 212–213; and WordPerfect Corporation, *1991 Annual Report* (Orem, UT: WordPerfect, 1991).
2. Elizabeth A. McCord, "The Business Writer, the Law, and Routine Business Communication: A Legal and Rhetorical Analysis," *Journal of Business and Technical Communication,* April 1991, 183.
3. McCord, "The Business Writer," 183, 193.
4. "Letters to Lands' End," *February 1991 Catalog,* (Dodgeville, WI: Lands' End, 1991) 100.
5. Based on Dana Milbank, "As Stores Scrimp More and Order Less, Suppliers Take on Greater Risks, Costs," *The Wall Street Journal,* 10 December 1991, B1.
6. Malcolm Forbes, "How to Write a Business Letter," International Paper Company, reprinted in *Strategies for Business and Technical Writing,* 3rd ed., ed. Kevin Harty (San Diego: Harcourt Brace Jovanovich, 1989), 116.
7. Based on Lisa Driscoll, "The New King of the Forest: International Paper," *Business Week,* 28 October 1991, 140–141.
8. John Markoff, "Recent Novell Software Contains a Hidden Virus," *The New York Times,* 20 December 1991, C2.

Chapter 9

1. René Nourse, interview with Mary Ellen Guffey, 3 March 93.
2. Raymond A. Dumont and John M. Lannon, *Business Communications,* 3rd ed. (Glenview, IL: Scott, Foresman/Little, Brown, 1990), 33.
3. Seth Faison, "Trying to Play by the Rules," *The New York Times,* 22 December 1991, sec. 3, 1.
4. "How to Ask for—and Get—What You Want!" *Supervision,* February 1990, 11.
5. Kevin McLaughlin, "Words of Wisdom," *Entrepreneur,* October 1990, 101.
6. Jeffrey Potts, "SBA Winner Profits From Survival Instinct," *USA Today,* 16 May 1991, B8.
7. Based on Bruce Horovitz, "Advertising Is Looking to Diversify," *Los Angeles Times,* 21 January 1992, D1.
8. "Fitness Center Gets Couch Potatoes Moving," *The Wall Street Journal,* 12 April 1991, B1.

Chapter 10

1. Tim Smith, interview with Mary Ellen Guffey, 15 March 1993. Other information from Kenneth Labich, "American Takes on the World," *Fortune,* 24 September 1990, 40–45; and AMR Corporation, *1992 Annual Report* (Dallas: American Airlines, 1992) 3–9.
2. *Customer Service Manager's Letter,* Prentice-Hall Bureau of Business Practice, 25 January 1992, 6.
3. William C. Himstreet, Wayne Murlin Baty, and Carol M. Lehman, *Business*

Communications, 9th ed. (Belmont, CA: Wadsworth, 1993), 477.
4. Betty Southard Murphy, Wayne E. Barlow, and D. Diane Hatch, "Manager's Newsfront," *Personnel Journal,* September 1991, 22.
5. "A 'Catch 22' in Honesty," *The Wall Street Journal,* 2 December 1990, F25.
6. Lauren Picker, "Job References: To Give or Not to Give," *Working Woman,* February 1992, 21.
7. Stephen B. Knouse, "Confidentiality and the Letter of Recommendation: A New Approach," *The Bulletin of the Association for Business Communication,* September 1987, 7.
8. Adapted from Terry McNally and Peter Schiff, *Contemporary Business Writing: A Problem-Solving Approach* (Belmont, CA: Wadsworth, 1986), 175–176.
9. Portions of this section are based on Rebecca Burnett Carosso, *Technical Communication* (Belmont, CA: Wadsworth, 1986), 354–374.
10. Based on "An Heirloom You Can Sit On," *Newsweek,* 23 December 1991, 61.

Chapter 11

1. Richard E. Eades, Jr., interview with Mary Ellen Guffey, 22 July 1992. Other information from *Where Research Is* (Rochester, NY: The Winters Group, 1991); and *Presenting . . . The Winters Group* (Rochester, NY: The Winters Group, 1991).
2. Daniel C. Arnsan, "Resources, Research, Results—Librarian and Instructor, Partners in Student Success," *Innovation Abstracts* 5 (February 1993): 1.
3. Christopher Velotta, "How to Design and Implement a Questionnaire," *Technical Communication,* Fall 1991, 390.
4. Robin Toner, "Politics of Welfare: Focusing on the Problems," *The New York Times,* 5 July 1991, 1.
5. Gerald J. Alred, Walter E. Oliu, and Charles T. Brusaw, *The Professional Writer* (New York: St. Martin's Press, 1992), 78.

Chapter 12

1. Theodore Downes-LeGuin, interview with Mary Ellen Guffey, 23 July 1992. Other information from RAND, *1992 Annual Report 1990–1991* (Santa Monica, CA: RAND, 1991).
2. Walter Wells, *Communications in Business* (Boston: PWS/Kent, 1988), 471.
3. Charlene Marmer Solomon, "Marriott's Family Matters," *Personnel Journal,* October 1991, 40–42.
4. Chuck Hawkins, "FedEx: Europe Nearly Killed the Messenger," *Business Week,* 25 May 1992, 124–126.

Chapter 13

1. Janet Marie Smith, interview with Mary Ellen Guffey, 24 March 1993. Other information from Janet Marie Smith, "Putting Together a Winning Team," *Working Woman,* October 1992, 28–30.

Chapter 14

1. Mary Piecewicz, interview with Mary Ellen Guffey, 31 March 1993. Other information from Hewlett-Packard, *1992 Annual Report* (Palo Alto, CA: Hewlett-Packard, 1992), 1–21.
2. Nancy Rivera Brooks and Jesus Sanchez, "U.S. Firms Map Ways to Profit From the Accord," *Los Angeles Times,* 13 August 1992, D1, D2.
3. Herman Holtz, *The Consultant's Guide to Proposal Writing* (New York: John Wiley, 1990), 188.
4. Based on Jane Applegate, "Weigh Freight Expenses Carefully," *Los Angeles Times,* 14 August 1992, D3.
5. Based on Joann S. Lublin, "Companies Use Cross-Cultural Training to Help Their Employees Adjust Abroad," *The Wall Street Journal,* 4 August 1992, B1.
6. Based on John R. Emshwiller, "Designer of Surfing Ride Catches a Wave of Success," *The Wall Street Journal,* 12 August 1992, B2.
7. Based on Barbara Ettorre, "Breaking the Glass . . . or Just Window Dressing," *Management Review,* March 1992, 16–22.
8. Based on Karen S. Sterkel, "Integrating Intercultural Communication and Report Writing in the Communication Class," *The Bulletin of the Association for Business Communication,* September 1988, 14–16.

Chapter 15

1. Jon Georges, interview with Mary Ellen Guffey, 4 December 1992. Other information from The Walt Disney Company, *1991 Annual Report* (Burbank, CA: The Walt Disney Company, 1991), 1–44; Walt Disney Imagineering, *Walt Disney Imagineering* (Burbank, CA: Walt Disney Imagineering); and Anthony Hatch, "Walt Disney Imagineering Facts," (Glendale, CA: Walt Disney Imagineering), 1–6.
2. Steven Grubaugh, "Public Speaking," *The Clearing House,* February 1990, 255.
3. Rod Plotnik, *Introduction to Psychology* (Pacific Grove, CA: Brooks/Cole, 1993), 484.
4. Some of the information presented in this chapter originated in Mary Ellen Guffey's *Essentials of Business Communication,* 2nd ed. (Boston: PWS/Kent, 1991), Chapter 14.
5. Wharton Applied Research Center, "A Study of the Effects of the Use of Overhead Transparencies on Business Meetings, Final Report" (Philadelphia: University of Pennsylvania, 14 September 1981).
6. Dianna Booher, *Executive's Portfolio of Model Speeches for All Occasions* (Englewood Cliffs, NY: Prentice-Hall, 1991), 259.
7. Raymond Slesinski, "Giving a Top-notch Executive Presentation," *Management,* April 1990, 16.
8. Ronald E. Dulek, John S. Fielden, and John S. Hill, "International Communication: An Executive Primer," *Business Horizons,* January/February 1991, 23.
9. Dulek, Fielden, and Hill, "International Communication," 22.
10. Kirsten Schabacker, "A Short, Snappy Guide to Meaningful Meetings," *Working Woman,* June 1991, 73.
11. Andrew S. Grove, quoted in Walter Kiechell, III, "How to Take Part in a Meeting," *Fortune,* 26 May 1986, 178.
12. Thomas C. Hayes, "Doing Business Screen to Screen," *The New York Times,* 21 February 1991, C1.
13. Hayes, "Doing Business," C5.
14. Anthony Ramirez, "Video Meetings Get Cheaper, and a Bit Better," *The New York Times,* 5 February 1992, C5.
15. Patricia A. LaRosa, "Voice Messaging Is Quality 'Lip Service,' " *The Office,* May 1992, 10.
16. "Did You Know That . . . ," *Boardroom Reports,* 15 August 1992, 15.
17. Michael Jacobson, quoted in "Garbage In, Garbage Out," *Consumer Reports,* December 1992, 755.

Chapter 16

1. Tania Romero, interview with Mary Ellen Guffey, 25 June 1992. Other information from Marriott Corporation, *1991 Annual Report* (Washington, DC: Marriott Corporation, 1991); *Marriott World* (Employee Communications and Creative Services, Spring 1992); and Mike Ruffer,

"Sharing a Vision for the '90s," *Insider* (newsletter for Residence Inn by Marriott), Spring 1992, 1.
2. Some of the information presented in this chapter originated in Mary Ellen Guffey's *Essentials of Business Communication,* 2nd ed. (Boston: PWS/Kent, 1991), Chapter 13.
3. J. Michael Farr, *The Very Quick Job Search* (Indianapolis, IN: JIST Works, 1991), 24.
4. Judith Schroer, "Seek a Job With a Little Help From Your Friends," *USA Today,* 19 November 1990, B7.
5. Manchester Inc. survey in *USA Today,* 1 November 1990, B1.
6. Carol Smith, "Starting Over in a New Career," *Los Angeles Times,* 15 September 1992, Careers sec., 3.
7. Dan Moreau, "Write a Resume That Works," *Changing Times,* June 1990, 91.
8. Quoted in Jacqueline Trace, "Teaching Résumé Writing the Functional Way," *The Bulletin of the Association for Business Communication,* June 1985, 41.
9. James Bates, "Pitfalls of the Resume," *Los Angeles Times,* 16 September 1991, 18–19.
10. "As Graduation Approaches . . . ," *Personnel,* June 1991, 14.
11. Diane Cole, "Ethics: Companies Crack Down on Dishonesty," *The Wall Street Journal, Managing Your Career supplement,* Spring 1991, 8.
12. "Managing Your Career," *National Business Employment Weekly,* Fall 1989, 29.
13. Joan E. Rigdon, "Deceptive Resumes Can Be Door-Openers but Can Become an Employee's Undoing," *The Wall Street Journal,* 17 June 1992, B1.
14. Marc Silver, "Selling the Perfect You," *U.S. News & World Report,* 5 February 1990, 70–72.
15. Harriett M. Augustin, "The Written Job Search: A Comparison of the Traditional and a Nontraditional Approach," *The Bulletin of the Association for Business Communication,* September 1991, 13.
16. J. Kenneth Horn, "Personnel Administrators' Reactions to Job Application Follow-up Letters Regarding Extending Interviews and Offering Jobs," *The Bulletin of the Association for Business Communication,* September 1991, 24.
17. Julia Lawlor, "Networking Opens More Doors to Jobs," *USA Today,* 19 November 1990, B7.
18. Farr, *The Very Quick Job Search,* 158.

Acknowledgments

Text, Figures, and Captions

pp. 4–5: interview with Renee Rodriguez used with permission. **p. 5:** photo caption based on Sara Lee Corporation 1991 Annual Report (Chicago: Sara Lee Corporation, 1991), 5. **p. 11:** Spotlight caption based on Sandra L. Kurtzig and Tom Parker, *CEO* (New York: W. W. Norton, 1991). **p. 22:** Spotlight caption based on Noel M. Tichy and Stratford Sherman, *Control Your Destiny or Someone Else Will* (New York: Bantam Doubleday Dell Publishing, 1993), as reported in "Jack Welch's Lessons for Success," *Fortune* (25 January 1993), 92. **p. 23:** Ethics box based on an article that first appeared in *Working Woman*, December 1991. Written by Craig Dellinger and Dan Rice. Reprinted with permission of *Working Woman* Magazine Copyright © 1991 by W. W. T. Partnership. **pp. 32–33:** interviews with Andrea Ciriello used with permission. **p. 36:** Spotlight caption based on Nancy K. Austin, "Why Listening's Not As Easy As It Sounds," *Working Woman* (March 1991), 46–47. **p. 37:** Career Skills box based on Mary Elwart-Keys and Marjorie Horton, "Collaborating in the Capture Lab: Computer Support for Group Writing," *The Bulletin of the Association for Business Communication*, June 1990, 38–44; and Ruth G. Newman, "Collaborative Writing with Purpose and Style," *Personnel Journal*, April 1988, 37. **p. 40:** Figure 2.3 based on "Understanding People Better Through 'Body Language,'" *The Book of Inside Information* (New York: Boardroom Classics, 1989), 192–193; Norma Carr-Ruffino, *The Promotable Woman* (Belmont, CA: Wadsworth, 1985), 191; and Walter Kiechel III, "How to Take Part in a Meeting," *Fortune*, 26 May 1986, 117–118. **p. 44:** Spotlight caption based on Minda Zeltin, "When 99 Percent Isn't Enough," *Management Review* (March 1993), 40–52. **pp. 58–59:** interview with Brian Finnegan used with permission. **p. 70:** Spotlight caption based on Judy Flander, "Catching Up With Katie Couric," *The Saturday Evening Post*, September/October 1992, 38–42. **p. 72:** Spotlight caption based on Tricia Drevets, "Her Personal Focus Is Personal Finance," *Editor & Publisher*, 13 May 1989, 46; and Jane Bryant Quinn, *Making the Most of Your Money* (New York: Simon & Schuster, 1991). **p. 74:** Spotlight caption based on Ingrid Abramovitch, "The Trust Factor," *Success* (March 1993), 18. **pp. 84–85, 86, 92–93:** from interview with Susanne Tully, used with permission. **p. 87:** Spotlight caption based on "Gerry Laybourne," *Working Woman*, November 1991, 89; and Kathleen Murray, "Tuned in to Kids, She Takes Nickelodeon to the Top," *The New York Times*, 14 March 1993, F8. **pp. 114–115:** interview with Louise Lague used with permission. **p. 118:** Spotlight caption based on "Sam Walton in His Own Words," *Fortune*, 29 June 1992, 98–106. **p. 119:** Spotlight caption based on Jeff Moad, "Mike Simmons: A CIO With No Apologies," *Datamation*, 1 August 1990, 73–75. **p. 120:** photo caption based on Kathy M. Kristof, "Mutual Funds Try Something New: Plain English," *Los Angeles Times*, 1 November 1992, D4. **p. 124:** photo caption based on Paul D. Zimmerman, "Neil Simon: Up From Success," *Newsweek*, 2 February 1970, 55. **p. 128:** Technology box based on Howard Eglowstein, "Can a Grammar and Style Checker Improve Your Writing?" *Byte*, August 1991, 238–242; Jean Harmon, "Say It Write!" *WordPerfect: The Magazine*, August 1992, 69–72; Rubin Rabinovitz, "New Windows Grammar Checkers Improve Error-Catching Rates," *PC Magazine*, 16 June 1992, 42, 44; Rubin Rabinovitz, "RightWriter for Windows: Works Smarter, Gains Ground on Grammatik," *PC Magazine*, 31 March 1992, 52; and Corey Sandler, "WordPerfect 5.2: New Polish for an Old Classic," *Windows Sources*, April 1993, 159–161. **pp. 138–139, 153:** from interview with Alice Blachly, used with permission. **p. 144:** Spotlight caption based on Mark H. McCormick, "Write on Target," *Entrepreneur*, February 1993, 60. **p. 156:** photo caption based on *Excellence Achieved* (Englewood Cliffs, NJ: Bureau of Business Practice, Inc., Prentice Hall, 1990), 37. **pp. 170–171:** Interview with Kenneth Kim used with permission. **p. 182:** John Fielden, "Clear Writing Is Not Enough," *Management Review*, April 1989, 51; Hal Fanner, as cited in *Boardroom Reports*, 15 January 1991; and Barrett J. Mandel and Judith Yellin, "Mastering the Memo," *Working Woman*, September 1989, 135. **pp. 194–195:** interview with Darin Richins used with permission. **p. 200:** Spotlight caption based on Malcolm Forbes, "How to Write a Business Letter," *Strategies for Business and Technical Writing*, Kevin J. Harty, ed., 3rd ed. (San Diego: Harcourt Brace Jovanovich, 1989), 116. **p. 215:** Cross Culture box based on Iris I. Varner, "Internationalizing Business Communication Courses," *The Bulletin of the Association for Business Communication*, December 1987, 9; Lennie Copeland and Lewis

Griggs, *Going International* (New York: Penguin Group, Plume Books, 1986), 104, 109; and Roger E. Axtell, *The Do's and Taboos of International Trade* (New York: Wiley, 1989, 249–250). **pp. 226–227:** interview with René Nourse used with permission. **pp. 232–233:** Career Skills box based on David W. Ewing, "Strategies of Persuasion," *Writing for Results* (New York: Wiley, 1979). Used with permission of the publisher. **p. 244:** Spotlight caption based on Bob Weinstein, "The Buck Stops Here: Going for Broke, Charles Schwab & Co.," *Entrepreneur*, February 1993, 127–131. **p. 243:** Spotlight caption based on Herb Kelleher, "Beware the Impossible Guarantee," *Inc.*, November 1992, 30. **p. 245:** photo caption based on Adam Bryant, "Advertising," *The New York Times*, 8 March 1993, C16. **pp. 256–257:** interview with Tim Smith used with permission. **p. 259:** Spotlight caption based on Andrew S. Grove, "The Fine Art of Feedback," *Working Woman*, February 1992, 28. **pp. 286–287:** interview with Richard E. Eades, Jr., used with permission. **p. 292:** Figure 11.2 based on William A. Bolger, "How to Start a Free Legal Services Plan for Your Group" (Gloucester, VA: National Resource Center for Consumers of Legal Services, 1987). **p. 300:** Spotlight caption based on John Case, "The Best Small Companies to Work for in America," *Inc.*, November 1992, 96. **p. 302:** Spotlight caption based on Tom Peters, *Thriving on Chaos* (New York: Knopf, 1991), 230–231. **p. 311:** Ethics box based on data from Gregg Easterbrook, "The Sincerest Flattery," *Newsweek*, 29 July 1991, 45–46; and William A. Henry, III, "Recycling in the Newsroom," *Time*, 29 July 1991, 59. **pp. 318–319:** interview with Theodore Downes-Le Guin used with permission. **p. 325:** Spotlight caption based on Mark R. Goldston, *The Turnaround Prescription: Repositioning Troubled Companies*, reported in "The Opportunity Finder," *Success*, March 1993, 80. **pp. 326–327:** Figure 12.5 based on Charlene Marmer Solomon, "Marriott's Family Matters," *Personnel Journal*, October 1991, 40–42; Suzanne Gordon, "Helping Corporations Care," *Working Woman*, January 1993, 30; and Karen Matthes, "Companies Can Make It Their Business to Care," *HR Focus*, February 1992, 4. **pp. 348–349:** interview with Janet Marie Smith used with permission. **p. 353:** Figure 13.2 based in part on Robert Half, "Mistakes People Make Interviewing People," *Boardroom Reports*, 15 April 1991, 10. **p. 356:** Career Skills box based on Pat R. Graves and Jack E. Murry, "Enhancing Communication With Effective Page Design and Typography," *Delta Pi Epsilon* Instructional Strategies Series, Summer 1990. **p. 357:** Spotlight caption based on Eileen Bedell, "Starting a Business Within a Business," *Working Woman*, February 1993, 40. **p. 360:** Spotlight caption based on Leslie Brokaw, "Twenty-eight Steps to a Strategic Alliance," *Inc.*, April 1993, 96–104. **pp. 378–379:** interview with Mary Piecewicz used with permission. **p. 386:** Spotlight caption based on Thomas Sant, "Powerful Proposals," *Entrepreneur*, February 1993, 54–55. **p. 390:** Spotlight caption based on Albert G. Holzinger, "How to Succeed by Really Trying," *Nation's Business*, August 1992, 50–51. **pp. 424–425:** interview with Jon Georges used with permission. **p. 427:** Spotlight caption based on Les Brown, *Live Your Dreams* (New York: Morrow, 1992). **p. 428:** Career Skills box based on Bert Decker, "Successful Presentations: Simple and Practical," *HR Focus*, February 1992, 19; and Lawrence Stevens, "The Proof Is in the Presentation," *Nation's Business*, July 1991, 33. **p. 433:** Spotlight caption based on Patricia O'Brien, "Why Men Don't Listen," *Working Woman*, February 1993, 58. **p. 436:** Spotlight caption based on Dianna Booher, *Executive's Portfolio of Model Speeches for All Occasions* (Englewood Cliffs, NJ: Prentice Hall, 1991), 252. **p. 441:** Figure 15.4 based on "Better Meetings," *Boardroom Reports*, October 1, 1991. **pp. 450–451:** interview with Tania Romero used with permission. **p. 455:** Career Skills box based on J. Michael Farr, *The Very Quick Job Search* (Indianapolis; JIST Works, Inc., 1991), Chapter Two. Copyright JIST Works, Inc. Used by permission of the publisher. **p. 456:** Spotlight caption based on Julia Lawlor, "Job Hot-line Caller Finds Work," *USA Today* (3 April 1991), 8B. **p. 460:** Spotlight caption based on "Anchoring California," *Transpacific*, March/April 1993, 34–35. **p. 462:** Figure 16.5 based on Yana Parker, *The Damn Good Résumé Guide* (Berkeley, CA: Ten Speed Press, 1989), 55. Used with permission of the author. **p. 480:** Career Skills box based on Mary Ellen Guffey, *Essentials of Business Communication* (Boston: PWS–Kent Publishing Company, 1991), 329. **p. 464:** Spotlight caption based on Walecia Konrad and Andrea Rothman, "Can Wayne Calloway Handle the Pepsi Challenge?" *Business Week* (27 January 1992), 92. **p. 469:** Spotlight caption based on "Give Your Résumé to a Computer," *Fortune*, 15 June 1992, 12.

Photo Credits

p. 1: Doug Menuez/Reportage. **p. 3:** Bruce Ayres/Tony Stone Worldwide. **p. 4:** Courtesy of Renee Rodrigues. **p. 5:** Courtesy of Dr. Mary Ellen Guffey. **p. 9:** Michael Abramson/Woodfin Camp & Associates. **p. 11:** Courtesy of The ASK Companies. **p. 21:** Hael/Photo Researchers, Inc. **p. 22:** Courtesy of The General Electric Company. **p. 31:** Jose Palaez/ The Stock Market. **p. 32:** Courtesy of The Travelers Companies. **p. 33:** © Chris Brown/Stock Boston. **p. 36:** Courtesy of Nancy Austin. **p. 44:** Photo by Brian Willar. **p. 49:** Courtesy of Hewlett-Packard. **p. 55:** Jose L. Pelaez/Stock Market. **p. 57:** Super Stock. **p. 58:** Courtesy of Brian Finnegan. **p. 59:** © Lands' End, Inc. Reprinted courtesy Lands' End Catalog. **p. 64:** Jim Pickerell/Stock Boston. **p. 70:** John Harrington. **p. 72:** Courtesy of Jane Bryant Quinn. **p. 74:** Michael Barley. **p. 76:** Tim Brown/Tony Stone Worldwide. **p. 83:** Courtesy of Hewlett-Packard. **p. 84:** Courtesy of Liz Claiborne, Inc. **p. 85:** © William Toufic. **p. 87:** Courtesy of MTV Networks. **p. 96:** Bachmann/Stock Boston. **p. 105:** Geer-Mink/ Tony Stone Worldwide. **p. 113:** Billy E. Barnes/Tony Stone Worldwide. **p. 114:** Courtesy of *People* Magazine. **p. 115:** © Tim Graham/Sygma. **p. 118:** Steven Pumphrey. **p. 119:** Courtesy of Mike Simmons. **p. 124:** Mark Burnett/Photo Researchers. **p. 135:** Doug Menuez/ Reportage. **p. 137:** Tony Stone Worldwide. **p. 138:** Photo by Lee Holden/Courtesy of Ben & Jerry's. **p. 139:** Photo by Lee Holden/Courtesy of Ben & Jerry's. **p. 144:** Sylvan Moson. **p. 151:** Stock Market. **p. 156:** Courtesy of LL Bean. **p. 169:** Robert Rathe/Stock Boston. **p. 170:** Courtesy of Ken Kim. **p. 175:** Ken Fisher/Tony Stone Worldwide.

p. 176: © 1986 David Burnett/Contact Press Images. **p. 181:** Super Stock. **p. 193:** Super Stock. **p. 194:** Courtesy of Darin Richins. **p. 195:** Courtesy of WordPerfect Corporation. **p. 200:** © E. Adams/Sygma. **p. 208:** Richard Palsey/ Stock Boston. **p. 211:** Richarfd Howard/ Offshoot. **p. 225:** Stock Market. **p. 226:** Courtesy of Rene Nourse. **p. 227:** © Burt Glinn/Magnum Photos, Inc. **p. 237:** Jeff Reinking/Picture Group. **p. 242:** Courtesy of Pitney Bowes. **p. 243:** Courtesy of Southwest Airline Company. **p. 244:** Menuez/Reportage. **p. 245:** Courtesy of Dr. Mary Ellen Guffey. **p. 255:** Tony Stone Worldwide. **p. 256:** Courtesy of American Airlines. **p. 257:** Courtesy of American Airlines. **p. 259:** Ed Kashi. **p. 261:** Richard Howard/Offshoot. **p. 264:** Courtesy of The Marriott Corporation. **p. 277:** Dennis Budd Gray/Picture Group. **p. 283:** The Stock Market. **p. 285:** Super Stock. **p. 286:** Courtesy of Richard Eades. **p. 287:** Phil Matt. **p. 298:** Tim Brown/ Tony Stone Worldwide. **p. 300:** Mark Katzman. **p. 302:** Courtesy of The Tom Peters Groups. **p. 305:** Courtesy of Hewlett-Packard. **p. 317:** Tony Stone Worldwide. **p. 318:** Courtesy of Theo Downes-Le Guin. **p. 319:** Courtesy of Dr. Mary Ellen Guffey. **p. 321:** Courtesy of Comaq. **p. 325:** Courtesy of Mark R. Goldston. **p. 328:** Courtesy of National Audubon Society. **p. 331:** Robert Frerck/ Odyssey Productions. **p. 347:** Bruce Ayres/Tony Stone Worldwide. **p. 348:** © 1992 Janice E. Rettaliata. **p. 349:** © Erik Kvalsvik. **p. 354:** Courtesy of First National Bank. **p. 357:** Courtesy of Beth Givens. **p. 360:** Doug Menez/Reportage. **p. 361:** Courtesy of Bechtel Corp. **p. 363:** Courtesy of Dr. Mary Ellen Guffey. **p. 377:** © Four By Five. **p. 378:** Courtesy of Mary Piecewicz. **p. 379:** Courtesy of Hewlett-Packard Company. **p. 384:** © Lawrence Manning/Woodfin Camp & Associates. **p. 386:** Courtesy of Thomas Sant & Associates. **p. 388:** Richard Howard/ Offshoot. **p. 390:** Courtesy of Roger Staubach. **p. 421:** Michael L. Abramson/Woodfin Camp & Associates. **p. 423:** Tony Stone Worldwide. **p. 424:** Courtesy of Jon Georges. **p. 425:** © The Walt Disney Company. **p. 427:** © 1993 Anthony Loew. **p. 433:** Ed Kashi. **p. 436:** Courtesy of Dianna Booher. **p. 440:** Charles Gupton/Stock Boston. **p. 442:** Courtesy of Hewlett-Packard. **p. 449:** Tony Stone Worldwide. **p. 450:** Courtesy of Tania Romero. **p. 451:** Courtesy of Marriott Residence Inn. **p. 454:** Super Stock. **p. 456:** Linda Sue Scott. **p. 460:** Courtesy of KNBC-TV. **p. 464:** Courtesy of Wayne Calloway. **p. 469:** Hank Delespinasse. **p. 479:** John Curtis/Offshoot.

Index

A

Abstract (executive summary)
  of formal proposals, 389, *398*
  of proposal reports, 385
Action
  letters for complying with requests for, 150–54
  letters for requesting, 144–45, *146*, 235–37
  listening process and, *35*–36
  motivating, in letters of application, 474–75
  motivating, in persuasive messages, 232–33, 245–46
  refusing requests for, 203–4, *205*
Action verbs in résumés, *462–63*
Active voice in sentences, 99
Adams, Diane, 363, *364*
Adaptation
  of messages for intercultural audiences, 48–50
  of messages for receivers, 13
  of negative messages, 202–3
Adaptation in 3-×-3 writing process, 60, *61*, 65–73
  checklist for, 72–73
  courteousness in, 70
  for letters, 143
  for memos, 174
  for oral presentations, *429*
  for persuasive messages, 229, 243
  positive language in, 69–70
  precise and vigorous language in, 72
  receiver benefits in, 66
  sensitive and bias-free language in, 68–69
  simplified language in, 70–72
  tone in, 65–66
  "you" view in, 66–68
Addresses on international letters, 160
Adjustments
  letters for granting, 155–58, *159*
  letters for requesting, 239–40, *241*
Age bias in language, 69
Akers, John, 17
Alphanumeric outline, 91, *92*, 93
American Airlines
  generation of goodwill toward, 256–57
  letter and memo to customer from, *15*
Analysis in 3-×-3 writing process, 60, *61*, 62–64
  identifying purpose of messages by, 62
  for letters, 143
  for memos, 174, *175*
  for negative messages, 202–3
  for oral presentations, *429*
  for persuasive messages, 228–29, 242–43
  for reports, 297–99, 320–28
  selecting correct communication form by, 64
Analytical reports, 360–72
  checklist for writing, 372
  feasibility reports, 289, 365–67
  functions of, 290
  justification/recommendation reports, 289, 360–65
  major components of, *94*
  manuscript format of, *295*, 296
  memo format, 290, 291, *294*
  organizing information in, *329*, 330
  research studies, 289, 369–72
  yardstick reports, 289, 368–71
Anderson, Robert H., 179
Announcements, writing formal, 274, 277
Anticipation in 3-×-3 writing process, 60, *61*
  of audience needs, 64–65
  for letters, 143
  for memos, 174
  for negative messages, 202–3
  for oral presentations, *429*
  for reports, 299–300
Appearance of persons and documents as nonverbal message, 42–43
Appendix
  in formal reports, 391, *406–7*
  in proposals, 386
Apple Computer, 34
Application forms
  filling out, 478
  letter requesting, 477
Appreciation, letters of, 259, *260*, 261
Ashton, Alan C., 194
ASK software company, 11
Attention-getting techniques
  in openings of letters of application, 470–73
  in oral presentations, 428
  in persuasive messages, 230, 243–44
Attitudes
  avoiding ethnocentrism in, 46
  beyond stereotyping in, 48
  developing tolerance as, 46–48
  good listening and positive, 36
Audiences
  anticipating needs of, 64–65
  holding attention of, in oral presentations, 428
  intercultural and international, 48–50, 436–38
  oral presentations and analysis of, 426–27
  organization pattern based on response of, 94, *95*, 96

Page numbers in *italics* refer to figures.

Audiences (*continued*)
of *People* magazine, 114–15
persuading, 229
primary and secondary, *65*–73
profiling, *65*
report organization based on, *291*, 299–300
spotlighting benefits to, 66
Austin, Nancy K., 36
Average, statistical, 322
Axtell, Roger, 49

B

Bad news. *See* Negative messages
Baltimore Orioles, 348–49
Bankers Trust Company, 357
Bank of America, 19, 23
internal messages at, 170–71
Bank of Boston, 119
Bar charts, *335*, *336*
Barriers to communication, 11–13, *24*
in organizations, 20–22
overcoming interpersonal, 13–14
overcoming organizational, 22–25
Bechtel Company, *361*
Bedell, Eileen, 357
Beltran, James, 155
Ben & Jerry's
customer response letters from, 138–39, *153*
mission statement, 161
Benchmarking, 439
Berle, Peter A. A., 328
Bibliography
in formal reports, 391, *405*
formats for, 310, *312*
Blachly, Alice, 138–39, *153*
Body
of formal reports, 390, *400–403*
of letters, 143
of letters of application, 473–74
of memos, 176
of oral presentations, 428–30
Body language as nonverbal message, 39, *40*
Booher, Dianna, 436
Brainstorming, 87
Brown, Les, 427
Bryan, John H., 4–5, 25
Budget section of proposal reports, 384–85
Buhler, Patricia, 238
Business communication
effect of E-mail on, 180
ethics of. *See* Ethics
international. *See* International business communications
oral. *See* Oral (two-way) communications
in organizations, 14–25
written. *See* Business writing; 3-×-3 writing process
Business plans, 289
Business writing. *See also* Letters; Memos; Messages; Reports
basics and goals of, 60
clear, as ethical goal, 77
five myths about, 8
humor in, 171
for intercultural audiences, 50, 160–61
law and. *See* Legal considerations
process and phases of. *See* 3-×-3 writing process
Bypassing as communication obstacle, 10, 12

C

Calloway, Wayne, 464
Calyx and Corolla, 360
Career path, choosing personal, 453–54
Career Track profiles
American Airlines, 256–57
Baltimore Orioles, 348–49
Bank of America, 170–71
Ben & Jerry's, 138–39
Dean Witter Reynolds, Inc., 226–27
Hewlett-Packard, 378–79
Lands' End, 58–59
Liz Claiborne, 84–85
Marriott Corporation, 450–51
People magazine, 114–15
RAND institute, 318–19
Sara Lee Corporation, 4–5
The Travelers insurance company, 32–33
Walt Disney Imagineering, 424–25
Winters Group, 286–87
WordPerfect Corporation, 194–95
Chambers, Kevin, 50
Change, cultural values and, 45–46
Channels of communication, 10–11
formal organizational, *19*–20
informal organizational, 20
Charts, 334–41
China, negative news presentation in, 215
Chronological résumé, 456, *457*, *466*, *468*
Chrysler Corporation, 22
Ciriello, Andrea, 32–33
Claims letters, 147–48, *149*, 150, 239–42
negative messages in, 209, *210*
Clarity, writing for, 116–17
Clean-Up Technology, 380
Closings
of letters, 143
of letters of application, 474–75
of memos, 176
of negative messages, 196, *197*, 201–2
Cluster diagram, 87, *90*, *91*
Cluster samples, 309
Coca Cola Company, 86, 302
Cohen, Ben, 138, *139*
Collaborative writing, 62, 104–7
computers for, 63
ground rules for, 106
obstacles to, 106–7
patterns of, 105–6
Comb Authorized Liquidators, 97
Combination style of résumés, 459, *467*
Comer, Gary, 58
Communication, 3–30
barriers to, 11–14. *See also* Barriers to communication
effect of E-mail on, 180
knowledge society and role of, 6–8
learning goals for, 3, 25–26
listening and, 34–38
nonverbal, 38–43
in organizations, 14–25
process of, 8–11. *See also* Messages
strengthening skills in, 25
Communication environment, 21–23
Communication skills
as job requirement, 6, *7*
listening as, 34–38
strengthening, 25
Communication styles, cultural differences in, 45
Compliance reports, 289, 357, *358–59*
Component, organizing report data by, 329
Composition in 3-×-3 writing process, *61*, 96–103
checklist for, 103–4
effective paragraphs, 100–103
first drafts, 96–97
forceful sentences, 97–100
of goodwill messages, 258
of letters, 144
of negative messages, 203
of oral presentation, *429*
of persuasive messages, 230–42, 243–48
using computers for, 62, 63
Compound prepositions, reducing, 118–19
Computers
composition process and use of, 62, 63
desktop publishing, 356
electronic databases on, 63, 86
grammar, spell, and style checkers, 8, 63, 126, 128
mail by. *See* E-mail
producing product charts with, 337
tabular data organized by, *321*

Conciseness, writing for, 117–19, 173
Conclusions
  drawing, from research data, 325–27
  in oral presentations, 430
  in report, 325–27, 390, *403*
Condolences, messages of, 263
Conferences
  situational reports on, 352, *353*, 354
  speaking in, 439–42
Confirmation memo, *186*, 187
Contracts, marketing information as legal, 77–78
Convenience samples, 309
Convention, organizing report data by prescribed, 330
Conventions, situational reports on, 352–54
Conversational language, 117
Correlations of variables, 323–24
Couric, Katie, 70
Courteous language, 70
Cover letters for job applications, 470–75
Crandall, Robert L., 256–57
Credibility and persuasive messages, 226–27, 232, 234
Credit
  documentation of sources as, 310–13, 523–27
  for others's ideas, 75, 311
  refusing customer, 209–11
Criteria, organizing report data by given, 330
Cross-cultural communication. *See* Intercultural communication; International business communications
Cross-tabulated data, 321
Cultural diversity, 44–46
Customer response letters, 150–58, 207–12
  for acknowledging customer orders, 154–55
  from American Airlines, *15*
  from Ben & Jerry's, 138–39, 140, *153*
  for complying with requests, 150–54
  denying claims, 209, *210*
  for granting adjustments and claims, 155–59
  handling order problems, 208
  from Lands' End, 58–59, *67*, 68, 200
  refusing credit, 209–11

D

Dangling phrases in sentences, 99–100
Data
  collecting, 86–89
  documenting, 310–13, 523–27
  ethics presentation of, 341, 342
  generating primary, 305–10
  illustrating, 334–43
  interpreting, 318–28
  locating secondary, 302–5
  organizing, 89–96, 328–33
  selecting types of, 302, *303*
Databases, electronic, 63, 86, 304–5
Dean Witter Reynolds, Inc., 226–27
Decimal outline, 91, *92*
Decoding messages, 11
Defamation, 197, 265–66
Delivery of oral presentations, 433–36
  handling fight-or-flight response in, 435
  method of, 433, *434*
  techniques of, 433–36
Desktop publishing, 356
Dictionaries, research using specialized, 304
Direct-mail sales letters, 243, 246–48
Direct pattern (frontloading) for organizing ideas, 94–95
  in letters, 142–43, 144–45, *146*, *153*
  in memos, 175, 176, 183
  in negative messages, 202
  in paragraphs, 100–101
  in reports, 290, *292–93*, *294*, 361, *362*
Disability bias in language, 69
Discover credit card, 97
Dr. Pepper cola, 10
Doctrine-of-relative-filth ethical trap, 73–74
Documentation of research data, 310–13, 523–27
Documents. *See also* Letters; Memos; Reports
  appearance of business, as nonverbal message, 42
  desktop-published, 356
  using computers for professional-looking, 63
Downes-Le Guin, Theodore, 318–19
Drucker, Peter, 6, 13

E

Eades, Richard E., Jr., 286–87
Echoing technique, 33
Electronic databases, 63, 86, 304–5
E-mail, 177
  confidentiality of, 182
  effect of, on international communications, 180
  memos by, 177–80
  open organizational communication and, 22–23
Emoticons, 180
Emotional interference as communication barrier, 12–13
Emotions, E-mail expression of, 179, 180
Empathy
  for audience's needs, 66, 68
  developing, 47
Employee empowerment, 439
Employees
  announcing bad news to, 212, *213*
  appearance of, as nonverbal message, 42–43
  letters of recommendation for, 265–67, *268*
  need for communication skills in, 6, *7*
  recognition of, 261, *262*, 263, 264
  sexual harassment of, 273
  warnings to, 269–72
Employment, 449–85
  follow-up letters and other documents for, 476–78
  interviewing for, 479–82
  learning goals on, 449, 482–83
  at Marriott Corporation, 450–51
  persuasive letter of application for, 470–76
  persuasive résumé for, 456–70
  preparing and searching for, 452–56
Encoding messages, 10
Encyclopedias, research using, 304
Endnotes, formats for, 310, *313*
Ends-justifies-the-means ethical trap, 74
English language for intercultural communication, 49, 50
Ethics, 73–77
  conflicting loyalties and, 75–77
  five common traps of, 73–74
  goals of ethical business communications, 74–75
  graphics and charts in reports and, 341, 342
  guidelines on business communication, 23
  indirect organization of ideas and, 97
  learning goals for, 57, 79
  letters of recommendation and, 265–66
  mission statements and, 161
  in oral presentations, 437
  persuasive messages and, 234
  plagiarism, avoiding, 311
  principles of, 73
  of résumé writing, 465
  rivalry as communication barrier and, 22
Ethnic bias in language, 69
Ethnocentrism, avoiding, 46
Evaluation, listening process and, 35

Evaluation in 3-×-3 writing process, *61*, 116, 128
of letters, 144
of memos, 174, 175
of negative messages, 203
of oral presentations, *429*
Experiments as data source, 87, 308–10
External organizational communications, 14, *15*. *See also* Letters
Exxon Corporation, 213
Eye contact as nonverbal message, 40–41

F

Fabergé USA, 325
Facial expression as nonverbal message, 41
Factoring in report writing, 299–300
Facts vs. opinions, 75
False-necessity ethical trap, 73–74
Favors
refusing requests for, 203–4
requesting, 235, *236*, 237
Fax cover sheet format, *521*, 522
Feasibility reports, 289, 324, 365–66, *367*
Federal Express, 325
Feedback, 11
customer complaints as, 155–56
encouraging organizational, 22–23
evaluating writing using, 129, 175
to listeners, 35–36
planning for, 14
Fidelity Investments, 120
Fight-or-flight response in public speaking, 435
Filtering as communication barrier, 21
Finnegan, Brian, 58–59
First draft, 96–104
Flow charts, *335*, 339, *340*
Focus groups, 87
Fog Index of readability, 123
Footnotes
format for, 310, *312*
in justification/recommendation reports, 363, *364*
Forbes, Malcolm, 140, 200, 209
Ford-Europe, 48
Foreign business communications. *See* Intercultural communication; International business communications
Foreign languages, learning, 48
Formal channels of organizational communication, *19*–20, 25
Formality, cultural values for, 45
Formal reports, 387–407
abstract or executive summary, 389, *398*
appendix, 391, *406–7*
bibliography, 391, *405*
body, 390, *400–403*
checklist for preparing, 393–94
conclusions, 390, *403*
cover, 388
introduction, 389–90, *399–400*
letter of transmittal, 388, *396*
list of figures, 389, *397*
recommendations, 390–91, *404*
references, 391, *405*
table of contents, 389, *397*
title page, 388, *395*
writing tips for, 391–92
Format
letters, *141*, 142, 160, 509–14
reports, 291, *292–95*, 296
source documentation, 310, 311, *312*, *313*, 523–27
Form letters, 8
personalizing, 206
Four Seasons hotels, 44
Frame of reference as communication barrier, 12
Frito-Lay Company, 464
Frontloading of main ideas, 94–95. *See also* Direct pattern (frontloading) for organizing ideas
Functional style of résumé, 456, 458

G

Gardener's Eden, 360
Gates, Bill, 64
Gender bias in language, 68–69
General Electric, 22
Georges, Jon, 424–25
Gestures as nonverbal message, 41
Global Settlement Fund, 357
Goldston, Mark R., 325
Goodwill, 16
generation of, by corporate news, 256–57
indicated in letters, 140–41
Goodwill messages, 256–63
appreciation and thanks, 259, *260*, 261
checklist for, 264
employee recognition, 261, *262*, 263, 264
learning goals on, 255, 277–78
response to recognition, 263
suggestions for writing, 258
sympathy, 263
Grammar checkers, 8, 63, 128
Grapevine as informal communication channel, 20, 25
Graphic highlighting
improving readability using, 121–22
in memos, 173–74, 176, *185*, 186
Graphics, 334–43
computer aids for, 63, 337
ethical, 341, 342
incorporating, 341–43
matching visuals to objectives, 334–43
with oral presentations, 431, *432*, 433
Greenfield, Jerry, 138, *139*
Grids for analysis of verbal data, *324*, 325
Grouped bar chart, *336*
Group writing. *See* Collaborative writing
Grove, Andrew S., 23, 259
Gunning Fog Index of readability, 123

H

Hall, Edward T., 42
Handbooks, research using specialized, 304
Handouts with oral presentations, 432–33
Headings
improving readability using, 122
in memos, 172, *173*
in reports, 332, *333*
Heart, Frank, 180
Hernandez, Gary, 469
Hewlett-Packard, proposal writing at, 378–79
Horizontal bar chart, *336*
Horizontal communication, 20, 24
Human resources information, avoiding lawsuits on, 78
Humor
in E-mail, 179, 180
in written messages, 171
Hurricane Andrew, *33*

I

Iacocca, Lee, 22, 176
IBM Corporation, 17, 97
Ideas
cluster diagram for creating, 87, *90*, *91*
grouping of, into patterns, 94–96
linking, in paragraphs, 102
positioning main. *See* Direct pattern (frontloading) for organizing ideas; Indirect pattern for organizing ideas
research and generation of, 86–89
in sentences, 98–99
Illustrations in reports, *335*, 341
Importance, organizing report data by, 329–30
Incident reports, *186*, 187
Indirect pattern for organizing ideas, 95–96
ethical considerations of, 97
in letters, 142
in memos, 176

in negative messages, 196, *197*, 200–201, 208
in paragraphs, 101–2
in persuasive messages, 229, *230*, 234
in reports, 290–91, *295*, 361, 363, *364–66*
Individualism, cultural value for, 45
Informal channels of organizational communication, 20
Information. *See also* Data
letters for complying with requests for, 150–54
letters for requesting, 144–45, *146*
refusing requests for, 203–4
Informational messages, 16, 62
memos, 87, *88*, 181–83
Informational reports, 288, 350–58
checklist for writing, 358–60
compliance, 289, 357–59
function of, 290
investigative, 288–89, 357
letter format, 290, *292–93*
major components of, *94*
organizing information in, *329*, 330
periodic, 288, 350–52
situational, 288, 352–57
Information industry, 6–8
Instructions, operational, 272–74, *275*
Intel Corporation, 23, 259
Intercultural communication, 44–50
adapting messages for intercultural audiences as, 48–50, 160–61, 436–38
checklist for improving, 50–51
comprehending cultural diversity as, 44–46
cultivating right attitude as, 46–48
learning goals for, 31, 51–52
nonverbal messages and, 41
women managers and, 47
Interest(s)
identifying personal employment, 452
in letters of application, 473–74
in persuasive messages, 231, 244
Interim reports, 354–57
Internal organizational communications, 14, *15*. *See also* E-mail; Memos
International business communications
E-mail as form of, 180
intercultural sensitivity in, 44–48
letters, 160–61
negative news in, 215
nonverbal messages and, 41
oral, 48–49, 436–38
questioning preconceptions about, 13–14
suggestions for oral, 48–50
suggestions for written, 50
International Sports Management Group. 144
Internship, letter requesting, 237, *238*
Interpretation of research data, 320–28
drawing conclusions, 325–27
listening process and, *35*
at RAND institute, 318–19
tabulating and analyzing research results, 320–25
writing report recommendations, 327–28
Interviews, employment, 479–82
behavior after, 482
behavior during, 481–82
follow-up letters after, 477–78
frequently asked questions in, 480
prior preparation for, 479, 481
Interviews, research, 86
guidelines for, 308
Introductions
to oral presentations, 427–28
to proposals, 380–81
to reports, 331, 389–90, *399–400*
Investigative reports, 288–89, 357
Investment information, avoiding lawsuits on, 77
Invitations, declining, 204–7
Involvement, good listening and, 36
"I/we" view, vs. "you" view, 66–68

J

Japan
cultural values in, 45
letters to and from, 160
negative news presentation in, 215
nonverbal messages in, 44
promotional brochures in, 13–14
status of businesswomen in, 47
Jargon, 71–72, 119
Job applicants
follow-up letters sent by, 476–78
letters of application sent by, 470–75
preparation for employment by, 452–56
refusal letters to, 214
résumé preparation by, 456–68
Job interviews, 479–82
Job market, 454–56
communication skills requested by, 6, *7*
networking to explore hidden, 455
Judgment samples, 309
Justification/recommendation reports, 289, 360–65
direct pattern for organizing, 361, *362*
indirect pattern for organizing, 361, 363, *364–65*, *366*
writing recommendations for, *327*, 328

K

Kal Kan Foods, 47
Kelleher, Herb, 243
Keukenhof Gardens, *363*
Kim, Kenneth, 170–71
KISS formula, 116–17
Knowledge workers, 6–8
Korzan, Kathleen, 469
Kraft Foods, 74
Kurtzig, Sandra, 11

L

Lague, Louise, 114–15
Lands' End, 58–59, 64
customer response letters from, *67*, 68, 200
Language
abusive, slanderous, or libelous, 197
avoiding lawsuits due to improper or unethical, 77–78
careless and indiscrete, 197–98
courteous, 70
hidden meanings in, 71
positive, 69–70
precise and vigorous, 72
revising to improve, 116–24
sensitive and bias-free, 68–69
simplified, 70–72
tone of, 65–66
Language skills
improving, 13
for intercultural communication, 48–50
lack of, as communication barrier, 12
Laun, Peggy, 300
Lawsuits, language for avoiding, 77–78
Laybourne, Gerry, 87
Legal considerations, 196–98
on abusive language, 197
adjustment/claims letters and, 155–56, 157
on careless language, 197
compliance reports and, 289, 357, *358–59*
good-guy syndrome and, 197–98
language and, 77–78
letters of recommendation, 265–66
proposals as legally binding, 378
for refusing customer credit, 209–11
Le Patch, 77
Letter of transmittal, 385, 388, *396*
Letters, 140–61
of appreciation, 259–61
characteristics of good, 140–42

Letters (*continued*)
to customers. *See* Customer response letters
direct pattern for, 142, *143*
as external communication, 14, *15*
form, 8, 206
format of, *141*, 142, 160, 509–14
goodwill, 256–63
informational report formatted as, 290, *292–93*
international, 160–61
learning goals on, 137, 162
legal considerations when writing, 155, 157
major components of, *94*
negative news in. *See* Negative messages
of recommendations, 265–68
reply, 150–58. *See also* Reply letters
reports formatted as, 291, *292–93*, 296
request, 144–48. *See also* Request letters
3-×-3 writing process applied to, 143–44, *146*, *152*
Letters of application, 470–75
building interest in body, 473–74
checklist for writing, 475–76
final tips on, 475
gaining attention in openings, 470–73
motivating action in closings, 474–75
Libel, 197
Library catalogs, research using, 302–3
Line charts, *335*, 338, *339*
Listening skills, 13, 34–38
checklist for improving, 38
dynamics of good listening, 36–37
with intercultural audiences, 49
lack of, as communication barrier, 12
learning goals for, 31, 51
listening process and barriers to, 34–36
poor listening habits, 37
reasons for poor, 34
at The Travelers insurance company, 32–33
Listen-to-report principle, 32–33
Lists
of figures in formal reports, 389, *397*
of figures in proposals, 385
improving readability using, 122
organizing ideas using, 89, 90
in procedure memos, 183
Liz Claiborne, Inc., 84–85
informational memo from, 87, *88*
recruitment brochure from, 89, *90*, *91*, 92, *93*
L. L. Bean Company, 156
Lotus Development Corporation, 77
Loyalties, ethics of conflicting, 75–77
Lucasfilms, 24

M

McBride, Teresa, 74
McCormack, Mark 144
McDonnell Douglas Corporation, 368
Manuscript format for reports, *295*, 296
Maps, *335*, 341
Margonine, Doris, 175
Marketing information, avoiding lawsuits on, 77–78
Marriott, Bill, 264
Marriott Corporation, 258
employment at, 450–51
research conclusions for study by, 325, *326*, *327*, 328
Mattel Corporation, 23
Mean, statistical, 322–23
Meaning in communication, 8–9
hidden, 71
Median, statistical, 322–23
Meetings, 439–42
conducting, 440–41
conferences vs., 439
participating in, 441
planned, 439–40, *441*
videoconferencing, 441–42
Memos, 172–89
analytical report formatted as, 290, 291, *294*
characteristics of successful, 172–74
checklist for writing, 187–88
confirmation, *186*, 187
electronic mail (E-mail), 177–80. *See also* E-mail
format, 520, *521*
information, 87, *88*, 89, 181–83
as internal communication, 14, *15*, 172
learning goals on, 169, 188–89
major components of, *94*
negative news in, 212, *213*
organization of, 175–77
persuasive, 237–39, *240*
procedure, 181–83
of recognition, 261, *262*, 263
reports formatted as, 291, *294*
request and reply, 183–86, 203–4, *205*
six cardinal sins of, 182
standard, 177, *178*
3-×-3 writing process for, 174–75, *178*
warnings sent as, 271–72
writing persuasive, 228–34
Messages
adaptation of, for intercultural audiences, 48–50, 160–61
adaptation of, for primary audience, 13, 65–73
analyzing purpose of, 62–64
anticipating audience for, 64–65
composing, 96–103
goodwill, 256–64
informational. *See* Informational messages
listening to, 34–38
negative. *See* Negative messages
nonverbal, 38–43
persuasive, 16, 62, 225–49
process of sending and receiving, 9–11
readability of, 121–24
revising, 116–21
sales, 242–48
special business, 265–77
Messaging. *See* E-mail
Microsoft Press, 64
Midas Mufflers, *245*
Mission statements, 161
Mode, statistical, 322–23
Money, refusing requests for, 203
Morrison, Lee, 469
Multiple line charts, 338, *339*

N

National Audubon Society, 328
Negative messages, 193–215
components of, 198–202
to customers, 194–95, 207–11
direct pattern for delivering, 202
goals in communicating, 196
indirect pattern for delivering, 196, *197*, 198, *199*, 200–201
in international communications, 215
learning goals, 193, 215–16
legal problems associated with, 196–98
in letters, 153–54
managing negative organization news, 212–14
refusing routine requests, 203–7
techniques for cushioning, 200–201
3-×-3 writing process applied to, 202–3
Networks, electronic, 180. *See also* E-mail
Newspapers, research using, 303–4
News releases, 274, *276*
Nickelodeon/Nick at Nite, 87
Noise as barrier to communication, 11
Nonprobability samples, 309
Nonverbal messages, 38–43
appearances of documents and individuals as, 42–43
body language clues in, 39, *40*
checklist for improving, 43–44
elements in, *39*
eyes, face, posture, and gestures as, 40–41

intercultural, 41, 44, 49
time, space, and territory as, 41–42
Note cards for oral presentations, 433, *434*
Noun phrases, overuse of, 120
Nourse, René, 226–27, 234
Numerical data
analysis of, 320–25
illustrating, 334, *335*

O

Objectivity as goal, 75
Observation, generating primary data by, 308–10
O'Connor, Sandra Day, 433
1-2-3 (software), 77
Openings
buffering, of negative messages, 196, *197*, 198–99
of letters, 142–43
of letters of application, 470–73
of memos, 175–76
of persuasive messages, 230–33
removing fillers in, 118
Openness, good listening and, 36
Operating reports, periodic, 288
Operational instructions, 272–74, *275*
Opinions, labeling of, 75
Oral (two-way) communications, 16–*17*. *See also* Oral presentations
in meetings and conferences, 439–42
selection of, vs. written communications, 18, 64
in telephone and voice mail, 442–45
Oral presentations, 426–38
checklist for, 438–39
ethics of, 437
for international and intercultural audiences, 48–49, 436–38
keeping audience attention in, 428
organizing content of, 427–30
polishing delivery of, 433–36
preparing effective, 426–27
visual aids and handouts with, 431–33
Orders
letters for acknowledging customer, 154–55
letters for requesting, 145–47
negative messages regarding, 208
Organizational communication, 14–25. *See also* Business writing
barriers to, 20–22
flow of, 19–20
forms of, 16–18. *See also* Oral (two-way) communications; Written (one-way) communication
functions of, 14–16
legal considerations of negative, 196–98
negative news to employees, 212, *213*
overcoming barriers to, 22–25
persuasive, 237–39
for refusing job applicants, 214
at Sara Lee Corporation, 4–5, 19, 22, 25
Organizational structure
charts illustrating, *335*, *340*, 341
flattening, to facilitate communication, 23
top-heavy, as communication barrier, 21
Organization chart, *335*, *340*, 341
Organization in 3-×-3 writing process, *61*, 89–96
computers used for, 63
grouping ideas into patterns as, 94–96. *See also* Direct pattern (front-loading) for organizing ideas; Indirect pattern for organizing ideas
for letters, 144
listing and outlining as, 89, 90–94
for memos, 175–77
for negative message, 203
for oral presentations, *429*
for persuasive messages, 229, *230*
for reports, 328–33
Orr, James, 22
Outlines, 89, 90–94
Overhead transparencies, 431, *432*
Owades, Ruth, 360

P

Paragraphs, 100–103
checklist for composing, 103–4
direct paragraph plan, 100–101
indirect paragraph plan, 101–2
linking ideas in, 102
one topic in, 100
organizing sentences into, 100
pivoting paragraph plan, 101
short, 103
transitional expressions between, 102, *103*
Parallelism, improving readability using, 121–24
Parenthetic notes, formats for, 311, *313*
Passion for Excellence, A (Austin), 36
Passive voice
in negative messages, 201
in sentences, 99
People magazine, 114–15
PepsiCo, 302, 464
Perception, listening process and, 34, *35*
Performance appraisals, 269, *270–71*
Periodicals, research using, 303–4
Periodic operating reports, 288, 350, *351*, 352
Persuasive messages, 16, 62, 225–49
credibility and, 226–27, 232, 234
ethical, 234
key components of, 230–33, *234*
learning goals, 225, 249
letters of application as, 470–75
résumé as, 456–68
sales messages as, 242–48
seven rules of, 232–33
3-×-3 writing process applied to, 228–29, *236*, 242–43, *247*
writing, for successful requests, 234–42
Peters, Tom, 302
Phelps County Bank, Rolla, Missouri, 300
Photographs, *335*, 341
Physical distractions as communication barrier, 13
Piecewicz, Mary, 378–79
Pie charts, *335*, 338, *339*
Pilot studies, 308
Pitney Bowes, 242
Pivoting paragraph, 101
Plagiarism, 75
Posture as nonverbal message, 41
Power and status as communication barrier, 22
Preconceptions, questioning communication, 13–14
Press releases, 274, *276*
Primary data, generating, 305–10
Primary sources, researching, 86–87
Printed forms for reports, 296
Privacy, zones of, 42, *43*
Probability samples, 309
Problem statement for reports, 297, 381–83
Procedures document, memos as, 181–83
Procter & Gamble, 117
Product charts, 337
Progress reports, 354, *355*
Proofreading in 3-×-3 writing process, *61*, 116, 125–29
of complex documents, 127
computer software for, 8, 63, 126, 128
of letters, 144
marks for, *127*
of memos, 174, 175
of negative messages, 203
of oral presentation, *429*
problem areas for, 125
of routine documents, 126
Proposals, 289, 380–86
checklist for writing, 386
components of formal, *381*, 385–86

Proposals (*continued*)
components of informal, 380–85
at Hewlett-Packard, 378–79
request for proposal (RFP), 380, 383, 385
Public schools, *319*
Public speaking. *See* Speaking skills
Publishing, desktop, 356
Punctuality, 41–42, 46
Purpose
of oral presentations, 426
of persuasive requests, 228–29
of reports, 297–99, 381–83
statements of, 298, 299

Q

Qualifications, evaluating personal employment, 452–53
Quality control movement, 439, *440*
Questionnaires, research, 87, 89, 306, *307*
Quinn, Jane Bryant, 72
Quota samples, 309
Quotations, using, 311

R

Racial bias in language, 69
RAND, 318–319
Random samples, 309
Range, statistical, 323
Rationalization as ethical trap, 74
Readability, 121–24
improving, 121–22
improving, with reader cues, 330–33
measuring, 123–24
Reasons and explanations in negative messages, 196, *197*, 199–200
Receivers of messages, 11. *See also* Audiences
adapting message to, 13
Recognition, writing memos of employee, 261, *262*, 263
Recommendation reports. *See* Justification/recommendation reports
Recommendations
in formal reports, 390–91, *404*
letters of, 265–67, *268*
writing report, *327*, 328
Record, permanent internal, 171, *186*, 187
Recruitment brochure, 89, *90*, *91*, 92, *93*
Redundancies, eliminating, 118
References
in formal reports, 391, *405*
formats for citing, 310–11, *313*
request for employment, 476
Rejection follow-up letters, 478
Reply letters, 150–58. *See also* Customer response letters
for acknowledging customer orders, 154–55
checklist for, 158–59
for complying with requests, 150–54
for granting adjustments and claims, 155–59
negative news in, 194–95, 207–12
to recognition or congratulations, 263
Reply memos, 183–84, *185*, 186
Reports
analytical. *See* Analytical reports
avoiding plagiarism in, 311
direct and indirect organization of, 290–91, *292–95*
documenting data in, 310–13, 523–27
formal. *See* Formal reports
formats of, 291, *292–94*, *295*, 296
functions of, 290
illustrating data in, 334–43
informational. *See* Informational reports
interpreting data in, 320–38
learning goals for, 285, 314, 317, 343–44, 347, 373, 377, 408
organizing data in, 328–33
proposals as, 289, 380–86
researching data for, 302–10
3-×-3 writing process applied to, 296–302
types of business, 288–89
writing style for, 296, *297*
Request for proposal (RFP), 380, 383, 385
Request letters, 144–48, 234–42
for adjustments and claims, 239–42
checklist for, 148–50, 242
for employment references, 476
for favors and actions, 235–37, *238*
for information and action, 144–45
letters for complying with, 150–54, 158
for making claims, 147–48
for placing orders, 145–47
Request memos, 183–86
persuasive, 237–39, *240*
refusing, 203–4, *205*
Requests, refusing routine, 203–7
checklist for, 207
for favors, money, information, or action, 203–4
invitations, 204–7
Resale information
in adjustment and claims letters, 157–58
in negative messages, 202
Research in 3-×-3 writing process, *61*, 86–89
electronic, 63, 86
formal, 86–87
informal, 87
for letters, 144
for memos, 174
for negative messages, 203
for oral presentations, *429*
for persuasive messages, 229
projects involving, 87–89
for reports, 302–10
Research studies
as analytical business report, 289, 369–72
at RAND institute, 318–19
at Winters Group, 286–87
Residence Inn, 450–51
Resistance, reducing, in persuasive messages, 231, 244–45
Résumés, 456–68
action verbs for, *462–63*
applying final touches to, 464–68
arranging parts of, 460–64
checklist for writing, 469–70
chronological style of, 456, *457*, *466*, *468*
combination style of, 459, *467*
computerized, 469
ethical considerations in writing, 465
follow-up letters after, 477, 478
functional style of, 456, 458
at Marriott Corporation, 450–51
skills style of, 456, 458
Retention, good listening and, 36–37
Revision in 3-×-3 writing process, *61*, 116–24
checklist for, 124–25
for clarity, 116–17
for conciseness, 117–19
of letters, 144
of negative messages, 203
of oral presentation, *429*
for readability and comprehension, 121–24
vigor and directness, 119–21
Richins, Darin, 194–95
Rivalry as communication barrier, 22
Rodriguez, Renee, career track profile of, 4–5
Romero, Tania, 450–51
Rosenberg, Richard M., 170
Rumor-control centers, 24

S

Saafir, Michael, 456
Safety information, avoiding lawsuits on, 77
Sales messages, 242–48
checklist for, 248
components of persuasive messages in, 243–48

included with negative messages, 202
proposals as, 380–86
3-×-3 writing process applied to, 242–43, *247*
Sampling, basics of, 309
Sant, Thomas, 386
Sara Lee Corporation, internal communication at, 4–5, 19, 22, 25
Schwab, Charles, 244
Scratch list, 89
Sculley, John, 34
Secondary data, locating, 302–5
Security Pacific National Bank, 170
Segmented line charts, 338, *339*
Segmented 100% bar chart, *336*
Self-deception ethical trap, 74
Self-publishing, 356
Senders of messages, 9–10
Sentences, 97–100
active voice in, 99
checklist for, 103–4
dangling phrases in, 99–100
elements of, 97–98
important ideas emphasized in, 98–99
organizing into paragraphs, 100
passive voice in, 99
short, 98
Service industries, communication skills and, 6–8
Sexual harassment, recognizing, 273
Shaklee Corporation, *237*
Sharp, Isadore, 44
Shea, Bill, 156
Simmons, Mike, 119
Simple line chart, 338, *339*
Simple random sample, 309
Simplified language, 70–72
Situational reports, 288, 352–57
progress and interim reports, 354–57
on trips, conventions, and conferences, 352–54
Skillsearch company, 469
Skills résumé, 456, 458
Slander, 197
Slides, 432
Smith, Janet Marie, 348–49
Smith, Tim, 256–57
Social interaction, space zones for, 42, *43*
Sony Corporation, 44
Southwest Airlines, 243
Space, nonverbal messages and use of, 42, *43*
Speaking skills, 423–48
learning goals for, 423, 445–46
at meetings and conferences, 439–42
for oral presentations, 426–38
proposal presentation at Walt Disney Imagineering, 424–25
for telephones and voice mail, 442–45
Special business messages, 265–77
announcements, 274, 277
learning goals on, 255, 277–78
letters of recommendation, 265–68
news releases, 274, *276*
operational instructions, 272–74, *275*
performance appraisals, 269, *270–71*
warnings to employees, 269–72
Spell checkers, 8, 63, 126
Staffing section of proposal, 384
Standard memos, 177, *178*
Statistical concepts, 322–23
Staubach, Roger, 390
Stereotypes, avoiding cultural, 48
Stratified random sample, 309
Style, writing
for reports, 296, *297*
software checkers of, 128
Subclusters of ideas, 89, *90*, *91*
Surface charts, 338, *339*
Surveys, research, 86–87, 305–8
guidelines for preparation of, 306, *307*, 308
letters requesting participation in, 235
sampling, basics of, 309
tabular presentation of data from, 320–21, *322*
at Winters Group, 286–87
Symbols for emotions, electronic, 180
Sympathy, messages of, 263
Synnott, Kathleen, 242

T

Table of contents
in formal reports, 389, *397*
in proposals, 385
Tables of numerical data
interpreting, 320–22
as report illustration, 334, *335*
Team writing, 62, 104–7
Technical writers, 8
Telephone calls, 442–45
making productive, 443
receiving productive, 444
voice mail and, 443, 444–45
at WordPerfect Corporation, 194, 195
Territory as nonverbal message, 42, *43*
Thanks, messages of, 259, *260*, 261
The Travelers insurance company, 32–33
3-×-3 writing process, 60–62, *129*
changing, 61, 65–72
collaboration on, 62, 104–7
computers and, 8, 62, 63, 126, 128
ethical and legal responsibilities in, 73–78
learning goals for, 57, 78–79, 83, 107–8, 113, 129–30
for letters, 143–44, *146*, *152*
for letters of appreciation, *260*
for letters of recommendation, 266–67, *268*
for memos, 174–75, *178*
for negative messages, 202–3, *205*, *213*
for oral presentations, *429*
for persuasive messages, 228–29, *236*, 242–43, *247*
phase 1 (analyzing, anticipating, adapting), 60, 62–73
phase 2 (researching, organizing, composing), 61, 86–107
phase 3 (revising, proofreading, evaluating), 61, 116–30
for reports, 296–302, *351*, *362*, *382*
for research surveys, *307*
Time
cultural values and orientation toward, 46
organizing report data by, 329
structure and use of, as nonverbal message, 41–42
Timeliness of messages, 258
Title page
for formal reports, 388, *395*
for proposals, 385
Titles of graphics and charts in reports, 343
Toffler, Alvin, 6
To-file reports, *186*, 187
Tokuda, Wendy, 460
Tolerance, developing attitudes of, 46–48
Tone
adapting messages for correct, 65–66
of goodwill, 140–41
in memos, 172, 181
Total quality movement, 439
Toys R Us, *277*
Transitions
in paragraphs, 102, *103*
in reports, 331–32
Trans World Airlines, 97
Trips, situational reports on 352–54
Trust, lack of, as communication barrier, 22
Truth-telling as goal in communication, 74–75
TRW Information Services, 209
Tully, Susanne, 84–85
projects of, 87–93
Twain, Mark, 13

U

UNUM insurance company, 22

V

Verbal signposts in oral presentations, 430–31
Vertical bar chart, *336*
Victoria's Secret, 97
Videoconferences, 441, *442*
Vigor, writing for, 119–21
Visual aids, 334–43
  computer aids for, 63, 337
  ethical, 341, 342
  improving readability using, 121–22
  incorporating, 341–43
  matching visuals to objectives, 334–43
  in memos, 173–74, 176, *185*, 186
  for oral presentations, 431, *432*
Voice mail, 443, 444–45
Volvo, 97

W

Wal-Mart Corporation, 118
Walt Disney Imagineering, proposal presentation at, 424–25
Walton, Sam, 118
Warnings to employees, 269–72
Welch, John F., 22
Winters, Mary-Frances, 287
Winters Group, 286–87
Wohl, Amy, 194
Women, intercultural sensitivity and status of, in business, 47
WordPerfect Corporation, 194–95
Words, purging empty, 119
Worker teams, 439
Work plan for reports, 300, *301*, 302
Works cited, formats for, 311, *313*
Writer's block, using computer to fight, 63
Written (one-way) communications, 16, *17*–18. *See also* Business writing; 3-×-3 writing process
  humor in, 171
  for intercultural audiences, 50
  selection of, vs. oral communication, 18, 64

X

Xerox Corporation, 19, 44, *354*

Y

Yardstick reports, 289, 368, *369–71*
"You" view in messages, 66–68

Z

Ziglar, Zig, 244